T0293210

The Origins and Dynamics of Inequality

Sex, Politics, and Ideology

JON D. WISMAN

OXFORD
UNIVERSITY PRESS

OXFORD
UNIVERSITY PRESS

Oxford University Press is a department of the University of Oxford. It furthers
the University's objective of excellence in research, scholarship, and education
by publishing worldwide. Oxford is a registered trade mark of Oxford University
Press in the UK and certain other countries.

Published in the United States of America by Oxford University Press
198 Madison Avenue, New York, NY 10016, United States of America.

Library of Congress Cataloging-in-Publication Data
Names: Wisman, Jon D., 1943– author.
Title: The origins and dynamics of inequality : sex, politics,
and ideology / Jon D. Wisman.
Description: New York, NY : Oxford University Press, [2022] |
Includes bibliographical references and index.
Identifiers: LCCN 2021031351 (print) | LCCN 2021031352 (ebook) |
ISBN 9780197575949 (hardback) | ISBN 9780197575963 (epub)
Subjects: LCSH: Equality—History. | Ideology. | Secularism. | Power
(Social sciences) | Evolutionary psychology. | Sexual selection.
Classification: LCC HM821 .W57 2022 (print) | LCC HM821 (ebook) |
DDC 305.09—dc23
LC record available at https://lccn.loc.gov/2021031351
LC ebook record available at https://lccn.loc.gov/2021031352

DOI: 10.1093/oso/9780197575949.001.0001

1 3 5 7 9 8 6 4 2

Printed by Sheridan Books, Inc., United States of America

Contents

Preface

I came of age in a period of declining inequality and rising optimism that social and economic justice would continue to expand. It was also an age in which the extent, pervasiveness, and meanness of inequality was becoming ever more conspicuous. Television brought poverty, and the civil rights and women's movements, into American living rooms, revealing the shocking unfairness and cruelty of economic, racial, and gender inequality. Why does it exist? Why, in a democracy, has it been tolerated?

The first of these questions was magnified for me by witnessing extreme inequality and harsh poverty during youthful visits to Haiti, Mexico, and closer to home, in remote Appalachian communities. At the same time, nightly television broadcasts revealed the horrific and murderous war that the wealthy United States was waging against the relatively impoverished people of Vietnam, who were seeking their freedom from foreign domination. Although it would be decades before inequality became a principal focus of my research, it lingered in my mind as a disquieting reality to which my thoughts often returned.

The fact that I spent my first 10 years in a happy, loving family in a house without running water on a farmlet in the Shenandoah Valley undoubtedly influenced my later thinking on inequality. We were poor, but not "living in poverty," in the sense that we were proud and locally esteemed. Moreover, there were no extreme differences in material well-being in the broader community. My boyhood recollections are of people interacting respectfully as social equals. Much later, reflections on these early childhood experiences stimulated my thoughts concerning inequality, relative social standing, and the material and social requisites for happiness.

While still a doctoral student in economics, I testified before Congress and coauthored an article on wealth taxation. Over the years, I researched and wrote on several issues related to inequality, but it did not become a principal research area until about 15 years ago, as I became increasingly disturbed by its uninterrupted progression since the 1970s. My research became more focused on inequality when my studies revealed its role in setting the conditions for the global financial crises of 2008 in real time as well as 1929

viii PREFACE

in economic history. So too did the difficulties it posed for dealing with the formidable threat of environmental devastation. As my research progressed, I also turned my attention to the differing institutional forms that inequality has taken over the course of time. I started to see an answer to the larger question of why inequality exists. It slowly became clear to me that the struggle over inequality has been the driving force of human history.

It also became increasingly clear that an adequate account of the origins and dynamics of inequality had yet to be written. But to expound a comprehensive explanation would require casting the net far wider than my home discipline of economics. It has, in fact, entailed drawing upon research not only in other social sciences and history, but also upon biology and, especially, evolutionary psychology.

That is a rough sketch of part of the genealogy of this book. The other part is my indebtedness to so many who have deeply influenced my understanding of the world.

It is, of course, impossible to trace the unfolding of one's ideas and modes of thinking. Too many influences fuse in mysterious ways. Nevertheless, Thelma Z. Levine, the professor who mentored me as an undergraduate philosophy major, stands out as a model of the life of the mind. My decades of friendship and prolonged discussions in a small reading group with philosophy professors Charley Hardwick, Jeffrey Reiman, and Philip Scribner contributed immeasurably to my intellectual development. In social economy, Professor Charles K. Wilber left an indelible imprint. And then there is my wife, Josette Andrée Denise Borgniet Wisman, a scholar in medieval French literature, from whom I have learned so much about scholarly domains well beyond those of my own research.

More concretely, in terms of the writing of this book, I am especially indebted to Charley Hardwick, Philip Lawton, Ugo Pagano, Jeffrey Reiman, and Josette A. Wisman for reading in full an earlier draft of the manuscript. They not only challenged interpretations and suggested improvements on many topics, but also offered detailed suggestions for improving syntax and style generally. Michael Cauvel, Eric Cheyfitz, Matthew Davis, Dennis Gilbert, Charles Larson, Jonathan Loesberg, Gabriel Mathy, Marie McGraw, Sikander Rahim, Nicholas Reksten, Stephanie Seguino, Howard Wachtel, and John Willoughby generously provided helpful comments on Chapter 1 and various other parts of the early manuscript.

I am also in debt to decades of bright and serious-minded undergraduate and graduate students at American University. Striving to assist them in developing their own understanding of our wonderful, exciting world has been a deeply rewarding adventure.

I celebrate James Cook, my editor at Oxford University Press, for seeing promise in this book and shepherding it through the review and acceptance process. Finally, I am deeply grateful to my dear friend, polymath Philip Lawton, who took on the editing for OUP as well as creating the index and assisting me with proofing, while offering incisive comments on the final version.

The publishers of the journals identified in the following have generously provided permission to draw upon limited portions of a few of my articles that reappear in several chapters of this book.

1) Chapters 4, 7, and 8: "Legitimating Inequality: Fooling Most of the People All of the Time," *American Journal of Economics and Sociology* 70(4), October 2011: 974–1013 (with James F. Smith).
2) Chapter 11: "Government Is Whose Problem?" *Journal of Economic Issues* 47(4), 2013: 911–38.
3) Chapter 12: "Inequality, Social Respectability, Political Power, and Environmental Devastation," *Journal of Economic Issues* 45(4), December 2011: 877–900.
4) Chapter 13: "Marx, the Predisposition to Reject Markets and Private Property, and Attractive Alternatives to Capitalism," *Forum for Social Economics* 48(3), 2019: 281–98. Published online May 2018.

Jon D. Wisman
Washington, DC
March 2021

1

Introduction

Inequality, Sex, Politics, and Ideology

Few who consider dispassionately the facts of social history will be disposed to deny that the exploitation of the weak by the powerful, organized for the purposes of economic gain, buttressed by imposing systems of law, and screened by decorous draperies of virtuous sentiment and resounding rhetoric, has been a permanent feature in the life of most communities that the world has yet seen.

—R. H. Tawney, *Religion and the Rise of Capitalism* (1926, 234)

In all known societies, at all times, the least wealthy half of total population own virtually nothing (generally little more than 5 percent of total wealth); the top decile of the wealth hierarchy own a clear majority of what there is to own (generally more than 60 percent of total wealth and sometimes as much as 90 percent).

—Thomas Piketty, *Capital in the Twenty-First Century* (2014, 336)

The form of law which I propose would be as follows: In a state which is desirous of being saved from the greatest of all plagues—not faction, but rather distraction—there should exist among the citizens neither extreme poverty nor, again, excessive wealth, for both are productive of great evil . . . .

—Plato, *Laws* (1988, Book 5)

Many observers of current world problems agree with President Barack Obama's statement that inequality is "the defining challenge of our time" (2013). This book claims more—that it has been the defining issue of all human history. The struggle over inequality has always been the underlying force that drives the history of humanity. Thus, the explosion in inequality in the United States and Great Britain over the past 45 years, and its less rapid growth in all other rich countries, has not been an anomaly. It is a return to the political dynamics by which elites have, since the dawn of civilization, taken practically everything for themselves and left all others with little more than the means with which to survive. Even after male workers in advanced capitalist countries in the nineteenth century gained the franchise and became the overwhelming majority of voters, inequality continued to increase. The only politically driven decline in inequality occurred over the 40 years between the 1930s and the 1970s. It is this that has been a historical anomaly.

Why has inequality characterized human societies since the rise of civilization? It is the project of this book to provide a comprehensive answer to this question. Before examining the explanatory framework of this answer, however, it is instructive to glance briefly at the history of inequality.

Inequality—most often, extreme economic and political inequality—has characterized human history since the rise of the state and the birth of civilization about 5,500 years ago, when superior military technology, military organization, and ideology enabled a few to subjugate all others. Premodern state societies became about as unequal as they could possibly be, near or on their "inequality possibility frontier," a concept developed by economist Branko Milanovic (2016) to designate an extreme at which elites take absolutely all output except subsistence—what producers need to barely survive and reproduce. To take more would be to kill the geese that lay the golden eggs.[1] Political scientist Carles Boix concurs: "By all measures an overwhelming majority of mankind lived at the margin of subsistence up until mid-nineteenth century. . . . Mean life expectancy [even as late as 1820] was slightly above twenty-six years. . . ." (2015, 202). A wealthy one percent and a few percent more of soldiers, administrators, and priests, along with some merchants, extracted virtually all surplus from an impoverished agrarian population (Scheidel 2017, 448).

This extreme inequality meant that a very small elite lived in relative luxury while all others lived at the edge of extreme material privation, often

---

[1] It should be noted that workers can be left with the wherewithal to survive and reproduce without being able to do so robustly or in good health. Economist and Nobel Laureate Angus Deaton reports that even with the enormous wealth being produced by the rise of industrialization in the eighteenth and early nineteenth centuries, in England working-class families had inadequate calories available for adults to maintain healthy bodily functioning and for their children to grow to their full potential (2013, 91).

falling from that precarious ledge into starvation when afflicted by poor harvests, natural catastrophes, social dysfunction, or war. At times producers lived above mere survival and reproduction, due to demographic collapses or increases in the demand for labor. Over the long haul, however, population growth and elites' political power pushed them inexorably back toward subsistence.

To understand this extreme economic and political inequality, it must first be recognized that it came quite late, only 5,500 years ago, and thus has existed for but a very short span, only the last 2 to 3 percent of the human story. Thus, contrary to widely held opinion, extreme material inequality cannot be claimed to be a naturally necessary part of the human condition.

Our species—*Homo sapiens*—has been in existence for about 200,000 years, and until the rise of the state and civilization, humans lived in relative political and economic equality. Before the adoption of agriculture about 10,000 years ago, practically all humans lived in nomadic forager societies,[2] finding food by hunting and gathering, as did other animal species, and living with high levels of economic and political equality. This was enforced by stone weapons technology that was relatively inexpensive and available to all, and to their ability to socially coordinate in coalitions against bullies. Leaders only existed during crises such as war, folding back among equals when calm returned.

Only with agriculture and eventually denser population concentrations did the need arise for more formal modes of social coordination, creating the social conditions in which chiefs could come forth. Chiefs bid for exceptional privileges by claiming special access and favor with spiritual or celestial forces. This ideological ruse provided them with certain privileges, most notably greater access to mates. However, it did not permit them to acquire significant wealth or even substantial political power. Indeed, their special status was fragile. A disastrous harvest could reveal the fraudulence of their claim of favor with divine powers, leading their societies to revert to a high degree of equality (Flannery and Marcus 2012).

Inequality gained permanence and completeness—on or approaching its inequality possibility frontier—with the rise of states and civilization. This occurred when elites could benefit from most, if not all, of three conditions. First, new, scarce, and expensive metal-based weapons and modes of martial organization and strategy provided them with sufficient military advantage

[2] The exceptions, as will be seen in Chapter 3, were a few sedentary fishing communities.

to demand tribute from producers and quell any resistance, even in the wake of failed harvests. Second, a sufficiently powerful ideology could convince most if not all members of society that inequality was the will of the gods, as it must be, and thus fair. Third, producers faced geographic or sociopolitical barriers that impeded escape, giving them little choice but to submit to their subservience. They essentially had nowhere to flee, all options being less attractive than that of their subservience. They were "caged."

Of these three conditions, ideology has received the least attention from historians and social scientists, even though it has been ever present and generally the most continuously commanding force maintaining social orders of inequality. What typically makes ideology sufficiently powerful for maintaining inequality is a deference to the views held by elites and fear that any substantial change would be for the worse. A powerful modern example makes this clear. Once the franchise became democratized and each adult member of society gained an equal voice, the ballot box could have been used to implement policies that would reduce or even eliminate inequality. That voters did not substantially do so is traceable to the superior power of the elite's ideology that unequivocally portrayed egalitarian measures as destructive of economic growth, social order, and freedom, and therefore in no one's interest.

However, it is possible that an elite's ideology can be delegitimated or seriously weakened. This occurred when chiefs, claiming special privileges due to a pretense of special favor with the gods, lost legitimacy in the wake of famines or other catastrophes. A more modern example is the heavy hit the ideology of elites took as a result of widespread suffering during the Great Depression of the 1930s. In this unique instance, in the United States and Europe, 40 subsequent years of democratically enacted policies substantially decreased inequality in income, wealth, and privilege. The uniqueness of this period is highlighted by the fact that the ideology underlying the policies that led to the financial crash of 2008 and the resulting "Great Recession" has not been seriously challenged. As this book goes to press, the explosion in inequality that dates to the late 1970s continues unabated. Whether it will be halted or reversed by the severe coronavirus pandemic that is currently ravaging economies and dramatically increasing the suffering and socioeconomic dysfunction caused by inequality remains to be seen.

Explaining the Origins and Dynamics of Inequality

All for ourselves, and nothing for other people, seems in every age of the world, to have been the vile maxim of the masters of mankind.
— Adam Smith, *The Wealth of Nations* (1776, 388–89)

The contemporary explosion in inequality has not gone unnoticed. It has drawn the attention of a growing number of citizens, politicians, and scholars. Students of inequality are creating a sort of inequality-research industry, generating a swelling number of books and articles providing better statistical data, historical analyses, causal explanations, and studies of its consequences for human welfare. Because noting all would almost be itself a book, mention here will be restricted to a few select works.

Notable books offering statistical studies of inequality include Thomas Piketty's two recent tomes, *Capital in the Twentieth Century* (2014a) and *Capital and Ideology* (2020), and Branko Milanovic's *Global Inequality: A New Approach for the Age of Globalization* (2016). Rich historical studies have appeared in Bos van Bavel's *The Invisible Hand* (2016), Carles Boix's *Political Order and Inequality* (2015), Kent Flannery and Joyce Marcus's *The Creation of Inequality* (2012), James C. Scott's *Against the Grain* (2017), and Walter Scheidel's *The Great Leveler* (2017). Among books that address inequality's consequences for human welfare are Richard Wilkinson and Kate Pickett's *The Spirit Level* (2009) and *The Inner Level* (2019), and Andrew Sayer's *Why We Can't Afford the Rich* (2015).

Although these works and very many others have greatly enriched our understanding of inequality, they have not provided an adequate theoretical account of its origins and dynamics. What they have most pointedly lacked is:

1) An understanding that the struggle over inequality has been the driving force of human history, even prior to the rise of substantial political and material inequality;
2) A grounding of the ultimate force generating inequality in human biology;
3) Recognition that politics, not economics, determines the degree of inequality;
4) An adequately detailed analysis of how elites' ideology legitimates inequality.

In contrast, the present book constructs a more complete explanatory framework for understanding why extreme economic and political inequality did not exist for the first 97 to 98 percent of human history but has characterized the human condition since the rise of states and civilization. Its central thesis is that the struggle over inequality has been the underlying force driving human history. This may partially appear obvious. People compete to be better and have more than others. Yet historians and social scientists have generally identified other forces as primary in driving history, such as technological advances, demographics, class conflict, war, religion, or the pivotal effects of great men. Whatever their validity, these other forces are proximate causes. As will be demonstrated as this book unfolds, the struggle over inequality is the ultimate causal force behind them.

This book's argument that the struggle over inequality has been the underlying force driving human history is built upon three key supporting claims. First, the ultimate driving force for inequality is found in our biology: the decisive competition that counts for sexually reproducing animal species is success in mating and thereby sending one's unique set of genes into future generations. This dynamic of sexual selection was extensively developed by Charles Darwin in his second major book, *The Descent of Man and Selection in Respect to Sex* (1871), and subsequently elaborated by evolutionary biologists. Regrettably, it has been largely ignored by historians and social scientists (excepting evolutionary psychologists). Yet this dynamic is critical for understanding social dynamics and history.

Among humans, coevolving with this dynamic of sexual selection has been resistance to inequality, expressing itself in an insistence on fairness. Until the rise of the state, this sense of fairness served as a constraint on sexual competition, preventing alpha males from monopolizing reproductive rights, as is the case with other primates. However, although humans appear to be hardwired with a sense of fairness, what is specifically understood as fair is culturally malleable. For instance, if a dominant ideology claims that another race or gender is innately inferior, and people embrace this ideology, then inequality between races and genders might be perceived as fair.

Biologically-driven to reproduce, humans compete for status that will make them attractive to potential mates. If properly channeled socially, this competition is positive. For instance, it can stimulate invention and innovation, generating technological change. But it might be channeled negatively such that some go to war to capture women or fame, or accumulate wealth and political power with which to exploit the weaker. Competition also occurs for excellence in knowledge, arts, sports, and even generosity. Those who excel in any of these domains are typically more attractive as mates. With appropriate social institutions, competition fuels human progress.

The second supporting claim for the thesis that the struggle over inequality has been the underlying force driving human history is that, because inequality is ultimately driven by the dynamics of sexual selection, and because humans are social and therefore political beings, inequality underlies all politics. Politics refers to how humans organize their relationships within and among groups. Politics always involves power, even when power is merely exercised through persuasiveness. The tension between sexual competition, on the one hand, and a sense of fairness, on the other, expresses itself through politics.

Although generally camouflaged by ideology, the struggle over shares of income, wealth, and privilege has, since the rise of states, been the principal defining issue of politics. Politics produces laws and social institutions to resolve tensions between competition and fairness. Although economists and other social thinkers typically locate the source of inequality in economic forces, ultimately the expression of these forces takes place in political contexts where the rules of the game are established. Politics can neutralize the distributional consequences of economic forces.

The third supporting claim is that, although physical violence remains the trump card in creating, maintaining, or increasing inequality, ideology has consistently been the most important inequality-sustaining political weapon on a day-to-day basis. Ideology almost makes it true that the pen (or the word) is mightier than the sword. The weaker must be led to believe that inequality is in their interest, and thus fair. Manipulating the strong sense of fairness is the essence of ideology. Ideology hoodwinks the losers into seeing fairness in conditions that in fact are contrary to their best interests. Like sexual selection, the concept of ideology has received inadequate attention from social scientists studying inequality.

Ideology justifies the gains of the stronger at the expense of the weaker. It is possible because humans, as reflective beings, must give meaning to their existence. This meaning is socially generated, and the component that legitimates inequality is ideology. The camouflage that masks the centrality of the struggle over inequality has been provided by dominant ideologies. Until modern times, they depicted inequality as some combination of the will of the gods, a celestial mandate, or in accordance with natural law. In modern times, inequality is principally legitimated as necessary for economic dynamism and therefore in everyone's interest, or attention has been deflected to other concerns such as foreign threats or cultural issues. Where substantial inequality exists, those with the most control over material and social assets possess determining advantages in generating and maintaining meaning systems or ideologies that justify their privileges.

These three claims in support of the thesis that the struggle over inequality is the driving force of history are set forth at greater length in the following sections. Then, Chapter 2 develops the theory of sexual selection and its importance for understanding the biological grounding of inequality. Chapters 4, 7, and 8 explore the dynamics of legitimation and especially its subcategory of ideology. Chapter 4 addresses legitimation theory, and Chapters 7 and 8 explore how it evolved, first at the end of the Middle Ages, and then with the maturation of economic science in the modern era. The claim that inequality is always political is demonstrated throughout the entire book.

The Dynamics of Sexual Selection

I don't know a single head of state who hasn't yielded to some kind of carnal temptation, small or large. That in itself is reason to govern.
—François Mitterand, quoted in Bobbi S. Low, *Why Sex Matters*
(2001, 57)

This book begins its exploration of the origins and dynamics of inequality by drawing upon the dynamics of sexual selection first noted in 1859 by Darwin in *The Origin of Species*, greatly elaborated in 1871 in his *The Descent of Man and Selection in Relation to Sex*, and further developed since that time within the disciplines of evolutionary biology and psychology. Thus "sex" is in the title of this book not explicitly to draw readers' attention, although all authors keenly hope their titles will do just that. Rather, it is to punctuate the central role of sex in the human story. At some level, everyone instinctively knows this. Sexuality saturates culture, although this same culture trains us to turn our attention most frequently in other directions. The critical importance of sex for understanding human history is the fact that sexual competition resides deep beneath politics. It propels competitive human action, and politics influences how this rivalry, countered by a sense of fairness, is expressed.

Understanding sexual selection and a sense of fairness in the human species is key for understanding our species' history.

Natural selection, through the competitive struggle for survival in the face of limited resources, is ultimately in service of reproductive success. Individual humans, like all sexually reproducing animals, must successfully compete for mates if their unique set of genes is to survive into the future. This competition for sexual selection is the ultimate driver of all expressions of competition. Saint Augustine characterized the three principal sins of fallen man to be lust for money, lust for power, and sexual lust. It took Darwin to make clear that the first two are driven by the third.

Humans strive to stand out, to be better than others, if not the best among them, so as to be attractive to the opposite sex. But, until recently in the human story, this competition was not expressed in the accumulation of wealth and political power. Instead, humans competed by being good hunters and gatherers, by being good warriors, or by being cooperative, generous, smart, artistic, humorous, and fun. However, following the rise of the state and civilization a mere 5,500 years ago, wealth, and especially political power, came to serve as the most potent magnets for sexual success. Their possession promised greater potential for mating and greater chances that resulting offspring would survive. Humans have, of course, continued to compete sexually through means that predated civilization. However, significant wealth and political power became capable of outplaying these earlier modes of competition. The reason, to repeat, is clear: choosing a mate possessing wealth or political power improves the likelihood that children will survive. Political power became a powerful aphrodisiac. As anthropologists Lionel Tiger and Robin Fox remark, "The political system is a breeding system. When we apply the word 'lust' to both power and sex, we are nearer the truth than we imagine" (1997, 182).

Humans evolved as a social species with a keen sense of fairness, and this provided them with a strong tendency to prefer equality.[3] Throughout most of human history—the period prior to civilization—the stone-age weapons technology for inflicting physical harm on others was equally available to all. Consequently, combined with the ability to form coalitions against potential alpha males, members of these societies could block anyone from

---

[3] Behavioral economists Ernst Fehr, Helen Bernhard, and Bettina Rockenback have found that aversion to inequality develops strongly between the ages of three and eight. Whereas between ages three and four, most children still behave selfishly, by the age of seven or eight, most prefer resource allocations that are more egalitarian (2008).

overzealously competing for sexual advantage through socially censured modes of behavior such as accumulating material wealth or seeking political power. They punished, even murdered, those who were boastful or who too blatantly asserted their own importance. Political power and the accumulation of material wealth were proscribed by their sense of fairness from the playing field for sexual competition. An imperative for food sharing also served as a powerful leveling mechanism. Sexual competition would have to be channeled through other forms of socially approved behavior that were generally in the best interest of the group. The behavior that provided status, making individuals attractive as mates and boosting the probability that their genes would make it into posterity, was that behavior which benefited the community and was therefore socially approved. In this manner, the genes that favored these modes of status-enhancing behavior were selected in human evolution.

Although competition is driven by the dynamics of sexual selection, political institutions channel this competition into specific expressions. It is in this sense that social inequality is political. How sexual competition unfolds and the character it takes are significantly determined politically.

All living things evolve within given environments to become equipped with the specific guidance mechanisms that are critical to their survival and reproduction. But even humans are not generally aware that their behavior is being steered toward these specific ends. For instance, humans intentionally eat to satisfy hunger and know that they must eat to survive. But they are not so keenly aware that their specific taste preferences evolved as guidance mechanisms to promote their good health for survival and reproduction. When people suffer the pain of loneliness, they are unlikely to realize that the reason they evolved to do so was to motivate them to seek the company of other members of their group, among whom they would be safer and thus better able to survive and reproduce. Likewise, although humans are aware that they compete for the attention and favors of mates and that they seek to satisfy their sexual urges, they are less aware, if aware at all, that the reason they possess these urges and compete with others to satisfy them is to enable their genes to survive into the future. As neuroscientist Jaak Panksepp notes, "It is a remarkable feat of nature to weave powerful sexual feelings and desire in the fabric of the brain without revealing the reproductive purpose of these feelings to the eager participant" (2004, Ch. 12).

Although physical characteristics substantially determine sexual attractiveness, culturally produced behavioral traits do so as well, the more so as humans mature into adults. These traits are especially valued to the extent that they provide status or certification of value. And because excellence in many socially approved arenas can provide this status, competition occurs in all of them. But participants are generally unaware that the dynamic of sexual selection lies behind this competition.

Although sexual competition ultimately drives inequality, the cultural dynamics generated by this competition established the conditions that eventually made humanity increasingly wealthy and free. In this, humans differed from all other animals. Sexual competition among male peacocks resulted in huge and elaborate tail feathers that increased the mating success of the most ostentatious but decreased their gender's actual physical fitness. Sexual competition among humans, by contrast, increasingly took cultural turns, manifesting itself in domains that increased humanity's success as a species. This competition generated knowledge, invention, innovation, cooperation, and generosity, which created the conditions for improving human welfare. Evidence of this progress is strikingly apparent practically everywhere in modern life. For instance, violence of humans against humans has declined throughout the human story; and in very recent times, extreme material privation has declined, average life expectancy has dramatically expanded, and more and more people are living in material affluence and political freedom.

Until recent centuries, the rise of states and the extreme inequality that accompanied them dramatically debased the lives of the overwhelming majority of humans. Due principally to poorer diets and social crowding, humans became shorter, more disease ridden, and shorter-lived than their pre-civilized predecessors. Most also became far less socially free. From a reproductive point of view, this situation was especially severe for low-status males. Elites acquired disproportionate sexual access to females, often in harems. This deprived the least privileged males of access to females and thus the possibility of sending their genes into the future.

Philosopher and cognitive scientist Daniel Dennett claims that Darwin's breakthrough in evolutionary biology has been the greatest scientific advance in history, surpassing in importance even Isaac Newton's much earlier breakthrough in physics (1995). Yet, as anthropologist John Tooby and psychologist Leda Cosmides lament, "nearly a century and a half after *The Origin of Species* was published, the psychological, social, and behavioral sciences remain largely untouched by these implications" (2005, 5). Instead, they have been captured by the Standard Social Science Model whereby "the mind is blank-slate like, and lacks specialized circuits that were designed by natural selection to respond differentially to inputs by virtue of their evolved significance" (2005, 6). The blank slate metaphor presumes that experience writes the full script for human behavior. Fortunately, in recent decades, psychology has substantially moved beyond behavioralism, whereby behavior was viewed exclusively as socially determined, to recognize what Darwin had made so clear: behavior is substantially guided by inherited traits that were selected in the course of evolution. Unfortunately, most other social sciences have been slow to follow.

Social sciences and human history necessarily concern human behavior, and it is imperative that scholars in these domains explicitly articulate what they take to be human nature. Yet rarely is this understanding made explicit. Presumably, these remiss scholars either see no need to do so, or they lack clear understanding of the deep forces steering the behavior of the actors they describe. Either is a mistake. It is imperative that works in social science and history come clean on what is understood as human nature. Further, only if human behavior were fully plastic, capable of being entirely directed by culture, might it be appropriate to ignore human biology. But, as cognitive scientist Steven Pinker (2002) and many others have made clear, this is not a tenable position. As biological beings, at the most fundamental level, how humans behave is a product of gene-culture coevolution, whereby changes in genes can lead to changes in culture and vice versa.[4]

For a work in social science or history to have adequate explanatory coherence, ultimately the biological character of humans must be recognized and made explicit. To be scientific, the social sciences should conform with the findings of the biological sciences that seek an understanding of what humans are first and foremost as living beings. It is for this reason that this study of inequality begins with the biological fact that humans are competitive because, as a sexually reproducing species, they must be. Biologically, sexual competition is the competition that ultimately counts. To ignore this is to condemn social and historical understanding to inadequacy.

---

[4] Biologist E. O. Wilson describes gene-culture coevolution more fully as follows: "Genetic evolution . . . affects cultural evolution. Conversely, cultural evolution affects biological evolution, by creating the environment in which the genes (the ones prescribing epigenetic rules) are tested through natural selection. Genes and culture are in fact inseparably linked. Changes in one inevitably force changes in the other, resulting in what has come to be called gene-culture coevolution" (1989, 37).

Pace Economists, Inequality Is
Always Political

There's class warfare all right, but it's my class, the rich class, that's making war, and we're winning.

—Warren Buffett (*quoted in* Stein 2006)

This book, in its exploration of the origins and dynamics of inequality, reveals the political maneuvers that have, since the rise of civilization, permitted elites to command most, if not all, of society's surplus by extracting virtually all output beyond that required for the producers' subsistence. This extraction of surplus was made possible by the fact that elites controlled political power that enabled them to hold the producers in various forms of bondage such as slavery, serfdom, and indebtedness. Although workers were no longer held in bondage by overt force under capitalism, until quite recently in rich countries, because they generally lacked ownership, control, or ready access to tools and resources, they had to pay most, if not all, of their surplus output to the capitalist owners for the right to work, and so survive. Thus, since the rise of the state and civilization, the basic dynamic of inequality has always been the same. Elites have held ownership or control over productive wealth such that workers were caged. They had no option short of starvation but to work for and render their surplus to elites.

Against this historical backdrop, as noted earlier, something unique occurred in the mid-twentieth century. Between the 1930s and the 1970s inequality significantly declined in today's rich countries, leading many to believe that the historical legacy of extreme inequality had come to an end and that the future promised ever-greater equality in wealth, income, and privilege. But then the trend unexpectedly reversed. Over the past 45 years inequality has exploded, especially in the United States and Great Britain, but significantly in virtually all countries around the world, including even the more socialized Scandinavian countries (Piketty 2020, 420–23).

This reversal crushes the optimistic expectations of those who believe that more equal societies are superior in virtually all respects. What has driven it? The current discourse typically identifies the causes as economic, due to some combination of technological change, globalization, inadequate education, and demographics. But these are proximate causes. They all take place within political frameworks that enable them to increase inequality.

Thus, these proximate causes could in principle be politically altered, or their effects could be politically neutralized.[5]

This mistake of focusing on proximate causes while ignoring underlying political forces is itself political. It masks the true cause of inequality and presents it as if it is natural, due to the forces of progress, just as in premodern times it was the will of gods. The science of economics has played a principal role in generating and disseminating this view that the ultimate causes of inequality are economic. This book is in agreement with economists Daron Acemoglu and James Robinson's observation that "while economic institutions are critical for determining whether a country is poor or prosperous, it is politics and political institutions that determine what economic institutions a country has." They rightly state, "Traditional economics has ignored politics, but understanding politics is crucial for explaining world inequality" (2006, 43, 68.)

Understanding the ultimate causes and dynamics of inequality requires moving beyond the narrow focus on economic forces that dominates contemporary mainstream economics. It requires the broader focus implicit in Marx's work whereby the development of an adequate understanding of social phenomena needs to search for the manner in which the scarcity-compelled struggle with nature for scarce resources influences and is in turn influenced by social relations, and the manner in which both are related to social consciousness (Wisman 2013c).[6]

Mainstream Economics Overlooks the Political

Economics has gained the title of Queen of the Social Sciences by choosing solved political problems as its domain.
—Abba Lerner, "The Economics and Politics of Consumer Sovereignty" (1972, 259)

In his 1955 presidential address to the American Economic Association, economist Simon Kuznets offered support for the hope that the historical

---

[5] Continental European workers have also faced the challenges of technological change and globalization. Thanks to compensatory government actions, however, they have suffered considerably less increased inequality than their American and British counterparts.

[6] Non-mainstream or heterodox economists have given due attention to the central importance of politics in accounting for inequality. However, their minority voices have been drowned out by mainstream economics' hegemonic dominance of the discipline.

pattern of extreme inequality had been broken and that growing equality would characterize humanity's future. In a conjecture he characterized as "perhaps 5% empirical information and 95% speculation, some of it possibly tainted by wishful thinking" (1955, 26), he surmised that, although inequality increases in the early stages of economic development,[7] at some more advanced level, inequality begins decreasing—an inverted U curve. Kuznets's reflections went public at about the midpoint of that unique period between the 1930s and the 1970s when inequality was declining. The science of economics thereby appeared to validate the hope and expectation that, in the end, economic growth would deliver lessened inequality. His conjecture came to be seen as "conventional wisdom" (Lantican, Gladwin, and Seale 1996, 243), "some sort of 'iron law' of development" (Srinivasan 1977, 15), "one of the most enduring and remarkable arguments in the history of the social sciences . . . [such that] by the end of the 1970s, the inverted U-curve process was universally considered a general statement of the historical and universal relationship between income inequality and economic growth" (Moran 2005, 209, 218).

Kuznets, however, did not believe that the shift toward greater equality would be driven by purely economic forces. He held that political and social forces are important, that political pressure for greater equality comes forth as the lower classes achieve greater social and political organization such that redistributive government intervention plays a role. However, he limited his analysis to mostly economic variables because "space does not permit the discussion of demographic, political, and social consideration that could be brought to bear . . ." (1955, 17–18). In closing his address, Kuznets noted that "it is inevitable that we venture into fields beyond those recognized in recent decades as the province of economics proper. . . . Effective work in this field necessarily calls for a shift from market economics to political and social economy" (1955, 28). Generally, political and social economists recognize that the economic is embedded in the political.

Apparently, few practitioners or anyone else paid much attention to Kuznets's concluding reflection.[8] As a consequence, the hypothesis that

---

[7] If worker wages are held at subsistence, or if workers do not share proportionately in the fruits of economic growth, then greater inequality necessarily accompanies economic growth.

[8] The misreading of Kuznets is widespread. Even economist Thomas Piketty, who has done so much to draw attention to inequality and who generally recognizes the importance of politics, mistakenly wrote in *Capital in the Twenty-First Century*, "According to Kuznets's theory, income inequality would automatically decrease in advanced phases of capitalist development, regardless of economic policy choices . . ." (2014b, 11).

rising inequality is a temporary side effect of economic growth came to serve as an ideology, justifying the conclusion that nothing really need be done to limit or reverse inequality. Morphed into "iron law," Kuznets's conjecture suggested that rising inequality in developing countries need not be of much concern since it is merely part of the story of successful economic development. This conveniently fit with the views of those who claim that inequality is positive for growth prospects: "Since only capitalists save and invest (at least to a significant degree), economic growth requires a change in the class distribution of control over these resources; hence, the wealth-generating advantages of inequality are not only to be expected, but inequality is actually seen as a necessary precondition to growth" (Moran 2005, 217). Notably, as if anticipating such arguments, Kuznets wrote of the need to "avoid the fatally simple remedy of [using] the population as cannon-fodder in the fight for economic achievement" (1995, 25).

Despite Kuznets's entreaty, cannon-fodder they were to be. It is ironic that a conjecture that Kuznets viewed as felicitous would support a passive attitude toward inequality. But that was clearly a consequence. As for the rich countries, because economic forces were presumably at work that will lead inequality continually to decline, vigorous redistribution measures can be viewed as less urgent or even unnecessary. Due to economic dynamics, inequality would "naturally" decline in due course with continued economic growth. Indeed, insofar as greater equality was viewed as a byproduct of economic forces in rich countries, then it might be concluded that there was in fact no redistributive role for public policy. The general view of economists has been that distribution, whether of income, wealth, or privilege, is a consequence of economic forces, not political policy. Kuznets's felicitous hypothesis wound up justifying leaving inequality off the economics research agenda as a problem that would solve itself.

Even in those rare instances when economists recognize a political dimension to inequality, they do so in a manner that continues to view economic forces as somehow or somewhat independent of the political world. Economist Joseph Stiglitz has written, "Markets, by themselves, even when they are stable, often lead to high levels of inequality" (2012, xiii). But markets are never to any substantial extent "by themselves." Substantial markets cannot exist and function without government provision of public goods such as law and order, security of private property, and legal sanctity of contract. Note, for example, that during the so-called Dark Ages in Europe, markets virtually disappeared because no states were powerful enough to define and enforce property rights.

An especially curious example is economist Thomas Piketty's thinking. Piketty peppers his influential book, *Capital in the Twenty-First Century*, with statements that distribution is ultimately an issue of politics. For instance, early in the book, he writes, "The history of the distribution of wealth has always been deeply political, and it cannot be reduced to purely economic mechanism. . . ." Later in the same book, he states, "In every country the history of inequality is political—and chaotic" (2014a, 20, 286). Yet he bases most of his theoretical analysis and much of his historical analysis, as well as his prediction of greater future inequality, on the rate of return on capital exceeding the rate of economic growth ($r > g$). He announces that this "fundamental inequality . . . sums up the overall logic of my conclusions" (2014a, 25). And this "fundamental inequality" appears to be what most reviewers and commentators have taken from his work, leaving them with the impression that, for this foremost authority on inequality, distribution is the consequence not of politics, but of pure economic dynamics.[9]

Likewise, taking their cue from mainstream economists, many other social thinkers give little or no role to politics in determining inequality. Political historian Jerry Muller, for instance, claims that the most recent surge in inequality "is not the result of politics, nor is politics likely to reverse it, for the problem is more deeply rooted and intractable than generally recognized. Inequality is an inevitable product of capitalist activity . . ." (2013). Muller appears not to recognize that "capitalist activity" takes place within political states that determine the rules of the game. Similarly, sociologist Peter Berger claims that "income distribution is a function of modern economic growth and is affected to only a limited degree by the institutional arrangements and policies of a society" (1986, 219).

The views of most contemporary economists have a parallel in the nineteenth-century belief in natural laws. It was common, as will be explored more fully in Chapter 8, for many earlier economists to view the distribution of income as a result of a natural law. Notable among them is John Bates

---

[9] In his more recent book, *Capital and Ideology*, Piketty makes his position clear: "Inequality is above all ideological." In another passage, he writes: "Inequality is neither economic nor technological; it is ideological and political." However, he continues by asserting: "I insist that the realm of ideas, the political-ideological sphere, is truly autonomous" (2020, 711, 7). This assertion cannot be correct. The spheres of material production, social relations, and social consciousness are always intertwined. To survive, ideas must be nested in nourishing social environments. This issue will be explored further in Chapters 4 and 7.

Clark, who wrote: ". . . the distribution of the income of society is controlled by a natural law, and that this law, if it worked without friction, would give to every agent of production the amount of wealth which that agent creates" (1908, v).

Curiously, when economists and historians examine pre-capitalist societies, the fact that those who labor are forced to give up their surplus to a ruling elite is generally understood in political terms. Thus, they take extreme inequality to be politically based. Slavery is due to the political power of slave-owners, and feudalism to the political power of landlords. However, when these scholars examine the same phenomenon within capitalism, they most frequently ignore political forces and ground inequality in economic dynamics. This tendency flows from a proclivity to see capitalism as a self-directing economic system wherein the political domain principally serves the function of the constable maintaining security and enforcing the laws. It ignores the distributional impact of the legal structure. Consequently, as economists Sam Bowles and Herbert Gintis put it, ". . . with some notable exceptions . . . economists have treated power as the concern of other disciplines and extraneous to economic explanation" (2007, 2).[10]

In a parallel manner, Karl Marx criticized classical economists for viewing all pre-capitalist societies as artificial, as human constructs, but capitalism as natural.[11] Yet, ironically, whereas Marx clearly understood the extent to which elites write the script within all societies, he frequently depicted them within capitalism as subject to its inherent laws of economic development. This suggests that even unconventional economists, like their mainstream counterparts, are so driven by the search for "universal laws" of economics

[10] Some social thinkers lodge the cause of inequality in neither the economic nor the political, but instead in the virtues of the rich and the personal failings of the less well-off. For instance, political scientist Ron Haskins claims that ". . . opportunity in America depends largely on decisions made by people who are free actors. . . . Unless young Americans begin making better decisions, the nation's problems with poverty and inequality will continue to grow. . . . Yes, the nation needs its safety net, but improvements in personal responsibility would have a greater and more lasting impact on poverty and opportunity" (2012, A15).
    Chapter 3 will explore in detail how the tendency to fault individuals rather than social institutions evolved within our species.
[11] Marx wrote of the "singular manner" in which, for classical economists, there were "only two kinds of institutions, those of art and those of nature. Feudal institutions are artificial institutions, those of the bourgeoisie are natural institutions. In this they resemble the theologians, who also establish two kinds of religion. Every religion but their own is an invention of men, while their own religion is an emanation from God. In saying that existing economic conditions—the conditions of bourgeois production—are natural, the economists give it to be understood that these are the relations in which wealth is created and the productive forces developed conformably to the laws of nature. . . . They are eternal laws which must always govern society. Thus there has been history, but there is no longer any" (1847, 147).

that they often become sidetracked from their customarily more interdisciplinary focus that accords a central role to politics. Recognizing that distribution is ultimately political and then letting economic forces rule the analysis might be the most striking parallel between Piketty's *Capital in the Twenty-First Century* and Marx's *Capital*.

*****

The claim that the nature of inequality and the manner in which it evolved are determined in the political sphere, and that historically, since the rise of civilization, elites have almost always controlled this sphere, does not mean that political measures have never been taken that benefit of the less well-off. After all, there is frequently a need to respond to their disgruntlement lest there be social unrest or rebellion. But such measures are usually blips in the continual advance of policies that pressure society in the direction of greater inequality.

Further, elites are by no means always of one mind, and this is especially true in modern times. Modern societies are less homogeneous than they were in the past, and, consequently, elites are often divided by religious and ethnic differences as well as differing secular values in the social realm. Indeed, many among the elite are leaders in support of progressive measures at their own expense that benefit the less privileged.

Most political issues are not specifically understood in distributional terms. Nevertheless, few measures taken by governments are without distributional consequences. This is as true in today's wealthy "democratic" nations as in history's despotic nations. As political scientist William Galston puts it, "The distribution of economic surplus is the daily business of normal politics in liberal democracies" (2018, 33). Understandably, on the whole, elites, who possess disproportionate political influence, spontaneously gravitate toward the formulation of public policies of which they are principal beneficiaries.

Oh, and what is the size of the elite? This varies historically and its definition is arbitrary, although often it is defined as the top one percent. In Piketty's words, "The top centile occupies a very prominent place in any society. It structures the economic and political landscape" (2014a, 277). But, of course, the wealth and power of the top one-tenth of one percent is yet far more impressive. And in recent decades, there has been an explosion in the ultra-rich: According to *Forbes*, whereas worldwide in 1987 there were 140 billionaires, in 2019 there were 2,153. These billionaires own more wealth than the 4.6 billion people who make up the bottom 60 percent of the planet's population. The wealthiest 20 Americans own as much as the poorest half of the US population (Scheidel 2017, 1).

The Critical Role of Ideology

All available sources agree that . . . 90 percent of wealth for the top decile and at least 50 percent for the top centile—were . . . characteristic of traditional rural societies . . . [and] whether such extreme inequality is or is not sustainable depends not only on the effectiveness of the repressive apparatus but also, and perhaps primarily, on the effectiveness of the apparatus of justification.

—Thomas Piketty, *Capital in the Twenty-First Century*
(2014, 262, 264)

Even in those instances when social scientists have heeded Kuznets's appeal to broaden analysis to political and social factors affecting distributional trends, the role of ideology has typically not received substantial attention. Yet, throughout history, the elite's superior influence over the generation and character of ideology, owing to their disproportionate control over resources and political power, has usually played a decisive role in maintaining their ability to appropriate most of society's surplus. Although violence has always been the most powerful political weapon, ideology has been the one most unswervingly employed. This does not necessarily mean that elites consciously conspire to craft ideologies that will legitimate their privileges. Instead, they gravitate spontaneously toward those ideas that support their interests. And because their privileges provide them with generally superior educations and greater knowledge, they are less readily mistaken as to what their best interests are.[12] However, it is important to note that most members of the elite sincerely believe that their ideals, and the measures that happen to be especially beneficial to them, are the objectively right ones, the ones that are in everyone's interest, the ones, even, that are in the best interest of

---

[12] Evolutionary psychology supports the view that elites are better able to manipulate ideology. Cognitive scientist Denise Cummins writes, "Social dominance has been found to correlate with deceptive ability and enhanced ability to decode nonverbal cues. Individuals who are perceived and rated as socially dominant are better at deceiving others, persuading others, and interpreting other's intentions" (2005, 682).

all of humanity. After all, everyone wishes to be of honorable character. As a rule, elites do not act in bad faith. This book is not a story of good guys versus bad guys.

Ideology is almost entirely ignored by economists and seldom given much importance even by historians. Notable exceptions are economic historian Douglass North and Piketty in his just published book, *Capital and Ideology* (2020). The former wrote:

> Without an explicit theory of ideology or, more generally of the sociology of knowledge, there are immense gaps in our ability to account for either current allocation of resources or historical change. In addition to being unable to resolve the fundamental dilemma of the free rider problem we cannot explain the enormous investment that every society makes in legitimacy. (1982, 47)

Yet, North equates ideology with beliefs or "shared mental attitudes," minimizing if not ignoring its role as an instrument of exploitation that enables the powerful to benefit at the expense of the weak. Although Piketty recognizes exploitation, his conception of ideology, much like North's, is defined without adequate precision fully to account for it.

What is judged as fair can be altered by ideology. Ideology is obfuscation and deception. It is a form of mystification that serves specific interests, legitimating the ability of the more powerful to gain at the expense of the weaker. It promotes a mistaken view of aspects of reality, most importantly social aspects and social relations. In doing so, it is a formidable instrument for creating and maintaining inequality.

This meaning of ideology follows that of Marx. Although Marx's theory of ideology is often dismissed as merely exhibiting his political biases, economist Joseph Schumpeter, from the other end of the political spectrum, thought otherwise: "Marx was the economist who discovered ideology for us and who understood its nature. Fifty years before Freud, this was a performance of the first order" (1954, 35). Following Marx, the use of the term *ideology* in this book differs from that found among positivists who contrasted ideology with science, where the latter meant thought that was empirically grounded. This opposition robs ideology of its specific meaning as an instrument of exploitation. Thus, the use of *ideology* in this book is more explicit, and more pointed, than the philosopher of science Karl Popper's use when he characterizes certain doctrines as "our own system of prejudices" and "ideological follies" (1966, 2:216–23).

Ideology is an aspect of legitimation understood as a set of beliefs concerning the nature of reality. Legitimation concerns how people mentally experience and understand their world. As such, it is neither positive nor negative. It is necessary that humans give meaning to their world. Ideology is a component of legitimation, one that presents a distorted picture of aspects of social reality and authorizes some to exploit others.

The critical importance of ideology might be better appreciated by noting that humans have produced three broad categories of tools to control their world. One way to summarize these categories is that *technology* promises more efficient control of the physical world, *social institutions* promise more efficient control or coordination of social processes, and *legitimation*, of which ideology is a subdomain, permits control of the mental world. That this is an overly simplified manner of classifying human tools is evident in that the categories are overlapping and functionally interrelated. Technology materially influences social processes and mental acts.[13] Institutions substantially influence technology and the mental sphere. And legitimation affects and partially controls everything humans do. An understanding of ideology—a component of legitimation—is essential for understanding the dynamics of exploitation and inequality.

The fact that highly unequal societies have endured for such long periods of time is significantly due to the ideology that justified the extremely unequal division of wealth and privilege. However, at times, economic, social, demographic, climatic, or other natural events brought on crises severe enough to threaten the elite's ideology and thus their right to rule. Nevertheless, their superior command over ideology eventually, and usually quickly, permitted them to reclaim legitimacy and society's surplus.

Inequality can be maintained by either physical or ideological force. Violence has often been necessary for establishing and solidifying a hierarchical social structure. Physical force has been used to prevent productive

---

[13] Note, for instance, the substantial impact of new media technology upon social consciousness, although it may be diminished as society adjusts to its initial stimulus. While this suggestion is highly speculative, fascism may have been facilitated by the rise and maturation or democratization of the radio; the radicalism of the 1960s with that of television; and current populism with that of the internet.

subordinates from fleeing, keeping them caged. However, brute force is relatively inefficient because it generates strong resentment and the constant threat of insurrection. It is also costly in terms of policing resources. A far more efficient and effective long-run strategy is for the elites to adopt and promulgate an ideological framework that convinces not only themselves but all beneath them of the moral and functional appropriateness of the existing social order. Those below are led to believe that their lesser status in terms of income, wealth, and privilege is as it should and must be, and thus that it is fair.

Over the past century or so, in countries where workers have gained substantial political power, elites have become limited in their ability to use violence against workers. Consequently, the effectiveness of their rule must rely more upon the degree to which their ideology is convincing to the larger population. As noted earlier, their command of this tool was significantly weakened as a consequence of the Great Depression of the 1930s. Just as droughts and other natural catastrophes in the distant past could delegitimize rulers' power, so too did the suffering of the Great Depression throw into question the laissez-faire ideology that had enabled elites to block reforms aimed at improving the welfare of workers and the poor generally. There consequently flourished doctrines such as those of economist John Maynard Keynes which legitimated state action favoring social policies that were beneficial to the greater population. Those policies reduced inequality over the subsequent four decades.

However, the history of the most recent four decades strikingly reveals how, even after a prolonged period between the mid-1930s and the mid-1970s, elites' command over ideology revived to operate as effectively as it always had in the past. It is this recapturing of ideology by elites that has foiled the optimistic expectations unleashed by Kuznets. As the French Enlightenment was wrong in overestimating the power of disinterested reason, so Marx was wrong in underestimating the ability of elites to retain (or regain) command of ideology.

With the exception of periods of extreme crises, inequality has always been adequately legitimated such that most people found it acceptable, even when it meant their own lives were filled with extreme hardship and misery. This was especially true if all other sufferers remained quiescent. As Tolstoy famously noted, there are "no conditions of life to which a man cannot get accustomed, especially if he sees them accepted by everyone around him" (1961, 700).

A Note on Social Science Fragmentation

For practical purposes, Political Economy is inseparably intertwined with many other branches of Social Philosophy. Except on matters of mere detail, there are perhaps no practical questions, even among those which approach nearest to the character of purely economical questions, which admit of being decided on economical premises alone ... [a truth] Adam Smith never loses sight of.
> —John Stuart Mill, *Principles of Political Economy*
> (1909, xxvii–xxviii)

In the social world, there is no division between that which is economic and that which is political, nor are there any divisions among the many domains addressed by social science's various disciplines. Any divisions that separate out aspects of social reality to form discrete intellectual disciplines are artificial and can be justified only insofar as they deepen and enrich understanding of that reality. Ideally, social scientists would remain ever aware that these divisions are fictive, created merely for heuristic purposes.

Regrettably, however, not only does awareness of the artificiality of disciplinary boundaries tend to slip away, but social forces other than the pursuit of truth often influence the way these divisions are drawn. This is precisely what has driven the division between the economic and political that has prevailed within mainstream economics since the late nineteenth century. Ideology has intervened such that the partition obfuscates far more than it clarifies. Underlying the analysis in this book is the contention that not only was the intentional separation of the economic from the political born from the womb of ideology, it also itself serves as political ideology.

By wide agreement, economics is first and foremost concerned with the existential problem of material scarcity. All living beings must succeed in acquiring the material wherewithal to survive and reproduce or they will perish, and their unique complex of genes will vanish with them. Without this basic success at the material level, humans can produce nothing else—no buildings, no roads, no music, no social science, no atomic bombs.

However, humans are a social species. Their struggle to survive and reproduce is not pursued by isolated individuals alone, but by individuals in concert with each other. And this orchestration is what politics means—organizing for the achievement of social or common objectives. Human beings must determine the rules of the game, a complex incentive structure that ideally steers behavior toward the accomplishment of desired social ends. It is for this reason that economics is necessarily political, an understanding not lost on those nineteenth-century pioneers in the discipline who called it political economy.

It is of course true that any specific aspect of reality might be examined in theoretical isolation from the larger whole of which it is a part. Indeed, this is necessary and occurs in all sciences. Accordingly, there is nothing inherently mistaken when economists isolate the market sphere for intense investigation. The problem arises when the discipline investigates too little else, or, when it does venture beyond the market sphere, it finds only the theory developed for understanding markets appropriate.

How This Book Unfolds

After setting forth the dynamics of sexual selection in driving the forces generating inequality, this book commences with a world-historical perspective, then shifts to Europe, and finally to the United States. The underlying reason for the broad initial focus is to capture the origins and dynamics of inequality without getting lost in excessive detail pertaining to all the world's regions. The initial focus is upon the evolution from the high degree of economic and political equality among hunter-gatherers to the extremely unequal societies that emerge with the rise of the state and civilization. The discussion then shifts principally to Europe, the first world area to experience sustainable economic growth with the rise of capitalism that would spread eventually around the globe. The next two chapters, although remaining broad in focus, principally concentrate on the United States to clarify the way the dynamics of inequality have evolved in recent times. The obvious reason is that the United States is not only history's richest and most powerful society, but also the one where the recent surge of inequality has been most extreme. The last two chapters prior to the conclusion focus on two specific issues that are critically linked to inequality: the challenge of ecological devastation, and the way in which attacks on capitalism's two principal social institutions of markets and private property deflect from the root problem of inequality and impede the development of an attractive alternative to exploitative capitalism.

*****

To assist the reader in grasping more fully what this book is about and how it unfolds, a brief glance into each chapter may be helpful. Chapter 2, "Blame It on Sex," addresses the ultimate driver of competition—sexual selection, the root biological force generating inequality. Like other animals, humans must solve the ecological problems necessary for survival and reproduction. Everyone exists only because their ancestors were successful in doing just that. They were the ones who, in competition with others, were the most effective in using the resources available in their environments to survive and reproduce. As humans have culturally evolved, what has enabled humans to stand out in their competition for mates has varied according to prevailing politically determined social institutions. These institutions set the incentive structure, providing guidance as to what kinds of behavior gain high status. High status is sexually attractive. Over history, the sources of status have varied. Individuals have achieved high status by being the best hunters and gatherers, the best warriors, the most cooperative, the most generous, and, since the rise of the state, the wealthiest and most politically powerful.

Chapter 3, "From Aboriginal Equality to Limited and Unstable Inequality," begins by noting that during the first 97 to 98 percent of the approximately 200,000-year history of *Homo sapiens*, when humans existed as hunter-gatherers and early agriculturalists, they lived with little political and economic inequality, due to the ready availability of stone weapons and the ability of the weaker ones to form defensive coalitions blocking bullies' attempts to amass political power. Their egalitarian incentive structure rewarded them for sharing food, child care, and practically everything else. The slow adoption of agriculture beginning about 10,000 years ago created the material condition on which a limited degree of social hierarchy could develop. About 9,000 years ago, chiefs arose by ideologically claiming special access to celestial powers to better assure the welfare of the community. They thereby gained greater access to material goods and mates. However, their legitimacy was fragile, readily upset by poor harvests or other catastrophes that delegitimated their ideology and returned their societies to economic and political equality.

Chapter 4, "The Dynamics of Religious Legitimation," examines legitimation theory and the ways in which religion has justified inequality throughout most of history. The rise of economic and political inequality generated social attitudes and beliefs that justified it, making it seem proper, natural, and consonant with the mandates of celestial powers. Elites' ideology presented this inequality as necessary and fair. Because religion also meets psychological and social needs, until modern times, religion played the major ideological role in legitimating inequality, social institutions, and behavior. Inequality and accompanying class or other group-based hierarchy can be maintained by either physical force or ideological persuasion. Physical force can be expressed as threat of imprisonment, torture, or death. But physical force generates resentment and expensive policing. Less costly, ideological control is generally expressed through the manipulation of social discourse. Thus, it is most effective for elites to embrace self-serving ideological systems that are convincing to themselves and to those below.

Chapter 5, "The State, Civilization, and Extreme Inequality," begins by discussing how agriculture set the preconditions for metallurgy and sophisticated military organization, facilitating the rise of the state and civilization in Eurasia about 5,500 years ago. Whereas earlier stone weapons, available to all, served to preclude the formation of elites and inequality, expensive metal weapons, superior organizational skills, and ideology enabled elites to subjugate all others and extract their surplus, leaving the latter with bare subsistence. This elite formed the state, that social agency with a comparative advantage in violence. Social hierarchy became hereditary and increasingly rigid, and inequality became extreme. Elites gained highly disproportionate sexual access to women, often enclosed in harems. Understandably, rulers would strive to appease potential internal usurpers by protecting their property rights and ability to extract surplus from their subordinates. Until the rise of capitalism and a bourgeoisie in Western Europe, this appeasement of potential usurpers and elites generally precluded robust and sustainable economic dynamism.

Chapter 6, "The Critical Break: The Bourgeoisie Unchained," shifts the book's focus from the whole world to Europe, where sustainable capitalist economic development first takes off. After Rome's disintegration, due to Western Europe's geography and level of military technology, no European state could gain a hegemony on power. The resulting intense and ever-present state competition fueled an arms race and technological innovation while keeping rulers in need of revenue. They found additional resources in the expanding commerce, manufacturing, and capitalist institutions that accompanied an emerging bourgeoisie. Consequently, uniquely in Europe a bourgeoisie sustainably managed to survive its own self-destructiveness and the hostility of a hereditary landed aristocracy. The growing muscle of the bourgeoisie expressed itself in increasingly successful demands for greater freedoms, privileges, status, and political power commensurate to their wealth.

The unique sustainable success of the European bourgeoisie and capitalist institutions constitutes a historical singularity, paving the way for today's riches and freedoms.

Chapter 7, "Theological Revolution and the Idea of Equality," examines how the transition in Europe from a predominantly agricultural society dominated by a landed aristocracy to an emerging commercial one with an expanding bourgeoisie gave birth to a reformulated expression of Christianity whose doctrines could better legitimate the new institutions and practices of commercial society. Whereas Catholicism provided an ideology that justified the landlords' capture of economic surplus, Protestantism legitimated the emerging bourgeoisie's ability to do the same. Protestantism's privileging of work and asceticism afforded social respectability to the bourgeoisie and ideological support for its capturing a share of society's surplus. It gave legitimacy to the harsh social treatment of a rising class of wage workers who had been separated from any ownership, control, or ready access to the means of production. Protestantism served as a transitional religion between a traditional agricultural world dominated by Catholic doctrine and a more modern commercial one dominated by secular thought.

Chapter 8, "The Shift toward Secular Ideology," begins by noting that following the rise of the state, religion served to legitimate societies' institutions, practices, and unequal distributions of income, wealth, and privilege. However, emerging capitalism and its expanding bourgeoisie in Western Europe challenged the Catholic Church's monopoly on truth and meaning, opening space for secular legitimation. The science of political economy increasingly evolved as a principal body of social thought legitimating inequality. This transfer from religion to political economy begins with the mercantilists and is mostly complete by the end of the nineteenth century. The principal inequality-legitimating doctrines of political economy include the utility of poverty, the justice of the invisible hand, the Malthusian population doctrine, the wages-fund doctrine, and the trickle-down thesis. Most of these doctrines take on more of a patina of "natural" science in the late nineteenth century, when the neoclassical revolution in economics attempted to sever economic science from morality and politics and to express itself technically with calculus.

Chapter 9, "Workers Gain Formal Political Power," addresses how industrialization and urbanization during the nineteenth century brought workers physically together where they could organize and petition through strikes and revolts for better wages, shorter working hours, limits to child labor, safer working conditions, education for their children, and most importantly, the franchise. Although inequality continued to increase, conditions for workers and their families began improving. Workers gained formal political power within government. Yet although workers acquired the vote and with it the potential for dramatically rewriting the rules of the game (because they held the overwhelming majority of votes), elites' ideology was effective in convincing them to restrain their political muscle. Nevertheless, elites' monopoly control over the political sphere had been broken. As a result, they could no longer as readily use violence to put down workers' demands. Their retention of disproportionate shares of income, wealth, and privilege would depend more fully upon the persuasiveness of their ideology.

Chapter 10, "From American Exceptionalism to the Great Compression," is the first of two chapters that address inequality in the United States since the end of the nineteenth century. The United States was an anomaly, beginning without clear class distinctions and with substantial egalitarian sentiment. Inexpensive land meant workers who were not enslaved were relatively free. However, as the frontier closed and industrialization took off after the Civil War, inequality soared and workers increasingly lost control over their workplaces. Worker agitation led to improved living standards, but gains were limited by the persuasiveness of the elites' ideology. The hardships of the Great Depression, however, significantly delegitimated the elites' ideology, resulting in substantially decreased inequality between the 1930s and the 1970s. Robust economic growth following World War II and workers' greater political power permitted unparalleled improvements in working-class living standards. By the 1960s, for the first time in history, a generation came of age without fear of dire material privation, generating among many of the young a dramatic change in values and attitudes, privileging social justice and self-realization over traditional material concerns.

Chapter 11, "Simon Kuznets's Happy Prognosis Crushed in an Ideological Coup," surveys the resurgence of laissez-faire ideology and the explosion in inequality over the past 45 years. It begins with economist Simon Kuznets's 1955 suggestion that, while inequality increases during early phases of economic development, in later stages it declines. However, this felicitous hypothesis has been contradicted by inequality's explosion since the 1970s. This explosion was energized by President Ronald Reagan's declaration in 1981 that "government is the problem." Turning popular sentiment against government was an ideological coup, because only government policies can decrease inequality. Government was not reduced in size or in its intervention into the workings of the economy, but policies shifted radically in favor of the wealthy. Taxes were cut for the rich, the economy was significantly deregulated, and welfare measures were trimmed. This chapter unfolds the dynamics that enabled laissez-faire ideology to strengthen and become more entrenched than ever before. It clarifies how this ideology managed to survive the Great Recession following the financial crisis of 2008, during and after which inequality has continued to explode.

Chapter 12, "Inequality, Conspicuous Consumption, and the Growth Trap," addresses the relationship between inequality and devastation of our habitat. Avoiding this fate is arguably the greatest challenge humanity has ever faced, and high inequality greatly impairs successfully addressing this threat. In societies in which fluid social mobility is believed possible, inequality encourages households to seek social certification and status through consumption. Rising inequality strengthens this dynamic. The institutions and behavior generated by the belief that ever-greater consumption brings ever-greater well-being reduce the potential for people to achieve social status and self-respect through more environmentally friendly domains such as democratized work and community. Inequality impedes responses aimed at reducing environmental damage by augmenting the political power of the wealthy, whose interests would be most harmed by measures to protect the environment. The wealthy benefit from pollution because their far greater consumption is made less expensive and their assets yield higher profits. They are also better able to shield themselves from the negative consequences of environmental degradation.

Chapter 13, "The Problem Is Inequality, Not Private Property and Markets," begins by noting that capitalism has always had vociferous critics, none of whom was more insightful than Marx. Marx recognized that although capitalism produced unprecedented wealth, behind its ideological patina of freedom, it was an exploitative social system wherein capitalists extracted workers' surplus. He and other critics also held capitalism's institutions of private property and markets to be corrupting. This has been a mistake. The problem is not these institutions in themselves, but the inequality that coevolved with them, providing elites with the political power to structure private property and markets so as to exploit producers. Marx believed that capitalism's evolution would eventually empower producers to take political power, and that once in power they would and should abandon these institutions. But these institutions are essential for economic dynamism and freedom. Blaming capitalism's institutions of private property and markets for the injustices and social irrationality that accompanied them is a mistake that hinders evolution of an alternative non-exploitative future that makes use of these institutions.

Chapter 14, "What Future for Inequality?" draws this book to its end by first noting that because the struggle over inequality is the principal defining issue of history, it will also be the defining issue of humanity's future. A brief survey is offered of reasons for pessimism and optimism concerning future inequality. On the side of pessimism, since the rise of the state 5,500 years ago, elites have almost always taken all of producers' surpluses, leaving them with bare subsistence. Only partial delegitimation of elites' ideology during the Great Depression led to 40 years of political measures that significantly reduced inequality. The resurgence of laissez-faire ideology and inequality over the past 45 years does not inspire optimism. Yet enormous progress has been made over the course of human history, and especially in the past several centuries. This has been especially impressive in the development of science and human critical faculties which privilege rule by reason. This book goes to press amidst growing awareness of inequality's unfairness and negative consequences for virtually all aspects of human well-being.

*****

Although this book develops historically, it is not intended primarily to be a treatise on history. Instead, history is used to elucidate the origins and dynamics of inequality, to clarify why it exists and how it came to be, and to explore, in its broadest outlines, the manner and extent to which it appears to have unfolded in a deterministic manner. Nevertheless, this book does provide a reinterpretation of human history, one in which the struggle over inequality is the principal defining issue.

Finally, a treatise such as this must come clean on a number of issues lest it be misunderstood as a diatribe on immorality and injustice. As noted earlier, this is not a history of good guys and bad guys. Humans are humans. They generally pursue their biologically and culturally generated self-interests. Whereas their foremost biological need is to ensure that their genes continue into future generations, the incentive structure determining how actors struggle to make this happen is substantially determined culturally, steered by social institutions.

Elites are driven to take as much surplus as possible for three reasons. First, members of elites within societies are in competition with each other for the pinnacle of status—a rivalry ultimately driven by sexual competition, although they do not typically recognize it as such. Second, they need resources to maintain their ability to extract the surplus from producers. And third, throughout most of civilized history, they were in military competition with other enemy elites, and to survive, they needed resources for their armies.

As noted earlier, humans evolved with a strong sense of fairness. This was accompanied by a disposition to judge the moral character of others. Early humans evolved within material and cultural environments that created similar incentive structures. Their social institutions appeared natural as opposed to human-created and thus, should something go wrong socially, the failure was not traced to social institutions. Instead, humans evolved to place blame with individuals.[14] In small bands, there was an evolutionary advantage in being able to evaluate trustworthiness. Life or death depended upon knowing whom to trust. The challenge of trust is made so difficult by the fact that humans evolved sophisticated means for deception. Behavioral ecologist Bobbi Low reports that "scholars are leaning more today toward the view that communication may be best understood if we view it as evolving to manipulate and deceive, rather than to transmit information" (2001, 177).

Accordingly, humans were predisposed to assess character. This evolved into the acute sense of justice and sensitivity to unfair treatment which continues to guide many of our attitudes and much of our behavior, even in a highly complex institutional world. The consequence is that when social institutions fail, such as with a financial crisis, people are strongly inclined to blame it on greedy and corrupt actors (bankers, corporate leaders, politicians) rather than the institutional structure—the politically determined rules of the game—that set the incentives for the behavior that is found at fault. Attention is focused on finding people morally deficient rather than seeking needed changes to social institutions. It is an understandable mistake. This book seeks to aid in fostering the insight necessary to overcome this reflex and move us forward toward the construction of appropriate institutions for a more humane future.

---

[14] Humans, due to their innate sense of fairness, are always keenly aware of the appropriateness of the behavior of others. Brain scans suggest the reason is that humans are innately hardwired for a sense of fairness or justice, and that this explains, for instance, why there is intense pleasure in imagining or actually taking revenge (Roach 2004).

2

Blame It on Sex

Power is the ultimate aphrodisiac.
— Henry Kissinger, quoted in Bobbi S. Low
(Why Sex Matters 2001, 57)

I've looked on a lot of women with lust. I've committed adultery in my heart many times.
— Jimmy Carter, quoted in *Playboy* (1976)

. . . courtship is the premier example of social behavior.
— Geoffrey Miller, *The Mating Mind* (2001, 13)

If you gain fame, power, or wealth, you won't have any trouble finding lovers, but they will be people who love fame, power, or wealth.
— Philip Slater, *Wealth Addiction* (1980, 73)

Whatever the proximate economic and social factors generating inequality, it is politics that determines its degree. Politics can in principle overrule or neutralize any other forces that are at work generating inequality. But because, since the rise of states, elites have disproportionately controlled politics, politics has overwhelmingly been the source of inequality. It is through politics that the social rules of the game are established and maintained, backed by physical force and legitimated by ideology.

It is not difficult to understand why humans seek political power. It provides considerable social advantages, notably status, typically the very highest status. But, more broadly, why do humans strive to outdo others in wealth, privilege, fame, or other markers of high status, all of which are useful for acquiring and retaining political power? The answer appears easy— possessing any of these status markers promises to make life more secure, comfortable, and interesting. Yet, there is a deeper reason lying within our biology. Our evolution has been driven by sexual competition, where success depends substantially upon social status. Since the rise of states and civilization, those with the greatest wealth and political power have enjoyed the highest status and, consequently, the greatest reproductive potential.

At some level, politicians may recognize this link between sex and politics. Psychologist John Pryor claims that for politicians, "thinking about power makes them think about sex, and thinking about sex makes them think about power" (1987, 271). However, aside from evolutionary biologists and possibly some politicians, the causal link between sex and political power is seldom recognized. Humans do not generally recognize the extent to which their behavior is driven by sexual competition because the psychological mechanisms that have evolved to guide much of our behavior chiefly operate beneath our conscious thinking. Further, because sexual competition underlies all competition, social attitudes and practices have culturally evolved to mask it.

Most social scientists and historians are also generally unaware of the deepest forces beneath human motivations. However, it is imperative that social sciences and history ground their analyses in the biological foundations set forth by Charles Darwin and subsequent evolutionary biologists. The reason, as behavioral economist Robert Frank correctly notes, is that "the Darwinian framework is the only scientific framework available for trying to understand why humans and other animals are motivated to behave as they do" (2011, 24).

In their magisterial study of inequality in early human societies, anthropologists Kent Flannery and Joyce Marcus ask whether the widespread existence of unequal societies is due to something innate in our species or to the limitations and biases of human logic (2012, 561). Although they remain agnostic as to the answer, this book does not. It argues for the former, the claim that the fundamental source of inequality is innate, located in our biology. This book rejects historian Michael Mann's contention that "there are no propositions that are valid across all societies other than utter banalities" (2012, 1:ix).

The ultimate driver of inequality is located in an evolved dynamic within our genetic makeup, in what Darwin called sexual selection. Sexual competition has always resulted in unequal access to mates, but, prior to the adoption of agriculture, it only rarely resulted in material or political inequality. About 9,000 years ago, with the development of agriculture and denser population settlements, sexual competition at times gave rise to relatively mild social inequality in chiefdoms. This means that if our kind—*Homo sapiens*—has been on earth for about 200,000 years, as is generally believed,[1] sexual competition did not result in any significant wealth and political inequality until its last 5 percent of existence. Extreme economic and political inequality came later, with the rise of the state and civilization about 5,500 years ago, during the last 2 to 3 percent of the human story.

Social popularity is a form of status, and it counts. Young children and, especially, teenagers sense this intensely, even if they do not grasp what deeply motivates it. The underlying driver is that individuals who receive greater positive social recognition are more sexually attractive and thus more likely to pass their genes into future generations. As behavioral ecologist Bobbi Low puts it, no matter the environmental context, among humans as "in most species there is a simple bottom line: reliably, higher-status males get more copulations and/or more off-spring than other males" (2001, 58). Among humans, positive social recognition can be acquired in many ways, from killing the most enemies and proving it by bringing back their heads, scalps, or genitalia, to writing the most beautiful poetry, painting the most beautiful pictures, winning the Tour de France, being the most generous, speaking with the greatest eloquence, being most fun to be around or, of course, becoming rich or winning elections. The bottom line is that human society and its history cannot be adequately understood without understanding the central motivating role located in the dynamics of sexual selection.

But if the social sciences and history must be grounded in evolutionary biology, and especially in the dynamics of sexual selection, to be theoretically adequate, as this book claims, why 150 years after Darwin's work has this not been the case? The reason is the dominance of behavioralism within social thought for most of the twentieth century. Behavioralism claimed that all behavior is socially conditioned, as opposed to driven, even in part, by instincts. Likely added to the failure to embrace sexual selection are the societal taboos and general uneasiness with sex. Cognitive scientist Pinker also notes that, for many on the left, appealing to biology to clarify social behavior has long been feared, and often vehemently attacked. For some, such as paleontologist Stephen Jay Gould and geneticist Richard Lewontin, it serves to justify the status quo by depicting racism, sexism, and eugenics as natural

---

[1] Recent findings in hominid paleontology suggest an earlier appearance, dating the first *Homo sapiens* to perhaps 300,000 years ago (Lawton 2020). This book retains the generally accepted dating of 200,000 years, awaiting further confirmation of the significant extension.

(Pinker 2002, 109). But fear that science might be misused as ideology must not smother the open search for truth.

Ironically, around the turn of the twentieth century, "Darwinian ideas," as historian Kimberly Hamlin points out,

> were invoked for radical as well as conservative political agendas. *The Descent of Man* and sexual selection theory, in particular, appealed to left-leaning reformers, including [Charlotte Perkins] Gilman and [Edward] Bellamy, because female choice promised to not only elevate the status of women but re-generate all of society—present and future—by refocusing attention on natural, as opposed to class-based, indicators of health and fitness and by restoring women's natural reproductive autonomy. (2014, 173)

Darwin's Dynamic of Sexual Selection

. . . only two topics can be of the least interest to a serious and studious mind: sex and the dead.

—W. B. Yeats, quoted in C. C. Barfoot,
(Barfoot 1995, 225)

For Darwin, species have evolved by natural selection such that their members behave to maximize their reproductive success—the "central theorem" of modern evolutionary biology (Lopreato 1984). The gene pool of a species consists of those genes that enabled their forebears to mate successfully. All sexually reproducing animals compete for sex, and humans are not excepted, even in the most equal society in other terms.

Recognition of the competition that occurs in sexual selection enabled Darwin to solve an enigma in his theory of natural selection, which views traits as selectively retained when they enhance chances of survival. The challenge was to explain the existence of evidently unfit traits such as the ornate and heavy male peacock's feathers, or the enormous racks of antlers found on stags. Such traits are expensive to grow and maintain. They make their owners less efficient in acquiring nourishment and avoiding predators. The huge tail on the peacock makes it difficult to pass through dense brush, as well as to take and stay in flight. The antlers of the stag (which are discarded and regrown each year) require huge investments in calories and minerals, and slow down flight.

The answer was a second mode of selection which Darwin called sexual selection. Sexual selection ". . . depends, not on a struggle for existence, but on a struggle between the males for possession of the females; the result is not death to the unsuccessful competitor, but few or no offspring" (1859, 88).[2] Thus, ". . . when the males and females of any animal have the same general habits . . . but differ in structure, colour, or ornament, such differences have been mainly caused by sexual selection" (1859, 89). These traits signal females as to which males to choose. They are advertisements of the male's fitness and thus signs of carrying healthy genes. Darwin elaborated that "the sexual struggle is of two kinds; in the one it is between the individuals of the same sex, generally the male sex, in order to drive away or kill their rivals, the females remaining passive; whilst in the other, the struggle is likewise between the individuals of the same sex, in order to excite or charm those of the opposite sex, generally the females, which no longer remain passive, but select the more agreeable partners" (1871, 566).

Each member of each gender is in competition with all others of the same gender in a zero-sum game as to whose genes will make it into future generations; that is, individuals of both genders must possess adequately attractive traits if their genes are to survive. For most animals, all these traits are genetically inherited, and they survive because they are viewed by sexual partners as indicating a good chance that their offspring will thrive. The peacock's feathers and the stag's antlers are selected in evolution because their carriers are preferred by females. They reveal to females that they must indeed be fit if they survive with such handicaps. Only the best nourished and healthiest peacocks can manage the feat of growing and carrying around such costly ornamentation. Only a very powerful stag could survive with such weighty and otherwise handicapping antlers—the "handicap principle" (Zahavi 1975; Zahavi and Zahavi 1999). But whereas these expensive tail feathers and antlers handicap their carriers' chances of physical survival, they enhance the potential for their genes to survive into the future by being attractive to females, by serving as "badges of status," by affecting "how much

---

[2] Darwin unfolded his theory of natural selection and took note of sexual selection in *On the Origin of Species by Means of Natural Selection*, published in 1859. He then greatly elaborated his concept of sexual selection in 1871, in *The Descent of Man, and Selection in Relation to Sex*. Darwin's achievement was extraordinary. Evolutionary biologists Adam Jones and Nicholas Ratterman write that "Darwin was correct about almost every topic related to sexual selection that he discussed" (2009, 1007).

recognition—prestige—others accord an individual" (Zahavi and Zahavi 1999, 55).[3]

Darwin's dynamics of natural selection and sexual selection can work against each other. For instance, a male might have a trait that is ideal for survival (favored by natural selection) but unappealing to females (disfavored by sexual selection), and he might therefore be unable to pass his unique set of genes into the future. Or the opposite might prevail: a male might have a trait that is exceptionally attractive to females, but which condemns him to death before he is able to mate. Accordingly, evolution will favor a balance or equilibrium that coevolves between these opposing forces (Prum 2017, 41–42).

Sexual competition can result in a wasteful arms race. Handicapping traits selected because of their sexual advantage may become especially harmful to all male members of the species since they become more vulnerable to predators and require more energy to maintain the handicaps.

It is, of course, possible that, rather than acting as a handicap, a sexually selected trait might turn out to benefit the survival of its carrier. As evolutionary psychologist Geoffrey Miller expresses this possibility, "Sexual selection works . . . as evolution's venture capitalist. It can favor innovations just because they look sexy, long before they show any profitability in the struggle for survival. . . . [Nevertheless] reproductive success is evolution's bottom line" (2001, 168, 155).

Within Darwin's theory of sexual selection, females are far from passive or powerless:

> The female could in most cases escape, if wooed by a male that did not please or excite her; and when pursued, as incessantly occurs, by several males, she would often have the opportunity, whilst they were fighting together, of escaping with, or at least temporarily pairing with, some one male. (Darwin 1871, 269)

---

[3] Darwin understood that sexual selection can be extremely complex, depending as it does "on the ardour of love, courage, and the rivalry of the mates, as well as on the powers of perception, the taste, and will of the female" (Darwin 1871, 296). Or, as ornithologist and evolutionary biologist Richard O. Prum puts it, ". . . the concept of subjective experience is absolutely critical to understanding evolution. . . . Sexual ornaments are aesthetic traits that have evolved as a result of mate choices based on subjective evaluations" (2017, 7, 9). The result of this complexity, as theoretical evolutionists Bram Kuijper, Ido Pen, and Franz J. Weissing have put it, is that "no single model has been able to capture all relevant aspects of sexual selection in a fully satisfactory way" (2012, 288).

The fact that females prefer males with certain characteristics will lead to the increasing prevalence of male genes with these characteristics in subsequent generations. In this manner, females direct the path of evolution. It was this empowerment of the female that drew the attention of feminists and progressives to Darwin's theory of sexual selection at the end of the nineteenth century. Hamlin writes, "The woman who did the most to popularize the feminist potential of Darwinian sexual selection was [an Edward] Bellamy disciple who went on to become the most influential American feminist thinker of the early twentieth century: Charlotte Perkins Gilman" (2014, 164). Prum also addresses the reason for feminists' attraction to Darwin:

> Unlike natural selection, which emerges from external forces in nature, such as competition, predation, climate, and geography acting on the organism, sexual selection is a potentially independent, self-directed process in which the organisms themselves (mostly female) were in charge. Darwin described females as having a "taste for the beautiful" and an "aesthetic faculty." (2017, 23)

Natural selection is driven by only one thing—reproductive success. Whereas natural selection occurs as a species undergoes mutations enabling a better fit to the opportunities and challenges of its environment, sexual selection occurs as a result of the way members of the species relate to one another. Those individuals who are unsuccessful in mating with a member of the opposite sex will have a unique complex of genes—their own—that will become extinct. As a consequence, Miller observes,

> . . . males of most species evolve to act as if copulation is the whole point of life. For male genes, copulation is the gateway to immortality. This is why males risk their lives for copulation opportunities—and why a male praying mantis continues copulating even after a female has eaten his head. (2001, 87)

The Human Cultural Dimension

> . . . *everything we do or have ever done—from demographics to economics to politics to religion—might be understood, more or less, as reproductive competition.*
> —Laura Betzig, "Roman Monogamy" (1992, 343)

Physical fitness indicators among humans that are important in mate selection include well-proportioned bodies, blemish-free skin, symmetrical faces, and, among males especially, size and musculature. Size and muscle generally suggest greater potential for successful hunting and effective protection. Physical characteristics of women that are attractive to men because they signal fertility potential include an ideal waist-hip ratio of 7 to 10: "A relatively narrow waist means 'I'm female, I'm young, and I'm not pregnant'" (Low 2001, 80). At times, corsets and bustles were used by women to attain or accentuate these measurements. These measurements are judged to be beautiful. Philosopher of art Denis Dutton points out that this waist-hip ratio "occurs in sexy women in art from Botticelli's *Birth of Venus* to Modigliani nudes" (2010, 142). These proportions were especially exaggerated in depictions of Hindu goddesses to imply supernatural sexuality and fertility. It is also noteworthy that of the more than 5,000 species of mammals, only human females have permanent and ample breast tissue, suggesting to mates that they can provide sustenance for their progeny (Prum 2017, 256).

Men have few morphological ornaments or physical "handicaps" like the peacock's tail or the stag's antlers because, during their evolution, females were more focused on social or cultural rather than physical characteristics. Culture plays a far more important role for humans than for other animals. Among humans, culture-guided behavior can outweigh the importance of physical size and other physical characteristics in predicting reproductive success.

Being a highly successful hunter or gatherer would signal a capacity to provide sustenance for offspring and thus would be found attractive. But, since at least the cultural explosion 30,000 to 60,000 years ago (Mithen 1999), being a gifted storyteller, engaging speaker, talented visual artist, gracious dancer, or fine singer[4] would have also been highly appreciated. Miller claims that the

> most distinctive aspects of our minds [evolved due to sexual selection, as a] magnificent sexual ornament. . . . Before language evolved, our ancestors could not easily perceive one another's thoughts, but once language had

[4] In modern times, evidence of the sexual attractiveness of popular musicians is offered by the near female hysteria at performances by Franz Liszt, Frank Sinatra, or later rock stars, some followed about by "groupies." Lemmy Kilmister, heavy metal rock star and lead singer for Motorhead, confessed: "I decided to pick up the guitar partly for the music, but girls were at least sixty per cent of the reason I wanted to play. . . . I discovered what an incredible . . . magnet guitars were . . ." (cited in Moyer 2015, 4).

arrived, thought itself became subject to sexual selection . . . [and] nobody has been able to suggest any plausible survival payoffs for most of the things that human minds are uniquely good at, such as humor, story-telling, gossip, art, music, self-consciousness, ornate language, imaginative ideologies, religion, and morality. (2001, 10, 18)[5]

It has been persuasively argued that what we define as art—as the aesthetically beautiful—evolved as a consequence of the dynamics of sexual selection (Miller 2001; Dutton 2010; Prum 2017). Cognitive psychologist Steven Pinker writes that "an eye for beauty . . . locks onto faces that show signs of health and fertility—just as one would predict if it had evolved to help the beholder find the fittest mate" (2002, 53). Sigmund Freud also linked aesthetics and sex: "The enjoyment of beauty produces a particular, mildly intoxicating kind of sensation. . . . Its derivation from the realms of sexual sensation is all that seems certain; the love of beauty is a perfect example of a feeling with an inhibited aim. Beauty and attraction are first of all the attributes of a sexual object" (1930, 16). Neurologist Amy Wax writes: "Men produced art because women liked it and found it sexually appealing. Women liked it because artistic expression is the quintessential form of wasteful display. . . . The pursuit of beauty requires both talent and the development of talent through sustained effort, which are costly and not easily faked" (2004, 545, 546).

Barring forced sex (rape),[6] individuals must sufficiently please at least one fertile member of the opposite sex if their genes are to survive into the future. They might do so with physical characteristics such as handsome faces or strong and well-proportioned bodies. Thus, there would be a tendency for these characteristics to be selected and survive into future generations.

---

[5] Miller's statement may underestimate the potential benefits of these mental processes and their products to individuals' and the group's survival. However, his reflections on listening and speaking appear to fully fit his argument: "Speaking costs the speaker time and energy, and brings information benefits to the listener, so it looks altruistic . . . [therefore] we should be a species of extremely good listeners and very reluctant talkers." But not only does this expectation run counter to evidence, it raises the question, can speaking properly be viewed as altruistic? Instead, suppose the capacity for language was selected because it provided a reproductive advantage. Rather than being altruistic, it would be the result of sexual competition: "Language puts minds on public display, where sexual choice could see them clearly for the first time in evolutionary history." Miller also notes that "human vocabulary sizes seem to have rocketed out of control. The average human English-speaker knows 60,000 words. . . . If language evolved in part through sexual choice as an ornament or indicator, it should be costly, excessive, luxuriant beyond the demands of pragmatic communication," thus not unlike the peacock's elaborate tail or the stag's antlers (2001, 346, 350, 353, 357).

[6] Wax reports that "the leading proponents of the 'rape is adaptive' view, regard rape as a last-ditch option, a desperate ploy for the sexually dispossessed" (2004, 585). Pinker agrees: "rapists tend to be losers and nobodies [and] coerced copulation is widespread among species in the animal kingdom, suggesting that it is not selected against and may sometimes be selected for. It is found in

But, because social behavior can be equally if not more important, those who act in a manner sufficiently attractive to the opposite sex will successfully mate, and the genes that carry these behavioral traits will be found in their offspring. This behavior becomes instinct-driven, the consequence of gene-culture coevolution (also called "dual inheritance theory"), which takes place when cultural changes make certain genetic adaptations sexually attractive or fitness-enhancing. The "desire and the object of desire coevolve with each other" (Prum 2017, 8).

Signaling for sexual selection can become highly complex, bizarre, and cruel. In China, for instance, wealthy families bound the feet of their daughters, rendering them crippled and unable to work or do much else beyond bearing children and being elegant. Males were attracted to them because, as wives, they signaled that their husbands were so wealthy they could afford a spouse incapable of being economically useful—a particularly harsh instance of conspicuous consumption noted by political economist Thorstein Veblen (1899). Being able to signal the wealth to afford such a wife would heighten the male's social standing and make him more attractive to potential additional mates. In Qing China (1644–1911), noblemen were polygynous and fathered more children. Similarly, a woman's paler skin in agricultural societies, where work was predominantly outdoors, suggested she did not need to work and was therefore of elite status. In industrial society, by contrast, where work moved predominantly indoors, a tan indicated that one has had the leisure to lie beneath the sun on a beach, or more impressively, on a yacht.

Sexual competition ". . . creates a psychological arms race in which the signaling capacity of one sex is pitted against the critical, discriminating powers of the other. That is why we have elevator shoes and push-up bras" (Dutton 2010, 152). Wax describes this wasteful behavior as follows:

> In general, the signals most likely to guarantee "truth in advertising" and thus to be found desirable are those that call upon extraordinary abilities, demand great effort, and are ostentatiously wasteful. Since only the most healthy and capable individuals can afford to make investments with little survival value, these displays will be difficult for low-fitness individuals to mimic without overly compromising their own survival chances. It follows that it will be in women's evolutionary interest to develop a refined

many species of insects, birds, and mammals, including our relatives the orangutans, gorillas, and chimpanzees. Rape is found in all human societies" (2002, 362, 367).

appreciation for the exercise of rare, expensive, and useless skills with no immediate fitness payoffs and to find such displays "sexy." And it will be in men's interest doggedly to cultivate those skills and display them at every opportunity. (2004, 544)

Dutton writes:

One of the best ways for the boy to prove he has resources is to give the girl something that is both expensive and useless. . . . If the male is serious, he will take the female to a lavish, overpriced restaurant serving mere smidgens of food. He will order champagne and make sure she notices his large tip. (2010, 153–54)

Or, as Miller puts it, "Romantic gifts are those that are most useless to the women and most expensive to the man" (Miller 2001, 329).[7]

The domain of Darwinian evolution has often been depicted as a cold, violent world of raw competition—*red in tooth and claw*. However, as political scientists John Alford and John Hibbing point out, ". . . evolution is agnostic about the methods (e.g., competition or cooperation) by which overall survival advantages are achieved" (2004, 709). Human sexual competitors are successful when their behavior gains them social status, making them attractive to mates. Such behavior might range from the bloody and murderous to the cooperative and generous. It depends upon what behavior a society's institutions favor for acquiring status. During the long evolution of the human species as foragers, both prowess and generosity were favored. Through gene-culture coevolution, behavior traits were selected. Happily, included within general welfare-enhancing social institutions were proclivities to share food, child care, defense, and practically everything else. In cooperativeness, humans stand out from other primates.

Paradoxically, cooperation can also be a form of competition. So too can generosity. Those who contribute less than others to collective welfare can be seen as less worthy, to be left out of cooperative exchanges, and therefore less attractive as sexual partners. By contrast, the contributions of the generous could be expected to be appreciated and reciprocated. The children of

[7] Veblen was right in viewing conspicuous consumption as wasteful, but in spite of his attempts to make economics a Darwinian evolutionary science, he failed to appropriate Darwin's theory of sexual selection and thus failed to understand the ultimate function of such wasteful expenditure (Wisman 2019).

those most appreciated would be most likely to receive the attention and care of others. For humans, being approved by others is of central importance. As Wax puts it, "If . . . self-sacrificial moral acts operate as fitness-indicating forms of sexual display—to put it bluntly, if women come to like generous men and want to sleep with them—then that is all that is required for these tendencies to take root and flourish in the human repertoire" (2004, 562). Dutton reports:

> On the serious question of choosing a mate, both men and women on average place *kindness* first on their respective lists, with both naming *intelligence* as number two. Men then will choose *physical attractiveness* . . . while women will tend to turn their priorities toward the man's *wealth or resources*. Other criteria on the list for both sexes are *exciting personality*, *adaptability*, *generosity*, *dependability*, *industriousness*, *creativity*, and a *sense of humor*. (2010, 144–45)

Sex, Violence, and War

Roman women loved a gladiator. At Pompeii they were commemorated as "heartthrobs" and "netters of young girls by night."
—Laura Betzig, "Roman Monogamy" (1992, 320)

A glance at the history of our species reveals that warfare was ever-present until modern times. But why would human societies war against each other? Clearly, if another group can be defeated, then their resources might become available to the victor. But before the advent of agriculture about 10,000 years ago, there was precious little of material value to take from other groups, excepting hunting and gathering territory, and for most of human evolution that was generally in abundant supply. Thus, the best strategy for hunter-gatherers would be to bluff belligerence, and should that fail, move on to new foraging territory rather than risk life and limb in contending with other groups. Or, as economists put it, from a material benefit-cost perspective, war would not be rational; flight trumps fight.

However, it appears that what might have been irrational from a purely material standpoint was not irrational in terms of reproduction. As Low points out, "Throughout evolutionary history, men have been able to gain reproductively by risky warfare; heroes gain status and access to women"

(2001, 217). In fact, this is true of our closest primate relative, chimpanzees, whose DNA differs from humans by only 1.1 percent (Maryanski 1994, 385). About 30 percent of all males among both human foragers and chimpanzees are estimated to have died in warfare (Keeley 1997, 174).

Among foragers, although defeating an enemy group might not yield much in the way of material resources, it did permit the theft of their women. Frequently, capturing women was a principal aim of war. Evolutionary psychologist David Buss provides a vivid report:

> Among the Yanomamö [a contemporary foraging-horticultural people in the Amazon rainforest], there are two key motives that spur men to declare war on another tribe—a desire to capture the wives of other men or a desire to recapture wives that were lost in previous raids.... It seemed silly to them to risk one's life for anything other than capturing women. (1994, 219–20)

Evolutionary psychologists David C. Geary, Jacob Vigil, and Jennifer Byrd-Craven note that among the Yanomamö, "... men who are skilled at political negotiations or are fierce warriors enjoy a higher social status than do other men.... These high-status men have more wives than other men, [and] receive food tributes from other families in their village" (2004, 30). Head-hunting and returning with scalps and genitalia demonstrated success in war.

The sexual spoils of war find expression in ancient texts. In the Old Testament, for instance, the following story is related in Numbers 31:9–35. After a victory against the Midianites where all the adult males were killed, as the Lord had commanded of Moses: "... the children of Israel took *all* the women of Midian captives, and their little ones, and took the spoil of all their cattle, and all their flocks, and all their goods." Moses instructed his troops as follows: "Now therefore kill every male among the little ones, and kill every woman that hath known man by lying with him.... But all the women children that have not known a man by lying with him, keep alive for yourselves." The total was "... thirty and two thousand persons in all, of women that had not known man by lying with him." Similarly, in Deuteronomy 20, God instructs the Israelites concerning military victory, "the women and the little ones, the livestock, and everything else in the city, all its spoil, you shall take as plunder for yourselves. And you shall enjoy the spoil of your enemies, which the LORD your God has given you."

In *The Rape of Troy*, Jonathan Gottschall characterizes archaic raids as follows: "... fast ships with shallow drafts are rowed onto beaches and seaside communities are sacked before neighbors can lend defensive support. The men are usually killed, livestock and other portable wealth are plundered, and women are carried off to live among the victors and perform sexual and menial labors" (2008, 1). In the *Iliad*, Achilles avows: "I have spent many sleepless nights and gone through bloody days in combat, fighting with heroes for the sake of their wives" (Homer 1847, 149).

Inequality and Polygyny

History is just one fucking thing after another.
—Alan Bennett, quoted by John Crace in
The Guardian (2006)

Ethnological studies of premodern cultures have found that over 80 percent allowed polygynous marriages, with about 10 to 15 percent of men having multiple wives (Schmitt 2005, 262; Geary, Vigil, and Byrd-Craven 2004, 38).[8] This estimate of relatively mild polygyny among humans is supported by the fact that men are only about 10 percent taller and 20 percent heavier than women. Gender size differences (dimorphism) among significantly more polygynous primates, by contrast, is over 50 percent (Schmitt 2005, 267). Mild polygyny is also corroborated by the fact that human males have small testes relative to their body size. Among animal species, testes are larger the greater the degree of dimorphism, and their size relative to body weight increases with polygyny (Betzig 1993, 56).

Mild polygyny characterized *Homo sapiens* when they lived in highly egalitarian hunter-gatherer societies, that is, during 95 percent of the species' 200,000 years of existence. In all societies that suffered a shortage of males, such as occurred after wars, polygamy could be expected to exist. More substantial polygyny began to appear about 9,000 years ago in the wake of the adoption of agriculture and the rise of ideologies legitimating inequality. It burgeoned, as did inequality, about 5,500 years ago with the rise of the state, when in Eurasia metal weapons, military organization, and ideology enabled the more powerful to subjugate the weaker. Politically dominant and

---

[8] The anthropological record shows that the 15 percent or so of societies that were monogamous were those with little difference among males in wealth or status (Henrich, Boyd, and Richerson 2012, 659).

wealthier males expropriated resources from the weaker and poorer to maintain large numbers of women, often in harems.

Within these highly inegalitarian societies, polygyny made women better off materially and most men worse off reproductively. Where there was extreme inequality among men, a woman's reproductive chances were generally greater as an additional wife of a wealthy or otherwise high-status male than as the wife of a poor male. This could be expected to influence patterns of inheritance. In polygynous societies, inheritance is strongly male biased since males' reproductive potential varies more than that of females, and male success is more dependent on possession of wealth. Health can also make a difference. Being an additional wife of a healthy rich man would have been reproductively superior to being the only wife of a disease-ridden poor man. However, where resource inequality among men is small, women choose to marry monogamously (Kanazawa and Still 1999).

Although exceedingly rare, polyandry has also existed. It occurred in less than one percent of premodern societies, mostly where inherited agricultural land could not be divided into economically viable plots to raise a family. Given these land-scarce conditions, brothers combined their inherited plots and jointly married a single woman to raise their offspring (Schmitt 2005, 263).

While in highly inegalitarian societies women might be reproductively better off as one of the wives of a wealthy man, the costs to women and their children in polygynous households or harems appear substantial. Evolutionary psychologists Joseph Henrich, Robert Boyd, and Peter J. Richerson find

> Co-wife conflict is ubiquitous in polygynous households. . . . A review of ethnographic data . . . reveals no case where co-wife relations could be described as harmonious. . . . Children from polygamous families experience higher incidences of marital conflict, household violence and family disruptions than do children of monogamous families. (2012, 665)

Given that polygyny reduces the supply of women available to non-elite males, it is hardly surprising that it would increase the latter's tendencies toward violence. It could be expected to increase the willingness of poorer men to participate in wars that could result in the theft of the enemies' women, and likewise to increase the incidence of murder and rape within societies (Kanazawa 2009, 27, 28). As psychologists Margo Wilson and Martin Daly write, ". . . any creature that is recognizably on track toward complete reproductive failure must somehow expend effort, often at the risk of death, to try to improve its present life trajectory" (1988, 163).

Accordingly, more polygynous societies are found to experience greater domestic civil disorder and civil wars, as well as the more authoritarian governments necessary to repress them. Islam is the only major contemporary religion that sanctions polygyny, and, accordingly, the practice is far more prevalent in Islamic nations. They have been found more likely to experience civil wars than Christian or Hindu nations (Kanazawa 2009, 31). Their governments also tend to be more authoritarian. The Middle East has the highest levels of inequality in the world (Piketty 2020, 405).[9] In polygynous societies, females are generally married at younger ages. They are also typically married to much older males who attempt to ensure their paternity by taking extreme measures to limit their wives' freedom, measures that are enforced by religious codes and authoritarian governments. Might polygyny, by making available females scarcer, help explain why so many Islamic jihadists become willing martyrs, and why some of their recruiters promise them 72 virgins in the afterlife?[10]

Shortage of females for other reasons can, of course, also result in greater violence. For instance, because of labor shortages, the American colonies imported indentured, predominantly male workers. Facing a severe shortage of women, once they had worked off their servitude the males were usually unable to find wives. They became an unruly, discontented, and rebellious bunch (Bailyn 2013).

Demographer Christophe Guilmoto foresees a "bachelor bomb" of over 37 million surplus men in India as a result of parental gender preference for males. Guilmoto anticipates that the imbalance will threaten social stability for decades to come as frustrated men grow more violent and gravitate toward right-wing nationalist organizations (Gowen 2018). Much the same fate might be in store for China as a consequence of its one-child policy and the accompanying parental preference for male offspring. Between 1988 and

---

[9] To put this in perspective, "the ratio of the top decile's share of income to that of the bottom 50 percent is roughly eight in Europe, nineteen in the United States, and thirty-five in South Africa and the Middle East" (Piketty 2020, 657).

[10] This promise is made in the *Hadith*, sacred sayings that are purported to have been pronounced by the prophet Muhammad. Hadith number 2,562 in the collection known as the *Sunan al-Tirmidhi* reads, "The least [reward] for the people of Heaven is 80,000 servants and 72 wives, over which stands a dome of pearls, aquamarine and ruby."

2004, crime rates nearly doubled in China as the male to female ratio rose markedly from 1.053 to 1.095 (Henrich, Boyd, and Richerson 2012, 662).

Differing Gender Reproductive Strategies

Society influences what we care about, but evolution has produced the fact that we care.
—Richard Wrangham, *The Goodness Paradox* (2019, 204–5)

Striving for reproductive success is the fundamental force ultimately driving behavior for both sexes. However, men and women maximize their chances of victory in different manners. They can, as Low puts it, "differ as much as peacocks and peahens in how they seek resources, what kinds of resources they seek, and how they use those resources. . . . Across societies, around the world, men's and women's days are spent differently" (2001, 113, 114). Wax writes that

> The prediction [of evolutionary psychology] is that women, as compared to men, will on average be more risk averse, less violent, less status-conscious, more nurturing, more oriented to relationships, less interested in mechanism and abstraction, and more attached to their children. Women will value monogamy and seek mates with status and resources. Men, in contrast, will have a greater taste for sexual variety, will value youth and beauty in women, will strive competitively to attain status and command resources, and will seek to control sexual access to their mates. (2004, 572)

Males can reproductively benefit from mating with many females since doing so increases the probability of their genes surviving into the future. They can consequently be expected to be more promiscuous. Females, by contrast, have a limited number of eggs and long gestation periods between births, providing little benefit from mating with multiple partners.[11] They can therefore be expected to be more discerning in their search for mates who are most likely to produce high-quality offspring. Whereas males compete more for quantity of sexual partners, females do so more for quality.

---

[11] Prostitution for which women receive resources to survive and care for offspring is an exception.

Internet hackers revealed 30 million American male, but only 5 million female, users of the Ashley Madison hookup site, which was crafted to enable discrete infidelity (Dewey 2015, 4). The 2010 census reported 138,053,563 adult males in the United States, suggesting that about 20 percent of American adult males pursued sex by subscribing just to this one site. The Ashley Madison website featured the slogan: "Life is short. Have an affair." In accord with the supposed relationship between political power and sex, Ashley Madison proclaimed Washington, D.C., as the cheating capitol of America. Chief executive Noel Biderman added, "The more successful you are, the more prone to cheating" (Andrews and Heil 2015, C2).

Psychologists Roy Baumeister and Kathleen Vohs report that studies show that:

> On every measure, men were found to display greater sexual motivation than women. Specifically, men think about sex more often, have more frequent fantasies, are more frequently aroused, desire sex more often (both early and late in relationships and outside of relationships), desire a higher number of sex partners, masturbate more frequently, are less willing to forgo sex and are less successful at celibacy (even when celibacy is supported by personal religious commitments), enjoy a greater variety of sexual practices, take more risks and expend more resources to obtain sex, initiate more goal directed behavior to get sex, refuse sex less often, commence sexual activity sooner after puberty, have more permissive and positive attitudes toward most sexual behaviors, are less prone to report a lack of sexual desire, and rate their sex drives as stronger than women. No findings indicated that women had a stronger sex drive than men on any measure. (2004, 342)

As Darwin noted, in the course of evolution, discerning female choice led to exaggerated male traits. These traits are typically physical among most species. But among humans the result of female choice predominantly tends to appear in forms of cultural achievement, as seen in the extremely intense competition to be viewed as the best, whether in accumulating resources, attaining political power, or excelling in sports, intellectual accomplishments, entertainment, or the arts.

Since the rise of states, men have competed principally by accumulating resources and political power. In a survey of 10,000 women in 37 different world cultures, Buss found that women put more value on a partner's financial prospects than did men (2011, 112). Geary, Vigil, and Byrd-Craven report, "Across age, ethnic status, and socioeconomic status, women preferred husbands who were better educated than they were and who earned more money than they did" (2004, 31). Buss notes that "ambition and industriousness, cues to resource acquisition, also tend to be valued more heavily by females than by males across cultures" (2011, 112). The reproductive advantages of these preferences seem clear. "In all cultures . . . studied," Geary, Vigil, and Byrd-Craven report, "the children of culturally successful men have lower mortality rates than the children of other men. . . . These are exactly the conditions that would result in the evolution of women's preference for socially dominant and culturally successful marriage partners" (2004, 30).

There is an interesting twist to Buss's survey. Although "males value physical attractiveness and relative youth in potential mates more than do females. . . . *Both* sexes ranked the characteristics 'kind-understanding and intelligent' higher than earning power and attractiveness in all samples" (Buss 1989, 12, 13). Nevertheless, Buss points out, "in each of the 37 samples, males prefer mates who are younger, which is consistent with the hypothesis that males value mates with higher reproductive capacity . . . [whereas] females prefer mates who are older than they are. Indeed, females appear to prefer a larger age difference (3.42 years older) than do males (2.66 years younger)" (1989, 9). On average, older males could be expected to possess greater command over resources, whereas younger women promise greater overall fertility.

In struggling to ensure that their genes survive into the future, males face a trade-off between maximizing the number of females they impregnate and ensuring the survival of their progeny. The more energy and resources they devote to having sex and impregnating multiple females, the less time they have for taking care of their offspring. If the females they impregnate cannot survive to birth their children and then successfully raise them, then the males' strategy fails. Successfully raising children also includes that they not become "losers" who are unable to find mates and thereby carry their parents' genes into the future. Parents have an interest not only in the welfare of their children, but in all future carriers of their genes.

In terms of reproductive success, men have an incentive to impregnate other males' wives. The cuckolded husband unknowingly rears the philanderer's child, leaving the philanderer free to sire children elsewhere, thereby increasing his chances of sending his genes into the future.

In contemporary times, between 10 and 15 percent of men (with a high of around 30 percent in southeast England) are reported to be deceived by their partners into rearing other men's children. The rates among hunter-gatherers are thought to have ranged between 2 and 9 percent (Geary, Vigil, and Byrd-Craven 2004, 33; Schmitt 2005, 266). This danger of investing in other males' offspring underlies the fact that evolution did not produce a high level of male parental care in almost all species. However, this does not preclude that most human males do not form caring and loving bonds with their children. Clearly, they typically do.

The risk men face as to their paternity has led them to undertake various strategies for restricting their mates' opportunities for sex with other males. This has included high bride prices for proven virgins (as a guarantee to a prospective husband that he will not raise another man's offspring from the start);[12] laws that severely punish, even stone to death, women found guilty of adultery; physical confinement; clothing that masks in public the sexual attractiveness of their wives; physical barriers to sex such as chastity belts or infibulation (suturing a woman's labia majora nearly closed to preclude penetration); and sexual mutilation or clitorectomy that reduces the woman's pleasure in sex.

Polygyny could be expected to exaggerate this control and abuse of females. Polygamous males have more women to shield from female-deprived males who would be motivated to take extreme risks to mate. This was especially evident in harems where women were cloistered, often behind high walls and, in some instances, male guards were castrated (eunuchs) so that they were incapable of impregnating females in the harem. Torture and death generally awaited males who trespassed onto this "property." Anthropologist Mildred Dickmann observes that

> it is precisely those societies with the greatest extremes between rich and poor . . . in which large numbers of beggars, outcasts, floater males, and celibates exist at the bottom while intense polygyny in the form of secondary wives, concubines, and harems occurs at the top that the most extreme forms of claustration, veiling, and incapacitation of women occur. (1981, 425)

---

[12] Pinker reports that "in no society are women and in-laws obsessed with the virginity of grooms" (2011, 397).

Obviously, the more resources or power that a male can command, the greater his potential to have others assist in caring for his offspring. A male with great wealth or power can pay others or command slaves to help with raising his children. Lactation suppresses ovulation, and, because the wealthy can afford to have wet nurses provide milk for their infants, the mothers are more frequently fertile and thus capable of bearing more children. Betzig reports that "rich English women of the sixteenth through eighteenth centuries who gave up their children to wet nurses were able to bear 20 or even 30 children, because the intervals between their births were closed from the roughly 4 years common in 'natural fertility' cultures to just over 1 year" (1993, 55).

Due to differing reproductive strategies, boys and girls are raised differently:

> Cross-culturally, boys engage more in rough-and-tumble play that prepares them for violent conflict, whereas girls are taught such values as sexual restraint, obedience, and responsibility—behavior sought by men in their wives. . . . [However], cross-culturally, the more women control important resources and exercise power, the less daughters are taught to be submissive. (Low 2001, 108, 109)

Pinker finds that "over the long sweep of history, women have been and will be a pacifying force" (2011, 43). Prum proposes that women can be expected to be less tolerant of violence than men because they can only produce a limited number of children, and thus the loss of one is more costly (2017, 292).[13]

The dynamics of sexual selection also help clarify why studies find males to be more biased toward short-run objectives, or in the language of economists, more prone to discount the future. The reason, Margo Wilson, Martin Daly, Stephen Gordon, and Adelle Pratt argue, is because men "are less likely than women to live to see the future and because immediate, even total, resource expenditure can pay off for a man (as mating effort) but is likely to be a disaster for a woman. For similar reasons, men may be expected

---

[13] Curiously, and offering conflicting evidence, political scientists Oeindrila Dube and S. P. Harish analyzed the reigns of 28 European queens between 1480 to 1913 and found a 27 percent increase in wars when they were in power, as compared to the reigns of kings (2015). However, the sample is too small to be statistically significant.

to disdain health risks more than women" (1996, 146). Because males privilege quantity rather than quality of offspring and spend less time and resources in long-term parenting, they seek resources, power, and status to appeal to females as quickly as possible. Efforts to gain the wherewithal for approval in the future is always possible, but given the future's uncertainty, these "long-term investment" efforts distract from current mating success and reduce the male's reproductive potential.

Recognizing what later researchers would document, Darwin claimed that "in civilized life man is largely but by no means exclusively, influenced in the choice of his wife by external appearances" (1871, 640). Consequently, as psychologists Sarah E. Hill, Christopher D. Rodeheffer, Vladas Griskevicius, Kristina Durante, and Andrew Edward White note, "the most frequent and effective tactic women use to attract or retain mates is enhancing their physical attractiveness. . . . Women spend significantly more time making themselves appear physically attractive compared with men" (2012, 276). This has produced surprising economic results. For instance, researchers have identified what they call the "lipstick effect": because fewer men have resources during a recession, women must compete more vigorously to locate a financially stable mate, and, to do so, they increase their purchases of beauty products. Although seemingly irrational, such behavior represents a deeper adaptive rationality. As Hill et al. remark, "Women's psychologies may have been shaped to respond to economic resource scarcity by allocating more effort into securing a financially secure mate in an environment where such mates are scarce" (2012, 288).[14] Accordingly, the more unequal a society, and thus the more dire the scarcity of men with resources to make promising fathers, the more time and expense women might be expected to spend to enhance their attractiveness.

[14] Further evidence is reported by Baumeister and Vohs: "In two studies of women's clothing fashions spanning 1885 to 1976, N. Barber (1991) found that skirt length covaried with the sex ratio, such that women wore shorter skirts when there were fewer men. Short skirts were also linked to high divorce rates (which also indicate higher female competition for men). Wearing short skirts is analogous to advertising one's wares, as a way of stimulating demand for one's product. It fits the economic analysis to suggest that sellers advertise more aggressively when demand is low. A cross-cultural survey of 185 countries showed that teen female pregnancy rates . . . are higher when men are relatively scarce" (Baumeister and Vohs 2004, 352).

Coalitions and Mating Advantage

The most common and durable source of factions has been the various and unequal distribution of property. Those who hold and those who are without property have ever formed distinct interests in society.
—Alexander Hamilton, James Madison, and John Jay,
The Federalist Papers (1787, II, 10)

Among many mammals, including humans, males have evolved to join together in coalitions to improve their chances of reproduction by acquiring resources and power more efficiently. Coalitions among males are reproductive strategies. Male baboons, for example, form coalitions explicitly to steal females from other groups. As noted earlier, men go to war for the same reason. Membership in political coalitions (parties) improves the probability of political success and the correspondingly high status that enhances reproductive success.

Coalitions can be highly fragile due to the fact, as primatologists and ethologists Frans de Waal and F. B. M. de Waal put it, "the unreliable, Machiavellian nature of the male power games implies that every friend is a potential foe" (2009a, 53). Members of coalitions often betray one another to gain reproductive advantage. Soap operas are not purely fictional in portraying friends sleeping with each other's spouses.

Women also form coalitions, but they do so primarily to acquire resources for themselves and their offspring. Low contends that "in our evolutionary history, men had more to gain from risky coalitions and high-stakes politics than women . . . [and thus the] rarity of women as major political figures is consistent with the hypothesis that men have evolved to make reproductive gains from striving in coalitions" (2001, 101, 201).

Group Selection

A strong argument can be made that our extraordinary intelligence, and much of our culture, derive from selection for ability to compete against each other (rather than against the physical environment), often as coordinated, cooperative groups.
—Bobbi S. Low, *Why Sex Matters* (2001, 176)

Darwin suggested that the proclivity among humans to cooperate and sacrifice for the benefit of others could underlie group selection, a sort of natural selection of groups: "A tribe including many members who, from possessing in a high degree the spirit of patriotism, fidelity, obedience, courage, and sympathy, were always ready to aid one another, and to sacrifice themselves for the common good, would be victorious over most other tribes; and this would be natural selection" (Darwin 1871, 159–60).[15] Yet, from the appearance of Richard Dawkin's *The Selfish Gene* (1976) until recently, the dominant view among evolutionary biologists and psychologists was that group selection could not have evolved through natural selection.

Today, however, an increasing number of scientists claim that the evolution of functionally organized groups, or *superorganisms*, has been vital for the evolutionary process (e.g., D. S. Wilson 2015; Bowles and Gintis 2013a; Stoelhorst and Richerson 2013; Prum 2017). Echoing Darwin, evolutionary biologist David Sloan Wilson claims that groups that include more altruists will generally perform better than those with fewer altruists, and that, therefore, the capacity for altruism evolved in the human species. Economists Samuel Bowles and Herbert Gintis concur: "genuine altruism, a willingness to sacrifice one's own interest to help others, including those who are not family members, and not simply in return for anticipated reciprocation in the future, provides the proximate explanation of much of human cooperation" (2013a, 198–99). Further, echoing Darwin's claim cited earlier, ". . . altruism increases the fitness of members of groups that practice it by enhancing the degree of cooperation among members, allowing these groups to outcompete other groups that lack this behavioral trait" (Gintis et al. 2005, 10).

But is it in fact truly altruism that has been instrumental in group selection? Bowles and Gintis define altruism as "helping in situations where the helper would benefit in fitness or other material ways by withholding help" (2013b, 8). If people are unaware that such helping enhances reproductive success, they may sincerely believe they are acting in a wholly unselfish manner, but theirs is not altruism in the largest sense. Instead, such behavior is an example akin to the handicap principle whereby an attribute such as the

---

[15] Also, in support of group selection, he wrote: "Selfish and contentious people will not cohere, and without coherence nothing can be effected. A tribe rich in the above qualities [including sympathy, fidelity, and courage] would spread and be victorious over other tribes: but in the course of time it would, judging from all past history, be in its turn overcome by some other tribe still more highly endowed. Thus the social and moral qualities would tend slowly to advance and be diffused throughout the world" (1871, 135).

male peacock's tail impairs its potential for physical survival while enhancing the potential for its own unique genes to survive into the future. As Miller puts it, "good moral character is sexually attractive and romantically inspiring. Conversely, liars and cheats are sexually repulsive—unless they have other charms that compensate for their flawed character. . . . Human altruism is . . . a sexual ornament" (2001, 293, 339). Miller continues:

> A sexual selection perspective allows us to explain sympathy, agreeableness, moral leadership, sexual fidelity, good parenting, charitable generosity, sportsmanship, and our ambitions to provide for the common good. . . . Morality is a system of sexually selected handicaps—costly indicators that advertise our moral character. . . . The rules of evolutionary biology demand that we find a hidden, genetically selfish benefit to our altruism. (2001, 293, 294, 295)

Thus, inequality in altruism can give those exhibiting greater concern for others an advantage in reproduction by increasing their sexual attractiveness.

The argument in favor of group selection holds that natural selection can occur simultaneously at multiple levels: genes, individuals, populations, and species. David Sloan Wilson writes, "Selfish individuals might out-compete altruists within groups, . . . [but] internally altruistic groups out-compete selfish groups. This is the essential logic of what has become known as multi-level selection theory" (2007, 328). Note that in cultural evolution, religions are group-level adaptations that induce people to behave for the good of the group, enabling groups in which religion has evolved to outcompete groups without religion (D. S. Wilson 2015). This has led some to suggest that, through gene-culture coevolution, the pull of religion became hardwired, an instinct (Wade 2009).

Modern Monogamy

> Polygyny, or reproductive inequality, requires economic and political inequality: a man with ten times as many women and children must either work ten times as hard to support them, or take what he needs from other men. Across space and time, polygyny has overlapped with despotism, monogamy with egalitarianism.
>
> —Laura Betzig, "Roman Monogamy" (1992, 310)

Polygyny results from inequality in access to females, and, as noted earlier, the anthropological record reveals that polygamy has existed in over 80 percent of human societies. It has also been more prevalent the greater the degree of economic and political inequality. Why, then, would monogamy come to be the norm (and most often the only legal possibility) in modern societies characterized by great inequality? The answer would appear to lie in the dynamics of group selection in the context of competition among complex states, where success depends upon sophisticated economies. Monogamous societies have stronger economies, providing them with military advantages to outcompete their even more unequal polygamous enemies (Henrich, Boyd, and Richerson 2012; Wilson and Gowdy 2015), an example of group selection at work.

Monogamy improves the prospects for more robust economic performance in several ways. Monogamous societies suffer less crime. Marriage reduces a man's probability of criminal activity by 35 percent. Even widowed or divorced men participate more in crime than do married men (Henrich, Boyd, and Richerson 2012, 661). Polygamous societies, by contrast, leave many young men with little prospect of finding mates, which increases their discounting of the future and, correlatively, their risky behavior. They are more likely to participate in criminal activities and civil disorder. It is noteworthy that there was a tenfold to fiftyfold decline in homicide in European societies between the late Middle Ages and the twentieth century as polygamy progressively declined (Pinker 2011, xxiv).

A consequence of a high level of polygamy is that it requires more despotic government and resources to inhibit crime and contain civil disorder. Such governments generally repress civil liberties, stifling the acquisition and diffusion of knowledge and thus dampening technological dynamism. For instance, the printing press that Gutenberg launched in 1440, and which quickly spread over all Europe, was banned in the polygamous Ottoman Empire until 1729.

Beyond reducing crime and violence, monogamy increases male parental investment, resulting in higher-quality children with more productive knowledge and skills (human capital), greater division of labor, more freely flowing information, more innovation, and so, more robust economic performance.

More dynamic economies increase a country's military strength. Because polygamous societies are more prone to economic stagnation, they tend to become vulnerable to defeat by stronger monogamous neighbors. The prevalence of monogamy in Europe contributed to the economic and military advantages that enabled its conquest of much of the world.

The successful spread of monogamy in Europe may also have been assisted by more egalitarian institutions and ideals that have deep roots in Western history. The rise of Christianity in Rome propagated belief in the basic equality of all humans. Nevertheless, despite this egalitarian religious heritage, it was a long time before the incidence of polygamy declined in Christian societies. In Western Europe, cultural prohibitions against polygyny, the democratization of access to mates, and the more equal potential to reproduce only emerged slowly during the Middle Ages (Geary, Vigil, and Byrd-Craven 2004, 38). Economist Deepak Lal contends that the rise of monogamous conjugal relationships accompanied by romantic love was unique to the West, distinguishing it from the marriage systems in other parts of Eurasia (2001, 89).

The rise of political democracy and monogamy reinforced each other. Male leaders seeking the votes of the poor would hamper their chance of success if they had multiple wives, thereby denying some of the male electorate reproductive potential. Both democracy and monogamy correlate with greater equality and less poverty, creating a larger pool of attractive potential fathers, encouraging women to choose to marry monogamously. The Islamic and polygamous Middle East leads the world in inequality and poverty (Habeeb 2018).

Although monogamy has deep historical roots in Europe, it is only in recent times that it has become the norm in most of the world. For instance, polygyny only became illegal in Japan in 1880, China in 1953, India in 1955, and Nepal in 1963 (Henrich, Boyd, and Richerson 2012, 657).

Low notes that "during west European history, as societies moved toward greater monogamy (reducing the potential rewards of power for men), politically powerful women seem to become more numerous (e.g., Mary Tudor, Elizabeth I, Mary of William and Mary, Queen Ann)" (2001, 212). She notes, however, that "in the few societies in which women wield substantial public power, as opposed to informal influence, there is no evidence of clear, direct reproductive gain" (2001, 211).The spread of monogamy may, however, help account for the decline in violence from war in modern times. The reproductive advantages that successful warriors had in earlier societies, extending back to humanity's earliest beginnings, may have largely disappeared. Warlike behavior, and violence generally, may have become unappealing in a potential mate. There is less fanfare celebrating war heroes, perhaps because wars themselves are less enthusiastically supported.[16] Might this help account for the rise in psychological difficulties that contemporary soldiers returning from battle zones are reported to suffer?

To be sure, polygyny has not exactly disappeared in today's relatively democratic and wealthy, yet considerably unequal societies. Wealthy and politically powerful men disproportionately have mistresses. Further, as divorce has become more socially acceptable and prevalent, men, and especially wealthy and high-status men, more frequently practice serial monogamy, a form of intertemporal polygyny. When their wives age beyond their reproductive prime, their husbands divorce and marry younger women who are more capable of bearing children.[17] This has been detrimental not only to the abandoned women but also to younger and especially poorer and lower-status men who find fewer women in their age cohort as potential mates. Geary, Vigil, and Byrd-Craven report that "serial monogamy has important reproductive consequence for men but not women . . . men but not women who engaged in serial monogamy had more children than their peers who stayed monogamously married" (2004, 38).

The development and widespread use of contraceptives and the more readily available possibility of abortion have modified the results of sexual competition.[18] In today's rich societies, the most socially successful men no longer parent the most offspring. Potential fertility is decreased by monogamy and artificial birth control. Families near the bottom of the social gradient have the most children. Nevertheless, it would appear that high-status men generally have more sex (Pérusse 1994). Although the sexual urge was selected during evolution because it enhanced reproductive success, most sex is not consciously sought for this reason. As to how to behave, humans, as well as other animals, generally act on proximate cues and are unaware of the ultimate reproductive motivation driving their desires and actions.

[16] In earlier times, it would have been inconceivable that a widely recognized war hero and politician in the United States, such as John McCain, could have been slandered, and that the slanderer, 2016 presidential candidate Donald Trump, could be elected president, and then continue to retain considerable political support despite referring to soldiers who died in wars as "losers" and "suckers."
[17] An ability to attract young and handsome "trophy wives" punctuates males' high status and desirability.
[18] Schmitt explains the demographic transition toward fewer children as follows: "In cultures with high mortality rates and unpredictable resources, the optimal mating strategy is to reproduce early and often. . . . In cultures that are physically safe and have abundant resources, mortality rates are lower and the optimal strategy is to invest heavily in fewer numbers of offspring. In safer environments, therefore, individuals should pursue a long-term strategy associated with more monogamous mating" (2005, 279).

What people identify as worthy of their competitive attention is what is socially recognized as yielding status. Throughout history, having a large number of children signaled sexual success and an ability to provide for them. Children also held forth promise that their parents would be cared for in old age. But as people became wealthier, parenting a large number of children served as a less powerful signal of success. Further, in addition to greater wealth, the evolution of old-age protections such as social security and pensions meant less dependence upon children for care in later life. As women received education and faced opportunities beyond caring for children and the household, they began to choose having fewer children. What provides social status is socially determined, and, as society changed, status came to be sought in other ways. It is thus an ironic twist that, although the proclivity for competitiveness is ultimately driven by sexual competition in the interest of genetic survival, success in reproduction, as opposed to having sex, declined in relative importance.

Fairness

Laws and government may be considered in this and indeed in every case as a combination of the rich to oppress the poor, and preserve to themselves the inequality of the goods which would otherwise be soon destroyed by the attacks of the poor, who if not hindered by the government would soon reduce the others to an equality with themselves by open violence.

—Adam Smith, *Lectures on Jurisprudence* (1763, 208)

As humans evolved, so too did their sense of fairness or "inequity aversion," which has served to restrain inequality and thus function for *reproductive leveling*. In fact, this sense of fairness appears to pre-date humans, insofar as it has been found, albeit in weaker expressions, among other primates and even dogs (de Waal 2009b). Capuchin monkeys will reject small rewards when they see other monkeys whom they perceive as undeserving getting more than they do (Brosman and de Waal 2002). Cotton-top tamarins will pull a lever to give more marshmallows (which tamarins love) to other tamarins who have rewarded them with marshmallows in earlier lever-pulls (Hauser et al. 2003).

Although the hypothesis has been contested (André and Baumard 2011), many studies have located the origin of this proclivity for fairness in the dynamics of group selection (e.g., Bowles and Gintis 2013b; Boyd and Richerson 2009). Among hunter-gatherers, food sharing was the norm. When food was scarce, fairness in sharing would be a matter of life or death. In addition, the ability to form coalitions (as well as the availability of stone weapons to all) enabled the weaker to block the stronger from unfairly gaining disproportionate access to women.

But whatever the specific origins of fairness, its impact on behavior is considerable and omnipresent. People experience this sentiment practically every day. How frequent the exclamation, "That's not fair!" Elections must be fair. Promotions and salary increases must be fair, as must access to universities. To be concluded, bargaining must be seen as fair. Sports must be played fairly. A sentiment of unfairness is strikingly on display in the rapid and spontaneous reaction of "road rage" to perceived or imagined disrespect on roadways.

All societies set rules for what constitutes fair competition for status and the reproductive advantages it conveys. Nowhere is this more systematically made clear than in sports. Sports are ritualized and rule-constrained social activities that enable individuals to demonstrate their high quality as mates. Outstanding individual performance is valued, but so, too, are cooperation and teamwork. Unfair play is penalized. But referees are also harshly berated for what fans perceive as mistaken, and therefore unfair, judgments of unfairness on the part of players ("bad calls"). Sports clearly illustrate that humans do not oppose competition per se, but instead its socially defined unfair expression. A reputation for playing fairly can be sexually attractive.

Humans evolved a much more acute capacity for detecting unfairness or injustice than for being logical. Although largely ignored by contemporary mainstream economics, it is noteworthy that Adam Smith—generally recognized as the father of modern economics—appreciated the critical importance of fairness for understanding human behavior and social dynamics:

Nature has implanted in the human breast, that consciousness of ill-desert, those terrors of merited punishment which attend upon [justice's] violation, as the great safe-guards of the association of mankind, to protect the weak, to curb the violent, and to chastise the guilty. . . . All men, even the most stupid and unthinking, abhor fraud, perfidy, and injustice, and delight to see them punished. (1759, 167, 171)[19]

"Ultimatum games" have been extensively used to reveal the importance of fairness. They are generally played by two people under conditions of anonymity: a "proposer" who makes an offer that can be accepted or rejected by a "responder." If the responder accepts the offer, they each walk away with the share offered by the proposer. For instance, if $100 is available and $30 is offered by the proposer and accepted by the responder, the proposer pockets $70 and the responder $30. If the offer is rejected, they both walk off with nothing. Neoclassical economics' self-interest postulate predicts that rational responders will accept any offer whatsoever, since to reject it means they get nothing. This game has been played around the world in the most varied cultures imaginable, and a threshold is always found below which the offer will be refused. This outcome clearly indicates that, rather than accepting what is viewed as an unfair offer, responders choose to refuse and accept nothing in order to punish the greedy proposer, who also gets nothing—altruistic punishment! It is common in a one-shot game for the proposer to offer a 50–50 split and for the responder to reject offers below 30 percent. The same outcome occurs in another experimental game, "public goods games," where participants often prove willing to incur a cost to themselves in order to punish free-riders (those who benefit from something without fairly sharing in its cost). The importance of fairness is accentuated by the fact that, when responders know that the proposer in the ultimatum game is a computer, they usually accept any offer whatsoever (Blount 1995).

Detecting injustice appears to lie at the core of human behavior. Indeed, brain scans locate an acute sensitivity to unfair treatment, offering evidence that humans are hardwired for a sense of fairness or justice. This explains, for instance, why there is intense pleasure in taking revenge, either in imagination or in actuality (Roach 2004). Thomas Aquinas held that souls in heaven "will see the punishments of the damned, in order that their bliss be that much greater" (Oriana 2016). Bowles and Gintis report evidence from neuroeconomics suggesting "that the brain processes the punishment of

---

[19] Moreover, Smith believed that a natural sentiment toward fairness was the source of the virtue of justice, which he saw as the "main pillar that upholds the whole edifice. If it is removed, the great, the immense fabric of human society . . . must in a moment crumble to atoms" (1759, 125). Similarly, political philosopher John Rawls claimed that "justice is the first virtue of social institutions, as truth is of systems of thought. . . . Laws and institutions no matter how efficient and well-arranged must be reformed or abolished if they are unjust" (Rawls 1999, 3).

defectors and the achievement of mutual cooperation much as it processes other pleasurable behaviors" (2013b, 39). People not only take pleasure in punishing those who have hurt or disrespected them, but also those who have treated others unfairly. Unfairness is a form of cruelty, and much entertainment (plays, films, etc.) exploits the audience's delight in seeing punishment meted out to its perpetrators. Evil is extreme, intractable unfairness.

Although humans appear to possess an innate sense of justice, just what is viewed as fair is influenced by what others view as fair, which in turn is influenced by a society's values, practices, and rules of the game. Those with the greatest ownership and control over society's resources exert the greatest influence upon what is understood as fair. The result is ideology that benefits them at the expense of those below. Thus, for instance, tax cuts that disproportionally reward a wealthy elite are accepted as fair by many unwealthy taxpayers because they are led to believe that everyone will benefit: the wealthy will use the extra income to make investments that will stimulate economic dynamism and create higher-paying jobs. Although this "trickle-down" argument has been repeatedly disproven, it continues to hold persuasive power due to the elite's greater command over society's media and educational institutions. The essence of ideology is manipulating people's strong sense of fairness so as to make foul seem fair.

Wealth Inequality and Sexual Selection

... it is chiefly from [the] regard to the sentiments of mankind that we pursue riches and avoid poverty. ... It is the vanity, not the ease, or the pleasure, which interests us.

—Adam Smith, *The Theory of Moral Sentiments* (1759, 112–13)

As a social science discipline, economics has typically viewed humans as principally motivated by income and wealth. This fits with the evolutionary view that humans seek resources to reproduce and ensure that their genes make it into the future. However, economists, like most other social scientists, do not generally view the pursuit of income and wealth as ultimately driven by the dynamics of sexual selection.[20] This is hardly surprising. As evolutionary psychologist Satoshi Kanazawa puts it:

[20] Among economists, the Reverend Thomas Malthus stands out in recognizing the central importance of sex. He claimed that "passions between the sexes" were with humans, like with animals

The fact that many of us do not think that [reproduction] is the ultimate goal of our existence or that some of us choose not to reproduce is irrelevant. We are not privy to the evolutionary logic behind our design, and no matter what we choose to do in our own lifetimes, we are all descended from those who chose to reproduce. None of us inherited our psychological mechanism from our ancestors who remained childless. Everything else in life, even survival, is a means to reproductive success. (2009, 26)

Although economists view humans as motivated to pursue income and wealth, over two centuries ago, the father of modern economics, Adam Smith, noted that these are proximate causes. Long before Darwin, Smith recognized a deeper cause: nature compels us to seek the approval of others, or what he more frequently called *social approbation*. But, preceding Darwin, he could not link his theory of approbation to the latter's dynamic of sexual selection. In *The Theory of Moral* Sentiments—which Smith considered to be the more important of his two books (Rae 1895, 436)—he argued:

Nature, when she formed man for society, endowed him with an original desire to please, and an original aversion to offend his brethren. She taught him to feel pleasure in their favourable, and pain in their unfavourable regard. She rendered their approbation most flattering and most agreeable to him for its own sake; and their disapprobation most mortifying and most offensive. (1759, 212)

Smith's understanding is paralleled in evolutionary biology. Biologist George Williams writes:

Simply stated, an individual who maximizes his friendships and minimizes his antagonisms will have an evolutionary advantage, and selection would favor those characters that promote the optimization of personal relationships. I imagine that this evolutionary factor has increased man's

generally, a fundamental drive, one that generated a tragic dynamic between population pressures and resources, resulting in widespread material privation. Darwin noted his considerable debt to Malthus. In his autobiography, he wrote: "In October 1838, fifteen months after I had begun my systematic inquiry, I happened to read for amusement Malthus on Population, and being prepared to appreciate the struggle for existence which everywhere goes on, from long-continued observation of the habits of animals and plants, it at once struck me that under these circumstances favorable variables would tend to be preserved and unfavorable ones destroyed. The result would be the formation of a new species" (Darwin 1887, 42–43).

capacity for altruism and compassion and has tempered his ethically less acceptable heritage of sexual and predatory aggressiveness. (1996, 95)

For Smith, it is this need for social approval that drives human behavior:

Humanity does not desire to be great, but to be beloved [and] . . . it is chiefly from regard to the sentiments of mankind that we pursue riches and avoid poverty. . . . The rich man glories in his riches because he feels they naturally draw upon him the attention of the world . . . and he is fonder of his wealth on this account than for all the other advantages it procures him. (1759, 276, 112, 113)[21]

Smith wrote at the outset of the industrial revolution that was unfolding within the womb of competitive capitalism. The accumulation of wealth to achieve status was appropriate to this social world. But it was not appropriate for humans during the first 95 percent of their history when they lived as foragers. Biologists Charles Lumsden and Edward O. Wilson report that "in hunter-gatherer societies such as the !Kung of the Kalahari, conspicuous attempts to improve personal status and to accumulate large quantities of personal goods are met with ridicule and hostility" (1983, 150–51). Moreover, in instances where wealth is sought, it is for the purpose of giving it away in search of approbation. Anthropologist Richard Thurnwald noted that, in early societies, "It is for social distinction that work is done, not for the acquisition of money or material goods, since these do not play the same intermediary role for acquiring reputation that they do in our society" (1932, 178). Similarly, anthropologist Bronislaw Malinowski commented on what motivates the Trobriand Islands' male to work: "He wants . . . to achieve social distinction as a good gardener and a good worker in general" (1922, 62).

The pursuit of wealth is not, thus, a universal human trait, but one that holds promise of status and reproductive success in social formations that appeared only in the last 2 to 3 percent of human history. After the adoption of agriculture and, especially, the much later capacity for metallurgy and

---

[21] Karl Polanyi, often identified as a father of economic anthropology, expressed a view conformable to that of Smith. An individual does not act "to safeguard his individual interest in the possession of material goods; he acts so as to safeguard his social standing, his social claims, his social assets. He values material goods only in so far as they serve this end" (1944, 46).

military organization, those who were able to command highly scarce metal weapons and coordinate sophisticated military organizations could control productive wealth and subjugate others.[22] This gave birth to the state, a novel social institution that could protect private property, thereby adding a new cultural force that would become central to human sexual selection. Those who possessed significant property would be more attractive as mates. They could provide more material security and, therefore, a greater likelihood that offspring would survive.

In capitalist countries, it is widely believed that substantial differences in income and wealth are essential to generate the incentives needed to achieve society's objectives. However, as will be seen in greater detail in Chapter 3, history indicates otherwise. Even modern non-capitalist societies have flourished through other non-material incentives, at least in certain domains. Although they are not well paid, doctors in Cuba provide the best healthcare for their populations as a whole of any country in Latin America. The Soviet Union had highly trained doctors, scientists, and mathematicians, even if it often paid them less than some manual workers (Roemer 2011, 92). It is, of course, true that only capitalism has produced both sustainable economic dynamism and a high degree of freedom. However, institutions that privilege ends other than income and wealth accumulation might equally well provide not only greater economic dynamism but greater freedom as well. This possibility is explored in Chapter 13.

Further, the differences that prove someone superior need not be large. The Olympic runner who wins by a mere 0.01 of a second still gets the gold medal and all the status that accompanies it. Material difference would also not need be great to have the same incentive effect. It would only need to be clear whose income or wealth was highest, or higher on average, to mark the highest rank. As pioneer neoclassical economist Alfred Marshall astutely observed, ". . . all the best business men want to get money, but many of them do not care about it much for its own sake; they want it chiefly as the most convincing proof to themselves and others that they have succeeded" (1890, 635).

---

[22] Although the central importance of metallurgy appears valid for Eurasia, as will be seen in Chapter 5, it needs to be amended to account for the early states in the Americas that did not develop metallurgy for weaponry.

Utopia's Limits

. . . very likely the utopian element in the human imagination is one of the driving forces of history, and humanity would be immeasurably impoverished if that element ever disappeared.
—Peter Berger, *The Capitalist Revolution* (1986, 222)

Understanding Darwin's theory of sexual selection is important for understanding the origins and dynamics of inequality. It is necessary not merely for explanatory completeness, but also for understanding humanity's social potential. It reveals that humans can be (and, for most of history, have been) motivated by ends other than income and wealth. It was in pursuit of other socially generated goals that they competed for recognition and therefore success in mating and sending their genes into future generations. Sexual selection also refutes the utopian belief in the possibility of a society in which competition and the pursuit of distinction could be eliminated. It puts the lie to such quixotic fantasies.

Utopians often viewed envy, jealousy, and competition as the consequence of social institutions, and especially private property. Eliminate private property, and humans, they claimed, would live in egalitarian harmony. In the early nineteenth century, for instance, entrepreneur and utopianist Robert Owen believed that "the fatal folly of distinction"—a result of insecurity and the need for protection—would disappear in a society of abundance without private property where everyone's needs were guaranteed. Because everyone fears for their very survival in capitalist society, they must be keenly self-interested. In his proposed communitarian society, by contrast, "all the natural wants of human nature may be abundantly supplied; and the principle of selfishness will cease to exist for want of an adequate motive to produce it" (quoted in Rosanvallon 2013, 125–26).

William Godwin went even further, believing that in his ideal utopia, even our sex drives would wither away as we transcended our animal origins. Aside from whether such transcendence is desirable, its possibility remains in the world of science fiction. All sexually reproducing animals, including humans, compete for sex. In doing so, humans strive to stand out, to be above others in whatever manner that is socially approved and therefore attractive to the opposite sex. No matter how equal a society might be in all other respects, sexual competition will lead to differential access to the opposite sex. In terms of evolutionary biology, this is the inequality that has always mattered the most.

Although humans are genetically programed to seek status and self-esteem, what provides these has varied considerably over the course of human history. As Chapter 3 will set forth in greater detail, depending upon the institutional rules of the game, status and self-worth might conceivably be provided just as well by generosity and civic virtue or community spirit as by wealth and political power. That is, even though what earns status is substantially determined by a society's institutions, the results of successfully attaining preeminence are the same cross-culturally.

Finally, the gender behavioral dimorphism, or different gender strategies, that have been pursued in the course of history need not foreclose the potential for gender equality. Arguably, women and men lived in a high degree of equality for 97 to 98 percent of human history, and extreme gender inequality only evolved with the extreme wealth and political power that attended the rise of states and civilization.

In contemporary societies, civilization's gender inequality is in retreat. Full sexual equality is increasingly embraced, and barriers to this goal are rapidly falling away. It is noteworthy, as Wax points out, that "commitment to the goal of sexual equality can also be understood as a component of sexual display" (2004, 577). Women may well consider males who exhibit gender-egalitarian attitudes and behavior to be sexy.

Sex Flashed and Repressed

One of the greatest Reasons why so few People understand themselves is that most Writers are always teaching Men what they should be, and hardly ever trouble their heads with telling them what they really are.
—Bernard Mandeville, *The Fable of the Bees* (1714, 77)

The claim that sexual selection is the ultimate cause of competitiveness, and thus the ultimate cause of inequality, may run counter to many readers' self-understanding. In concluding this chapter, therefore, it may be helpful to note again the degree to which humans are unmindful of the way their genetic heritage surreptitiously steers their behavior. With regard to sex, this shortcoming in self-knowledge persists despite the fact that sexuality pervades Western cultural practices, both blatantly and covertly. It shares with violence top billing in our entertainment, from soap operas to the Metropolitan Opera, from pop to classical music, from pulp fiction to the literature of the classic canon. It is endlessly exploited in commercial advertising. Navigating interactions with the opposite sex begins at practically the earliest ages and continues throughout life. From an evolutionary perspective, all of this is understandable. Humans evolved to be continuously preoccupied with sex, because if they fail to mate, their unique set of genes faces oblivion. All sexually reproducing life forms are instinctively driven to struggle to send their genes into posterity. Although humans are keenly aware of their interest in sex, they rarely recognize the biological cause of this compelling interest.

From early childhood, almost everyone is conscious of their actions that are intended to impress members of the opposite sex. They are also aware that members of the same gender are in competition with each other in this pursuit. Everyone knows that at times this competition can be extreme. However, few if any are aware of the extent to which striving for excellence in practically any activity is ultimately driven by Darwin's dynamic of sexual selection. The reason is that humans are generally cognizant of proximate as opposed to ultimate clauses. And, as Pinker points out,

> the distinction between proximate and ultimate causation is indispensable in understanding ourselves because it determines the answer to every question of the form "Why did that person act as he did?" To take a simple example, ultimately people crave sex in order to reproduce (because the ultimate cause of sex is reproduction), but proximately they may do everything they can not to reproduce (because the proximate cause of sex is pleasure). (2002, 54)

Anthropologist Jared Diamond remarks, "Perhaps our greatest distinction as a species is our capacity, unique among animals, to make counter-evolutionary choices" (1998, 62). Note, for example, that some humans remain celibate for religious reasons. This may be extreme: theologian, scholar, and "steely ascetic" Origen (184–254 AD) castrated himself to remove the temptation of sex. He also sold his non-Christian books to remove the temptation of philosophy (Hobart 2018, 56–57). Evolutionary biologists David Sloan Wilson and John Gowdy point out that "thinking in terms of ultimate causation is one of the most important tools in the evolutionary toolkit" (2013, S5).

Human society requires cooperation and internal peace. Precisely because of the centrality of sexual competition in human behavior, considerable cultural practices (in addition to our innate sense of fairness) have evolved to mask or soften its expression. Human sexual competition is far less often demonstrated in physically fighting than is the case among many other mammals. Humans are the only animal that has come to hide its genitalia. Taboos on nudity are enforced by punitive laws. Why? It is understandable that when humans migrated into cold climes, they would need to cover their bodies. But prior to becoming "civilized" in recent times, naked savages were reportedly common in warm climes. But what happened that could explain the injunction to cover sex organs? Might it have been to dampen sexual competition? Could it be that once elites gained sexual competitive advantage through wealth and political power, they had an interest in repressing sexual competition where with nudity they might be disadvantaged? Darwin hypothesized that naked body skin evolved as a sexually selected aesthetic trait (Prum 2017, 253), one which, of course, would favor natural nakedness. Anthropologist Maxine Sheets-Johnstone suggests that uprightness, or bipedalism, may have evolved in part by making the display of the penis more evident (1990).

Members of "polite society" find words referring to sex acts or genitalia offensive, and either avoid them entirely or substitute lighthearted euphemisms. In all known human societies, sexual activities have been accompanied with restrictions and rules. Clearly, most of these were not designed merely to limit population growth. Moreover, social attitudes have evolved to highlight the value of cooperation and to downplay sexual competition, depicting humans as driven by more "noble" motives. Evolutionary psychologists Satochi Kanazawa and Mary C. Still note, for instance, that

> human actors believe that they are choosing to mate with the ones they love
> and desire, not the ones with characteristics that increase their reproduc-
> tive success (measured by the number of grandchildren). Human actors
> are not usually conscious of the evolutionary logic behind their emotions.
> (1999, 46)

The repressed character of sexual competition is evident in that it has not received significant attention in social thought. Until recent decades, this was true even in psychology, although Freud notoriously placed it center stage.[23]

---

[23] Freud wrote: "We said that man, having found by experience that sexual (genital) love afforded him his greatest gratification, so that it became in effect a prototype of all happiness to him, must have

Surprisingly, however, while he cited Darwin over 20 times, as noted earlier, he did not focus on Darwin's dynamic of sexual selection, in spite of the fact that it was well known in the late nineteenth century. Note, too, that the popular reaction to Freud's emphasis on sex was highly negative.

It is telling that the theory of sexual selection that Darwin laid out with such clarity came under withering attack immediately after its appearance, spearheaded by Alfred Russel Wallace—Darwin's cofounder of the theory of natural selection. Wallace claimed that sexual displays served as "honest" indicators of their hosts' fitness and therefore that sexual selection is merely a form of natural selection—the "honest signaling" paradigm. Consequently, for almost a century, Darwin's theory of sexual selection received relatively little attention. Curiously, it began to reappear among evolutionary biologists when the women's movement gathered steam in the 1960s and 1970s and more women began studying and contributing to biology (Prum 2017, 33–41; Miller 2001, 57ff).

been thereby impelled to seek his happiness farther along the path of sexual relations, to make genital erotism the central point of his life." Although "the gratification of instincts is happiness," civilization required the subordination of happiness, and especially sexual pleasure, to work and social restraint, and thus "our so-called civilization itself is to blame for a great part of our misery, and we would be much happier if we were to give it up and go back to primitive conditions," even though sublimation of the sexual instinct (that is, repression of the libido to the benefit of cultural pursuits) is "what makes it possible for higher psychical activities—scientific, artistic or ideological—to play an important part in civilized life" (1930, 31, 13, 19, 28). One of Freud's wayward disciples, Wilhelm Reich, claimed genital orgasm to be the antidote to every neurosis and the cure for many physical diseases.

3

From Aboriginal Equality to Limited and Unstable Inequality

For the poor shall never cease out of the land.

—Deuteronomy 15:11

What is honored in a country will be cultivated there.
—Plato, *The Republic* (1968, Book viii)

Chapter 2 explored how humans are compelled by their biology to compete for social status. The reason they do so is because high status is sexually attractive to potential mates. The unique set of genes of those who are chosen to mate are more likely to survive into the future. These surviving genes carry the proclivity to pursue social status into future generations.

This chapter begins with a brief sketch of the biological evolution of our species, *Homo sapiens*. It then examines how a high degree of economic and political equality characterized almost all of our species' history. Only with the adaption of agriculture and denser populations did a limited degree of inequality develop.

Such expressions as "the poor shall never cease" have led people to believe that societies are invariably made up of rich and poor, and that inequality is an inherent feature of the human condition which always has existed and always will. But this is not true. Strikingly, material and social equality prevailed during almost all of the human story. For 97 to 98 percent of *Homo sapiens*'s approximately 200,000 years of existence, during which period humans evolved to possess basically all the genetic makeup that continues to define their traits and behavior today, humans lived in virtual material and political equality, surviving as hunters and gatherers and then as early agriculturalists.

Until the adoption of agriculture about 10,000 years ago, humans lived as foragers, searching for food, much like other animals. They were overwhelmingly nomadic and highly egalitarian. The 2 percent of exceptions were stationary communities with formal class structures characterized by wealth and political distinctions. Their sedentary condition was due to fishing on food-rich waterways.[1]

Following the adoption of agriculture, humans became increasingly settled. In some instances, religious ideology enabled the appearance of chiefs who acquired special privileges, and especially greater access to women. However, their position was threatened and frequently overthrown when catastrophe, in the form of failed harvests or natural disasters, delegitimated the ideology upon which their claim to special status relied. They lacked the weapons and organizational clout to retain their privileges when their legitimacy dissipated, and their societies tended to return to political equality.

The Genetic and Early Cultural Evolution of Humans

Genes hold culture *on a* leash.
—Edward O. Wilson, *On Human Nature* (1978, 167)

Over the course of human evolution, distinct physical and psychological characteristics were genetically and culturally selected to permit survival and reproductive success. All species, to survive and reproduce, evolve toward fitting their environments, and the longer the time to adjust and the more stable the environment, the more perfect the fit. If new environments evolve and endure for sufficiently long periods, evolutionary biology predicts that species will evolve to exploit and fit them. This dynamic underlies the evolution of our humanoid ancestors, who diverged from other primates about 6 million years ago. They presumably developed to exploit the environmental niche of savannahs created by climate change that cooled Africa, reduced forest habitats, and expanded grasslands.

---

[1] For example, coastal settlements such as those in the Pacific Northwest of North America accumulated wealth, developed hierarchies, and even produced slavery, mostly of women and children. Their populations could be dense with occupational specialization, resource ownership, and military structure (Flannery and Marcus 2012, 72–80; Garfield, von Rueden, and Hagen 2019, 6).

Life on the savannahs was purportedly so determinative that physicist and science writer James Trefil claims, "The human brain, that marvelous instrument we all carry around in our skulls, evolved for one purpose and one purpose only: to allow our ancestors to survive on the African savannah millions of years ago" (2014, B6). Evolutionary psychologist Satoshi Kanazawa identifies a "savannah principle," according to which "[the] human brain has difficulty comprehending and dealing with entities and situations that did not exist in [this] ancestral environment" (2009, 26). The savannah principle suggests that humans are poorly adapted to the radically different environment of the contemporary world.

The human brain changed rapidly to fit the savannah environment. Biologist Edward O. Wilson claims it was "the most rapid evolutionary change known in any advanced organ system of the biosphere" (2014, 49). As this brain evolved, it came to exhibit the characteristics of political economist Thorstein Veblen's wasteful conspicuous consumption. This was due, according to evolutionary psychologist Geoffrey Miller, to sexual competition:

> Our brains are only 2 percent of our body weight, but they consume 15 percent of our oxygen intake, 25 percent of our metabolic energy, and 40 percent of our blood glucose. . . . If we view the human brain as a set of sexually selected fitness indicators, its high costs are no accident. . . . Sexual selection made our brains wasteful, if not wasted: it transformed a small efficient ape-style brain into a huge, energy-hungry handicap spewing out luxury behaviors like conversation, music, and art. (2001, 134)

Over almost the entire six-million-year period since humanoids began separating from other primates, our human ancestors survived by hunting and gathering, essentially living from hand to mouth. They lived in small groups, searching for food and shelter while attempting to evade predators and groups of enemies. As with other sexually reproducing animals, males competed for access to females, and females competed for the highest-quality males, ensuring that the genes for successful competitiveness were passed into the future. Their social structure for well over half of this initial period was likely hierarchical, much the same as the configuration observed in other bands of primates. Alpha males used their physical strength and guile to gain disproportionate control over resources and access to females. They were, of course, constantly challenged by beta males fighting for the alpha males' privileged reproductive status.

However, over much of the second half of their history as hunter-gatherers, humans lived in a relatively high degree of equality. The dominant hypotheses trace this development to cultural change. Culture is that part of the environment that is created by humans. It has historically been an increasingly important part of humans' environments (and one that has historically altered far more rapidly than their physical environment, although climate change is now advancing with untoward speed).

The specific changes that led to highly egalitarian conditions were the development of tools and more sophisticated social coordination. Toolmaking dates to about 3.7 million years ago (McPherron et al. 2010). Many of the tools that served to increase the productivity of hunting, gathering, and food preparation could also serve as weapons for potential use against other humans. This early period of cultural change marks the birth of the weapons technology that will play a central role in determining the degree of inequality within societies.

Early human species and other primates are unable to throw objects with force and accuracy. However, about 2 million years ago, human shoulders underwent changes that enabled them to throw stones and other projectiles with greater precision and energy. Thus, stone, bone, or wood weapons could be thrown from a safe distance, enabling the bullied to kill those who were physically stronger and seeking greater shares of food or women. The invention of spears, and much later bows and arrows, further increased the effectiveness of weaponry as a means to eliminate bullies. This ability to throw lethal projectiles from a distance also allowed humans to hunt big game more safely.

In terms of social relations, these earliest weapons required individuals to avoid overly upsetting others, lest they provoke a murderous response. The same rudimentary social skills enabled individuals to form coalitions, enabling the weaker to coordinate their forces against males vying for alpha status or special privileges.[2] Thus, tools and coalitions compressed the earlier ape-like male hierarchy.

---

[2] Chimpanzees are our closest relatives, and, although they lack equalizing tools, beta chimpanzees have been witnessed forming alliances to overthrow dominant alpha males by force. Nevertheless, they have remained highly inegalitarian and hierarchical. Because outside their group they would be killed by members of other groups, they could only escape their rank by struggling to move up. Alpha males physically abuse rival beta males, who in turn abuse those below them (Flannery and Marcus 2012, 58, 37). Bonobos, another less violent close relative, also maintain hierarchical rankings.

Constraining alpha male behavior meant that size and strength became less important in reproductive success, leading to a reduction in dimorphism (the size differences between males and females). Fossil records of prehuman hominins indicate that dimorphism was substantial, not unlike that found among other primates where alpha males prevailed. But, accompanying the ability to use stone weapons and form coalitions against bullies, this dimorphism began to diminish, suggesting that violent competition between males for females was declining and that there was more pairing off of one male, one female (Klein 2009, 197). This would naturally tend to reduce male-to-male aggression and thus expand the potential for cooperation. Sexual acts also became less public, moderating a provocation for male rivalry. Nevertheless, mild polygyny existed, often the result of a shortage of males due to warfare and, as will be seen in the following, the superior success of some warriors.

Leaders could arise in times of crisis, but anthropologists Kent Flannery and Joyce Marcus report that even they "were generous, modest, and diplomatic, because their constituents were too skilled at alliance-building to put up with bullies. The fate of a bully was to be lured into the bush and shot with poisoned arrows" (2012, 59). The cooperative killing of violent individuals was critically important in our self-domestication. It eliminated the most violent genes from posterity. This domestication was furthered by women choosing less violent mates, providing selective pressure toward lower reactive aggression (Wrangham 2019).[3]

Humans are competitive due to the dynamics of sexual selection, but their evolving ability to form coalitions favored cooperative behavior. So too did the fact that cooperative behavior can provide status and thus reproductive success. Thus, genes for both competition and cooperation were selected in human evolution. In respect to cooperation, human foragers are far more cooperative than other primates, sharing food, child care, and practically everything else.

---

[3] Much later humans domesticated plants and animals, but from humanity's beginnings they also domesticated themselves. As political scientist and anthropologist James C. Scott puts it, ". . . we are as much a product of self-domestication in both intended and unintended ways as other species of the domus are products of our domestication . . . [for example] the spread of sedentism transformed Homo sapiens into far more of a herd animal" (2017, 83). Further, what we domesticated, domesticated us in turn. Botanist Michael Pollan provides a delightful discourse on the manner in which four domesticated plants—apples, tulips, marijuana, and potatoes—domesticated their domesticators (Pollan 2002).

Excepting the 2 percent of foragers who were sedentary, early humans lived in freedom with relatively little social or material inequality and, thus, without domination by more powerful individuals or social groups. They lived democratically. Cultural anthropologist Christopher Boehm describes their social conditions as follows:

> All nomadic foragers are egalitarian, a pattern that makes the adult males, and sometimes also the females, into equals as household heads. They are politically egalitarian to the degree that named leadership roles are lacking or devoid of authority, status differences among politically autonomous household heads are muted, and individuals who try to influence group decisions must do so very circumspectly. . . . Alpha-male types are not allowed to flourish, even though the tendency to engage in status rivalry and seeking dominance persists and can still be expressed within carefully circumscribed limits. (1997, S104)

Although forager groups lacked hierarchy, at times, leaders were needed, especially to confront external threats. Their selection was rapid and spontaneous, according to confidence in their ability to gain the support of members, provide coordination, and, where necessary, monitor effort and mete out rewards and punishments. Thus, leader-follower relationships appear to have evolved to better carry out collective action (von Rueden et al. 2014, 539). However, when emergencies were resolved, leaders folded back into the band as equals. Leaders faced increased risk of injury and death, but as Miller notes, "Leadership is like hunting . . . : it provides a common good that looks purely altruistic until one considers its sexual attractiveness" (2001, 320).

Because older men generally had more experience in battle, they were more readily chosen to lead in war expeditions. For instance, among the Amazonian Yanomamö, there is no social hierarchy, and, in peacetime, no leaders. However, when war breaks out, older seasoned men who have demonstrated their skills by having killed many enemies and brought back their scalps, heads, or genitalia as proof, are chosen to lead (Low 2001, 224). They were the "first among equals"—in addition to being seasoned warriors, they were verbose, skilled hunters, and knowledgeable about tribal lore (Neel 1980).

Paleolithic Women and Men

There was little division of labor beyond that due to sex. Whereas gathering was predominantly done by females, hunting was almost exclusively a male preserve, as is the case with chimpanzees (Stanford 2001). Because females generally carried suckling infants, they were far less mobile for hunting. Children needed to be carried in nomadic forager societies until they were about four years old and could walk fast enough to keep up with the group.

Anthropologist Helen Fisher claims that our Pleistocene ancestors likely had sequential medium-term sexual relationships of about five years each (1994). Miller concurs: "During prehistory, there were fewer economic incentives to stay together, fewer distracting entertainments to replace lost romance, and fewer ways to insulate oneself from new sexual opportunities" (2001, 189).[4]

Among almost all mammals, mothers bear the burden of child care with little assistance from fathers. The basic reason is that males could not be certain of their parentage, and thus the probability of their genes passing into future generations would be higher if their energies were spent attempting to inseminate other females. As seen in Chapter 2, whereas females maximize quality, males maximize quantity. Thus, like with other primates, human females and their children formed the basic social unit. Miller reports that

> women clustered together for mutual help and protection. . . . The traditional view that females needed males to protect them from predators has been challenged by an increased understanding of primate and hunter-gatherer behavior. . . . An ancestral female would have been much safer in a group of a dozen sisters, aunts, and female friends than with a single male in a nuclear family. . . . Ancestral women could protect one another from harassment and rape, just as other female primates do. From a female's point of view, a strong male partner could be a mixed blessing. He could fend off unwanted attention from other males, but he could also beat you up if he got jealous or angry. (2001, 190–91)

---

[4] Miller adds: "Historically, humans did not begin to put up with lifelong marriage until they could no longer live off the land, property inheritance became the key to children's survival, and couples had economic incentives to continue cooperating long after they were no longer on speaking terms" (2001, 189).

Did men then play no role in childrearing? Miller embraces the hypothesis that men assisted mothers with caring for children in order to earn sexual favors. If a man provided assistance to a mother in looking after what could well be other men's children, he might please her and gain sexual privileges. Paternal attention might then be a form of courtship (2001, 194). This does not, however, preclude that males formed strong bonds with children. The fact that they have done so with their own and those adopted throughout recorded history suggests that they did so as well in prehistoric times.

Religion

No human society has ever been found that is without religion. The fact that religion has been culturally universal strongly suggests it provided survival value. The predominant view is that it evolved because it provided for better group cohesion.

Among foragers, sacrificing for the community was promoted by the extent to which it was composed of close relatives. In a genetic sense, a sacrifice for other members of a kinship group would be an act of nepotism because it increases the likelihood that some of the genes carried by kinfolk will be represented in future generations. Although most members of smaller bands might have family ties with one another, bands as large as 50 might be more diverse. Religion could help provide social cohesion that extends beyond those related by kinship. Note that in religions about which we have detailed information, social relationships are metaphorically described in the language of kinship. Devotees are brothers and sisters, a family with god as father, suggesting that religion served as a glue of fictive kin (Crippen and Machalek 1989).

The foremost function of religion, E. O. Wilson claims, is that "individuals are persuaded to subordinate their immediate self-interest to the interests of the group" (quoted in Flannery and Marcus 2012, 63). Religions' mores, taboos, sayings, and shaming practices served as cultural mechanisms to subdue self-interest and produce more harmonious group living. As economists would express this, religions enable societies to deal more handily with free-riders (individuals benefiting from public goods without paying their fair share). For instance, all religions embrace something more or less equivalent to the Ten Commandments of Abrahamic religions. If adherents truly believed in the necessity of abiding by these commandments,

their society would be less burdened by social discord and the expenses necessary to maintain social peace and goodwill. That would free resources for
the welfare of the community, including defense or aggression against other
groups. This would partially explain the absence of atheistic societies: less
effective in dealing with free-rider problems, they would disappear when
outcompeted by societies made more cohesive and efficient by religion.

Clearly, religion serves other purposes as well. Historian Willie Thompson
likens religion to an "intellectual Swiss army knife" that was culturally
selected because, in addition to promoting social cohesion, it performed
other functions, such as making sense of reality and offering solace in the
face of suffering and death (2015, 114).

It has been suggested that, in the process of gene-culture coevolution,
humans became hardwired for religion (E. O. Wilson 1978). As discussed
in Chapter 2, gene-culture coevolution theory views genetic and cultural
evolution as mutually interdependent. Genes set the conditions for cultural
expression, but over time, where a cultural practice provides survival advantage to the group and its members, the genes that privilege this cultural
expression are carried into future generations. Accordingly, religion would
provide groups with greater cohesion and therefore improved potential for
survival. Its members' genes would carry this proclivity for religion into the
future.

The religion of foragers reflected their high degree of social equality. There
were no priests or ecclesiastical hierarchy. All practiced their religion with
equal authority.[5] Their religious rituals were generally ad hoc, held when adequate resources permitted a large group to live together for a while. They typically danced in a circle without leaders, where the uniformity of participants
spontaneously interacting with each other gave expression to their equality
(Garfinkel 2003, 100). Further, their religion was animistic, viewing all of reality as imbued with spirituality, and thus suggesting that all elements of the
world stand to each other in a fundamental sort of equality.

---

[5] Anthropologist Richard Wrangham describes an exception. Among nomadic hunter-gatherers,
the least egalitarian has been found to be the Australian Aboriginals where elderly men of about
50 years of age monopolize young wives. Their ability to do so presumably results from their absolute
control over religious beliefs. This appears to be the rare instance among foragers in which religion is
used as ideology to enable some to gain at the expense of others. However, these elderly males apparently do not exert power in other manners (2019, 305). But then there would be no reason to do so
since they accomplish the ultimate competitive end of sexual advantage.

Health and Quality of Life

Although possessing little, hunter-gatherers were generally healthier than humans would be again before the twentieth century. Their nutritional needs evolved to fit the food resources of their environments. Their diet was highly diverse. They consumed a wide variety of animals and plants, so that micronutrient deficiencies, and the diseases associated with them, were uncommon. This makes sense: in stable conditions, living things evolve toward perfectly fitting the nutritional potential of their environments. Like those of other animals, humans' taste preferences were selected to guide them toward consumption of a nutritious and ideally balanced diet.

Because they were nomadic, they left their waste behind. Thus fecal-oral transmission, the contamination of food or water by human excrement that devastated later sedentary agricultural communities, was infrequent. They had contact with fewer people and thus suffered fewer of the "crowd diseases" that afflict sedentary populations whose far less varied diets provide less resistance to diseases (Diamond 2012, 294, 299). Political scientist and anthropologist James C. Scott notes that "virtually all the infectious diseases due to microorganisms specifically adapted to *Homo sapiens* came into existence only in the past ten thousand years [since the adoption of agriculture], many of them perhaps only in the past five thousand [since the rise of the state and civilization]" (2017, 102).

Although average life expectancy was only about 30 to 40 years, this was due to high infant mortality. Those who survived their first five years had a good chance of reaching 60, and some made it to 80 (Harari 2015, 50–51). All in all, they lived longer than subsequent humans until quite recently in human history. Foragers were also taller and stouter than later agriculturalists. Because the latter suffered inadequate nutrition, their children grew to be smaller so as to require fewer calories in their nutritionally limited environments.

The nomadism of foragers meant that the accumulation of a substantial surplus above subsistence was not possible. Their limited specialization also resulted in glacially slow technological and cultural change. Since the earliest appearance of *Homo sapiens*, cultural change has been geometrically unfolding in its complexity. But the pace in the earliest periods was extremely slow, and then not always smooth. It sped up between 70,000 and 30,000 years ago, during and after a "cultural explosion" or "cognitive revolution"—what archaeologist Stephen Mithen calls "the big bang of human culture" (1999,

15)—that left evidence in the form of art,[6] more complex technology, and religion.

Although others date it much earlier (for example, Wrangham 2019), linguists Robert Berwick and Noam Chomsky maintain that "the capacity for language and thinking symbolically emerged suddenly about sixty thousand years ago, remaining basically unchanged since" (2017, 53–88). During this period, *Homo sapiens* migrated out of Africa eventually to populate practically the whole planet. It is also during this time frame that bows and arrows, needles, boats, and oil lamps were invented. Cognitive skills and language became capable of transmitting information about things that do not exist, at least materially, such as spiritual forces. Historian Yuval Harari claims that this capacity "to speak about fictions is the most unique feature of Sapiens language" (2015, 21, 24). He also characterizes this "cognitive revolution" as "the point when history declared its independence, [and afterwards] historical narratives replace biological theories as our primary means of explaining the development of *Homo sapiens*" (2015, 37–38).

Anthropologist James Suzman argues that prior to this revolution, humans "lacked the ability to muse about the mysteries of life, praise gods, and curse spirits, tell funny stories, paint decent pictures, reflect on a day's events, . . . sing long songs, or make clever excuses to get out of a chore." But after the cognitive revolution, they were "behaviorally modern" (2021, 125). As human culture became increasingly sophisticated, people lived ever more in a world of their own creation to which they had to adapt themselves. Humans, through the dynamic of gene-culture coevolution, increasingly determined the conditions of their own evolution, or, as the title of anthropologist V. Gordon Childe's book puts it, *Man Makes Himself* (1936). Their cultural suppleness enabled them to spread all over the globe, with its highly varied climates, flora, and fauna, while remaining essentially the same species. However, it was only after the Neolithic revolution—the adoption of agriculture about 10,000 years ago—that the pace of cultural change

---

[6] Very recently, an abstract pattern, a crosshatch of red lines like a hashtag, has been found on a rock chip in a cave in South Africa dating back 73,000 years. This now stands as the first evidence of the use of symbols that store information outside the human brain. The big bang in symbolic art about 30,000 years ago is most striking in the cave paintings of Chauvet, Altamira, and Lascaux, as well as carvings of human figures such as the Venus of Willendorf or the Loewenmensch. And this art was extraordinarily complex. It is reported that when Pablo Picasso viewed the cave paintings at the Lascaux caves in the Dordogne region of France, he declared in reference to the modern art he so actively participated in creating that "we have discovered nothing" (J. P. Miller 2018).

dramatically sped up, and the intervening time since has been too short for it to have greatly affected humanity's genetic makeup.[7]

The fact that there was relatively little material and political inequality among hunter-gatherers does not mean that inequality did not exist. As detailed in Chapter 2, all sexually reproducing animals compete for sex. Humans are not excepted, and they will deploy every socially acceptable advantage available, even in the most equal society in other terms. In this fundamental biological sense, sexual competition meant that human societies were never, and never could be, purely egalitarian.

However, it was imperative that their self-interest in success in sexual competition be channeled into behavior that was socially valued. Social approval was essential for attracting mates. Therefore, what would *appear* as egoism, ambition, or greed had to be repressed. Flannery and Marcus claim that "foragers knew that as long as they suppressed ambition and greed, they could be well thought of" (2012, 66). More correctly stated, they needed to conceal their ambition and greed, perhaps even from themselves. Evolutionary biologist Robert Trivers offers the interesting hypothesis that self-deception evolved as a trait in our prehistoric environment to enable us better to hide the truth from others by suppressing the signs of deception, such as shifty eyes or sweaty palms (1985, 415, 416).

It was also imperative that others be treated with appropriate generosity. This meant not just sharing, but also not shaming others by giving something so valuable that they could not reciprocate, thereby generating status inequality. The properly generous were considered superior in virtue, which gave them more access to mates and thus more offspring (Flannery and Marcus 2012, 561).

Because foragers were nomadic, they had few material possessions of economic value beyond stone tools and clothing. Nevertheless, they often possessed items that could be characterized as "conspicuous consumption," providing a degree of social prestige. Most notable were beads, earrings, pendants, and necklaces. Body piercing and other forms of body art were also common. As early as 70,000–80,000 years ago, humans were drilling seashells to make necklaces and painting themselves with natural pigments

---

[7] The ability to digest milk as adults is one of the best-documented examples of genetic evolution due to cultural changes since the adoption of agriculture (Holden and Mace 2009). Nevertheless, there have only been 240 human generations over this period and only 160 since digesting milk by adults became widespread, likely too short a period for more substantial genetic change in the human species (Scott 2017, 86).

such as red ocher and white pipe clay (Flannery and Marcus 2012, 6). Tattoos and scarring could confer status because acquiring them signaled courage and fortitude to tolerate pain and risk infection. Although such items and practices have no obvious evolutionary survival advantage, and indeed such practices could increase the chances of infection and death, they could be of service for sexual selection, much like the peacock's tail or the stag's antlers. In the case of humans, these cultural practices were art, intended to attract the attention of potential mates (Miller 2001; Dutton 2010; Prum 2017).

The dynamics of sexual selection have also been credited with powering the evolution of human language. Language permits humans to know each other more profoundly than any other human capacity. Those capable of speaking with sophistication and eloquence reveal intelligence, which confers status, increasing the attractiveness of the speaker to potential mates.

A final observation on the quality of life among Jean-Jacques Rousseau's supposed "noble savages" highlights their lack of privacy and their forced conformity. Political scientist Carles Boix writes that

> ... in stateless communities every one of their members monitors everyone else constantly, talking about and judging them in public, and sanctioning harshly any individual deviation from their common expectations about what constitutes good behavior—even to the point of ostracizing or killing those who defy societal norms. (2015, 8)

However, even after the rise of the state and civilization, and until recent times, humans continued to live without much privacy, and all societies enforce a substantial degree of conformity.

Sharing and Equality

Beyond taking up weapons and forming groups to oppose bullies, these stateless forager and early agricultural communities evolved a vast array of social practices, values, and rituals to equalize the distribution of material resources and political power in accordance with their sense of fairness.

Hunters and gatherers would typically exploit an area until it was well picked over and then move on, often following the migratory routes of animals. They shared food such that no one starved unless virtually all did so.

Unlike hierarchically structured primates that ate their food as they came upon it, humans brought their food back to encampments and shared it with others. Anthropologist David Graeber notes, "The obligation to share food, and whatever else is considered a basic necessity, tends to become the basis of everyday morality in a society whose members see themselves as equals." He goes on to point out that "early missionary accounts of native North Americans almost invariably include awestruck remarks on generosity in times of famine, often to total strangers" (2012, 98).

Explorer and anthropologist Peter Freuchen gave a classic report of this attitude toward food sharing among foragers. A Greenlander returned from a hunt empty-handed and found that a successful hunter had left him a few hundred pounds of walrus meat. His attempt to thank him was met with indignation:

> Up in our country we are human! And since we are human we help each other. We don't like to hear anybody say thanks for that. What I get today you may get tomorrow. Up here we say that by gifts one makes slaves and by whips one makes dogs. (1961, 154)

Hunter-gatherers held to a rule that all meat be distributed so as to preclude that an especially skillful hunter might gain social power and sexual privilege by controlling its allocation. Groups used ridicule and social pressure to thwart anyone from developing a sense of superiority. Arrogance or boastfulness was belittled. Even when a hunter had been exceptionally successful, he was expected to be humble and self-deprecatory, presenting his success as the result of collective effort, thereby dampening blatant sexual advantage. Boehm adds:

> In effect, the group intimidates its stronger, more gifted, or more assertive members to keep them in line, but at the same time it uses them, in strictly limited ways, for purposes of leadership or meat procurement. . . . When foragers suppress upstarts who would like to dominate their peers, they are thinking about food resources in addition to personal political autonomy. (1997, S104, S112)

Sharing was so important that foragers had to refrain from saving lest they be suspected of selfishly hoarding it (Flannery and Marcus 2012, 549). Anthropologist Richard Lee reports:

The most serious accusations one !Kung can level against another are the charges of stinginess and the charge of arrogance. To be stingy, or far-hearted, is to hoard one's goods jealously and secretively, guarding them "like a hyena." The corrective for this is to make the hoarder give "till it hurts"; that is to make him give generously and without stint until everyone can see that he is truly cleaned out. In order to ensure compliance with this cardinal rule the !Kung browbeat each other constantly to be more generous and not to hoard. (1979, 458)

Economist Angus Deaton speculates that "our current deep-seated concerns with fairness, as well as our outrage when our norms of fairness are violated, are quite possibly rooted in the absence of storage options for prehistoric hunters" (2013, 76).

In addition to its reproductive leveling effect, sharing food within the group constituted a form of social insurance, since luck in hunting and gathering could vary considerably for an individual over time. It was better to share one's bounty today so that others would reciprocally share their future successes. Anthropologist Polly Wiessner claims that for an individual hunter, sharing could serve as a form of investment. She observes that after a period of successful hunting, a !Kung male may take it easy for a period, taking advantage of his built-up reciprocal obligations (1982, 68).

Graeber additionally identifies a deeper motivation for sharing: "... sharing is not simply about morality, but also about pleasure. Solitary pleasures will always exist, but for most human beings, the most pleasurable activities almost always involve sharing something: music, food, liquor, drugs, gossip, drama, beds. There is a certain communism of the senses at the root of most things we consider fun" (2012, 99).

Sharing and cooperation generally require a degree of trust, and thus there was an evolutionary advantage in the ability to determine trustworthiness. Judging character was of utmost importance. Humans were selected not for abstract reasoning per se, but for a form of social reasoning that serves to interpret the motivations and intentions of others before responding or taking action. It has been suggested that the human ability to reason evolved in large part for evaluating the arguments of others (Mercier and Sperber 2011).[8]

---

[8] Neurobiologist Terrence Sejnowski writes, "Yes, we can learn how to think logically or follow rules, but only after a lot of training, and most of us aren't very good at it" (2018, 37).

Gossip is talk between at least two people about others, who are not pre-sent. It accounts for about two-thirds of conversation, and our preoccupation with it had, and still has, important survival advantages (Emler 1994; Harari 2015). Life or death can depend upon whom to trust. Language may have evolved in part because of its potential for the transmission of information concerning whom to trust. Low points out that, in game-theory contexts, "the more that people could communicate, and the more they could punish cheaters . . . the more they cooperated and the better their payoff" (2001, 191).[9] Cognitive scientist Steven Pinker claims, "Our hypersociality comes about because information is a particularly good commodity of exchange that makes it worth people's while to hang out together" (2003, 29).

The evolutionary advantage of being able to determine trustworthiness that evolved in hunter-gatherer societies clarifies why many people today are so drawn to tabloid-like material, rather than to issues that physically and materially affect them, such as highway safety, or tax and spending bills. People often give more rapt attention to political scandals than to the details of politicians' policy stances.

Scott points out that "historically, the subsistence safety of hunters and gatherers lay precisely in their mobility and the diversity of food sources to which they could lay claim" (2017, 64). Nevertheless, when starvation did occur, it was not faced alone by individuals or families since food was shared by all members of the group. All in society suffered starvation's ravages, leading political and anthropological economist Karl Polanyi to remark, "It is the absence of the threat of individual starvation which makes primitive society, in a sense, more human than market economy, and at the same time less economic" (1944, 164). To be well off in early societies was to be among others with whom resources are shared. Among the Nunu people of Zaire, the word for a poor person is the same as for a person alone (Harms 1999, 65).

Trust was also essential for the evolution of trade, evidence for which dates back about 50,000 years, within the time span of the presumed "cognitive revolution." Peaceable trade between groups depended on mutually trusting outsiders and holding a degree of confidence in their behavior. It is remark-able that trust-dependent trade evolved when humans generally viewed all strangers as enemies. As will be seen later, however, their normally homicidal

[9] Political economists Samuel Bowles and Herbert Gintis report that ". . . evidence indicates that solitary individuals rarely attempt to punish those who violate social norms. When punishment occurs, it is usually collective, and partly for this reason conveys a message of peer condemna-tion . . . groups with more punishers can sustain more cooperation" (2013, 149, 148).

relationship with outsiders was driven by the dynamics of sexual competition, which could conceivably be overruled by the benefits of trade. In addition, the procurement of foreign goods might confer sexual advantages on the traders.

Children were raised to cooperate, share, and trust each other within the group. These values were communicated through adult behavior and storytelling that emphasized the subordination of individuals' needs to those of the group. Anthropologist Jared Diamond reports that "children's play involves cooperation rather than winning and losing . . . [and that in New Guinea, for instance] children learn to share, and not to seek an advantage for themselves." Their cooperative behavior provided them with a form of social maturity. He notes how Westerners "are struck by the emotional security, self-confidence, curiosity, and autonomy of members of small-scale societies, not only as adults but already as children" (2012, 204, 91, 208). Contemporary research finds that trust within societies varies inversely with the degree of inequality (Wilkinson and Pickett 2019).

Recall Kanazawa's claim that our mentality and psychological needs were formed on the savannah. Researchers have found that modern humans suffer from the suppression of many deep sentiments, such as cooperation rather than competition, and sharing rather than hoarding, that evolved during our early tribal existence. Benjamin Franklin noted the curious phenomena that Indians did not voluntarily join civilized society, and that Whites rescued from Indian captivity soon expressed disgust at "our manner of life" and tried to return to their former captors. They chose the egalitarian and communal nature of primitive life over that of colonial civilization. What humans need is a sense of being necessary, useful, and thus appreciated. This may help clarify why rear-echelon troops are more likely to suffer from post-traumatic stress disorder (PTSD) than combatants, who account for only about 10 percent of the armed forces (Junger 2016).

Work and Leisure

It seems ironic that when technology was at its most primitive level, and humans possessed the least control over nature, work was not viewed negatively. Historians and anthropologists inform us that, prior to the rise of states, people did not clearly distinguish between work time and leisure time. Indeed, the distinction did not exist. Frequently the vocabularies of these peoples did not include a distinct word for work (Curle 1949, 41). Anthropologist Joffre Dumazedier has described this lack of a clear differentiation between work and leisure as follows:

> In the earliest known societies, work and play alike formed part of the ritual by which men sought communion with the ancestral spirits. Both these activities ... had the same kind of meaning in the essential life of the community. Religious festivals embodied both work and play. Moreover, work and play were often combined.... "Leisure" is not a term that can be applied to societies of the archaic period. (1968, 248–49)

Similarly, historian Keith Thomas reports that the Dogons of the Sudan

> employ the same words to indicate both cultivating the ground and dancing at a religious ceremony, for to them both are equally useful forms of activity. Technique and ritual are thus bound up together, each an indispensable means of maintaining the preservation and unity of the group. (1964, 51)

It was long believed that the reason a work-leisure distinction was not found among primitive peoples is that the scarcity problem was so harsh as to preclude the very possibility of leisure time. However, since the 1960s, anthropologists have rejected the view that hunting and gathering peoples never rested from an unrelenting struggle just to survive. Apparently, such peoples enjoyed a great deal of time that was not devoted explicitly to meeting their material needs.

A striking example is provided by the !Kung. Although dwelling in one of the least hospitable environments imaginable, the Kalahari desert, they reportedly spent only between 12 and 19 hours per week in activities directly related to subsistence (Lewin 1978, 95). Anthropologists have found similar hours of work for other hunter-gatherer peoples. It is this short workweek, imposed by necessity, that prompted anthropologist Marshall Sahlins to refer to foraging peoples as "the original affluent society": "Hunter-gatherers consume less energy per capita per year than any other group of human beings.... To accept that hunters are affluent is therefore to recognise that the present human condition of man slaving to bridge the gap between his unlimited wants and his insufficient means is a tragedy of modern times" (1974, 3).[10]

---

[10] Benjamin Franklin noted that the Indians of the Iroquois Confederacy viewed the "laborious manner of life" of the colonists as "slavish and base," revealing them to be hostage to "infinite

An important reason why work was not viewed in paleolithic societies as intrinsically unpleasant is that it was not coerced by unequal social power. Aside from sexual divisions of labor necessitated by biology and environmental conditions, all shared more or less equally in scarcity-driven tasks. No parasitic class lived off the labors of others. As anthropologist Marvin Harris puts it: "People did what they had to do, but the where and when of it was not laid out by someone else. No executives, foremen, or bosses stood apart, measuring and counting" (1991, 101).

The dynamics of evolution suggest that activities necessary to meet basic needs would be selected to be gratifying to better motivate their accomplishment, just as taste preferences were selected to guide appetites toward nutritious foods, and sex was selected to be pleasurable to better ensure reproduction. Note that later elites have found (as have recent non-elites) great enjoyment in the primordial activity of pursuing game, as Adam Smith remarked: "Hunting and fishing, the most important employments of mankind in the rude state of society, become in its most advanced state their most agreeable amusements, and they pursue for pleasure what they once followed from necessity" (1776, 100–1). Relatedly, one might also mention cooking on an outdoor grill. Agriculture that was not socially coerced may have been similarly rewarding. Note the widespread enjoyment of gardening in modern times. In the United Kingdom, for instance, in a population of 64 million, 27 million partake in "leisure" gardening (Evergreen Garden Care 2020). Many productive activities of early humans, such as cooking, woodworking, pottery, knitting, sewing, weaving, and leather work, are much later practiced as hobbies.

Aristotle wrote in *Politics* that, "it is the business of nature to furnish subsistence for each being brought into the world; and this is shown by the fact that the offspring of animals always gets nourishment from the residuum of the matter that gives it its birth" (1962, 28, 1258a). Aristotle's attitude appears to extend back to the very earliest humans. Anthropologist Rodney Needham points out that the behavior of hunter-gathering peoples exhibited "a confidence in the capacity of the environment to support them, and in their own ability to extract their livelihood from it" (quoted in Leakey and Levin 1978, 106). They did not view themselves as involved in a struggle with

Artificial wants," whereas the Indians possessed only "few . . . wants," which could be satisfied by "the spontaneous productions of nature with the addition of very little labor, if hunting and fishing may indeed be called labor when Game is so plenty." Thus, compared to the colonists, the Indians enjoyed an "abundance of leisure" (cited in Suzman 2021, 244).

nature, but as living harmoniously in it. Just as foragers shared with each other, they viewed their environment as sharing with them, as opposed to presenting them with a challenge of scarcity (Suzman 2021, 147).

Hunters were capable of extreme effort, pursuing game for days on end with little rest (Leo Marx 2000). But, once the hunt had succeeded, they would be idle until their food supplies were used up. Perhaps this capacity, if not preference, for hard labor followed by idleness has remained with humanity. Historian E. P. Thompson notes of free workers in the seventeenth century that "the work pattern was one of alternate bouts of intense labour and idleness, wherever men were in control of their own working lives," and he writes that, because this "pattern persists among some self-employed— artists, writers, small farmers, and perhaps also with students—today, [it] provokes the question whether it is not a 'natural' human work-rhythm" (1963, 73).

It is also claimed that the rewarding complexity of work life has been diminished over the course of history. Scott writes that, compared

> with the life world of the hunter-gatherer . . . the life of farming is comparatively far narrower experientially and, in both a cultural and a ritual sense, more impoverished. . . . It is no exaggeration to say that hunting and foraging are, in terms of complexity, as different from cereal-grain farming as cereal-grain farming is, in turn, removed from repetitive work on a modern assembly line. Each step represents a substantial narrowing of focus and a simplification of tasks. (2017, 20, 90)

Cross-cultural psychologist John Berry also reports greater cognitive complexity among foragers than agriculturalists. For instance, the former are better able to analyze parts and wholes. Not surprisingly, agricultural peoples are less independent and more conformist than hunter-gatherers (1976). Harari concurs:

> . . . at the individual level, ancient foragers were the most knowledgeable and skillful people in history. There is some evidence that the size of the average brain has actually *decreased* since the age of foraging. Survival in that era required superb mental abilities from everyone. When agriculture and industry came along people could increasingly rely on the skills of others for survival, and new "niches for imbeciles" were opened up. (2015, 49)

Murderous Warriorhood as Sexual
Competition

Nature, red in tooth and claw.
  —Alfred Lord Tennyson, *In Memoriam* (1895, Canto 55)

Rousseau famously asserted that "nothing can be more gentle than [a human] in his primitive state.... The example of the savages . . . seems to confirm that mankind was formed ever to remain in it, . . . and that all ulterior improvements have been so many steps . . . towards the decrepitness of the species" (1755, 161–62). The simplification of work noted earlier would support Rousseau's claim. Rousseau envisioned the primeval man as one who lived in a pacific state of nature, and was therefore "a free being, whose heart is at peace, and body in health," during an era he considered "the best for man" (1755, 150, 167).

However, although early humans may have been smarter in work, and more egalitarian, cooperative, and generous within their social units, their existence should not be overly romanticized. Foragers lived in dangerous environments, inhabited not only by large predator animals, but also by other belligerent bands. In fact, their experience was far removed from that of Rousseau's imaginary noble savage. Hunting and gathering peoples were anything but peaceable beyond their own group and, as their technical skills evolved, so too did their weapons. The personal, social, and tactical skills necessary for bringing down prey were well-suited for inflicting death in war.

Until fairly recently, the dominant view was that foragers' warring was infrequent and quite limited in scope, resulting in few deaths and injuries. This view prevailed in spite of Darwin's observation in the *Descent of Man* of his making contact with Fuegians, who "like wild animals lived on what they could catch; . . . had no government, and were merciless to every one not of their own small tribe . . ." (1871, 398). Apparently ignoring this observation, as well as that of others describing their encounters with foragers, the reasoning was that bands' meager material wealth would have offered other groups little incentive to attack. Further, unless there was a shortage of promising hunting and gathering territory, groups would not so readily risk death or injury in battle. An economic form of reasoning was believed to have prevailed, one balancing the risk of death from starvation against the risk of death in battle. And because these nomadic groups could usually move on to other territories, conflict was believed to have played out chiefly in the form of bluffing, as opposing groups attempted to convince each other of their fighting superiority and willingness to do battle.[11] But, when push came to shove, fleeing was a more rational choice than fighting.

Recognition of a more powerful motivation for belligerence has challenged this highly "economistic" view of weighing material benefits against costs. Extensive evidence suggests that warfare in pre-agricultural societies was incessant, driven more by the sexual rewards of capturing women and the sexual attractiveness of being a successful warrior than by economic advantage. Those warriors who succeeded in killing enemies mated with more women and sired more children, thereby passing more of their murderous genes into future generations—a biological basis for the observation that "many societies believed that the taking of a head could add to one's life force" (Flannery and Marcus 2012, 553). Particularly successful male warriors were more likely to have multiple wives, although usually not more than three or four. Anthropologist Napoleon Chagnon calculated that among the Yanomamö, those who killed had an average of over two and a half more wives and more than three times as many children (Diamond 2012, 163). Because of the egalitarian character of these societies, a male would be unlikely to command enough resources to care for a larger number of wives and children. Also, because of the high mortality among males, "polygynous marriages soak up any 'extra' women" (Henrich, Boyd, and Richerson 2012, 659). Polygamous men in forager societies have been estimated at less than 20 percent of all males (Otterbein 1994).

Violent routes to prestige included leading warriors into combat, killing numerous enemies, and returning with captives, heads, scalps, genitalia, or other body parts as proof of success. Flannery and Marcus report that among the Konyak Naga in northeastern India, "Men who had taken heads received special tattoos and were allowed to wear a brass pendant in the form of a trophy head. . . . Warriors returning to the village with enemy heads were greeted enthusiastically, bathed, and honored with dances" (2012, 51, 204).

Low notes that ". . . if a man avoids several possible opportunities, or behaves in ways perceived as cowardly on the raids, he becomes the butt

---

[11] Bluffing is common among animals. Various displays to seem bigger, stronger, and more ferocious are meant to convince potential enemies that an attack would be costly if not fatal. For instance, fangs show and hair stands up on many animals, giving the impression of larger size. Humans stand tall, puff up their chests, and stiffen their muscles. Economist John von Neumann, founder of game theory, claimed that "real life consists of bluffing, of little tactics of deception, of asking yourself what is the other man going to think I mean to do. And that is what games are about in my theory" (cited in Harford 2016).

of jokes, and other men may begin to make sexual overtures to his wife" (2001, 224). Flannery and Marcus report that among some peoples, "a man who had beheaded no one was considered such a wimp that he had trouble getting a wife" (2012, 105). They report the case of an Incan general who had lost a number of battles being sent women's clothing, which he was forced to wear upon returning to Cusco (2012, 538). After head-hunting was forbidden by conquering modern societies, complaints such as the following were expressed: "Once we had leaders who lined the walls of our men's house with enemy skulls, but now we are reduced to squabbling like girly men" (Flannery and Marcus 2012, 51).

Darwin wrote that "with savages . . . the women are the constant cause of war both between members of the same tribe and between distinct tribes" (1871, 871). Anthropologist and historian Laura Betzig reports that "the evidence suggests that in virtually all societies, women are a significant cause of male conflicts of interest" (1986, 26).[12]

In this manner, a genetic proclivity for warlike behavior was presumably selected, even though many warriors were killed. Most hunter-gatherer societies were patrilocal (wives are sought from outside the band to live with the husband's family). Consequently, many, if not most, of the males in the band were relatives. If one were killed, some of his genes—those shared with his relatives—would still pass into future generations, exemplifying the same evolutionary dynamic that underlies kin altruism. Interestingly, our closest primate relatives, chimpanzees, whose genome is almost 99 percent identical to humans, are also patrilocal and share this propensity for murderous raids on other groups. None of this, of course, is incompatible with successful warfare yielding economic benefits. Annihilating one's enemies also meant reduced competition for scarce resources.

To minimize risks, such warfare was often carried out as raids, ambushes, and surprise attacks. The ideal was to gain or protect territory and to exterminate the opponent so as to preclude revenge. It was noted in Chapter 2 how a sense of fairness underlies a desire for revenge, a human emotion that ranks among the most powerful, comparable in strength with jealousy, anger, grief, and fear. Humanity's murderous evolution may have reinforced this emotion. Homer's Achilles described experiencing revenge as "far sweeter than flowing honey welling up like smoke in the breasts of man" (1847, Book

---

[12] Betzig quotes Confucius's dictum that "disorder does not come from heaven, but is brought about by women" (1986, 26).

18). Criminologist Fiona Brookman found that revenge was a motivation for 34 percent of British homicides (2003). An appetite for vengeance would be selected over the course of human evolution since those who successfully took murderous revenge on their enemies would gain a greater probability of surviving to pass on their genes to posterity.

According to anthropologist Lawrence Keeley, 65 percent of pre-agricultural societies were at war continuously, and 87 percent fought more than once a year. As many as 10 percent of a band's population might perish in a single raid. To limit revenge, they typically killed their enemies, taking no prisoners except women. It has been estimated that about 30 percent of males were killed in warfare, about the same rate as for chimpanzees (1997, 174). Peace might prevail during certain times and periods, but these interludes appear to have been infrequent and short-lived (LeBlanc and Register 2004, 8). This history of constant warfare and its high rate of casualties may help explain why males reportedly discount the future more than do women.

Boys were raised to know how to fight and to survive attacks. To help eliminate qualms about killing, enemies were frequently depicted as sub-human. Religion also evolved to legitimate hostile attitudes toward outsiders. Sociologists Timothy Crippen and Richard Machalek note that "perhaps more powerfully than any other human behavioral mechanism, religions divide 'in-groups' and 'out-groups' " (1989, 76–77).

Given the sex-driven incentive for warlike behavior, peace between groups would have been difficult to achieve and fragile without an overarching centralized government to enforce it. Although warriors took only female prisoners, occasionally they dragged a male enemy back to the village to be tortured to death. William Bradford of the *Mayflower* pilgrims observed of the natives of Massachusetts:

> Not being content only to kill and take away life, [they] delight to torment men in the most bloody manner that may be, flaying some alive with the shells of fishes, cutting off members and joints of others by piecemeal and broiling on the coals, eat collops of their flesh in their sight while they live. (quoted in Steven Pinker 2011, 44)

Yet hostility did not characterize all contact with other groups or tribes. The practice of gift-giving with non-kin neighboring peoples frequently existed, with the expectation that gifts of approximately equal value would at some point be given in return. Such gift-giving created good will and also served as a form of social security. There could be resource-sharing in especially challenging periods when food was scarce. There were even instances in which these trading partners were made honorary kinsmen (Flannery and Marcus 2012, 548).

However, as noted earlier, it was imperative that gifts not be so grand that trading partners be shamed by not being able to reciprocate with gifts of equal value. Such attitudes and practices served to prevent anyone or any clan from gaining an edge in inequality. A guarded effort was made to prevent reciprocity from degenerating into a sense of indebtedness, because, as Flannery and Marcus write, "The loss of face created by asymmetrical exchange could lead to blood feuds, and blood feuds could increase the scalping and head-hunting" (2012, 553). For this reason, Graeber claims, "...religious traditions often insist that the only true charity is anonymous—in other words, not meant to place the recipient in one's debt" (2012, 109). After the adoption of agriculture, most farming tribes continued these forms of intergroup generosity and non-competitive gift giving (2012, 66–87, 98, 553).

How do the warring tendencies of early humans square with the self-domestication that tended to reduce violence? Self-domestication resulted from the cooperative killing of violent individuals within the group, thereby reducing their genes' prevalence in future generations. Because this occurred within the group, it strengthened the community by favoring more cooperative behavior. Killing outsiders was also celebrated as a practice that fortified the community. Self-domestication thus appears to have lessened murderous behavior inside the community while reinforcing it outside. However, because groups became ever larger over subsequent history, overall violence decreased.

The Adoption of Agriculture and the Rise of Limited Inequality

Why anyone not impelled by hunger, danger, or coercion would willingly give up hunting and foraging or pastoralism for full-time agriculture is hard to fathom.
—James C. Scott, *Against the Grain* (2017, 18)

The success of a species is measured by its population growth; an increasing population signals success, a declining one, failure. Among humans, technological advances such as fire and hunting tools increased available food, and more children survived. But greater population density also meant that foraging grounds could be more rapidly depleted. The result was shorter and less healthy humans who had to spend more time procuring food (Deaton 2013, 77).

Along with climatic changes brought about by the end of the last ice age, increases in population and more sophisticated technology in both foraging and husbandry are believed to have encouraged humans to take up agriculture—the Neolithic revolution.[13] Economist Ester Boserup advanced a "backs-to-the-wall" hypothesis: agriculture, she claimed, was a forced choice because the superior option of continuing foraging was no longer viable (1965). Although Boserup's hypothesis has been challenged and alternatives offered, there is inadequate evidence to resolve the debate convincingly (Boix 2015, 111ff).

It has also been claimed that humans became sedentary prior to adopting agriculture. Scott argues that in Mesopotamia, where the transition is believed initially to have occurred, foragers first became sedentary because the wetlands abounded in food; "planting and livestock rearing as *dominant* subsistence practices were avoided for as long as possible because of the work they required" (2017, 96).

Although some primitive agriculture appears to have been practiced long before the Neolithic revolution, perhaps as much as 40,000 years earlier, it was done as a supplement to foraging (Flannery and Marcus 2012, 7). The adoption of agriculture as a principal means of subsistence[14] is generally dated to about 10,000 years ago. Most early agriculturalists were semi-nomadic, practicing "slash and burn" or "shifting agriculture," burning off an area of

---

[13] Around 20,000 years ago the ice of the last glaciation began melting, and by 8000 BC temperatures had risen to a point where they stabilized and persisted. The end of the last glacial period also witnessed a surge in atmospheric carbon dioxide, which increases the photosynthesis rate and lowers the photorespiration rate (Suzman 2021, 188–89). The end of the last ice age marks the beginning of the Holocene era that has provided a relatively warm and stable climate, enabling humans to extract more energy from their environments, thereby setting conditions in which population could grow and social and economic development could more readily evolve. Yet world population remained very low. Evolutionary biologist David Sloan Wilson and economist John Gowdy report that "for 95–99% of our existence as a species, the worldwide human population was under 4 million and may have dropped to a few hundred thousand at some points" (2015, 43).

[14] An interesting alternative or complementary hypothesis is that humans first cultivated cereals for making beer, which is not only nutritious, but also intoxicating and germfree. Only sedentary agriculture could ensure a year-round supply. Supposedly, beer enhanced ceremonies and strengthened social bonds (Courtwright 2019; Slingerland 2021).

forest and cultivating it until the soil was exhausted, and then relocating to new forests, while continuing to forage.

The more complete adoption of agriculture was the most transformative of all revolutions. It was a transition from searching for food, much like all other animals, to producing food in a controlled manner. It set in motion the cultural foundations underlying a sustained progression toward greater social complexity, technological dynamism, and ever greater inequality. Agriculture was a precondition for the rise of the state and civilization, private property, subjugation, and extreme inequality, all of which, paradoxically, were eventually to establish the preconditions for the material wealth and freedom of the contemporary world.

Food in the form of grains and domesticated animals could be stored, creating the potential for wealth accumulation. Whereas reproductive success for men in hunter-gatherer societies correlated with their success in hunting and war, status and thus the degree of reproductive success in agricultural and pastoral societies evolved to include control of and rights to cultivatable land and herd animals (Fieder and Huber 2012, 192). And as these communities grew in size, so too did the need for more sophisticated social organization, or formal government.

It is not fully correct, however, to associate a right to the exclusive use of productive property with inequality. *Pace* Rousseau and Marx, a right to productive property did not automatically or inexorably entail social inequality. In pre-state societies, for instance, households with subsistence family plots remained more or less socially equal as long as ample land was available. Plot size would depend upon the household's capacity to farm it. As will be seen in Chapter 5, substantial inequality only evolved with the rise of states that protected elites' ability to own and control access to all productive property, leaving others with no attractive options but to accept subordination and exploitation. They had to work for the wealthy elites or starve. Without alternatives, they were "caged."

With farming, life became more settled, enabling mothers to care for more children than was possible among nomadic foragers. Further, grain diets softened by cooking enabled children to be weaned earlier, permitting pregnancy at shorter intervals. High-carbohydrate diets also boost ovulation and thus the frequency of pregnancy (Scott 2017, 114). But it was principally improvements in agricultural productivity that boosted population density. Whereas population density among foragers averaged 0.05 persons per square mile, it increased in the Levant to about 35 per square mile following the adoption of agriculture. It rose as high as 155 per square mile with intensive irrigated agriculture.

Progress for foragers had been constrained not only by the social organization necessary for their nomadism, but also by their inability to accumulate wealth and the limits to their division of labor. With sedentism, non-portable wealth, such as land, buildings, and workshops, could be accumulated. Agriculture also permitted the accumulation of food surpluses, enabling some to eat without farming. This change freed them to engage in the development and production of other goods, services, and cultural artifacts. Villages expanded into towns and eventually cities. The increasingly refined division of labor additionally nourished technological advances.

A forager economy is typically depicted as an "immediate return labor investment system," whereas agriculture, by contrast, is viewed as "delayed return" (Woodburn 1980). Although this sharp delineation has been challenged by Scott (2017),[15] the incontestably delayed returns of agriculture entailed that the producers were relatively trapped geographically, meaning that survival would be difficult should they leave their investments. Consequently, living in agricultural settlements made producers more vulnerable to domination by those who could acquire disproportionate power. Unlike foragers, they could not so readily pick up and leave. Further, the greater their harvests or stock of animals, the more they would be targets for outside pillagers, and therefore face a need to fight rather than flee. Their risky position would make them more willing to enter into Douglass North's presumed contract with a state that would give them protection in exchange for a portion of their surplus (1982).[16]

Planting and herding increased what economist Alfred Marshall called humans' telescopic faculty—their orientation to the future. Whereas much of the economic existence of forager peoples was mostly short-run, centered on consuming the food from a few days of hunting and gathering, agriculturalists had to embrace a far longer time horizon. As anthropologist James Suzman relates, "To produce food requires that you live at once in the

---

[15] Scott points out that hunter-gatherers were far from the "immediate return" peoples they have generally been depicted to be: "All mass capture—gazelle, fish, and bird migrations—involve elaborate, cooperative advance preparations: the building of long narrowing 'drive corridors' to a killing ground; building weirs, nets, and traps; building or digging facilities for smoking, drying, or salting of the catch. These are delayed-returned activities par excellence" (2017, 65–66).

[16] The neoclassical economic perspective of viewing this arrangement as a contract suggests that participants are "free to choose," when in fact the "contract" offered by the state was more like organized crime's "offer you can't refuse." The coercion necessary for the creation of the state will be explored in Chapter 5.

past, present, and future. Almost every task on a farm is focused on achieving a future goal or managing a future risk based on past experience" (Suzman 2021, 236). Over an agricultural cycle, they had to plan and save for planting and animal breeding. They had to be strictly disciplined in the sense that, no matter how hungry they might become, they could not eat their seed corn or breeding animals, lest they starve in the next agricultural cycle. Religious beliefs and practices often facilitated this harsh discipline. A notable, albeit much later, example is the Christian Lenten period of belt-tightening that traditionally preceded the birthing of domesticated animals.

To cohere peaceably, all societies must possess some form of organization. Living in small bands with no leaders or hierarchy, forager societies organized themselves in spontaneous and participatory ways. They evolved as natural social units for self-regulation. Many agricultural societies remained egalitarian and did without formal decision-making structures for thousands of years. However, due to free-rider problems that were less susceptible of spontaneous resolution, densely populated agricultural societies required more formal organizational complexity.

The need for self-defense prompted members of early agricultural communities to coalesce into tribes that were substantially united by kinship and culture. In the next stage, if population density continued to increase, these tribes merged into chiefdoms, where some social coordination was performed by a centralized leader with a supporting entourage. This rising organizational complexity begins appearing about 4,000 years before the arrival of the state, civilization, and extreme inequality.

The Ethnographic Atlas data set includes more than 1,100 societies. The data reveal that, while practically no foraging community had a leader, approximately 58 percent of societies practicing extensive agriculture and 77 percent with intensive agriculture were chiefdoms (Boix 2015, 101, 109, 44). These leaders benefited from what Flannery and Marcus call "achievement-based inequality." Although population growth, climatic improvement, and intensive agriculture facilitated the rise of this form of inequality, they did not make it inevitable (Flannery and Marcus 2012, 553).

Achievement-based village societies arose around 9,000 years ago in the Near East, 4,500 years ago in the Andean mountains, and 3,500 years ago in Mexico (Flannery and Marcus 2012, 552). They enabled some men to achieve prestige but limited their ability to accumulate wealth or exercise significant political power. Indeed, Graeber reports, "observers often remarked that in terms of personal possessions, a village chief was often the poorest man in the village, such was the pressure on him for constant supply of largesse" (2012, 113). Their reward came in the form of greater reproductive potential.

In some agricultural societies, ambitious men achieved greater prestige by showing exceptional leadership in raiding and head-hunting. Alternatively, they did so by rising in religious achievement such as making sacrifices or sponsoring other ritual events. Costly or painful sacrifices demonstrated their dedication to what the community viewed as most sacred. Among these sacrificial practices, scarring was common. Far more extreme were excruciating acts such as "suspension of oneself by skewers through the flesh" (Flannery and Marcus 2012, 173), or "chopping off a finger joint, circumcising or subincising (splitting lengthwise) the penis, or spilling one's blood by cutting one's nose or tongue or penis or inside the throat or other body part" (Diamond 2012, 330, 331). Low points out:

> As in sexual selection (in which females are likely to require expensive, unbluffable displays of quality and willingness to commit), in social selection we frequently require evidence of a willingness to be a good group cooperator, even—or especially—when that is likely to be expensive. (2001, 167)

Individuals might also achieve status by being especially skilled in entrepreneurial exchange. The greater the distance from which trade goods came, and thus the greater the danger in their procurement, the more prestigious the trader. In addition to making religious sacrifices and importing prized goods from afar, high-status males might borrow food and property from kinsmen to sponsor events such as ritual feasting or to oversee the building of ceremonial lodges, stone monuments, and other public structures (Flannery and Marcus, 2012, 121, 176). Diamond contends that it was status competition among the elite of Easter Island that led to the creation and erection of the 397 mammoth legless statues of human male figures, the largest of which was 70 feet tall and weighed 270 tons. They were transported and erected without cranes, wheels, metal tools, or draft animals (2006, 79–135).

A more common (and frequently mentioned) example of sacrifice in pursuit of prestige is that of the "big man" who hosted a feast so splendid, or gave a gift of such value, that his rivals would be shamed because they could not match his largesse. This was a clear change from the life of foragers, where shaming was unacceptable and punished. Whereas individuals in hunting and gathering societies were strictly barred from publicly displaying superiority, achievement-based agricultural societies permitted an open, albeit still limited, display of preeminence.

It is noteworthy that big men did not exploit others by forcefully misappropriating their surpluses. Nor did they accumulate significant wealth beyond what they intended to give away. They "were rich for what they dispensed and not for what they hoarded" (Fried 1967, 118). They worked hard and convinced others to aid them in their endeavors.

Nevertheless, the big men's successes enabled them to have two or three wives (Flannery and Marcus 2012, 99, 101). The more wives they possessed, the more gardens they had from which to draw food for gifts or feasts that could humiliate rivals. More wives also meant, of course, more offspring. Harris depicts "bigmanship" as follows:

> to achieve *mumi* [big man] status is every youth's highest ambition. A young man proves himself capable of becoming a *mumi* by working harder than everyone else and by carefully restricting his own consumption of meat and coconuts. Eventually, he impresses his wife, children and near relatives with the seriousness of his intentions, and they vow to help him prepare for his first feast. If the feast is a success, his circle of supporters widens and he sets to work readying an even greater display of generosity. . . . [His followers] remain loyal as long as their *mumi* continues to maintain or increase his renown as a "great provider." (1991, 104–5)

A big man would retain his prestige until he could not match a feast mounted or gift given by a rival. Anthropologist Marcel Mauss studied the potlatch, or gift-giving feast, practiced by Indians on the northwest coast of North America. He characterized the power game behind the potlatch as follows:

> The motive for these excessive gifts and this reckless consumption, the senseless loss and destruction of property is in no way unselfishly motivated. Among chieftains, vassals, and followers a hierarchy is established by means of these gifts. Giving is a way of demonstrating one's superiority, of showing that one is greater, that one stands higher . . . ; to accept, without reciprocating or giving more in return, means subordinating oneself, becoming a vassal and follower, sinking deeper. (quoted in Schivelbusch 1993, 173)

There are parallels in modern societies where the recipients of gifts are generally the least powerful and most passive, such as children and, frequently, women in male-dominated societies. The German expression for reciprocating a gift is *sich revanchieren*, an expression linked to the idea of revenge. Accordingly, philosopher Friedrich Nietzsche characterized gratitude as follows:

> The reason why the powerful man is grateful is this: his benefactor, through the benefit he confers, has mistaken and intruded into the sphere of the powerful man, now the latter, in return, penetrates into the sphere of the benefactor by the act of gratitude. It is a milder form of revenge. Without the satisfaction of gratitude, the powerful man would have shown himself powerless, and would have been reckoned as such ever after. Therefore, every society of the good, which originally meant the powerful, places gratitude amongst the first duties. [Jonathan] Swift propounded the maxim that men were grateful in the same proportion as they were revengeful. (1878)

Typically, however, as Flannery and Marcus point out, the big man's economic privileges and political authority were strictly limited by the community: "Many agricultural village societies resisted every attempt to increase inequality. They found a way to let talented people rise to positions of prominence while still preventing the establishment of a hereditary elite" (2012, 153). Successful men were not permitted to accumulate property, and they were encouraged to lead by example, as opposed to exercising substantial political power (Flannery and Marcus 2012, 176). They were pressured to give away accumulated valuables or make them available to the community. Their behavior gave the appearance of generosity rather than self-interest, although, because successful men had greater access to the opposite sex, a fundamental reproductive self-interest was always in play.

The status of high achievers was legitimated by the clan's religious cosmology. Religion, which had previously supported social equality, was reformulated to justify inequality. Eventually, a class of priests arose that structured and controlled rituals, while claiming special access to supernatural forces. "The communal dances ceased. The songs were silenced. The shamans were marginalized as witch doctors or sorcerers.'" (Wade 2009, 78)

High achievers claimed a special place in ritual leadership because, they declared, their ancestors were present at creation. As religion was transformed into an ideology justifying inequality, their higher liturgical status provided them with what biologically has always been the bottom line—greater potential for reproduction and, thus, more progeny. It is notable that the deities who presumably rule over hierarchical societies often have a hierarchy of their own; this arrangement tacitly suggests that the unequal human social order is divinely ordained. These early examples of religion serving to justify differences in rank foreshadow the central importance ideology will come to have in making inequality acceptable, not only to the elites who are its direct beneficiaries, but also to the ordinary people who bear the cost.

Yet, there persisted strong resistance to sanctioning superiority in any domain other than the ritual hierarchy. Flannery and Marcus affirm that there remained "constant pressure to give away your possessions to others, and if you began to act superior, you would be ridiculed even by your own relatives" (2012, 181). They also find that most attempts to establish achievement-based societies "ended with a return to egalitarian behavior" (2012, 551).

Hereditary Inequality

It is in the age of shepherds. . . that the inequality of fortune first begins to take place, and introduces among men a degree of authority and subordination which could not possibly exist before. It thereby introduces some degree of that civil government which is indispensably necessary for its own preservation.
—Adam Smith, *The Wealth of Nations* (1776, 674)

Hereditary chiefdoms and rank inequality appeared in Mesopotamia between 7,300 and 7,000 years ago, and in Peru and Mexico between 3,200 and 3,000 years ago (Flannery and Marcus 2012, 207). Rulers and elites claiming hereditary superiority acquired the power to take larger shares of practically everything desirable, including a greater number of wives. Again, a religious cosmology legitimated their claim of higher status. Inequality was said, in religious language, to be in conformity with what is cosmically correct. Sociologist of knowledge Peter Berger describes this religious legitimation as follows:

The political authority is conceived of as the agent of the gods, or ideally even as a divine incarnation. Human power, government, and punishment thus become sacramental phenomena, that is, channels by which divine forces are made to impinge upon the lives of men. The ruler speaks for the gods, or is a god, and to obey him is to be in a right relationship with the world of the gods. (1967, 124)

In this manner, religious ideology presented the extra share of everything desirable that accrued to rulers and the nobility as an allocation condoned by higher forces and, thus, indisputably suitable. The elite were the agents or servants of gods or celestial powers, and, as philosopher and cognitive scientist Daniel Dennett points out,

> . . . *accepting inferior status to an invisible god is a cunning stratagem,* whether or not its cunning is consciously recognized by those who stumble upon it. Those who rely on it will thrive, wittingly or otherwise. As every subordinate knows, one's commands are more effective than they might otherwise be if one can accompany them with a threat to tell the bigger boss if disobedience ensues. (2006, 172)

In addition to privileged access to women and goods, religiously legitimated status endowed chiefs with political power and afforded them a limited monopoly over the use of violence to maintain internal peace and ensure that all members of society behaved appropriately. It is important to note that their power stemmed from the legitimating ideology, as opposed to command over superior military technology or organization. The stone-age armaments they possessed were virtually the same as those available to their subordinates, the very projectiles that had served as an equalizing force in forager societies.

Their power and wealth permitted leaders to appear generous, thereby gaining the support and admiration of those from whom they were appropriating surplus. Thus began, *in embryo*, a dynamic that would repeat itself throughout subsequent history. An elite acquires political and economic power to appropriate the surplus from producers, frequently leaving them with the mere wherewithal physically to survive, and then uses a part of this surplus to persuade the dispossessed of the elite's generosity. Well-known and thoroughly documented instances include the Greco-Roman world, where wealthy citizens would make munificent endowments for festivals and games. With the rise of Roman Christianity, the wealthy provided funds to the Church for highly visible structures. Contemporary examples are not hard to find. Thanks to the relative monopoly of government-granted intellectual property rights, some high-tech entrepreneurs have gained extraordinary wealth, enabling them to become renowned philanthropists who are celebrated as friends of the least privileged. Charity has always had this character: those who own or control the means of production charge workers a premium for the privilege of indispensable access to their productive wealth. It is then easy for them to appear generous toward those they have effectively deprived of part of the value of their labor.

Former British prime minister Tony Blair succinctly captured charity's utility for elites: "We need philanthropy to lessen hostility toward the rich" (quoted in Sayer 2015, 285). There's also the "feel good" effect that Warren Buffett, one of the world's wealthiest individuals, describes as follows:

> As more lives and communities are destroyed by the system that creates vast amounts of wealth for the few, the more heroic it sounds to "give back." It's what I would call "conscience laundering"—feeling better about accumulating more than any one person could possibly need to live on by sprinkling a little around as an act of charity. (quoted in Sayer 2015, 287)

Achievement-based prestige exploited the fact that generosity had evolved as a virtue and was rewarded in egalitarian forager societies. When population density within agricultural societies required more formal social coordination, hereditary nobility additionally exploited human susceptibility to belief in supernatural forces. Religious activity in achievement-based societies typically took place in big men's houses or public areas; in hereditary societies, this activity shifted to temples where only specially educated priests—often rulers—had privileged access. Clan ancestors and lesser spirits were relegated to the background as deities, and celestial powers claimed the foreground (Flannery and Marcus 2012, 295).

The special access to divine forces claimed by hereditary chiefs was viewed as legitimate to the degree that it was believed to ensure the well-being of their societies. For instance, the Hunza chiefs of today's northern Pakistan claimed dominion from a sacred life force that empowered them to melt glaciers, replenishing rivers and bringing vital rain to crops. But, should droughts reveal the sham character of these supposed powers, the chiefs could be overthrown or even assassinated (Flannery and Marcus 2012, 355).

Hereditary aristocrats signaled their status through displays of sumptuary goods. Thus, for instance, among the Konyak Naga, only high-status women could wear their hair long and dress in red-and-white-striped skirts, while the elite men had elaborate facial tattoos not permitted to lower-status men. In the Oaxaca Valley of Mexico from 3,200 to 2,900 years ago, elites deformed their infants' heads to signal their aristocratic ancestry (Flannery and Marcus 2012, 202, 230). Whereas modesty was always prevalent in hunter-gatherer societies, "Heroic chiefs and warriors tended to talk themselves up [and practiced] a highly developed art of boasting . . . just as consistently as those in egalitarian societies talked themselves down. . . . As endless epics, sagas, and eddas attest, heroes become heroes by making others small" (Graeber 2012, 117, 209).

Class endogamy—restricting marriages within classes to class members—served to preserve an ideology of the superiority or purity of the nobles. However, because degrees of nobility would hierarchically descend below the ruler, there was continual competition to "marry up." Warriors who had proven their superiority in battle might receive grants of land and be allowed to marry women of a higher class (Flannery and Marcus 2012, 336). Class endogamy could lead societies to relax incest prohibitions, especially for those at the very top. For instance, Hawaiian chiefs married their own sisters or half-sisters, whose mana would bolster their offspring.

The powers rulers claimed by virtue of their special relationship to celestial powers could be even more extraordinary than melting glaciers. For instance, the highest chief in the Samoan archipelago pretended to belong to the lineage of the first to descend from the Sky God who had mated with mortal women to produce a semi-divine elite. In his presence, subjects would prostate themselves because, report Flannery and Marcus, "His glance could wither fruit on the tree. His body, his house, his personal possessions, and even the vessels from which he ate were so charged with mana as to be dangerous . . . [while he] symbolized order in a world plagued by disorder." The exceptional privilege this religious ideology legitimated is evident in the fact that one Samoan ruler maintained a harem of 200 women (2012, 317, 318, 315, 348). Obviously, to provide for such a huge harem and the resulting offspring, the ruler had to extract a substantial surplus from producers.

As noted earlier, these early hereditary aristocracies were often fragile. They did not possess the superior military organization or technology that would be adequate to back up their power should their ideological legitimacy crumble, for example, in the event that a crop failure should gainsay their pretention to celestial favor. Flannery and Marcus note instances in some Asian societies where aristocracies were overthrown from time to time because "a long-standing desire for equal treatment . . . periodically overcame hereditary privilege." Some societies cycled "back and forth between hereditary privilege and equality" (2012, 159–60; 192). More stable arrangements would have to await the development of metallurgy or more effective organizational structures that would equip the rulers' military forces to back them up when their legitimacy was discredited. As Boix puts it:

> Broadly speaking, the power ratio is more favorable to producers and self-defense when military technologies are simple. As long as the production of violence is labor intensive and does not rely on sophisticated weaponry such as chariots, horses, and heavy armor, plunderers have little comparative advantage over producers and can subjugate very few peasants or farmers at a time to extract rents from them. However, once military technologies become more complex, the comparative advantage of would-be predators in the production of violence tends to increase. (2015, 174)

Chapter 5 will recount how metallurgy developed in Eurasia to provide rulers with decisive weaponry that would sustain their ability to extract surplus from producers, even when their religiously backed legitimacy collapsed in the face of crop failures or other catastrophes. The advent of this military technology heralds the rise of the state and civilization about 5,500 years ago.

Restricted Control of Property

> *The great and chief end . . . of men's uniting into commonwealths and putting themselves under government is the preservation of their property.*
>
> —John Locke, *The Second Treatise of Government* (1689, 7)

Restricted or private rights to property, in the sense that some people hold exclusive possession of and control over productive resources such as land, evolved with hereditary inequality.[17] It radically transformed human behavior. Generally, among foragers, no one starved unless all did. And, because

---

[17] The English word "private" comes from the Latin *privatus*, which means "restricted." In this sense, private ownership is wholly, and only, an institution of exclusion, and institutional exclusion is a matter of organized power.

they lived somewhat hand to mouth, they lived substantially in the present. Early agriculturalists also remained highly egalitarian, and sharing resources was common (Bogaard, Fochesato, and Bowles 2019, 2). But the rise of restricted property meant that those who possessed it might eat while others starved. A radical form of insecurity was born where what is most fundamental—food and the right to life—might be available to only some, and the most likely to possess it would be those who owned or controlled property. To survive, those without property would have to work with the land or other resources that belonged to the owners. They were exploited to the extent that to survive they had to hand over the surplus of their labor to the owners of the means of production with which they had to mix their labor.

Although religious ideology would present this inequality as appropriate—indeed, mandated by the highest celestial powers—a latent sense of fairness, manifested as resentment, could create the potential for insurrection. In face of this possibility, property owners would also live with a sense of insecurity. The existence of restricted property also means everyone must look out more carefully for themselves, as opposed to thinking first of the community's well-being. In addition, confronted with material insecurity, they become less present-oriented: they worry and fear for the future. Many religions changed to capture and legitimate this transformed time horizon, downplaying the importance of this woeful temporal life and promising a blissful existence after death for those who work hard, obey their superiors, and abide by society's norms. This sacred vision, of course, privileged the elites.

This chapter has introduced early examples of inequality legitimated by religious ideology. The next chapter explores in greater depth the dynamics by which religions and other doctrines subsequently evolved as powerful ideological instruments, justifying the elites' taking all, or practically all, of the producers' surpluses.

4

The Dynamics of Religious Legitimation

The stability of any society requires an ideological superstructure to legitimize the rules of the game.

—Douglass North and Robert Paul Thomas,
"The Rise and Fall of the Manorial System:
A Theoretical Model" (1971, 182)

The ideas of the ruling class are in every epoch the ruling ideas: i.e., the class which is the ruling material force of society is at the same time its ruling intellectual force. The class which has the means of material production at its disposal, has control at the same time over the means of mental production, so that thereby, generally speaking, the ideas of those who lack the means of mental production are subject to it.

—Karl Marx, *Economic and Philosophic Manuscripts of 1844* (1978, 172)

As seen in Chapter 3, a few sedentary fishing communities had significant inequality prior to the adoption of agriculture. The first agricultural societies to reveal a notable degree of inequality appeared in sedentary agricultural societies about 9,000 years ago. This inequality was legitimated by religious ideologies that justified it as proper, natural, and in accordance with the mandates of celestial powers. Religion was transformed from legitimating and reinforcing equality within hunter-gatherer societies to validating as yet unstable forms of inequality in some pre-state agricultural societies. The dynamics whereby inequality was justified in these first socially inequitable agricultural societies will be essentially the same in all subsequent unequal societies. With the rise of central government, ideology backed by the state's monopoly on violence will become the unremitting means for legitimating and maintaining inequality, even until today.

Ideology, an expression of legitimation, has played a central role in the evolution of asymmetrical, exploitative power relationships. Yet, the role of legitimation in human history has received relatively little attention. This chapter examines the dynamics of social legitimation, focusing especially on the way its ideological component has served to justify inequality. Subsequent chapters will examine the role played by ideology in specific historical contexts.

Physical Force versus Ideology

When plunder becomes a way of life for a group of men living together in society, they create for themselves in the course of time a legal system that authorizes it and a moral code that glorifies it.
—Frédéric Bastiat, *The Law* (1850)

Social thinkers since Machiavelli (1469–1527) have recognized that class inequality and other forms of group-based hierarchy can be maintained by either physical or ideological force. Physical force can be expressed as threat of death, torture, mutilation, imprisonment, or the elimination of all kin. Ideological force, by contrast, is generally expressed through the manipulation of social discourse.

Physical force has often been necessary for initially establishing and solidifying exploitative social relationships and hierarchical social structures. Slaves had to be captured, societies had to be credibly threatened to provide tribute, peasants had to be forced to give up a portion of their harvests or herds. Overt brute force, however, is relatively inefficient in the long term: because it generates strong resentment and the constant threat of insurrection, it requires costly policing resources. A far more efficient and effective long-run strategy is for elites to embrace an ideological system that convinces "both themselves—and more important, members of subordinate groups—of the moral and intellectual legitimacy of the existing social order" (Sidanius and Levin 2001, 309). Ideology reduces the costs of physical repression and terror. It has always been the most effective day-to-day political weapon for maintaining the elite's ability to take the producers' surplus. When ideology has proven insufficient, states protecting elites' interests have always resorted to violence. As political philosopher Thomas Hobbes put it, "when nothing else is turn'd up, clubs are trumps" (1651, xvii).[1]

The fact that ideologies benefit elites does not mean that elites sit around conference tables and craft clever doctrines to justify their privileges and pacify those they exploit, although on occasion they might do just that. But more likely is that they would naturally embrace those ideas floating around in social thought-space that serve their interests. The metaphor of biological evolution is helpful for clarifying the process by which this occurs.[2]

Ideas are in a constant state of evolution. As genetic mutations continually occur in the biological world, so too do new ideas—mutated thoughts—continually spring forth within social thought-space. In both domains, almost all mutations are condemned to perish. They do not find adequately nourishing environmental niches to enable survival and reproduction. Most biological mutations make their carriers less fit for their environments. Similarly, most new ideas are seen by others as uninteresting or outlandish. Thus, either the ideas are ignored, or those expressing them are mocked or even persecuted (imprisoned, tortured, burned at the stake). But occasionally a mutation emerges into a nourishing environmental niche, survives, and spreads. Because cultural change is generally far more rapid than ecological change, new cultural niches are more frequently created, offering potentially fertile environments for new ideas, institutions, and practices. Thus, social and cultural evolution can make room for ideologies that serve convincingly to legitimate the power and privilege of elites. Elites did not so much create their privilege-legitimating ideologies as seize them from the swirl of ideas that were "in the air."

Within this evolutionary metaphor, an ideology that legitimated inequality would not only be readily embraced as true by its privileged beneficiaries, but perhaps be even more willingly accepted as valid by its victims. A large study conducted by social psychologists John Jost and colleagues

---

[1] In the maintenance of inequality, the existence of a tradeoff might be expected between surplus spent on ideology and force in maintaining inequality. Although on thin evidence, economist Thomas Piketty reports that during the Edo era in Japan prior to the Meiji Restoration, Shinto priests and Buddhist monks accounted for one to one-and-a-half percent of the population and the warrior class three to four percent. By contrast, in France and the United Kingdom during the sixteenth to eighteenth centuries, proportionately, the religious class was larger and the warrior class smaller (2020, 383).

[2] The metaphor of ideas evolving by a process parallel to genetic evolution was expressed by Herbert Spencer in *A System of Synthetic Philosophy: First Principles,* published in 1910 (2008). It was expressed more recently by Richard Dawkins in *The Selfish Gene* (1976). Dawkins proposed the word "meme" as a basic unit of thought evolution to play a role similar to "gene" in biological evolution.

finds that, "contrary to their own self-interest, members of disadvantaged groups were more likely to provide ideological support for the system than were members of advantaged groups" (2003, 20). For these less fortunate, it might provide meaning for their suffering, or even a promise that a far superior future awaits them in an afterlife. Because religion offers solace in face of suffering and death, when in the control of priests, it became a powerful instrument for social control. The threat of harsh supernatural justice, such as an eternity burning in hell, could compel people to obey what priests tell them is the will of gods.

The wealth, political power, superior education, and status of the elite, and thus their social influence, enable them to establish attitudes and social institutions that communicate their self-serving doctrines to those below them. Further, research suggests that elites are especially adept at duping their victims. Cognitive psychologist Denise Cummins reports that "social dominance has been found to correlate with deceptive ability and enhanced ability to decode nonverbal cues. Individuals who are perceived and rated as socially dominant are better at deceiving others, persuading others, and interpreting other's intentions" (2005, 682).

Persuading the exploited that their condition was as it must and should be was made easier for much of history by the fact that political elites often were also the high priests, their societies' intellectuals. But even when priests were a separate caste or class from the rulers, they were usually beholden to the elite's political power and wealth. Accordingly, it is not surprising that both ruling elites and ruled masses typically embrace the same ideology, even though it vindicates the former taking the latter's surplus. Psychologists Jim Sidanius and Shana Levin write that

> almost all perspectives on legitimizing ideologies suggest that their power is derived from their consensuality . . . legitimizing ideologies are believed to be effective in regulating group-based inequality because they are often endorsed by dominants and subordinates alike. All other things being equal, the greater the degree to which both dominants and subordinates agree on the veracity of hierarchy-enhancing legitimizing myths, the less physical violence will be necessary to keep the system of stratification intact. (2001, 316)

History reveals that, excepting periods of extreme crises, inequality has always been adequately legitimated. Most people found it acceptable, even when it meant that an exploitative elite caused their lives to be filled with extreme hardship and misery. This was especially true if all other sufferers remained quiescent.

Legitimation as Existentially Necessary

Make the lie big, keep it simple, keep saying it, and eventually they will believe it.

—Attributed to Joseph Goebbels, Hitler's propaganda minister

Humans evolved with a strong innate sense of fairness. This predilection, along with inexpensive stone weapons and the ability of the weaker to form coalitions, served to maintain a high degree of political and economic equality during humans' first 97 to 98 percent of existence as foragers and then early agriculturalists. However, the adoption of agriculture created conditions that enabled the embrace of ideas justifying inequality, making clear that ideology can alter what is judged as fair.

Ideology is deception. It is a form of mystification that legitimates the ability of the more powerful to gain at the expense of others. For the sake of clarity, this use of the term *ideology* follows that of Marx, as opposed to its virtual loss of specific meaning in modern discourse. As sociologist Daniel Bell put it, "In the twenty-five years since *The End of Ideology* was published, the concept of ideology has unraveled completely. What is considered an ideology today? Ideas, ideals, beliefs, creeds, values, *Weltanschauungen*, religions, political philosophies, systems, linguistic discourses—all have been pressed into service" (1988, 321). Ideology has been stripped of the specific meaning Marx gave it as a tool of exploitation. Regrettably, when social scientists and historians make use of the term, it is typically in this meaning-impoverished sense. Economist Thomas Piketty's use of the term *ideology* in his new extraordinarily rich book on inequality, *Capital and Ideology* (2020), unfortunately suffers from this deficiency.

Ideology, in the original sense provided by Marx, projects a distorted understanding of aspects of reality, most importantly including social relations. In doing so, it is a powerful instrument for creating and maintaining inequality. However, ideology is not the only component of legitimation, and inequality is not the only social condition that is legitimated. Viewed most broadly, social legitimation is the process by which social knowledge explains and justifies prevailing social reality. Legitimation per se is neither good nor bad. It is unavoidable. Our instincts do not furnish us with full guidance as to how to behave in our world. It is human culture that supplements our instincts to provide us with fairly complete and stable relationships. Humans are the only animal whose culture requires symbolically maintaining a sense of "appropriate" or "right" action (Berger and Luckmann 1967, 48).

Typically, legitimations are both cognitive and normative in character. That is, they purport to inform us not only what *is* but what *ought to be*. Although the greater part of legitimation occurs pre-theoretically in religious or secular expression as "an assemblage of maxims, morals, proverbial nuggets of wisdom, values and beliefs, myths, and so forth" (Berger and Luckmann 1967, 65), a substantial degree of legitimation occurs at the theoretical level. Inequality has been predominantly legitimated by religion throughout most of history, and increasingly in modern times by the social sciences, most notably mainstream economics.

Legitimations need not be literally true: "the issue of 'truth' is essentially irrelevant to an ideology's ability to legitimate and justify group-based social inequality: ideologies can serve as legitimizing instruments regardless of whether they are 'true' or 'false' in any epistemic sense" (Sidanius and Levin 2001, 310–11). There will, nonetheless, be an understandable insistence on the supposed truth value of legitimization systems, whether they are provided by religion or science.

Social psychologists Elizabeth Haines and John Jost note that "providing justification makes people feel more comfortable with inequalities of status or power, even when they are in a relatively disadvantaged position. Thus, reasons and justifications serve a placating function when it comes to the preservation of power" (2000, 222–23). Further, empirical research in system-justification theory by Jost et al. finds that "members of disadvantaged groups are even more likely than members of more advantaged groups to provide ideological support for the very social system that is responsible for their disadvantages" (2003, 30). Yet more striking, "people may be more willing to accept relatively illegitimate accounts than is commonly assumed . . . [and the authors] found that people misremembered the explanations that were given to them as more legitimate than they actually were" (2000, 232).[3] This finding confirms South African leader Steve Biko's

---

[3] For instance, their research reveals that "poorer Southern Blacks were more likely than wealthier Southern Blacks to endorse the legitimizing myth that hard work leads to success. In short, people

remark that "the most potent weapon in the hands of the oppressor is the mind of the oppressed" (Peters 2018).

Sociologists of knowledge Peter Berger and Thomas Luckmann formulated a conceptual model of the dialectical relationship between humans and their social creations. The model is constructed around three existential conditions: culture as a human creation; culture as objective reality; and humans as cultural products. Corresponding to these three conditions are three dialectically related processes or "moments" relating to human mental creations: externalization, objectivation, and internalization. Externalization is the process whereby humans, because of their "instinct-poverty," create a stable cognitive environment for their conduct and survival. They create the meaning of their world. The second moment of this dialectic, objectivation, is the process whereby human products become habitualized and institutionalized so as to take on an objectivity or facticity which appears to be independent of their human authorship. That is, humans lose awareness that they created it.[4] The third moment, internalization, is the process of socialization whereby human products, once objectified, turn back to form and control their human creators.[5]

Applied to exploitation, this model explains that humans externalize their thought in setting forth an ideology that justifies the prevailing distribution of income, wealth, and privilege. The ideology then comes to be seen as the will of the gods or as part of the inherent nature of reality—the way it must be, as opposed to the way it was humanly designed. The ideology thus becomes "objective," a fact or set of facts seemingly existing independently of

whose self-interest would have been served the most by rejecting the myth of meritocracy clung most fervently to this system justifying belief" (2003, 29, 26).

[4] This second moment involves reification, by which is understood "the apprehension of human phenomena as if they were things, that is, in non-human or possibly suprahuman terms. Another way of saying this is that reification is the apprehension of the products of human activity as if they were something other than human products—such as facts of nature, results of cosmic laws, or manifestations of divine will. Reification implies that man is capable of forgetting his own authorship of the human world, and further, that the dialectic between man, the producer, and his products is lost to consciousness. The reified world is, by definition, a dehumanized world. It is experienced by man as a strange facticity, an *opus alienum* over which he has no control rather than as the *opus proprium* of his own productive activity" (Berger and Luckmann 1967, 89).

[5] Berger gives three examples: "Man invents language and then finds that both his speaking and his thinking are dominated by its grammar. Man produces values and discovers that he feels guilt when he contravenes them. Man concocts institutions, which come to confront him as powerfully controlling and even menacing constellations of the external world" (1967, 9). Marx focused on yet another: workers create capital (machines, etc.), which, in a capitalist regime, serves as an instrument of their exploitation.

its creators. Finally, this ideology sets limits on human thought and action. Humans are socialized to live by the mandates of the ideology. According to Berger, this dialectic between humans and their products constitutes what we mean by alienation: "The essence of all alienation is the imposition of a fictitious inexorability upon the humanly constructed world. . . . Men then live in the world they themselves have made as if they were fated to do so by powers that are quite independent of their own world-constructing enterprises" (1967, 95). Thus, by forgetting their authorship, humans become alienated from their own creations and are ruled by them.

Ideology, Poverty, Repression, and Resistance to Change

> . . . out of the hundreds of logical premises that could be used to justify inequality, a handful worked so well that dozens of unrelated societies came up with them.
>
> —Kent Flannery and Joyce Marcus,
> *The Creation of Inequality* (2012, xi)

An extraordinary power of legitimation is that it establishes what Haines and Jost call "status quo biases," whereby people tend to favor the prevailing option and to avoid choices that require change. This bias is especially understandable among the very poor, for whom the prospect of famine is ever-present. Because they are normally on the verge of starvation and have only the wherewithal barely to survive, they predictably resist change: it might push them over the edge.[6]

Thus, historically, the poor have generally been highly averse to almost any change, whether in production techniques or social arrangements. This helps clarify why the pace of technological change remained so glacially slow

---

[6] Political economist Thorstein Veblen ventured so far as to contend that the exploited poor were so debased and conservative because they lacked even the energy to contest the given: "the institution of the leisure class acts to make the lower classes conservative by withdrawing from them as much as it may of the means of sustenance, and so reducing their consumption, and consequently their available energy, to such a point as to make them incapable of the effort required for the learning and adoption of new habits of thought. . . . The abjectly poor, and all those persons whose energies are entirely absorbed by the struggle for daily sustenance are conservative because they cannot afford the effort of taking thought for the day after to-morrow; just as the highly prosperous are conservative because they have small occasion to be discontented with the situation as it stands today" (1899, 204). "History . . . teaches that abject misery carries with it deterioration and abject subjection" (1919, 443).

for most of human history. Just as traditions must be preserved, so too must the ideas that legitimate them. Anthropologist Bronislaw Malinowski wrote of the conservatism of traditions in the following terms:

> Let us realize that in primitive conditions traditions are of supreme value for the community and nothing matters as much as conformity and conservatism of its members. Order and civilization can be maintained only by strict adhesion to the lore and knowledge received from previous generations. Any laxity in this weakens the cohesion of the group and imperils its cultural outfit to the point of threatening its very existence. (1992, 39)

Behind this desire for stability and resistance to change is a fear of turmoil. Berger and Luckmann write, "*All* social reality is precarious. *All* societies are constructions in the face of chaos."[7] Further, psychologists John Blanchar and Scott Eidelman point to empirical support for the fact that the longer the status quo has been perceived to exist, the more it is embraced (2013, 238).[8] What people have generally wanted is calm and secure lives in which to raise their children. That is the mandate of biology, to pass on one's genes. When faced by material and social insecurity, it is understandable that people would favor stability and only be moved to opt out under severe duress. Accordingly, system legitimation theory finds that they accept and defend the status quo to lessen uncertainty and to alleviate social and psychological uneasiness.

Economic historian Douglass North writes, "order reduces uncertainty and therefore has some common characteristics that are considered a 'good' in themselves and individuals and groups in society have frequently knowingly accepted authoritarian order in preference to disorder" (2010, 105). Rebellions have, of course, occurred, but generally only when the threat of starvation becomes extreme. A well-known example is the French

---

[7] "Society is the guardian of order and meaning not only objectively, in its institutional structures, but subjectively as well, in its structuring of individual consciousness. . . . It is for this reason that radical separation from the social world, or anomy, constitutes such a powerful threat to the individual" (Berger 1967, 21).

[8] Psychiatrist and political philosopher Franz Fanon wrote, "Sometimes people hold a core belief that is very strong. When they are presented with evidence that works against that belief, the new evidence cannot be accepted. It would create a feeling that is extremely uncomfortable, called cognitive dissonance. And because it is so important to protect the core belief, they will rationalize, ignore and even deny anything that does not fit in with the core belief" (1967, 194). Fanon's point calls to mind philosopher of science Thomas Kuhn's analysis of how a scientific paradigm resists refutation by conflicting evidence (1970).

Revolution, which began in a period of economic crisis when spiraling inflation was pushing the price of the population's staple food, bread, beyond their reach, driving them to the edge of actual starvation.

It is also noteworthy that the ideology of the elite has always benefited from a proclivity of people to admire the privileged, a penchant that caught Adam Smith's attention:

> We frequently see the respectful attentions of the world more strongly directed towards the rich and the great, than towards the wise and virtuous. We see frequently the vices and follies of the powerful much less despised than the poverty and weakness of the innocent . . . [indeed] the fascination of greatness . . . is so powerful, that the rich and the great are too often preferred to the wise and the virtuous. (1759, 126)[9]

Veblen was also of this view. He believed that because the elite are emulated, their ideology carries special weight: "The fact that the usages, actions, and views of the well-to-do leisure class acquire the character of a prescriptive canon of conduct for the rest of society, gives added weight and reach to the conservative influence of that class. It makes it incumbent upon all reputable people to follow their lead" (1899, 200). Legal scholar J. M. Balkin observes: "to some extent, individuals can choose what beliefs and cultural skills they will internalize. They may choose to adopt beliefs and behaviors of powerful and influential people because they believe this selection will make them seem influential and powerful" (2003, 84).

It should be noted that imitating successful people is rational insofar as it saves on learning costs. The rich are obviously successful, and imitating their behavior and adopting their attitudes and beliefs may enhance one's chances of also becoming rich. Sexual selection would favor those learners who have been successful in evaluating effective behavior in achieving status and then imitating it. Those of high status have greater reproductive success. Game theory experiments show that a winning strategy is to copy high-status winners, even in contexts where their behavior is not an obvious source of their status (Low 2001, 154).

---

[9] Smith further argued that the "disposition to admire, and almost to worship, the rich and the powerful, and to despise, or at least, to neglect, persons of poor and mean condition . . . is . . . the great and most universal cause of the corruption of our moral sentiments" (1759, 126).

The Predominant Role of Religion

Philosophy is questions that may never be answered. Religion is an-
swers that may never be questioned.
>   —Anonymous, cited in Daniel Dennett,
>   *Breaking the Spell* (2006, 17)

The end of worship amongst men is power.
>   —Thomas Hobbes, *Leviathan* (1967, 237)

Societies cannot survive and flourish without their members' willing identification with the group and commitment to its values. Sociologist Morris
Zelditch explains:

> The problem of any kind of polity . . . is to find a basis of loyalty that is
> voluntary but not purely instrumental; that does not depend only on ra-
> tional self-interest or purely on personal preferences . . . legitimacy is always
> a matter of voluntarily accepting that something is "right," and its conse-
> quence is always the stability of whatever structure emerges from the pro-
> cess. (2001, 37, 40)

In pre-modern traditional societies, religion served as the predominant if
not nearly exclusive means of legitimation. Religion provides a status to prevailing social institutions that transcends their human character. As Berger
has expressed this,

> Religion legitimates social institutions by bestowing upon them an ulti-
> mately valid ontological status, that is, by locating them within a sacred and
> cosmic frame of reference. . . . The fundamental "recipe" of religious legiti-
> mation is the transformation of human products into supra- or non-human
> facticities. (1967, 33, 89)

In this manner, social institutions are accorded the stability and inevita-
bility that are ascribed to the ultimate spiritual and material realms. They
are not alterable since they cannot be improved. They must be accepted.
Because they are identified with the ultimate reality of the universe, their denial appears evil or the consequence of madness: "To go against the order of
society as religiously legitimated . . . is to make a compact with the primeval

forces of darkness" (Berger 1967, 39). Rulers are chosen by and in service to the gods. Therefore, to challenge rulers was equivalent to blasphemy, punishable by the gods. Although this punishment might be threatened to occur in an afterlife, rulers as the agents of gods could be counted upon to deliver it as an auto-da-fé (an act of faith) in this life. All school children learn of the witches and heretics burned at the stake, but many other ingenious and cruel punishments have been practiced in defense of religion.

Psychologically, religious legitimation of social institutions provided individuals with enormous solace by giving them an ultimate sense of meaning, rightness, and order. Further, religious consciousness is "a behavioral trait that attaches individuals to one another by means of intensely sublime emotional experiences. The joy of religious celebration is both real and profound" (Crippen and Machalek 1989, 76). This began with the evolution of religion when it reinforced the equality of humans within forager bands. Inequality and class stratification were provided with legitimacy by hitching onto this joy and solace. Inequality, as with all else in society, was the will of the gods, executed by their appointed representatives on earth, and therefore the way it must be. Because religious legitimation gave sacred meaning to social reality, it provided the poor with a meaning for their poverty, as well as providing the rich with a meaning for their wealth.

As noted in Chapter 3, no atheistic society has ever been located. This is understandable. All religions embrace moral imperatives not unlike the Ten Commandments of the Abrahamic religions. If society's members truly believe in the necessity of obeying these injunctions, then public order and internal peace can be more efficiently provided, thereby reducing policing costs and freeing scarce resources for more productive activities. Further, religion adds to a society's identity and cohesion, while justifying hostility toward outsiders and making it more unified against their threats. These advantages of lower policing costs and greater cohesion gave religious societies a competitive advantage over those lacking religion, and over time, the latter would become extinct. Evolutionary biologist David Sloan Wilson (2003) develops an extended argument for the thesis that religion evolved to improve cooperative behavior within groups. His reasoning presupposes the possibility of group selection discussed in Chapter 2.

Although religion first evolved in the highly egalitarian world of hunter-gatherer societies, it continued to perform the functions of lowering policing costs and generating social cohesion after the adoption of agriculture. But as greater inequality appeared within more densely populated societies, religion came to be used to buttress rulers' authority and to justify their wealth and power. Because modern states justify inequality through social science doctrines, religion plays a lesser role in these societies, as will be seen in Chapter 8. Nevertheless, religion still serves to offer solace and social cohesion. Indeed, religion tends to regain importance in periods of rising insecurity, stress, and social discord.

Anthropologist Jared Diamond elaborates on the public-good benefits of religion:

> Besides justifying the transfer of wealth to kleptocrats, institutionalized religion brings two other benefits to centralized societies. First, shared ideology or religion helps solve the problem of how unrelated individuals are to live together without killing each other—by providing them with a bond not based on kinship. Second, it gives people a motive, other than genetic self-interest, for sacrificing their lives on behalf of others. (1999, 278)

Similarly, biologist Edward O. Wilson points out that "religion is superbly serviceable to the purposes of warfare and economic exploitation [because it is] above all the process by which individuals are persuaded to subordinate their immediate self-interest to the interests of the group" (1978, 175). As noted in Chapter 3, because of its critical social utility, Wilson embraces the view that through gene-culture coevolution, an attraction to religion has become genetically hard-wired in the human species (1978).[10]

A tendency to sacrifice one's own self-interest for the group evolved during the long period of hunting and gathering, when little inequality existed. These forager groups were typically patrilocal, meaning that men remained in the group and their wives came from outside. Consequently, males within the group were often kin-related, such that if a warrior lost his life, some of his genes would still survive in his kin and could be passed down to future generations.[11] Further, sacrifice benefited the whole band. After extreme inequality and rigid hierarchy evolved with the rise of the state, this same proclivity served the elites in their exploitation of those below, who sacrificed their lives while the elite disproportionately harvested the benefits. Both before and after the rise in inequality, religion served to justify the sacrifices

---

[10] For a detailed account of this belief, see Nicholas Wade's *The Faith Instinct* (2009).

[11] The fact that within patrilocal societies wives came from outside the band and thus only shared genes with their children may have favored the greater risk aversion that is purported to exist among females (Baumeister and Vohs 2004, 342).

and to comfort their loved ones. As Berger expresses it: "Men go to war and men are put to death amid prayers, blessings, and incantations. The ecstasies of fear and violence are, by these means, kept within the bounds of 'sanity,' that is, of the reality of the social world" (1967, 45).

Upon the rise of inequality, religion became more sententious and advanced the formalization of certain behaviors. Diamond characterizes some of these as follows: "standardized organization, preaching political obedience, regulating behavior towards strangers by means of formal moral codes, and justifying wars—were absent in small scale societies, [but] appeared with the rise of chiefdoms and states" (2012, 355).

Within religious legitimation, appropriate behavior must be in accord with rules, which come to be understood as determined by supernatural agents or gods. Children are raised to respect and believe in the authenticity of the rules expressed in codes of behavior similar to the Ten Commandments of the Abrahamic faiths. These rules typically applied only to behavior toward others within the chiefdom or state. "Thou shalt not kill" within the same political unit, but outsiders seen as enemies could be killed with the full blessing of the spiritual forces, even to the point of genocide and the enslavement of the enemies' women and children. Note, for instance, the admonition in the Old Testament book of Deuteronomy (20:12–15):

> If they refuse to make peace and they engage you in battle, lay siege to that city. When the LORD your God delivers it into your hand, put to the sword all the men in it. As for the women, the children, the livestock and everything else in the city, you may take these as plunder for yourselves. And you may use the plunder the LORD your God gives you from your enemies.[12]

As will be seen in Chapter 5, with the important exception of reducing the risk of death from violence, the rise of the state decreased the well-being of all

---

[12] The following chapter, Deuteronomy 21:10–14 lays out ethical guidance for the treatment of captured women:

> When you go out to war against your enemies, and the LORD your God gives them into your hand and you take them captive, and you see among the captives a beautiful woman, and you desire to take her to be your wife, and you bring her home to your house, she shall shave her head and pare her nails. And she shall take off the clothes in which she was captured and shall remain in your house and lament her father and her mother a full month. After that you may go in to her and be her husband, and she shall be your wife. But if you no longer delight in her, you shall let her go where she wants. But you shall not sell her for money, nor shall you treat her as a slave, since you have humiliated her.

but the ruling elites. The producers worked longer hours, their nutrition became less varied, they suffered more infectious diseases, and their life spans were shortened. Perhaps worse, they were at the mercy and whim of the more powerful, who might brutalize and enslave them.

Although foragers often believed in an afterlife, their focus was seeking assistance from spiritual powers for practical help with worldly problems arising in hunting, defense against their enemies, and the health of their families. Religion was a communal experience, and it was accessible and understood by everyone, reflecting and reinforcing their equality. The supernatural world was accessed through dreams and trances, often with the kinetic help of dances.

With state religions, by contrast, a priesthood claimed unique access to spiritual wisdom and used it to justify the privileges of the elite as the mandates of supernatural forces. The definition and control of religion became the monopoly of priests. Priests were the ones who knew the sacred secrets, and because they served the interests of the ruling elites, they controlled, or at least interpreted, the knowledge that legitimated society's hierarchy of wealth and privilege. In Berger and Luckmann's description, "the 'lay' member of society no longer knows how his universe is to be conceptually maintained, although, of course, he still knows who the specialists of universe-maintenance are presumed to be" (Berger and Luckmann 1967, 212). The priests preserved their control over meaning by using rituals and even language that was not comprehensible to the general lay population. A striking instance is the use of Latin in Catholic services until 1965. A fetish was made of religious mysteries to which only the priests had access. Their complexity and impenetrability served to awe believers, revealing the limits of their possible understanding, and masking the social function of providing justification for the unequal distribution of wealth, income, and privilege.[13]

Given producers' degraded life conditions, it is not surprising that state religions shifted the focus from life in this material world to a higher spiritual realm. The imperative was to work hard, keep quiet, respect your

---

[13] All religions where gods are omnipotent, omniscient, and caring for humans, face the problem of evil, why there must be suffering and death. It is noteworthy that salvation religions evolved with a Manichean character, providing a safety valve for gods who could avoid culpability by identifying an evil force to take blame for all the horrors of existence, albeit at the cost of putting into question their omnipotence. Not unexpectedly, rulers appeal to the same strategy wherever possible, blaming famine, pandemic, or social dysfunction on internal or foreign evil forces.

superiors, and obey the rules, and the reward would be everlasting bliss in heaven or higher status in a subsequent reincarnation. Little matter if material conditions are rude and life filled with hardship and suffering; what is important is the eternal spiritual life that follows physical death.

State religions with priesthoods also led to horrific practices such as sacrificing children or enemies as necessary to appease the gods. Anthropologist Marvin Harris claimed that the religion of pre-Columbian Aztecs justified sacrificing up to 20,000 captured enemies daily. Sacrificing young virgin girls was presumably a form of population control, disguised as a mandatory practice to appease the gods (1991).

Ruling elites enjoyed lives that were far less arduous, and this too had to be legitimated. As was seen in Chapter 3, religious cosmologies evolved to depict achievement-based elites as chosen by gods. They were presumed to have the power to intercede with gods or other forces on behalf of the welfare of the entire society, to bring rain and ward off plagues and locusts. It was supposed that their privileged relationship with the spiritual world enabled them to exert control over the weather, the fertility of the land and the livestock, and the well-being of their subjects. It is not surprising, then, that their right to rule was most contested when the rains failed to come, harvests were very poor, and the people they ruled faced starvation.

It is because religions served to legitimate domination, exploitation, and inequality that Marx declared religion to be "the opiate of the people" (1843, 73), the drug that lulled them into docile acceptance of their exploited condition with the promise of happiness in the hereafter. Yet the fact that legitimation may serve to augment or preserve the privileges of the elite does not entail that the world should be broken down into the guilty and the innocent. Elites have always believed the doctrines that further their interests. They do not view them as self-serving ideologies. As political economist Joan Robinson aptly put it, "No one . . . is conscious of his own ideology, any more than he can smell his own breath" (1962, 41). They believe that it represents the will of the gods or, in the modern era, that it accords with the laws of economic science. And they typically believe such doctrines to be in the best interests of everyone, even the poor. As for the poor's acceptance of an unjust status quo, cognitive dissonance theory finds "that people who suffer the most from a given state of affairs are paradoxically the least likely to question, challenge, reject, or change it" (Jost et al. 2003, 13).

Religious Ideology in Its Most Perfect Expression:
Hinduism's Caste System

Hinduism represents the pinnacle of the powers of ideology in human experience to date.

—Michael Mann, *The Sources of Social*
Power (2012, 1:302)

What is surely one of the most extreme and effective instances in which inequality was legitimated by religion occurred in India. A frozen religious stratification assigned everyone a fixed rank and function in society. Brahmanism was brought to India in the second millennium BC by light-skinned Aryan conquerors of dark-skinned Dravidians. These invaders embraced a perfectly rigid hereditary caste system that served to perpetuate their dominance and induce the acquiescence of the lower classes. This religious ideology enabled the Aryan conquerors to control the land and exploit workers in the labor-intensive agriculture of the Indo-Gangetic Plain. Hinduism spread in India when princes came to see it as representing superior civilization and learned of its extraordinary potential for social control. They invited Brahmans to serve as "social engineers" to set up the system within their territories (Berger and Luckmann 1967, 118).

Rigid caste-determined occupations meant that individual families or groups could not readily flee to establish new settlements. To do so, they would need goods and services produced by members of other castes, who would probably be unwilling to join them. They were trapped in service of their Aryan superiors (Lal 2001, 29–30).

According to Hindu doctrine, everyone's status is determined by his or her karma or behavior in previous lives, and, in this sense, everyone deserves his or her current status. If good karma is expressed in this life, then promotion to a higher caste in a next life becomes possible through reincarnation.[14] Castes are endogamous—people must marry within their caste. The higher

---

[14] Historian Michael Mann reports that "between about 200 B.C. and A.D. 200, *The Book of Manu* attained its final holy form. It gave the instruction of the creator of the universe to the first man and king, Manu. It explained caste status as the consequence of *Karma* accumulated in earlier incarnations. Essential duty was to fulfill the karma, the duties, the path to be followed, of whatever position one is born into. To die without longing or desires realizes Brahman, eternal truth. Whatever is, is holy" (2012, 1:357).

the caste, the purer, and care must be taken to avoid pollution by improper contact with those below.[15]

Good karma was understood to mean a resigned and obedient life, wherein individuals carried out the duties appropriate to their social position. All other forms of personal achievement were intrinsically unacceptable. Economic historian Eric Jones characterizes caste membership as "the limiting case of rigidified institutions" where "personal achievement is excluded in principle" (2000, 103–4). This system precluded occupational mobility, helping account for relative economic stagnation.

This static world was depicted as ideal, a perfect world in which everyone and everything has its proper place, where everything, including poverty, is sacred. Thus, to contest the status quo was to violate the sacred order and thereby to condemn oneself to a yet lower and more miserable status in the next life. And, of course, there was no good reason to be dissatisfied with one's condition, no matter how miserable. It is fair because it is just desert in this life for behavior in past lives and a necessary stage in one's spiritual development.[16] As Berger puts it,

> the life of the individual is only an ephemeral link in a causal chain that extends infinitely into both past and future. It follows that the individual has no one to blame for his misfortunes except himself—and conversely, he may ascribe his good fortune to nothing but his own merits. (1967, 65)

Moreover, one's current status is merely temporary, only this short lifetime. A virtuous life will ensure a better deal next time. Through future reincarnations, with patience and obedience, everyone will eventually arrive at perfection. Best to get there as soon as possible and thus avoid further deprivation and pain. An incentive to proper behavior was the possibility within this cosmology to return more miserably as less than human. Indeed, the status assigned to the outcasts (Dalits or Untouchables), those at the very bottom of the hierarchy, was closer to that of animals than to humans (Berger and Luckmann 1967, 102).

[15] The Hindu term for social class is *varna*. The term *caste* was derived from the Portuguese word *casta*. It designated pure or not mixed. (Mann 2012, 1:349).

[16] Thus, capturing the sense of V. Gordon-Childe's quip, "Magic is a way of making people believe they are going to get what they want, whereas religion is a system for persuading them that they ought to want what they get" (1947, 37).

There were four broad castes (*varnas*). At the summit were the priests (*Brahmins*), next the warriors (*Kshatriyas*), third, the merchants (*Vaishya*), and, below them, the peasants and workers (*Shudra*).

The Brahmans, the highest caste, were those who know the nature of ultimate reality. They serve as the bridges between humanity and the forces that control the universe. The rest of the population was to remain ignorant of such matters. So jealous were the Brahmans of their monopoly on esoteric knowledge that

> the Laws of Manu . . . set down that any Sudra (lowest caste, assigned to farming and material production) who so much as listened in on the teaching of the law or sacred texts should have molten lead poured into their ears; on the occasion of a repeat offense, they should have their tongues cut out. (Graeber 2012, 255)

The existence of rigid caste divisions also militated against the downtrodden taking collective action against their exploiters. First, except for the *Dalits* or Untouchables at the bottom, others higher up could feel some degree of superiority. The rigid division also worked against rebellious coordination across caste lines. A striking example of the barrier to cross-caste coordination is recounted by historian Joyce Appleby:

> In 1973, a bus carrying eighty-six persons was trapped in floodwaters southwest of New Delhi. A passerby waded out to the bus with a rope that he had tied to a truck, asking the passengers to haul themselves to safety. But since the passengers belonged to two different castes, they refused to share the same rope, preferring to stay in the bus as it was swept away. (2011, 388)

Even today, only 5.8 percent of Indian marriages take place between individuals of different castes. According to caste-system historian Uma Chakravarti, murders of lower caste sons-in-law are carried out in the name of tradition and family honor, because cross-caste marriages "destabilize the entire system" of inequality (Slater 2019, n.p.).

Mann writes, "Chinese travelers to India from Gupta times onward were astonished at its peace and order, which they thought did not depend on police control, criminal justice, taxation, or forced labor. 'Every man keeps to his hereditary occupation and attends to his patrimony,' said Hiuen Tsang in the seventh century" (2012, 1:358). Although religious ideology reduced the need for costly policing, its rigidity constrained the potential for economic dynamism. Economic historian Joel Mokyr characterizes Hinduism as "a fiendishly clever and almost failure-proof incentive system to protect the status quo" (1990, 172).

Although most extreme in its conservatism, Hinduism was not unique in its disavowal of the material world and its power to legitimate inequality. Confucianism, Daoism, and Chinese Buddhism similarly depicted a static world where no significant improvement in material life was possible, beyond that accompanying a religiously and morally well-ordered life. These religions turned the individual inward toward a state of consciousness where material considerations were no longer of great importance. For most of its history, Christianity did not stand apart from this passivity toward the material world,[17] which shielded elites from disgruntlement, on the part of the populace, with extreme inequality in income, wealth, and privilege.

From Doctrinal Plasticity to Rigidity

Until the invention of writing, religion had a plasticity that enabled it to evolve with the exigencies of evolving social practices. Its specific character was entrusted to human minds, which themselves are remarkably plastic. Language, and perhaps especially poetry and song, could provide it with a bit of intertemporal stability. So too could monuments, statuary, and other forms of symbolic art. But over time, religion would be highly fluid, changing with social needs and practices. Thus, in response to the adoption of agriculture, the egalitarian religion of hunter-gatherers mutated into religion that legitimated inequality, first in achievement-based societies and hereditary chiefdoms, and then in states, and finally empires.

With the advent of writing, religious doctrines and practices could be captured in texts and thereby given significantly greater fixity, providing doctrines with a degree of permanency in the face of changing social needs and practices. This is highly visible among contemporary fundamentalists who hold the ancient written sacred texts as literally and precisely capturing the word and will of their gods.[18]

[17] Christianity will be considered in later chapters where its importance for legitimating medieval inequality, and later, capitalism, will be addressed in the context of the broad social and economic development of the West.

[18] Even in the modern and rich United States, according to a recent Gallup Poll, about one in four Americans believe the Bible to be the literal word of God (Quinn 2017, B2).

The issue is, of course, not so simple, as was recognized by German theological and biblical scholar Friedrich Schleiermacher in the early nineteenth century. He pointed out that because biblical texts were written at such a cultural remove from contemporary lives, their words cannot be taken literally, but instead must be interpreted, thus laying the foundation for *hermeneutics*, the science or art of interpretation.

Not surprisingly, fundamentalists and many others ignore the interpretative dimension. Consequently, the texts which they take literally tend to make their thinking highly conservative. But secular documents of the past, such as constitutions and laws, also hold a strong conservative sway. In the history of the birth and maturation of capitalism, these traditionalist forces worked against the rising power, first of a bourgeoisie, and later of a working class.

The next chapter, Chapter 5, will explore the second greatest revolution in human history—the rise of the state, civilization, and extreme inequality.

5

The State, Civilization, and
Extreme Inequality

Till there be property there can be no government, the very end of which is to secure wealth and to defend the rich from the poor.
— Adam Smith, *Lectures on Jurisprudence* (1763, 404)

Thousands of years of history boil down to a simple truth: ever since the dawn of civilization, ongoing advances in economic capacity and state building favored growing inequality but did little if anything to bring it under control.
— Walter Scheidel, *The Great Leveler* (2017, 391)

. . . the ostensible serious occupation of the upper class is that of government, which, in point of origin and developmental content, is also a predatory occupation.
— Thorstein Veblen, *The Theory of the Leisure Class* (1934, 247)

As discussed in Chapter 3, a degree of inequality, legitimated by religion, arose in some agricultural communities as population density increased. However, those who achieved higher status to become leaders lacked military force to solidify their privileges. Their special status was, therefore, fragile, and their legitimacy was prone to crumble in the face of poor harvests or other calamities. These modestly unequal communities often returned to a high level of equality.

Extreme and enduring exploitation and inequality only came into existence with the rise of the state and civilization about 5,500 years ago (the last 2 to 3 percent of human history). Technological advances in metallurgy, superior military organization, and ideology empowered elites to gain ownership and control of the means of production. All others were forced into subservient roles to access the productive resources necessary for survival. The cost for this access was the elite owners' appropriation of the workers' surplus, the output they produced in excess of what they needed for survival. Over the course of civilization, workers surrendered their surplus by serving as slaves, serfs, indentured servants, indebted peasants, and wage earners.

The first states arose in the riverine valleys of southern Mesopotamia, Egypt, the Indus Valley, and China. But state populations represented only 25 million, or about one-third of the world's population, around the year 2000 BC. Two-thirds still lived as "barbarians"—non-state peoples (Scott 2017, 14).

Typically, control over the means of production enabled elites to extract all, or practically all, of the surplus workers produced beyond that necessary for subsistence. Thus, state societies were about as unequal as they could possibly be, near or on what economist Branko Milanovic (2016) calls their "inequality possibility frontier." Wealthy owners, representing one percent of the people, and a few percent more of soldiers, administrators, priests, and a few merchants extracted virtually all surplus from an impoverished agrarian population (Scheidel 2017, 448). As a rule, state violence was necessary to create exploitative institutions, but ideology legitimating those institutions generally sufficed to maintain them.

While the ultimate driving force of competition and exploitation is to be found in the dynamics of sexual selection, it is political institutions that channel how competitive behavior is expressed. Politics resolves the tension between sexual competition and a sense of fairness. However, in an unequal society, the ideology of the stronger manipulates the sense of fairness to their benefit, and they resort to violence when their ideology fails.

Substantial exploitation and inequality could arise only if surplus food could be produced. As productivity in agriculture improved, cultivators acquired the ability to produce more than was necessary for their own subsistence. However, producers would have little incentive to produce more than enough to meet their basic needs unless they were compelled to do so.[1] Indeed, if fleeing were an option in face of exploitation, rulers would have to maintain what political scientist and anthropologist James Scott calls "a delicate balance between maximizing the state surplus on the one hand and

---

[1] This was clearly recognized by Adam Smith: "A person who can acquire no property, can have no other interest but to eat as much, and to labour as little as possible. Whatever work he does beyond what is sufficient to purchase his own maintenance can be squeezed out of him by violence only, and not by any interest of his own" (1776, 365).

the risk of provoking the mass flight of subjects on the other." To maximize exploitation, the state had to inhibit and punish flight. The earliest legal codes testify that they did just that (2017, 152–53).

The surplus expropriated from agricultural producers supported rulers, priests, soldiers, traders, and workers who were no longer employed in tilling the land. Non-agricultural workers specialized in the production of various goods and services that were not available in earlier social formations. That is, the expropriated surplus enabled greater division of labor, the process of specialization that Adam Smith identified, much later, as the fundamental dynamic for economic growth.

The division of labor made it possible for workers to engage in particular occupations, such as making shoes, carts, and tools. This specialization by craft, in turn, fostered the development of larger towns and cities. Denser population centers gave birth to a "collective brain" that results from an increased frequency of human interactions. The result was greater techno-logical dynamism, or what evolutionary geneticists Adam Powell, Steven Shennan, and Mark G. Thomas call the "invention of invention" (2009, 1299). Population growth and new technologies propelled cultural change as never before, although the accelerated pace still remained glacially slow relative to later ages.

A new challenge facing agriculturalists was that their accumulated wealth in the form of domesticated animals, harvests, or cultivated land could be stolen, threatening the owners with starvation. Typically, the optimal strategy for hunter-gatherers had been to flee rather than fight an all-out war over resources. Their mobility and the availability of uninhabited or thinly populated foraging territory provided them with an escape route.[2] The oppo-site, however, held for sedentary agriculturalists, whose resources were sub-ject to theft. The protection of farming communities was especially critical since they were ready targets for nomadic peoples still living by hunting and gathering.

Because both predator and prey possessed the same military technology, early agricultural communities were fairly successful in defending them-selves without substantial centralized political authority. But ever greater population density created new challenges of coordination and social con-trol as well as the need for more organized defense. Political power became

---

[2] As will be recalled from Chapter 3, their incessant warring is believed to have been driven by sexual rewards as opposed to conquest of resources.

increasingly sophisticated, shifting from "big men" to chiefs, and then, with superior metal weapons and military organization, to kings and, eventually, emperors.

This chapter explores the rise of states and civilization and the consequences for inequality and the quality of life for the overwhelming majority of people.

The State's Comparative Advantage in Violence

... there is no known historical instance of a political state not founded in circumstances of war. The state is indeed hardly more than the institutionalization of the war-making apparatus.
—Robert Nisbet, *The Social Philosophers* (1973, 101)

With agriculture and increasing population density, a niche evolved for political actors who could provide a degree of social coordination, maintain internal peace, and organize defense against external threats. To a limited extent, this role was performed first by big men and then by chiefs. Because military technology was fairly simple, relatively inexpensive, and widely available, substantial social inequality did not accompany these early forms of more centralized authority. If, however, a small group gained exclusive access to superior military technology or military organization, they could deploy it to force workers to produce a surplus for their benefit. In Eurasia, this superior military capability became notably available with the development of metallurgy. Copper swords, helmets, and shields revolutionized warfare, enabling a coalition of specialized warriors to seize control of political power and productive resources. This set the conditions for the rise of the state and civilization.

The toughest band of organized thugs in control of this new scarce and expensive military technology subdued and subjugated the weaker.[3] These

---

[3] It is evidence of Rousseau's acute mind that in the mid-eighteenth century he recognized inequality to follow upon the ability of labor in agriculture to produce a surplus and that of thugs to develop metallurgy. He did so in his winning entry in the Dijon Academy's 1753 essay contest on the question, "What is the origin of inequality among men, and is it authorized by natural law?" He wrote, "... from the moment one man needed the help of another, as soon as it was thought to be useful for a single person to have provisions for two, equality disappeared, property was introduced, labor became necessary, and vast forests were changed into smiling fields which had to be watered with the sweat of men, and in which slavery and misery were soon seen to germinate and grow with the crops.... Metallurgy and agriculture were the two arts whose invention produced this great revolution" (1755, 76).

warriors acted not unlike a modern-day mafia or protection racket, extorting resources from producers in exchange for safety from hostile outsiders and from each other. This "contractual" offer could not be refused. Thus was born the state, run by a powerful elite with a comparative advantage in violence, enabling them to live on the surplus production of the masses. And religion gave them the highest level of legitimacy.

This understanding of the state as the social actor with a comparative advantage in violence was first expressed by sociologist Max Weber (1921a) and further developed by economic historian Douglass North (1982). The state provides protection in return for taxes or tribute. Accordingly, the state is (or more correctly, its directors are) self-interested, seeking maximum benefits like all other economic actors. Yet, the state is also unique: it has the special advantage of being able to mete out more violence than any other competing actor or group of actors. With the rise of the state, as historian Michael Mann has put it, "The gigantic protection racket of political history began: 'Accept my power, for I will protect you from worse violence—of which I can give you a sample if you don't believe me'" (2012, I:100).

As an economic actor, the state will strive for the greatest degree of monopoly power to preserve its privilege and to extract the greatest amount of surplus in return for its services. Like any monopoly, it will attempt to take whatever measures are necessary and possible to eliminate competitors, using force and ideology to suppress free speech, free press, and assembly, while depicting enemies, whether domestic or foreign, as subhuman, or driven by evil forces of darkness, or as terrorists.

The more successful the state becomes at maximizing revenue, however, the more it invites competition. Like a firm's profits, its revenues signal the potential rewards to be had by a successful competitor. Those best positioned and equipped to compete from within the society would be groups with adequate resources to hire and arm their own thugs and generate popular support for their brand. To appease them, the state would protect their property and uphold their right to expropriate surplus from producers. The state could also offer concessions in the form of tax breaks or special privileges to the most powerful and, therefore, the likeliest and most menacing competitors. In economic terms, the state uses discriminatory pricing, or discriminatory exploitation, charging different prices (e.g., tax rates) according to class membership, so as to maximize revenues. Consequently, taxes would fall most heavily on those with the least ability to organize and threaten the state—those at the bottom, the producers. A well-known example of this discriminatory exploitation set the stage for the French Revolution. In the old regime, the First and Second Estates (the clergy and the nobility) were exempt from taxation, placing the tax burden on the Third Estate (the rest of society, and especially the peasants).

Marx and Engels called the state the executive committee of the ruling class because, in return for their loyalty, it defended the property and privileges of its most powerful domestic competitors from the workers they exploited as well as from foreign enemies. Or, as Adam Smith expressed it much earlier, "Civil government ... is in reality instituted for the defense of the rich against the poor, or of those who have some property against those who have none at all" (1776, 674).

The state's monopoly on violence is always relative. Potential substitutes, whether internal or external, constrain the state and its closest supporters from taking the maximum amount of surplus from producers. Pure democracy would exist where the availability of substitutes is virtually infinite, since all citizens would possess equal political power. No one, of course, pretends that pure democracy is possible, but the concept awakens us to the fact that democracy in practice is always relative, on a spectrum from none to total (Wisman 2017).

The greater the threat posed by competitors, the more states must spend on defense. The necessary funds have to be drawn from their societies' surpluses, thus reducing the excess available to elites and drawing resources away from potentially productive investments promising greater economic dynamism. As resources for waging war or maintaining internal order are extracted from producers, incentives to work hard, save, and invest are weakened. More heavily taxing for defense would also lessen popular support for the regime and risk making a competitor more attractive. Thus, a vicious cycle may result whereby increased taxation for defense leads to a weakened economy, a consequently smaller tax base, and a pressing need to raise taxes even higher. At some point, this self-reinforcing downward spiral may motivate the populace to support a competitor.

Geography also plays a critical role in determining the degree of a state's monopoly power. Boundaries that are arduous to cross with armed forces would reduce outside competition and thus enhance the state's potential for a high degree of monopoly. Not only would it be costlier for foreign forces to invade, it would also be more difficult for domestic rebels to benefit from external assistance. An extreme example is the extent to which pharaonic Egypt was isolated from potential enemies by desert and the Mediterranean

Sea.[4] Egypt developed in a long, narrow trench, carved by the Nile, varying in width from 5 to 20 kilometers, that supported the ancient world's highest concentration of people.[5] The surrounding harsh desert made it a fitting example of what historian Karl Wittfogel called "oriental despotism" (1957), since escape for the producers was all but impossible. They were geographically trapped. Outside the Nile's fertile flood plain, the desert was highly inhospitable to human beings. Further, troop movements on the Nile could quickly suppress domestic revolts along the narrow riverine valley. After the limits of irrigation were reached, Egypt's geography also meant that population growth increased its density.

Throughout history, natural barriers and hostile peoples in surrounding territories often made producers' escape from exploitation extremely difficult, if not impossible. They were, as Mann puts it, caged: "The decisive feature of these ecologies and of human reactions to them was *the closing of the escape route*. Their local inhabitants, unlike those in the rest of the globe, were constrained to accept civilization, social stratification, and the state" (2012, I:75).[6]

Egypt's geographic isolation permitted its ruler and a small elite to extract virtually all surplus from producers. The pharaoh, as absolute sovereign, held all property rights, with the backing of a highly centralized bureaucracy to meter output and maximize appropriation of the society's surplus (North 1982, 98). From 2850 to 2190 BC, almost 700 years, the pharaoh was held to be the god Horus, the life force or son of Re, the sun god. So effective was this legitimating ideology that he had no standing army, "few traces of internal militarism, repression of popular revolts, slavery, or legally enforced statues" (Mann 2012, I:109). The pharaohs' success in convincingly portraying themselves as gods, combined with Egypt's geography, afforded it one of the most extreme levels of exploitation among the earliest states.

---

[4] Physically isolated, Egypt suffered few substantial external attacks until later competing empires, such as the Persians, Macedonians, and Greeks, managed to combine large-scale land and sea operations.

[5] Agriculture began in the Nile Valley between 7,000 and 6,000 years ago, 3,000 to 4,000 years after it started in Mesopotamia. At the beginning of the Holocene era about 12,000 years ago, rainfall in North Africa dramatically increased, making lands to the east and west of the Nile more attractive for hunting and gathering and early dispersed agriculture. Increasingly, however, people moved into the Nile Valley when lower rainfall turned these adjacent areas into desert (MacEachern 2010).

[6] Within riverine civilizations, the producers may have been least caged in the Indus Valley in what is now Pakistan. The surrounding jungle made escape far easier and thus stratification and inequality were likely less pronounced. However, as their written language has yet to be deciphered, relatively little is known of their social structure.

At the other end of the spectrum are the much later classical Greek city-states, where mountainous terrain severely limited the usefulness of the heavily armed war chariots that served to centralize and maintain political power in riverine valleys. Over 1,000 Greek city-states formed between 750 and 500 BC. Despite continual warfare, geography worked against any one city-state subjecting all others.

The rugged terrain and the resulting competition among city-states meant that political institutions and social structures were more horizontal and less vertical or hierarchical. The proximity of comparable city-states with similar cultures offered workers substitute locales to which they could flee, making their exploitation far more challenging. The result was greater equality and even a degree of democracy. For example, Mann describes the Spartans:

> All adult Spartan males were hoplites, possessed an equal amount of land (in addition to whatever they inherited), and were entitled to participate in assemblies—although this coexisted with a degree of oligarchy and aristocracy . . . [they emphasized] strong collective discipline and equality. (2012, I:203)

The political consequence was striking. Mann states, "Never before (and rarely subsequently) had peasant farmers ruled a civilized society, and by binding majority votes, after free discussion, in public meetings" (2012, I:203; 198).

Classical Greece also possessed iron metallurgy, and the relative abundance of iron ore meant that comparatively inexpensive and, thus, more abundant iron armaments became available to far more actors than had been the case with more scarce and expensive copper and bronze equipment. Affordable iron weapons enabled the hoplites—citizen soldiers—to be heavily self-armed.

Competition among city-states curbed the extent to which ideas and inventions could be censored or stifled. If there were repression in one locality, intellectuals could escape to adjoining city-states, increasing the potential for science and philosophy to flourish.[7] Borrowing the alphabet from Phoenicia, Greece became the most literate culture in early history.[8]

---

[7] As will be discussed in Chapter 6, significant geographic frontiers and nation-state competition also played critical roles in the much later "European Miracle" (Jones 1987).

[8] The Phoenicians were a great trading community and most likely devised the alphabet for more efficient trade accounting.

Rome's later growth and unparalleled expansion were a consequence of its expanding comparative advantage in violence. It subdued its neighbors at an ever-greater remove, taking slaves from their populations, confiscating their lands, integrating some peoples into the empire, and demanding tribute from others. Its extraordinary success is attested by its thousand-year existence. But just as Rome's rise was predominantly due to its comparative advantage in violence, its demise, North contends, was due to the loss of that advantage: ". . . the *reasons* for the Roman Empire's existence simply disappeared as its military advantages evaporated and the large-scale state no longer provided for the protection and enforcement of property rights . . . [it was] perhaps the most striking watershed that exists in economic history" (1982, 123).

Why did Rome's comparative advantage weaken? In large part because it was no longer able to deal successfully with the challenge that, as we have seen, all states face. Fighting off foreign and domestic competitors requires considerable resources. If the state raises taxes, rulers lose some popular support as people transfer their allegiance to enemies promising better protection and other state services for less taxes. The state might borrow instead of raising taxes, thus pushing the problem into the future, but this assumes that moneyed interests continue to find the regime creditworthy. When severely challenged, the state may be forced to confiscate goods, in particular, livestock and grains to feed its armies, thereby further weakening the citizens' loyalty. Higher taxes and, especially, confiscation discourage citizens from working diligently and encourage them to hoard and hide their assets in unproductive forms, such as precious metals and jewelry. A less productive economy means a shrunken tax base and, thus, less potential revenue for the state. This downward spiral might last for decades, if not—as in the case of the Roman Empire—for centuries.

Inequality also contributed to the fall of Rome in another way. Economists Daron Acemoglu and James Robinson argue that Rome fell, in part, because its elite became increasingly rent-seeking, pursuing wealth and income by manipulating political rights and associated economic privileges rather than by creating new productive wealth:

> . . . the success of the Goths, Huns, and Vandals against Rome was a symptom, not the cause of Rome's decline. . . . Rome's increasingly extractive political and economic institutions generated its demise because they caused infighting and civil war. (2012, 167, 168)

In other words, Rome declined because increasing inequality gave its elite citizens ever greater political power to craft social institutions that enabled them to extract ever more surplus from producers. They spent their wealth on items of conspicuous consumption, such as huge estates, fine clothing, and lavish banquets. The result was economic stagnation and internal strife. Of the 20 emperors who ruled between AD 235 and 284, 18 died violently.

The case of Rome is extreme but by no means unique. Another example of a state's rapacity in discouraging productive activity was reported by English explorer William Dampier in the 1680s among the Mindanao in the Philippines:

> These people's laziness seems rather to proceed not so much from their nat-ural inclinations, as from the severity of their prince (an Islamic sultan), of whom they stand in great awe: for his dealing with them arbitrarily, and taking from them what they get, this damps down their industry, so they never strive to have anything but hand to mouth. (quoted in Jones 1987, 163)

The Anatomy of the Earliest Civilizations

> *Laws and government may be considered in this and indeed in every*
> *case as a combination of the rich to oppress the poor, and preserve to*
> *themselves the inequality of the goods which would otherwise be soon*
> *destroyed by the attacks of the poor, who if not hindered by the govern-*
> *ment would soon reduce the others to an equality with themselves by*
> *open violence.*
>
> —Adam Smith, *Lectures on Jurisprudence* (1763, 208)

Although *civilization* has been variously defined (Mann 2012, I:74ff), it is used here to denote a complex society characterized by urban develop-ment, social stratification, and extreme inequality imposed by a cultural elite possessing a high degree of monopoly control over violence and ideology. Kingdoms and oligarchic states, and thus civilization, originally appeared around 5,500 years ago. The first six of these pristine major civilizations, in terms of dates of appearance, were Mesopotamia, Egypt, the Indus Valley, Yellow River China, Mesoamerica, and Andean America.

The earlier rise of civilizations in Eurasia may have been facilitated, as anthropologist Jared Diamond (1999) has argued, by its relatively high availability of domesticable plants and animals, and by the fact that it was the biggest continent with the greatest population spread more or less along the same east-west band. Here again geography has an impact: the dissemination of domesticated plants and animals, production techniques, and, indeed, general knowledge is more readily possible for populations living at roughly the same latitude. By contrast, people on continents with north-south axes, such as Africa or the Americas, were separated by climatic differences as well as geographic barriers. The most culturally backward peoples were found in mountains or on small isolated islands.[9] Diamond provides the example of the aboriginal Tasmanians, living on a small isolated island for 30,000 years without fire, axes with handles, boats, or even sewing needles (1999, 312).[10]

The six earliest major civilizations are considered pristine in the sense that they were the first such social organizations. They formed through warfare among chiefdoms, each one struggling for survival and attempting to subdue others rather than become their subjects. This warfare could go on for centuries without resolution. The push toward consolidation as kingdoms followed upon the comparative advantage in violence provided by metal weaponry and superior military organization. It was expedited by a generally common cultural heritage such as their pantheon of gods, festivals, rituals, etc. All six civilizations evolved from societies that practiced alluvial farming in riverine valleys dependent upon irrigation, which in Mesopotamia predated civilization by perhaps two millennia.

Rivers facilitated communications and political control. Information and soldiers could move more efficiently on waterways. Rivers also reduced the cost of trade and increased the gains from comparative economic advantage. Raw materials such as wood and stone often had to be transported from great distances. Meat, hides, and other goods produced by surrounding peoples also traveled at lower costs on waterways. These early civilizations' riverine geography also provided early agriculturalists with favorable food sources. Mesopotamia, for instance, possessed a delta offering fish, fertile soil

---

[9] This does not mean that all island cultures remained backward. The Minoan civilization flourished between about 3000 BC to about 1450 BC on the island of Crete and other Aegean Islands. However, its culture was continually nourished by contacts with other civilizations on the highly trafficked Mediterranean Sea.

[10] The claim that Tasmanians lacked fire has been challenged by historian Rebe Taylor (2008).

resulting from regular flooding, migratory birds, and migratory land animals that followed the river routes.

Humans had settled in riverine valleys when they still were foragers because of these plentiful and diverse food sources. As population density
increased, however, they became increasingly dependent on cereal crops
and intensive cultivation. This move to grains was legitimated by religion.
Scott observes that "in virtually all early agricultural settings the superiority
of farming was underwritten by an elaborate mythology recounting how
a powerful god or goddess entrusted the sacred grain to a chosen people"
(2017, 7). It may also have been, at least partially, forced by the arrival of the
state. What is noteworthy about grain, as Scott makes clear, is that it is easily
taxed. Root crops such as potatoes, sweet potatoes, or cassava are buried and
thus lend themselves to concealment. In addition, they are harvestable over
longer periods. Grains, by contrast, are harvested at once, visibly and durably stored, and easily transported—characteristics that simplify taxation.
In some instances, archaic states even mandated a uniform planting time
for grain. Almost all states relied on grains, because they are "best suited to
concentrated production, tax assessment, appropriation, cadastral surveys,
storage, and rationing. . . . History records no cassava states, no sago, yam,
taro, plantain, breadfruit, or sweet potato states" (2017, 133, 21).

Because grains could be planted at the same time, they would also mature
at about the same time, making it easy for tax officials to monitor harvests
and confiscate the states' part. This, Scott finds, made grains "the premier
political crops." Grains also have higher value-to-volume and -weight ratios,
keeping down the costs of storage and transport (2017, 134, 130, 131).

Writing appeared about 3100 BC. Most early writing developed as a technology of social control. For example, it was used for accounting purposes
such as recording taxes or listing war captives and female slaves. A late
Sumerian farm manual stresses how to discipline workers, with emphasis
on "whips, goads, and other disciplinary instruments to keep both laborers
and beasts working strenuously and continuously" (Mann 2012, I:154). Early
writings also mention bounty hunters specializing in tracking and recapturing runaways. As further evidence of writing's social-control functions,
when civilizations collapsed, centralized authority dissolved, and the need
for tax and other administrative records disappeared. In these circumstances,
writing and literacy shrank, and perhaps in some instances even vanished.
Such shrinkage occurred with the Greek Dark Ages between 1200 and 800

BC. Outside religious establishments, literacy largely died out in Western Europe after the disintegration of the Roman Empire (Scott 2017, 147–48).

In agrarian societies, agricultural productivity determined the maximum amount of surplus that could be extracted from farm workers. High agricultural productivity had the obvious benefit that fewer cultivators could support larger workforces in manufacturing, bureaucracy, the priesthood, and, especially, the army. Agricultural productivity has varied greatly across cultures. For instance, in ancient Egypt, thanks to its fertile riparian flood plain, one peasant farmer could produce five times the amount required for his family's subsistence. By contrast, a Mayan peasant farmer—lacking, among other things, draft animals—could only produce twice the basic needs of his own family (Diamond 2006, 164). To increase the available surplus, rulers would prefer larger populations on more extensive lands, a strong incentive for colonialism.

Just as agricultural productivity sets a clear limit on the maximum size of a society's army, so too is its military reach limited by its ability to transport food to the troops. Historian Donald Engel estimates that soldiers could carry their own provisions for about two and a half days. Pack animals would be necessary for longer campaigns, but five days were likely the limit (1980). In terms of distance, Mann contends that soldiers could carry enough food to march about 90 kilometers. Pack animals such as oxen, mules, horses, and donkeys could carry additional food, but they too needed to be fed, and within about 150 kilometers they would consume all the fodder they could carry. Thus, unless human or animal food could be acquired along the way, the range of an army was quite limited. Water transportation, where available, could greatly extend these bounds (2012, I:26; 136). Lacking either water transportation or pack animals, the Mayan society suffered political division and constant war among its small kingdoms. Consequently, it never evolved into an integrated empire (Diamond 2005, 165).

The first city, Uruk, arose among the Sumerians around 3500 BC and grew to a population reaching 10,000 spread over about three-quarters of a square mile (Neal and Cameron 2016, 27). Flannery and Marcus speculate that the Sumerians may also have been the first society in which private property existed, and that this ownership became ever more concentrated in the hands of nobles as they foreclosed on unpaid loans held by peasants. As a result, the debtors were reduced to serfs or sharecroppers. In Sumer, slaves were owned by rulers, temples, and private citizens. Most were war captives, although some impoverished families were forced to sell their children into slavery (2012, 475, 480, 413).

Over the 700-year period preceding the reign of Sargon of Akkad (2334–2279 BC), the 12 principal city-states of Mesopotamia were transformed into kingships. This evolution is attributable to increasingly sophisticated weaponry and military organization, which enabled a rising concentration of political power. Sargon created the first empire by unifying the scattered city-states and defeating enemies over a geographic area of several hundred kilometers (Mann 2012, I:162).

Empires were characterized by colonialism and heightened ethnocentrism, racism, and religious intolerance. Earlier hunter-gatherers and achievement-based farmers believed that different ethnic groups had been created by different celestial spirits, and they generally were tolerant of these differences (K. Flannery and Marcus 2012, 558). Hereditary societies within states, by contrast, exploited these differences in the interest of social control.

Kingdoms emerged from wars of conquest between competing chiefdoms; empires, from wars between rival kingdoms. The basic dynamic was similar. War, or its constant threat, forced each society to attempt to subdue its rivals, lest they themselves be subjugated. Such state competition fueled innovation in social organization, productive technology, and military hardware. Successful innovations allowed for larger and denser populations and greater per-capita energy production, resulting in larger and more powerful sociocultural systems that replaced or absorbed smaller and less powerful ones.

The hypothesis that there are deterministic stages of cultural evolution is controversial. Nonetheless, the development trajectories of peoples around the globe have been strikingly similar. Population size, means of subsistence, degree of political centralization, and social stratification appear to be correlated. With low population density, hunter-gatherer societies exhibited a high degree of equality, whereas complex systems of social hierarchy have been the norm in densely populated states. Flannery and Marcus note that ". . . out of the hundreds of possible varieties of human societies, five or six worked so well that they emerged over and over again in different parts of the world" (2012, xi). Although there was no communication between Eurasia and the Americas, they developed in similar ways: sequentially from foragers to tribes to chiefdoms and, eventually, centralized states and empires. In the later stages came social stratification, priesthoods, accounting, bureaucrats, armies, slaves, serfs, architecture, astronomy, and writing. Harris has indicated how the Aztecs and Incas of the new world were independently evolving toward political and social institutions that bear striking similarity to those that took shape earlier in Eurasia. In fact, the lack of large domesticated animals to pull plows and carts might have been a crucial factor in both the developmental lag and the principal differences. Without animals for traction, the technology of the wheel was not developed, although it existed for children's toys in Mexico (Harris 1989, 488ff). To that might be added the lack of metallurgy in the ancient Americas.

Hereditary Aristocracy

From the hour of their birth, some are marked out for subjection, some for command.
                                        —Aristotle, *Politics* (1962, Book 1, 1254a)

The rise of hereditary societies predates the state. Hereditary ranking first appeared in achievement-based societies, became class-stratified with the rise of the state, and reached its most extreme point during the era of early empires. Rulers and elites by birth expropriated not only the economic surplus but also a disproportionate number of women, often in harems.

Hereditary inequality served to freeze privilege. The rich and powerful had originally gained their advantages because they were indeed more powerful and skillful, but they came to believe they were innately superior, and so did the subjugated. Religions provided class stratification with legitimacy, typically by foisting the power structure of society on the cosmos, and in so doing they *politicized nature* (Frankfort et al. 1977). Early states were theocracies ruled by political-military-religious elites.

The superior talents that had enabled elites to acquire command over others were often wanting in their offspring. Over time, kings and other hereditary nobles might prove to be incompetent, or even mentally deficient, often due to inbreeding. However, their privileged position gave them every chance to compensate for any natural deficiencies. The entire hierarchical structure of privilege depended upon preserving the legitimacy of their status.

Hereditary societies became increasingly rigid in their stratification as sharper delineations were made between classes. The most extreme outcome was division into castes, and the most extreme example, as discussed in Chapter 4, was Hinduism. However, social division into castes existed throughout Eurasia and Africa, and it often continued into modern times. It built upon three elements: occupational exclusiveness, hereditary descent, and exploitation (W. Thompson 2015, 66).

Agriculture, Civilization, and Quality of Life

> *As soon as the land of any country has all become private property, the landlords, like all other men, love to reap where they never sowed, and demand a rent even for its natural produce. The wood of the forest, the grass of the field, and all the natural fruits of the earth, which, when land was in common, cost the labourer only the trouble of gathering them, come, even to him, to have an additional price fixed upon them. He must then pay for the license to gather them; and must give up to the landlord a portion of what his labour either collects or produces.*
> —Adam Smith, *The Wealth of Nations* (1776, 49)

With the rise of the state, societies were generally divided into essentially two classes: a small, wealthy elite and a large, poor producer class comprising slaves, serfs, debtors, or peasants. The elite represented about 2 percent of the population in pre-revolutionary China and about 15 percent in pre-modern Western Europe.[11] They lived off the surplus created by the producer class, who overwhelmingly worked in agriculture and lived at the edge of mere subsistence (Jones 1987, 4).

It was the development of agriculture that set the material preconditions, not only for the evolution of the state, but also for extreme inequality, social domination, and hence social unfreedom. Rousseau was correct when he claimed that, with civilization, the powerful "irretrievably destroyed natural liberty, established for all time the law of property and inequality . . . and for the benefit of a few ambitious men subjected the human race thenceforth to labour, servitude and misery" (1755, 122).

Following the adoption of agriculture, and especially with the evolution of the state, the general quality of life dramatically declined for the vast majority of people in these societies. Agriculturalists suffered poorer diets, more diseases, shorter stature, and shorter life spans than did hunters and

---

[11] The fact that 15 percent shared the surplus in Europe whereas 2 percent did so in China accounts for the opulence of the Chinese elite that so bedazzled Western visitors and reveals its extreme concentration of economic and political power.

gatherers. They became victims of a host of diseases transmitted from their domesticated animals (Diamond 1999).[12] Human skeletons became weaker as bones became less dense (Feltman 2014, A3). Skeletons from Greece and Turkey reveal that, after the adoption of agriculture, average height declined from 5'9" to 5'3" for men and from 5'5" to 5' for women. Life expectancy at birth fell from about 26 years to 19 (1987: 65). Among hunter-gatherers, about 5 percent lived past age 50; among early agriculturalists, about one percent.

Echoing Rousseau and surely only half in jest, Diamond asserts that the adoption of agriculture was "the worst mistake in the history of the human race" (1987). Was the fall depicted in Genesis a metaphor for this "mistake?" (Pollan 2002). Others, such as anthropologist Claude Lévi-Strauss, have also claimed that human well-being has been in decline since the Neolithic period (Schiffman 2017). Historian Willie Thompson writes: "Kafka's novels and Munch's famous painting 'The Scream' are frequently quoted to characterise the twentieth century—but rather they do so also for the entire historical narrative since the Neolithic revolution" (2015, 245). When the Sioux Indians took possession of horses brought to North American by the Spaniards, they abandoned agriculture to become nomadic hunters, mostly following buffalo herds. Scott writes:

> There is massive evidence of determined resistance by mobile peoples everywhere to permanent settlement, even under relatively favorable circumstances. Pastoralists and hunting-and-gathering populations have fought against permanent settlement, associating it, often correctly, with disease and state control. (2017, 8)

Prior to agriculture, sexual competition was generally expressed in ways that supported cooperation and the general well-being of the community. The egalitarian community determined what forms of competition were appropriate and thus meritorious. In seeking approval, and the status it conferred, individuals strove to be the best providers of food and the best defenders

---

[12] Paleontologist Tim Flannery writes, "The scale of disease transfer in the early cities must have been overwhelming: we share twenty-six diseases with poultry, thirty-two with rats and mice, thirty-five with horses, forty-two with pigs, forty-six with sheep and goats, fifty with cattle, and sixty-five with our oldest companion, the dog. In the majority of cases, the transfer was one-way—humanity is a 'dead end' for most infections. In effect, a new ecology was taking shape in the first cities, within which diseases and parasites did as well as, if not better than, the city's human and animal inhabitants" (2020, 32).

of the community. They competed to be seen as generous and cooperative because others would appreciate and requite such deserving behavior. The promise of reciprocation from a grateful community would improve their offspring's chances of thriving and, in turn, becoming attractive to potential mates. At the same time, egalitarian pre-agricultural societies repressed, and harshly punished, individuals' or groups' attempts to seek status by amassing wealth or political power.

Within forager groups, virtually no one starved unless all did. But the establishment of state-enforced private property was a watershed that radically rechanneled human behavior. People became more competitive for life's necessities. Those who did not own or control property could no longer look to the community for their fundamental requirements, food and livelihood. Even those who possessed property had to live with the fear of losing it. Out of this insecurity, everyone would wish to possess more property for security and self-protection. And, of course, those who possessed property would be more attractive to potential mates, giving them greater success in passing their genes into the future. While reproductive success in hunter-gatherer societies accompanied success as warriors, hunters, and gatherers, status and hence reproductive potential in agricultural and pastoral societies correlated with ownership of land and livestock.

In a world of highly unequal property ownership, elites possessing property would benefit if the less fortunate—especially those living in misery and on the verge of starvation—viewed the present material world as not so very important. As seen in Chapter 4, religion evolved into ideological expressions that devalued the material world in favor of a more appealing afterlife, which could be best attained by obedience to authority and acceptance of the status quo.

Is it the case, then, that the adoption of agriculture and the evolution of the state represented an unambiguous decrease in the quality of life for the masses—humanity's "worst mistake," as Diamond put it? There is evidence that violence generally became less pervasive. Cognitive psychologist Steven Pinker argues that with the rise of civilization "came a reduction in the chronic raiding and feuding that characterized life in a state of nature and a more or less fivefold decrease in rates of violent death" (2011, xxiv). Diamond writes of his astonishment at learning that "trench warfare, machine guns, napalm, atomic bombs, artillery, and submarine torpedoes produce time-averaged war related death tolls so much lower than those from spears, arrows, and clubs . . . [due in part to the fact that] state warfare is an intermittent exceptional condition, while tribal warfare is virtually continuous" (2012, 140).

Whereas Pinker documents the decline in overall violence accompanying the rise of the state, he also cites the work of sociologist Steven Spitzer that "has shown that complex societies are more likely to criminalize victimless activities like sacrilege, sexual deviance, disloyalty, and witchcraft, and to punish offenders by torture, mutilation, enslavement, and execution" (2011, 57). Did harsh state religions and punishments help account for reduced violence? Cultural anthropologists Benjamin Purzycki et al. report that "cross-cultural data sets show that larger and more politically complex societies tend to have more supernatural punishment and moralistic deities." However, they also appear to have made people more cooperative and trusting (2016, 227, 228).

Economic historians Richard Steckel and John Wallis speculate that perhaps the reason there was little retreat back to hunting and gathering was that while "the attraction of an agrarian society was not a higher physical standard of living, it was a safer life and thus, presumably, of greater utility" (2007, 3). However, Steckel and Wallis apparently presume that there was free choice as to whether to remain in agriculture or return to foraging. In fact, as will be shown in more detail in the following, producers were often forced into states as slave labor, and producers were variously "caged" to prevent their escape. In the extreme, the eyes of prisoner-slaves might be gouged out to preclude their fleeing (J. Diamond 2012, 146).[13]

It should be noted that not all scholars are convinced that the rise of the state decreased total violence. Sociologist Norbert Elias, for instance, claimed that the reduction in tribal conflicts found among foragers must be weighed against the violence the state used against its subjects, through state wars, suppressing rebellions, and most notably the systematic violence against slaves and women, the latter suffering the subjugation of patriarchal households (1939). Although women were often forced to join the harems of the elite, poor men were the greatest losers, being deprived of the possibility of mating. This too benefited the rulers, insofar as men who are unable to find mates tend to be highly violent and thus able candidates for the rulers' armies. Anthropologist and historian Laura Betzig offers support for Elias's

---

[13] Some slave work did not require sight. This could be true for sex slaves and those such as the Old Testament's Samson (Book of Judges, chapters 13–16. These are Bible chapters, not chapters of this book).

position. Early states tended to fall under the control of despots "who are guaranteed to get their way in conflicts, who can kill with impunity, and who have large harems of women at their disposal. . . . When it came to violence, then, the first Leviathans solved one problem but created another. People were less likely to become victims of homicide or casualties of war, but they were now under the thumbs of tyrants, clerics, and kleptocrats" (1993, 58).

As noted in Chapter 3, primatologist Richard Wrangham claims that through execution of furiously and reactively violent individuals dating back perhaps as much as 300,000 years, humans self-domesticated to become less ferocious as a species. This domestication surely continued with civilization and may have accelerated as the state arrogated and centralized the power to execute miscreants. As with domesticated animals, the unruly ones would have been eliminated. Not only could disorderly humans be killed, they could alternatively be castrated, or sent to mines, quarries, into forestation, or other outposts where they would not have the opportunity to reproduce and send their genes into future generations.

Finally, Scott emphasizes the extent to which early states needed to cage their populations. Such caging of agricultural producers may have been especially necessary in the earliest period of state societies since "epidemiologically, this was perhaps the most lethal period of human history." Sedentism created ideal "feedlots" for pathogens (2017, 97, 100). Consequently, extensive measures were instituted and enforced to hold on to producers. Surviving evidence, for instance, are the Old Babylonian legal codes that extensively address the problem of returning escapees to their tasks, as well as punishing them to discourage others from fleeing. Scott notes sinologist Owen Lattimore's claim that the great walls of China were built as much to keep Chinese taxpayers in as to keep barbarians out (2017, 30, 155). With the high toll from crowd diseases and the need for producers' surpluses, keeping the producers trapped was essential for the early states' survival.

Producers had good cause to abscond. Should they succeed in doing so, they would escape, not only from the diseases that plagued cities, but also from the unfreedom and grueling compulsory work to produce output that would be expropriated. Indeed, greater equality and improved quality of life followed when states collapsed. Recall that, after the fall of the Roman Empire, ordinary people enjoyed not only greater freedom but also improved health, as evidenced by greater height and stronger teeth and bones (Scheidel 2017, 266).

In the world of nomadic hunter-gatherers, all of nature was humanity's commons. In time, increasing population density and evolving military technology enabled ever-greater privatization of humanity's commons. Yet, until the beginnings of modernity, most people lived beyond the clutches of states (Scott 2017), and thus in a world of commons where natural resources were not owned or controlled. However, as civilized history unfolded, population density and more sophisticated technologies enabled the extension of state control and increasing privatization of the commons. Today, practically all habitable land has been privatized or has come under state restrictions that preclude free non-state human habitation. With advances in patent law, knowledge itself is increasingly privatized. Economist Ronald Coase argued that the assignment of property rights only matters because of positive transaction costs (1960). However, what his much-celebrated thesis overlooks is that property rights also matter because they enable owners to exploit non-owners.

The very word *civilization* has always connoted a positive development for humanity. It has been endlessly celebrated as lifting humans out of a state of barbarity or savagery. Scott points out that

> from Thomas Hobbes to John Locke to Giambattista Vico to Lewis Henry Morgan to Friedrich Engels to Herbert Spencer to Oswald Spengler to social Darwinist accounts of social evolution in general, the sequence of progress from hunting and gathering to nomadism to agriculture (and from band to village to town to city) was settled doctrine. (Scott 2017, 9)

But until modern times, this sequence has not been progress for the overwhelming mass of humanity. Scott writes:

> It would be almost impossible to exaggerate the centrality of bondage, in one form or another, in the development of the state until very recently. As historian Adam Hochschild observed, as late as 1800 roughly three-quarters of the world's population could be said to be living in bondage.... [The] well-being of a population must never be confounded with the power of a court or state center. It is not uncommon for the subjects of early states to leave both agriculture and urban centers to evade taxes, conscription, epidemics, and oppression. (2017, 155–56; 211)

Why Elites and Rulers Must Maximize
Surplus Extraction

Peasants are like sesame seeds: the harder you squeeze, the more they render.

—Feudal Japanese maxim

Although ruling elites lived lives of relative luxury, they did not have unfettered use of the full extracted surplus for their own extravagance. Their struggle to capture the entire surplus was compelled by three forces, only the first of which occasions profligacy. Ruling elites require, first, high status; second, political power; and, third, control over the prevailing ideology.

The elite were in a constant struggle with one another for the very pinnacle of status. As we have seen, the human preoccupation with status or relative social position makes good sense from an evolutionary perspective. Those with higher status, whatever its socially valued source, possess disproportionate access to resources and members of the opposite sex. The combination of more material goods and more potential mates enabled them to have more and better-cared-for progeny, and thus better chances of winning the biological race to send their genes into the future. A proclivity for seeking status would thus be naturally selected. Or, as economist Robert Frank has put it, "falling behind ones local rivals can be lethal" (2005, 183). And especially so for the future of one's genes.

Since the rise of civilization, much of the competition for status has been manifested in conspicuous consumption, the point of Adam Smith's "baubles and trinkets" thesis for the decline of aristocratic power in late medieval Europe and Thorstein Veblen's focus on wasteful spending in late nineteenth-century America.[14] Otherwise wasteful expenditure, not unlike the male peacock's tail or the stag's heavy rack, communicated to others, and especially to potential mates, how very worthy one must be. For example, household staff providing personal services could serve the purpose of conspicuous consumption, as Veblen remarked: "The possession and maintenance of slaves employed in the production of goods argues wealth and prowess, but the maintenance of servants who produce nothing argues still higher wealth

---

[14] Smith contended that late medieval aristocrats competed through conspicuous consumption for status, impoverishing themselves and enriching a rising commercial class that would slowly take away their power and privilege (1776, 389–92). Veblen's analysis of the waste of resources in extravagant conspicuous consumption was crafted during America's Gilded Age (1899).

and position" (1899, 63). Relentless competition for status pressured elites to squeeze as much surplus as possible from their productive subordinates.

The second reason for maximum exploitation is that, to survive politically, ruling elites needed to command as much wealth and control as much power as possible. They needed resources to protect themselves not only from domestic and foreign contenders for their privileged status, but also from those who might rebel against their surplus extractions. The threat of warfare with neighbors was ever present, and the best defense was generally offense. As Prussian military theorist Carl von Clausewitz famously said, "So long as I have not overthrown my opponent I am bound to fear he may overthrow me. Thus I am not in control; he dictates to me as much as I dictate to him" (1989, 77). The constant threat of war fueled an arms race, requiring resources for the maintenance of soldiers, fortifications, and weapons. Rulers were caught in a dilemma: if they fell behind in the arms race, they could be conquered, but an increase of their state's power could provoke their enemies to attack preemptively. Thucydides described how the rise of Athens's power instilled fear among the Spartans, prompting them to go to war before Athens became even stronger. Over the past 500 years, dominant nations have seen the rise of major competitors as such a threat that they preemptively went to war in 12 of 16 cases (Allison 2016).

The third reason rulers need the entire available surplus is to maintain the ideological infrastructure that preserves social peace by legitimating the status quo. This infrastructure consisted principally of expensive physical structures such as temples, pyramids, cathedrals, and priests garbed in costly raiment. To be vigorous and convincing, ideologies needed to be delivered in awe-inspiring manners to generate respect, and outlays for the ideological apparatus could be large. Economist Thomas Piketty reports that, on the eve of the French Revolution of 1789, the Catholic Church's share of national output was about 25 percent (2020, 89), much of which was essential for legitimating the status quo.

To reinforce their ideology, the elite also needed to spend resources to signal their superiority, and thus their right to rule. They were far better nourished, clothed, and sheltered than the masses, and they received the best healthcare. Accordingly, they were on average taller and more robust. They exhibited fewer signs of ill-health such as deformed bodies, facial pimples or blemishes, and open or poorly healing wounds. And they were cleaner. Their inherent superiority was there for all to see. Even as late as 1800, cadets at the British military academy of Sandhurst were six centimeters taller than regular army soldiers (Clark 2009, 184). As social psychologists John Jost and Brenda Major note, ". . . members of low status groups are more likely to accept the legitimacy of their own inferiority and display outgroup favoritism when there is a clear, well-established, non-overlapping status-related difference between their own group and a higher status outgroup" (2001, 21).

The Absolutist State

Power tends to corrupt, and absolute power corrupts absolutely.
—John Dalberg-Acton, Letter to Bishop
Mandell Creighton, April 5, 1887

The term absolutism characterizes a state free of constraints imposed by a legislature, a judiciary, religious institutions, or economic classes. States ruled by monarchs legitimating their rule as a divine right, by dictators, and more generally by autocrats have been referred to as absolutist states. Absolutism is frequently associated with France's Sun King, Louis XIV (1643–1715), who famously asserted *L'état, c'est moi* (I am the state). But, despite its widespread use, *absolutism* is a misnomer. Because a state's monopoly on violence is always relative, so too is its power. It is never absolute. Retaining the word as it is commonly used, however, absolute monarchs portrayed themselves as embodying the entire nation in their persons, and, until modern times, they typically claimed a divine mandate to do so. They sought to appear as above all factions, to be non-partisan, to represent the best interests of everyone. When Napoleon seized full power, he declared that he stood above the divisions, wearing neither the red heels of the aristocracy nor the red liberty caps of the revolutionaries (*ni talon rouge, ni bonnet rouge*).

Nonetheless, for most of history since the rise of the state, a thin wealthy elite needed to be appeased because their command over resources could fund violent opposition to rulers. They conformed more closely to Marx's characterization of the state as an executive committee of the ruling class. This description especially held where the aristocracy elected the ruler.

Rulers continually sought to constrain the power of elites, just as any monopolist struggles to curb or, if possible, eliminate all competition. To that end, rulers might give favor to other classes. Against the interests of elites, states could use debt cancellation and land redistribution to reduce the threat of peasant rebellion or flight, thereby retaining them to pay taxes and serve in armies. One of the first records of such debt cancellation was that of Hammurabi in Babylon in 1761 BC (Graeber 2012, 217). In another notable example, the Greek lawmaker Solon abolished debt and slavery in 594 BC.

In medieval Europe, Tudor monarchs pursued legal changes that increased landownership among the common people. Monarchs at times sided with peasants against landlords by cancelling debt, redistributing land, or opposing enclosures. Henry VII blocked lords from evicting tenants holding 20 or more acres, thereby favoring the "middle people" (Sitaraman 2017, 55). With the expansion of markets at the end of the Middle Ages, as will be recounted at greater length in Chapter 6, rulers could gain greater independence from aristocrats by supporting and thereby gaining revenues from emerging commercial activity. The amount of surplus in a society at any moment is fixed, and the more the state could constrain the landlords' exploitation of producers, the more remained for the state to gather as taxes.

In recent history, relative freedom from the constraints of a ruling class appears to have been the condition of the Soviet state, although the leaders' prerogatives were somewhat limited by the broad membership of the Communist Party, whose members enjoyed certain privileges. Stalin's murderous purges of the late 1930s served to consolidate his own power as well as that of the state. He had earlier abolished private property in land and had collectivized agriculture in an effort to redeploy agricultural surplus toward industrialization. As owner of practically all land and capital, the state held virtually uncontested political power, not unlike the pharaohs of ancient Egypt.

The state, with its monopoly on violence, offers protection, and nothing legitimates and empowers the state more effectively than war or the risk of imminent war. Because leaders receive greater loyalty and respect from the populace when external aggression threatens, they face an all-but-irresistible temptation: they benefit if they can convincingly keep alive the perception of such a menace. They can even be expected to craft measures against other powers that will provoke and sustain a limited amount of real threat (Wisman 2020). As philosopher Friedrich Hegel put it, "peoples involved in civil strife . . . acquire peace at home through making war abroad" (1958, 295). Far from being the product of a social contract, the state arose due to its monopoly on violence, and its struggles against external enemies, real or conjured, gave it legitimacy.[15] It is the temptation to fabricate the existence of

---

[15] Social contractarians from Thomas Hobbes and John Locke to Douglass North depict rational self-interested agents freely giving up some of their sovereignty to a state for their mutual well-being. But this presumed free choice is closer to that faced by the Mafia's "offer you can't refuse."

a foreign menace that prompted Samuel Johnson to declare that patriotism is the last refuge of scoundrels.

Examples of states enhancing their power through warlike behavior are endless, but many readers may find two twentieth-century instances familiar. A hostile capitalist West made the continual threat of foreign aggression convincing to the peoples of the Soviet Union after 1917. In the wake of the Bolshevik revolution, the English, French, and Americans sent an expeditionary force to unseat the Bolsheviks. Thereafter, except for a brief period during World War II, Western capitalist countries' hostility toward the Soviet Union was unrelenting. The use of atomic bombs on Japanese cities furnished the Soviet peoples with unambiguous evidence as to the magnitude of the threat they faced—the extremes to which the United States might go to achieve its objectives. A similar dynamic played out in Cuba after 1961, legitimating Castro's dictatorial powers. In both the Soviet Union and Cuba, the hostility of capitalist countries justified concentrated political power and restrictions on citizens' rights. More recently, the 9/11 terrorist attacks had a similar effect in the United States. They generated wide support for an unpopular president whose very election was viewed by many as a sham and a so-called Patriot Act that compromised civil liberties (Wisman 2014a). As war historian John W. Dower puts it, just as December 7, 1941, was "a political godsend for President Roosevelt . . . September 11 proved to be a windfall for President Bush" (2010, 138).

It is because of the extraordinary power of external threats to create internal cohesion that the military component of government often retains considerable legitimacy, even when overall trust in the state is low. In the United States, for example, in a June 2014 Gallup Poll, only 30 percent of the population expressed confidence in the Supreme Court, and 7 percent in Congress. Fully 73 percent considered corruption to be rampant in government. However, 80 percent expressed confidence in the armed forces (Gylfason 2015, 332).

Military Organization, Weaponry, and Inequality

The power of making laws was long vested in those—and still is vested in their descendants—who followed no trade but war, and know no handicraft but robbery and plunder.
   —Thomas Hodgskin, *The Natural and Artificial Rights of Property*
Contrasted (1832, 32)

Since the invention of tools, military technology has played a central role in the struggle over inequality. As noted in Chapter 3, many tools useful in hunting and gathering could serve equally well as weapons. Made of readily accessible materials such as stone, bone, and wood, they acted as equalizers, preventing individuals or groups from acquiring political or economic power. These early weapons, along with the potential for weaker members of the community to form coalitions, also played a role in the self-domestication of humans. Eliminating alpha males who could monopolize access to resources and females created a more peaceful and cooperative species (Wrangham 2019). Later, however, military weaponry crafted from metals played a decisive role in the rise of states and extreme inequality in Eurasia. Military historian John Keegan estimates that 10 chariots, each with a driver and an archer, could slay 500 enemies in 10 minutes! (2004, 165–66).

However, although they were highly efficient on relatively flat terrain, chariots could not operate smoothly in hilly topography such as that of Greece, whose power expanded with the new technology of smelting iron ore. Iron is far more abundant than copper or tin, and cheaper iron weapons, shields, and armor became available to producers after about 1200 BC. Such equipment enabled non-elites to defend themselves more effectively against aristocratic power, but it also let outlaws prey upon states and their residents.

As will be seen in Chapter 6, expensive horses and the stirrup have been credited with creating the conditions for feudalism in Europe, and gunpowder and cannons were important in its demise. Superior armaments also played a central role in the Atlantic slave trade. Firearms sold by Europeans in exchange for slaves greatly enhanced the ability of African ruling elites to increase their power over their subjects and capture yet more slaves to bring to the coast for sale from the seventeenth century onward (Boix 2015, 169). However, not all instances of increasingly concentrated political power and inequality appear to be traceable to "hard" weapons technology. The rise of achievement societies and chiefdoms was not made possible by changing armaments, but instead by religious ideology and the need for greater social coordination that accompanied increased population densities.

Boix's claim that ". . . human communities only witnessed the emergence of centralized political institutions after war technologies became sophisticated enough—at around 3000 BC or five millennia after the domestication of plants and animals" (2015, 128) appears to hold for Eurasia. It does not, however, apply to the Americas, where kingdoms and empires arose without metal armaments or horses. Indeed, the technology available to the rulers' armies was based on inexpensive stone, bone, and wood that differed little from the resources available to the general population. Highly centralized political power in the Americas appears to have developed from a combination of superior organizational skills and ideology. As evidence of the extraordinary power of ideology in pre-Columbian America, historian Álvaro Enrique reports:

> War in Mesoamerica, unlike in Europe, was a highly ritualized process, determined by the calendar and agreements between specific groups. Cities did not have defenses—there were no ramparts, no moats, no castles—because the dates and locations of battles were agreed on beforehand, during the brief period in the calendar when the Nahua belief system allowed for fighting. (2018, 45)[16]

Thus, military superiority does not appear to depend upon superior technology alone. Superior organization and effective ideology appear at times to have accomplished the same thing. As for ideology, states spend considerable resources to communicate the state's power, glory, and worthiness. Religious rituals combined with displays of pomp and expensive monuments provide legitimacy to concentrated political power. They absorb a considerable portion of all societies' surplus, making less available to rulers and elites for other ends. Rulers have continually emphasized that their power protects the people from disasters, notably including foreign aggression and internal chaos.

Modes of Surplus Extraction

[T]here are some people, some of whom are naturally free, others naturally slaves, for whom slavery is both just and beneficial.
—Aristotle, *Politics* (1962, 1255a 1–2)

---

[16] These seemingly ritualized wars suggest a strategy of rulers to enhance their subjects' cohesion and loyalty by accentuating foreign menaces in a manner similar to that depicted in George Orwell's dystopian novel *1984*.

As hunter-gatherers for 95 percent of their history, humans coordinated their activities to survive without formal political institutions, private ownership of the means of production, exploitation, or political and economic inequality. Only since the rise of the state and civilization, about 5,500 years ago, has significant private or state ownership of nature (land) and capital (stored-up labor) emerged within societies. Elites' monopoly ownership and control of productive wealth has meant that others gain access to the means of production only on the condition that they surrender all output in excess of the minimum required for survival. They have done so by means of labor services, portions of crops, and money.

Differing historical conditions have supported varying systems of exploitation such as slavery, debt bondage, feudalism, and in recent centuries, capitalism. To maintain these social orders, the state created, protected, nourished, and legitimated exploitative social institutions and ideologies. While the state and elites have struggled over their respective shares of producers' surpluses, they have generally been unified in the coordination necessary to maintain its extraction. This has been true for that taken both from domestic producers and from those in external militarily weaker societies.

Interstate exploitation, called tribute, is found in two arrangements. The first is seen where conquered peoples have been required to make periodic payments to the victors or suffer the further infliction of violence and destruction. The second is observed where weaker peoples make payments in exchange for protection from other potential enemies. Even in mutual defense alliances, the stronger state could exact tribute from its partners. Tribute payments usually came in forms that had high value-to-weight ratios such as gold and luxury goods, or in the form of animals and slaves capable of transporting themselves over land or cheaply in boats. Some powers ruled almost exclusively on the economic basis of tribute from surrounding peoples, such as during the almost two and a half centuries (1237–1480) that Tatar-Mongols drew surplus from Russian states.

In predominantly agricultural economies, landlords constituted the ruling class, and laws, customs, and ideology tied agricultural workers to the land as slaves, serfs, indebted peasants, and indentured servants. In all instances, they were caged, unable to escape their exploited condition. This section provides a brief summary of these dominant modes of surplus extraction. It concludes with the exceptional instance of capitalism, where "free" labor is no longer legally tied to the land but has continued to be caged, de facto, in systematic exploitation.

Slavery

The economics of slavery are clear. Capturing and exploiting slaves offers high returns. Apart from precious metals and some jewelry, conquering armies could cart off little of value from poor countries. What had considerable value was land and humans capable of labor and procreation. The land could not, of course, be carried off, but, because they could walk, slaves could be driven over land in coffles at low cost. Water transportation, where available, was also relatively inexpensive.

Raising children is extremely expensive. They are dependents whose feeding and care absorb material resources and, especially, time that might otherwise be used for more immediate gain. Only after years of dependency does the next generation's labor start to cover their upkeep. For a society, raising children is an investment in potentially productive labor for its collective future. For parents, children represent an investment for care in old age—children are the principal way to provide for senescence in kinship groups. To capture slaves is to steal this investment. Taking female slaves also represented a reproductive windfall for the male conquerors who, by mating with them, increase the probability that their genes will survive into the future.

The economic and reproductive utility of slavery for elites is evidenced by the tardiness of its legal abolition. For example, slavery was proscribed in New York State in 1827; France and Denmark in 1848; the United States as a whole in 1865; Brazil in 1880; Saudi Arabia in 1962; the Sultanate of Muscat and Oman in 1970; and Mauritania in 1981. The International Labour Organization estimates that, although slavery is no longer legal, 40.3 million humans—25 percent of whom were children—lived in conditions of slavery in 2016. Most were sex slaves (Swarens 2018).

Because slaves experience the extreme unfreedom of being bought and sold as commodities, slavery is the most debased condition possible for workers. Slaves are treated in much the same manner as other forms of property. Families can be broken up and their members, children as well as adults, sold as individuals. Female slaves can be raped, an extreme form of physical, mental, and emotional abuse that also deprives them of choice as to the male parentage of their children.[17] And just as whips and goads were

---

[17] Graeber reports that "in ancient Ireland, female slaves were so plentiful and important that they came to function as currency . . . slave girls also served as the highest denomination of currency in

used to discipline horses and oxen, so were they used to control and castigate slaves. Indeed, slaves were subject to treatment far worse than that accorded livestock: they could be tortured and killed to set an example for other slaves.

Slavery has been ubiquitous for most of history since the rise of states. Scott claims that all ancient states were slave states; slaves constituted at least 30 percent of their populations and as much as 50 percent in Athens and Sparta. "[S]laving was at the very centre of state-making" (2013, 14, 15). In French and British colonies at the end of the eighteenth century, the proportion of slaves to population reached as high as 90 percent (Piketty 2020, 217–20).

Early agrarian states needed labor to cultivate fields, build monuments, serve as soldiers, and bear and raise children. The toll taken by crowd diseases in cities required that their populations be continually replenished, making the capturing or purchasing of slaves essential to states' economic and political power. War was at times undertaken as much for acquiring slaves as for other ends. Scott reports that

> . . . most South-East Asian early state chronicles gauge the success of a war by the number of captives marched back to the capital and resettled there. The Athenians and Spartans might kill the men of a defeated city and burn its crops, but they virtually always brought back the women and children as slaves. And . . . a slave merchant caravan trailed every Roman war scooping up the slaves it inevitably produced. . . . Wars between states became a kind of booty capitalism, where the major prize was human traffic. The slave trade then completely transformed the non-state "tribal zone." Some groups specialised in slave-raiding, mounting expeditions against weaker and more isolated groups and then selling them to intermediaries or directly at slave markets. (2013, 14)

Selling people as slaves was far more profitable than working them and capturing their surplus.[18] A slave trade flourished when elites had nothing of value to exchange for the imported goods they sought. For instance, until

---

Medieval Iceland, and in the Rig Veda, great gifts and payments are regularly designated in 'gold, cattle, and slave girls'" (2012, 128, 408).

[18] Only after Britain employed its navy to end the slave trade to the Americas did African slave-exporting rulers turn significantly to using slaves in domestic agriculture, exporting a portion of the surplus as a substitute for slaves to acquire desired imports (Tylecote 2016, 735).

modern times, European elites had little of value other than precious metals and slaves to exchange for the luxury goods they desired from the East. By the mid-eighth century, Venice had established a thriving slave trade, buying Europeans and selling them to the Moors in Northern Africa. Between the sixteenth and eighteenth centuries, more than a million Western Europeans were enslaved and sold to Arab merchants (Appleby 2011, 126).

African autocrats and elites desired both foreign luxury goods and richer countries' advanced weapons, but they lacked a valuable export commodity other than slaves. Consequently, there was a long history of slave trading across the Sahara between East Africa and the Arabian Peninsula and later from West Africa across the Atlantic. The huge quantities of muskets that Europeans brought to Africa to exchange for slaves solidified the African rulers' despotism and lowered the cost of capturing yet more slaves (Boix 2015, 170).

Until modern times, one of the principal spoils of war was young women and girls taken as slaves. Males usually faced death and thus were fortunate to be taken as slaves. Social thought legitimated their sad fate. Even progressive John Locke held that "captives taken in a just war [had] forfeited their lives and, with it, their liberties [and were therefore] subjected to the absolute dominion and arbitrary power of their masters" (quoted in Losurdo 2014, 24). He was, however, apparently "the last major philosopher to seek a justification for absolute and perpetual slavery" (Davis 1999, 45).

Descriptive examples of captured female sex slaves often appear in ancient literature. Classics scholar Moses Finley reports that the sexual availability of slaves to their masters "is treated as a commonplace in Graeco-Roman literature from Homer on; only modern writers have managed largely to ignore it" (1980, 95). Pinker writes that "for the heroes of the *Iliad*, female flesh was a legitimate spoil of war: women were to be enjoyed, monopolized, and disposed of at their pleasure" (2011, 5).

When European powers conquered the Americas, they faced a huge imbalance in factors of production: abundant fertile land but scarce labor. The indigenous peoples were highly susceptible to European diseases and difficult to enslave since they could escape into non-European-controlled territories. One response was to bring in indentured servants from Europe; another was to import slaves from Africa. Approximately 12.5 million men and women were shipped as slaves from Africa, with about 10.7 million arriving in the Americas. The remainder perished in the crowded and unsanitary ship holds.

Wherever slavery existed, it was legitimated by ideology. Aristotle argued that "the lower sort are by nature slaves, and it is better for them as for all inferiors that they should be under the rule of a master" (1962, 1254a). Although Christianity embraced a concept of universal humanity where all are equal in the eyes of God, "Church Fathers from Paul to Jerome unanimously accepted slavery, merely advising slaves to be obedient to their masters and masters to be just to their slaves—true liberty, after all, was not to be found in this world anyway" (P. Anderson 2013, 133–34).

In the wake of the French Revolution,

> the trade-and exchange-conscious [Anne Jean Marie René] Savary was able to come to terms with the institution of slavery by pointing out that the "cultivation of tobacco, sugar and indigo . . . does not fail to be advantageous" to the slaves because of "the knowledge of the true God and of Christian religion which is supplied to them as a kind of compensation for the loss of liberty." (Quoted in Hirschman 1997, 62)

Although the country was founded on the principle that all humans are created equal, slavery had little difficulty finding legitimation in the United States. Eleven of the first 15 presidents were slaveowners. The enslaved were not equal after all. They were childlike and needed their masters to civilize and protect them. And adding to this rationalization, historian Joyce Appleby points out, "the unattractive personal traits that slavery instilled in children and their parents—indolence, insolence, sluggishness, lethargy— were exactly the qualities that were used to justify enslavement" (2011, 134).

Religions willingly accepted slavery in North America. Witness the fact that the Catholic Church was among the largest institutional slaveholders in America. In 1838, Georgetown University, a Jesuit institution, sold 272 slaves to settle debts, even though families were broken up and many individuals were sent to Louisiana to labor under the harsh conditions of gang slavery on cotton and sugar plantations (N. Anderson and Svrluga 2016). Southern churches of practically all denominations owned slaves.

Serfdom

Serfdom shared many similarities with slavery. Both existed primarily in predominantly agricultural economies. In both there was bondage, slaves to their owners, serfs to the land where they were ruled over by landlords. (The Latin phrase *glebae adscripti*—bound to the earth—described their situation in medieval Europe.) In both instances, the condition was generally hereditary. Children of slaves or serfs would also be slaves or serfs. Although serfdom is often associated with Europe in the Middle Ages, variants existed around the world.

But there were also distinct differences between slavery and serfdom. Whereas slaves were chattel, not unlike domesticated animals, serfs were viewed as persons and members of society. Unlike slaves, serfs had a right to be on the land and could not be sold. Slaves were typically aliens, imported from abroad. Usually they were racially or ethnically different, facilitating legitimation and aiding in the recognition and return of runaways. As private property, they possessed no civil rights. Serfs, by contrast, were generally indigenous and not racially and ethnically unlike the landlords. Where political authority above the landlords existed, serfs might find some protection against landlord abuses. Finally, in those instances where slaves were permitted families, the families could usually be broken up and their members sold separately. Serfs, by contrast, formed family units that endured, with descendants inheriting rights to parental land.

Serfdom tended to exist where state power was relatively weak and landlords owned or controlled safely habitable land. Weak state power usually resulted in several conditions that were ill-suited for slavery. New slaves could not so readily be acquired through conquest, nor would runaways be as easily identified and recaptured. Moreover, without a strong state, trade routes could not be well protected, so there would not be well-developed markets within which slaves and their output could be traded. Substantial markets can only exist where transactions can be protected by state power.

In these demographic and political conditions, landlords acted as proto-states. They offered serfs law and order on manorial estates, as well as protection within their castle walls from external enemies. They also provided a degree of social security by maintaining food stocks to weather disasters. Serfs might run off and try to survive in the "no man's land" between and beyond manors, but doing so meant giving up the protection the manor provided. Further, recaptured runaways often faced punishment, or even torture and death, to set an example for others, as was common in Eastern Europe's more extreme form of serfdom.

These micro-states were frequently at war with one another. To limit such conflict, landlords often entered general accords that barred bidding for one another's serfs and providing sanctuary to runaways.

In medieval Europe, low population density, distances, and insecurity meant that transaction costs were too high for markets to form. Thus, there were few if any markets in which agricultural output could be sold. Consequently, landlords needed a way to appropriate serfs' surpluses that did not depend upon money as a medium of exchange. Although landlords might have required rent in the form of a portion of the serfs' output, forcing serfs to spend a portion of their labor time (typically two or more days of *corvée*, or unpaid labor, per week) working the landlords' land provided them with greater control over what was produced. Serfs could also be compelled to work on community projects such as roads, forests, and, in certain instances, mines. With the remainder of their time they worked their own plots for their own subsistence.

The paucity of markets also underlay why producers were tied to the land as opposed to being free laborers. Without substantial labor markets, landlords would be unable to hire replacement workers should their workers strike during critical times such as planting and harvesting. If serfs were not bound to the land, labor discord could lead to ruin.

The condition of serfs varied considerably depending upon local conditions. Where labor was in short supply, they received better conditions from lords attempting to discourage them from running away to towns or to other manors where better terms were available. By contrast, where labor was relatively abundant and towns relatively weak politically, the status of serfs could approximate that of slaves. This was the case in much of Eastern European serfdom.

Although serf women were not typically raped at will by superiors, the *droit du seigneur* allegedly allowed feudal lords to have sexual relations with subordinate females. A practice of *jus primae noctis*, or "right of the first night," was apparently common (although disputed) during the European Middle Ages. It permitted the lord to spend the first night with the bride of a marrying couple. This brutal custom comports with Darwin's dynamic of sexual selection, where powerful males strive to inseminate as many women as possible to ensure the future of their specific genes. All the better if another male must raise the resulting children.

Economic historian Richard Tawney wrote of the debased character of producers under feudalism in the following terms:

The very essence of feudal property was exploitation in its most naked and shameless form, compulsory labor, additional *corvées* at the very moments when the peasant's labor was most urgently needed on his own holding, innumerable dues and payments, the obligation to grind at the lord's mill and bake at the lord's oven, the private justice of the lord's court. (1926, 56)

Yet, despite the shamelessness of feudal exploitation, the Catholic Church participated without reservation. In fact, peasant revolts in Germany were more frequent and bitter on ecclesiastical estates (Tawney 1926, 119).

Debt Bondage

Interest-bearing debt arose during the early appearance of civilization and debt bondage has existed practically ever since. As elites captured disproportionate shares of land, others were often left with too little to sustain them in years of poor harvests. To survive, they had to borrow from the elite. The terms of repayment were generally usurious and too burdensome to meet, with debt bondage resulting whereby they were forced to labor for the creditor. Worse, indebtedness could entail slavery. At times, children of the debtor were taken into slavery or prostitution to settle their parents' debts.

Anthropologist David Graeber writes:

For thousands of years, the struggle between rich and poor has largely taken the form of conflicts between creditors and debtors . . . [and] for the last five thousand years, with remarkable regularity, popular insurrections have begun the same way: with the ritual destruction of the debt records. (2012, 8)

Finley claimed that behind revolts in the ancient world was the call, "Cancel the debts and redistribute the land" (quoted in Graeber 2012, 8).

Not unexpectedly, debtors were blamed for their fate. In some Indo-European languages, the word *debt* is related to the words for "sin" or "fault." This was also true for the Inca language (W. Thompson 2015, 86).

Indentured Servitude

Indentured servitude is a form of unfree labor created by a contract in which the worker agrees to labor for an employer for a specified number of years to pay off a debt or other obligation. It is not unlike debt bondage. It is a kind of term-limit slavery, insofar as the contract, and hence the worker, could often be sold to another employer. In the North American colonies, it was called "white slavery." Like slaves, they could be severely punished for failing to work diligently or attempting to escape. When the specified years of contract were completed, the worker was free.

Indentured servitude played a major role in populating the American colonies with Europeans in response to the shortage of labor where land was abundant and cheap. Impoverished Europeans could obtain transportation to colonial America in return for a contractual agreement to work for a specified number of years as indentured servants. The ship's captain would sell the contracts to a landowner or manufacturer who would work the newcomers for a specified period of five to seven years. It has been estimated that between one-half and two-thirds of white immigrants to the American colonies came as indentured servants between the 1630s and the American Revolution (Galenson 1984). After the Civil War, it was outlawed by the Thirteenth Amendment to the US Constitution.

Employers continually complained that indentured servants were as lazy, unruly, and rebellious as fully free workers. Given the abundance of land, free workers generally could not be paid starvation wages, abused, or caged. Although the colonies had been formed as businesses and were expected to operate profitably, their governors found the colonists highly uncooperative, and profits were rare. Consequently, Virginia planters turned to importing African slaves (Bailyn 2013). Because of their skin color, black slaves could be more effortlessly hunted down and returned to their owners. They were more easily caged.

Ultimately, the North American labor supply problem was solved by the huge number of children that families brought forth, giving support to Malthus's claim that where resources are available, population will increase.

"Free Labor"

Primitive accumulation was the term Marx used to characterize the evolution of capitalism's two dominant institutions of private property and markets, and the separation of workers from ownership, control, or free access to the means of production, and the concentration of that ownership within the capitalist class. Although feudal serfs were exploited, at times brutally, they were secure in their right to live in a community on productive land. They had the security of belonging to a community where, as a rule, no one starved unless all did, and they had access to the resources they needed for survival. But with the evolution of capitalism, producers lost their supportive communities and rights to productive wealth. For this reason, economic geographer David Harvey has suggested that "accumulation by dispossession" is a more fitting term for the process Marx called "primitive accumulation" (2003, 137).

The consequence of the capitalist class's monopoly ownership and control of the means of production is that propertyless workers had to contract with them for access and survival. The worker became "the slave of other men who have made themselves the owners of the material conditions of labour. He can only labour by their permission and hence only live by their permission" (Marx 1875, 526). Marx, however, was not the first to view wage labor as a form of slavery. In the first century AD, the Roman statesman, lawyer, and philosopher Cicero wrote: "Unbecoming a gentleman . . . and vulgar are the means of livelihood of all hired workmen whom we pay for mere manual labour, not for artistic skill; for in their case the very wage they receive is a pledge of their slavery" (1913, Book 1: 42). Or, as Graeber expresses it, ". . . wage labor [is] effectively the renting of our freedom in the same way that slavery can be conceived as its sale" (2012, 206).

The progression of primitive accumulation, combined with the evolution of its core institutions of private property and markets, was not the free and peaceful process depicted by capitalism's champions. Instead, it drew on

> the power of the State, the concentrated and organized force of society, to hasten, hothouse fashion, the process of transformation of the feudal mode of production into the capitalist mode, and to shorten the transition. Force is the midwife of every old society pregnant with a new one. It is itself an economic power. (Marx 1867b, I:823–24)

Classical economists depicted markets as sites of freedom. In a market exchange, all participants appear free and in an important sense equal. No exchange of goods or services can take place without the willing agreement of both participants, and they are equal in the sense that each possesses the power to break off the exchange by refusing the terms. A market society, where so much human interaction takes place through commercial transactions, appears to be highly attractive in that it makes human relationships appear to be consensual and free. However, as Appleby argues, "the adjective 'free' as in 'free enterprise' serves the ideological purpose of masking the coercion in capitalism" (2011, 24). It is, of course, true that workers were liberated from the medieval lord's control, but they "became sellers of themselves only after they had been robbed of all their own means of production, and of all the guarantees of existence afforded by the old feudal arrangements" (Marx 1867b, 1:786).

In a highly unequal society in which one class holds ownership and control of the means of production and all others must contract with them for the right to work, workers are hardly free in more than a formal sense because, if they cannot locate an owner to employ them, they face privation or even starvation. For this reason, the philosopher and anarchist Pierre-Joseph Proudhon proclaimed that "property is theft." He viewed private property as an artifice created by the elite to serve as a device for extracting the surplus produce of workers.[19]

Thus, the freedom of labor markets, so celebrated by mainstream economists, is spurious. The myth serves an ideological function. There is an illusion of "freedom because both buyer and seller of a commodity, say labour-power, are constrained only by their free will [although the worker] is compelled to sell himself of his own free will" (Marx 1867b, 1:95). But this compulsion is hidden because "direct force, outside economic conditions, is of course still used, but only exceptionally" (Marx 1867b, I:809). It is because markets appear as sites of freedom, and because direct forceful subjugation is not used against the wage worker as it was against the slave and serf, that wage workers are perceived as free.

But did not workers freely choose among employers and work conditions? Not in a meaningful sense since early industrial jobs required little skill beyond that possessed by children, and competition among capitalists and

---

[19] In fact, Proudhon was not against private property per se. He opposed the exploitation that results from its concentrated ownership. He advocated the union of workers with the productive wealth with which they labored.

an excess supply of labor bid wages and work conditions down to the same common level in all workplaces. The workers' freedom of choice was only to work for these wages and in these work conditions or starve. But was the worker not free in consumption? No, because subsistence wages meant that they could only purchase the cheapest goods necessary for survival. Worker freedom was an illusion.

During early capitalism, becoming free of feudal fetters did little to improve workers' standards of living. Indeed, the opposite appears true. During feudalism, serfs had a right to be on the land to which they were also tied. They also belonged to communities which provided substantial material, social, and psychological support. As producers were pushed off the land by enclosures or pulled into urban areas in expectation of better lives, they were separated from their supportive communities. In industrial cities, households were socially isolated, even though they were crowded into dirty, crime-filled slums where they had to compete for available jobs. Moreover, real wages generally declined in Western Europe between 1500 and 1800. The fact that workers had to work longer hours and that more members of the household had to work to make ends meet testify to the increased hardship. Conditions appear to have been generally harsher in England than on the continent. In England, the workday increased from 12 hours in 1700 to 14–18 hours in 1800 (Willensky 1961, 34), while the average number of workdays a year increased from 250 to 300 (Appleby 2011, 106). Families also had to substitute cheaper foodstuffs such as potatoes and maize for nutrition.

Conditions for workers appear to have declined yet further once the industrial revolution took off in earnest. For instance, Manchester weavers earned 15–20 shillings a week in 1780 but only 5–6 shillings a week 40 years later (Deane 1965, 146, 244). Manchester and its textile mills became renowned for the severe and inhumane circumstances many came to associate with capitalism. Worker wages supported only the most miserable life conditions, and worker discipline was draconian. For instance, for a mere minute's tardiness a spinner would lose a quarter of a day's wages (E. P. Thompson 1963, 201). Upon visiting Manchester, de Tocqueville wrote: "Civilization works its miracles and civilized man is turned back almost into a savage" (quoted in Hobsbawn 1968, 67–68). Throughout Europe and much of the world, the name "Manchester" conjured up a human-created hell on earth for workers.

Historian Willie Thompson writes that "total reliance on wages was initially regarded as a disgrace by the workforces first subjected to it and only submitted to when all other potential sources of legal income had been closed off" (2015, 190). Historian Keith Thomas concurs, claiming that pro-letarianization was viewed as extreme human debasement. For centuries, dependence on wages was considered unfit for humans, and certainly unsuit-able for free people. Thomas writes that "in the seventeenth century . . . wage labourers were thought to have 'lost their birthright': even Levellers excluded them from the franchise" (1964, 63). Social philosopher Lewis Mumford characterized life in these new urban environments in the following terms:

> In the city, new ways, rigorous, efficient, often harsh, even sadistic, took the place of the ancient customs and comfortable easy-paced routine. Work itself was detached from other activities and canalized into the "working day" of unceasing toil under a taskmaster; the first step in the "managerial revolution" which has reached its climax in our day. Struggle, dominion, mastery, conquest were the new themes; not the protectiveness and pru-dence, the holding fast, or the passive endurance of the village. (1961, 27)

Economist Angus Deaton has found that

> the population of Britain in the eighteenth and early nineteenth centuries consumed fewer calories than they needed for children to grow to their full potential, and for adults to maintain healthy bodily functioning and to do productive and remunerative manual labor. People were very skinny and very short, perhaps as short as at any previous (or subsequent) time.

Life expectancy at birth also appears to have declined (2013, 91, 82). Deaton goes on to note that

> There were more public latrines in Ancient Rome than in Manchester during the Industrial Revolution. When the same sources that provided drinking water were used to dispose of feces, the fecal-oral link that had been a problem since the Neolithic revolution was amplified to industrial strength. Life expectancy in the cities—as is still the case in some poor coun-tries today—fell far below life expectancy in the countryside. (2013, 94)

There was apparently fresh water available, but it was used by factories as a source of power, and elites had little interest in supporting taxes to pay for clean water for their workers (2013, 97). It was not until the second half, or even the final third, of the nineteenth century that real worker wages appear to have begun rising (Piketty 2014, 7–8). The reason for their rise, as will be seen in Chapter 9, was the increasingly insurrectional behavior of workers that frightened elites and the state into pursuing reforms.

Economist John Hicks claimed that "the principal reason why free labour displaced slave labour was that in the conditions when the change occurred, free labour was cheaper" (1973, 131). This seems true insofar as, unlike slave-owners or landlords whose workers were held as assets or tied to the land, capitalists had little investment in their workers, who required little or no training. If a slave died, the owner suffered a capital investment loss. If a slave was too ill or stunted or weak to work productively, the owner lost income. Likewise, the landlord had an interest in the health and productivity of his serfs or indebted peasant workers, from whom surplus was extracted. But for the capitalist, if a worker should die or become too weak to be sufficiently pro-ductive, there was no loss beyond inconvenience, because there were always replacements to be drawn from what Marx termed the "reserve army of the unemployed."[20] And this army was continually being replenished, in early capitalism by population growth and the enclosures that pushed peasants off the land as well as by peasants who fled feudal conditions. In the maturing capitalism of the early nineteenth century, the reserve army of the unem-ployed was continually nourished by labor-displacing technological change.

Acemoglu and Robinson view the potential for economic development as consequent to the replacement of extractive economic and political institutions by inclusive ones. However, the evolution of more inclusive ec-onomic and political institutions accompanying capitalism, as they present them, did not put an end to extractive ones. What they did, as will be seen in the next chapter, was break the ability of aristocratic landlords to capture as great a share of society's economic surplus and to block dynamic change.

Revolt of the Downtrodden

The peasants of all lands recognize power and they salute it, whether it's good or evil.

—Andrei Codrescu, "The Posthuman
Dada Guide" (2019)

---

[20] Economic historians Robert Fogel and Stanley Engerman find that in terms of health and mate-rial well-being, southern slaves in the United States were on average better off than wage workers in the North (Fogel and Engerman 1995).

Chapter 4 examined the role of ideology in pacifying the exploited so that they would remain acquiescent no matter how miserable their condition might be. But at times the oppressed did revolt. This section examines how their own conservatism and the threat of harsh reprisals combined to discourage rebellion.

Historian Marc Bloch contended that "peasant revolts were as natural to traditional Europe as strikes are today" (1970, 170). However, few historians seem to agree. Jacques Le Goff, for instance, claimed that, rather than insurgency, "the habitual form of peasant struggle" was instead individual "passive resistance. . . . The silent guerrilla warfare of looting on the lord's lands, poaching in his forest, burning crops, refusing to pay dues . . . leading sometimes to flight and desertion" (1997, 373). Scott has also argued that "the emphasis on peasant rebellion is misplaced" (1987, 29).

The downtrodden tend to be conservative. Barely subsisting, they cannot afford the luxury of taking action or risking change that might push them over the edge into starvation. On this extreme precarity, Annales historian Fernand Braudel reported:

> France, by any standards a privileged country, is reckoned to have experienced 10 *general* famines during the tenth century; 26 in the eleventh; 2 in the twelfth; 4 in the fourteenth; 7 in the fifteenth; 13 in the sixteenth; 11 in the seventeenth and 16 in the eighteenth. . . . This could be said of any country in Europe. (1982, 1:74)

Historian Eric Jones reports that "in China there was a drought- or flood-induced famine in at least one province almost every year from 108 B.C. to A.D. 1911" (1987, 19). It is thus to be expected that the poor would be conservative and typically resigned to their fate.

Prevailing ideology legitimated hierarchy, existing social institutions, and extreme inequality to such an extent that even the poor could not readily imagine a possibly superior social world. Political scientists Raj Desai and Harry Eckstein note that, when conditions provoked them to revolt, they looked to recovering what they had lost, as opposed to achieving some visionary future: "Visions of radical change, of some sort of a new better world, played no part in historic peasant violence. Hierarchy and inequality, privilege and subordination, were regarded as in the unalterable nature of things" (1990, 446, 47). Further, they point out, immobility, subordination, lack of choice, and the very unfamiliarity with making choices (due to kinship, religiousness, client-patron relationships, and little or no experience with formal organization), all worked against peasant rebels regardless of the urgency of their demands. (1990, 454)

On the relative absence of slave and worker revolts in the United States, historian Eugene Genovese observes that "only those who romanticize ... the laboring classes would fail to understand their deep commitment to 'law and order.' Life is difficult enough without added uncertainty and 'confusion'" (quoted in Dubofsky 1986, 217).

Nevertheless, where workers were living near the extreme edge of material privation, failed harvests or tax increases could delegitimate the prevailing rulers and provoke revolt. For instance, the Great Rising of AD 1381 (Tyler's Rebellion) was triggered by the imposition of a poll tax upon peasants who were already living at bare subsistence. Although rising food prices have often sparked insurgency, historian and sociologist Pierre Rosanvallon notes that "in France, rage against the tax collector accounted for 40 percent of seventeenth- and eighteenth-century rebellions, a far higher proportion than bread riots" (2013, 166).

If revolts were relatively infrequent, it is in good part because reprisals were severe to the point of murderous savagery. Given the likelihood of ferocious retaliation, the classic free rider problem predisposes people to settle for the *status quo* rather than rising up to protest social conditions. A revolt or revolution is a public good. Participants face possible imprisonment, torture, and death, yet nonparticipants cannot be excluded from any potential benefits. Thus, from the individual's perspective, it is certainly safer to let others protest and face the possible consequences. If their collective action should succeed, then the risk-takers and the free riders will benefit alike.

All the same, individuals do take part in insurrections. They have been driven to revolt by the prospect of seeing their families starve. They have also been driven by a sense of fairness and the experience of solidarity in fighting injustice. Participants can be rewarded for their courage by the strong approval of their suffering community. Much like soldiers, they are heroes, even if they are often doomed. And, as may be recalled from Chapter 2, hidden deeply beneath the pursuit of approbation and high status is the ultimate drive for reproductive success.

Police states are not merely a modern phenomenon. Most of "civilized" history has witnessed people living under the arbitrary exercise of extra-judicial power. Anyone attempting to foment opposition was easily found out—often by compensated informers—and cruelly punished, including by torture before death. An agitator's entire family could be slaughtered, wiping out their genetic heritage and setting a terrifying example for other potential renegades. In some extreme instances, entire villages and their inhabitants were destroyed. Remnants of oubliettes or dungeons—generally deep holes, covered by hatches or grills, into which people were tossed to live in their own filth and survive on whatever food scraps were tossed down—have been found around the world. Historian Willie Thompson reports:

> Mutilation was commonly practiced; branding, eye gouging, amputation of various limbs and body parts, and, a favorite of medieval European rulers from Byzantine emperors to the princes of northern Europe, blinding accompanied by castration, for the purpose of degradation as well as in-tense pain and loss of function. (2015, 107)

In suppressing Spartacus's slave revolt, Rome killed about 100,000 participants (E. P. Thompson 1963, 81). When peasants revolted and were captured in Normandy in the mid-eleventh century, Count Raoul had their hands and feet cut off and then returned them to their families as a memo-rable reminder that acquiescence is best (Piketty 2020, 66). A major revolt in Flanders took place between 1323 and 1328 in the wake of expropriations of peasant lands, rising debt burdens, and mounting inequality. Princes and nobles from all over Western Europe joined to quash it with an army of 3,000–4,000 mounted noblemen and 12,000 soldiers and foreign merce-naries. Over 3,000 insurgents were executed, some of whom had their arms and legs broken and were burned with hot irons before being executed (Bavel 2016, 178).

Even seemingly mild offenses to the elite could provoke their murderous wrath. Historian R. C. Padden reports that among the Aztecs,

> Montezuma was a god, and no mortal might err in his presence or temple and live to tell of it. . . . If detected in treason against a lord or the state [an individual] was tortured to death, his family and descendants enslaved to the fourth generation, his fields sown with salt, his house pulled down. (1970, 82, 94)

Sinologist Jacques Gernet depicts imperial China as having "one of the cruelest systems of justice that has ever existed," helping to account for the fact that relative peace held in the Chinese countryside for 2,000 years. Rebellions were provoked by great famines, but "the repression was terrible" (1979, 61).

Moreover, there is no evidence that revolts ever improved the distribution of wealth or the general lot of peasants, although the peasants themselves were unlikely to know this. Examining modern times, Scheidel reports that greater inequality has tended to follow civil wars in developing countries (2017, 7).

In rural agricultural societies, the workers (slaves, serfs, indebted peons, and peasants) were scattered over the landscape, making communication and organization difficult for them. In addition, the authorities were alert to signs of discontent and acted effectively to avert seditious conduct. As will be seen in Chapter 9, nineteenth-century industrialization and urbanization changed all this. Workers were brought together in urban factories and slums where communication and organization became far easier. Escape in the maze of slum alleys was also easier. These conditions created the potential for democratic control of the state.

Political Power and Reproduction

Reproductive inequality was made possible by economic inequality; and economic inequality was made possible by political inequality.
　　　　—Laura Betzig, "Sex, Succession, and Stratification
　　　　　　in the First Six Civilizations" (1993, 72).

Civilization gave rise to extreme inequality not only in material goods and political power, but also in males' access to females. Between the rise of civilization and the modern era, economically and politically powerful men established harems, corroborating Darwin's thesis that the ultimate driver of competition aims at success in reproduction. A thesis of this book is that politics is the realm in which the most powerful vie for the greatest reproductive success. The most despotic rulers' harems gave them sexual access to many hundreds of women. Renowned examples include the biblical King Solomon, who "loved many foreign women, together with the daughter of Pharaoh, women of the Moabites, Ammonites, Edomites, Sidonians, and Hittites. . . . He had seven hundred wives of royal birth and three hundred concubines" (Kings 11:1, 3). Genghis Khan allegedly sired hundreds if not thousands of children. His paternity was reportedly due not just to his many wives, but also his penchant for rape. Historian Evan Andrews reports that

> according to a famous 2003 genetic study, around one in 200 living men carry a form of the Y chromosome that may have originated with the Great Khan himself. If true, that would mean that 0.5 percent of the world's male population are his direct descendants. (2014)

Morocco's seventeenth-century Emperor Moulay Ismail the Bloodthirsty is reported to have fathered 700 sons and, presumably, a comparable number of daughters (J. Diamond 1998, 37).

Within autocratic societies, kings or emperors had the largest harems. At lower levels of the political hierarchy, the size of harems varied according to the degree of power held. As states became larger and more complex due to conquests and rising population density, greater hierarchization evolved and top-level harems grew bigger. Anthropologist Laura Betzig provides the following sketch:

> The political hierarchy parallels the reproductive hierarchy in most human societies. Dominant men in groups with no formal hierarchies have as many as 3 women at a time in their harems, heads of societies with one-level hierarchies have as many as 10, heads of societies with two-level hierarchies have as many as 100, and heads of societies with three-or more-level hierarchies may have 1,000 or more women at a time in their harems. As each new harem is added at the top, women are taken from growing numbers of unmated men at the bottom. (1993, 53)

In China, princes possessed hundreds of women; generals, 30 or more; upper-class men 6 to 12; and middle-class men, 3 to 4. In the case of the Inca Empire, the legal code specified the permitted number of women in harems at each level of the power hierarchy. Betzig reports that

> by Inca law, "principal persons" were given 50 women; leaders of vassal nations, 30 women; heads of provinces of 1 hundred thousand, 20 women; governors of 100, 8 women; petty chiefs over 50 men, 7 women; chiefs over 10 men, 5 women; chiefs over 5 men, 3 women; and the "poor Indian" took whatever was left. (1993, 42)

Rulers chose young, pretty, and healthy virgins for their harems. These girls would be cared for in the harem's nursery until reaching puberty. Parents often freely gave their daughters to rulers, judging that in such extremely unequal societies they might fare better in the protected harems where they would be safe and well fed. The fact that any grandchildren would be of the rulers' blood line also increased the possibility that their genes would survive into the future.

Women in harems were virtual prisoners. They were typically guarded by eunuchs and "Amazon women" and were not permitted to leave or receive visits from even family (the word *harem* means "forbidden"). Any male guilty of adultery with a member of a harem was subject to the worst torture. Betzig writes that

> the single starkest deterrent against approaching noble women was the one Incans thought up. For "violation" of women of the Inca (women of the king's harem), or of the Sun (the king's cloistered kinswomen), the man and his wife, children, kin, and servants, along with all of the inhabitants of his village and all of their flocks, should be put to death.... The village was to be pulled down and the site strewn with stones. (1993, 51)

Some rulers had the menstrual cycles of their harem women monitored so as to better judge ovulation and optimize the chance of fertilization. Other mating strategies included

> monitoring the health and fertility status of harem women, carefully allocating their limited supplies of semen, using wet nurses and others to help raise their children, hiding the women in their harems inside concealing clothes and formidable fortifications, and at the same time having relatively unrestricted access to other men's women. (Betzig 1993, 37–38)

Rulers typically were formally monogamous in that they married only one "legitimate" wife who bore their rightful heirs to simplify succession. Because there was often insistence that the wife be of noble blood, inbreeding was common, and in some instances rulers married their sisters (Betzig 1993, 61–63). This appears to have been especially true in societies such as Egypt and the Inca where rulers were considered divine (K. Flannery and Marcus 2012, 333, 531).

Clear markers of nobility were desirable, and some measures to create them could be extreme. For instance, many cultures practiced cranial deformation of noble children, generally intended to suggest the look of the gods. This was a trait that ordinary people could not readily fake.

To ensure that the dowries of nobles' wives were passed down to a nobleman's children, widows were not permitted to remarry. (An exception might be marriage to one of his brothers.) Another solution in some empires was to kill wives upon their husbands' deaths (Betzig 1993, 64).

Among polygynous humans, high-status males parent far more offspring than high-status females. This accounts for the practice of leaving most assets and titles to sons, often in the form of primogeniture.[21] Thus, whereas high-status families in polygynous societies might have more descendants if they invest preferentially in sons, low-status families might do so by favoring daughters. Because of polygamy, demand for females will be high, and low-status sons may not be able to locate mates. Thus, as behavioral ecologist Bobbi Low points out, "the more polygynous the society, the more should boys be taught to strive. Variance in reproductive success increases for men as degree of polygyny increases, and very few men may be extremely successful while many men fail entirely just as in other polygynous species" (2001, 108).

A polygynous male must either inherit or acquire resources to provide for his wives and children. One who did not inherit but had only a few wives could conceivably support his family by working very hard. But if he had many wives and children, his only option would be to amass the political power or material resources to exploit the labor of others. Thus, the more polygynous a society, the greater the likelihood that it will be despotic to permit the degree of exploitation necessary for elites to support a great number of wives and offspring. The degree of inequality will parallel the degree of polygamy. Exploitation enabled polygyny, which in turn required exploitation.

Polygamy considerably devalued women's status. For instance, as noted earlier, in some kingdoms, wives could be expected to accompany the ruler into the afterlife. As polygamy and harems absorbed large numbers of women, fewer were available as mates for lower-class men, whose specific

---

[21] Muslim society presents an interesting exception to primogeniture. According to the Koran, when a Muslim merchant dies, at least two-thirds of his wealth must be split among surviving family members, who could be numerous due to polygamy. This helped impede the evolution of feudal relations in Islamic societies. Because it also worked against the long-run survival of large firms that capture economies of scale, it may also have served to brake economic dynamism (Kuran 2004).

genes would not survive into future generations. In terms of reproduction, non-elite males were the biggest losers. It is noteworthy that polygamy often generated political instability as the offspring of elites, claiming the same rank, competed for power.

The Debasement of Labor

Whenever the legislature attempts to regulate the differences between masters and their workmen, its counsellors are always the masters.
—Adam Smith, *The Wealth of Nations* (1776, 142)

As was seen in Chapter 3, among hunters and gatherers, work was not viewed negatively. In fact, they did not distinguish between work and leisure. The effort required to meet their needs was not considered unpleasant. Given the dynamics of evolution, this is entirely predictable. Activities that favored survival and reproduction would be selected to be pleasurable to direct energies toward these ends. Thus, just as evolution would select as tasty those foods that were nutritious, and the pursuit and act of sex would be highly pleasurable, so, too, the activities needed to procure nutrition and maintain general well-being could also be expected to be pleasurable.

It is noteworthy that the activities of foragers (their "work") was far more complex than that of later agriculturalists. Anthropologist James Suzman contends that the de-skilling or the step-down in complexity from foragers to agriculture was as big as the step-down from agriculture to industrial assembly-line work (2017). Nevertheless, work in early agricultural societies, where inequality remained low, continued to be viewed positively. Typically, work was seen not merely as a means of gaining subsistence, but also as a wellspring of sociality and a religious way of maintaining harmony with the natural world.

Attitudes toward work changed radically with the rise of civilization, the development of social hierarchies, and the subjugation of producers to those who owned or controlled the land. More and more work became socially coerced, and it was robbed of variety with greater division of labor.

As will be seen in Chapter 6, arguably the Christian view of work had an impact on the character of Western Europe's development. Work had been viewed positively in antique (pre-classical) Greek and Hebrew societies, the two main cultural sources of Christian thought. In both of these instances (as in other societies at similar levels of development) there was social stratifi-cation but little division of labor. The principal reasons were that population pressures had yet to lead to extensive privatization of the commons, substan-tial markets, the enserfment of poorer farmers, and substantial state power. The primary social unit was the kinship group and the primary production unit was the household.

In the world depicted by Homer, even the nobles worked. For instance, *The Odyssey* refers to King Odysseus's work skills, while his wife Penelope was a weaver (Homer 1944, 233). Even many of the deities worked. This is all the more surprising in that slavery existed in Homeric society. However, there does not appear to be any substantial difference in the work performed by slaves and free workers. Slaves are reported to have been part of households and generally well-treated (Finley 1980).

A similar attitude toward work prevailed in early Hebrew thought. Even the leaders and rabbis worked. Moreover, work is central to the creation story. According to *Genesis*, it was through God's work that creation was ac-complished, and God took the seventh day to rest—a detail which suggests that the work of creation was arduous. In a sense, then, work was another way in which humans were created in the image of God. As God's work was good, so too was that of his children. Through work, they would continue his project.

Yet *Genesis* is ultimately ambivalent about work. It depicts work as God's curse cast on humans for their insubordination—their daring to taste from the tree of knowledge:

> And unto Adam he said, Because thou hast hearkened unto the voice of thy wife, and hast eaten of the tree, of which I commanded thee, saying, Thou shalt not eat of it: cursed is the ground for thy sake; in sorrow shalt thou eat of it all the days of thy life.... In the sweat of thy face shalt thou eat bread, till thou return unto the ground. (*Genesis* 3:17, 19)

This textual passage lent support for negative views of work held at times by both Jews and Christians. The story of the fall might also be interpreted as the transition from the easy work-life of hunter-gathers to the heavier demands of agriculture.

In both late Greek and Hebraic cultures, as population pressures increased and metal weapons empowered rulers, the state evolved to replace the house-hold as the principal social institution of power and authority—society transitioned from rule by kinship to rule by the state. So long as power resided in households, work was viewed positively. These households were large kinship groups that were mostly self-sufficient. But as power shifted from households to states, the division of labor expanded, along with markets and increased social stratification.

With the rise of the state and civilization, it was freedom from work that conferred nobility. The appropriate domains for "noble" action were warfare and politics. The elites' concern was not with improving production so much as increasing the means of procuring tribute and booty. Even as late as the mid-nineteenth century, aristocratic De Tocqueville wrote: "I do not wish to speak ill of war; war almost always enlarges the mind of a people and elevates their character" (de Tocqueville 1840, 2:268).

Work became socially compelled and thus seen negatively as it was performed increasingly by subservient peoples and slaves. It came to be viewed as unfree and beneath the dignity of full humans (Geoghagen 1945, 15). Aristotle wrote:

> . . . a state with an ideal constitution—a state which has for its members men who are absolutely just and not men who are merely just in relation to some particular standard—cannot have its citizens living the life of mechanics or shopkeepers, which is ignoble and inimical to goodness. Nor can it have them engaged in farming: leisure is a necessity, both for growth in goodness and for the pursuit of political activities. (1962, 1328b–29)

Plutarch praised Archimedes for "regarding mechanical occupations and every art that ministers to needs as ignoble or vulgar, he directed his own ambition solely to those studies the beauty and subtlety of which are unadulterated by necessity" (quoted in Mokyr 1990, 196).

Even trade and commerce were predominantly performed by resident aliens. Many of those who worked and were not slaves were foreigners, peoples viewed as barbaric and inferior. Work carried out by subjugated people was inherently degrading.

The seeds for a renewed positive view of work were planted in early Christianity. This new religious doctrine was nourished by Rome's ethnically diverse lower classes, which it drew together by minimizing their differences and focusing on their common humanity. Christ's doctrine of brotherly love places emphasis on the inherent value and dignity of each individual, regardless of status, race, ethnicity, or origins. It established what would later become so important as the universal humanity postulate during the Enlightenment—all humans are equal. Indeed, the scriptures often appear to privilege the poor and, by extension, those who work; for example, "It is easier for a camel to enter through the eye of a needle, than for a rich man to enter the Kingdom of God" (Matthew 19:24). Jesus was the son of a carpenter and is himself referred to as one (Mark 6:3). Paul, a leather worker or saddler (Acts 18:3), praises work for making independence and self-respect possible. Work also enables charity: ". . . by so laboring ye ought to support the weak and to remember the works of the Lord Jesus, how he said, it is more blessed to give than to receive" (Acts 20:35). To work was to do God's will, or, as Saint Benedict put it, "*Laborare est orare*," to work is to pray.

However, work would not always be viewed positively within Christian societies. Although a favorable view was kept alive within monasteries, this was not the case within broader, hierarchically rigid Christendom. As will be seen in Chapter 7, Protestantism's later expression of Christianity will significantly renew a positive view of work that will legitimize the rising power and status of the bourgeoisie.

*****

In the next chapter—Chapter 6—the book's focus shifts to Europe, the first world area to experience sustainable capitalist development, which ultimately delivered the abundance and freedom of contemporary times.

6

The Critical Break

The Bourgeoisie Unchained

Conflict over income and power, and indirectly over institutions, is a constant in all societies.

—Daron Acemoglu and James Robinson,
Why Nations Fail (2012, 431)

The sustained economic development that transpired in Western Europe has been appropriately characterized by economic historian E. L. Jones as *The European Miracle* (1987). Although not literally a miracle, it required an extraordinary convergence of geographic and historical factors. Europe's geography provided a resource-rich environment and a high degree of access to water transportation. More importantly, its division by geographic barriers impeded any state from subjecting the others. Europe's historical legacy included a powerful Church that provided a degree of cultural unity and a lingua franca that facilitated commerce and the advancement of knowledge. Christianity was also pregnant with modern attitudes toward labor and equality. The remnants of a Roman legal system facilitated the creation of efficient property rights and contracts. A devastating demographic crisis helped break the landlord class's historical hold over economic and political power. And new military technology in the form of the cannon enabled rising states to centralize political power by blasting away feudal fortifications.

Central to the miracle was the rise in Western Europe of a commercial and manufacturing class, a bourgeoisie. Never before had a bourgeoisie forced a sustainable sharing of political power with the traditional landed aristocracy, then assumed practically the whole of that power without subsequently destroying its own achievement. This rising class would not only be a driving force for capitalist dynamism and sustainable economic development, but it would also eventually create the conditions in which the producers could bid successfully to share political power.

This chapter will demonstrate that understanding the struggle over inequality is essential for constructing a coherent account of the genesis of sustainable economic development—the "European miracle."

European Feudalism

[Rentiers] grow richer, as it were in their sleep, without working, risking, or economizing. What claim have they, on the general principle of social justice, to this accession of riches?
   —John Stuart Mill, *Principles of Political Economy* (1909, 818)

Disintegration of the Roman Empire swept away most of the fundamental institutional arrangements that had enabled extraordinary centralized political power and a relatively high standard of living for the elite. Rome's demise left in its wake the vast wilderness of a sparsely populated Europe with relatively primitive social relations.

Attempts to re-establish more centralized political authority, most notably by Clovis (466–511) and Charlemagne (742–814), were continually thwarted. Beginning in the eighth century, hordes of invaders assaulted Europe from three directions: Muslims from the east and south, Vikings from the north, and Magyars from the east. In 711, Muslims from North Africa invaded Spain, displacing the Visigoth Kingdom. By 732, they crossed the Pyrenees into France, but were repelled at Poitiers. Muslims conquered Sicily, Corsica, and Sardinia, taking effective control of the Mediterranean. Vikings invaded the British Isles, conquered Normandy, and raided settlements down the Atlantic coast and into the Mediterranean, ravaging Spain, Italy, and Byzantium. In the ninth century, Magyar nomads crossed the Carpathians, raiding Central Europe and extracting tribute. They continued into northern Italy, southern Germany, and France as far west as Orleans in 937.

Land was abundantly available, but it was valuable only when protected and worked. Much of Europe returned to isolated villages inhabited by semi-autonomous and thus relatively free farmers. Without centralized authority to safeguard elites' ability to appropriate their surplus, most producers' lives likely improved after the fall of Rome (Scott 2017; Scheidel 2017).

Farmers and villages within this wilderness could generally defend themselves against roving bandits and other potential enemies who were not significantly better trained or armed than the residents. But this changed with the introduction of military technology that gave the bandits a distinct advantage. Horses were expensive and generally beyond the means of peasant farmers. Historian Lynn White (1966) argued that when horses were paired with the stirrup—an innovation borrowed from the nomads of the Asian steppes—mounted bandits gained a decisive advantage for subjugating those without horses. Stirrups were critical because, without them, riders could be easily dislodged from their steeds. Thus, they could not be heavily armed. The stirrup better fixed the rider in the saddle, providing him with the stability to wield heavy armaments.[1] Well-armed and even armored horsemen could now easily pillage the countryside. Because horses and iron were scarce and expensive for rural dwellers, peasant communities could not equip themselves for adequate defense.

In the formation of feudalism, a warrior class survived by pillaging, raiding, and demanding tribute and ransom. Warfare was small in scale but ubiquitous. Military historian Jan Verbruggen estimates that "ten riders were mechanically equal to a hundred foot-soldiers" (1997, 188).[2] The new military technology of horses, stirrups, iron weapons, and armor within sparsely populated Europe created the conditions for subjugation. Roving bandits settled down, subjugated producers, expropriated their surplus, and blocked their escape options by means of feudalism or slavery.

Feudalism in Western Europe—the manorial system—began emerging in the ninth century, expanded from the tenth century on, and reached its zenith in the twelfth and thirteenth centuries. The earliest evidence is found between the Loire and Rhine rivers, the southern Low Countries, Western Germany, and the Po Valley of northern Italy. Manors were ruled by equestrian warrior aristocracies who dominated Europe throughout the Middle Ages. Politically, feudalism remained highly fragmented and unstable. The military power of most kings, the most prominent of the noblemen, was not adequate for dominating and controlling dispersed feudal lords. Jurisdictions were constantly contested and renegotiated, typically by war.

---

[1] It should be noted that Whyte's stirrup thesis is not without critics. See Farndon (2010).
[2] The importance of the horse in warfare is well captured by anthropologist Jared Diamond's assertion that "only with the introduction of trucks and tanks in World War I did horses finally become supplanted as the main assault vehicle and means of fast transport in war" (1999, 91).

Between manors, due to the danger of marauders, few or no social, political, or economic transactions occurred.

The Mafia parallel with feudalism's formation is striking. Facing the threat of heavily armed horsemen, formerly autonomous farmers and villages were now in need of more substantial protection. Some of these marauders, much like organized criminals in later times, engaged in a protection racket enforced by the threat of violence: they took it upon themselves to defend the hapless local people, and, in return, they demanded a portion of their output. The foundations of feudalism were thus established. A lord with his armed knights offered protection in exchange for a significant part of the serfs' labor. Feudal manors served as micro-states, providing defense, law and order, and basic services to its inhabitants. Only tenuous ties were maintained with any larger centralized political authority.

Mounted horsemen had their greatest advantage on open, flat terrain. Their superiority was far less decisive in dense forests, mountains, or marshlands. Consequently, the thick forests in Sweden and Norway precluded the development of feudalism, enabling a free peasantry to participate in their own governance (Boix 2015, 156). Nor did feudalism succeed in marshlands such as those of Friesland or parts of the Netherlands. Mountainous areas such as Switzerland or the highlands of Serbia, Bosnia, and Montenegro also lacked ruling aristocracies because their geography did not permit mounted raiders an adequate military edge to subjugate peasants.

The microstates that evolved by forcefully subjugating peasants generally ranged in size between 1,200 and 1,800 acres, with populations between 50 and 200 individuals. The feudal manors were highly autonomous as production units, meeting their food needs by growing their own crops, raising animals, milling their grain, baking their breads, and brewing their beer. They also wove cloth and forged plows and other metal instruments.

The lord's demesne generally constituted 25–30 percent of the arable manor's land. Lords might have multiple manors. Some manors were ecclesiastical and tended to be far larger. There, too, labor was enserfed and exploited.

Life, especially for serfs, was rude and often harsh. Their cottages were one to two rooms in size, windowless, often made of mud and wattle, with a thatched roof and a chimney hole. About one-third of infants died before age five. Harvests failed about one in six years, and epidemics often broke out, especially in times of malnutrition when the people's resistance to disease was weakened. Although serfs were the dominant exploited class, some slavery continued to exist.

Because all surrounding manors possessed similar resources and produced essentially the same products, there were limited gains to be had from trade. Further, trade would face the danger of bandits in no man's lands. Consequently, trade was dangerous, making transactions costs—the costs of exchanging goods (transferring property rights)—very high and thus precluding the formation of organized markets. With markets sparse, so too was money. Consequently, the landlords' interest was to have their serfs work their land several days each week, often as many as three, as opposed to taking a portion of their output or requiring money payments. These labor rents provided landlords with more control over what was produced than would have been the case if they expropriated a portion of their serfs' output, which might require negotiation with the serfs when landlords wished to consume a different mix of goods in the next season. Thus, neither land, labor, nor its products were commodities.

As a warrior class, lords and knights held a high degree of monopoly on violence in their immediate vicinity. There were few substitutes for their protection racket. Although serfs might run away to chance life in no man's lands, they would face considerable danger in lawless wildernesses. They would also run the risk of recapture by the Lord's goons, euphemistically called knights, and face severe punishment or execution that was intended to dissuade others from attempting to escape. Serfs were virtually caged.

Low population density, the state of weapons technology, and geography meant that the viable size of political units was very small. Castles became practically impregnable. Nevertheless, lords and their knights lived in an environment of great insecurity.[3] Neighboring lords and knights could fear their aggression or covet their powers. Adam Smith characterized the violence of the late Middle Ages as follows:

> After the institution of feudal subordination, the king was as incapable of restraining the violence of the great lords as before. They still continued to make war according to their own discretion, almost continually upon one

---

[3] The conditions that led to feudalism in Europe occurred elsewhere. For instance, at the time of Confucius (551–479 BC), comparable widespread insecurity reigned in China. Sinologist H. G. Creel reports that "aristocrats had little enough security. The people had none. They were chiefly farmers, commonly virtual serfs. They had few if any rights as against the nobility; in practice they were taxed, worked, expropriated, scourged, and killed by the aristocrats, with almost no check save the fact that if goaded too far they might rebel" (1951, 24).

another, and very frequently upon the king; and the open country still continued to be a scene of violence, rapine, and disorder. (1776, 388)

Historian Barbara Tuchman similarly emphasized the violence of the feudal environment:

> These private wars were fought by the knights with furious gusto and a single strategy, which consisted in trying to ruin the enemy by killing and maiming as many of his peasants and destroying as many crops, vineyards, tools, barns, and other possessions as possible, thereby reducing his sources of revenue. As a result, the chief victim of the belligerents was their respective peasantry. (1987, 8)

The ideological sheen overlaying the knights' behavior was the concept of chivalry. Cognitive scientist Steven Pinker notes that

> . . . to maintain the credibility of their deterrent threat, knights engaged in bloody tournaments and other demonstrations of macho prowess, gussied up with words like *honor, valor, chivalry, glory*, and *gallantry*, which made later generations forget they were bloodthirsty marauders. (2011, 67)

Beginning in the eleventh century, a form of chivalric literature evolved, depicting knights as driven by paternalistic concern for the weak and by romantic love of women (Priestland 2012, 27)—yet another example of ideology's unfailing presence and characteristic resourcefulness in legitimizing the power, privileges, and behavior of elites. The warrior attitudes of the aristocracy endured long after the end of feudalism, serving to justify large landowners' claims of high status, privilege, and superior qualifications by birth. As economist Albert Hirschman notes, ". . . anyone who did not belong to the nobility could not, *by definition*, share in heroic virtues or violent passions" (1997, 63).

Increasing population density, evolving modes of organization, and advancing military technology gradually made larger political entities both possible and necessary. A fuller hierarchy of feudal political powers evolved, providing layers of authority such as castellanies, baronies, counties, or principalities standing between the manors' lords and the distant monarchy. At each level, attention was focused on maintaining peace among those political entities below. However, these hierarchical structures were unstable. Growth in population density and concentrated military power enabled states to emerge. The first states in Western Europe formed around AD 900. There were about 5,000 states in the fourteenth century, 500 in 1600, and only 30 by 1950.

It is useful to contrast the social and geographical conditions that enabled the subjugation and caging of European peasants with the conditions that left producers relatively free in colonial North America. In the early seventeenth-century Jamestown settlement, for instance, the Virginia Company owned all the colony's land but did not succeed in coercing the peasant settlers to work diligently for mere subsistence rations. The reason is that the surrounding territory was sparsely populated with land available to colonists who dared chance it. Unlike the well-armed mounted horsemen in Europe, the indigenous population had neither horses nor as sophisticated weaponry as the settlers brought with them. Consequently, the Virginia Company had no choice but to allow the producers a high degree of freedom and provide them with adequate incentives to work hard and invest. They could not be easily caged and forced to give up their entire surplus so long as there was land to which they could flee and where they would not be at too great a military disadvantage vis-à-vis potential Indian enemies. The evolution of colonial political institutions reflected this situation: they distributed power more equally. Abundant land would undergird the evolution of America's relatively high degree of producer freedom until the end of the nineteenth century and the closing of the American frontier, bringing the availability of abundant cheap land to an end.

Population Growth and the Expansion of Trade

After declining in the wake of Rome's collapse, Europe's population began expanding, increasing from about 20 million in 950 to 54 million in 1348 (Anderson 2013, 190). Vast empty spaces became more densely populated, bringing potential trading partners closer together and making it easier to protect roads and trade. Transactions costs—the cost of forming markets—were lowered, stimulating trade and the growth of urban centers.

With property rights better defined and enforced, lower transactions costs meant that gains from manufacturing and commerce became more attractive, and far less dangerous, than gains from plunder. And, whereas plunder had been a negative-sum game (one in which the amount gained by winners was less than the combined losses of winners and losers), commercial activity became a positive-sum game in which everyone's position could be improved.

However, should their numbers and wealth increase too much, merchants who traded in these growing markets could pose a threat to the aristocracy's power and privilege. Consequently, predominantly aristocrat-controlled agrarian societies attempted to curb the rising power of a commercial class. The dominant ideology depicted commercial activity and markets as corrupting, realms of sinfulness, and thus inappropriate for the participation of full members of society. Markets were claimed to cultivate self-interest and greed, and, in today's language, to produce zero-sum outcomes where someone's gain was offset by someone else's loss. Because the output of society tended to be seen as rather fixed in quantity, a newly made rich man was a *mangeur d'hommes*—a devourer of others (Landes 1969, 129).[4] Due to aristocratic hostility and ideology, history records few premodern societies where markets steadfastly served dominant roles in the exchange and allocation of output. Rarer still were those within which substantial markets existed for land, labor, and capital, the factors of production.

Because participation in trade and finance was disdained, these commercially vital functions were substantially restricted to resident aliens who could not share in the privileges of full citizenship and, thus, could not challenge the privileged status of the aristocracy. Resident aliens were typically prohibited from owning land, the most important form of wealth, ownership of which was necessary for political power and high status in predominantly agricultural societies. No matter how wealthy resident aliens might become, because their market behavior was considered sinful and their social standing was marginal, their wealth could be confiscated, and they could be exiled or killed.

Metics (resident aliens) had predominantly provided trade and financial services in classical Greece. Jews would do so in medieval Europe. Because Jews were generally not permitted to own land or take part in most professions, they were denied practically any means of survival other than

---

[4] This view persisted until early modern times. For instance, as late as 1697, mercantilist economist Charles D'Avenant had not yet grasped that domestic exchange offers more than zero-sum outcomes. He claimed that domestic trade within the nation did not augment a nation's wealth, but instead merely changed the relative wealth of its inhabitants. Foreign trade, by contrast, could add to a country's wealth, but again, only in a zero-sum game among nations (Roll 1974, 66). This view of markets as static zero-sum institutions played a role in blocking the evolution of the idea of economic progress.

trading and lending at interest. Characterized as usury, lending especially ensured that they would be villainized and hated. They were frequently scapegoated for systemic social dysfunctions, exiled, sometimes murdered, and their wealth was subject to confiscation.

So long as the landed aristocracy could limit the power of a commercial class, markets posed little threat to systems for tying labor to the land and thereby maintaining aristocratic control of wealth and political power. However, as markets expanded, more Christians began participating in commercial activity, stimulating the rise of trading centers and towns. Between the tenth and fifteenth centuries, the number of towns in Europe increased from approximately 100 to 5,000, with the greatest growth occurring during the second half of the twelfth and the thirteenth centuries (Pounds 1974, 101). Market expansion was greatest in areas where landlords had less authority, such as borderlands between feudal units (Jones 1987, 91).

Insofar as towns might provide serfs with an alternative to life on the manors, they curbed the lords' ability to exploit them, to expropriate their full surplus. To run away to a town was to become in a certain sense "free," no longer bound to the land and the tyrannical control of the lord. Town labor markets were "thicker," making it easier for employers to find workers and enforce labor contracts. If workers were to strike, replacements could be more readily found in towns than in the countryside, making it possible to discipline workers with the threat of dismissal.

Many towns in feudal Europe were largely self-governing. They had considerable autonomy from both the nobility and the Church, making them somewhat unique for an agrarian economy (North 2010, 138). They were typically dominated by merchant families who used their political power to grant themselves special trading rights and monopolies (Rosenberg and Birdsell 1987, 60). This contrasted with town governance in most societies in which landed elites predominantly held political power. In China, for instance, towns were ruled by landowners or mandarin bureaucrats who resided in the towns.

Although the relative autonomy of towns in Western Europe served to erode the landlords' power, landlords were not consistently opposed to them. After all, towns provided not only new consumer and producer goods, but also sometimes new sources of revenues in the form of taxes where towns fell within their jurisdictions (North and Thomas 1971, 792).

Economists generally view free labor (wage labor) as more productive than unfree labor insofar as it is easier to provide incentives for wage workers to encourage them to work diligently. Why, then, did landlords not use free workers as opposed to unfree slaves and serfs? The geographical dispersion of land meant that labor markets in rural areas remained thin. If landlords were to use free labor (wage contracts), they could suffer a severe loss if workers were to strike at critical time-sensitive junctures of the agricultural cycle such as planting and harvesting. They would not be likely to find replacements. Thus, landlords continued to prefer binding workers to the land (vertical integration in the economists' lexicon). However, the continual expansion of markets and towns created options for runaway serfs. Eventually, the thicker labor markets of towns also increased the potential for landlords to find replacement wage workers should a labor strike occur.

As will be seen in the following, the inability of the aristocracy to restrain the expansion of markets and the rise of an ever more powerful bourgeoisie entailed that, uniquely in Western Europe, with its particular geography, capitalism would emerge in a sustainable manner to deliver economic dynamism and to set the pre-conditions for the eventual evolution of democratic freedom and lessened inequality. If state power had continued to be adequately controlled by the landed aristocracy, as was the case in most feudal and slave societies, then the evolution of a sizable and powerful bourgeoisie could have been thwarted.

As towns expanded, households began meeting a few of their needs through purchases in markets. Although families continued to produce most of what they consumed, the spread of markets made households more market-oriented, affecting practically all aspects of social life. Prior to this market expansion, behavior and attitudes were guided by traditional religious, communal, and political institutions that limited the occasions when people were called upon to exercise the sort of free choice or free decision-making necessary in markets. The spread of markets increased their participation in buying and selling, and therefore the need to make rationally self-interested choices and decisions. This does not mean that they had no prior experience with self-interested calculations, but instead that in markets they had to make decisions in a more conscious and deliberate manner. They had to be conscious of their own self-interest and accept a greater degree of responsibility for their decisions, lest shrewder market participants take advantage of them.

Nevertheless, traditional morality continued to denigrate the pursuit of self-interest, and especially calculating self-interest, as cultivating sinful behavior. Chapter 7 will describe how views of commercial institutions and behavior would change with the transformation of ideology brought forth by the Protestant Reformation.

The Decisive Demographic Crisis

The population collapse that began in the fourteenth century has widely been identified as the triggering event creating the conditions for the rise of capitalism in Western Europe (e.g., Dobb 1947; Duby 1974; DuPlessis 1997; Moore 1966; North 1982). It did so by raising the bargaining power and wages of labor, decreasing rents to the detriment of the landlords' economic and political power, while simultaneously empowering a rising bourgeoisie.

This demographic catastrophe was preceded by population growth in Western Europe from about 20 million in AD 950 to about 54 million in 1358. Land became more scarce, and average peasant household holdings fell from around 100 acres in the ninth century to 20–30 acres in the thirteenth (Anderson 2013, 190, 186). Diminishing returns in agriculture began appearing in the twelfth century (North 1982, 133). Diets became less balanced and more carbohydrate-dense and protein-poor as the commons were overexploited, leading to restrictions on the number of animals a family could pasture as grazing lands were turned to cereal production. Fewer animals also meant less manure and thus decreased soil fertility. Heavy carbohydrate diets increased fertility, thereby further fueling the population expansion.

Population growth raised the labor-land ratio, decreasing the relative price of labor and raising that of land. This increased landlords' power and decreased that of cultivators. Consequently, lords intensified their exploitation of their serfs and peasants by imposing additional fees, threatening violence to increase rents, and seizing communal lands, thereby pushing medieval society perilously close to its "inequality possibility frontier" (Milanovic 2016). Serfs and peasants often collectively resisted these measures, sometimes with proto-strikes. They appealed to higher political authority, where available, to curb the lords' abuses and demands for more surplus (Anderson 2013, 187). The state, in its struggle with the landed aristocracy for shares of the surplus, often sided with the peasants. Its interest was in maximizing revenues, more of which would, of necessity, come predominantly from the landlords' rents because the producers were already living at bare subsistence. Offering some degree of assistance to the producers could also help limit the potential for peasant revolts by presenting the state as just and caring for the least privileged—"long live the king!"

The demographic crisis of the fourteenth century was due to many convergent forces: less balanced diets made the population less resistant to disease and thus more vulnerable to the ravages of the Black Death; climatic deterioration brought colder and wetter winters that reduced agricultural output; and general scarcity provoked war that lasted for more than a century—the Hundred Years War—further disrupting agricultural output.

The democratic collapse reduced Europe's population by 25 to 40 percent, perhaps 50 percent in England and Wales (Scheidel 2017, 296–97). Consequently, the labor-land ratio significantly declined, raising the relative price of labor and decreasing that of land. Worker welfare was also increased by falling food prices. For instance, real wages doubled between 1349 and 1390 in Flanders and rose by 50 percent in England and Italy (van Bavel 2016, 12). Workers' diets became better balanced with more protein as land was shifted from growing crops to raising livestock. With better diets, people became healthier and grew taller (Scheidel 2017, 91).

Workers' power was further augmented by the expansion of town-based commerce, which increased the demand for labor and thus put upward pressure on wages and working-class living standards. The landlords' power was compromised by the fall in food and land prices and the fact that they had to compete with urban employers for scarce labor.

Whereas the fourteenth century, especially its second half, was a demographic catastrophe due to famine, plague, and war, the fifteenth century witnessed a recovery that featured considerably altered institutions. Western Europe began to take on the economic and political characteristics of the nascent modern world.

The rise of markets, commerce, and manufacturing motivated landlords to evict cultivators and enclose the land. The incentive worked as follows. An expanding textile industry raised the demand for and price of wool, making sheep husbandry increasingly remunerative. Landlords could let sheep graze if they forced most peasants off the land, retaining only the workforce necessary for pasturage, shearing, and raising the crops needed for the lord's household and livestock. Economic historian-anthropologist Karl Polanyi reports that enclosed land was worth two to three times unenclosed as "sheep turned sand into gold." The enclosures, he claimed, had "appropriately been called a revolution of the rich against the poor. . . . The fabric of society was being disrupted; desolate villages and the ruins of human dwellings testified to the fierceness with which the revolution raged" (1944, 34, 35).

The enclosures that took place in early capitalism carried forward the private appropriation of common or social wealth that had been proceeding since the rise of the state and its protection of the elite's ownership and control of productive wealth. By way of maintaining perspective, this privatization of social wealth continues to today, where it principally occurs with government-assigned intellectual property rights—private ownership of knowledge.

Although the landlords' enclosures were continually resisted, often by the Crown, they came to be legitimated on the twin grounds of morality and economic efficiency. The dominant ideology claimed that "common rights encourage idleness by offering a precarious and demoralizing livelihood to men who ought to be at work for a master" (Tawney 1926, 215). Thus, the enclosures were clothed in the ideology that they were "designed to eliminate idleness, intemperance and riotous behaviour, and to render the poor sober and respectable" (McNally 1993, 20).

Continuing for centuries, enclosures played an important role in generating a proletarian urban workforce. In England they reached their peak in the late fifteenth and sixteenth centuries, although as late as 1700, about one-fourth of arable land was still held as commons, precluding it being sold or mortgaged (Bogart and Richardson 2011, 247). It has been estimated that in the early sixteenth century in Holland and eastern England, about 50 percent of the labor force worked for wages (Tylecote 2016, 732). About half of all small farmers in seventeenth-century England had too little land to get by on without supplementing their incomes with wage labor in industrial employments (McNally 1993, 17), becoming thereby semi-proletarianized.

In England, between 1086 and 1640, the percent of peasants not tied to a manor increased from 6 percent to 40 percent, and the number of landless peasants increased from 66,000 to 2,200,000 in an end-of-period population of 5.6 million (Lachmann 1987, 129). At the end of the seventeenth century, statistician Gregory King found that over half of the English population depended upon some form of charity to get through the year (Appleby 2011, 82).[5]

---

[5] Polanyi writes: "It was in the first half of the sixteenth century that the poor first appeared in England; they became conspicuous as individuals unattached to the manor, or to any 'feudal superior' and their gradual transformation into a class of free laborers was the combined result of the fierce persecution of vagrancy and the fostering of domestic industry which was powerfully helped by a continuous expansion of foreign trade" (1944, 104).

Brutal methods were often involved in this conversion of common into private property. In the early nineteenth century, when the transformation was nearing its completion in England, entire villages were razed to the ground, forcing peasants into the proletarian workforce. The entire process continued to be propelled by the rapidly expanding textile industry (Losurdo 2014, 121).

Despite their relative loss of power to the growing merchant class, landlords remained the dominant political force, and laws and practices that served their interest continued to be enforced. This power manifested itself in virtually all domains of social life. Political economist Michael Perelman offers an especially striking example in the enforcement of game laws in England:

> A commoner's punishment for killing animals was harsh, to say the least, even when the purpose was to prevent the creatures from destroying a farmer's crop. Infractions of the law met with penalties that ranged from execution to incarceration, which was more common, or transportation to Australia, which was even more common. . . . The Game Laws were an important tool of primitive accumulation, preventing self-provisioning, thereby forcing people to enter the labor market in order to subsist. This pressure increased the supply of labor and lowered wages. (2012, 55–56)

The privatization of resources, of which the enclosures of the commons stand out in history, is ongoing, albeit with ever less to privatize, excepting knowledge, as noted earlier. Anthropologist Heather Remoff reflects that

> although some degree of privatization of land has occurred in all civilizations around the world, there were generally loopholes that allowed the poor to glean grain left in fields after the harvest, to catch fish in rivers, or to collect firewood for cooking and heating. But in recent centuries those exceptions have been closed off, leaving the poor with less access to nature than was previously the case. . . . By the time the process was complete, exclusive rights to the private ownership of land were formalized in law. Today, most people accept the unrestricted private ownership of natural resources as an inevitable part of living in society, but, in fact, it is a violation of our deepest biological needs and rights. (2016, 896)

An extreme example is where impoverished people blackened their faces to remain undetected while collecting wood, mushrooms, and hunting game on landed estates. The Black Act of 1723 in England made this a capital offense. The tall dense hedges still found in the English countryside originated as fences to keep gleaners out. The privatization of all commons caged producers such that they had no alternative to wage labor, no matter how low the wage or degrading the working conditions.

The Growth and Role of Semi-Autonomous Towns

Stadtluft macht frei (town air makes you free).
— Late medieval German dictum

Although landlords continually posed a threat, the towns of northern Italy gained considerable freedom as early as the eleventh century. Thanks to its formidable military, Milan, for instance, did so by 1035. To protect themselves from feudal suppression, and especially from the Hohenstaufen Holy Roman emperors, in 1167 northern Italian cities formed a mutual defense pact—the Lombard League—whose most prominent members were Venice, Florence, Genoa, and Milan. These allied independent city-states had their own court systems and legal structures to enforce property rights and contracts. Commerce and capitalist institutions flourished.

However, as economic and social historian Bas van Bavel demonstrates (2016), these early capitalist institutions in northern Italy faced destruction as the capitalist class that had shepherded them into existence became ever wealthier and politically powerful. In order to claim larger portions of society's surplus, they used their political power to transform social institutions to provide them with greater potential for rent-seeking, at the cost of stifling growth. (The goal of rent-seeking is to gain income by manipulating the political setting, rather than by creating new productive wealth.) They used their rents increasingly to compete among themselves for high status through conspicuous consumption, rather than channeling them into productive investment. Although their spending stimulated the flowering of Renaissance art, it diverted funds from other, potentially more economically beneficial uses. The decay of Italy's early capitalist institutions was also fueled by a decline of trade following the fall of Constantinople to the Turks in 1453 and the closing of the eastern Mediterranean trade routes.

Towns north of Italy also joined together for self-protection. For instance, in 1354 an alliance called the *Zehnstädtebund* (*Décapole* in French) was formed by ten Imperial cities of the Holy Roman Empire in the Alsace region[6] to protect their autonomy and maintain their rights in a political environment controlled by the landed aristocracy and the Church. The *Zehnstädtebund* provided for mutual defense and proto-democratic constitutions. It endured until 1679 when Alsace was annexed to France. Its formation and longevity were evidence of the rising power of a commercial bourgeoisie.

A yet more formidable example of strategic cooperation was the Hanseatic League of towns and cities along the northern coast of Europe. Beginning in the thirteenth century, towns controlled by merchants developed naval fleets and sought alliances with other towns to defend themselves against landlords' attempts to curb or eliminate their autonomy. Their first general Diet, or deliberative assembly, met in 1356 in Lübeck to formulate official accords. Although they were largely free politically and had their own legal systems and their own armies, the towns in the Hanseatic League maintained allegiance to the Holy Roman emperor, albeit without recognizing obligations to the local nobles. The League waged war, signed treaties, regulated economic activity, and raised revenues. At its height, it united almost 100 cities. It lasted about three centuries. Its decline paralleled the rise of Dutch and English trading power, the rising power of the Swedish Empire, and the closing of certain trade routes by the Ottomans.

Cheap water transportation linking large geographic areas was critical to the success of cities that belonged to the Lombard League in the Mediterranean basin or the Hansa on the North Sea and the Baltic. The conditions that favored these cities were generally absent elsewhere; comparable examples of relatively independent city-states are not found in the Asian or Muslim worlds (Rosenberg and Birdsell 1987, 59). The extent of their relative autonomy, or their degree of self-governance, has its closest parallel in the Greek city-states that had much earlier flourished in the Mediterranean between the sixth and fourth centuries BC. After the Lombard League and the Hanseatic League faded, relatively inexpensive water transportation privileged towns on the European Atlantic seaboard, providing them with

---

[6] Haguenau, Colmar, Wissembourg, Turckheim, Obernai, Kaysersberg, Rosheim, Munster, Sélestat, and Mulhouse.

resources to resist the military pressures of absolutism, the Church, and aristocratic landlords.

Military organization and technology, even if primitive, were important to towns' autonomy from aristocratic and ecclesiastical attack. Urban militia could successfully hold back the landlords' heavy cavalry charges by forming tightly closed columns and deploying long pikes against mounted horsemen. The prosperity of a town could enable it to maintain food stocks and equip a few thousand soldiers with the latest military equipment, however unsophisticated it might have been. The landlords, by contrast, were constrained by their limited ability to furnish their cavalry with food and supplies at a distance from their manors.

However, the development and spread of firearms offered a limited reversal of this ability of townspeople to defend themselves against aristocratic forces. Where such arms could be afforded, they permitted knights an advantage over the town's pikemen (Boix 2015, 165).

Over the long term, especially as their costs declined, firearms revolutionized warfare. They also posed a considerable threat from below, and concerted efforts were undertaken to keep firearms out of the hands of the working class. For instance, in England in 1515, possession of firearms was not permitted to those with revenues below £200 a year. The Teutonic Order and Sweden outlawed possession of guns by peasants in the sixteenth century. These prohibitions, as well as the costs of firearms, increased the exploitative potential of the landlords over their peasants and that of the bourgeoisie over their wage workers (Boix 2015, 165).

An appreciation of the uniqueness of bourgeois towns' independence in Western Europe and the condition of producers can be gained by noting the fate of their counterparts in Eastern Europe. Economic historian David Landes writes that ". . . the further east one goes in Europe, the more the bourgeoisie takes on the appearance of a foreign excrescence on manorial society, a group apart scorned by nobility and feared or hated by (or unknown to) a peasantry still personally bound to the local *seigneur*" (1969, 129). Whereas serfdom was coming to an end during the fourteenth century in Western Europe, it intensified in the following century in the East, where towns were fewer and weaker. Consequently, the demographic collapse had the opposite outcome. Landlords were incited to "cage" peasants who lacked alternatives. Peasant rights were crushed, and they were reduced to serf status. Landes describes the landlords' power as follows:

Anywhere east of the Elbe, for example—in Prussia, Poland, Russia—the local lord enjoyed so much authority over the population that abusive treatment even of those residents who were nominally free, let alone the unfree serfs, was widespread and unrestrainable. In these areas of seigneurial autonomy, moreover, conditions actually grew worse from the sixteenth to the eighteenth centuries, as the spread of commercial agriculture enhanced the incentive to exploit the weak. (Landes 1969, 17–18)

The enhanced power of the aristocracy in the east, aided by firearms, led to the crushing of commercial towns. In areas such as Poland and Russia, merchants were deported as towns became military and administrative centers under the control of princes. Historical sociologist Perry Anderson notes that "in the German-colonized lands of Brandenburg, Pomerania and the Baltic . . . deurbanization was so complete that as late as 1564, the largest single town in Brandenburg, Berlin, numbered a pitiful 1,300 houses" (2013, 254). The defeat of towns enabled the imposition of an extreme form of serfdom. For instance, in Brandenburg and Poland, serfs' obligatory labor services on the lords' lands could run as high as five or six days a week (Anderson 2013, 262). By 1494 landlords had the right to hang runaway serfs without a trial (2013, 252, 255). The suppression of the towns and their bourgeoisie foretold backwardness and ensured that a commercial class, and eventually capitalism, could not evolve as it had in the West.

Two further aspects of the destruction of the bourgeoisie in Eastern Europe merit note. One is that increased trade with the West enabled the importation of many desired manufactured goods, precluding the need for their local production and, therefore, forestalling the formation of an indigenous bourgeoisie. Second, the migration of Jews into the East ensured the performance of many commercial and financial functions without the threat posed by having these tasks provided by a native bourgeois class. Those who partook in commerce were vilified. But because Eastern European societies feared that without economic development they would be at the mercy of the West, they admitted Jews who could provide these economic functions. The result was that Eastern European towns had large Jewish populations. For instance, in 1900, there were over 200,000 Jewish residents in Budapest, where they represented more than a quarter of the city's inhabitants. Budapest was second only to Warsaw, which had Europe's largest Jewish community (Muller 2003, 259, 260). Should Jews become too powerful, or threatening in any other manner, they could be checked by expropriation or pogroms.

In Western Europe, workers were at times able to retain a portion of their surplus. This could result from a labor shortage such as that following the demographic shock of the fourteenth century, or from increased demand for their services due to competition between the rising bourgeoisie and the landed aristocracy. However, because of the political power of elites, the long-run tendency was for surplus extraction to push workers' livelihoods back toward bare subsistence, just as had been the prevalent case from the rise of the state and civilization 5,500 years ago. For instance, in the wake of the demographic collapse of the fourteenth century, the aristocracy and the nascent bourgeoisie used the evolving nation-states to set what were effectively wage ceilings. The Ordinance of Labourers of 1349 and the Statute of Labourers of 1351 in England outlawed collective bargaining and required workers to accept what they were paid in 1346. Artisan prices were also fixed at pre-crisis levels. Similar laws were promulgated on the Continent.[7] These measures were essentially wage freezes that prevented the landlords' and employers' competition for workers from driving up wages that would reduce the surpluses available for appropriation. Although these laws were not highly effective, they stand as another example of elites using their blatant command over political power to maximize their exploitation of producers.

These wage controls also demonstrate that, in spite of their many conflicts of interest, the aristocracy and emerging bourgeoisie could coordinate in using the rising nation-state to enact legislation to their mutual benefit.[8] Nevertheless, more often their divergent interests led them to struggle to limit each other's power and privileges. Landlords appealed to the state to suppress peasant revolts, which usually occurred near powerful urban centers. Bourgeois-dominated towns, by contrast, often supported and assisted the rural rebellions (Anderson 2013, 205).

Attempts to return producers to conditions prevailing prior to the demographic crisis brought forth notable peasant revolts. In 1358, a peasant revolt called the *Grande Jacquerie* was set off in northern France by military requisitioning and pillage during the early phase of the Hundred Years' War.

---

[7] In later centuries, wages were often controlled by statutes empowering local jurisdictions to establish boards or agencies, composed mainly of landlords, to fix wages annually for agricultural and artisan work. It was not until 1813 that maximum wage legislation was repealed in England.

[8] Van Bavel writes that after the Black Death, "the Florentine city council passed what probably were the most oppressive labour laws in Europe. These laws—directed against rural labourers—froze wages, forced labourers to buy their food at high prices from urban vendors, and restricted their mobility, forcing them to stay on the burgher-owned farms. Those labourers and sharecroppers who did leave and violated these laws were designated as rebels, to be buried alive" (2016, 119). In this manner, producers faced the choice of virtual slavery or horrible deaths.

A massive peasant revolt took place in England in 1381 in response to the authorities' enforcement of a poll tax to support England's military needs. Before their defeat, rebels briefly captured most of London.

Later peasant revolts followed landlords' appropriation of the commons. Notable among them was the German Peasant War of 1524–1525, the greatest insurrection in continental Europe prior to the French Revolution. Market relations also disturbed customary relationships and unsettled the overarching meaning system. Development economists Raj Desai and Harry Eckstein point out that "markets disrupt the safety of traditional mutual rights and obligations and plunge peasants into what is, for them, an unfamiliar world . . . leaving [them] unshielded against the vicissitudes of vast, impersonal markets." In addition, as Desai and Eckstein write, "the breakdown of church authority during the Reformation provided peasants with the occasion to attempt, by violent means, to redress long-standing grievances" (1990, 443–44, 447).

There were also two notable revolts by craft masters and workers. In 1309, the masters and weavers of Ghent seized and held power for a short period. In Florence in 1378, under the pressure of heavy taxation, famished wage workers revolted and briefly seized power. These and other revolts were suppressed with extreme brutality (Anderson 2013, 203).

The rise of the bourgeoisie alongside the state and the aristocracy meant that three interests now fought over shares of the producers' surpluses. Although the state held a monopoly on violence, it needed to use it with caution. If it did not sufficiently satisfy the most powerful interest groups in its realm, it could sow the seeds of their revolt. The bourgeoisie's ability to wrest economic and political power from the aristocracy in Western Europe generally unfolded through largely peaceful dynamics. Both classes continually attempted to ally the broader body of people behind their cause. In Catholic countries, the aristocracy drew support from the Church.

The bourgeoisie's growing success in this class struggle created the conditions for capitalist economic development with dynamics that would eventually lead to democracy by requiring the extension of political rights to workers. But enabling this sustained success of Europe's bourgeoisie was its unique geography.

Europe's Felicitous Geography and the Nation-State

In Asia they have always had great empires; in Europe these could never subsist. Asia has larger plains; it is cut into much more extensive divisions by mountains and seas . . . in Europe, the natural division forms many nations of a moderate extent. . . . It is this which has formed a genius for liberty; that renders every part extremely difficult to be subdued and subjected by a foreign power . . . [in contrast] there reigns in Asia a servile spirit.

—Charles Montesquieu, *The Spirit of Laws* (1748, 269)

Europe's unique geography played a critical role in setting the stage for the evolution of capitalism. A large number of geographical barriers separated the peoples who would populate evolving nation-states, making conquest of one by another difficult. Two large islands, England and Ireland, are blessed with the equivalent of enormous moats that made invasion nearly impossible. Indeed, the British Isles have not been successfully invaded since the Norman conquest of 1066 and the Dutch invasion of 1688.[9] Peninsulas also provide a measure of protection, and Europe possesses five large ones: Greece, Denmark, Norway/Sweden, Italy, and Iberia. The last two also benefit from the difficulty of traversing the Alps and Pyrenees mountains. Parts of the Netherlands is made up of marshland. These natural barriers made invasion exceedingly costly. Only to the east did lesser barriers such as the Vosges Mountains and the Rhine River invite less costly invasion. These same geographic barriers to invasion also generated distinct ethnic and linguistic zones that enabled each nation's leaders to appeal to a sense of shared identity.

Because of this geography, after the fall of Rome, no political power succeeded in gaining sustained political hegemony over Europe. It was not for lack of trying. Clovis, Charlemagne, Napoleon, and Hitler all attempted, in vain, to win political control of Europe. Europe's unique geography and military technology made it impossible. There could be no *Pax Europa*. Political states would remain in continual and intense competition.

Early or proto-states—mostly baronies and principalities—began emerging around AD 900, and about 5,000 existed in the fourteenth century. With advances in military technology and increased population density, the number of states declined over subsequent centuries. About 500 political units remained at the beginning of the seventeenth century, 200 in 1800, and

---

[9] Protestant nobles invited William of Orange to organize an invasion to assist in the overthrow of Catholic King James II, an event that is curiously often omitted from English histories, especially in British schools.

fewer than 30 in 1953 (Wright 1942, 215; Richardson 1960, 168–69). Hostile state competition stimulated an arms race which produced technological spillovers to non-military sectors. Because offense is often the best defense, evolving nation-states tended to maintain belligerent relations. The fact that no nation could subdue its neighbors meant that Western Europe would not pass from kingdoms to empire. The empires that these nations were to form would subjugate peoples outside of Western Europe.

Europe possesses other geographic advantages. It has relatively high rainfall, meaning that cut forests can recover quickly, and overgrazing is less likely to lead to desertification. There was abundant potential energy in the form of forests, coal, and falling water. Northern winters helped limit endoparasitic infestations that plagued so many southern regions. Europe faced relatively few geophysical catastrophes, such as earthquakes, tsunamis, and volcanos, and climatic misfortunes, such as floods, droughts, typhoons, and hurricanes (Jones 1987). Europe is exceedingly rich in coastline. Its convoluted coasts and islands yield 22,000 miles (37,000 kilometers) of coastline, the equivalent of the world's circumference. Riverbanks, coasts, and deltas offer extraordinarily rich and regular caloric harvests, and iodine from seafood boosts fertility. Abundant coastlines and navigable rivers mean that produce could more readily be transported by the most efficient and cheapest means of transportation, reducing the costs of forming markets and offering the benefits of comparative advantage.

Southern Europe borders on the Mediterranean basin. No other part of the world possesses anything as significant for providing relatively inexpensive transportation between zones with such differing comparative advantages. It also enabled contact with differing cultures, facilitating the acquisition of their ideas, science, technology, and culture. Incidentally, these substantial advantages put a premium on eliminating pirates, which Greece and Rome had done with considerable success, and later states would continually struggle to do.

Europe's geographic advantages, and especially its relatively isolated physical regions, enabled nation-states to develop in what Jones characterizes as "a purely European form which has been exported to parts of the world that had hitherto known only tribalism" (1987, 127). The power of most earlier states varied inversely with distance from the capital. The nation-state differs in that its law is practically as effective at the edges as at the center, again favored by Europe's many natural geographic barriers.

Intense state competition provided a hotbed for cultural evolution. Within states, differing cultural practices and institutions could evolve, like mutations in differing environmental niches in the biological sphere. Over time, state competition would favor selection of the superior mutations. This competition also made it difficult for any state to suppress novel thoughts or inventions. Cross-national transmission was made easier by the shared cultural framework of Christianity and, relatedly, Latin, the dominant language of European intellectuals prior to modern times. France attempted to bar the printing press to slow the dissemination of radical ideas, but manuscripts were sent abroad for publication, outflanking the prohibition while depriving France of an important industry. Within short order, France permitted printing within its own borders, albeit under the censors' eyes. The same state competition made it difficult to stamp out ideas deemed subversive by rulers and religious authorities. Repressed or fearful intellectuals often sought sanctuary in neighboring states. Some well-known examples include Dante Alighieri, Réné Descartes, John Locke, Voltaire, and Karl Marx.[10]

States encouraged population growth for a supply of soldiers, greater food output, a larger tax base, and the replenishment of cities that continually suffered population loss due to crowd diseases. An enlarged population usually meant more surplus for rulers and elites to expropriate. Concern with population was not, of course, new. It was captured in some ancient religious texts. For instance, the Mosaic sexual code of the Old Testament rigorously proscribed non-procreative sex. Most religions also prohibit abortion and infanticide. But the extreme bellicosity and constant threat of war between Europe's nation-states led to what economist Eli Hecksher characterized as an "almost frantic desire to increase population" (1934, 2:158).[11] A diverting example is that in 1695, the English Parliament passed a measure that placed a tax on bachelors. This legislation had an unintended consequence insofar as reducing the population of single males shrank a ready pool of potential military recruits who would be optimally prone to the violence required of soldiers. Further, married men are less likely to participate in crime, weakening rulers' claim to be all that stands between citizens and social chaos (Henrich, Boyd, and Richerson 2012, 667).

[10] Although China's state-led development had produced an approximately equal level of economic development by the fifteenth century, its geography did not privilege political fragmentation, denying intellectuals with radical ideas ready refuge in neighboring political states (Mokyr 1990, 236).

[11] Between 1500 and 1800, France and Britain were at war 50 percent of the time, and Spain warred with its enemies 80 percent of the time (Ferguson 2012, 37).

China's Geography and Absolutism

China's geography presents very modest internal barriers. Consequently, unlike Europe, it was politically unified as early as 221 BC, and it has mostly remained so since that time. This geography and political connectedness gave it certain timely advantages. It could capture the economic benefits of a huge land mass. It also became relatively unified culturally.

However, this geography also enabled the concentration of political power in an absolutist state which could block the development of a bourgeoisie, thereby thwarting the economic development that sustainably took off in Europe. This came about despite the fact that by 1500 China was the most technologically advanced country in the world. It had invented gunpowder, blast furnaces, the compass, printing and paper, clocks, and paper money. Its bureaucrats were well trained.[12] It might be expected that such accomplishments were due to the evolution of markets and commerce, as would later occur in the West, but this was not the case. China's impressive technological achievements were attributable to state-led development.[13]

Chinese rulers had always maintained a hostile stance toward markets and merchants. They feared the political instability that might result from a growing class of merchants and manufacturers. Rulers' enmity toward the merchant class also stemmed in part from the fact that their wealth could be hidden and easily moved about, thwarting the tax collector. Ideology dating back to Confucius (551–479 BC) depicted the accumulation of private wealth from trade or manufacturing as profoundly immoral. But, here as elsewhere in premodern societies, aristocratic interests understood that wealth gained through markets could threaten their status and privilege.

---

[12] The fact that entry into China's civil service required passing competitive examinations is an interesting expression of its absolutism insofar as it was based on merit rather than birth, clearly revealing a degree of independence from the aristocratic class with its "born-to" status.

[13] Economic historian Joel Mokyr provides the following description of China's state-directed technological dynamism:

> The Chinese imperial government generated and diffused new technologies in rice cultivation, including better (drought resistant) varieties, owned the great foundries that were central to its iron industry, developed and built the great junks with which the Chinese sailed along the African East Coast in the fifteenth century, and encouraged the use of cotton, better implements, and hydraulic techniques. Clockmaking technology was wholly monopolized by the emperor. The authors of the great treatises on agriculture such as Wang Chen and Hsü Kuang Chhi, as well as the inventor of the use of mulberry tree bark in papermaking, were government bureaucrats (2004, 223).

China developed a state-owned and -managed merchant fleet with ships that were four times larger than those used by Columbus to cross the Atlantic. State trade missions sailed out to South Asia, Arabian lands, and the east coast of Africa. However, by decree in 1433, shipbuilding ceased and all foreign trade came to a halt. Wary that foreign trade would destabilize the political order, China isolated itself, and "belief in the utter superiority of the 'Heavenly Kingdom,' as they styled it, predominated in Chinese culture" (Appleby 2011, 9). China virtually stagnated for the next five centuries as extensive population growth swallowed productivity gains and held living standards near or at subsistence. China's humiliating defeats during the Opium Wars (1839–1842 and 1856–1860) seriously posed the question whether to change course, but little change would occur before the twentieth century.

The decree of 1433 ending foreign trade reveals the fragility of economic development directed by an absolutist state. The limits of absolutist state-led development would again become evident in the state socialist experiments of the twentieth century.

War, Nation-State Revenue Needs, and Bourgeois Ascendancy

The art of taxation consists in so plucking the goose as to obtain the largest possible number of feathers with the smallest possible amount of hissing.

—Attributed to Jean-Baptiste Colbert[14]

Late medieval nation-states emerged in an environment in which war rather than peace was the norm as they continually struggled to subdue their feudal rivals and hold hostile neighboring states at bay. State revenue needs could increase fourfold in times of war (North 2010, 141). Thus, monarchs were constantly facing indebtedness and fiscal crises.

Monarchs relied on revenue from their own manors and from the feudal fees owed by their vassals, which often came in the form of military

[14] Translated by the author from: "L'art de l'imposition consiste à plumer l'oie pour obtenir le plus possible de plumes avant d'obtenir le moins possible de cris."

service.[15] Any increased demands by the monarch upon vassals would constitute a violation of the traditional social contract. It could compromise the vassals' loyalty or turn it in favor of the state's competitors. These vassals could individually be as powerful as the Crown and, when joined together, more powerful. They could, and at times did, ally with foreign powers to overthrow the Crown. Consequently, raising their taxes was perilous. Until the state gained adequate military advantage to more fully subjugate the nobility, it needed to locate alternative revenue sources.

The state could be expected to place the tax burden upon those least likely to revolt. This was usually the peasants, but if they were already living at bare subsistence, nothing remained to appropriate. Nevertheless, states, desperate for revenue, did at times raise impoverished peasants' taxes, at the risk of provoking an insurrection. The massive peasant revolt in response to the English poll tax of 1381 is a notable example.

Further, the state was continually in conflict with landlords for greater shares of increased surplus consequent to productivity gains. Any increase taken by the state left less for landlords. Therefore, landlords, pretending to care for the poor, could be expected to oppose any increase in taxes on cultivators. And the state would oppose any further extractions by landlords, similarly feigning concern for the poor.

New sources of revenue emerged with the rise of a merchant class accompanying markets as they spread across Western Europe. States could borrow from an increasingly wealthy bourgeoisie. They could sell the merchants trading rights or monopolies for annual payments. Towns could be granted trading privileges. Guilds could be easily taxed in exchange for exclusive rights of monopoly conferring the power to exclude competitors. Alternatively, alien merchants could be sold legal rights and exemptions from guild restrictions. Foreign trade, relatively easy to tax, was encouraged. These new and expanding revenue sources gave states an interest in protecting, to some degree, the towns' independence from the nobility and Church. It was this unique state support for a rising bourgeoisie and its institutions and practices within a political environment of continual interstate competition that enabled capitalism eventually to flourish and endure in Western Europe.

---

[15] Prior to the rise of a money economy, in addition to military service, the Crown's court appropriated resources from its vassals by circulating among them as their guests, consuming their goods and services. The later evolution of a money economy enabled monarchs to collect their dues in money form, permitting the court to remain stationary and construct a more formidable power base.

Although the practice of granting monopolies was an important source of immediate revenue for the state, it came at the long-run cost of dampening competition that could increase efficiency and economic dynamism and, thus, raise the level of future state revenues. Similarly disadvantageous for long-term growth were other revenue options where the burden to constituents was not so immediately apparent, such as increasing the public debt or debasing the currency. However, the state's focus is necessarily upon surviving the present; if it cannot survive the short run, it will not see a long run. This necessity of near-term survival has repeatedly braked state actions that would establish institutions and practices favorable to economic dynamism. It is remarkable that the European miracle occurred nonetheless.

France developed into a nation-state as a response to the problems posed by the Hundred Years' War (1337–1453). The challenge was to establish law and order and take back the half of the kingdom that had been captured by England and the Burgundians. But the French Crown faced formidable internal competitors. During the fourteenth and fifteenth centuries, the dukes of Burgundy were even more powerful than the French king, and sometimes they even colluded with England. The king also faced the threat that other powerful vassals could unite against his authority (North 1982, 139).

As noted earlier, the state's comparative advantage in violence is greatly dependent upon military technology, and new technologies can significantly realign power relationships. Examples addressed in earlier chapters included the critical importance of inexpensive stone weapons in blocking the rise of rulers and maintaining equality among foragers, of metallurgy in furthering the rise of states, and of stirrups and mounted warriors in creating feudalism. The rapid spread of the cannon in the mid-fifteenth century played a comparable role in the rise of the nation-state by making feudal castle fortifications obsolete. The cannon's destructive power was so great that in 1449–1450, Charles VII of France recaptured Normandy from England, destroying about 60 fortifications in 369 days.[16] He also created Europe's first post-feudal standing army.

The cannon played a comparable role in England. After 1485, Henry VII succeeded in disarming the aristocracy and thereby centralizing the state's monopoly on violence. This was followed in the 1530s by Thomas Cromwell's

---

[16] The arrival of the cannon also brought an end to the Byzantine Empire. The fortifications of Constantinople had withstood over a thousand years of periodic siege but fell under heavy cannon attack by Ottoman Turks in 1453. The largest Austrian-made cannon weighed 16.8 tons, was 17 feet

measures to create a bureaucratic state, one where power would reside more in state institutions than in the family of the monarch. Further centralization of power came when Henry VIII broke with the Church in 1553, expropriated its lands, and abolished the monasteries, putting about a quarter of all English landed property onto the market and achieving a revenue windfall for the Crown. This was an extraordinary gamble, not only because the Church's excommunication meant eternal damnation, but also because the rupture risked alienating subjects' loyalty. After this break, says economist Deepak Lal, "the church-state was dead and the nation-state was born" (2001, 86).

The term *mercantilism* came to be applied to the economic doctrines and policies, widely held between approximately 1500 and 1750, that were supportive of increasing state power in European nations. These doctrines and policies reflected growing awareness of the extent to which military prowess depended upon economic conditions. It was not sufficient merely to adopt and improve upon the military hardware or battle tactics of more powerful rivals. It was also important to have a robust, expanding economy to support a growing population capable of producing more output, weapons, soldiers, and surplus.

Some social thinkers even came to believe that increasing commercial relations between nations could decrease their tendencies to engage in warfare. Montesquieu, for instance, lamenting the almost constant state of war during the seventeenth and eighteenth centuries, claimed that "the natural effect of commerce is to lead to peace. Two nations that trade together become mutually dependent: if one has an interest in buying, the other has one in selling; and all unions are based on mutual needs" (quoted in Hirschman 1997, 80).

Booty from the New World also played a role in the rising fortunes of the bourgeoisie. The influx of gold and silver from the Americas created the most rapid and longest inflation in Europe's history, with prices rising between 150 and 400 percent during the sixteenth century. Inflation greatly shifted command of resources in favor of the rising bourgeoisie as the prices of manufactured goods rose more swiftly than did wages and rents. Landlords found their fortunes falling, and workers' living standards were pushed down toward subsistence. The gains came in the bourgeoisie's profits—a dynamic called profit inflation resulting from price increases outpacing a rise in wages.

---

long with a diameter of just under 3.5 feet, and could project a 1,300-pound marble shot at a range of one-and-a-half miles.

Much of the precious metal pillaged from the Americas flowed to Spain's elites, who spent much of it on luxury and manufactured goods from the rest of Europe. These same metals then flowed out of Europe by the same dynamic. Although Europeans imported luxury goods from the East, they had little to offer in return, because their products were relatively crude and little sought by Asian elites. Consequently, Asians demanded payment in specie, bleeding much of Europe's gold to temples in India and its silver to China.

Practically anything that could be sold in markets could be taxed. Nevertheless, the most valuable of all resources remained land. By and large, however, land was not alienable (that is, not available for exchange through markets). Much land was held in "equitable estates," preventing it from being bought, sold, mortgaged, or leased (Acemoglu and Robinson 2012, 198–99). In addition, aristocratic landlords generally resisted the commodification of land that had been in their families for generations and was crucial to their identity, status, titles, privileges, and influence. Accordingly, their political power over centuries had led to the creation of institutional impediments to land's commodification, such as entails that enforced primogeniture, the transfer of control from one generation to another through the eldest son.

Ever in need of revenues, states had an interest in the commodification of land, and early measures to bring it about date back as far as the end of the thirteenth century. In England, peasants were formally granted the right to sell land in 1290 and nobles in 1327 (North 1982, 141). The result was continual weakening of the fundamental institutional support for the aristocratic landlords' power.

But the greatest force breaking down traditional impediments to the exchange of land for money was that impoverished aristocrats were forced to sell. Given the deep-rooted legacy of high status attached to land possession, it is not surprising that many greatly successful merchants and bankers aspired to become landlords themselves. Indebtedness often compelled landowners to sell their holdings to the willing buyers they found in the rich merchant class. And the new owners typically put the land to better economic use, as Adam Smith noted: ". . . merchants are commonly ambitious of becoming country gentlemen, and when they do, they are generally the best of all improvers" (1776, 384).

Although the state found a new source of revenue in expanding commerce and manufacturing, attempting to tax the wealth and activities of the bourgeoisie faced an important constraint. Unlike land, financial capital is mobile: it can take flight, go abroad, flee to a more attractive jurisdiction. Due to its immobility, land had always been a reliable and predictable tax base. Labor, too, was largely stationary, usually tied to the land or locale, and thus readily targeted for taxation. But whereas the tax bases of land and labor were highly inelastic with respect to tax rates (as tax rates increased, the amount to tax did not proportionately decrease), not so with capital. The supply of capital was elastic to tax rates (as tax rates increased, the amount to tax proportionately decreased more) because the providers of capital can seek less burdensome taxes abroad. Capital is a moving target.

The mobility of capital became an important brake on the power of the state. It provided the new class with an unprecedented degree of leverage against state power. If wealth could fly abroad in response to excessive taxation, the bourgeoisie could command friendlier policies from rulers eager to keep it at home. This was alleged to promote better governance, as Montesquieu recognized. Because "invisible wealth" could be sent anywhere "without leaving a trace," rulers were "compelled to govern with greater wisdom" (quoted in Hirschman 1997, 72).[17] This constraint on the state's power would also make the bourgeoisie more open to democracy.

Apparently, Montesquieu was correct. This "greater wisdom" appears to have resulted in policies that led to more effective law and order and internal domestic peace. Whereas in the fourteenth and fifteenth centuries, 26 percent of male aristocrats died of violence, this fell into the single digits by 1800. Pinker records that England in the twentieth century was 95 percent less violent than it had been in the fourteenth century (2011, 82, 61).[18]

States, realizing that growing commerce and manufacturing increased their tax base, provided the bourgeoisie with greater protections and privileges. They established and enforced property rights that reduced the cost of market activity and brought forth productive incentives. More sustainable economic growth was the consequence. Economic historian

---

[17] Adam Smith equally noted that "commerce and manufactures gradually introduced order and good government, the liberty and security of individuals . . . who had before lived almost in a continual state of war with their neighbours, and of servile dependence upon their superiors" (1776, 385).

[18] This fall in violence has also been attributed to the rise of monogamy, which in turn stimulated commerce. Evolutionary biologists Henrich, Boyd, and Richerson claim that the ". . . historical patterns in pre-modern England during the lead up to the industrial revolution . . . [indicate] that reducing the pool of unmarried men and levelling the reproductive playing field would have decreased crime, which would have spurred commerce, travel and the free flow of ideas and innovations. Greater security would have reduced transaction costs and both public and private security expenditures. Instead of engaging in risky status-seeking endeavours, low-status males would be more likely to marry, thus becoming risk-averse and future-oriented and focus on providing for their offspring in the long run. Higher status males, instead of seeking to attract additional wives, would make long-term investments and attend to their offsprings' security" (2012, 666).

Douglass North claims that these institutional changes set the stage for tech-nological change, as opposed to the other way around (1982, 157).

The increasingly empowered bourgeoisie pressured the state to do more than define and enforce property rights. It also pressured the state to produce infrastructures such as roads, bridges, ports, standardized measures, and money, as well as other actions that decreased transactions costs—the costs of exchanging property rights through markets.

Impediments to Market Expansion

> The capitalist system presupposes the complete separation of the la-bourers from all property in the means by which they can realize their labour.... The so-called primitive accumulation, therefore, is nothing else than the historical process of divorcing the producer from the means of production. It appears as primitive, because it forms the pre-historic stage of capital and of the mode of production corresponding with it.
>
> —Karl Marx, *Capital* (1867, 1:714)

The rigidities that stood in the way of market expansion were extensive. Jones lists them as:

> ... gild regulations, monopolies (other than those to encourage the impor-tation of new trades or to shelter infant industries), an excessive schedule of holy days, sumptuary legislation, monasticism (which tied up labour and sometimes forbade the exploitation of mineral rights and woodland), settlement laws, price controls, and taboos and religious sanctions on eco-nomic behaviour or even on the study of science and technology. (1987, 96)

A few of these impediments are addressed in this section, and others later in this and subsequent chapters.

Craft guilds produced the marketable goods fabricated within premodern agricultural societies, while merchant guilds bought and sold goods. Guild membership was often hereditary. Guilds held monopolies over their segments of production and trade within their local jurisdictions. They served as fraternal brotherhoods with strict codes of both professional and personal conduct. Their power over their own members was wide-ranging and commonly extreme. Sociologist Max Weber wrote of the policing power of Chinese guilds as follows: Their "criminal power was draconic; a breach of regulations led to lynch justice on the part of the guild members and even in the nineteenth century there were executions for violations of the set maximum number of apprentices" (2003, 231). Although generally far less severe, guilds were present in all substantial medieval towns in Europe. Paris, for instance, with a population of about 80,000 at the end of the thirteenth century, had 128 guilds with 5,000 masters and 6,000 to 7,000 journeymen (Tawney 1926, 30).

Their extensive regulations controlled price, quality, production technology, number of apprentices, and entry (which was, as noted, often hereditary). These regulations impeded innovation or entrepreneurship more generally.[19] In Europe, the first such associations were merchant guilds dating back to the ninth century. Evidence of craft guilds dates to the early twelfth century.

As markets expanded in the late Middle Ages, a challenge to the guilds' monopolies developed in the form of rural production in peasant cottages. This cottage industry, also known as proto-industry or the putting-out system, took place in the countryside, beyond the jurisdiction of the guilds. It acted as a corrosive acid slowly dissolving the guilds' power and privilege. Capitalists arranged with peasant families to set up the productive machinery needed to carry out some aspect of production, such as spinning or weaving, in their cottages. The capitalists supplied the materials and picked up the output from cottage workers when their stage of production was completed, transporting it to other cottages for subsequent stages.

The putting-out system nourished the growth of a bourgeoisie fairly free from restrictions. It also enabled society to engage and exploit underutilized labor. Workers in these cottages were generally still engaged in agriculture, where less labor is necessary for fairly long periods between fall harvests and spring planting. By working for the circulating capitalists during these agricultural downtimes, they not only supplemented their incomes, but also increased society's aggregate output by making use of unused labor time.[20]

---

[19] Guild regulations serve as examples of how a community's (in this case the guild's) sense of fairness can result in rules of the game that constrain competition and maintain community goodwill to the benefit of its members.

[20] Capturing underutilized labor is one of the major challenges of economic development. Visitors to poor countries are invariably struck by the number of men idling in small groups in towns and villages with obviously no productive outlet for their time. They are removed from any ownership,

In the late Middle Ages, the rising commercial and manufacturing sectors' need for labor was encumbered by laws and customs that had evolved over centuries to serve the interests of the landlord class. But as these non-agricultural sectors grew in economic importance, so too did their political power, eventually enabling them to push with increasing success for laws that restricted landlords' ability to hold laborers against their wills. Once freed from involuntary labor in agriculture, workers migrated somewhat more easily to places offering higher wages and more favorable living conditions. Nevertheless, regions attempted to hoard their labor by measures such as settlement laws that forced workers to remain in their home parish or district and helped keep their wages near the subsistence level. Employers were generally concerned that external demand for labor would put upward pressure on wages, and landlords were particularly concerned that inadequate labor would be available during their peak seasons of planting and harvesting.

Monopolies were common because granting them provided a ready source of income for the Crown. A scholar in the early seventeenth century reported that a typical Englishman lived "in a house built with monopoly bricks . . . heated by monopoly coal. His clothes are held up by monopoly belts, monopoly buttons, monopoly pins. . . . He ate monopoly butter, monopoly currants, monopoly red herrings, monopoly salmon, monopoly lobsters" (quoted in Appleby 2011, 40). A century and a half later, ever the critic of monopolies, Adam Smith railed against this rent-seeking (gaining income by manipulating the political setting, rather than by creating new wealth): "the cruellest of our revenue laws, I will venture to affirm, are mild and gentle, in comparison of some of those which the clamour of our merchants and manufacturers has extorted from the legislature, for the support of their own absurd and oppressive monopolies" (1776, 612).

There was also strong opposition to exporting food out of local jurisdictions. In periods of extreme food shortages, these exports, initiated by speculators, could lead to famines and social strife. But even in more abundant years, an export-driven shortage in local supplies would put upward pressure on food prices and wages. It took, as Polanyi (1944) made clear, an ever more powerful nation-state to break these local restrictions, and as it did so, it privileged the interests of the increasingly powerful bourgeoisie.

control, or ready access to the means of production, and those who possess that ownership or control have inadequate incentives to employ them. They are a wasted productive resource for these economies. They are also denied the income and dignity of being productive members of their societies.

Polanyi notes the importance of distinguishing between three geographically different markets: local, internal, and long distance. Local markets, where local producers exchange goods to meet their needs, are community-oriented. They have existed since ancient times and are still prevalent around the world, especially in less wealthy countries. They usually feature locally produced and manufactured goods. Long-distance markets have also existed since antiquity, serving to provide goods that are locally unavailable, principally due to geography and climate. Salt is a classic example.

In contrast to local and long-distance markets, internal markets between local jurisdictions within the same general polity faced substantial barriers. For instance, guilds, to protect their interests, established regulations that prohibited the importation from neighboring areas of the goods they themselves produced. Polanyi describes how, over several centuries, the state took measures to break these local restrictions on trade that impeded the development of internal markets. In this manner, he demonstrates the state's critical role in the creation of national economies and the rise of capitalism. Polanyi's account contradicts the customary laissez-faire story that attributed the rise of capitalism to the decline of state interventions into the economy. More correctly expressed, state intervention did not decline, but instead expressed itself increasingly in ways that favored the bourgeoisie and economic dynamism.

Urbanization, Wages, and the Degradation of Women

Although the expansion of commerce and manufacturing exerted upward pressure on wages, counterforces continually pulled them back toward subsistence levels. In addition to the dampening effect of measures such as maximum wage legislation and settlement laws, population growth and the enclosure movement tended to hold down wages. Despite the demographic crises of the fourteenth and seventeenth centuries, over the long haul, population expanded in step with agricultural output, increasing the supply of labor and pressing wages downward. Landlords' fencing off their lands for sheep grazing pushed cultivators into the urban proletariat, increasing the supply of labor and constricting wages in cities and towns.

Wages had substantially risen in the wake of the Black Death in the mid-fourteenth century, but, by 1600, real wages had fallen to half their level right after the plague ended. Strikingly, the Gini coefficient for income inequality soared from about 0.5 in the early fifteenth century to almost 0.8 in the eighteenth century. (On the Gini index, zero represents perfect equality and 1, perfect inequality.) Even by the onset of World War I, real wages remained lower than they had been around 1400 (B. van Bavel 2016, 111, 128, 135).

The enclosure movement continued for centuries, and those who were pushed off the land generally migrated to towns to seek work as wage-laborers. But life in the premodern countryside was harsh for most workers, and many voluntarily left the land in search of better situations. Not all the serfs who stole away from their manors headed to towns; some joined bands of marauders. Yet life on feudal estates was not always intolerable, and the manors generally offered greater security than runaways would find in urban centers or the lawless wilderness. Workers had a traditionally recognized right to be on their manorial land, where they had access to the means for survival. Further, there was a greater sense of community on the manor: few starved unless all did.

Town life was often harder than life in the countryside. Although workers in towns were free of feudal fetters, and sometimes better off materially, their work was less secure. They were packed more tightly together in unsanitary slums and suffered higher death rates from diseases that spread in crowded conditions. Crimes took place more frequently, and violence was generally more prevalent, as were drunkenness and prostitution. Moreover, inequality was greater in towns than in the countryside (van Zanden 1995).

Town work was more onerous and unpleasant than that in agriculture. With the exception of gang slavery, agricultural workers had substantial control over the timing, pace, and intensity of their work. Wage laborers, in contrast, were required to spend long hours, on a schedule determined by their bosses, performing repetitive tasks that were frequently dangerous. Lack of punctuality, irregular attendance, and inattention were severely punished. Workers were made subservient first to the clock (DeGrazia 1962, 315),[21] and then, with rising mechanization, to the rhythmic pace of machinery. In agriculture and crafts, work was diverse and task-directed, whereas with industrial work it became repetitive and time-directed. Wage work provided progressively fewer vents for creativity and self-esteem, and fewer occasions

---

[21] Mechanical public clocks came forth in the fourteenth century, first where labor markets were increasingly prevalent, such as northern Italy and the Low Countries, due to pressure by entrepreneurs on town governments. They enabled better control of the workday. Workers had to show up for work at designated hours or suffer fines or dismissal. Rebellious workers often tried to silence the clock bells (van Bavel 2015, 75).

to earn the approbation of others through the quality of one's work. Whereas during antiquity and the Middle Ages almost half the days of the year were "holidays" (generally religious), with the rise of capitalism this number decreased dramatically (Willensky 1961).

Proletarianization and urbanization also transformed gender relations in a manner that relatively disempowered women. In pre-industrial work, husband and wife generally worked as a partnership, first as foragers and later in agriculture and handicraft industry. Although their tasks varied, they had similar work and social schedules. As discussed in Chapter 5, anthropological and historical evidence reveals that, with the exception of gang slavery and socially coerced labor, work was not generally viewed as unpleasant prior to the rise of wage labor.

In early industrialization, by contrast, work became socially organized, with orders coming down from superiors. Wives and even children often needed to work in factories and mines for households to earn enough for bare subsistence.[22] Much later, when workers gained greater political power and higher wages, males became wage workers outside the home, leaving wives to handle household tasks and care for the children. The earlier teamwork in production ceased. Because males earned and controlled money, and household needs had to be met increasingly through the market, the males' domestic power was enhanced and that of their spouses diminished. Women became more dependent.[23] Their social status also weakened as their participation in activities perceived as "economically productive" declined in an increasingly monetized and industrialized economy (Tilly and Scott 1988, 144–45). Living quarters were generally too small for extended families, making women virtual prisoners of the household because they could not leave young children unattended. The separation of work and leisure or family activities lessened familial bonds (Vanek 1980, 429).

---

[22] The debased condition of working-class women is attested to by the need of some to prostitute themselves. Even in the late nineteenth and early twentieth centuries, studies have found that between 5 percent and 15 percent of working-class women in urban areas engaged in prostitution to supplement their meager incomes at some point in their lives (Baumeister and Vohs 2004, 348).

[23] Historians Louse Tilly and Joan Scott (1988) provide detailed support for the manner in which women's participation in activities perceived as "economically productive" declined as an economy industrialized (1988, 144–45). Historian Joseph Interrante points out that "many, if not all, of the village-centered institutions sold goods and provided services—food, clothing, education, health care, entertainment—which farm women had produced or performed themselves, and over which farm families had retained a close and immediate control. Metropolitanism [accompanying industrialization] interrupted that relationship and thus represented a reorganization of the social relations of consumption" (1979, 158).

In northern Europe of the thirteenth century, especially in the Low Countries, some women responded to their subservient status, as well as to a shortage of men due in part to war and the Crusades, by joining together in *béguinages* (Simons 2003). Their members, the Beguines, belonged to Christian lay religious orders. They lived in semi-monastic communities but did not take formal vows. Although strongly religious, their freedom is striking for the period. They were free to accumulate property and free to take it with them if they left. Although weaving and dying textiles were often their main occupations, they also taught children and helped the poor. Some *béguinages* became quite large, the number of women reaching the thousands in Ghent, which was walled with a moat, had two churches, a brewery, and an infirmary.

Despite their relative freedom, the Beguines were at times persecuted. For instance, in 1311, Pope Clement V accused them of fostering heresy. They also suffered under popes John XXII, Urban V, and Gregory XI. During the Protestant Reformation of the sixteenth century and during the French Revolution, they came under further attack. Nevertheless, a few Belgian *béguinages* survived until the early twentieth century, notably those of Bruges, Lier, Mechelin, Leuven, and Ghent, the last counting a thousand members in 1905 (Simons 2003).

The Bourgeoisie's Pursuit of Status

Few tricks of the unsophisticated intellect are more curious than the naïve psychology of the business man, who ascribes his achievements to his own unaided efforts, in bland unconsciousness of the social order without whose continuous support and vigilant protection he would be as a lamb bleating in the desert.
—Richard Tawney, *Religion and the Rise of Capitalism* (1926, 221)

Humans evolved to seek the highest status available, and as will be recalled from Chapter 2, the ultimate cause is to be found in the biological dynamics of sexual selection: the genetic proclivity to seek status was selected during human evolution and passed from generation to generation down the ages. Although generally unaware that reproductive success is the underlying goal of their quest for preeminence, those who acquired high status found more mates and parented more offspring. As seen in Chapter 3, with the adoption of agriculture and the subsequent evolution of more organized societies, hereditary privilege emerged in the upper social class. This meant that status became ascriptive, ascribed by birth, according to the status of one's ancestors. This became the norm with the rise of the state and extreme inequality.

Little vertical mobility existed in these societies. Everyone had their "born-to" status. As Aristotle put it, "From the hour of their birth, some are marked out for subjection, some for command" (1962, 1254a). This was their identity. "Born-to" status had huge consequences for inequality, making it virtually unalterable. Prior to the French Revolution, there was widespread recognition of three biologically transmissible relations of power: monarchy, aristocracy, and manual laborers or slavery. Even within formal law there was unequal treatment. For instance, courts meted out more severe punishment for harm done to a nobleman than to those socially below the aristocracy (Spruyt 1994, 141).

A typical example of this "born-to" ideology is provided by French nobles prior to the Revolution who believed themselves a race apart, having descended from the conquering Franks, not the defeated Gauls. De Tocqueville remarked of such aristocrats that "they scarcely even think of themselves as belonging to the same humanity" (quoted in Rosanvallon 2013, 12). They saw themselves as sharing the same "blue blood." Therefore, any attempt to eliminate hereditary rank would constitute an assault on their very biology.

Societies characterized by ascriptive hierarchy viewed society as comparable to a living organism, composed of parts with differing and unalterable functions. Accordingly, all classes of society must perform those functions naturally given to them, whether it be ruling, warring, or doing manual labor. As Tawney put it, "Each must receive the means suited to its station, and must claim no more. . . . Between classes there must be inequality; for otherwise a class cannot perform its function, or . . . enjoy its rights" (1926, 23). Practically no paths were available for raising one's status, and any attempt to do so was discouraged, if not reprimanded.

The rise of capitalism and the bourgeoisie upset this established social order. Whereas ascriptive status gave permanence to hierarchy by privileging the past over the present, the emerging bourgeoisie, by contrast, located its status in the unfolding present of its members' achievements. This performance mentality would be nourished in Protestantism's values of hard work and asceticism, as will be explored more fully in Chapter 7.

Expanding markets threatened the ideology of "born-to" social relationships where everyone's social position and fitting behavior are highly fixed. Smart rational calculation in markets can turn good profits, and, if it is persistently pursued, the manufacturer, trader, or financier may become rich. In this manner, a rising commercial class, a bourgeoisie, began to accumulate wealth, and as it did so, it sought social recognition commensurate with its new command of resources. It began to petition for equal status with the aristocracy. Its success in doing so entailed that the ground for status be shifted from birthright to personal achievement. Ascriptive status was forced to yield space to achievement status (undergirding meritocracy in contemporary times). Vertical mobility became increasingly possible: one might rise in status through cleverness and diligent effort. Evolving philosophy legitimated social mobility. For instance, John Locke's notion that at birth the mind is a *tabula rasa*, a blank slate, "undermined a hereditary royalty and aristocracy, whose members could claim no innate wisdom or merit if their minds had started out as blank as everyone else's" (Pinker 2002, 5).

It is in view of the potential for vertical mobility that traditional ideology, legitimating the privileges of the aristocracy, depicted markets as corrupting and their profit-seeking participants as vulgar, selfish, and greedy. Such ideology could help them retain their privileged status by describing the bourgeoisie as enemies of morality and public welfare.

The aristocracy also used other tactics to block the bourgeoisie's quest for equal status. They did so most visibly in the domain of conspicuous consumption, for example, wearing the most fashionable and expensive clothing. Prior to the expansion of markets, only the aristocracy possessed surplus resources with which to engage in competitive conspicuous consumption. They did so among themselves, out-spending one another in the quest for the highest prestige.

Sumptuary laws—especially those laws that prohibited lower classes from wearing the garments of classes above them—proliferated in the late Middle Ages in Europe, but especially multiplied as the bourgeoisie grew between the fourteenth and seventeenth centuries (Jones 1987, 97). There were even special courts enforcing these dress codes. Sumptuary laws were not restricted to dress. They could apply to practically anything that might indicate rank. For instance, under James the First of Scotland (1406–1407), men under the grade of baron were prohibited from consuming baked meats and pies. Anthropologist Jack Goody writes that within class societies, "What one ate became seen as constitutive of the very quality of persons, giving rise to sumptuary legislation which saw to it that people consumed the foods appropriate to their status and not those of higher groups" (1998, 129). Dietary sumptuary regulations provided additional assurance that elites consumed the highest-quality foods.

Sumptuary laws were not new. They had existed wherever elites became apprehensive that the consumption behavior of an ascendant class might compromise their status by appropriating their marks of distinction. The biblical Book of Leviticus offers a compendium of such rules. Sumptuary restrictions could provoke anger and resistance. During peasant uprisings of the Tokugawa period (1603–1868) in Japan, for example, the right to wear leather-soled footwear was restricted (Borton 1968). Members of the increasingly prosperous merchant class of this period were prohibited from wearing jewelry and the distinctive clothing of the aristocracy and samurai, and were disqualified from owning certain objects of fine art. Merchants in the Ottoman Empire were denied the privilege of wearing furs, which were reserved for the aristocracy and high government officials (Hunt 1996, 353).

Adam Smith's famous "baubles and trinkets thesis," purporting to account for the demise of feudalism, shows how rising markets and conspicuous consumption eroded the aristocratic monopoly on economic and political power. As commerce expanded, it presented landlords with a growing number of new luxury goods that had no utility (baubles and trinkets) beyond that of impressing their fellow landlords with their wealth and refinement. Smith wrote: "With the greater part of rich people, the chief enjoyment of riches consists in the parade of riches, which in their eye is never so complete as when they appear to possess those decisive marks of opulence which nobody can possess but themselves" (1776, 172). The amount that a lord and his dependents could consume had long served as an obvious status signal. Expensive but useless novelties could additionally allow members of the elite to express themselves, reveal their imagination, or evoke their fine sensibilities. Needless to say, self-expression, imagination, and sensitivity could enhance their status and raise their potential for attracting mates and siring children.

During the feudal era, the cultivators' obligations to the lords were principally paid in the form of labor services. But money was the efficient medium that lords needed to purchase the new goods, notably including baubles and trinkets, made available by expanding trade. Landlords were tempted to convert labor rents owed them into money, and, in so doing, they frittered away their wealth and stature. As though anticipating Marx's conception of a class digging its own grave, Smith said of the aristocracy that "for the gratification of the most childish, the meanest and the most sordid of all vanities, they gradually bartered their whole power and authority" (1776, 389).[24]

Towns thus put constant pressure on the embattled nobles to realize their rents in monetary form. The consequence was a steady commutation of dues into money rents and increased leasing-out of the demesne to peasant tenants. This conversion of serf labor services into money rents had been slowing occurring since as early as the tenth century (Neal and Cameron 2016, 63), but it picked up speed as commerce expanded, and it reached near completion in the wake of the demographic crisis. By the sixteenth century, Western European feudalism had been replaced by new social relationships between landlords and tenant farmers, sharecroppers, and wage laborers (North and Thomas 1971, 780).

The bourgeoisie's pursuit of respectability and social prominence opened yet another revenue source for states. Monarchs granted and sold noble titles. Such titles conferred inferior status to traditional titles, giving rise to a distinction between *noblesse d'épée* (literally, nobility of the sword, meaning "born-to" rank) and *noblesse de robe* (Crown-granted or purchased rank, whose holders were permitted to wear the aristocratic garments). Such was the state's need for revenue that in Spain, not only noble titles, but also offices were sold, and sometimes they were made hereditary. Even immunity from justice was for sale (Acemoglu and Robinson 2012, 221).

The slowly evolving victory of acquired over ascribed status was punctuated by the French Revolution and the founding of the American Republic. In France, the Revolution of 1789 abruptly abolished most institutional remnants of feudalism, including the nobility and clergy's exemption from taxes. In the short three years between 1789 and 1792, absolute monarchy was destroyed, and a democratic republic was established where all adult

---

[24] The continuation of Smith's passage on this "childish" behavior of the landlords fit into Smith's conception of an invisible hand whereby the behavior of individuals produces unintended and beneficent consequences: "The merchants and artificers, much less ridiculous, acted merely from a view to their own interest, and in pursuit of their own pedlar principle of turning a penny wherever a penny was to be got. Neither of them had either knowledge or foresight of that great revolution which the folly of the one, and the industry of the other, was gradually bringing about" (1776, 391–92). David Hume also took account of the felicitous consequences of the landlords' conspicuous consumption: "When luxury nourishes commerce and industry, the peasants, by a proper cultivation of the land, become rich and independent; while the tradesmen and merchants acquire a share of the property, and draw authority and consideration to that middling rank of men, who are the best and firmest basis of public liberty. These submit not to slavery, like the peasants. . . . They covet equal laws, which may secure their property, and preserve them from monarchical, as well as aristocratical tyranny" (1955, 28–29).

men were declared innately equal and accorded uniform political participation with the right to vote. The Revolutionaries intended to sound the
final knell of all "born-to" aristocratic privileges. On June 19, 1790, a decree
eradicated all titles of nobility. There could be no displays of coats of arms
before residences. Many aristocrats fled (about 12 percent), and the guillo-
tine beheaded almost one percent. In 1797, the Directory stripped nobles of
French citizenship. In the Revolutionaries' quest for equality, even *Monsieur*
and *Madame* were to be replaced by *Citoyen* and *Citoyenne*.

Similarly, nobility was denied legal status in the new American republic,
as were primogeniture and entails. The Declaration of Independence of 1776
opened with "the self-evident truth" that "all men are created equal," and
Sections 9 and 10 of Article I of the Constitution adopted in 1789 prohibits
the US government or its states from granting any "Title of Nobility." In short
order, the newly founded US republic demonstrated what theretofore had
been considered impossible—that a society without nobles could function,
even very well.

Nevertheless, in Europe, no matter how rich a member of the bourgeoisie
might become, the aristocracy held the pinnacle of social status. As Appleby
writes:

> Noble and gentry families were the celebrities of the premodern world.
> They contributed learning, taste, style, and their glamorous presence to
> major public celebrations. They were the only candidates for high positions
> at court, or in the military, or in the church. (2011, 32)

The status of an aristocrat could not be matched by a bourgeois, no matter
the latter's mountain of wealth, or as Adam Smith put it, "Upstart greatness is
every where less respected than ancient greatness" (1776, 672). Aristocracy
was due to noble birth, not crass money-grubbing.

Even today, prestige and privilege continue to be the fruits of high "born-to"
status. Those raised in "old wealth" are not only far more likely to be wealthy,
but they also receive superior educations, especially in the arts, which serve
as a showground of choice for competitive conspicuous display—a marker
of refined sensibilities (Bourdieu 1984). Those of old wealth are still highly
sought after as marriage partners. They are above the vulgarity sometimes associated with those who have amassed wealth through hard work. The label
nouveaux riches still stings.

The Church's Legacy

Since Judaism made Christianity possible and gave it the character of a religion essentially free of magic, it rendered an important service from the point of view of economic history. For the dominance of magic outside the sphere in which Christianity has prevailed is one of the most serious obstructions to the rationalization of economic life. Magic involves a stereotyping of technology and economic relations.
—Max Weber, *General Economic History* (2003, 265)

The Catholic Church served as the major unifying force within Europe for over a millennium. It was a lonely center of literacy. Its Latin provided a lingua franca, a single language in which Churchmen and educated elites could communicate across an otherwise linguistically diverse Europe. Latin lowered the cost of knowledge dissemination, aided the comprehension of laws, and facilitated the carrying forth of commerce. Thus, Europe was doubly blessed, first by its geography that fueled rigorous state competition, and second by the significant degree of cultural integration provided by its dominant religion.

In spite of its otherworldliness, Christianity espoused views that were favorable to economic development. The earliest religions were animistic, seeing spirituality residing in all of reality. People, animals, plants, land, mountains, rivers, and all else in nature were sacred. Animism could put certain parts of nature off limits and unavailable for economic exploitation. However, the religion of ancient Israel located spirituality in a solitary transcendental being, God. The rest of reality was stripped of its sacredness, in a momentous step that Weber called "the disenchantment of the world." This desacralization of nature was carried forth in Judaism's two daughter religions, Christianity and Islam.

Rather than living in harmony with all of reality—indeed, as a part of nature—people who adhered to these Abrahamic religions could be understood, in the image of their transcendent creator, as spiritually standing above and outside nature. This station had been determined at the time of creation: "And God said, Let us make man in our image, after our likeness; and let him have dominion over the fish of the sea, and over the fowl of the air, and over the cattle, and over all the earth, and over every creeping thing that creepeth upon the earth" (*Genesis* 1:26). Thus, when Europeans were

Christianized, the land and resources which earlier religions had deemed sacred were released from their hallowed restrictions and made available for human economic use.

As noted in Chapter 5, Christianity viewed work as willed by God, and essential not merely for physical survival, but also for human fulfillment and the completion of God's creation. This outlook ran counter to the Greek and Roman view of work as that which was to be done by less-than-fully-human slaves because it was beneath the dignity of a free person. Many of the earliest adherents to Christianity in Rome were workers, and part of the attractiveness of this new religious doctrine was its view of the nobility of labor (Wisman 1998).

However, later Catholic thought—in a manner reminiscent of most Greek and Roman philosophers—considered work to be divided into higher and lower forms. For Christians, the higher form was spiritual reflection and contemplation, directed, accordingly, to the more important concern of the eternal hereafter. The lower form of work was viewed as servile, to be performed by inferior beings, because it was involved with the transient present (Pieper and Schall 1963, 21). This attitude legitimated Catholic orders' practices of slavery and serfdom on Church properties.

Yet the monastic orders, a strong force within Christianity, continued to extol the virtues of all work. With the decline of urban centers that followed the disintegration of the Roman Empire, these orders became not only important carriers of learning but also the vanguard of much technological progress. Members worked, and their work was understood as the fulfillment of divine will. St. Benedict, for instance, argued that all work, whether mental or menial, was a duty. Idleness, by contrast, was an invitation to sin.[25] In addition to meeting physical needs, the purposes of work were to provide discipline and enable charity. By ennobling work, the monastic orders weakened a cultural barrier to technical invention and innovation.

---

[25] On Christianity and the dignity of work, Mokyr writes:

> In the fourth and fifth centuries, a belief that productive labor was virtuous started to take root. In about 530 A.D., St. Benedict, founder of the Benedictine order, wrote the Benedictine Rule, which earned him the unlikely accolade of being "probably the pivotal figure in the history of labor" (White 1969, 63). Idleness is the enemy of the soul and to labor is to pray, taught St. Benedict. . . . Because monks belonged to the educated classes—indeed *were* the educated classes for centuries—there is some basis to White's belief that "for the first time the practical and the theoretical were embodied in the same individual . . . the monk was the first intellectual to get dirt under his fingernails" (1969, 65). By establishing the moral acceptability of physical labor and production, the Benedictine Rule was the first challenge to the classical notion that identified work with depravity. Benedictine monks had enormous influence on medieval life, playing a major

Christianity was universalist. Christ's doctrine of brotherly love places emphasis upon the inherent value and dignity of each individual, regardless of his or her origins or station. Everyone is equal in the eyes of the one and only God. As Lal has put it, "Christianity's great innovation was to combine the monotheism of Judaism with a new claim to universalism" (2001, 76). This universal character moved beyond tribal religion whose members claimed a special relationship with their divinity as a "chosen people." Christianity's postulate of universal humanity corresponded with the ethnic diversity of those who embraced the faith in Rome. They had come to Rome, often as slaves, from disparate parts of the Roman Empire and conquered territories. This idea of a universal humanity not only equipped Christianity to proselytize widely, it also planted a seed that would, in time, mature as a claim for secular as well as spiritual equality.[26]

Ever perceptive, Tocqueville observed how Christianity's spiritual equality would seep into secular thought: "Christianity, which made all men equal in the sight of God, will not shrink from seeing all citizens as equals in the eyes of the law. . . . It took the coming of Jesus Christ to make people understand that all members of the human race are by nature similar and equal" (quoted in Rosanvallon 2013, 16). The philosopher Friedrich Hegel set forth a similar understanding of Christianity's legacy for the cultural development of Europe. He contended that the history of individual human freedom began in classical Greece, where it was conceived as limited to a few. The next major breakthrough, he claimed, came with Christianity, which recognized all humans as free because they were all equal in the eyes of God. Hegel's vision of the subsequent history of Western civilization can be interpreted as the slow working out in the secular realm of this Christian recognition of the universal freedom and dignity of all humans before God (Houlgate 2005).

Although Christianity was pregnant with conceptions such as the dignity of work and human equality that would be important for Europe's economic "miracle," in many ways it served more as an impediment to progress. It

role in education, in agriculture, in land reclamation, and in the techniques of arts and crafts (1990, 203–4).

[26] It is noteworthy that Christianity was not unique in its universal humanity postulate. During the Hellenistic period, for example, commercial activity flourished, giving rise to a middle class and radical views that would not reappear in the secular world until the later development of capitalism. The Stoics of that era embraced a universal humanity postulate according to which all humans are by nature equal. They also viewed work as noble. Classics scholar A. A. Long claims that they exerted considerable influence on nascent Christianity: "Many of the Christian fathers were more deeply affected by Stoicism than they themselves recognized" (1974, 107).

advanced a static conception of the material world and legitimated the social structure and practices of the Middle Ages. It downplayed the elite's harsh exploitation of the many by depicting this temporary life of suffering on earth as unimportant in comparison to an everlasting life of bliss in the hereafter. Christianity also described markets as both reflecting and generating selfishness. It thus opposed the institutions and values central to capitalism: competition, market-determined prices, interest on loans, and alienable property. As will be discussed in Chapter 7, it would take a theological revolution—the Protestant Reformation—to reconcile Christianity with the attitudes, behavior, and institutions of capitalism.

A Historical Singularity

> . . . it is far from obvious that, had western Europe never existed, or had it been wiped out by Genghis Khan, that some other society would have eventually developed X rays, freeze-dried coffee, and solar-powered desk calculators.
>
> —Joel Mokyr, *The Lever of Riches* (2004, 286)

The European landed aristocracy failed to curb the expansion of market activity and towns, and the rise of a competing class that would eventually predominate in social and political power.[27] Because this new order became sustainable, it marks a turning point in history. No longer could Europe's landed elite appropriate most of society's surplus and stifle economic dynamism. The unchaining of the bourgeoisie set the conditions for sustainable economic growth and, in due time, democracy. The sustainable triumph of Europe's bourgeoisie stands as a historical singularity.

As will be examined in Chapter 9, the unshackled bourgeoisie created the conditions in which formal working-class political power could arise. Numerous social thinkers, notably including Friedrich Hayek and Milton Friedman, have suggested a link between the extent of market penetration within a society and its general level of political freedom. However, they may

---

[27] Although rising markets contributed to the decline of the aristocracy over the long haul, at times the aristocracy benefited from trade in ways beyond having access to a wider variety of goods, especially when granted special privileges by the Crown. For instance, during the reign of Louis XIV in France, Jean-Baptiste Colbert initiated and oversaw government-controlled industry and trade, of which the aristocracy was the main beneficiary.

not have fully appreciated the importance of the conflicting class interests that accompanied the rising power of the bourgeoisie.[28]

The struggle of the bourgeoisie was the beginning of the movement toward the democratization of the political sphere, and it took centuries for the bourgeoisie to wrestle control of the state from the aristocracy. But this expansion of control over the political sphere was essential for constraining the political power of the traditional ruling elite. Only then could the potential for economic dynamism be released. For poor countries, this remains as true today as ever it was. Economists Daron Acemoglu and James Robinson explain that poor countries are poor "precisely because [they] have been ruled by a narrow elite that have organized society for their own benefit at the expense of the vast mass of people. . . . Countries such as Great Britain and the United States became rich because their citizens overthrew the elites who controlled power and created a society where political rights were much more broadly distributed" (2012, 3).

Recent scholarship by historian Bas van Bavel provides the background for a fuller understanding of the reasons why the European miracle was a historical singularity. In *The Invisible Hand? How Market Economies Have Emerged and Declined since AD 500*, he demonstrates the way in which the rising economic and political power of a bourgeoisie enabled the expansion of factor markets. He presents three case studies of pre-industrial countries: Iraq in the fifth to seventh century, Italy in the tenth to twelfth century, and the Low Countries in the eleventh to thirteenth century. These increasingly capitalist societies achieved robust economic dynamism for extended periods. Ordinary people became better organized and won greater freedom as the traditional elites' monopoly of political power was broken. However, in each case, increasingly rich capitalist elites gained ever more political power to transform the rules of the game (social institutions), opening the way to highly remunerative rent-seeking. They increasingly used their wealth to purchase political influence and engage in financial speculation as opposed to productive investment. They also competed vigorously for the pinnacle of status through conspicuous consumption, especially in villas

---

[28] As with Marx, political scientists Evelyne Huber, Dietrich Rueschemeyer, and John D. Stephens recognize the importance of class conflict in the rise of freedom. Their research leads them to conclude that "the shift in the balance of class power to be the most important factor accounting for the positive correlation between development and democracy . . ." (1993, 74–75). Contemporary China, with its expansive market system and dramatic economic dynamism under totalitarian rule, is the most striking example putting in question the presumed link between markets and political freedom.

and art.[29] The consequences were, first, stagnation, and then severe secular declines in the economic well-being of these three countries.[30] In a more cursory manner, van Bavel examines how these dynamics also unfolded in the later experiences of Great Britain and are currently playing out in the United States. In all these instances, what happened was that "the market economy was ... taken hostage by these elites, through their growing economic weight and also their hold on state power" (2016, 271).

The lesson of van Bavel's analysis appears to be that, after having broken aristocratic power and created robust economic growth, the bourgeoisie ends up using its greater political power to alter institutions so as to enable its own rent-seeking, and, in so doing, it kills the goose that lays the golden eggs.

Given these dynamics of capitalist self-destruction, how did Europe as a whole manage to create enduring capitalist-driven economic development? If these devastating rent-seeking dynamics occurred in Italy, the Low Countries, and Great Britain, why did they not manifest themselves in Europe as a whole so as to abort its miracle? The answer appears to lie in the fierce state competition that was fostered by its unique geography. No state could acquire a hegemony over all of Europe, but all states had to remain economically robust to ensure that none of their competitors did so. European nations became aware that they needed to become and remain economically strong to avoid being conquered. Moreover, to maintain a balance of power, they had an interest in not permitting severely weakened economies—such as Italy and, to a lesser extent, the Low Countries—to be swallowed by more powerful neighbors. Europe as a whole managed to endure even while some of its members faltered. If a nation slipped and lost its leadership, others were there to continue the upward progress.

Mokyr's view of Europe's technological dynamism appears to support this view. He notes how Europe was privileged by its geography as follows:

... most societies that have been technologically creative have been so for relatively short periods ... [but] because Europe was fragmented it does not

---

[29] Thus, ironically, art most flourished in Abbasid Iraq, the Italian Renaissance, and the Dutch Golden Age when these economies were in decline, driven by the status-competitive conspicuous consumption of an increasingly rich rent-seeking bourgeoisie.

[30] It was in Italy that Europe's sustainable economic dynamism began, but "Italy lost its economic primacy by 1500, and it would even drop to the bottom of the economic hierarchy in Europe in the following centuries. Because of the high levels of inequality, the effect of this decline on real wages and average standards of living was probably even more pronounced" (van Bavel 2016, 135).

hold for the continent as a whole. It is as if technological creativity was like a torch too hot to hold for long; each individual society carried it for a short time. So long as there was another nation or economy to hand the torch to, however, some light source illuminating the landscape has been glowing in Europe more or less continuously since the eleventh century. (2004, 276)

7

Theological Revolution and the Idea of Equality

Modern man, on the whole, is rarely able, with the best will in the world, to imagine just how significant has been the influence of religious consciousness on conduct of life, "culture," and "national character."

—Max Weber, *The Protestant Ethic and the Spirit of Capitalism* (1905, 122).

Humans are conscious beings, capable of being aware of themselves, thinking about thinking, and editing their own thoughts. A consequence is that they develop meaning or legitimation for their behavior. In fact, they must do so, even if without conscious intention. Legitimation explains and justifies prevailing social reality. It gives meaning to what is and guidance as to what ought to be. Accordingly, legitimation is both factual and moral. As was seen in Chapter 4, religion evolved to serve as the principal social institution legitimating the human world, and generally did so with near monopoly force until the rise of secular thought in modern times.

In traditional societies, religious legitimation militated against the idea of economic growth and development in several ways. First, it understood social reality as constituting a part of a divine project, rendering a degree of sacredness to the given, to what already exists, as opposed to what might be brought about through change.[1] This resistance to change accords with

---

[1] If the religion depicts its god as omniscient, omnipotent, and omnibenevolent, then its creation must be perfect and any attempt or even thought to change it would be not only misguided, but blasphemous.

the conservatism of those for whom survival is precarious. Second, the most important reality, or part of reality, was not the earthly or material domain where suffering and death occur, but the otherworldly or spiritual realm. In its extreme expression, religion advocated *contemptus mundi*, an outright rejection of this sinful world. Energy is properly expended in striving for progress in spirituality or, in salvation religions, pursuing eternal spiritual life, rather than struggling for material progress in the base physical world where life is impermanent. Third, in traditional societies, all thought is consistent, or must be made consistent, with the overarching religious cosmology. New social phenomena, as well as seeming advances in knowledge, must be conformable to and explainable by the sacred beliefs and texts, or, as economic historian Richard Tawney put it, ". . . all activities fall within a single system, because all, though with different degrees of immediateness, are related to a single end, and derive their significance from it" (1926, 24). Social phenomena that are inconsistent with such texts must be opposed; ideas that are at odds with the sacred doctrines must be suppressed as heretical and their propagators punished, if not killed.

As social conditions evolve, the character of religion also changes. This was seen in Chapter 3 as the adoption of agriculture established the material and social conditions within which hierarchies could develop. As chiefdoms and classes arose, beliefs were transformed from the equality-reinforcing convictions of foragers and early agriculturalists to the teachings and rituals overseen by a religious priesthood claiming special access to spiritual forces. Priests participated in reorienting religious doctrines to serve the ideological function of legitimating inequality.

This chapter addresses the way Christianity was transformed as Europe underwent its long-drawn-out transition from a predominantly agrarian economy commanded by landlords to a commercial one increasingly dominated by a bourgeoisie. The altered class-driven power relations, institutions, and practices required legitimation that traditional Catholicism was ill-suited to provide, forcing Christianity to undergo a profound revolution in the form of Protestantism.[2]

---

[2] Recognition of a relationship between changing social conditions and religious expression dates back to Montesquieu, who suggested that the English "had progressed the furthest in three important things, piety, commerce, and freedom," and emphasized the debt of the third to the first. Much later, sociologist Max Weber famously related the second to the first (1905).

The Pre-Modern Antipathy toward Markets

The medieval theorist condemned as a sin precisely that effort to achieve a continuous and unlimited increase in material wealth which modern societies applaud as a quality, and the vices for which he reserved his most merciless denunciations were the more refined and subtle of the economic virtues.

—Richard Tawney, *Religion and the Rise of Capitalism* (1926, 38)

Christianity was nurtured in the Roman Empire, and, because it evolved to legitimate Rome's hierarchical institutions and practices, it is unsurprising that its own organizational structure became hierarchical. This tiered structure was also a good fit for legitimizing the medieval social system that would later develop in Europe. Catholicism's pyramid of authority placed the pope at the top and cardinals, archbishops, bishops, monsignors, priests, and laymen sequentially lower in rank. In the medieval world, it would be roughly paralleled, with country variations, by emperors, kings, dukes, earls, barons, lords, peasants, and serfs and slaves.

Between the fall of Rome and the late Middle Ages, the Church existed in a world where, although there was change in basic social institutions, it was limited. This relative stability of medieval social relations allowed the Church's doctrines to calcify. They became rigid and ill-suited to the dynamic changes that were to accompany the rise and spread of markets. Thus, although Catholic doctrine evolved to fit the legitimation needs of the institutions and the ruling landowning class in medieval European societies, it was poorly equipped to do the same for the emerging institutions and practices of capitalism.

Along with its firm hierarchy, the enormously complex nature of the Church's dogmas impaired its capacity to respond in a supple manner to social change. A massive body of Church doctrine had evolved to supplement the sacred texts, and, as noted in Chapter 4, once doctrines are written down, they become more impervious to alteration. The strikingly inflexible character of Church doctrine is evident in the fact that, while financial markets spread throughout Europe and grew to be vital to its economic dynamism, both canon law and often civil law in Catholic countries condemned taking interest on loans until the eighteenth century. Charging interest remained generally censured for some time afterward (Muller 2003, 11).[3]

Catholicism was uncomfortable with profits, interest, alienable property, competitive markets, and even money. But why? As noted in Chapter 6, aristocratic landlords grounded their privileges in their noble birth, and the societies they dominated likewise depicted everyone else's status as a "born-to" condition. Status was given, not earned or achieved, and it could not be changed. Religion evolved to serve as an ideology legitimating this unalterable hierarchical inequality. The problem with markets is that they put "born-to" status hierarchies in danger. Those who work hard and are clever in markets might become wealthy and improve their relative social standing. They might even become richer than the aristocratic landlords and use their wealth to undermine hereditary status relationships and usurp the aristocracy's political power and privileges. Accordingly, in aristocratic, landlord-dominated societies, a strong anti-market animus prevailed.

Commercial activity also grated upon the Church's vision of society as harmonious and caring. It is manifest that the interests of participants in market transactions are conflictual, the buyer seeking the lowest price, the seller the highest. Even if an exchange benefits both willing parties, its process represents opposed interests. Catholic thought therefore characterized markets as base and corrupting, requiring behavior that was inappropriate for a full member of the community, much less a dignified and morally righteous one.

This disdain for markets was expressed by countless scholars dating back to antiquity. In the early Confucian conception of four social orders, merchants were at the bottom. In Plato's *Republic*, Socrates asserts that "the more men value money-making, the less they value virtue" (1968, Book 1). Aristotle wrote that "citizens should not live a vulgar or a merchant's way of life, for this sort of way of life is ignoble and contrary to virtue" (1962, 1328, b38). Both Plato and Aristotle expressed the prevailing ideology in the premodern understanding of market-based exchanges: markets result in zero-sum outcomes, where someone's gain is someone else's loss. It is, therefore, inherently unfair. As Aristotle expressed this, trade is "justly to be censured, because the gain in which it results . . . is made at the expense of other men" (1962, 1258a, 28). Augustine contended that "to wish to buy cheap and to sell

---

[3] Proscribing the taking of interest was common in premodern societies. Following the Quran's prohibition, this remains true in contemporary Islamic nations.

dear is common, but it is a common vice" (quoted in Tawney 1926, 180). The biblical book of Ecclesiastes says, "As a stake is driven firmly into a fissure between stones, so sin is wedged between selling and buying" (27:2). And, as shown earlier, this contempt for markets extended into the Christian era. Markets cultivate undue concern with money and material possessions, the desire for which, according to Augustine, is "one of the three principal sins of fallen men" (Suttle 1987, 460). He even declared that "business is in itself an evil." St. Jerome claimed that "a man who is a merchant can seldom if ever please God" (quoted in Tuchman 1978, 37).[4]

As a result of anti-market ideology, the determination of the terms of trade during the medieval era appeared to be based upon custom, usage, and law rather than the negotiation of traders within markets. For example, the customary price of an item might be considered the fair price. Traditional status relationships were grounded in the expectation that prices and rates of return would be honest and fair. Higgling and haggling in markets were prone to violate the imperative that prices be just, because the wiliest participant might command the better deal. Note that Mercury was not only the Roman god of commerce and profit, but also the god of deceit and thievery. This view lasted until long after the end of the Middle Ages. Anthropologist David Graeber reports that even ". . . in the century or two before [Adam] Smith's time, the English words 'truck and barter,' like their equivalents in French, Spanish, German, Dutch, and Portuguese, literally meant 'to trick, bamboozle, or rip off'" (2012, 34).

The continual expansion of impersonal, competitive markets progressively shattered the traditional sense of community. Rather than seeing oneself and others as part of a moral community, in the increasing market encounters, buyers and sellers came to see themselves as standing alone, one against the other, on opposite sides of the market. Market participants shrewdly look to their own self-interest, or, as Nietzsche wrote, they develop ". . . the custom of comparing, measuring, and calculating power against power" (1887, 70).

Catholicism, like most religions in landlord-dominated societies, viewed calculating self-interest as sinful and socially unacceptable. Without proper checks, it could lead to greed, one of the seven deadly sins. Behavior should be directed to the well-being of others. Although markets may not actually

---

[4] Not all expressions of anti-market attitudes were clearly religious or in terms of ethics. Julius Caesar, privileging warriorhood, viewed participation in commerce as tending toward the "effeminization of the spirit" (McCloskey 2007, 262).

THE ORIGINS AND DYNAMICS OF INEQUALITY

make their participants more self-interested, they compel them to become more conscious of it. To not lose out, they must make market decisions in a rational calculating manner, being aware of their own best interest. If charity for their trading partners guides their market decisions, they will lose out to more coldly calculating self-interested traders. Should their charitable behavior persist, markets will send them away in financial ruin.

This anti-market ideology was highly useful to the aristocratic landowning class. Its arguments served to curb the rise of commercial activity and reduce the threat to their commanding position atop rigid hierarchical societies. Further, by casting traders in an unflattering light, the ideology could legitimate the expropriation of assets or even the destruction of the merchant class. Chapter 5 described how this was carried out in Eastern Europe beginning in the fifteenth century.

Because the prevailing ideology was antagonistic toward markets, they were, to a considerable extent, relegated to resident aliens, especially Jews in Europe. Consequently, those who engaged in the unsavory activities of trade and finance were also ethnically different. Christians of all classes viewed them with suspicion, if not odium. "The merchant . . . enjoyed the double unpopularity of an alien and a parasite" (Tawney 1926, 37). Historian David Priestland writes that "German folktales were full of simple, honest peasants using violence to get their own back against clever, deceitful Jewish traders" (2012, 50). Markets require money, and "in early medieval iconography money was often connected with excrement and portrayed as filthy and disgusting . . . [and] Jews themselves were often depicted as foul-smelling" (Muller 2003, 10).[5]

Protestantism Filling a New Ideological Niche

> Riches are only dangerous when they tempt us to idleness and sinful indulgence; and striving for riches is only dangerous when it is done with the aim of later leading a carefree life of pleasure.
> —Max Weber, *The Protestant Ethic and the Spirit of Capitalism* (1905, 110)

---

[5] Political scientist and historian Jerry Muller writes that "St Bernard of Clairvaux, the leader of the Cistercian order in the middle of the twelfth century, referred to the taking of usury as 'jewing' (*judaizare*), and chastised Christian moneylenders as 'baptized Jews'" (2003, 10).

Although the Church railed against commerce and profit-making, it doggedly pursued its own mercenary interests. Tawney writes: "From the middle of the thirteenth century a continuous wail arises against the iniquity of the Church, and its burden may be summed up in one word, 'avarice.' At Rome, everything is for sale" (1926, 32). Martin Luther's critique of the sale of indulgences—boons purporting to shorten the length of time a soul would have to spend in purgatory—was an attack on the Church's corruption in commodifying salvation.

Despite religions' condemnation of profit-making and markets generally, the continuing expansion of commerce inevitably drew Christians into its sphere. The temptation to grow rich by turning a profit became increasingly seductive as the opportunities multiplied. But Christians who entered the marketplace found themselves behaving in a manner that conflicted with the religious value system they shared with their community of faith, the identity group in which they had been born, baptized, and raised. They risked suffering not only the disapprobation of their communities, but also what psychologists call cognitive dissonance, an uncomfortable awareness that their behavior stood at odds with their internalized beliefs and attitudes. This tension created a niche, an *environmental legitimation space*, where convincing doctrines that could recast their market behavior as proper and virtuous would be favored, or, in Darwinian terms, "selected." Their social and psychological condition would be much improved by a new variant of their faith that was less hostile to the market sphere and more congenial to nontraditional ways of thinking and acting in the new commercial order. The personal stakes were high. As psychologist Elliot Aronson puts it, "When a person reduces his dissonance, he defends his ego, and keeps a positive self-image" (1989, 135).

The metaphor of biological evolution helps clarify the extraordinary success of the Protestant Reformation. As discussed in Chapter 4, just as mutations continually occur in the biological world, so, too, do new ideas—mutated thoughts—continually spring forth in the social world. In the domains of both biology and ideas, however, almost all mutations are condemned to perish by the environmental conditions into which they emerge. Without nourishing physical environments, biological mutations cannot survive and reproduce. The same dynamic holds for new ideas. Without nourishing cultural and socioeconomic environments, most innovations will be dismissed as stupid or uninteresting, and some will be attacked as the bizarre or dangerous products of deranged or evil minds.

Certain new ideas that were viewed as offensive or threatening to those with social and political power were likely to be considered heretical. Their authors might be exiled, imprisoned, tortured, or condemned to a horrible death, for instance, by being burned at the stake. In both the biological world and the world of ideas, almost all mutations fail to find salubrious environmental niches where they can survive and reproduce or spread.[6]

It is noteworthy, in this context, that new ideas contesting aspects of Catholic doctrine and practice were hardly unprecedented. There were significant attempts to reform the Roman Catholic Church before Luther came onto the scene. Most notable were the movements led by Peter Waldo, excommunicated by Pope Lucius III in 1184; John Wycliffe, a fourteenth-century scholastic philosopher whose heretical writings were posthumously banned by the Council of Constance in 1415; and Jan Hus, burned at the stake in 1414. But these earlier variations on (or mutations of) Christianity—these earlier *protests*—came forth in inopportune places and times, before sufficiently hospitable niches had evolved. But the Protestant Reformation launched by Martin Luther in Germany and Jean Calvin in Switzerland had the good fortune of taking place when the times were ripe. Environmentally friendly political, social, economic, and cultural niches were maturing, and, despite its most strenuous efforts, the Church could no longer suppress the new ideas.[7] A rising bourgeois class stood in need of new doctrines that would reconcile their core religious beliefs with the novel institutions and practices in which they were thriving. They needed a modified Christianity that would free them from cognitive dissonance and the disapprobation of their priests and fellow citizens. The transition was radical, but far from total. They could remain good Christians and embrace most of the dogmas of traditional Christianity. In this manner, the *protest* doctrines expressed by Luther and, especially, Calvin found a fertile habitat within which to survive, reproduce, and spread over most of northern Europe.[8]

[6] Herbert Spencer was novel in recognizing this character of the world of ideas: "Ideas wholly foreign to [a] social state cannot be evolved, and if introduced from without cannot get accepted, or if accepted die out. Hence the advanced ideas when once established act upon society: yet the establishment of such ideas depends on the fitness of society for receiving them. Practically the popular character and social state determine what ideas shall be current" (quoted in Sweezy 2001).

[7] A similar interpretation was expressed by historian Max I. Dimont: "Though Protestantism had begun as a strictly religious reform movement, the people behind the new economic forces seized the Reformation and bent it to their own economic needs. . . . As the modes of production changed, the people responsible for these changes searched for a state that would legalize what they were doing and for a religion that would sanctify it. They adopted the Protestant religion and made it embrace the capitalist state. The two went hand in hand like bride and groom" (2004, Chapter 6).

[8] Although the theological doctrines of both Luther and Calvin served to establish a legitimating framework for emerging capitalism, there were substantial and important differences in their

The basic attitudes and values that differentiated Protestantism from Catholicism were those generated by market expansion. Montesquieu was one of the first intellectuals to recognize the mentality and behavior that markets cultivate:

> the spirit of commerce brings with it the spirit of frugality, of economy, of moderation, of work, of wisdom, of tranquility, of order, and of regularity. In this manner, as long as this spirit prevails, the riches it creates do not have any bad effect. (quoted in Hirschman 1997, 71)

In an important sense, Protestantism served as a transitional religion between a predominantly traditional agricultural world dominated by aristocratic landlords and legitimated by Catholic doctrine, and a more modern commercial one dominated by the bourgeoisie and legitimated by secular thought. In doing so, it constricted the sphere of the sacred. Sociologist Peter Berger writes:

> Protestantism may be described in terms of an immense shrinkage in the scope of the sacred in reality, as compared with its Catholic adversary. . . . Protestantism ceased praying for the dead. . . . [It] divested itself as much as possible from the three most ancient and most powerful concomitants of the sacred—mystery, miracle, and magic. This process has been aptly caught in the phrase "disenchantment of the world" [and] God's sovereign grace [is] the only true miracle in the Protestant universe. (1967, 111, 112)

Expanding markets had freed more and more people from feudal limitations but had isolated them in economic insecurity. They were forced to focus relatively more on material survival and relatively less on spiritual truths. To survive in competitive markets, individuals had to place greater weight on

contributions to what became the Protestant world. As Tawney noted, "Whereas Lutheranism had been socially conservative, deferential to established political authorities, the exponent of a personal, almost a quietistic, piety, Calvinism was an active and radical force. It was a creed which sought not merely to purify the individual, but to reconstruct Church and State, and to renew society by penetrating every department of life, public as well as private, with the influence of religion" (1926, 91). Also highlighting their differences, Muller writes that "Luther's economic thought, reflected in his *Long Sermon on Usury* of 1520 and his tract *On Trade and Usury* of 1524, was hostile to commerce in general and international trade in particular, and stricter than the canonists in his condemnation of moneylending. John Calvin took issue with the Scholastic view of money as sterile, and permitted the lending of money up to a fixed maximum rate of 5 percent, but remained hostile to those who lent money by profession, and banished them from Geneva" (2003, 12).

their own judgment and make decisions and often behave contrary to the dictates of traditional morality. Thus, survival itself required a more secular view of reality.

Although Protestantism generally evolved most rigorously where capitalism was emerging most robustly, this was not always the case. For instance, market expansion undergirded Renaissance Italy, where the people remained overwhelmingly Catholic, although leading intellectuals of the time tended to think in secular terms. The niches in which Protestantism thrived had more dimensions than the rise of commercialism alone. For instance, Protestantism developed along fault lines of Germanic and Romance languages.[9] These linguistic differences, and the ethnic differences that accompanied them, may have affected groups' predispositions to embrace or reject Protestantism. But much more important may have been the disparate character types that developed in two distinct climatic regions. Peoples who lived in the harsh climate of the North would naturally be more receptive to a religious sanctification of hard work and asceticism. Their survival depended upon both. They faced long, hard winters, and, no matter how hungry they might be in the months before spring, they had to exercise self-control not to eat the seed corn or the animals pregnant with offspring. Should they yield to the temptation to do so, even at the edge of starvation, their future was doomed. The unforgiving climate of the North matched the severely judgmental Protestant God and the discipline he demanded. The impact of these cultural and climatic variables arguably complemented the effect of rising commercialism in forming socioeconomic niches favorable to Protestantism.

Until very recent times, rulers could not retain political power without the support of religious leaders. Indeed, during much of early civilization, state authority and religious authority were fused in priest-rulers, even to the point of rulers portraying themselves as gods. After the fall of Rome, political authority became fragmented, leaving the Catholic Church as the only institution recognized throughout Europe. This privileged monopolistic command over religious authority empowered it to grant or deny legitimacy to political rulers.

The Church provided European rulers with legitimacy for hundreds of years, and, as the only available legitimator, it charged a monopoly price. In exchange for religious validation, rulers had to concede a degree of political power and permit the Church to hold considerable control over economic

---

[9] Although Calvin was francophone, his influence was predominantly in Germanic linguistic areas.

resources, especially land. The state also awarded tax exemptions and allowed the Church to take part of the surplus as tithes (one-tenth the value of output). In competition with rulers and landlords, the Church struggled to appropriate as much surplus as possible, not only from its tithes, but also from the slaves and serfs it exploited on its extensive lands, and from the voluntary contributions of the faithful.

The extraordinary wealth of the Church bears witness to its success in garnering surplus, and that success testifies, in turn, to the exceptional importance of ideology. The Church's portion of the surplus was, in large part, what the Church extorted from the state and the landowning aristocracy in exchange for the ideology that enabled them to exploit the cultivators. Indeed, it was the Church's avaricious attempt to extract yet more surplus through the sale of indulgences that triggered Luther's decisive move toward rupture.

The growing popularity of the new religious doctrines tempted rulers with the prospect of switching their allegiance from the Catholic Church to the far less costly Protestant alternative for their own legitimation. This constituted another favorable characteristic of the niche in which the Reformation would thrive. Protestantism promised Europe's bellicose nation-states the larger share of surplus they needed. Military demands incessantly pressured rulers to find new sources of revenue. Confiscating the Church's property— especially the substantial landed wealth held by monasteries—offered them a tempting windfall. Religious competition in the market for legitimation not only lowered its cost, it also served to strengthen the state's autonomy and authority.[10] Secular rulers also benefited from another aspect of the ongoing cultural change: university students increasingly prepared to enter public administration rather than religious offices. Building construction shifted relatively from religious to secular structures (Cantoni, Dittmar, and Yuchtman 2017).

Of the two main variants of Protestantism, Lutheranism and Calvinism, the latter held greater potential for legitimating commercial institutions and practices. Tawney describes the social environment in which Calvinism thrived and rapidly reproduced as follows:

---

[10] Although the rise of Protestantism reduced the cost of religious legitimation, it also decreased its effectiveness and created space into which secular doctrines such as those of Mercantilism could arise and complement religion's ideological functioning. Chapter 8 shifts attention to the rise of these secular legitimating doctrines.

Like early Christianity and modern socialism, Calvinism was largely an urban movement; like them, in its earlier days, it was carried from country to country partly by emigrant traders and workmen; and its stronghold was precisely in those social groups to which the traditional scheme of social ethics, with its treatment of economic interests as a quite minor aspect of human affairs, must have seemed irrelevant or artificial. As was to be expected in the exponents of a faith which had its headquarters at Geneva, and later its most influential adherents in great business centers, like Antwerp with its industrial hinterland, London, and Amsterdam, its leaders addressed their teaching, not of course exclusively, but none the less primarily, to the classes engaged in trade and industry, who formed the most modern and progressive elements in the life of the age. (1926, 293)

Competition for Truth and Meaning

For first of all we must prepare a Natural and Experimental History, sufficient and good; and this is the foundation of all; for we are not to imagine or suppose, but to discover, what nature does or may be made to do.

—Francis Bacon, *Novum Organon* (1620, 127)

Throughout the Middle Ages, the Church served as the custodian of knowledge and meaning, holding monopoly power over both. It also had a virtual monopoly on literacy, which not only helped enforce its intellectual hegemony, but also made its clerics useful to political authorities for administrative work. Should the laity have a pressing question concerning any aspect of reality or spirituality, it was to the Church that they turned. The Church had all the answers, and those answers were definitive. Any further inquiry was viewed as "adultery of the soul."[11]

Challenged by the Reformation and the rise of science, the Church did not relinquish its monopoly on truth and meaning without a ferocious fight. It relentlessly persecuted and prosecuted heretics. The tendency to respond with violence to actual or potential opposition is, of course, common to all

---

[11] A parallel is found in the decline of the Islamic Golden Age when an extreme religious view gained strength claiming that since all knowledge is contained in the Quran, further scientific investigations are pointless, if not sinful. Accordingly, education was reduced to memorizing the Quran.

power, including that over thought. Monopolists will always strive to liquidate all competitors. In Europe, between 1550 and 1700, over 80,000 persons were prosecuted for witchcraft, and about half of them were executed, often by being burned at the stake (Becker, Pfaff, and Rubin 2016, 39). Many Protestants suffered torture at the hands of the Catholic hierarchy, yet, when they gained the upper hand, they willingly inflicted torture and death on their own heretics and enemies. Conversely, peace reigns when monopoly power is unopposed. There is no evidence of widespread prosecution of witches or other heretics during the so-called Dark Ages when the Catholic Church held an uncontested monopoly.

Doctrinal competition became more widespread and intense with the growth of commercial society. The Church countered by launching the formidable Inquisition to retain its monopoly control. The Inquisition began in twelfth-century France to eliminate the Cathars and the Waldensians. It also targeted the Spiritual Franciscans, the Hussites, and the Beguines. It expanded and greatly intensified its battle when the Protestantism Reformation and secular science came onto the scene. Although continually losing terrain, it sustained this struggle into the early nineteenth century.

The breakdown of the Church's monopoly on truth and meaning portended far-reaching consequences for the development of human knowledge. No longer was learning forced to be consistent with the Church's dogma. Skepticism of all traditional authority—including questions about who had the right to rule—could be voiced more safely.

This skepticism expressed an epistemological problem: How can we have confidence that our knowledge claims are correct? The Church had provided a solid foundation for answering this question with conviction. But knowledge competition destroyed that confidence. The implications were enormous. How could there be certainty about anything, including ethical values? The loss of an authoritative source of knowledge and a solid basis for thinking and acting was profoundly distressing. But there was also a positive outcome: this uncertainty kept the doors wide open for unimpeded inquiry.[12]

---

[12] Bacon's empiricism and Descartes's rationalism were the most concerted and influential early secular attempts to resolve the knowledge crisis created by the waning of the Church's monopoly over truth and meaning. But their resolutions were soon found inadequate, and ever since, the search for a way to provide a solid foundation for our knowledge claims has been a dominant concern of philosophy. The last influential attempt at resolution was logical positivism. But logical positivism was discredited and fell into disfavor over a half century ago. The epistemological crisis unleashed by the Church's loss of monopoly control over truth and meaning endures (Wisman 2001).

The spirit of inquiry (and the self-confidence to seek answers) advanced with the expansion of literacy that Protestantism greatly stimulated by encouraging people to read the sacred texts for themselves. Previously, churchmen alone could read the scriptures, a stricture that was reinforced by the use of Latin. With the advent of Protestantism, the sacred texts were translated into the vernacular. The spread of the printing press also made them more widely and inexpensively available.

With the rise of knowledge competition, religion came, over time, to conform ever more comfortably to the mandates of competitive capitalism.[13] The Protestant Reformation altered social rules and practices in ways that were felicitous for economic dynamism. Religion was, as Tawney wrote, "converted from the keystone which holds together the social edifice into one department within it, and the idea of a rule of right is replaced by economic expediency as the arbiter of policy and the criterion of conduct" (1926, 228).

Protestantism was also supportive of science in its more secular outlook on the world. In this sense, it helped recover aspects of secularization that had been conveyed in the ancient books of the Old Testament but repressed by the ascendancy of Catholicism. Berger writes:

> Catholic Christianity, both Latin and Greek, may be seen as an arresting and retrogressive step in the unfolding of the drama of secularization, although it preserved within it (at least in the Latin West) the secularizing potential, if only by virtue of its preservation of the Old Testament canon.... The Protestant Reformation . . . may . . . be understood as a powerful reemergence of precisely those secularizing forces that have been "contained" by Catholicism, not only replicating the Old Testament in this, but going decisively beyond it. (1967, 124)

The loss of the Church's monopoly on truth and meaning paralleled and reinforced the loss of the aristocracy's monopoly on status. In both instances, basic foundations were severely weakened: what to believe in matters of faith and morals, and how to think, dress, and behave in society, where prestige is positively correlated with sexual attractiveness. (Recall the biological imperative to send one's genes into the future.) As markets expanded and the

---

[13] Religion, like other commodities, had to be marketed. Children almost invariably retain the religious affiliations of their parents, at least nominally, but in growing up they inevitably become aware of other options. Given customers' strong brand loyalty, the commodity of religion had to be produced, packaged, and peddled all the more energetically.

new commercial class gained the ascendancy, the Church and the aristocracy grew less influential. The state became correspondingly stronger.

Prior to the rise and spread of markets, the Church relied on secular power to guarantee its monopoly position. The Church's monopoly power was most secure where it was assisted by secular authorities in enforcing its doctrinal claims, punishing heretics, and banishing rivals. The Church and political rulers generally maintained a symbiotic relationship, with the Church providing legitimation for the rulers' right to secular power (e.g., acknowledging the monarch's divine right to rule) in exchange for the rulers backing up the Church's religious monopoly and permitting it to capture a substantial share of society's surplus.

The doctrinal rigidity of Catholicism handicapped its ability to coordinate efficiently with the rising nation-state that evolved with and was nourished by commercial expansion. The availability of a cheaper substitute for legitimation—Protestantism—empowered the state to force the Church to make concessions, such as relieving elites from paying tithes or adhering to other religious obligations (Becker, Pfaff, and Rubin 2016, 12). If the Church took less of society's surplus, there remained more for elites to expropriate or the state to tax away. In addition, the state itself came to stand in competition with the Church as a source of truth and meaning. States are always censoring, but, as society changed, the European nation-states relied less on the Church to legitimate their censorship. However, in reducing the Church's power, it became more difficult to control thought effectively.

Protestantism "attracted believers and princes by lowering prices in the market for salvation and for legitimacy" (Cantoni, Dittmar, and Yuchtman 2017, 11). However, for these lower prices to become available, a new class embracing Protestantism had to come into existence and be of such importance that rulers would protect their religion from the Church's repression. It is this new class's need for respectability and status concordant with their wealth that provided the "protest" religions with the specific contours they came to express.

Hard Work and the Bourgeoisie's Social Status

It is better that a man should tyrannize over his bank balance than over his fellow-citizens; and whilst the former is sometimes

denounced as being but a means to the latter, sometimes at least it is
an alternative.

—John Maynard Keynes, *The General Theory of
Employment, Interest, and Money* (1936, 374)

The two principal elements of what sociologist Max Weber called "the
Protestant ethic" were hard work and thriftiness. Both are grounded in the
rising bourgeoisie's quest for social status. Behaving in socially approved
ways is a prerequisite for achieving status. From an evolutionary perspective, those with higher status enjoy disproportionate access to resources and
members of the opposite sex, enabling them to have more and better cared-
for progeny who will carry their genes into the future. Thus, in Darwinian
terms genes favoring conformity with conventional standards of behavior
are "selected" for transmission down the generations. Humans are innately
predisposed to conduct themselves in accordance with their community's
values and expectations.

Protestantism's work ethic played a critical role in securing social status
for the rising bourgeoisie. In doing so, it contributed to the nourishing environment in which Protestantism thrived. The bourgeoisie in Europe owed
its rising status not to birth, as was the case with the aristocracy, but to work,
which aristocrats considered demeaning. It is not surprising, then, that the
religion that rose to support the institutions and behavior of this new class
would especially honor work.[14]

The privileged position of work was characteristic of both the Lutheran
and Calvinist expressions of Protestantism. But Calvinism had a special
twist, holding that God had determined in advance whether each individual
would be saved or damned. In Calvin's words, "By the decree of God, for the
manifestation of His glory, some men . . . are predestined unto everlasting
life, and others foreordained to everlasting death" (quoted in Weber 1905,
70). No actions on the part of the individual could change the outcome. This

---

[14] Further evidence that the values espoused by Protestantism resulted from their utility in legitimizing rising capitalist institutions and behavior is the fact that these values also come forth in other
cultures where a significant merchant class emerges. A strong Calvinistic-like work ethic developed in Japan among merchants as their power and status rose in the seventeenth century (Landes
1998, 363). There, too, an emerging hard-working bourgeoisie sought status in a social world where
the highest status was conferred by birth. Historian David Priestland identifies other instances of
"merchant-friendly" religions: "Buddhism, Jainism, and some forms of Islam also appealed to
merchants for similar reasons: they all rejected wasteful ceremony and priestly hierarchy and often,
with them, martial glory and aristocratic display. They also valued literacy and encouraged laypeople,
not just priests, to read sacred texts" (2012, 47).

doctrine of predestination or election left individuals in the agonizing position of not knowing whether they were among the saved or the damned.

Understandably, all would seek some hint of their fate. It could be expected that worldly success would be seen as a sign of God's favor, and poverty as the opposite. And hard work offered the best chance of achieving material success in an evolving commercial world. In this manner, spiritual insecurity endowed Protestantism's work ethic with special force. As Tawney wrote, "success in business is in itself almost a sign of spiritual grace, for it is proof that a man has labored faithfully in his vocation, and that 'God has blessed his trade'" (1926, 204).

Catholicism had disparaged the pursuit of material success. Its teaching is exemplified by New Testament passages such as 1 Timothy 6:8–10: "If we have food and clothing, we shall be content with that. Those who want to be rich are falling into temptation and into a trap and into many foolish and harmful desires, which plunge them into ruin and destruction. For the love of money is the root of all evil. . . ." In Matthew 10:17, a rich man approaches Jesus and asks: "Good Teacher, what must I do to share in everlasting life?" Jesus answers: "Go and sell what you have and give to the poor; you will then have treasure in heaven. After that, come and follow me." Or again in Matthew 19:24: "No servant can serve two masters. Either he will hate the one and love the other or be attentive to the one and despise the other. You cannot give yourself to God and money." Such scriptural passages capture what was generally the premodern view concerning acquisitiveness, and especially commerce. Note, for instance, Aquinas's agreement with Aristotle that "trade, insofar as it aims at making profits, is most reprehensible, since the desire for gain knows no bounds but reaches into the infinite" (quoted in Muller 2003, 8).[15]

This devaluation of wealth-seeking comported with the Church's view that behavior should uphold the moral conditions of the just order. These ideas jointly served ideologically to legitimate the privileged position of elites at the top of a frozen status hierarchy. Material well-being is secondary to appropriate behavior as determined by one's social position within the community, and any challenge to the established social order is an affront to justice.

---

[15] Aquinas and other Schoolmen of the late Middle Ages struggled to make Catholic doctrine more concordant with evolving commercial institutions and behavior. Their attitudes became more relaxed toward private property, markets, and even the taking of interest on lent money. Although their work had an effect within the Church's intellectual community, there is scant evidence that it filtered down to the understanding of everyday practicing Catholics or even to the front-line priests who adhered to, taught, and preached the scriptures to them.

Distributive justice requires that shares be appropriate to individuals' social ranks. Wealth, in particular, was considered appropriate for those whose "born-to" status placed them among the elite. But good Christians were not to attempt to increase their wealth and improve their social status. To do so was to be guilty of "the cardinal sins of *avaritia* (avarice) and *luxuria* (lechery)" (Muller 2003, 8).

Further, the premodern presumption was that society's total material wealth is fixed, so anyone's gain is someone else's loss. Thus, wealth-seeking behavior generates social discord. Consequently, the hard work that enabled members of the bourgeoisie to improve their material status could not win ecclesiastical approval. The social cost of the Church's devaluing entrepreneurial behavior that might raise someone's relative position was to stymie incentives and stifle potential economic growth. It is understandable, then, that members of the rising bourgeoisie would find themselves drawn toward a reformulated version of Christianity that would ennoble work while enabling them to embrace the most central elements of their traditional faith. This is precisely what Protestantism did. Work became a calling, a duty set by God, as opposed to a selfish means of getting rich. The magnitude and durability of the turnabout in attitudes toward acquisitiveness is evident in Samuel Johnson's striking proclamation, in the mid-eighteenth century, that "there are few ways in which a man can be more innocently employed than in getting money" (quoted in Appleby 2011, 91).

While the first component of the Protestant ethic was hard work, the second was asceticism. Self-denial constrained consumption and made savings available for investment, which further augmented the material success resulting from hard work. Protestantism was not troubled by wealth as long as it was not squandered on frivolous consumption. Asceticism made it clear that one's wealth was not earned for sensual ends: "The most urgent *task* was the eradication of *uninhibited* indulgence in instinctive pleasure" (Weber 1905, 81).[16] This made the accumulation of wealth more consonant with traditional Christian values hostile to materialism in general and wealth-seeking in particular. Asceticism gave early Protestants a shield behind which they could accumulate wealth in fulfillment of an obligation to

---

[16] This was especially extreme with sexuality: "For Puritanism, sexual asceticism differs only in degree, not in principle, from monastic asceticism, and since it also applies to conjugal life, is more far-reaching than the latter. For even in marriage, sexual intercourse is *only* permissible as the means willed by God for the increase of his glory, in accordance with the command: 'Be fruitful and multiply'" (Weber 1905, 107).

God, as opposed to doing so in the interest of physical pleasure or in pursuit of status through conspicuous consumption. Wealth would not, therefore, draw attention away from God. The combination of hard work and frugality provided a bridge between spirituality and worldly affairs.

Asceticism also legitimated inequality. Weber claimed that

> . . . the power of religious asceticism made available to [the businessman] sober, conscientious, and unusually capable workers, who were devoted to work as the divinely willed purpose in life. In addition, he was given the comforting assurance that the unequal distribution of this world's goods was the special work of the providence of God, who by means of these distinctions, and his "particular" grace, was working out his secret purposes, of which we know nothing. (1905, 119)

Although the virtue of asceticism barred the bourgeois from seeking status through conspicuous consumption, wealth nevertheless communicated one's good standing because material success signified having worked hard and saved. Importantly, accumulated wealth could also be interpreted as a sign that one had been chosen for eternal salvation. By contrast, the inherited wealth of the aristocracy was seen as encouraging idleness. In fact, the positive view of work and its corollary, a negative attitude toward inheritance, eventually penetrated predominantly Catholic countries as their bourgeoisie expanded. Early modern society's predilection for earned wealth over inherited wealth persists in today's embrace of meritocracy.

Nonetheless, the aristocracy lived on, continuing to believe that work was beneath their dignity and thus suitable only for lesser humans. Political economist Albert Hirschman writes that "the very contempt in which economic activities were held led to the conviction, in spite of much evidence to the contrary, that [such activities] could not possibly have much potential in any area of human endeavor and were incapable of causing either good *or evil* on a grand scale" (1997, 58). Even as late as the mid-eighteenth century a French essayist, the marquis de Vauvenargues, claimed that "a man of quality, by fighting acquires wealth more honorably *and quickly* than a meaner man by work" (quoted in Hirschman 1997, 58). The aristocracy continued to view military and political service as the only fitting occupations for nobility. These views would long survive among the landed aristocracy.

The Protestant ethic evolved into a code of conduct that would guide members of the commercial class in their pursuit of social approbation, respectability, and status. It provided tradesmen and manufacturers with "a sense of dignity and righteousness, armor in a world of anticommercial prejudices." It made "a new kind of man—rational, ordered, diligent, productive [and] it generalized [these virtues] among its adherents, who judged one another by conformity to these standards" (Landes 1998, 176, 177). These virtues also made behavior more predictable and reliable.

Luther, by holding that the best way to serve God is by performing one's occupation as well as possible, swept away the idea—common to classical antiquity and the Catholic Church—that contemplation is superior to work. Privileging work gave worldly expression to the concept set forth in Genesis that nature exists to be transformed by human ingenuity and labor. The human calling was not to spend one's life in thought, but to tame and craft the material world to meet human purposes in accordance with God's plan. Humans had been created in the image of a working God, and their obligation was to participate in furthering God's creation. This celebration of work devalued attempts to acquire status through contemplation, just as the elevation of asceticism discouraged conspicuous spending.

By privileging work and rejecting the aristocracy's pursuit of status through conspicuous consumption, Protestants, in principle, if not always in practice, refused to play the status game according to traditional aristocratic criteria. Their quest for social status was to be differently exercised. And it would be grounded in a powerful moral stance, one that was appropriate to a commercial world. Bourgeois morality emphasized self-discipline, hard work, frugality, creditworthiness, caution, trust, and sobriety.

The need to project an image of prudence and sobriety was, of course, critical to the merchants' and financiers' success as businessmen. Such behavior communicated trustworthiness. It also led them to find fellowship within coffee shops as opposed to ale houses.[17] As cultural historian Wolfgang Schivelbusch puts it, "Coffee awakened a drowsing humanity from its alcoholic stupor to middle-class common sense and industry—so seventeenth-century propaganda would have it" (1993, 34). Coffee houses sprung up everywhere in the Protestant world as places to read newspapers, gather information, and conduct business. Around the year 1700, for instance, there were about 3,000 coffee houses in London, approximately one for every 200 people (1993, 51).

---

[17] "From the seventeenth century on, the bourgeoisie found unrestrained drinking increasingly offensive ... [and increasingly so such that] [i]n Victorian England stopping in at a pub became almost as scandalous as visiting a brothel" (Schivelbusch 1993, 148).

Among the nobility and in Catholic southern Europe, by contrast, chocolate was the preferred drink. Schivelbusch writes:

> Aristocratic society preferred to drink its chocolate at breakfast. Ideally it was served in the boudoir, in bed if possible. . . . Whereas the middle-class family sat erect at the breakfast table [and drank coffee], with a sense of disciplined propriety, the essence of the chocolate ritual was fluid, lazy, languid motion. If coffee virtually shook drinkers awake for the workday that lay ahead, chocolate was meant to create an intermediary state between lying down and sitting up. Illustrations of the period nicely portray this ideal of an idle class's morning-long awakening to the rigors of studied leisure. (1993, 92)

Further, whereas coffee was presumed to suppress erotic urges and favor work, chocolate was believed to serve as an aphrodisiac (Schivelbusch 1993, 92).

Competitive markets compel merchants to be ever on the lookout for the best deal. The origins of their counterparties in commercial transactions are of minor importance; it matters little if they are of higher or lower status, or of a different ethnicity, religion, or race. What counts is the best price. Accordingly, merchants have an interest in treating all market participants with the respect due their equals. Merchants esteemed tolerance, friendliness, and politeness, expressing an easygoing cordiality that enabled them to trade with anybody. They disparaged the aristocratic tendencies toward arrogance, showiness, and anger. They favored reason over passions. Philosopher David Hume, for instance, held that those of "middle station" were more prone to follow "the calm voice of reason," since "the great are too much immersed in pleasure, and the poor too much occupied in providing for the necessities of life." Only those of the middle could exercise the virtues of "generosity, humanity, affability, and charity" (1742, 5, 5). Similarly, long before Weber set forth his famous thesis, Friedrich Hegel understood Protestantism as exchanging the Catholic vow of poverty for a commitment to "the activity of supporting oneself through reason and industriousness, and rectitude in economic relations and in the use of one's fortune" (quoted in Muller 2003, 150).

Notable social critics commented on the place of tolerance in commerce. Jonathan Swift reported that in the Commonwealths and other free countrys one may see in a see port, as many relligions as shipps. The same god is there differently whorship'd by jews, mahometans, heathens, catholiques, quackers, anabaptistes, which write strenuously one against another, but deal together freely and with trust and peace, like good players who after having humour'd their parts and fought one against another upon the stage, spend the rest of their time in drinking together. (quoted in Muller 2003, 28)

Writing to a friend in Paris, Voltaire claimed of the market-oriented city of The Hague that "the opera here is detestable . . . but in its stead I watch Calvinist ministers, Arminians, Socinians, rabbis, and Anabaptists who talk together quite miraculously, and with every reason."[18] Voltaire further wrote:

Come into the London exchange, a place more respectable than many a court. You will see assembled representatives of every nation for the benefit of mankind. Here the Jew, the Mohametan and the Christian deal with one another as if they were of the same religion, and reserve the name "infidel" for those who go bankrupt. (quoted in Muller 2003, 27–28, 29)

Commercial deals appeared as exercises in freedom as well as tolerance. For an exchange to take place, both buyer and seller must agree. Each is equally free to say no. This contrasts with the coercion inherent in the state's taxation and tribute, the aristocrats' rent and fees, and the Church's tithes.

With the Enlightenment, Protestantism's stern austerity began to yield to a more relaxed attitude. Wealth-seeking even came to be seen as an ethically appropriate pursuit that contributes to happiness. By the latter half of the eighteenth century, Adam Smith would write in *The Theory of Moral Sentiments*, "The happiness of mankind, as well as of all other rational creatures, seems to have been the original purpose intended by the Author of nature, when he brought them into existence." The view that the goal of human life is happiness followed upon the naturalization of providence that accompanied the Enlightenment, thereby changing the human

---

[18] The highly commercialized economy of the Netherlands became one of the most open to intellectual dynamism, not only welcoming dissidents from other countries, but also welcoming foreigners generally. Appleby writes that "Holland became an intellectual center, offering refuge to dissenters, freethinkers, and a raft of cranks. The book trade flourished, fostered by the high rate of literacy in the Netherlands as well as the freedom to publish writings banned in surrounding countries. Of some one hundred thousand people living in Amsterdam, a third of them were foreigners; Portuguese, Jews, Belgians, and refugees from all over Europe" (2011, 46).

relationship to God. Smith continued, ". . . by acting according to the dictates of our moral faculties, we necessarily pursue the most effectual means for promoting the happiness of mankind, and may therefore be said, in some sense, to co-operate with the Deity, and to advance as far as in our power the plan of Providence" (1759, 166). Earlier, humans were to find fulfillment in single-minded service to God. But in God's natural world, as opposed to the spiritual realm, humans seek happiness in terms of secular pleasures and avoidance of pain, ends to which nature itself is conducive.[19] In *The Wealth of Nations*, Smith recognized that the conscious goal of an individual in seeking wealth is that person's own security, but he proposed that the simultaneous pursuit of wealth by many individuals benefits all society. Thus, individuals are "led by an invisible hand to promote an end which was no part of [their] intention" (1776, 485). Such ideas about happiness and the constructive social effects of individuals' self-serving actions in the natural world favored an optimistic view of human fate. Indeed, already at the outset of the eighteenth century, the Earl of Shaftesbury (Cooper) understood philosophy to be "the Study of Happiness" (1714).

The Poor Are to Blame for Their Poverty

> Everyone but an idiot knows that the lower classes must be kept poor
> or they will never be industrious.
> —Arthur Young, quoted by E. S. Furness in *The*
> *Position of the Laborer in a System of Nationalism* (1920, 118)

The poor had been doctrinally privileged within Catholicism. Accordingly, charity was central to the Church's mission. Indeed, Catholic communities took care of the poor in the thirteenth century to an extent that would not be matched until the twentieth (Tierney 1959, 109). Studies have suggested that the Church may have allocated up to a third of its revenues to aiding the poor. As much as half of the populations of some pre-Reformation towns may have been receiving Catholic assistance (Becker, Pfaff, and Rubin 2016, 16).

---

[19] Tawney wrote: "The law of nature had been invoked by medieval writers as a moral restraint upon economic self-interest. By the seventeenth century, a significant revolution had taken place. 'Nature' had come to connote, not divine ordinance, but human appetites, and natural rights were invoked by the individualism of the age as a reason why self-interest should be given free play" (1926, 152–53).

Graeber notes that "by the thirteenth century, the great intellectual debate was between the Franciscans and the Dominicans over 'apostolic poverty'—basically, over whether Christianity could be reconciled with property of any sort" (2012, 290). Private property did not yet have the inviolable character it was to acquire later with capitalism. It was accepted reluctantly, at best, and only with considerable reservations. In particular, private property was subject to a moral principle under which the owner held it in "trust" for God's greater designs. Aquinas went so far as to claim that, in the case of dire privation, it would be appropriate for an impoverished individual to "succor his own need by means of another's property, by taking it either openly or secretly" (quoted in Noell 2006, 156). Rather than esteeming the rich, Catholic teaching favored the poor: "Blessed are you poor, for yours is the Kingdom of God. Blessed are you who hunger, for you shall be satisfied. Blessed are you who weep, for you shall laugh" (Luke 6:20–21).

In contrast to Catholicism, Protestants in early capitalist society stigmatized the poor, especially those who, deprived of access to land or capital, often faced difficulty in finding employment. Protestantism viewed poverty as due not to social or economic conditions, but to the personal failings of the poor. Consequently, the Catholic virtue of charity gave way under Protestantism to a reduced level of concern for the poor. This view of poverty relieved the owners of productive wealth from any strong sense of responsibility to provide assistance to the poor, either individually through private charity or collectively through social welfare policy. To survive, the poor would have to find someone to hire them. The unemployed were forced to accept any form of employment, no matter how onerous, dangerous, demeaning, or ill-paid. Those unable to find jobs, or unwilling to accept those available, were treated harshly. In England, for instance, the Statute of 1536 powerfully illustrates the resulting severity toward those who were out of work. It subjected them on the first discovered offense to a public whipping in the nude, and on the second offense to whipping plus the loss of part of their right ear. On third offense, the unemployed person who was still disinclined to "put himself to labor like as a true man oweth to do [was exposed to] pains and execution of death" (Byrne 2010, 42).[20]

---

[20] A pamphleteer wrote in 1646 that "the general rule of all England is to whip and punish the wandering beggars" (Cited in (Tawney 1926, 219). In 1649, an Act was passed to provide an enterprise with the power to apprehend vagrants and to offer them the choice of a whipping or work. A generation later, politician Andrew Fletcher of Saltoun proposed that they be "sent to the galleys" (Tawney 1926, 220).

The Calvinist expression of Protestantism legitimated an especially un-charitable attitude toward the poor. According to its doctrine of election, because God had chosen the saved and the damned, one's poverty was presumably the will of God.[21] The 1647 Westminster Confession of Faith conveys a vivid sense of this doctrine: "By the decree of God, for the manifes-tation of His Good, some men and angels are predestinated unto ever-lasting life, and others foreordained to ever-lasting death" (Herztberg 1966, 53). Weber noted that "the analogy between the predestination of the few (which is, in human terms, 'unjust') and the distribution of wealth (which is equally unjust, but equally willed by God) is very clear" (1905, 200). Tawney added, "A society which reverences the attainment of riches as the supreme felicity will naturally be disposed to regard the poor as damned in the next world, if only to justify itself for making their life a hell in this" (1926, 222). Their poverty was necessary, Calvin maintained, because only if workers were kept poor would they remain obedient to God (Weber 1905, 119).

Early Protestants were "nurtured in a tradition which made discipline of character by industry and self-denial the center of its ethical scheme." Luther "denounced the demands of the beggars as blackmail" (Tawney 1926, 221, 220). The poor are not to be aided, lest charity prolong their dependency:

> That the greatest of evils is idleness . . . that the truest charity is not to en-ervate them by relief, but so to reform their characters that relief may be unnecessary—such doctrines turned severity from a sin into a duty, and froze the impulse of natural pity with the assurance that, if indulged, it would perpetuate the suffering which it sought to allay. (Tawney 1926, 221)

Reformation-era attitudes toward wealth and poverty survived well into modern times. Baptist minister Russell Conwell's best-selling book, *Acres of Diamonds*, sold 10 million copies to a US society of about 22 million households in 1915. Its extraordinary success strikingly captured the still-robust attitudes of Protestantism toward hard work, wealth, and the poor in early twentieth-century America:

---

[21] Calvinism was not unique among Abrahamic religions in adhering to predestination. Berger points out that "conceptions of divine predestination . . . developed in all the major branches of the Biblical tradition, though with particular ferocity in Islam and later in Calvinism" (1967, 75).

I say that you ought to get rich, and it is your duty to get rich. . . . Some men say, "Don't you sympathize with the poor people?" Of course I do, or else I would not have been lecturing all these years. But the number of poor who are to be sympathized with is very small. To sympathize with a man whom God has punished for his sins, thus to help him when God would still continue his punishment, is to do wrong, no doubt about it. (2004, 17)

By blaming the poor for their miserable condition and thereby dispensing the well-off from the need to be charitable, Protestantism left the bourgeoisie with more surplus to save and invest, and thus to become ever wealthier. This rejection of charity released an ideological brake on their ability to capture and use the full surplus for their own ends. Further, Protestant attitudes toward the workers insisted that wages must be kept low, ideally at subsistence, since with higher wages, workers would work less, permitting them free time and more income to spend on alcohol and other forms of sinful debauchery. Subsistence wages were essential to help the poor save their souls. Thus, low wages and poverty were in everyone's interest—the "utility of poverty."

Individualism and the Idea of Equality

All rational action is in the first place individual action. Only the individual thinks. Only the individual reasons. Only the individual acts.
       —Ludwig von Mises, Socialism: An Economic and Sociological
                                                Analysis (1988, Ch. 5)

Protestantism was the form of Christianity that European capitalism needed. Largely at ease with capitalist institutions and practices, it provided them with legitimacy. This is hardly surprising insofar as it evolved into a niche that was being created by the emerging institutions and behavior that would mature into capitalism. And, importantly, it provided social approval and self-respect to a new bourgeois class. Protestantism and aborning capitalism developed symbiotically, continually supporting and reinforcing each other.
    The evolving socioeconomic world at the end of the Middle Ages was indeed ripe for a religious movement such as the Reformation. In fact, Reformation ideas spread swiftly throughout Germany within months of the initial circulation of Martin Luther's famous Ninety-five Theses in 1517.

(Dittmar and Meisenzahl 2016, 6).[22] Their rapid dissemination was boosted by the fact that political power was highly dispersed in Germany, making it more difficult for the Church to coordinate with rulers to suppress heresy. Fortuitously, the propagation of Reformation thought was also greatly aided by widespread adoption of the printing press over most of Western Europe. The importance of the printing press was not lost on Luther, who claimed it "God's highest and ultimate gift of grace by which He would have His Gospel carried forward" (quoted in Becker, Pfaff, and Rubin 2016, 18). A study of sixteenth-century European cities found that Protestantism was significantly more likely to be adopted in those that had a printing press by 1500 (Rubin 2014).[23]

Protestantism's view of individuals as standing alone before God mirrored the growing individualism of capitalism. As individuals were pushed and pulled from the traditional communities that had provided social and psychological support, they stood increasingly alone as wage-workers in a competitive world. The defining character of individuals was less their social being, as Aristotle had seen it, but instead their individuality. As philosopher-sociologist Lucien Goldmann put it, the individual came to be seen both by himself and others as "an independent element, a sort of monad, a point of departure" (1973, 18).

Workers, however, were unlikely to celebrate their new individualism and freedom. They had been freed, as capitalism's acolytes would continually insist, from feudal fetters, from what was often the control of tyrannical landlords. However, they were also untied from communities that had provided a sort of social insurance by seeing to it that no one starved unless all did. Moreover, feudal serfs and peasants had a right to be on the land, and that right gave them access to productive wealth with which they could mix their labor to survive. The freed unfettered workers, by contrast, were freed of any ownership, control, or ready access to productive wealth. Consequently, they had to find some owner of means of production willing to provide them employment, lest they suffer extreme privation or even starvation. Those who found employment typically worked for very low wages, and many were crowded into unsanitary, crime-ridden urban slums. Those who failed to find

---

[22] The proximate cause of the Ninety-five Theses was the Church's efforts to raise revenues by selling indulgences—payments to the Church to reduce time spent in Purgatory for sins and thus speed entry into Heaven. They could be purchased for both the living and the dead. Ironically, whereas the Church looked askance at markets, it created one for salvation.

[23] Other forces aiding the success of the Reformation in Germany include the favorable attitude of intellectuals and students and the fact that the Church and the Habsburgs were preoccupied with the threats posed by the Ottomans.

employment wound up as destitute urban and rural beggars or criminals. It is hardly surprising, then, that surrounded by this social world, Thomas Hobbes would depict the natural state of humans as "solitary, poor, nasty, brutish, and short . . . a warre as is of every man against every man" (1651, i. xiii.9). Economic historian Douglass North writes of how people were

> increasingly cut off from the personal ties that had produced a common set of values. Informal agreements had to be replaced with formal contracts; the consequent structure of impersonal market organization encouraged the very behavioral characteristic that posed the Hobbesian dilemma [whereby] a formal set of rules evolved to constrain behavior in market exchange but also created conditions in which there was a large pay-off to disobeying those rules. (1982, 182)

Luther's view of the condition of humans as sinners was as harsh as Hobbes's secular view:

> Christians are rare in this world; therefore the world needs a strict, hard, temporal government that will compel and constrain the wicked not to rob and to return what they borrow. . . . Let no one think that the world can be ruled without blood; the sword of the ruler must be red and bloody; for the world will and must be evil, and the sword is God's rod and vengeance upon it. (quoted in Graeber 2012, 321)

Weber claimed that the Reformation meant "*for each individual,* a feeling of tremendous inner *loneliness* . . . [for] the most crucial concern of life . . . eternal salvation, man was obliged to tread his path alone. . . . No one could help him" (1905, 73). For Protestants the comforting Catholic Church—Holy Mother Church, as the Catholics called it—no longer stood between them and their God.

Luther was little mindful of the individual's social condition. He directed his attention instead to their spiritual condition: all stand individually before their God. No intermediaries were either necessary or desirable. He viewed as corrupt the Church's maintenance of an elite privileged class of priests who pretended to have special access to God and claimed the power to mediate between laypeople and their God. Luther held that the priesthood held no powers not vested in laypeople, and thus the entire Church hierarchy existed contrary to God's will. Similarly, Calvin challenged the power of the Church to grant salvation. God alone elected some to be saved. For Protestants, gone was the soft forgiveness through confession offered by Holy Mother Church intervening on their behalf with God the Father. Individuals might consult the clergy for advice and guidance, but not turn to them for salvation. That responsibility was theirs as individuals, standing alone before God.

Market transactions are essentially contracts between buyers and sellers coming to agreement on the terms of exchange. Thus, the expansion of markets within an increasingly commercial society meant that humans would relate to one another more and more through contracts. This experience nourished an evolving conception of society as consisting of contractual social relationships, a conception which is reflected in the emphasis that Protestants, and especially Puritans, placed upon the "covenant" between God and man. This emphasis revealed their affinity for the Old Testament, where the Jews had entered into a covenant with their God. For Puritans, all social relationships—within their churches, between husband and wife, between individuals and God, and among businessmen—came to be viewed as contractual relationships between freely acting individuals. A Puritan minister described the contract as "the highest human bond . . . an agreement between equals . . . fully voluntary and unforced on both sides" (quoted in Waltzer 1974, 301).[24]

Although punctuated by major power-shifting events (e.g., the Glorious Revolution and the French Revolution), the rise of the bourgeoisie's power was gradual. It led to greater power sharing, creating what economists Daron Acemoglu and James Robinson call pluralist institutions (2012, 306–8). These institutions embodied mechanisms of compromise that facilitated the resolution of discord without violence. They represented the evolution of the rule of law as opposed to the whim of rulers. Further, as Acemoglu and Robinson point out,

Once in place, the notion of the rule of law not only kept absolutism at bay but also created a type of virtuous circle: if the laws applied equally to everybody, then no individual or group . . . could rise above the law, and common

[24] Yet, many early secular observers expressed an uneasiness with what they feared were the consequences of human interaction becoming reduced to contractual agreements. For instance, although Montesquieu was highly supportive of the new evolving commercial order, he expressed concern nonetheless that community, hospitality, and other "moral virtues" would be lost as commerce monetizes all human relations (Hirschman 1997, 80).

people accused of encroaching on private property still had the right to a fair trial. (2012, 308)

Nonetheless, this expanding bourgeoisie encountered continual resistance to its quest for political power and social recognition commensurate with its wealth. The aristocracy's reaction to a presumptuous rising bourgeoisie could be extreme in its cruelty. For instance, in the early sixteenth century, Margrave Casimir of Brandenburg-Ansbach gouged out the eyes of 58 burghers who, following a revolt, had "refused to look at him as their lord" (Graeber 2012, 325).

Despite its disparaging attitude toward the poor, Protestantism projected a latent message of egalitarianism, especially through its privileging of work. All must work, and, in this, they are equal. Although spiritual salvation was bestowed only by grace or election, responsibility for the economic and social fate of individuals in this world was theirs alone.[25] Hard work could raise their status. Thus, class division could no longer be so readily viewed as divinely ordained or naturally given. Instead, Protestantism implied that vertical mobility depended solely upon the individual's industry.

Implicit in this understanding is that all humans are created equal and it is up to each to make something of life. What might be called a secular universal humanity postulate evolved (a spiritual one already existed in Christianity), whereby all humans everywhere are equal. At the end of the seventeenth century, as noted earlier, John Locke's theory that each human brain is a *tabula rasa*, a blank slate on which experience is written, implied that all are born equal. By the eighteenth century, growing numbers of social thinkers were giving expression to this equality. French economist and statesman Anne-Robert-Jacques Turgot maintained that "the original aptitudes are distributed equally among barbarous peoples and among civilized peoples; they are probably the same in all places and at all times" (2010, 88). Hume agreed: "Mankind are so much the same, in all times and places, that history informs us of nothing new or strange in this particular. Its chief use is only to discover the constant and universal principles of human nature" (1909, 14). So too did Adam Smith: "the difference between the most dissimilar characters . . . seems to arise not so much from nature as from habit, custom, and education" (1776, 16).[26]

---

[25] "In its early days, capitalism needed workers who were willing to subject themselves to economic exploitation for the sake of their conscience" (Weber 1905, 201).

[26] Smith elaborated: "The difference of natural talents in different men is, in reality, much less than we are aware of; and the very different genius which appears to distinguish men of different

Alongside the idea of equality came the idea of citizenship. The bourgeoisie strove to soften, if not eliminate, hereditary hierarchies of rank. Status is not given but earned.[27] Humans should be free to contract with others. They should not be subordinate. Any threat that this idea of innate equality might lead to a redistribution to those below seemed remote, given the command of political and economic power shared by an elite composed of landlords and the bourgeoisie. The bourgeoisie merely sought the same rights, privileges, and status as the aristocracy. They had no more intention than the aristocrats of sharing their advantages or their fortune with the working and peasant classes socially beneath them. Indeed, they actively and continually attempted to block any extension of their gains to those below.

Arguably, it was the expansion of markets that most cultivated an ideal of equality. As noted earlier, inherent in the act of exchange—even if only latently—is the idea of human equality. As economist John Hicks put it: "The mercantile system is not hierarchical; buyer and seller are on a level; why should one be master and one servant? The master-servant relation does not fit" (1973, 122). In fact, a notion of equality is the first ruling principle of exchange: in the judgment of the participants, each must receive at least the equivalent for what he or she gives up. Should this principle of equivalence not hold, free exchange would cease, or continue under political force (in which case it would no longer constitute free exchange), and the natural reaction of one participant would be to exit the market.

But there is more to the relationship between markets and equality in a post-barter economy where money is the medium of exchange. The use of money inculcates the idea of equality: ". . . money introduced a democratization of desire. Insofar as everyone wanted money, everyone, high and low, was pursuing the same promiscuous substance" (Graeber 2012, 190).

At this level, the idea of equality spills over from the commodities to the participants. Whether in the hands of a lord or those of a peasant, the same

---

professions, when grown up to maturity, is not upon many occasions so much the cause as the effect of the division of labour. The difference between the most dissimilar characters, between a philosopher and a common street porter, for example, seems to arise not so much from nature as from habit, custom, and education. When they came into the world, and for the first six or eight years of their existence, they were perhaps very much alike, and neither their parents nor playfellows could perceive any remarkable difference..." (1776).

[27] It is in the Netherlands and England that the bourgeoisie first achieves respect without reference to birth. Philosopher Terry Pinkard notes that "the English 'gentleman' represents the way in which one can be a 'true individual' independently of one's past. . . . The idea of the 'gentleman' is a man of uncertain ancestry" (1996, 114).

amount of currency taken into the market buys the same quantity of goods. What occurs in an exchange of goods for money is, thus, governed by rules that are completely independent of the participants' personal characteristics. Each enters the market with freedom and self-interest. Because a market transaction cannot be concluded without the voluntary assent of both buyer and seller, they are equal in a very real sense. Either can kill the deal.

The conception of equality also got an early boost from one of history's greatest technological innovations, Johannes Gutenberg's printing press with movable type. Introduced in Mainz in 1445, the printing press is the technological innovation often considered to mark the beginning of the modern world. It spread rapidly: to Strasbourg in 1460, and soon thereafter to Rome, Venice, Florence, Milan, Turin, and London. Fifty years after Gutenberg's death, there were printing presses in every European country except Russia. Everywhere it came into use, literacy rapidly expanded. By 1500, 20 million books had been printed. Although most were religious books in Latin, many were written in the vernacular and addressed secular issues (Mann 2012, I:446).

Protestantism significantly advanced the spread of more egalitarian doctrines by means of the printing press. In particular, Luther used the new medium of print deliberately to restore religion to the center of individual life and society by translating the Bible into German, publishing the New Testament in 1522 and both the Old and New Testaments and Apocrypha in 1534. His translation of the New Testament was widely successful, making him the most published author since the invention of the printing press (Pettegree 2015). Luther also disseminated a large number of his sermons in German as pamphlets, giving ordinary people access to religious ideas previously available only to a small elite. The printing press so dramatically reduced the cost of information that Protestantism could more reasonably insist that all have equal access to the Holy Scriptures, reinforcing the central teaching that all have equal standing in an unmediated relationship to God. By the mid-sixteenth century, about half a million of Luther's Bibles had been printed (Acocella 2017, 71).

This latent idea of equality also found expression in the modern conception of the state as first formulated by Hobbes. The state traditionally drew its legitimacy from religion. However, as markets increasingly became the locus of social interactions, Hobbes's conception of the state as a social contract gained traction. Just as market contracts unite the interests of discrete individuals in exchange, so the collective whole is tied together by an overarching social contract. Market exchanges imply equality because both participants equally hold the power to say no. Similarly, the fact that all members of society freely, rationally, and self-interestedly enter into the social contract implies a basic equality: each one has an equal voice. The state is desacralized, becoming nothing more than an agreement of free and politically equal individuals to give up some of their sovereignty for the sake of peace and security. The state was humanized: the product of humans, not gods.

In effect, the legitimation of state power was turned on its head. In traditional societies, legitimation is top-down. At the top, political power draws its authority from the sacred framework of religion above. At the bottom, economic activity must comply with both political and religious authority. But, as commercial activity expanded, society came to be steered more and more by markets. Accordingly, the state began seeking to derive its power and legitimation from below, from the domain of economic activity. Thus, the state started to collude with the rising merchant class. In return for special privileges, prizes, and monopolies, merchants provided the state with tax revenues, credit, and contracts for the provision of public goods, especially for defense. Eventually, with the rise of laissez-faire ideology, the state's internal role will be conceived as the limited one of a constable, maintaining peace by protecting life and private property.

The general notions of a social contract, individualism, and equality increasingly informed political discourse. They are pervasive in the writing of the social contractarians, whether explicitly expressed or implicitly assumed. Locke, for example, made clear that in a natural state, prior to political institutions, humans lived in equality. In answer to his question "what estate men are naturally in?," he answered, "A state . . . of equality, wherein all power and jurisdiction is reciprocal, no one having more than another, there being nothing more evident [than that they] should also be equal one amongst another" (1975, ii: 4). His labor-based defense of private property also suggests not only individualism, but also equal access to productive resources: "As much land as a man tills, plants, improves, cultivates and can use the product of, so much is his property. He by his labour does, as it were, enclose it from the common." Property, then, is anterior to the existence of the state: "The great and chief end . . . of men's uniting into commonwealths and putting themselves under government is the preservation of their property" (1689, 36; 71).

In the mid-seventeenth century, a political movement in England called the Levellers argued for general social equality. Its members advocated popular sovereignty, equality before the law, religious tolerance, and democratic suffrage, the last captured in a famous speech by Colonel Thomas Rainsborough:

> I think it clear that every man that is to live under a government ought first by his own consent to put himself under that government; and I do think that the poorest man in England is not at all bound in a strict sense to that government that he hath not had a voice to put himself under. (quoted in Wolin 2010, 251–52)[28]

By the time of the French Revolution, the idea of equality had become central to progressive political discourse. Louis Roederer, a leading figure of the French Revolution's National Constituent Assembly, reported that "the emotion that stirred the first outburst of the revolution, aroused its most violent effort, and obtained its greatest successes was the love of equality. . . . The first motive of the revolution was impatience with inequalities" (quoted in Rosanvallon 2013, 4). To overcome status by birth, French revolutionary Michel Le Peletier proposed that children of the ages 5 to 12 be taken from their families and placed in schools he called "houses of equality" where all would be given "the same clothes, the same food, the same instruction, and the same care." Their futures would therefore depend upon "only talent and virtue" (quoted in Rosanvallon 2013, 249). Far from seeing a conflict between liberty and equality (as do today's conservatives), the French revolutionaries held them to be inseparable. Historian and sociologist Pierre Rosanvallon writes that Bertrand Barère, a prominent member of the National Convention, "set the tone for the French Revolution's efforts to build a society of individuals" with the pronouncement that "anything that

---

[28] Tawney sets forth the demands of the Levellers and the more radical Diggers as follows:

The program of the Levellers, who more than any other party could claim to express the aspirations of the unprivileged classes, included a demand, not only for annual or biennial Parliaments, manhood suffrage, a redistribution of seats in proportion to population, and the abolition of the veto of the House of Lords, but also that "you would have laid open all enclosures of fens and other commons, or have them enclosed only or chiefly for the benefit of the poor." Theoretical communism, repudiated by the leading Levellers, found its expression in the agitation of the Diggers, on whose behalf Winstanley argued that, "seeing the common people of England, by joynt consent of person and purse, have caste out Charles, our Norman oppressour the land now is to returne into the joynt hands of those who have conquered, that is the commonours," and that the victory over the King was incomplete, as long as "wee . . . remayne slaves still to the kingly power in the hands of lords of manors" (1926, 212).

may establish the dependence of man on man should be proscribed in a republic" (2013, 29).

The central importance that capitalism and Protestantism give the individual is even reflected in philosophy. This was noted earlier in Locke's conception of the mind as a blank slate at birth. There is also a striking parallel between the individual point of view in Descartes's epistemology and Hobbes's social theory. Descartes locates the problem of epistemology in the claim of an individual mind to know what is exterior to it. Similarly, Hobbes sees the problem of social order from the point of view of the insecure individual within society. Both reformulate thought by shifting from the perspective of tradition and authority to that of rational autonomous individuals facing the world on their own.

Like philosophy, cultural productions increasingly reflected a secular world of free and equal individuals. The individual, each equal to all others, came to be seen as Protagoras's measure of all things. To emphasize the individual was to emphasize equality. Music began to express bourgeois ideals as opposed to those of the aristocracy. Operatic reform began in the 1730s, reflecting middle-class ideas. Rousseau, himself an accomplished musician, viewed Baroque opera seria as artificial and elitist. The new opera, opera buffa, "pitted street-smart servants and members of the lower class against negatively portrayed members of the upper class" (Greenberg 2006, 135). Equality was becoming a subtext in all cultural media.

Visual art was also transformed as the bourgeoisie rose to dominance. In the Enlightenment, artists turned for inspiration to classical Greece and Rome, the birthplaces of truth and reason in the Western world. Art became an expression of rationalism. This change from earlier motifs shows up most strikingly where the power transition from aristocratic dominance was most abrupt, such as in the Eastern European cites of Prague, Budapest, Vienna, and Riga.

The Enlightenment initiated a movement—by historical standards, a rather swift one—from a theological to a secular orientation. A consensus developed that authority originates not with tradition, but within each individual, from what the seventeenth-century theologian and scientist Blaise Pascal called the "law of the heart." People shifted from concern with how they might be saved to consideration of how they might be happy. They transitioned from a preoccupation with the duties appropriate to their rank in society to a focus on personal fulfillment. Musicologist Robert Greenberg notes, for instance, that "Beethoven combined the Enlightenment spirit of individuality and the spirit of revolutionary change that characterized Europe at the time. Music, for Beethoven, was a form of self-expression and in keeping with the Enlightenment's emphasis on 'the 'right' of individuals to pursue 'happiness,' meaning self-realization" (2006, 147, 150).

8

The Shift toward Secular Ideology

. . . each new class which puts itself in the place of one ruling before it, is compelled, merely in order to carry through its aim, to present its interest as the common interest of all the members of society, that is, expressed in ideal form: it has to give its ideas the form of universality, and present them as the only rational, universally valid ones.
— Karl Marx, "The German Ideology" (1845, 67–68)

The last chapter explored how the expansion of commerce and markets created an environment in which the Protestant Reformation could thrive, stimulating the rise of individualism and equality as ideals. This chapter addresses how these European economic and doctrinal transformations, and the mentality they generated, also created thought space in which non-religious or secular meaning systems could flourish. Secular doctrines, especially in political economy, increasingly complemented religious ones in legitimating inequality, and would eventually replace them in advanced capitalist nations. Economist and theologian A. M. C. Waterman asserts that it was not until the 1880s that economists no longer found it necessary to reconcile their theories with Christian theology (2008, 136).[1]

The rise of secular legitimation was already strikingly evident in 1513 with the publication of philosopher Niccolo Machiavelli's *The Prince*, the first Western book in more than a millennium without biblical quotations or references to the writers of antiquity. It urged that politics be free from both ethical and theological considerations, and that knowledge be used opportunistically: ". . . it is necessary for a prince, who wishes to maintain

---

[1] This decline in religion's role in legitimating societal conditions was accompanied by its appropriation of a greatly reduced share of society's surplus. Economist Thomas Piketty reports that whereas in the United Kingdom, France, and Spain, the clergy represented about 3 to 3.5 percent of all adult males in the sixteenth and seventeenth centuries, their number fell to less than 1 percent in the nineteenth and twentieth centuries (2020, 157).

himself, to learn how not to be good, and to use this knowledge and not use it, according to the necessity of the case" (1513, 56). *The Prince* became a bestseller.

Machiavelli's later *Discourses*, written in 1517 but only published in 1531, suggested that religion is not so important for its truth as for its utility in manipulating the people, whether to deceive them or to inspire them to sacrifice their lives for the state. He expressed approval of the use by Roman consuls of religious language even when they themselves thought it false. He also noted that fear of divine punishment would help keep citizens and soldiers loyal to their rulers. Although Marx is generally considered the first student of ideology, that honor might rightfully be bestowed upon Machiavelli.

The long-drawn-out shifting of the legitimation of inequality from religious to economic doctrines began as rising nation-states in a bellicose environment started to recognize that their military power and survival were dependent upon a strong economic base. Called Mercantilism, the economic thought that developed between 1500 and 1750 matured with the expansion of capitalist institutions. Mercantilism may be said to have laid the groundwork for modern economics insofar as it expressed many of the economic doctrines that would become part of Adam Smith's path-breaking 1776 work, *The Wealth of Nations*. Economics, wearing the mantle of science, gradually evolved to serve as the dominant ideological instrument for legitimating inequality, a role it continues to perform today.

As explained in Chapter 7, human interaction was progressively understood to operate according to impersonal social laws, as opposed to codes of morality. In the Middle Ages, most people lived in parishes where economic relations were predominantly personal, and therefore appeared to be properly governed by the participants' shared moral principles. However, with the rise of markets, larger-scale organizations, and distant trade, economic relations became impersonal and therefore more abstract, and could more readily be articulated and understood as operating according to laws rather than moral principles. Five distinct inequality-legitimating doctrines were advanced as natural social laws during the heyday of Mercantilism and the later era of classical political economy. They were the utility of poverty, the justice of the invisible hand, the Malthusian population doctrine, the wages-fund doctrine, and the trickle-down thesis. These ideology-laden doctrines are addressed in turn in the following.

The Utility of Poverty

> ... to make society happy, it is necessary that great numbers should
> be wretched as well as poor.
> —Bernard de Mandeville, *The Fable of the Bees* (1714, 1:194)

As will be recalled from the last chapter, the Catholic Church had attempted to limit the extent to which the rich captured the surplus by insisting upon a moral obligation of charity.[2] Protestants were less favorable to the idea of aiding the least fortunate, lest it discourage them from working. Thus, the doctrine of the utility of poverty—the idea that unrelieved need would compel the poor to work—was implicit in their view that the poor's laziness and proneness to debauchery were the source of their misery.[3] It should be noted that such differences between Catholics and Protestants were to wane as the commercial forces that had played a role in molding Protestantism exerted their influence on Catholicism as well. Eventually, even among Catholics, as philosopher Terry Pinkard observes,

> the cult of charity [was] transformed into a repressive, puritanical means of social control [as] beggars and other vagabonds [came to be viewed as] completely lacking in "virtue" and whose poverty was to be explained by their lack of such "virtue" [and thus they] were to be forcibly housed, given exhortational religious and moral lectures, and fed and clothed badly in order to "reform" them, all in the name of Christian charity. (1996, 103)

The widespread Mercantilist view that the poor are by nature slothful and unwilling to work justified extreme measures to force them into useful employment. For instance, as noted in Chapter 7, England's Statute of 1536 subjected vagrants to public whipping in the nude on the first offense, whipping plus loss of part of an ear on the second, and execution on the third. Even as late as the mid-eighteenth century, when the Enlightenment was gaining

---

[2] Among other major religions, this is also true of Islam and Buddhism. Hinduism, by contrast, found no grounds for charity since one's current station in life was justified: it was determined by behavior (karma) in previous incarnations.

[3] "Advanced by men of religion as a tonic for the soul, the doctrine of the danger of pampering poverty was hailed by the rising school of Political Arithmeticians as a sovereign cure for the ills of society. For, if the theme of the moralist was that an easy-going indulgence undermined character, the theme of the economists was that it was economically disastrous and financially ruinous" (Tawney 1926, 222). Some pre-Mercantilist secular thinkers had also opposed higher wages, claiming that they result in idleness and luxury consumption (Johnson 1932, 718).

momentum, Adam Smith's revered teacher Francis Hutcheson advocated a sort of penal slavery for those found guilty of vagrancy (Losurdo 2014, 6).

This presumption that workers are lazy by nature underlay the doctrine of the utility of poverty. It legitimated the need to maintain wages at subsistence, the lowest level they can reach if the working class is to survive. This view, which Protestants expressed in religious terms, was increasingly articulated in secular terms. For instance, Daniel Defoe, author of *Robinson Crusoe*, contended that the poor must be compelled to work. Any sort of public assistance would merely indulge them in their indolence. Similarly, political economist Bernard de Mandeville wrote: "Every Body knows that there is a vast number of Journey-men . . . who, if by Four Days Labour in a Week they can maintain themselves, will hardly be persuaded to work the fifth" (1714, 1:509). Mandeville also wrote:

> It would be easier, where property was well secured, to live without money than without poor . . . who, as they ought to be kept from starving, so they should receive nothing worth saving . . . [the poor] have nothing to stir them up to be serviceable but their wants, which it is prudence to relieve, but folly to cure. (1714, 1:193, 194)

Later, in America, Benjamin Franklin expressed a similar view: "I am for doing good to the poor, but I differ in opinion about the means. I think the best way of doing good to the poor is not making them easy in poverty, but leading or driving them out of it" (2017, 358).

The utility-of-poverty doctrine contends that, should wages rise above mere subsistence, workers will work less because they can meet their consumption needs by working fewer hours.[4] As the Reverend Joseph Townsend asserted,

> Hunger will tame the fiercest animals, it will teach decency and civility, obedience and subjection, to the most perverse. In general it is only hunger which can spur and goad them [the poor] on to labor. (quoted in Polanyi 1944, 113)

---

[4] This doctrine is partially captured by what modern economists refer to as the backward-bending supply curve of labor, which presumes that if wages rise above some level, workers will work less, or technically that the income effect will outweigh the substitution effect (Wisman 1989).

Therefore, higher wages would result in lower output, making the whole of society poorer. Quite understandably, those who held that poverty was useful never mentioned that higher wages would reduce the appropriable surplus or diminish the rate of exploitation. Further, and quite critically at a time of intense nation-state conflict, less national output would weaken the state. The central thrust of Mercantilist doctrine was to advise and legitimate the rising nation-state (Heckscher 2007). It was the economics of state-building.

The utility-of-poverty doctrine justified state intervention to hold down wages. It legitimated state-enforced maximum wages capping what employers could legally pay, thereby ensuring that the working class would retain little surplus beyond mere subsistence. Political economist William Petty, a contemporary of Adam Smith, thought wages should be legally fixed so that they "should allow the labourer but just the wherewithal to live" (quoted in Roll 1974, 106). Of course, wages fixed at subsistence favored profits and guaranteed extreme inequality. It will be recalled from Chapter 6 that maximum wage legislation first appeared in the wake of the population collapse that reduced the supply of labor and put upward pressure on wages in the fourteenth and fifteenth centuries.

Workers should not only be kept poor, they should also be unschooled, lest they become discontent with their physically demanding menial labor and their rude living conditions. As Mandeville put it, to ensure that cheap, docile, and obedient labor not disappear, it is ". . . requisite that great Numbers of them should be Ignorant as well as Poor" (1714, 1:288). Some otherwise progressive thinkers of the French Enlightenment, such as Louis-René Caradeuc de La Chalotais and Denis Diderot, expressed a similar opinion. La Chalotais claimed that "for the good of society, people's knowledge must not extend beyond its occupation." Diderot disparaged the "false learning that makes people stubborn [and] the foolish ambition of parents determined to save their children from their subaltern occupations" (quoted in Rosanvallon 2013, 106, 107). Curiously, the English Civil War, the French Revolution, and the Russian Revolution all occurred when literacy levels reached about 50 percent (Stone 1969).

Undoubtedly, those who argued that workers needed to be kept poor and ignorant lest they not work were sincere in their beliefs. They were not merely constructing ideological justifications for an elite's right to appropriate the full surplus. Nonetheless, whether or not they saw the connection, the utility-of-poverty argument loaned itself to justifying low wages. In addition, there appears generally to have been a certain animus toward the poor, evident in contradictory arguments against allowing them to earn too much. Cleric and political economist Nathaniel Forster, for instance, advocated wage caps to limit luxury consumption by the working class due to "a perpetual restless ambition in each of the inferior ranks to raise themselves to the level of those immediately above them" (1767, 41). Workers were reviled both for lacking ambition and for having aspirations.

In any event, Mercantilist thought practically viewed the overwhelming majority of humans as beasts of burden to be kept alive for productive work. The utility-of-poverty doctrine even stood behind a proposal to tax workers to force them to work longer hours for their subsistence. For instance, in 1750, churchman and political economist Josiah Tucker advocated the imposition of a high tax upon necessities to decrease the real wage rate and thereby increase work effort (1966, 32, 36–38).

To appease the elite's social conscience, it was further argued that the workers' poverty was in their best interest, because having either more income or more free time would result in sinful dissipation. Tucker claimed that

the men are as bad as can be described; who become vicious, more indigent and idle, in proportion to the advance of wages, and the cheapness of provisions: Great numbers of both sexes never working at all, while they have any thing to spend upon their vices. (1966, 31–32)

A half century later, the Reverend Thomas Malthus was of the same opinion: "even when they have an opportunity of saving they seldom exercise it, but all that is beyond their present necessities goes, generally speaking, to the ale-house." All money above subsistence would be spent on "drinking, gaming, and debauchery" (1798, 34), ruining their health and risking their souls. Low wages were thus in everyone's best interest, properly understood— the "utility of poverty."

To force the poor to work, begging also had to be controlled. In 1786, Townsend acknowledged that although solving the problem of poverty could be left to public policy, he thought it better that "the poor might safely be left to the free bounty of the rich, without the interposition of any other law" (quoted in Lepenies 2013, 451). He reasoned that, if the poor were to invoke the beneficence of the rich, they would have to prove themselves worthy by being respectful and industrious. Political economist Charles Dunoyer, a leading ideologue for the July Monarchy (1830–1848) in France, viewed poverty and inequality as an essential disciplining force for the non-poor as well:

It is a good thing that society provides its inferior stations into which families that behave badly may fall and from which they may not rise unless
they behave well. Misery is that awesome hell. It is an inevitable abyss, sit-
uated alongside the mad, the dissolute, the debauched, and all the other
species of vicious men, to keep them under control. (quoted in Rosanvallon
2013, 93–94)

Not all social thinkers embraced the utility of poverty argument, but most
did. Adam Smith was one of the few exceptions:

The wages of labour are the encouragement of industry, which, like every
other human quality, improves in proportion to the encouragement it
receives.... Where wages are high ... we shall always find the working-men
more active, diligent and expeditious, than where they are low. (1776, 81)

Further, he argued that low wages result in low levels of nutrition and a
constrained ability to work (1776, 81ff).[5]

Although Smith's views were generally charitable toward the poor, the
greater number of earlier and later social thinkers, including his disciples,
endorsed harsh policies toward the less fortunate. They continued to embrace the utility-of-poverty argument, maintaining that nothing can be done
to help the poor without making them and everyone else worse off. Of the
English Poor Laws that, however heavy-handed, were intended to relieve
poverty, political economist David Ricardo asserted: "The principle of grav-
itation is not more certain than the tendency of such laws to change wealth
and vigor into misery and weakness . . . until at last all classes should be
infected with the plague of universal poverty" (1819, 86).

---

[5] With characteristic insight, Adam Smith saw through the ideology and practices that benefited
the rich at the expense of the poor. An example of his keen awareness of how laws and attitudes were
biased against the interests of workers is his observation that "the masters, being fewer in number,
can combine much more easily; and the law, besides, authorizes or at least does not prohibit their
combinations, while it prohibits those of the workmen.... We rarely hear ... of the combinations
of masters; though frequently of those of workmen. But whoever imagines, upon this account, that
masters rarely combine, is as ignorant of the world as of the subject. Masters are always and every
where in a sort of tacit, but constant and uniform combination, not to raise the wages of labour above
their actual rate.... [Further] [m]any workmen could not subsist a week, few could subsist a month,
and scarce any a year without employment. In the long-run the workman may be as necessary to his
master as his master is to him; but the necessity is not so immediate" (1776, 66).

The Justice of the Invisible Hand

Thus every Part was full of Vice, Yet the whole Mass a Paradise.
—Bernard de Mandeville, *The Fable
of the Bees* (1714, 24)

Adam Smith is generally recognized as the father of modern economics. This credit comes to him for having conceptualized an economy in which the forces of supply and demand, left to themselves, harmonize individuals' self-interests and thereby guide the economy as a whole toward stability and prosperity. Borrowing from the Physiocrats of the French Enlightenment, Smith played an important role in applying the mechanistic Newtonian cosmology of natural law to the social world. Markets came to be seen as natural phenomena, behaving according to natural laws not unlike those that govern the physical world. Because the natural was equated with the good, natural laws should be allowed to function without constraint.

According to this laissez-faire approach, markets would allocate resources efficiently if people were left alone to follow their self-interest. Because it was natural, the distribution of income, wealth, and privilege that flowed from untrammeled market processes was also just. No government intervention was necessary or appropriate to adjust market outcomes. In particular, no assistance need or should be offered to the poor. This outlook accorded with many Enlightenment thinkers' view that nature is not just physical but also normative: the natural world, of which markets are a part, is as it ought to be. This notion dates at least as far back as 1736, when Bishop Joseph Butler claimed that the laws of nature and the laws of morality are the same (Butler 1736).

Unnatural and therefore immoral inequality could exist where the spontaneous functioning of free markets was distorted by monopoly privileges granted by corrupt governments. Indeed, the classical school of French and Scottish Enlightenment economists accused Mercantilist governments of actively intervening in, and thereby perverting, markets' natural processes. Examples would be wage regulations or the granting of monopolies. The result was economic inefficiency and injustice. Some proponents of this natural law cosmology claimed that, if free markets were allowed to operate naturally, society would tend toward equality. For instance, Nicolas de Condorcet, a prominent Enlightenment philosopher, wrote:

It is easy to prove that fortunes tend naturally toward equality, and that excessive differences of wealth either cannot exist or must promptly cease, if
the civil laws do not establish artificial ways of perpetuating and amassing
such fortunes, and if freedom of commerce and industry eliminate the advantage that any prohibitive law or fiscal privilege gives to acquired wealth.
(quoted in Piketty 2014, 363–64)

For the French revolutionaries, inequality is impermissible unless it serves
the common good. Consequently, according to Article One of the 1789
Declaration of the Rights of Man and the Citizen, "Social distinctions can be
based only on common utility" (Piketty 2014, 422).

That the market nexus was natural seemed indisputable. After all, the
market economy is nothing other than the sum product of innumerable
decisions on the part of free individuals. Anything that fetters this free interaction of individuals must be viewed as unnatural, the abnormal product of
prejudice, corruption, and tyranny. It is little wonder, then, that free markets
came to be seen as necessary for a society of rational, self-determining individuals, and government intervention came to be seen as wholly objection-
able. Unlike Marx, the French and Scottish Enlightenment economists failed
to recognize that once land and capital (stored-up labor) become the privately owned property of a small elite, those without ownership are caged,
trapped in a social condition where they must sell their labor power to the
owners or starve. Because they sell their labor power in markets, and because
those markets were viewed as sites of freedom where buyers and sellers reach
contractual agreements of their own free will, the workers' oppressed state
was concealed beneath the patina of free-market philosophy.

Many of the French and Scottish Enlightenment writers who embraced
natural law cosmology deemed it to have been created by an all-good and all-
wise God. They were deists, believing that a perfect God could only create a
perfect world, one which did not require ongoing divine intervention. Thus,
in what appeared to be secular doctrine, religious legitimation continued to
play its backup role.[6] Nevertheless, natural law cosmology was a significant
advance toward secularization, whereby social institutions and practices became increasingly divorced from religious symbols and meaning. Natural

---

[6] It is, of course, but a short step to an atheist view that this cosmos came to be by natural processes,
or that it was simply the way nature had always been. Principal Enlightenment figures such as Paul-
Henri Thiry, Baron d'Holbach, and Denis Diderot were known for their atheism.

law cosmology progressively distanced natural explanations of phenomena from divine causes and justifications.

Doctrinally, it is conceivable that this separation of the secular from the sacred finds its roots in the separation of church and state that characterized Christianity, as delineated by Jesus's injunction in Matthew 22:21 to "render to Caesar the things that are Caesar's; and to God the things that are God's." The actual separation that begins in Europe, as was seen in Chapter 7, accompanied the spread of markets and the related ascendancy of the bourgeoisie. Together, they created legitimation space for the rise of Protestantism, natural science, and the resulting knowledge competition. With no universally accepted authority over truth and meaning, the realms of politics and social thought became increasingly freed from religion.

Of critical importance to economics is the natural-law view that, in pursuing their own narrow self-interests, individuals unintentionally further a felicitous social outcome, as if, in aggregate, their actions were guided by "an invisible hand." Most traditional religions had considered pursuing one's self-interest sinful. Now it became morally, socially, and "scientifically" respectable. The deliverance of self-interest from moral opprobrium was another way in which the social world continued to sever its ties to religion.

Implicit in the metaphor of an invisible hand is the idea of unintended consequences. As noted earlier, it is not the intention of individual market participants that a more dynamic and robust economy result from their self-interested actions. They are merely looking out for their own well-being. All then can be left to the harmonious self-regulation of the natural social world. Individuals follow their natural self-interests, and natural social laws do the rest.

This concept of unintended consequences was elaborated and widely popularized in the twentieth century by sociologist Thomas K. Merton (1936). It evolved into a line of attack against government intervention during a period in which laissez-faire ideology was out of favor and public policy initiatives to end the suffering caused by the Great Depression grew more and more popular. The basic thrust of the unintended consequences argument is that, due to the sheer complexity of the social world, the full aftereffects over time of any significant government action cannot be predicted and are likely to be harmful. A laissez-faire approach is more prudent. In this manner, the doctrine of unintended consequences extends and complements that of the invisible hand. Government must be kept at a minimum, providing nothing more than national defense and domestic law and order (notably including the protection of the existing distribution of private property). The doctrine of unintended consequences was given its fullest ideological expression by twentieth-century economist Friedrich Hayek, whose ideas were seconded by philosopher of science Karl Popper in his political writings. It continues to underlie the political stance of free-market libertarians.

Building upon Smith's metaphor of an invisible hand, Hayek also put forth the argument that the market economy is a "spontaneous order" which emerges organically through a process akin to natural selection in the biological world. It was socially selected because those societies in which it evolved became more dynamic and prosperous. The market economy provides for "a more efficient allocation of societal resources than any design could achieve" (quoted in Petsoulas 2001, 2). It does so by generating the information necessary for actors to make rational decisions. No government's planning system could ever match this achievement (Hayek 1991, 6).

The related doctrines of the metaphorical invisible hand, unintended consequences, and the spontaneous order of natural processes highlight the necessity of giving individual self-interest free rein in unrestricted markets to achieve the ideal social results. The market nexus cultivates individuals' self-reliance. It requires utmost vigilance on the part of both buyers and sellers as to their own self-interests, lest they be defrauded, ruined, and impoverished. Indeed, in any exchange, it is not enough for participants to keep their own interests in mind; they must be rationally or calculatingly self-interested to a degree that is at least equal to the competition they face. If they take into account moral considerations such as charity for the other, the public good, or social considerations such as the status of the other, they will lose out. Of course, a pretense of charity or of deference might be "good business," but as such it is merely part of cunning and calculating self-interest. That is, market participants may deceive others, or even delude themselves, to think that they are trading in the interest of all. It is in the trader's self-interest to pretend not to be self-interested. But the pretense is usually, on reflection, transparent—hence the ill repute of traders in premodern societies. Recall that Mercury was the Roman god of thieves and tricksters as well as merchants.

By the end of the eighteenth century, the open pursuit of self-interest was gaining wide acceptance as a vital force that must be unleashed to enable economic dynamism, a view given scientific validity by political economy. Voltaire offered that it is impossible for a society to be formed and lasting without self-interest as it would be to produce children without carnal desire or to think of eating without appetite, etc. It is love of self that encourages love of others, it is through our mutual needs that we are useful to the human race. That is the foundation of all commerce, the eternal link between men. Without it not a single art would have been invented, no society of ten people formed. (quoted in Muller 2003, 35)

Although secularism was on the rise, and the science of political economy increasingly became the principal ideological construct serving to legitimate inequality, a new strain of religion developed in support of the prevailing social order. Evangelical movements, arising in religious revivals in Anglophonic countries in the eighteenth century, married the harsh Protestant view of the poor with the argument that God's plan for an orderly society was manifest in the automatic workings of the laissez-faire market system. The free workings of the market served to reward the good hardworking Christian and punish the slothful sinner. Central to the evangelical doctrine was the idea of original sin. The true purpose of life on earth was to redeem ourselves of our innate sinfulness, our proclivity to yield to the pleasures of the flesh. Thus, poverty was part of the divine plan, an incentive to force the poor to work hard, save, and live virtuous lives. Those who achieved higher status served as moral examples; they demonstrated that the incentive system works. They had earned their wealth and social standing.

Evangelicals played a significant role in the elimination of the old English welfare system in which parishes had taken responsibility for care of the poor. The fullest flowering of laissez-faire policies in England came with the Poor Law Amendment of 1834. It nationalized welfare and established a punitive stance toward the poor, a stance generally advocated by political economists[7] and evangelicals alike. Workhouses were set up to house and regulate the unemployed and their families. It is clear that the rules of many workhouses

---

[7] The Poor Law Commission was headed by the notable political economist Nassau Senior. Sentiments among political economists were generally exceedingly hostile to the Poor Laws. Tawney captures their views by fusing quotations from political economists: "The Poor Law is the mother of idleness, 'men and women growing so idle and proud that they will not work, but lie upon the parish wherein they dwell for maintenance.' It discourages thrift; 'if shame or fear of punishment makes him earn his daily bread, he will do no more; his children are the charge of the parish and his old age his recess from labour or care.' It keeps up wages, since 'It encourages willful and evil-disposed persons to impose what wages they please upon their labours; and herein they are so refractory to reason and the benefit of the nation that, when corn and provisions are cheap, they will not work for less wages than when they were dear'" (Tawney 1926, 222).

were not intended to improve the lives of the indigent, as "the jail-like work-house, forcibly separated husbands, wives and children in order to punish the poor for their destitution, and discourage them from the dangerous temptation of procreating further paupers" (Hobsbawn 1968, 69–70). Daniel Defoe claimed appreciatively that the workhouse in Bristol "has been such a Terror to the Beggars that none of [them] will come near the city. . . . Inmates of work houses often deliberately make themselves guilty of any crime what-soever in order to go to prison" (quoted in Losurdo 2014, 70). De Tocqueville wrote with approval that they were "the most horrendous and repugnant [spectacle] of misery. . . ." He went on to explain, "It is obvious that we must make assistance unpleasant, we must separate families, make the workhouse a prison and render our charity repugnant" (quoted in Losurdo 2014, 69, 72). Their conditions were so atrocious that "poor people were known to sell the shirts off their backs to avoid the workhouse" (Garraty 1978, 84).[8]

The Malthusian Population Doctrine

Men multiply like Mice in a barn if they have unlimited Means of Subsistence.

—Richard Cantillon, *Essay on the Nature of*
Trade in General (quoted in Routh 1975, 66)

Thomas Malthus wrote his most famous work, *On Population,* at a time when elites throughout Europe dreaded potential attacks on their privileges in the wake of the French Revolution of 1789. With its radical call for a new order grounded in *liberté, égalité, et fraternité,* the revolution spread great fear of the lower classes among European elites, especially when Robespierre gained power and the Reign of Terror erupted.[9]

In this climate of anxiety, elites saw any extension of democracy as a move toward the chaos of irrational mob rule that would ultimately result in the

---

[8] Harsh treatment toward the poor was expressed in the legal code. Social philosopher Domenico Losurdo reports that in England, "from 1688 to 1820, the number of crimes carrying the death pen-alty increased from 50 to between 200 and 250, and they were almost always crimes against property. While attempted homicide was regarded as a petty crime until 1803, the theft of a shilling or handker-chief, or the illegal clipping of an ornamental bush, could entail hanging; and one could be consigned to the hangman even at the age of eleven" (2014, 77).

[9] Piketty shares this interpretation: "It is impossible to understand Malthus's exaggeratedly somber predictions without recognizing the way fear gripped much of the European elite in the 1790s" (2014, 5).

confiscation of their wealth, suppression of their privileges, and a descent into universal poverty. The typical response was to limit political participation to property owners. They rejected claims that all humans are by nature equal, insisting that elites are manifestly superior as well as indispensable for sustaining and developing civilization. Malthus was very much of this mind.

The doctrinal genealogy of the Malthusian population doctrine runs as follows. The Reverend Robert Wallace—a friend of Adam Smith's—rejected the optimistic and egalitarian sentiments of the Enlightenment on the grounds that greater equality resulting from higher wages or charity would result in "excessive population" and the impoverishment of all. Wallace, and many others, embraced the claim that political economist Richard Cantillon had expressed at the outset of the eighteenth century, captured in the epigram that opened this section. In an attempt to refute Wallace, William Godwin (1793) set forth a determined defense of the French Enlightenment's belief in full equality and the perfectibility of society. In 1798 the cleric and political economist Thomas Malthus set out to refute Godwin and other utopians by expanding upon Wallace's argument. The full title of his vastly influential work is *An Essay on the Principle of Population, as it affects the future improvement of society with remarks on the speculations of Mr. Godwin, M. Condorcet, and other writers.*

The theory Malthus expounded was rooted in his explicit rejection of the Enlightenment's faith in the power of reason to improve the lot of all humanity. So strong was the Enlightenment's belief in reason that the Physiocrats "expected their ideal system of political economy to be enacted by enlightened statesmen, as a result of the persuasiveness of their arguments" (Hirschman 1997, 99). But Malthus vigorously contested the Enlightenment thinkers' claim that humans are rational. They are not predominantly ruled by reason, he argued, but rather by their passions. In a colorful passage, Malthus wrote, "The cravings of hunger, the love of liquor, the desire of possessing a beautiful woman, will urge men to actions. . . ." (1798, 92). And this proclivity to act on the impulses of the appetites is especially true of the poor.

With this background, the kernel of Malthus's doctrine may be summarized as follows. Driven by passion, most importantly including sexual urges, "population, when unchecked, increases in a geometrical ratio. Subsistence increases only in an arithmetic ratio" (1798, 9). Underlying this bleak prognosis is the fact that the supply of land is ultimately fixed. Thus, to improve the lot of the poor through higher wages or welfare measures would only enable them to produce more children, pushing cultivation to lower-productivity marginal land and lowering general economic well-being. Consequently, an argument for greater equality "offends against the cause of truth" (1798, 6). He noted that "the principle argument of this *Essay* only goes to prove the necessity of a class of proprietors and a class of labourers" (1798, 104). The poor, the far greater part of humanity, are condemned by the laws of nature to live at the edge of starvation, and, in fact, often starve: "It has appeared, that from the inevitable laws of our nature some human beings must suffer from want. Those are the unhappy persons who, in the great lottery of life, have drawn a blank" (1798, 74).

It is noteworthy that Malthus was an ordained minister in the Church of England, and his views reveal the enormous distance Christian doctrine had traveled from the Catholic view of the poor as "blessed." This expanse is especially evident in the following passage from the second edition of his *Essay on Population*:

> A man who is born into a world already possessed, if he cannot get subsistence from his parents, on whom he has a just demand, and if the society does not want his labour, has no claim of *right* to the smallest portion of food, and, in fact has no business to be where he is. At nature's mighty feast there is no vacant cover for him. (1803, 531)

This impolitic language, excised from later editions, exposes how easily it was accepted as natural that other humans could be denied access to the means of production necessary for their survival. Malthus's view of the poor lends support to sociologists Peter Berger and Thomas Luckmann's contention that

> in the period following the Industrial Revolution . . . there is a certain justification in calling Christianity a bourgeois ideology, because the bourgeoisie used the Christian tradition and its personnel in its struggle against the new industrial working class, which in most European countries could no longer be regarded as "inhabiting" the Christian universe. (1967, 123)

Malthus's population doctrine generated a quietist attitude toward the poor: "No possible sacrifices of the rich, particularly in money, could for any time prevent the recurrence of distress among the lower members of society, whoever they were" (1798, 31). Nothing can be done. Inequality and the misery of the poor are part of the divine scheme.[10] Malthus's population doctrine laid the responsibility for poverty on the poor themselves. They failed to control their passions, especially their sexual appetites. The rich need suffer no guilt and concede no obligation to be charitable. The money they might have squandered on misguided charity is put to better use in profitable investments that increase both their wealth and society's salutary inequality.

Malthus's influence persisted despite vehement criticism.[11] The surplus population doctrine he recrafted would go on to serve for 70 years as a principal legitimation of inequality. It was typically used to block public programs to help the poor and unemployed. In the 1860s, the notable political economist Henry Fawcett contended that "granting a legal right to employment at the ordinary wage" would be a mistake "because there would be no check on population" (1863, 245–47).

Toward the end of the nineteenth century, it became clear that improved living standards were not increasing workers' family size, and the threat of Malthusian overpopulation went into remission. Yet it would resurface again in the late 1960s and early 1970s in response to food shortages and starvation in several poor countries. Famines occurred against a backdrop of a post–World War II population explosion in what was then called the "third world" and a growing concern that natural resources were running out. This neo-Malthusian view was reflected in the widespread success of *The Population Bomb* (Ehrlich 1968) and *Limits to Growth* (Meadows 1972). The affluent

---

[10] Yet, Malthus's God is still good: "The partial pain ... that is inflicted by the supreme Creator ... is but as the dust of the balance in comparison of the happiness that is communicated, and we have every reason to think that there is no more evil in the world than what is absolutely necessary.... Evil exists in the world not to create despair but activity. We are not patiently to submit to it, but to exert ourselves to avoid it" (1798, 141, 142). Although Malthus presented his thesis as a secular one, its ties to religion remain strikingly evident.

[11] And the criticism was indeed severe. Historian Steven Shapin reports:

The assault on Malthus and his doctrines continued through the 19th century and beyond. Cobbett called him a "monster in human shape," saying that he had never "detested" anyone as much as Malthus. Carlyle found his views "dreary, stolid, dismal, without all hope for this world or the next; Nowhere ... is there any light; nothing but a grim shadow of Hunger; open mouths opening wider and wider; a world to terminate by the frightfullest consummation; by its too dense inhabitants, famished into delirium, universally eating one another." Secular socialists accused Malthus of immorality as well as error: Engels condemned his work as a "repulsive blasphemy against man and nature"; Marx accounted it "a sin against science" and a "libel on the human race"—little more than an apology by a "parson of the English State Church" for his own class interest.... Shelley argued that Malthus was "the apostle of the rich" and that his work was "calculated to lull the oppressors of mankind into a security of everlasting triumph." He characterized Malthus's work as "the political bible of the rich, the selfish, and the sensual" (2014, 26, 29).

would have to become accustomed to watching passively the victims of famine on their televisions. Nothing could be done. Food aid to poor countries should cease because it would fuel the population explosion.

Malthus added two other justifications for inequality, and especially for the existence of a non-producing landlord class. Unlike most members of the Classical School who believed the economy to be automatically self-adjusting, Malthus held that under certain conditions there could be a "glut" of commodities due to "ineffectual demand." First, for demand to be adequate such that all that is produced is sold, "There must . . . be a considerable class of persons who have both the will and power to consume more material wealth than they produce . . . [and] [i]n this class the landlords no doubt stand preeminent" (1820, 400). Second, the elite status of this leisure class is merited, because its behavior and consumption have led to the development of "all the noblest exertions of human genius, all the finer and more delicate emotions of the soul" (1798, 103). Further, he wrote that "it is an historical truth which cannot for a moment be disputed, that the first formation and subsequent preservation and improvement of our present constitution, and of the liberties and privileges which have so long distinguished Englishmen, are mainly due to a landed aristocracy" (1820, 380). Preservation of this unproductive class was thus the key, not only to macroeconomic stability, but also to retaining and furthering the benefits of civilization itself.

The Wages-Fund Doctrine

Writers of all views and parties, conservatives and liberals, capitalists and socialists invariably referred to social conditions under the Industrial Revolution as a veritable abyss of human degradation.
—Karl Polanyi, *The Great Transformation* (1944, 39)

Classical economists, drawing from the Physiocratic conception of *avances* (advances, that is, wages paid before production has been completed), argued that there was a fixed fund of capital out of which wages could be paid. This "wages fund" was made up of previously produced items that labor consumes, such as food, housing, and clothing. This fund was fixed by output in the previous period, thus carrying the implication that any attempt to raise general wages would be futile. The wages fund doctrine meant that combinations of workers (labor unions) could not increase the welfare of the working class as a whole, since if they were successful at raising the wages of their own members, it would be at the expense of other workers. In this manner, the wages-fund doctrine became a powerful ideological weapon against struggles of workers to organize to hold on to a share of their surplus. In England, it gave "scientific" legitimacy to the Anti-Combination Acts of 1799 that had been legislated to curb the rising power of the working class. Even John Stuart Mill embraced the doctrine until 1869. He eventually publicly rejected the doctrine in a review of a book by political economist William Thornton (1869), who proved the theory invalid. In doing so, Mill recognized that wage levels were dependent upon the relative bargaining power of the laboring and capitalist classes. A greater wage share could come out of the consumption expenditures of elites. Curiously, Mill's recantation of the wages-fund doctrine was not incorporated into the 1871 revision of his highly popular and influential *Principles of Political Economy*, thereby prolonging its ideological impact.

The "Trickle-Down" Thesis

If you feed enough oats to the horse, some will pass through to the road for the sparrows.
   —John Kenneth Galbraith, "Recession Economics" (1982).

Since the beginning of Classical economics, a "trickle-down" thesis has powerfully served to justify inequality. Economic dynamism is credited to saving and investing, and it is claimed that only the well-off carry out these functions. Thus, greater equality would reduce savings, and therefore investment, and therefore economic growth. Because everyone benefits from a dynamically growing economy, inequality benefits even the poor. The benefits trickle down to everyone, because, when the wealthy invest their savings, they raise demand for workers, increasing employment and putting upward pressure on the wage level. In another common metaphor, a rising tide lifts all boats.

Even social thinkers and political economists such as John Stuart Mill and Alfred Marshall, who sincerely sympathized with the poor, nonetheless argued that any substantial lessening of inequality would sap the springs of capital accumulation, leaving the poor and everyone worse off in the future.

More recently, as will be explored more fully in Chapter 11, the trickle-down doctrine became central to a resurgence of laissez-faire ideology expressed in supply-side economics' advocacy of tax cuts for the rich. The theory that tax relief favoring the wealthy raises the level of savings, investment, and economic growth was endorsed by Ronald Reagan in the United States and Margaret Thatcher in Great Britain.[12]

The wages-fund doctrine was abandoned toward the end of the nineteenth century. The other four inequality-legitimating doctrines of classical political economy (the utility of poverty, the justice of the invisible hand, the Malthusian population doctrine, and the trickle-down thesis) have, with varying frequency and intensity, continued to serve as ideological tenets justifying inequality in the distribution of income, wealth, and privilege.

A More "Scientific" Economics

> . . . the notion of 'individual marginal productivity is . . . something close to a pure ideological construct on the basis of which a justification for higher status can be elaborated.
>
> —Thomas Piketty, Capital in the
> Twenty-First Century (2014, 331)

In the last three decades of the nineteenth century, mainstream economics was reformulated in an attempt to make it more scientific. This entailed a restriction in scope and an emphasis on marginal change, permitting its theoretical expression to draw upon calculus. In doing so, it began to take on the "look" of Newtonian physics. One of its champions, economist George Stigler, famously claimed that economics was transformed "from an art, in many respects literary, to a science of growing rigor" (1941, 1). This reformulation of economics is often called both the *marginalist revolution* and the *neoclassical revolution*.

---

[12] The starkest modern statement of the trickle-down thesis was offered by Austrian economist and libertarian Ludwig von Mises: "Inequality of wealth and incomes is the cause of the masses' well-being, not the cause of anybody's distress. Where there is a 'lower degree of inequality', there is necessarily a lower standard of living of the masses" (1990). Von Mises held strong class views: in a congratulatory note to Ayn Rand upon the publication of *Atlas Shrugged* in 1957, he expressed little esteem for the greater part of humanity: "You have the courage to tell the masses what no politician told them: you are inferior and all the improvements in your conditions which you simply take for granted you owe to the efforts of men who are better than you" (quoted in Frank 2012, 147).

This remake also involved an attempt to sever economic science from its earlier "Classical" orientation that understood economic phenomena in terms of social classes and political power, while drawing on history to clarify complex economic dynamics. This older approach had been called political economy. The new brand dropped the "political" and became simply "economics," or, as its proponents imagined, pure economic science. Its prominent use of calculus and its focus on the marginal change that calculus is adept at expressing resulted in a primary emphasis on market phenomena. This model enabled economists more consistently to depict market participants as motivated by their shrewdly rational self-interest in maximizing their utility. Contemporary mainstream economics is built upon the theoretical foundation laid by this methodological and substantive "revolution." Indeed, it is often still referred to as neoclassical economics.

Presumably divorced from politics and other social dynamics, this supposedly more scientific economics was to be free from ideological contamination. In this, however, it patently failed. Far from objective, the new economics was as thoroughly ideological as the old. And, as will be seen in the following, it legitimated inequality with equal, if not greater, adroitness.

Marginal analysis made it possible to construct a theoretical model that presumes to measure the contribution of each additional unit of a factor of production—typically understood as land, labor, and capital—to the value of the final product. This added value is often understood as the appropriate and just income for that factor. For instance, the addition to total revenue of the last hour of labor determines the just wage for that hour.

In the preface to his highly influential book, *The Distribution of Wealth*, John Bates Clark asserted, "It is the purpose of this work to show that the distribution of income of society is controlled by a natural law, and that this law, if it worked without friction, would give to every agent of production the amount of wealth which that agent creates." A few pages later, Clark restated the workings of this natural law in terms of each factor of production: "free competition tends to give to labor what labor creates, to capitalists what capital creates, and to entrepreneurs what the coordinating function creates" (1908, v, 13). As ideology legitimating inequality, neoclassical economics shares a feature with Hinduism. It depicts what you get as what you deserve, and, most impressively, what you get is your responsibility. You chose your fate in the decisions you made about education and how hard you were willing to work, just as in Hinduism everyone's present condition depends upon their karma or behavior in previous lives.

Within this theoretical framework, all get what they deserve, the just return for what they contribute to the total value of society's economic output. This idea was already implicit in the natural law cosmology of the "invisible hand." What neoclassical analysis added was analytical rigor to make the case quite explicit and theoretically clear. The morality suggested by Adam Smith's invisible hand was dressed up in scientific-looking apparel. Free-market capitalism is just. Most mainstream economists would not likely say this outright. To do so would be to violate a supposed boundary between positive and normative economics. Nevertheless, the effect is the same. The theory implies that the distribution of income effected by free-market capitalism is as it should be.

The political and social power that had been important in classical political economy no longer figured into this analysis. Power relations are issues outside of the new, more scientific economics. Indeed, within this analytic framework, they would not likely ever come to mind. Whereas the distribution of income and property were critical to classical political economy, neoclassical economics pays them relatively little attention, despite the fact that inequality is crucial not just to everything economic, but also to everything social.

Fully lost, then, was any perspective that might resemble that of Marx's political economy. For Marx, the fundamental character of capitalism was located in its specific form of inequality, whereby an elite owned and controlled all capital (stored-up labor) and natural resources (land). Workers, who had no ownership, control, or unimpeded access to productive wealth, were forced to contract with the elite owners if they were to work and survive. For this right to work, workers had to pay the high price of their surplus, the value of what they produced in excess of what they needed for their meager subsistence. Neoclassical theory pretends that the owners of the means of production pay the workers, when, in fact, the workers pay the owners of capital and resources the surplus output of their labor in exchange for the privilege of using them. Many of the faults found with capitalism are the direct result of this special form of inequality. These include poverty, debased and alienated work, and macroeconomic instability. These will be addressed more fully in Chapter 13.

The inequality-justifying character of neoclassical economics finds support, especially in the United States, from three complementary currents of contemporary thought: libertarianism, the belief in fluid vertical mobility, and the view of government as incompetent.

Neoclassical economics and libertarianism share common intellectual roots in the Western Enlightenment tradition that sets the autonomous individual at the center of the social world.[13] But, whereas Enlightenment thinkers generally viewed liberty and equality as inseparable, both neoclassical economics and libertarianism typically see them as antithetical.

Both see markets as essential social institutions for individual freedom.[14] Libertarianism's ethical foundation is the single, broadly conceived, and inviolable right of self-ownership. For libertarians, this has come to mean that individuals have a right to dispose of both their persons and their legitimately acquired property as they choose. Therefore, libertarianism proscribes interfering with the right of individuals to do as they please with themselves or their property. Inequality is not a problem. It is the natural consequence of freedom. Justice never permits the state to take legitimately acquired property from some individuals in order to give it to others, no matter how great the benefits to recipients relative to the costs to donors. All such transfers would involve confiscation or coercive taxation and thus constitute an unacceptable infringement of the right to self-ownership. It must be observed, however, that what constitutes legitimately acquired property is defined by states that are typically controlled by those who own most property, a fact that is almost always conveniently ignored by libertarianism's proponents. And as Honoré de Balzac quipped, "behind every fortune lurks a well-hidden crime."[15]

The belief in fluid vertical mobility holds that, by dint of hard work, anyone can make it to the top. It reinforces neoclassical economics' claim that

---

[13] Many of the most distinguished intellectual defenders of inequality—such as the late economist Milton Friedman and his colleagues in the Chicago School—appear to blend neoclassical and libertarian arguments as complementary, and freely mix them in their writings for general audiences, e.g., Friedman's *Capitalism and Freedom* (1962), and *Free to Choose* (1980).

[14] Historian of economic thought Miya Tokumitsu summarizes the genealogy of this conception of freedom:

> The notion that personal freedom is rooted in free markets . . . originated with the Levellers in seventeenth-century England, when working conditions differed substantially from today's. The Levellers believed that a market society was essential to liberate individuals from the remnants of feudal hierarchies; their vision of utopia was a world in which men could meet and interact on terms of equality and dignity. Their ideas echoed through the writing and politics of later figures like John Locke, Adam Smith, Thomas Paine, and Abraham Lincoln, all of whom believed that open markets could provide the essential infrastructure for individuals to shape their own destiny. An anti-statist streak runs through several of these thinkers, particularly the Levellers and Paine, who viewed markets as the bulwark against state oppression (2017, 54).

[15] "Le secret des grandes fortunes sans cause apparente est un crime oublié, parce qu'il a été proprement fait" (*Le Père Goriot*).

in capitalist society all economic actors get their just desserts. The system is fair. This idea that one's place in the social hierarchy is the individual's responsibility has especially deep roots in US culture. For much of its history, thanks to abundant land and the arrival of immigrants fleeing Europe's rigid class structure, there was greater social mobility in America than anywhere else on earth. Consequently, Americans more readily take credit for their successes and find the poor responsible for their poverty.[16] In this land of opportunity and abundant resources, poverty was easily understood as the fault of the poor themselves: due to their lack of diligence, they brought too little value into the marketplace.

Laissez-faire ideology was also strengthened by President Ronald Reagan's identification of government as *the problem*, a view that has become ever more widely embraced since the end of the 1970s (Wisman 2013a). It claims that government is corrupt and incompetent and therefore should be minimized, a position that bolsters the ideology of laissez-faire economics. Political scientists Susan Pharr and Robert Putnam have found empirical support for the perception that trust in government has declined: "The onset and depth of this disillusionment vary from country to country, but the downtrend is longest and clearest in the United States where polling has produced the most abundant and systematic evidence" (2000, 8). In the mid-1950s, three-quarters of Americans agreed with the statement, "You can trust the government to do the right thing most of the time"; only 10 percent agreed 50 years later (Wade 2012, 33). This hostility toward government has legitimated cuts in welfare and public goods that benefit the less well off, thus enabling elites to capture more income, wealth, and privilege.

The Keynesian Anomaly

> ... *economics is essentially a moral science and not a natural science.*
> *That is to say, it employs introspection and judgment of value.*
> —John Maynard Keynes, The General Theory
> of Employment, Interest, and Money (2012, I:297)

---

[16] It should be noted that since the recent explosion in inequality, multiple studies have found that there is less vertical mobility in the United States than in other rich societies such as Canada, Sweden, Germany, Spain, Denmark, Austria, Norway, Finland, and France (Jäntti et al. 2006; d'Addio 2007; Hertz 2007; Mishel, Bernstein, and Allegretto 2007; Mazumder 2005; Bowles and Gintis 2002; Solon 1992).

It is by no means the case that all economists and economic theories have served to legitimate inequality. This is especially true among heterodox economists who attempt to construct alternative theories to those of the mainstream. But mainstream economists, even those who identify excessive inequality as one of capitalism's major failings, address it relatively infrequently in their analyses. Political economist James Galbraith points out that of the 848 subcategories of economic journal articles in the classification codes of the *Journal of Economic Literature*, only five relate to income inequality (2019, 1).

John Maynard Keynes stands out as a major exception among mainstream economists. He believed he was working within the mainstream when he formulated a macroeconomic theory in which inequality plays a central role. However, mainstream economics began reverting to a pre-Keynesian laissez-faire orientation in the mid-1970s, and many American economists no longer view Keynes as "mainstream," or even as an important economist.

Keynes's economics matured during the Great Depression of the 1930s. In the face of massive unemployment and a dramatic contraction in production, the prescription of the then-prevailing mainstream of economic theory was to leave the economy alone so that prices could adjust and bring forth a spontaneous return to dynamism and full employment. Free markets would do the job. Keynes challenged this thinking. Under certain conditions, markets will not self-correct and revert to a stable equilibrium. To grasp why, he focused upon economic aggregates such as total demand, investment, savings, consumption, and employment. He concluded that the crisis was due to inadequate total demand, and that government intervention in the form of greater spending was necessary to restore the economy to full employment. But he added a special radical kicker: inequality was part of the problem. Because the less well-off spend a larger percentage of their incomes, redistributing income to them would increase total consumption and thereby help protect the economy from falling into recessions or depressions due to insufficient demand.

Keynes also claimed that a science of economics could not be value-free, permitting him to continue to wear the mantle of science when he claimed that "the outstanding faults of the economic society in which we live are its failure to provide for full employment and its arbitrary and inequitable distribution of wealth and incomes" (2011, 372).

Keynes's view of inequality challenged the trickle-down economics that has dominated economic and political thinking since the beginning of modern economics more than 150 years ago. Keynes characterized the legitimating function of laissez-faire doctrine as follows: "That it could explain much social injustice and apparent cruelty as an inevitable incident in the scheme of progress, and the attempt to change such things as likely on the whole to do more harm than good, commended it to authority" (2011, 33). In its place, Keynes provided legitimacy for government intervention to maintain full employment and to reduce inequality, not merely in the name of justice, but for the well-being of the economy and, therefore, all of society. He reversed the ideological embrace of trickle-down theory, which legitimated inequality, by describing greater equality as generating greater economic stability and dynamism—a trickle-up theory.

Keynesian economics was highly influential—and generally considered part of mainstream economics—for more than 30 years. Inequality lessened while Keynesianism was in favor, demonstrating the power of economics to influence public policy. Thus it contradicted neoclassical economist George Stigler's assertion that "economists exert a minor and scarcely detectable influence on the societies in which they live" (1982, 63). Keynes claimed just the opposite:

> ... the ideas of economists and political philosophers, both when they are right and when they are wrong, are more powerful than is commonly understood. Indeed, the world is ruled by little else. Practical men, who believe themselves to be quite exempt from any intellectual influences, are usually the slaves of some defunct economist. Madmen in authority, who hear voices in the air, are distilling their frenzy from some academic scribbler of a few years back. (1936, 383)

Its peak influence occurred during the decade of the 1960s. Ironically, the doctrine encountered heavy weather as it was gaining its fullest acceptance (in 1971, President Richard Nixon was the first prominent Republican to embrace Keynesian economics). By the late 1970s, mainstream economists began returning to pre-Keynesian laissez-faire economics, endorsing public policies that would fuel the explosion of inequality that has taken place over the past 45 years. Chapter 11 will examine in detail this resurgence in inequality-legitimating laissez-faire ideology that emerged under the banner of "supply-side" economics.

The next chapter, Chapter 9, will explore how industrialization and urbanization, brought about by maturing capitalism, enabled workers to gain a degree of formal political power, potentially allowing them to retain a larger share of their surplus.

9

Workers Gain Formal Political Power

*When masters combine together in order to reduce the wages of their
workmen, they commonly enter into a private bond or agreement, not
to give more than a certain wage under a certain penalty. Were the
workmen to enter into a contrary combination of the same kind, not to
accept of a certain wage under a certain penalty, the law would punish
them very severely.*

—Adam Smith, *The Wealth of Nations* (1776, 142)

Since the rise of civilization, the state and a thin elite class have expropriated the surplus from low-status agricultural producers. Sporadically, producers revolted or offered concerted resistance, especially when extractions
increased, or where war or poor harvests pushed their material conditions
beneath those necessary for survival. However, there was no inherent dynamic whereby these struggles would transform society in any particular
manner, or even the nature of the struggle itself. Rebellions were brutally
suppressed, and exploitation continued as before.

The struggle between landlords and cultivators manifested itself in practically all domains of social existence. For instance, during feudalism,
cultivators appealed to public justice, where available, to rectify excessive seigneurial impositions, or pressured lords for rent reductions, or engaged in
chicanery to conceal quantities of produce. Lords fabricated new dues, used
violence to secure rent increases, or laid claim to commons or disputed lands.
Until the rise of capitalism, the state was generally beholden to a landed aristocracy. It was this class that commanded resources that could be deployed
to challenge the state's monopoly on violence. Consequently, the state had to
appease this class by permitting its members to capture a substantial share of
producers' surplus, at the cost of having less to tax away.

The rise of capitalism created the conditions for the first system-
transforming class struggle. It occurred, as was seen in Chapters 6 and 7,

between a rising commercial and manufacturing class and the aristocratic landlords. It fueled the transition from feudalism to capitalism.

The landed aristocracy was forced to share power and influence over the state with an increasingly wealthy bourgeoisie, a new commercial class made up of traders, manufacturers, and bankers. To retain the loyalty of both the aristocracy and the bourgeoisie, the state protected their property and interests. This protection often entailed violently curbing the aspirations of workers, especially by crushing revolts and putting down strikes. Three social interests—the state, the aristocracy, and the bourgeoisie—now participated in a struggle, each one vying to maximize its share of society's surplus. Below their level, the producer class endeavored to retain enough output to stay healthy, and, if possible, a bit more. Because of bourgeois-driven economic growth, when not absorbed by population growth, there was more surplus over which to fight.

The political dynamics unleashed by the inability of the landed aristocracy to hold in check the rising power of a bourgeoisie were unprecedented. There had been earlier instances where a commercial class had gained the upper hand in sharing political power with landed aristocracies, such as Iraq in the fifth to seventh century, Italy in the tenth to twelfth century, and the Low Countries in the eleventh to thirteenth century. Chapter 6 recapitulated key points in Bas van Bavel's studies of these cases (2016). In each instance, growing inequality enabled the thriving bourgeoisie to gain ever-greater political power. The bourgeoisie then set about transforming social institutions to create opportunities for rent-seeking (attempting to gain income by means of political machinations rather than by investing to create new productive wealth). They channeled their increased income into financial speculation, as opposed to productive investment, and partook in massive conspicuous consumption through purchases of land, villas, and art. The consequences were, initially, stagnation, and then severe secular declines in the economies of these three countries.

Uniquely in Western Europe, as discussed in Chapter 6, geographic conditions meant ever-present competition among states. It resulted that, should capitalism begin to self-destruct in one country, it would continue to survive in some neighboring states. Thus, in Europe as a whole, an empowered bourgeoisie gained adequate political power to shepherd the continuing maturation of capitalism. This unleashed capitalism created an industrialized and urbanized working class that could, in its own turn, successfully organize under the umbrella of bourgeois values and bid for a share of political power. The workers' ultimate goal was to reduce inequality. This was the second system-transforming class struggle. The first pitted an emerging commercial class against the landed aristocracy; this one set workers in opposition to capitalists. This second initiative gained momentum during the nineteenth century, establishing the conditions for democratic freedom and enabling workers to retain a portion of the surplus.

Workers could not be walled off from the contagious bourgeois ideals of universal humanity and equality. Workers were motivated to revolt not only by their miserable social and material conditions, but also by the bourgeois ideals that exposed the injustice of those conditions. They saw that the existing structure of society was neither divinely ordained nor required by nature, and they began to challenge the class system itself. This was new. When earlier peasants revolted, they generally did not do so because they envisioned the possibility of another, more just social order. They did so because, ill-housed and chronically undernourished, they suffered material deprivation. As sociologist J. Craig Jenkins writes, "Peasants rebel because of threats to their access to an economic subsistence, not because of the particular form of class relations in which they are enmeshed" (1982, 487).

Nonetheless, nourished by early bourgeois values, there were some relatively early cases where groups of workers or artisans called for a radical restructuring of society. In the mid-seventeenth century, a wave of social revolts occurred in urban England. The most notable of these uprisings were initiated by the Levellers, who included small tradesmen, yeomen, and other small producers in control of their means of production. Their most extreme contingent, the Diggers or True Levellers, advocated abolishing the markets for land and labor, and transferring property to communal ownership. The Levellers met defeat, first in 1647, and then by Cromwell in 1649 (Bavel 2016, 213). It is only in the nineteenth century that industrialization and urbanization enabled workers to organize effectively and to force society to give them better deals.

Intensifying Worker Militancy

It is the credible threat of a revolution by the population that ultimately pushes the elites to democratize.
—Christian Houle, "Inequality and Democracy" (2009, 592)

The extraordinary economic and political successes of the bourgeoisie worsened inequality as elites captured the fruits of economic growth, usually leaving producers barely enough to survive. But growth also set in motion forces that would further democratize political power and ultimately promise to lessen inequality. In particular, industrialization and urbanization made it easier for insurgent workers to communicate and assemble. In earlier agricultural economies, producers were spread over the countryside as slaves, serfs, and peasants. Distances between them hampered communications, limiting both the spread of radical ideas and the capacity to organize. Radicals in rural areas could also be easily identified, isolated, and eradicated. By contrast, maturing nineteenth-century capitalism brought workers together in factories and urban slums where they could find common cause. In this environment, ideas could circulate faster, and their propagators could remain better hidden among the urban masses. Workers could come to see that their dehumanizing work and miserable living conditions were due, not to the natural order, but to capitalism itself and the exploitation it engendered. They could come to see that the state was not divinely ordained but, rather, an instrument used by the ruling elites to enforce subjugation. They could rally in revolt, often spontaneously, without traveling far from their dwellings, and, when attacked, they could disperse down narrow alleys and hide away in the slums.

Social observers began to grasp what was going on as early as the end of the eighteenth century. Philosopher and historian John Millar, a contemporary of Adam Smith, noted the suitability of large urban centers for worker revolts. In such settings

> a great proportion of the people are easily roused by every popular discontent, and can unite with no less facility in demanding a redress of grievances. The least ground of complaint, in a town, becomes the occasion of a riot; and the flames of sedition spreading from one city to another, are blown up into a general insurrection. (quoted in Hirschman 1997, 90)

By the mid-nineteenth century, when Marx was writing, industrialization and urbanization had considerably advanced beyond the stage that existed in Millar's time. There was, accordingly, greater potential for the working class to organize, demand redress, and threaten violence against the elite's state. This was a rude awakening for the ruling elite, because, as political economist Maurice Dobb notes, earlier social theories "held no inkling of an historical role for the working class. Such a role was quite foreign to bourgeois conceptions, and its introduction was at once transforming and, to traditional notions, distinctly shocking" (1967, 528). Working-class agitation for a better deal frightened elites. Historian and sociologist Pierre Rosanvallon writes that "throughout the nineteenth century, people were obsessed with the possibility that a new period of revolutionary turmoil might be on the horizon" (2013, 173).

Marx was far from alone in writing about the fundamental unfairness of the existing order. Stimulated by Enlightenment ideals of equality, freedom, and brotherhood, utopians and socialists explored more just alternatives to capitalism and attempted to organize movements for creating these alternatives. Their writings energized leaders of worker movements who championed their visions of a fairer and more humane society. For the first time since the rise of the state and its concomitant, systemic exploitation, producers began to grasp their own power to create radically alternative social arrangements that promised them better lives.

The evolution of an urban industrial working class brought with it organized, and at times violent, resistance to long workdays, low wages, child labor, unhealthy working conditions, and the lack of education for working-class children. When workers got together, conversation often turned to their conditions. As the coffee house had been the important meeting place for the bourgeoisie since the seventeenth century, the tavern was to serve that function for the proletariat in the nineteenth century. Whereas coffee was believed to kindle rationality, sobriety, and individualism, alcohol arouses the proletarian ideals of collectivity and solidarity. Alcohol can increase trust and a sense of community (Slingerland 2021). In England, the first worker associations met in public houses. Pubs also served as information centers during strikes and revolts. Philosopher Karl Kautsky claimed that "without the tavern, the German proletariat has not only no social but also no political life" (quoted in Schivelbusch 1993, 166).

From the very beginning of the industrial revolution, elites controlling the state succeeded in having worker associations outlawed. For instance, in France, the ordinance Le Chapelier of 1791 banned all associations of workers in the same profession. Organizations of workers were outlawed in England by the Combination Act of 1799, which remained in force until 1824. Political economist Karl Polanyi reported that "between 1793 and 1820, more than 60 acts directed at repression of working-class collective action were passed by Parliament" (1944, 81). Worker associations were also illegal in the United States until *Commonwealth v. Hunt* in 1842.

Nevertheless, workers persisted in joining together, even if illegally. But the state, in service to elites—increasingly composed of bourgeois—violently curbed worker aspirations, especially in putting down strikes, riots, and insurrections. The resources the state brought to this task were often massive, and the punishments meted out to workers were ferocious. For instance, to put down the Luddite disturbances,

> the government sent an armed force of twelve thousand soldiers to quell the rural riots, a force greater than that which the Duke of Wellington took with him to Spain to fight Napoleon. Parliament followed up by adding frame breaking to the list of capital crimes [meriting execution], which already numbered in the hundreds. (Appleby 2011, 153)

However, repression proved inadequate. Eventually, to reduce and, hopefully, eliminate the threat of violence, the elite-controlled state began pacifying the working class with various benefits and, importantly, with the franchise. Both strategies for calming revolutionary fervor resulted in higher living standards for workers. Although conceding benefits was immediately costly to elites—lowering the amount of surplus they could appropriate—the alternative of violent revolution threatened to be far worse. They also realized that providing workers with nonviolent means of influencing the political process would inhibit the ability of revolutionary-minded dissidents to rally large numbers in violent actions (E. N. Muller and Seligman 1987, 444). Writing of the 1930s in America, labor historian Melvyn Dubovsky notes that "what workers most often experienced in common—participation in the political system—was precisely what most effectively diluted militancy and radicalism" (1986, 215). Tocqueville (1835) had foreseen this calming effect of participation a century earlier when he observed that the political inclusion of disgruntled groups served to quiet social resentment. He was well aware that conservative French elites' vociferous opposition to extending the franchise had been followed by devastating urban riots.

In the end, as political scientists Evelyne Huber, Dietrich Rueschemeyer, and John D. Stephens note, "the bourgeoisie often comes around to support democracy once it turns out that its interests can be protected within the system" (1993, 75). Arguably, there may also have been some understanding among elites that their superior command of ideology could limit their losses. In addition, the threat that democracy represented was lessened by the fact that, should voters attempt to impose confiscatory taxation, the bourgeoisie could send its wealth abroad.

Nonetheless, some continued to back the state's use of violence to quell social unrest. President Theodore Roosevelt offered that "the sentiment now animating a large proportion of our people can only be suppressed . . . by taking ten or a dozen of their leaders out, standing . . . them against a wall, and shooting them" (quoted in Hofstadter 1989, 216).

Democracy has, of course, always been justly feared by elites, and most vehemently among the aristocracy and the wealthiest of the bourgeoisie. The reason is clear. As political scientists John Kane and Haig Patapan put it, "Democracy is at root a revolt against the rank ordering of society. . . . The leveling instinct of democracy is principally directed against the arrogance of inherited or entrenched power" (2012, 32–33). Political scientist Carles Boix characterizes democracy as a mechanism of decision in which, to a large extent, everything is up for grabs at each electoral contest. The majority of the day may choose to redraw property rights or alter the institutional and taxation landscape, thus dramatically reorganizing the entire social and economic fabric of the country (2006, 4).

The landed upper class had always been democracy's most consistent and ferocious opponent. Its animus was first directed against the claims of the bourgeoisie for political representation. The aristocracy also knew that they had long been depicted by most political economists as parasites. Adam Smith memorably described them as people who "love to reap where they never sowed" (1776, 49). It is unsurprising, then, that opposition to democracy would be strongest among the aristocracy. Nineteenth-century art and culture historian and defender of patrician values, Jacob Burkhardt proclaimed, "I know too much about history to expect anything from the despotism of the masses but a future tyranny, which will mean the end of history" (quoted in A. Green 2008, 17). By the second half of the nineteenth century, however, the aristocrats' remaining economic and political power was rapidly slipping away.[1]

Neither the aristocracy nor the bourgeoisie imagined the franchise could be extended to the working-class rabble, and, as that day approached, they lived in fear of dispossession by mob rule. The rise of capitalism and the

---

[1] Nevertheless, Huber, Rueschemeyer, and Stephens note that "in four of the five Western European countries in which large landholders played a significant political role toward the end of the nineteenth century—Germany, Austria-Hungary, Spain and Italy—democratic regimes collapsed in the interwar period" (1993, 77).

bourgeoisie's struggle for political power and status brought forth ideals that would underpin democracy, such as individual freedom, equality, and government as a social contract. But democracy was not given to the working class under the banner of these ideals, as is often claimed. Instead, it was fought for in the streets and won by the working class's continual threats of violence against the elite's state.

Greater democratization at the ballot box progressively curbed the elite's ability to muster state support for the use of violence against workers. To retain their economic and political power, elites had to rely more heavily on ideology. They had to convince the masses that the self-interest of the elites was in fact the self-interest of everybody. This, of course, they had always done. Less and less, however, could they back up their ideology with intimidation.[2]

In a fictive world without ideology, individuals might be expected to gravitate spontaneously toward political and economic doctrines that uphold their interests. The options would fall across the spectrum of political parties from right to left, with wealthy individuals generally supporting political parties that represent their interests on the right and poorer individuals generally supporting parties that represent theirs on the left. However, individuals come to the task of discerning their best interests and choosing a political affiliation with widely unequal assets. In the play of ideology, the wealthy are dealt the best cards. In addition to far greater material assets, they have the best educations and the most gifted friends and acquaintances. These privileges make them on average more astute in judging their interests and more successful in attaining them than less fortunate citizens. Indeed, their more sophisticated mental worlds mean that they are less likely to be fooled as to precisely what their self-interests are, while presenting them to all others as fair. In their competition for status, the rich naturally gravitate toward ideologies favoring measures that bring them ever greater shares of society's income, wealth, and privilege. Their competition among themselves for the pinnacle of status compels each of them to seek the greatest share

[2] However, economist Gerald Friedman reminds us that violence remained a major response in the United States, especially in the latter part of the nineteenth century: "Repression, rather than conciliation, was the method chosen by most American government officials to deal with large strikes and with rising labor militancy. Following the 1877 railroad strike, most states reorganized their national guards, and both the guard and the regular army were increasingly active in later labor disputes, intervening over 500 times between 1877 and 1903.... Where state power was insufficient, businessmen filled the gap with private force, including lynch mobs, armed Pinkerton guards, and quasi-public bodies like the Pennsylvania Coal and Iron Police" (1988, 14–15). Perhaps the less vehement response to violence against strikers in the United States, as compared to Europe, stems from the former's lack of a strong socialist party and anti-capitalist sentiments threatening revolution.

of everything considered valuable—the enduring mandate of biology that rewards people of distinction with material well-being and greater access to mates.

Democracy did not come forth full-blown overnight, but instead in bits and pieces over a protracted period. The franchise spread as states were forced under the threat of violence to relax voter restrictions such as property owner-ship, evidence of paying taxes, or literacy. Nevertheless, by historical standards, its rise was extraordinarily swift. Male suffrage came relatively early in the United States, although there, too, it has run up against the constant friction of restrictions. But in the Europe of 1870, only Switzerland had a substantial degree of democracy: the franchise was shared with male producers. Other countries that are often thought to have been democracies, including Britain, the Netherlands, and Belgium, had elements of democracy, such as com-peting parties and parliaments, but used income or property rights that mili-tated against extending the right to vote to the working class. Fifty years later, by 1920, almost all Western European countries had granted the franchise to their entire male adult citizenry. This extension paralleled the intensifica-tion of worker protests that accompanied industrialization and urbanization. The non-agricultural workforce in these economies grew by one-third to one-half, reaching on average about 61 percent of the total workforce (Huber, Rueschemeyer, and Stephens 1993, 76).

Rosanvallon contends that "the idea of democracy introduced a much more significant *intellectual* break in the concept of humanity than did the idea of so-cialism . . . the utopia of an economically egalitarian society was formulated long before the idea of political equality appeared" (2013, 36). The franchise implied full political equality in the sense that every vote counted the same and that all are presumed equally capable of weighing what constitutes the common good and what is just and unjust.

The abolition of slavery also coincided with the rise of worker power and the spread of the idea of human equality. As doctrines of equality became ever more entrenched in social consciousness, the idea of the innate superi-ority of the elite weakened, and indeed would ultimately become politically unacceptable. Great Britain ended slavery both at home and in its colonies in 1833, the end of slavery in France followed in 1848, in the Netherlands in 1863, the United States in 1865, Spain in 1886, and Brazil in 1888.[3] The notion of universal humanity gained greater strength and everyone, slaves

---

[3] The last country to legally outlaw slavery was Mauritania in 1981, although no laws were passed

included, became more fully "humanized," recognized as members of the same human family. Claims to racial superiority also receded, albeit much more slowly and far less completely.

Industrialization not only degraded the quality of work, but also relatively disempowered women. As was seen in Chapter 6, prior to the proletarianization of workers, husbands and wives generally worked as partnerships, first as foragers and later in agriculture and handicraft industry. But when men began to work in factories, women were often left to care for the home and children. Because males brought home and controlled money, and because household needs had to be met increasingly through the market, the males' domestic power was enhanced and that of their spouses weakened. And because urban workers' living space was generally too cramped to accommodate extended families, women became virtual prisoners of the household, unable to leave young children unattended. However, just as urbanization brought workers more closely together where they could organize, so, too, it put women in contact with others who were also experiencing industrialization's gender inequality. Women educated each other, organized, and began to petition for a better deal. The women's suffrage movement was one of the major outcomes. Women won the full right to vote in the Netherlands in 1917, Germany in 1918, the United States in 1920, the United Kingdom in 1928, France in 1944, and Italy in 1945.

Quelling Revolutionary Impulses with Reforms and the Franchise

The task of elitism in the so-called age of democracy was not to resist democracy but to accept it nominally and then to set about persuading majorities to act politically against their own material interests and potential power.

—Sheldon Wolin, *Democracy Incorporated* (2010, 234)

to penalize its continued practice. Incidentally, when England and France abolished slavery in their colonies, bending to the political pressure of their elites, legislation passed requiring taxpayer-financed compensation of slave-owners for their capital losses. The compensation burden inflicted on Haiti equaled 300 percent of the value of its national income in 1825. Not until 1950 was Haiti freed of this heavy crippling handicap to its economic development (Piketty 2020, 217–20). Freed slaves everywhere never received compensation for their years, if not their entire lives, of suffering the most abject condition of labor.

The following examples more fully characterize the threat of worker insurrection and the response of ruling elites in a few European nations.

Due to property qualifications, less than 2 percent of the British population enjoyed the right to vote in 1831. In the ensuing year, the franchise was extended, following "unprecedented political unrest, including the Luddite Riots from 1811–1816, the Spa Fields Riots of 1816, the Peterloo Massacre in 1819, and the Swing Riots of 1832" (Acemoglu and Robinson 2000, 1182–83).[4] Also to quell worker militancy, England introduced the 10-hour working day in 1847. The franchise was extended again after the revolution of 1848, and yet again in 1867 following a heightened threat of violence due to a severe economic downturn. By 1884–1885, about two-thirds of English men were entitled to vote. England effected each extension by progressively relaxing property qualifications.

The expansion of the franchise led to welfare measures paid for by increased taxes that fell heavily upon elites. Taxes as a percent of national income doubled between 1870 and 1900 (Acemoglu and Robinson 2000, 1167, 1191). Yet, England continued to lag behind other European countries in providing a welfare system. Although inequality continued to rise—the richest one percent owned 70 percent of total wealth at the beginning of World War I—real wages more than doubled between 1860 and the 1920s (Bavel 2016, 227, 225).

In France, universal male suffrage accompanied the Revolution of 1789, but it was whittled down to virtually nothing in subsequent decades. In its attempt to re-establish the *ancien régime* after the 1830 revolution, the Orleanist monarchy set forth a number of decrees known as the July Ordinances. One of them excluded even the commercial middle class from elections. It limited the franchise to a mere 0.75 percent of the population, mostly landowning aristocrats (Acemoglu and Robinson 2000, 1184). However, in the 1830s and 1840s, the specter of a "social conflagration akin to Saint Bartholomew's Day in the Wars of Religion was frequently raised," heightening awareness among elites that, to avoid further revolutionary violence, reforms would need be made (Rosanvallon 2013, 173).

The years 1847 and 1848 brought severe economic hardship across Europe. The potato blight and poor grain harvests dramatically raised food prices at

---

[4] It is insufficiently recognized that the Luddites protested not just against the loss of jobs and incomes created by new textile machinery, but also against the degraded character of work that also accompanied its introduction.

a time of high unemployment, creating widespread hunger and destitution. All of Western Europe exploded in the Revolutions of 1848. There was widespread fear among elites that, without reforms, revolutions would abolish their privileges and put an end to their way of life.

In the wake of the revolutions of 1848 and the collapse of the Orleanist monarchy in 1849, universal suffrage was promised to all French males and became law after Louis Napoleon Bonaparte seized power in 1851 and declared himself emperor. Nevertheless, continued concern with looming worker insurrection over the next half-century led France to further reforms. Notable among them was the creation in 1898 of compulsory workmen's compensation insurance requiring payment to injured workers regardless of fault. This represented, as Rosanvallon puts it, socialization of the very idea of responsibility (2013, 195).

Because substantial capitalist institutions came relatively late to Germany, traditional paternalistic values remained widespread, especially in comparison with England's laissez-faire ideology. Nevertheless, working conditions for the urban proletariat in Germany were generally as harsh as elsewhere in much of industrializing Europe. To house, feed, and clothe their families, wives and children typically needed to enter the workforce. They often worked in conditions of heat, deafening noise, and choking dust in poorly ventilated factories for 12 or more hours per day, six days a week. The wear and tear on their bodies condemned most workers to old age by 40, often mutilated and infirm. They typically spent their last years in dire poverty. The socialist promise of liberation from this fate understandably resonated with a great number of workers.

Otto von Bismarck's understanding of the need to appease workers to maintain social peace was already evident during the Revolution of 1848, when he proclaimed that "the factories enrich individuals, but they create a mass of poorly nourished proletarians, who by virtue of the insecurity of their existence have become a threat to the state" (quoted in J. Z. Muller 2003, 172). The franchise was extended with property restrictions after the 1848 revolution and greatly extended in 1867.

In the decades after he became chancellor in 1871, Bismarck proceeded to launch the foundations of the welfare state. In a speech before the Reichstag on March 20, 1884, he justified his insistence for social welfare reforms in the following terms:

... the actual complaint of the worker is the insecurity of his existence; he is unsure if he will always have work, he is unsure if he will always be healthy and he can predict that he will reach old age and be unable to work. If he falls into poverty, and be that only through prolonged illness, he will find himself totally helpless being on his own, and society currently does not accept any responsibility towards him beyond the usual provisions for the poor, even if he has been working all the time ever so diligently and faithfully. The ordinary provision for the poor, however, leaves a lot to be desired.... (Images and History 2018)

Reforms became especially urgent after Germany's Social Democratic Party embraced a Marxist program in 1875. To counter the threat it posed, between October 1878 and late 1903, Bismarck invoked pre-capitalist paternalism—the state is the nation's caring parent—and successfully advanced social programs that largely defanged worker militancy: worker accident insurance in 1879; compulsory health insurance in 1883, jointly paid for by employers and workers; old-age and disability insurance, combined with mandatory retirement in 1890; the Workers Protection Act of 1891; and the Children's Protection Act of 1903. Although these measures largely quelled working-class revolutionary fervor, in 1912 the Social Democrats became the most powerful party in parliament.

As industrialization and urbanization spread to other European nations, so too did worker militancy. Males gained the franchise and significantly improved working conditions, wages, and social support measures that put a safety net, albeit a paltry one, beneath workers. The state assumed responsibility for much of what had earlier been viewed as the domain of charity. The state presented itself as an agent for social solidarity, and often as paternal caretaker, while workers came to see their hard-won benefits as rights.

Several other reforms were especially noteworthy. One was the democratization of education for workers' children. In England, for instance, in a mere 30 years (between 1870 and 1900), school enrollment of 10-year-old children soared from 40 percent to 100 percent (Acemoglu and Robinson 2000, 1191). More surprising, in the late nineteenth and early twentieth centuries, almost all advanced capitalist countries enacted progressive income and inheritance taxes. They came into effect in Germany and Japan in the 1890s and most other industrial countries between 1910 and 1920. Initially, they were taxes on the wealthy. Rates were as high as 50 to 90 percent at the very top

(Piketty 2020, 559). Between 1900 and 1920, many countries also legislated wealth and inheritance taxes.

Also striking was the state's response to the abysmal condition of workers' health. Migrants to urban areas lived in severely crowded hovels without sanitary facilities, surrounded by disease, crime, and violence. The misery of the slumdwellers was not only more extreme than the deprivation which had afflicted the rural poor, it was also more visible, and it evoked a strong political reaction.

During the late eighteenth and first half of the nineteenth centuries, elites often took more than surplus from workers, drawing from the minimum they needed for good health.[5] Consequently, diets of workers' families were insufficient for children to grow to their full potential, or for adults to be fully productive. Economic historian Robert Fogel found that, at the time of the French Revolution, the poorest 10 percent of the population lacked adequate calories to carry out work, and the second lowest decile could not perform more than three hours of undemanding work daily (1994). Economist Angus Deaton reports that working-class children in England were very short and skinny, with life expectancy of only about 40 years. By 1850 the gap in life expectancy between the aristocracy and the general population had widened to 20 years (2013, 83, 91). Economic historian John Komlos reports that upper-class 16-year-old boys in England were 8.6 inches taller than their lower-class counterparts (2007). Clearly, elites were expropriating more than the surplus above subsistence, leaving the working class living on less nutrition than necessary for physical well-being.

The threat of revolution by an increasingly organized working class raised wages and forced public authorities to institute improvements in sanitation and water supplies. Better nutrition due to higher wages, and cleaner drinking water due to public services, enabled children to grow taller and stronger. By the end of the nineteenth century, working-class families

---

[5] Economist Thomas Piketty reports that

> ... all the historical data at our disposal today [for England and France] indicate that it was not until the second half—or even the final third—of the nineteenth century that a significant rise in the purchasing power of wages occurred. From the first to the sixth decade of the nineteenth century, workers' wages stagnated at very low levels—close or even inferior to the levels of the eighteenth and previous centuries ... available historical studies ... suggest that capital's share increased by something like 10 percent of national income, from 35–40 percent in the late eighteenth and early nineteenth centuries to around 45–50 percent in the middle of the nineteenth century (2014, 7–8; 225).

benefited from substantial advances in diet and health. This progress, combined with improvements in medical care, allowed life expectancy at birth in England and Wales to increase from 40 in 1850 to 45 in 1900 and to 70 by 1950 (Deaton 2013, 83). Deaton captures the dynamic as follows:

> Whenever health depends on collective action—whether through public works, the provision of health care, or education—politics must play a role. In this case, the (partial) removal of one inequality—that working people were not allowed to vote—helped remove another inequality—that working people had not access to clean drinking water. (2013, 98)

As will be recalled from Chapter 1, empirical evidence led Simon Kuznets (1995) to infer that, although inequality increases in the early stages of economic development, it begins to decrease at some more advanced level. However, Piketty's recent statistics suggest that, while worker well-being increased as the franchise expanded, inequality did not start to fall until the 1930s (2014).[6] Prior to the Great Depression, workers were receiving a larger absolute amount of economic output, yet inequality continued to trend upward.

The rise of working-class living standards above bare subsistence signaled that all major social actors came to share in society's surplus, albeit highly unequally. For the greater part of history since the rise of the state and civilization, the state and a thin aristocracy competed for the surplus they appropriated from the workers, usually leaving the producers with virtually none. With the rise of capitalism, a bourgeoisie entered into this competition, still leaving workers with little or none. When more recently the working class gained formal political power, it too could successfully compete to retain a portion, even if a small one, of the surplus they produced. The extreme inequality in this sharing has been principally due to elites' ongoing control over ideology.

---

[6] Historian Walter Scheidel reports that in the United States the share of income accruing to the top one percent increased from 10 percent in 1870 to 18 percent in 1913 (2017, 109). This was despite the pro-labor reforms of the Progressive Era that improved worker welfare. The elite were simply taking the lion's share of the economic growth dividend. Workers' improved welfare and the 40-year decline in inequality beginning in the 1930s were, as will be explored in Chapter 10, due to the Depression-fueled delegitimation of the laissez-faire ideology that had guided public policies resulting in greater inequality.

Ideology—The Powerful and Perennial
Political Weapon

When twenty years ago a vague terror went over the earth and the word socialism began to be heard, I thought and still think that fear was translated into doctrines that had no proper place in the Constitution or the common law.

—Oliver Wendell Holmes, quoted by Felix Frankfurter
in "The Constitutional Opinions of Justice Holmes"
(2013, cited in Abrams 2009)

Excepting severe crises, elites have almost always been successful in convincing the workers below them that what was more narrowly, and perhaps more obviously, in the interests of elites served the interests of workers just as well. Workers would see how they benefit from the prevailing order if only they would take a broader view of social relations and economic forces. In those instances when events delegitimated elites' ideology and workers revolted, the state resorted to force to maintain the elites' privileged status. Typically, elites regained the ability to legitimate their status quickly. But progressively greater democratization at the ballot box diminished the ease with which elites could call upon the state's policing power to curb the aspirations of workers, especially in putting down strikes. The new challenge was to maintain their privileges when their ideology could no longer as easily be backed up with state violence.

Marx and Engels famously wrote, "The executive of the modern State is but a committee for managing the common affairs of the whole bourgeoisie" (1848a, 475).[7] Yet they also believed that the ruling class would behave in a self-destructive manner, or as they put it, "dig their own graves," by letting capitalism's presumed "contradictions" build until an increasingly revolutionary working class would overthrow the capitalist state and institute socialism. However, they failed to foresee that, when threatened with insurrection, the elite-controlled state would placate workers by conceding

---

[7] Although the idea that historically the state served the interests of the wealthy is generally associated with Marx, it was expressed much earlier by Adam Smith: "Laws and government may be considered in this and indeed in every case as a combination of the rich to oppress the poor, and preserve to themselves the inequality of the goods which would otherwise be soon destroyed by the attacks of the poor, who if not hindered by the government would soon reduce the others to an equality with themselves by open violence" (1763, 208).

the necessary benefits, and even the franchise, to defuse their revolutionary fervor. Counter to Marx and Engels's expectations, this committee of the bourgeoisie was generally savvy enough to do what was necessary to appease a revolutionary working class. By acquiring the power to better their lot peaceably within the system through the democratic political process, workers came to see more forceful and extreme actions as no longer necessary or desirable. Such costly incendiary actions lost their urgency and legitimacy within the working class itself.

If the decisive role of ideology is ignored, it could be said that the working class had achieved what Marx and Engels called its "first step"—the victory of democracy. Because the working class would then possess an overwhelming majority of votes, it could rewrite the social script in its interest. Marx and Engels expressed the process as follows:

> . . . the first step in the revolution by the working class . . . is to raise the proletariat to the position of ruling class, to win the battle of democracy. The proletariat will use its political supremacy to wrest, by degrees, all capital from the bourgeoisie, to centralize all instruments of production in the hands of the State. (1848b, 490)

But, within Marx's understanding of ideological control, it is hardly surprising that the working class would be unable to progress to the second step of socializing ownership of the means of production. Within Marx's own terms, they did not—could not—have the requisite ideological authority:

> The class which has the means of material production at its disposal, has control at the same time over the means of mental production, so that . . . the ideas of those who lack the means of mental production are subject to it. (1845, 172)

The bourgeoisie had been able to take political power from the aristocracy because it came to control capital, the principal evolving means of productive wealth, and, crucially, to embrace an ideology appropriate to this ownership. Nothing parallel to this occurred for the proletariat. They achieved a substantial measure of political power, but without command over the means of production, which, Marx suggested in the preceding passage, is key to commanding "the means of mental production." The elite, the ownership class, continued to hold sway over ideology.

Elites discovered that democracy could be contained and was not, therefore, to be overly feared after all. This was a surprise. As Polanyi relates, "Inside and outside England, from Macaulay to Mises, from Spencer to Sumner, there was not a militant liberal who did not express his conviction that popular democracy was a danger to capitalism" (1944, 226). But elites' command over ideology appeared to be sufficient to limit the risks of democracy and so to check the resulting dreaded social transformation. Nevertheless, since workers began to gain the franchise, elites have attempted exclude as many as possible from exercising this right.

Thus Marx's expectations were thwarted. Nonetheless, at the end of the nineteenth century and the beginning of the twentieth, workers used the state to advance their collective interests on an unprecedented scale. The state had been transformed from the executive committee of the ruling class to a social agency with the ability to limit, or in the extreme case eliminate, the elites' appropriation of disproportionate shares of income, wealth, and privilege.

Without revolution, the working class had in principle gained power to reconfigure society. That workers did not substantially do so is testament to the control the bourgeoisie retained over ideology. They retained this control in part because they were able to exploit the workers' susceptibility to the doctrines legitimizing inequality that were expressed by the science of economics, as explored in the previous chapter. However, another set of doctrines came forth in the second part of the nineteenth century to buttress the economists' rationalizations. These are addressed in next section.

Seeming accidents also play a role in the fate of ideologies. As will be seen in the next chapter, elites in the United States were better equipped to reverse the rising worker power of the Progressive Era when fortuitous events during and after World War I delegitimated the labor movement.

Social Darwinism, Racism, Nationalism, and Protectionism as Ideology

As worker militancy gained momentum, elites' ideological arsenal was strengthened by additional doctrines: social Darwinism, racism, nationalism, and protectionism. Social Darwinism and racism served to turn workers domestically against each other. Nationalism and protectionism served to turn workers of different nations against each other, while suggesting that, within a country, workers and the elites who exploit them should unite in the face of external enemies.

Social Darwinism rose to prominence in the late nineteenth and early twentieth centuries when workers' intensified militancy was gaining them better working conditions, higher wages, education for their children, and the franchise. The pseudo-scientific character of social Darwinism allowed it to fold into the natural law cosmology that underlays laissez-faire economics. It depicted society as naturally competitive. If left unfettered, much as laissez-faire doctrine insisted, the innate drive to compete for survival and domination would bring about greater economic and social progress. The doctrine presumed that, as in the biological world, so too in the social world, the fittest would thrive and the unfit perish—that is, if the laws of nature were left to work unhindered. Thus, for the progress of humanity, society should not block this natural dynamic. It should be underlined that, whereas Darwin rejected the idea that evolution unfolds in a teleologically progressive manner, social Darwinists held that unimpeded social evolution inexorably improves society and its members.

This social Darwinism was most visible in the competition among firms, where the fittest organizations earn profits and expand while the less fit undergo bankruptcy and disappear. Some claimed that this same dynamic should be left free to sort out workers as well as businesses. Superior workers are rewarded with high incomes. The most unmotivated and inefficient workers wind up unemployed and poor. They are either indolent, and thus personally to blame for their failure to find jobs and work hard, or they are unfit. Social Darwinism's most extreme expression was the eugenics movement that advocated selective breeding and compulsory reproductive sterilization of the unfit.

More generally, successful workers with good jobs and living incomes could look upon the unemployed and the lowest-paid workers as unfit due to flaws in their character or biology. Elites could then count upon these better-off workers to join them in opposing higher taxes to support public measures to assist those who would not or could not rise to the demands of the competitive workplace. This view often comported with racism, portraying some groups as biologically or ethnically inferior. To intervene in the dynamics of natural social selection in any manner would be counterproductive, impeding social progress. This theory served as a powerful force in opposition to demands for social reforms. As historian Richard Hofstadter notes, although the ideas behind social Darwinism were not new, they served to provide validation for laissez-faire ideology, giving "the force of a [new] natural law to the idea of competitive struggle" (1992, 171).

As social Darwinism gained ideological momentum, so too did the notion of meritocracy.[8] Although it had long been used to legitimate inequality, it became increasingly prominent in political discourse as workers gained the franchise. As Piketty expresses this, ". . . the survival instinct of the upper classes . . . led them to abandon idleness and invent meritocracy, without which they ran the risk of being stripped of their possession by universal suffrage" (2020, 711).

At the end of the *Communist Manifesto*, Marx and Engels implored all the world's workers to join together in their struggle for liberation: "Working men of all countries, unite! . . . The proletarians have nothing to lose but their chains" (1848b, 500). But opposition to elites' rule could be softened if workers of one nation could be taught to see workers of other nations as enemies—the infamous divide-and-conquer strategy of nationalism. Nationalism has, as historian Willie Thompson observes, "proved to be the most pervasive of modern ideologies, generating a sense of identity and loyalty across wide spectra of society, and it has a clear quasi-religious dimension" (2015, 150). It depicted the nation "as a deep horizontal comradeship" (B. Anderson 2006, 24). Questioning Marx and Engels's belief that workers would unite worldwide, political economist Thorstein Veblen recognized that they might instead "sink their force in the broad sands of patriotism" (1919, 442).

In France, for instance, toward the end of the nineteenth century, workers' attention was redirected from demanding a fairer share of national income to safeguarding the country against "alien" workers. This took on a "violently xenophobic and anti-Semitic" character. As Rosanvallon puts it, "The transition from revolutionary radicalism to ultranationalism was one of the period's most striking examples of ideological and political reclassification" (2013, 144). This ideology emphasized protecting "national labor" against immigrant workers, and, to give it substance, advocates proposed that employers using foreign workers be subject to a special tax. Street demonstrations grew in the 1890s with attacks on Italian immigrants, and, in the north of France, on Belgians. Although socialist parties and labor unions

---

[8] Although the term *meritocracy* only came into use in the 1950s, the idea that everyone gets their just deserts according to their efforts was prominent in Western social thought since early capitalism and the Protestant Reformation. In a more cosmological expression, it also existed within Hinduism, as was seen in Chapter 4.

opposed such actions, they were powerless to stop them (Rosanvallon 2013, 147).

Identifying unfair foreign competition can also play an ideological role by generating a kind of solidarity not unlike that of patriotism. It can be used to persuade workers that their interests and those of their firms' owners are the same, thus reducing class conflict. In the late decades of the nineteenth century in France, "protectionism developed into a full-blown political culture. The movement had its newspapers, such as *Le Protectionniste* (1879) and *Le Travail national* (1884) and its champions" (Rosanvallon 2013, 141). It fed on the argument that protectionism sheltered the workers' wages and farmers' prices. The larger goal "was to establish a national identity that could compensate for social divisions. . . . The split between capital and labor [could] be replaced by a new idea of collective solidarity against a foreign threat" (Rosanvallon 2013, 141).

Workers in the United States also joined in racism against the influx of Chinese workers—the "yellow peril." A referendum on Chinese immigration passed with overwhelming support in California in 1879. Even members of the Workingmen's Party and Knights of Labor participated in physical attacks on Asian workers (Rosanvallon 2013, 163). In 1882, Congress passed the Chinese Exclusion Act, the first law restricting immigration by race or nationality.

The effectiveness of turning workers against each other in terms of race and ethnicity has borne fruit for elites. Transnational research by economists Alberto Alesina and Edward Glaeser finds a strong correlation between social homogeneity and redistributive policies. The more racially and ethnically heterogeneous the society, the less its expenditures on social programs (2006). As further evidence, ". . . across the United States, the states with the smallest percentage of African Americans in their population offer the most generous social benefits" (Rosanvallon 2013, 163).

Another face of nationalism was imperialism.[9] Magnate and politician Cecil Rhodes apparently understood quite clearly how imperialism could extinguish the embers of worker revolt in famously claiming, "He who would avoid civil war must be an imperialist" (quoted in Rosanvallon 2013, 142).

---

[9] Imperialism was, of course, far more than a means of calming revolutionary fervor. It promised cheap raw material imports and markets for exports. In an extraordinary show of cooperation among the imperial powers, German chancellor Bismarck convened a conference in Berlin in 1885 peacefully to carve up Africa into spheres of exploitation, although the European nations presented their missions as bringing Christianity and civilization to barbarians.

As Rosanvallon puts it, "Colonialism . . . counterbalanced and camouflaged domestic inequalities by depicting the nation as a community in confrontation with the rest of the world" (2013, 143). Governments flattered citizens by claiming that as a nation they were special. As public intellectual Gilbert Murray observed in 1900, each country seemed to be asserting: "We are the pick and flower of nations . . . above all things qualified for governing others" (quoted in Kennedy 2001, 211). Sociologist Domenico Losurdo links the surge of imperialism to workers' increasing political power. He writes, "In Europe extension of the suffrage in the nineteenth century proceeded in tandem with colonial expansion and the imposition of forced labour on peoples or 'races' deemed barbarous or childlike" (2014, 343).

Patriotism and war have always served to unify people with conflicting interests. Rulers throughout history have identified foreign threats to distract and better fleece their subjects, prompting Samuel Johnson to claim that "patriotism is the last refuge of the scoundrel" (April 7, 1775). Rulers rarely achieve as high a degree of loyalty from their subjects during peace as during war. Consequently, facing worker insurrections or other forms of acute social unrest, leaders representing the interests of the elite might even be expected to craft measures against other powers to provoke a limited amount of real threat. As will be recalled from Chapter 5, Hegel noted that "peoples involved in civil strife . . . acquire peace at home through making war abroad" (1821, 295). Similarly, de Tocqueville wrote: "The sword of war cuts to the heart. But what a mighty influence this struggle has on the political and social body! What a unity of sentiment and endeavor it creates" (quoted in Losurdo 2014, 287). Biologist John Alcock claims that warlike behavior evolved because of its social utility, and that "paradoxically, war depends on the cooperative, group-bonding, authority-accepting aspect of human behavior" (1978, 24–25). Historian Volker Berghahn claims that the ruling elite in pre–World War I Germany became increasingly warlike in part to deflect and mollify the growing challenge of Germany's working-class movement (1993). A century ago, journalist Randolph Bourne observed that "War is the health of the state. . . . A people at war become in the most literal sense obedient, respectful, trustful children again, full of that naïve faith in the all-wisdom and all-power of the adult who takes care of them" (quoted in Bacevich 2013, B3).

Yet, despite the tendency of war or the threat of war to mollify internal conflict, worker militancy has often strengthened in wartime. This has especially been true where sacrifices are seen to be unfairly allocated, with members of the working class suffering loneliness, deprivation, mutilation, and death while capitalists reap exceptional profits. This was the case during and immediately after World War I in Europe. The Bolshevik Revolution in Russia inspired workers' parties and movements all across Europe to rise up in revolt. In Germany, the Spartacist uprising included a general strike and an armed struggle. In Hungary, the government was overthrown, and the Hungarian Soviet Republic was proclaimed. At the Peace Conference in March 1919, Lloyd George warned, "All of Europe is in a revolutionary state of mind" (quoted in Rosanvallon 2013, 188).[10] Union membership from the beginning of the war to its end doubled in Great Britain, tripled in Germany, and quadrupled in France. Consequently, reforms were undertaken and politicians strived to convince workers that the state was not an instrument in service of the elites, but rather a force for improving the lives of all citizens. As will be seen in the next chapter, American workers also became more militant during World War I, albeit much to the subsequent thwarting of their interests.

Early in the twentieth century, the United States became the world's most powerful economy. Among industrially advanced societies, it also became the most inegalitarian over the course of that century: Piketty reports that ". . . the United States was less inegalitarian than Europe in 1900–1910, slightly more inegalitarian in 1950–1960, and much more inegalitarian in 2000–2010" (2014, 324). For these reasons, Chapter 10 and Chapter 11 will focus predominantly, although not exclusively, on the American experience. Looking farther ahead, the final two chapters prior to the conclusion focus on specific issues that are critically linked to inequality: the challenge of ecological devastation (Chapter 12) and the misplaced attacks progressives frequently make against the social institutions of markets and private property, impairing the development of attractive non-exploitative alternatives to laissez-faire capitalism (Chapter 13).

---

[10] The assumption of political power by the Bolsheviks meant that the "specter of communism" was no longer simply a theory. In a review of John Maynard Keynes's *The Economic Consequences of the Peace*, Veblen wrote that ". . . the central and most binding provision of the Treaty (and of the League [of Nations]) is an unrecorded clause by which the governments of the Great Powers are banded together for the suppression of Soviet Russia. . . . Bolshevism is a menace to absentee ownership; and in the light of events in Soviet Russia it became evident, point by point, that only with the definitive suppression of Bolshevism and all its works, at any cost, could the world be made safe for that Democracy of Property Rights on which the existing political and civil order is founded" (1920, 468, 470).

10

From American Exceptionalism to the Great Compression

The demand for equality has lain at the epicenter of the major up-
heavals that have erupted on the American political scene: the
Revolution, the Jacksonian era, the Civil War and Reconstruction, the
Populist-Progressive period, the New Deal and the tumultuous 1960's
and 1970's.
  —Sidney Verba and Gary R. Orren, *Equality in America* (1985, 21)

So far, this book has unfolded as follows. After addressing the biological
roots of inequality—found in the dynamics of sexual selection as developed
by Darwin—it has focused on the struggle over inequality as the underlying
force driving all human history. This exploration began with a world-historical perspective to capture the social origins and dynamics of inequality
without getting lost in excessive regional detail. The discussion then shifted
principally to Europe, the first area to experience sustainable capitalist economic growth that has subsequently spread around the globe and unleashed
the dynamics that are increasingly making the world's peoples rich and free.
This chapter and the next continue to take a broad view but center principally on the United States in order to show how the dynamics of inequality
have evolved in recent times. The reasons for this choice may be obvious.
The United States is not only history's richest and most powerful society, but
also the most unequal among rich countries. It is additionally the society in
which the recent surge of inequality has been most extreme.

The North American experience radically differed from the European in
two opposing ways. At one extreme, its extensive slavery, especially in the
brutal gang form that prevailed on Southern plantations, represented the
cruelest and most extreme form of inequality. At the other, until the end of

the nineteenth century, far more egalitarian conditions existed for freemen, especially in the North, than in Europe.[1]

American slavery, predominantly in the South, and the free labor that generally characterized the North are both linked to abundant land that was forcefully stolen through murderous campaigns from the aboriginal owners who held it in tribal commons. From its earliest colonization, America was land-rich but labor-poor. Importing slaves from Africa was an early response, beginning just 12 years after the founding of Jamestown in 1607. Almost 11 million African slaves arrived on North American shores, and, at the time of their emancipation in the 1860s, they constituted almost 13 percent of the US population. Another response to the labor shortage was the importation of indentured servants. Between one-half and two-thirds of white immigrants to the American colonies between the 1630s and the American Revolution came as indentured servants—a time-limited form of slavery, often referred to as "white slavery." The abundance of cheap land limited the ability of elites to subjugate and exploit them when their five to seven years of servitude were complete.

Skin color played a critical role in the differing conditions endured by the permanent and hereditary slaves brought out of Africa versus those undergone by the temporarily subjugated indentured servants of European origin. The former were more easily "caged," because runaway black slaves could be fairly easily identified and recaptured. Indentured servants of European origin could blend into the predominantly white population of freemen. Further, in terms of ideology, those from Africa could more readily be depicted as inferior and therefore appropriately enslaved.

There was considerable commerce between the Northern and Southern states. For instance, Southern cotton fed Northern textile mills. Nonetheless, the slave South and the free North existed almost as two separate countries within the same republic, and the federal government significantly treated them as separate. This sense of separateness contributed to the willingness of the South eventually to attempt secession from the Union.

Because this chapter is principally focused upon the dynamics of inequality in the United States between the end of the nineteenth century and the mid-1970s, it devotes little further attention to the barbaric US experience

---

[1] In England and the Netherlands, the Gini coefficient for income inequality (where 0 is perfect equality and 1 is perfect inequality) at the end of the eighteenth century was near 0.60, about what is found today in Brazil, Haiti, or South Africa, whereas it was near 0.45 in the United States (Lindert and Williamson 2016, 39; Tables 2–5).

of slavery. The nature of slavery in the US South largely conformed to the dynamics of slavery throughout history that were discussed in Chapter 5. That chapter also described how ideology legitimated Southern US slavery with the same facility as it had always justified slavery since the rise of the state and civilization. Although it is beyond the scope of the present chapter to examine this topic in depth, the consequences of slavery for inequality in the United States have been far-reaching. The aftereffects of slavery have been catastrophic for African Americans and gravely damaging to potential working-class progress. Racism and the extreme and continual exploitation of the descendants of slaves have condemned most to a subaltern class.[2] The racism that continues to divide American workers has impaired attempts to delegitimate the elite's ideology and has thwarted the development of a unified labor movement. It has thus impeded political action that could substantially reduce inequality in wealth, income, and privilege.

Egalitarian Values in Pre-Industrial North America

> . . . the best state for human nature is that in which, while no one is poor, no one desires to be richer, nor has any reason to fear being thrust back by the efforts of others to push themselves forward.
> —John Stuart Mill, *Principles of Political Economy* (Mill 1909, 748–49)

In North America, notions of equality pervaded the social, economic, and governmental spheres, first during the colonial period and then in the early Republic. Titles of nobility were specifically prohibited in the Constitution (Article I, Section 9). In a speech in September 1848, the historian and early political scientist Alexis de Tocqueville reported,

> You will see there a people among whom conditions are more equal than they have ever been among us; among whom the social structure, the customs, the laws, everything is democratic; among whom everything comes from the people and returns to it, and where, nevertheless, each individual

---

[2] The average white household possesses 13 times more net wealth than the average African American household.

enjoys an independence that is fuller, and a liberty that is greater, than in any other time or place on earth. (quoted in Losurdo 2014, 170)

Yet, there was a peril for those at the bottom. Abundant and cheap land, combined with a strong Protestant ethic, implied that anyone who worked hard could "make it" in America. Therefore, those who failed were lazy, and they alone were responsible for their fate. In this setting, the law treated criminals harshly, as evidenced by conditions in American prisons. De Tocqueville continued, "It must be acknowledged that the American prison regime is severe. While US society affords the example of the most extensive liberty, this country's prisons offer a spectacle of utter despotism" (quoted in Losurdo 2014, 192).

Nonetheless, egalitarianism continually advanced in the new republic. Historian and sociologist Pierre Rosanvallon summarizes this movement as follows: "In America one can speak of a *continuous revolution*. The thirty years between the presidencies of George Washington and Andrew Jackson were notable for a steady rise of the egalitarian ethos. Federalist ideas gradually receded while 'republican' ideas gained strength" (2013, 61). By 1815, 7 out of 20 states had universal white male suffrage (Black and Sokoloff 2006, 77). All states abolished property requirements for voting by 1856. In five states—Massachusetts, Rhode Island, Delaware, North Carolina, and Pennsylvania—only taxpayers were eligible to vote, but that restriction was eliminated by 1860 (Engerman and Sokoloff 2005, 898).

It should be noted that the development of democracy in America ran counter to the intentions of those who crafted the first guiding documents. Political scientist Sheldon Wolin writes that ". . . the Founders, almost without exception, believed that democratic majority rule posed the gravest threat to a republican system. It stood for collective irrationality or, as Madison put it, the 'wishes of an unjust and interested majority'" (2010, 229). In addition, small farmers and members of the urban middle classes were not unanimously pro-democratic (Huber et al. 1993, 77).

American elites, like their European counterparts, feared democracy and continually pressured states to reduce or eliminate the voting rights of the less well off. For instance, Connecticut passed the first literacy test in 1855. Adopted in 1870, the Fifteenth Amendment prohibited federal and state governments from denying a citizen the right to vote on the basis of "race, color, or previous condition of servitude"; after it came into effect, literacy tests spread all over the country. They only became illegal when outlawed by

Congress in 1975. Even today, measures are continually undertaken to disen-franchise those likely to vote against the elite's interests. Statutes purportedly intended to "protect the integrity of elections" are designed to make voting more difficult for racial and ethnic minorities and the poor generally.

Underpinning the spirit of American democracy was the fact that, at the birth of the United States as a nation, most non-slave workers owned the tools and resources with which they worked. In the early American re-public, about two-thirds of the white population owned land. Even as late as 1850, about 70 percent of the free workforce was self-employed (Lebergott 1964, 139). Owning and controlling the means of production, and working without bosses, self-employed people place great importance on defending their freedom by participating in political decision-making (Lane 2001). Yet, the harshly judgmental views of the poor that held sway in the land of oppor-tunity led many to oppose voting rights for all.

Abraham Lincoln claimed in an address before the Wisconsin State Agricultural Society in 1859 that "the prudent, penniless beginner in the world labors for wages awhile, saves a surplus with which to buy tools or land for himself, then labors on his own account another while, and at length hires another new beginner to help him" (USDA n.d.). Lincoln's understanding was widely embraced. Self-employment is the ideal. It enables workers and their families to be economically free of subservience to an elite class that owns productive wealth. It gives them freedom from bosses.

Abundant cheap land made it possible for workers to achieve greater self-sufficiency than wage labor would permit. Scholar and educator Noah Webster remarked in 1787 that due to "small inequalities of property ... every man has the opportunity of becoming rich" (quoted in Sitaraman 2017, 69). In Europe, the means of production were owned by a small elite class and work conditions and pay were draconian.[3] In America, where arable land was inexpensive, workers were not caged; they had an alternative to wage labor. Available cheap land also meant that, to retain workers, employers had to provide tolerable work conditions and keep wages relatively high.

---

[3] Writing in the mid-nineteenth century of European working conditions, political economist William Thompson wrote: "The productive labourers, stript of all capital, of tools, houses, and materials to make their labour productive, toil from want, from the necessity of existence, their re-muneration being kept at the lowest, compatible with the existence of industrious habits" (1850, 133). Twelve-hour working days became the norm in mid-nineteenth century Europe (Appleby 2011, 152). During a period in the 1860s, workers in a Manchester factory put in 84-hour weeks on average, or 14 hours daily in a six-day work week (Menand 2016, 97).

Economic historian Jeremy Atack reports that "visitors to America in the middle of the nineteenth century were little short of amazed at the dress and manner of the working person" (2014, 564). Charles Dickens noted in 1842 of the textile mill girls of Lowell that they "were all well dressed: and that phrase necessarily includes extreme cleanliness . . . they were healthy in appearance, many of them remarkably so, and had the manners and deportment of young women; not of degraded brutes of burden. . . . [Yet] [t]hey labour in these mills, upon an average, twelve hours a day" (quoted in Atack 2014, 564).

To lay claim and control over Western territory, the government took measures to populate it with non-Indian Americans. The Land Ordinance of 1785 and the Homestead Act of 1862 were explicitly designed for this end. That these laws were enacted testifies to the political power collectively exercised by common people. Had they had less influence, these lands might have been sold for a pittance to moneyed interests who could then hire wage labor to work them. There was also considerable support for an America constituted of yeoman farmers and shopkeepers. This was Thomas Jefferson's widely shared ideal.[4] He held that the unemployed should be granted 50 acres of land to be independent (Sitaraman 2017, 73).

The Homestead Act was also motivated by a need to maintain social order on the East Coast, where most immigrants settled. It was believed that cheap Western land would act as a safety valve, attenuating the unemployment problem—and thus lessening the potential for worker unrest—in Eastern cities. This safety valve depended upon the continued availability of cheap land. Historian Frederick Jackson Turner argued, however, that inexpensive land had disappeared by the 1890s. Population growth and land settlement erased the great open American frontier. Turner lamented that the result would be an erosion of the egalitarian conditions and values that the open frontier had spawned (1921).

Loss of the frontier, and relentless industrialization, trapped workers. No option remained but to work for the owners of the means of production. Unfree labor cultivates unfree political attitudes. Political psychologist Robert Lane reports that research has found that "self-directedness in work is associated with nonauthoritarianism, assumption of moral responsibility for one's own acts, trust in others, self-esteem, and lower anxiety"

---

[4] Thomas Jefferson "in his draft constitution for Virginia, written in 1776, . . . proclaimed that lands be distributed so that each adult would own 20 hectares of land in full property" (Bavel 2016, 229).

(1991, 242). Workers with jobs that permit them a significant degree of autonomy also tend to be culturally liberal, whereas those who are bossed about and micromanaged tend to be more authoritarian (Kitschelt 1994, 12–18). Historian Eric Foner reports that, for many late nineteenth-century Republicans, "A man who remained all his life dependent on wages for his livelihood appeared almost as unfree as a southern slave" (1995, 17).

The "Progressive Era" in America

The absence of effective state, and, especially, national restraint upon unfair money-getting has tended to create a small class of enormously wealthy and economically powerful men, whose chief object is to hold and increase their power. The prime need is to change the conditions which enable these men to accumulate power which is not for the general welfare that they should hold or exercise. . . . Therefore, I believe in a . . . graduated inheritance tax on big fortunes, properly safeguarded against evasion and increasing rapidly in amount with the size of the estate.

—Theodore Roosevelt, "The New Nationalism"
(Quoted in O'Mara 2017, 32)

From its earliest colonization until the Civil War, America had been predominantly an agricultural economy. This began changing rapidly after the Civil War as industrialization accelerated. Industrialization dramatically increased inequality, conforming to the dynamic that Kuznets (1955) attributed to the earlier phase of economic development. Inequality would necessarily rise if wages remained at subsistence and all the gains of economic growth flowed to an elite. This was largely the case between 1870 and 1910, when the share of income captured by the richest one percent rose from 10 percent to 18 percent (Scheidel 2017, 109). Public policies that helped fuel this explosion in inequality were legitimated by the laissez-faire ideology that gained strength following the Civil War.

As in Europe, industrialization was accompanied by urbanization. Between 1870 and 1910, the percent of Americans living in urban areas doubled from 23.2 percent to 46.3 percent (R. J. Gordon 2016, 98). As seen in the previous chapter, industrialization and urbanization generated greater worker cohesion and demands for reforms. Such demands led to exceedingly violent confrontations between workers and the state. The fact that the United States lacked a strong socialist party and clamorous Marxist calls for revolution[5] may have emboldened the state and the elite to meet strikers with murderous force. More workers were killed during strikes in the United States than in any other country but Russia. Historian Michael Mann reports that, between 1872 and 1914, 16 striking workers were killed in Germany and about 35 in France. In the same period, 500 to 800 were killed in the United States, a toll exceeded only by the 2,000–5,000 who died in Russia (1993, 2:653).

At the cost of deaths, maimings, and financial hardships, strikes brought results in workers' favor. Early evidence of workers' mounting political power was the 1892 law that mandated an eight-hour day for firms with federal or state government contracts (US Department of Labor 1962, 83). A severe economic crisis in 1893 generated a sharp reaction against laissez-faire ideology and further empowered a growing Progressive movement.[6] Despite rising inequality, workers' participation in control of the state improved significantly the quality of their lives. Economic dynamism created a larger pie, and workers were successful in holding on to some of their surplus, enabling many to live above bare subsistence.

Improvements in workers' lives came about in part because a 60 percent increase in union membership during the first decade of the twentieth century and unemployment that rarely exceeded 5 percent (Historical Statistics of the United States) gave workers greater political clout. The average workweek declined from 57.3 hours to 54.9 hours. And, for the period from 1890 to 1914, real wages for factory workers increased by 37 percent (Rees and Jacobs 1961). This wage growth occurred despite downward pressure on wages due to huge inflows of immigrant labor, frequently hired to replace strikers. Economists Timothy Hutton and Jeffrey Williamson estimate that

---

[5] This lack of a strong socialist party has been linked to racism. Legal scholar James Grey Pope writes: "During the late nineteenth and early twentieth centuries, when the working classes of Europe were building durable and resilient socialist movements, the American working class was hopelessly split along racial lines" (2016, 1590). In his now classic 1906 book, *Why Is There No Socialism in the United States?* (1976), among other reasons, Werner Sombart credits labor market segmentation by race, ethnicity, and gender.

[6] Laissez-faire ideology, which had remained dominant from the end of the Civil War until about 1900, declined in legitimacy under attack by the Progressive movement between 1900 and the end of World War I. It then returned in full force between the end of World War I and the onset of the Great Depression. The New Deal and World War II significantly delegitimated laissez-faire ideology under assault by a strong labor movement, mistrust of bankers and industrialists, and support for governmental intervention. However, as will be discussed in the next chapter, laissez-faire ideology powerfully resurged in the 1970s.

the competition from new immigrants retarded real wage growth by about 6 to 9 percent between 1890 and 1914 (1995).

During the "Progressive Era," attitudes favorable to the working class flourished. This was evident in the broad popularity of books by social critics such as Henry George's *Progress and Poverty* (1879), Edward Bellamy's *Looking Backward* (1888), Thorstein Veblen's *The Theory of the Leisure Class* (1899), Upton Sinclair's *The Jungle* (1906), and the muckraking journalism of Ida Tarbell. Pro-labor sympathies fueled enactment of Progressive Era policies benefiting workers.

Politically, President Theodore Roosevelt took advantage of the increased support for labor and reduced inequality. He campaigned for giving the franchise to women, a minimum wage, an interdiction on child labor, and federal insurance covering "the hazards of sickness, accident, invalidism, involuntary unemployment and old age" (Marmor 2014). He also supported the right of workers to unionize, and called for the creation of a national industrial commission with powers to regulate industries participating in interstate commerce. He envisioned that this commission would have the power to set wage standards and prices on commodities such as oil (Chace 2005). The Roosevelt administration's pro-labor policies included regulating the use of injunctions in labor disputes and urging arbitration rather than military force to resolve strikes (Wynn 1986, 87), and initiating greater government oversight of large corporations. A workmen's compensation system for certain federal employees was established in 1908. By 1909, all but six states had established a minimum age for factory work, and by 1913, 19 had eight-hour-day laws for those under 16. Two constitutional amendments increased democracy: the Seventeenth Amendment of 1913 allowed for the direct election of senators by voters rather than their selection by state legislatures, and the Nineteenth Amendment of 1920 gave women the right to vote. Campaign finance reforms passed, and government employees became increasingly professionalized.

A movement opposing anticompetitive business combinations that had gained force in the late nineteenth century gained renewed support from Roosevelt's "Trust Busting." It was also backed by President Woodrow Wilson, who wrote in 1913: "If monopoly persists, monopoly will always sit at the helm of government. I do not expect to see monopoly restrain itself. If there are men in this country big enough to own the government of the United States, they are going to own it" (quoted in Acemoglu and Robinson 2012, 323).

Workers' enhanced political power was also evident in other domains. By 1900, 16 states provided for factory safety inspections. By 1916, 40 states had disability compensation programs, most of which survived constitutionality challenges (Robertson 2000, 48, 233). In 1913, the Department of Labor was established to promote the interests and welfare of workers, giving labor a voice inside government. Pushed by progressive reformers, legislation created a vast array of public goods that benefited the broad population, such as schools, playgrounds, parks, and public transportation.

Public outrage at the level of collusion between politicians and corporations led to the Tillman Act of 1907, which banned corporate political contributions in federal campaigns. Unease with corporate political power also prompted 22 states to enact their own laws prohibiting corporations from making political campaign contributions in their states. In 1909, Congress passed the Publicity Act that mandated disclosure of political contributions. Twelve states enacted measures requiring supervision of lobbyists. This new "system of governance" had the intention of regulating the behavior of corporations and their wealthy owners, effectively promoting the general interest of labor (Gould 1996, 76).

At the outset of the twentieth century, the Progressive movement battled for taxes to fall mainly on rent, other kinds of income from property, and high incomes. The Sixteenth Amendment, ratified in 1913, gave Congress the power to tax income "from whatever source derived, without apportionment among the several states." This overrode an 1895 Supreme Court decision that had declared an income tax unconstitutional (interestingly, the income tax was strongly supported by the temperance movement because it lessened the government's dependence on alcohol taxes). Whereas only the richest one percent initially paid the tax, to help pay for World War I, the uppermost 5 percent did by 1917, with the highest marginal income tax rate set at 67 percent (Blakey 1917). In 1916, Congress passed an estate tax that applied only to the very wealthy. The top estate tax rate would remain between 70 and 80 percent until the 1980s (Piketty 2014, 507).

These diverse efforts to contain the power of corporations and improve the lot of workers make it evident that Progressive Era writers, activists, and political leaders thought it vitally important to reduce inequality. Economist Irving Fisher asserted in his 1919 presidential address to the American Economic Association that the increasing concentration of wealth was the nation's foremost economic problem (Piketty 2014, 506).

World War I and Labor's *Faux Pas*

A State divided into a small number of rich and a large number of poor
will always develop a government manipulated by the rich to protect
the amenities represented by their property.
                          —Harold Laski, quoted by Rodrigue Trembley
                             in "A Long Economic Winter Ahead" (2010)

In his presidential campaign speeches, Woodrow Wilson strongly emphasized that the nation's well-being depended upon labor's well-being.
Although the Socialist Party never gained more than 6 percent of the vote in
a presidential election, its popularity nevertheless pulled the political center
of gravity leftward. Its strength from 1901 to 1917 made it the only sustained
third party of any significance in twentieth-century America. In 1917, Wilson
became the first president to deliver an address at an American Federation of
Labor (AFL) convention. He proclaimed that labor's condition was not to be
"rendered more onerous by the war" and that, in disputes, "[labor is more]
reasonable in a larger number of cases than the capitalists" (quoted in Wynn
1986, 96). It was common for companies to reject mediation in labor disputes
and to "flatly refuse" to cooperate with suggested proposals from labor or
other sources (Montgomery 1987, 348).

During World War I, maintaining a high level of output was imperative,
and preserving peaceful labor relations was critical to this goal. As Mary
van Kleeck, coauthor of a policy statement issued by the Office of the Chief
Ordnance, put it, "industrial history proves reasonable housing, fair working
conditions, and a proper wage scale are essential to high production" (quoted
in Wynn 1986, 195). The idea of conscripting income and wealth was even
put before Congress. As one congressman put it, "Let their dollars die for
their country too" (quoted in Rosanvallon 2013, 187).

In return for government support, labor was expected to work diligently
and not walk out during the war. However, as the war unfolded, profits
increased and real wages began a slight downward trend (Douglas 1996,
219). In response, organized labor became ever more militant and defied
expectations, using "the strike weapon as never before." Between 1915 and
1918, the number of work stoppages tripled and strikes "raged with singular intensity" in the munitions and armaments industry (Dubofsky 1996,
129), resulting in a 10 percent fall in labor productivity (Brody 1993, 12).

A particularly significant blow to labor's power came with the breaking of a strike in the steel industry in 1919.

Labor Busted and Surging Inequality

> *The country is governed for the richest, for the corporations, the bankers, the land speculators, and for the exploiters of labor. The majority of mankind are working people. So long as their fair demands— the ownership and control of their livelihoods—are set at naught, we can have neither men's rights nor women's rights. The majority of mankind is ground down by industrial oppression in order that the small remnant may live in ease.*
>
> —Helen Keller, quoted by Andrew Belonsky in
> "Video: Helen Keller Tells It" (Quoted in Belonsky 2018)

By the war's end, forces were in motion to restore the persuasiveness of the elite's ideology. Labor's failure to fulfill its informal wartime "no strike" pledge was depicted as unpatriotic, just when the Russian Bolsheviks were introducing an alternative to capitalism. In a "Red Scare" environment, labor's struggles were increasingly portrayed as part of a communist conspiracy to turn the United States into a Western version of the Soviet Union. Commercial interests embarked on a campaign to demonstrate the patriotism of business and the dangers inherent in labor's intransigence. The Bolshevik Revolution's creation of a socialist society gave the rich the leverage they needed to delegitimate anything critical of free-market capitalism. The "Red Scare" between 1917 and 1920 was used to purge leftist thinkers and tarnish movements for greater social equality. Progressives were branded as foreign-directed, godless, and a threat to all that Americans held dear. Political economist Fred Lee writes that in academia, "trustees and presidents in cooperation with the business community set up spy systems in their universities and colleges to identify the radical, un-American professors and students for dismissal; and a movement was launched to scrutinize economic textbooks for breaches of loyalty." He continues, "economics departments with too many progressives (as at the University of Washington) were restructured and placed in conservative business schools; and businesses threatened not to donate to universities that retained faculty with radical economic views" (2009, 31).

The election of 1920 turned over the White House to the Republican Party until the election of 1932, with the result that business interests dominated national policy. The ascendant laissez-faire ideology of the rich legitimated busting labor's bargaining power. Flowing out of this ideology were arguments to reduce the size of government, implement tax cuts for the rich, deregulate the economy, and leave unregulated the newly evolving credit instruments.

With labor unions viewed negatively, the courts issued as many anti-labor injunctions during the 1920s as they had during the entire period from 1880 to 1920 (Bernstein 1966, 200). The Supreme Court ruled minimum wage legislation in the District of Columbia unconstitutional in 1923. Undergirding these court decisions was the doctrine of "freedom of contract"—the claim that because all enter the market contract freely, it should be inviolable. The right of workers to organize was suppressed, and "everywhere, it was open season on anyone who dared to talk union" (Zieger 1995). Unions affiliated with the American Federation of Labor were harassed, as were leftist organizations of all sorts (Edsforth 1998, 247).

President Calvin Coolidge and Treasury Secretary Andrew Mellon energetically campaigned to cut taxes massively on the highest incomes. During the 1920s, only the very highest portion of the income distribution was subject to federal income taxes. Thus, the large tax cuts undertaken in 1921, 1924, and 1926 benefited only the wealthy. Marginal tax rates that had been as high as 75 percent on net income above $500,000 were reduced to 25 percent on incomes above $100,000 (Smiley 1998, 218). Meanwhile, other tax "reforms" reduced corporate taxes.

Fortifying the reinvigoration of laissez-faire ideology, the soaring inequality of the 1920s meant that the very rich had more resources with which to influence public opinion and state policy. Armed with these economic resources, their education, and their command over essentially everything, the rich embraced and disseminated self-serving ideologies that became ever more convincing to a majority of the electorate. Their disproportionate control over the media, educational institutions, and think tanks made this outcome inevitable.

Because the elite constitute only a small part of the electorate, they could win elections only if political attention could be diverted from economic to cultural issues and/or their self-serving economic policies could be successfully presented as in everyone's interest. Cultural issues were handily available. The 1920s saw political combat over such issues as Darwinian evolution, prohibition of alcohol, nativism (blaming social problems on immigrants), and the growing and increasingly militant Ku Klux Klan.[7]

The American free-enterprise system was trumpeted as promoting the values of "social harmony, freedom, democracy, the family, the church, and patriotism." Advocates of government regulation of business were characterized as subversive (Carey 1996, 27). The Progressive Era had witnessed the rise of regulatory agencies, but, after the war, the regulated exercised increasing control over the regulators. In economist John Hicks's assessment, "Business control of government, so marked throughout the decade of the 1920s, made the regulation of business by government a farce" (1960, 232). Thus, when the second great American merger movement took off during the second half of the 1920s, little response came out of the Justice Department. By 1929, about half of all corporate wealth was controlled by 200 corporations (McElvaine 1993, 37). Price fixing, although illegal, also brought little government response.

A new media technology—the radio—greatly assisted the dissemination of pro-business ideology. The first regular radio broadcast took place in November 1920. By 1928, 12 million sets served 40 million listeners in a US population of 120 million (Blanning 2008, 204–5). Because radio stations were private ventures dependent upon advertising, they were necessarily beholden to the business point of view, and ". . . in search of advertisers were at great pains not to give offense" (Hicks 1960, 174). So completely did business dominate the climate of opinion during the 1920s that Roger Babson, a powerful investment advisor and the founder of Babson College, claimed that business had conquered "the press, the pulpit and the schools" (quoted in Cochran and Miller 1961, 343–44).

In addition, academic economists increasingly corroborated free-market ideology, thereby lending "scientific" support to policies benefiting the elite. The mainstream economic canon was decidedly favorable to unfettered and thus unregulated markets, even when greater inequality was the consequence.

---

[7] This diverting of attention to cultural issues is evident in Calvin Coolidge's rejection of "the appeals of the American Jewish Committee for a clear-cut denunciation of the Klan during the campaign of 1924" (Edsforth 1998, 265). At its peak in the 1920s, the Klan claimed as members one of every six eligible Americans and was the country's largest private organization, evidence of the deeply entrenched racism that impeded the rise of a unified labor movement. It was not only a movement in the South, but its tentacles extended into the North, with, for instance, 50,000 members in Chicago, 38,000 in Indianapolis, and 35,000 in Philadelphia (L. Gordon 2017). The culture wars of the 1920s moderated once the extreme hardship of the Great Depression refocused attention on the economic struggle for income and jobs.

The decade of the 1920s appeared to be broadly prosperous. Growth of overall economic output averaged 5.9 percent per year between the end of the recession in July 1921 and August 1929, despite two mild recessions (1923–1924; 1926–1927). However, the real prosperity of the 1920s was reserved for the wealthy. Per capita income for the lowest 93 percent of the non-farm working class decreased by 4 percent from 1923 to 1929 (Holt 1977), while the share of total income received by the richest 5 percent increased from 24.3 percent in 1919 to 33.5 percent in 1929. By 1928 the richest 10 percent received 46 percent of total income. Over the decade, the disposable income of the top one percent of taxpayers rose 63 percent (Livingston 2009, 38). Whereas there were about 7,000 millionaires in 1922, by 1929 there were about 30,000 (Phillips 2008, 11).

Because of the wealthy's increased command over society's dominant ideology, the losers—the overwhelming majority of Americans—did not use their dormant political power to stop the heist. Through the democratic process, they could have forced the creation of compensatory measures to succor workers harmed by technological change or international trade. Taxes could have been restructured in their favor, and public services that benefit them, such as public transportation, day care, schools, healthcare, and public recreational facilities, could have been greatly expanded and improved. However, the wealthy's successful reassertion of laissez-faire ideology resulted in the majority believing that such measures would not inure to either their own or the country's benefit. The seemingly robust economy, low unemployment, the booming stock market, and new consumer goods suggested that the laissez-faire policies touted by the dominant ideology were indeed beneficial for all. If some were not prospering, they were presumed to be at fault for failing to work hard and save.

Depression and "The Great Compression"

So distribution should undo excess, and each man have enough.
—Shakespeare, *King Lear* (Act 4, Scene 1, line 71)

History reveals that only rarely has inequality been sustainably challenged, even when it has been extreme. Revolts did occur, usually in spontaneous response to acts or events that endangered the poor's already precarious survival. But only rarely have challenges resulted in anything other than harsh

338 THE ORIGINS AND DYNAMICS OF INEQUALITY

repression. The state, with its comparative advantage in violence, enforced the property rights of elites, and, working together, they expropriated the producers' surplus. The rarity of challenges has been in good part due to the extraordinary legitimating power of the elite's ideology.

Worker strikes and threatening protests before and during the Progressive Era led to public measures that improved worker household welfare, but failed to halt the rise in inequality accompanying economic growth. The Great Depression of the 1930s proves to be the historical exception to the failure of worker protest to reverse rising inequality. Uniquely, it resulted in public policies over the subsequent 40 years that lessened inequality and vastly improved living conditions for most of the population. The ideology that enabled the rich to take ever larger shares for themselves during the 1920s had steered the economy into severe systemic dysfunction (Wisman 2014b). Not only did that ideology create the preconditions for the financial crisis of 1929 and the subsequent economic collapse, it also impeded implementation of the policies necessary to end it.

Although historians still debate the reasons for the depth of the Great Depression, there is broad agreement that two serious public policy mistakes were made. First, following the stock market crash of 1929, the Federal Reserve System permitted the money supply to contract, creating a liquidity crisis, bank failure, and deflation. Second, blaming unfair foreign competition, Congress passed the Smoot-Hawley Tariff Act of 1930, the most protectionist legislation in US history. These two misguided reactions helped transform a financial crisis into a full-blown depression, the worst in US history.

As surveyed in the previous chapter, the social dislocation that followed upon extensive proletarianization, urbanization, and technology-generated unemployment during the nineteenth century had a profound radicalizing impact upon industrial workers all over the maturing capitalist world. The crisis of the 1930s similarly mobilized workers in the United States, especially as it reached its depth in 1933 with official unemployment rising to 25 percent (a recent estimate puts it closer to 50 percent; Gans 2014, 56). Half of all banks folded, destroying the life savings of countless households. The response in 1933 to escalating protests prompted the federal government, in a "New Deal," to legislate the National Industrial Recovery Act, including the Federal Emergency Relief Act and the Civilian Works Administration (CWA).

Labor historian Melvyn Dubofsky notes that "the Great Depression and the New Deal had wrought a veritable political revolution among American workers. Masses of hitherto politically apathetic workers, especially among first-generation immigrants and their spouses, went to the polls in greater numbers" (1986, 212). In the 1930s, the Congress of Industrial Organizations (CIO), a federation of unions, orchestrated mass labor actions in support of demands for shop floor democracy, wealth redistribution, public ownership of utilities, public investment, and economic planning (Fraser 2015). Labor protests and organization surged between 1934 and 1939. In 1934, workers engaged in general strikes that shut down several major cities, pressuring Congress to sanction collective bargaining and move toward the creation of the Social Security Act of 1935.[8]

Widespread suffering during the Great Depression called laissez-faire economic policies into question. As free-market economists Milton and Rose Friedman put it, the Depression "discredited [and] shattered the public's confidence in private enterprise" (1988, 458, 462). It also challenged the prevailing economic theory that legitimated the laissez-faire policy stance, making space for the Keynesian revolution. In consequence, inequality in income, wealth, and opportunity lessened during the subsequent four decades. This development was guided by economic doctrines that depicted greater equality as positive and active government intervention as essential for a prosperous and fair economy. Only government could guarantee workers a "New Deal."

As the Depression lingered on, Franklin Delano Roosevelt became increasingly supportive of workers. In his presidential campaign of 1936, he advocated a wealth tax. He also advocated marginal income tax rates as high as 79 percent, stiffer inheritance taxes, and greater taxes on corporate profits. He declared in his presidential address of 1936 that the rich "economic royalists" formed an "autocracy" that sought "power for themselves, enslavement for the public" (quoted in Kennedy 2001, 227–82).

The delegitimation of the elite's ideology ushered in 40 years of political programs that benefited the general population. The most outstanding of these measures reducing inequality and improving conditions for the broad population included, most notably, workers' rights to bargain

---

[8] Francis Townsend, a California physician, proposed that everyone over the age of 60 be given a monthly pension of $200 both to eliminate their poverty and to stimulate the economy by increasing consumer demand. This became known as the Townsend Plan, which gained considerable populist support and served to stimulate the initiative of Roosevelt and his Democratic Congress to pass the Social Security Act of 1935.

collectively, Social Security, unemployment insurance, minimum wages, the GI Bill, Medicare, Medicaid, Food Stamps, public housing and rent subsidies, Project Headstart, the Job Corps, the Occupational Safety and Health Administration, the Consumer Product Safety Commission, the Mine Enforcement and Safety Administration, and the Environmental Protection Agency. Public goods benefiting the working class, such as schools, parks, playgrounds, and public transit, were vastly expanded in quantity and quality. And the percent of Americans living in poverty declined dramatically from about 30 percent in 1950 to 11 percent in 1973.

Highly progressive income taxation also reveals the government's intent to redistribute wealth in the interest of greater equality. The highest marginal income tax rates were, in percentage terms, 1929, 24 percent; 1936, 79 percent; 1942–1943, 88 percent; 1944–1945, 94 percent; 1946–1950, 91 percent. Top marginal tax rates remained in the upper 80 percent range from 1951 until 1964, and 70 percent from 1965 until 1981. The top marginal rate averaged 81 percent between 1932 and 1980 (Piketty 2020, 447). In 1940, the estate tax was raised to 70 percent, with a $40,000 exemption. In 1941, it was again raised to 77 percent.

Whereas the top one percent of households in 1929 received 22.5 percent of all pre-tax income (including capital gains), they received only 9 percent by the late 1970s (Piketty and Saez 2006). What economist Arthur Burns termed a "revolutionary leveling" (Williamson 1991, 11), and economists Claudia Goldin and Robert Margo called the "Great Compression" (1992), between the 1930s and the mid-1970s seemed to confirm Kuznets's conjecture that inequality would decrease in the later stages of economic development. Wealth distribution returned to a state that had disappeared in the decades after the Civil War. Public policies, made possible by the delegitimation of laissez-faire ideology benefiting the rich, drove this redistribution.

A sense of the political pressure to create a more equal society is strikingly evident in Lyndon Johnson's State of the Union Address in 1964:

> This administration today, here and now, declares unconditional war on poverty in America. I urge this Congress and all Americans to join with me in that effort. It will not be a short or easy struggle, no single weapon or strategy will suffice, but we shall not rest until that war is won. The richest Nation on earth can afford to win it. We cannot afford to lose it. (quoted in Jencks 2015, 82)

For a short while, this war appeared headed for a quick victory. Whereas in 1964, 19 percent of Americans were living in poverty, in a mere five years, this number fell to 11 percent of the US population (Jencks 2015, 82).

The New Deal and subsequent legislation favoring workers might have achieved far more for the general population had racial segregation in the South not blocked its leftward tendencies. For instance, in return for Southern support, the Social Security system was formulated to exclude domestic and agricultural workers, a huge percent of whom were not only poor but also black. The South's white population appeared willing to support leftist legislation so long as it posed no threat to segregation and the low wages and quiescent labor force that racism facilitated. Southern fear that labor legislation would threaten segregation generated strong support for the substantial restraints put upon the labor movement by the Taft-Hartley Act of 1947.

The racism underlying segregation served as a powerful ideology benefiting the better-off Southern elites. By pitting white against black workers, it effectively blocked the potential for an effective labor movement in the South. Tragically, organized labor often supported the racism that divided and severely weakened American workers' struggle for a better deal. A declaration by an official of the American Federation of Labor (AFL) during the 1930s expresses the extreme character of this racism:

> I consider the Negroes poor union men. You know as well as I do that they are shiftless, easily intimidated and generally of poor caliber. . . . What should have happened is what is being done in Calhoun County, Illinois, where Negroes are not allowed to stay overnight. As a result there are no Negroes there and no Negro problem. (quoted in Dubofsky 1986, 210)

The results for Southern workers were low wages, poor health, and substandard education for whites as well as blacks. Given these conditions, productivity remained low, condemning much of the South to the status of a less-developed nation. Martin Luther King Jr. clearly recognized the way racism served as an ideology benefiting the elites. He expressed this in his address at the conclusion of the Selma to Montgomery March on March 25, 1965:

> Racial segregation as a way of life did not come about as a natural result of hatred between the races immediately after the Civil War. There were

no laws segregating the races then. And as the noted historian, C. Vann Woodward, in his book, *The Strange Career of Jim Crow*, clearly points out, the segregation of the races was really a political stratagem employed by the emerging Bourbon interests in the South to keep the southern masses divided and southern labor the cheapest in the land. You see, it was a simple thing to keep the poor white masses working for near-starvation wages in the years that followed the Civil War. Why, if the poor white plantation or mill worker became dissatisfied with his low wages, the plantation or mill owner would merely threaten to fire him and hire former Negro slaves and pay him even less. Thus, the southern wage level was kept almost unbearably low. (Olenda 2015)[9]

World War II

In 1939, 10 years after the onset of the Great Depression, 11 percent of the US workforce—6.2 million workers—remained unemployed. Two years later, as the United States entered World War II, unemployment was halved, and by 1944, the unemployment rate fell to an unprecedented one percent. What happened?

The US government began massive deficit spending and—a fact far less noted in the political and economic literature—it effectively became an employer of last resort when it placed over 10 million Americans in uniform and added another two million to the Department of Defense and other agencies. War-stimulated demand employed an additional 5 million Americans. In all, employment increased by 17 million (Vatter 1985, 16–17), boosting the total labor force by 18 percent. In other words, war-related hiring created a negative unemployment rate of about that magnitude. This expansion drew minorities and women into the active workforce, breaking through racial and gender barriers that had traditionally excluded them.

By creating full employment, the war created de facto what Roosevelt had wished to create de jure. He had proposed that "Employment Assurance"

---

[9] Much earlier, in 1872, Horace Greeley, founder of the *New York Tribune*, wrote: "We have stricken the (slave) shackles from four million human beings and brought all laborers to a common level not so much by the elevation of former slaves as by practically reducing the whole working population, white and black, to a condition of serfdom. While boasting of our noble deeds, we are careful to conceal the ugly fact that by an iniquitous money system we have nationalized a system of oppression which, though more refined, is not less cruel than the old system of chattel slavery" (quoted in Coogan 2018).

be part of the Social Security Act. In 1943, a "New Bill of Rights" was proposed, but not adopted. It would have entailed the "formal *acceptance by the Federal Government of responsibility* for insuring jobs at decent pay to all those able to work regardless of whether or not they can pass a means test." In his 1944 State of the Union address, Roosevelt advocated an "economic bill of rights" that would include the "right to a useful and remunerative job" and the "right to earn enough to provide adequate food and clothing, and recreation." The original draft of the Full Employment bill of 1945 affirmed that "all Americans able to work and seeking work have the right to useful, remunerative, regular, and full-time employment" (Rose 2013, 170). Had this language been retained, it would have obliged the federal government to guarantee employment, essentially to become *employer of last resort*.

It is noteworthy that guaranteeing employment at a living wage would have redefined the character of capitalism. Although it would not have eliminated the separation of workers from ownership and control of the tools and resources with which they work, it would have dampened considerably its harshest consequences. It would have substantially changed the social power between the owners of the means of production and workers. Employers would have to offer better-paid, more interesting, and safer work to attract employees from the pool of those within a guaranteed work program. It would have led to lessened inequality, while creating a floor of security, and it would also have assured workers the dignity of being productive members of society. It would have eliminated poverty, the social costs of lost output, decayed human capital, crime, decayed neighborhoods, and welfare expenditures that accompany unemployment. That guaranteed employment has only very rarely been included in worker demands is traceable to the dominance of the elites' ideology that blames the victims by depicting those without jobs as lacking motivation (Wisman and Cauvel 2021).

World War II was a war of mass mobilization and, as political scientist Walter Scheidel (2017) observes, such wars serve as great levelers of wealth, income, and privilege. This happens because political leaders gain legitimacy and thus power at the expense of elites during times of war. For example, as noted earlier, marginal income tax rates were raised to 94 percent. War also heightens a sense of solidarity, consensus, and sharing that works against the individualistic ideology of the rich, the ideology that all individuals are alone responsible for their fates. In this manner, World War II further delegitimated laissez-faire ideology and nourished the solidarity and the egalitarian social ethic that were generated by the Great Depression.

The war had been extraordinarily expensive, increasing the federal debt (held mostly by the wealthy) to a record of about 120 percent of gross domestic product. Following the war, a surge in consumer spending driven by pent-up demand generated inflation, devaluing the real value of this public debt and, thus, decreasing wealth inequality. The period 1945 to 1980 witnessed "financial repression" in which real interest rates (market rates adjusted for inflation) were on average negative, helping to liquidate the immense public debt (Reinhart and Sbrancia 2011). This devaluation of the public debt represented a massive transfer of resources from the wealthy bondholders to the general taxpayer. Earlier, when elites held more complete control of political power, inflation was almost nonexistent. Public debt therefore held its value and served as a means by which elites could safely preserve their wealth with interest income.

Although they recognize that the state must have adequate resources to defend the elites' property rights, the wealthy have always had a Janus-faced relationship with the state's raising funds by issuing debt. On the one face, borrowed money put more resources and thus power in the hands of the state with which elites compete for shares of society's surplus. On the other, elites preferred that the state borrow from them rather than tax them. In societies where producers lived at bare subsistence, a state could only acquire additional resources from the elite, either by outright confiscation, taxation, or borrowing. Elites would clearly prefer the last option. Further, money loaned to the state provided interest at low credit risk. No other agency in society had as much promise of making good on its debts as the state. Its comparative advantage on violence generally assured that it could impose and collect taxes to pay off the bondholders (although states did at times go bankrupt).

For elites holding public debt to win, inflation must be contained because, as noted previously, it erodes the real value of bonds (and debt generally). This is why, in the trade-off between inflation and unemployment, they identify the former as "enemy number one." However, since the rise of bourgeois political dominance, and prior to World War I, inflation had typically been near zero. Indeed, for much of the nineteenth century, deflation, which increases the value of debt, was more common. Inflation has largely been a twentieth-century phenomenon that accompanied workers' growing influence over public policy (Piketty 2014, 103). That is, the reason for twentieth-century inflation was the rise in workers' political power, which they exerted in favor of full employment rather than low inflation.

Although elites benefit from holding public debt, they nonetheless ideologically war against it as a means to force government to reduce spending on programs that benefit the less fortunate. But, in fact, their opposition is considerably more muted when the national debt is raised by public policies that benefit them, for instance, the radical tax cuts in their favor over the past 45 years. As noted earlier, wealthy elites would prefer that government support its spending by borrowing from them as opposed to taxing them.

Unparalleled Prosperity and the Birth of Postmaterialist Values

Democracy is first and foremost about equality: equality of power and equality of sharing in the benefits and values made possible by social cooperation.

—Sheldon Wolin, *Democracy Incorporated* (2010, 61)

The three decades following World War II witnessed extraordinary economic and social progress. Between 1946 and 1976, gross domestic product grew an average of 3.8 percent per year and unemployment averaged 5 percent. Over this period—often called the Golden Age of Capitalism[10]—the United States became a more egalitarian society. Inflation-adjusted per capita income increased by about 90 percent overall, but it rose only about 20 percent for the richest one percent of the population. According to the US Census Bureau, between 1947 and 1968 the Gini index for income inequality fell to 0.386, the lowest ever recorded. Workers held considerable political power, thanks to powerful unions, to which almost one in three workers belonged in 1948. Home ownership increased from 43.6 percent of households in 1940 to 64.4 percent in 1980, thanks in good measure to the GI Bill, which financed a fifth of all new homes built between the end of the war and 1966. Thanks also to the GI Bill, 2.3 million veterans went to college, almost all of them the first in their families to do so (Sitaraman 2017, 202).

Understandably, from the very end of World War II, elites attempted to reverse the progression of egalitarian social policies that had been launched in the 1930s. Their greatest success was the Taft-Hartley Act of 1947, passed by

---

[10] This dynamism also characterized Europe, where it is often called *les trente glorieuses*, "the thirty glorious years."

Congress over President Harry Truman's veto. The act permitted states to ban union shops, and prohibited unions from engaging in secondary boycotts. It also prohibited unionization of foremen or low-level supervisors.

A Red Scare, generated in the wake of World War II in the form of McCarthyism, demonized the political aspirations of workers. Legal scholar and historian Ganesh Sitaraman reports that "between 1947 and 1956, more than five million federal employees were screened by an anticommunist loyalty program; twenty-five thousand were subjected to an FBI full field investigation; and twenty-seven hundred were dismissed" (2017, 195).

The Red Scares in the wake of both world wars represented an opportunistic ideological tactic to delegitimate the sense of solidarity and egalitarianism that had been generated by wartime sacrifices. Solidarity and egalitarianism were ideologically recrafted to represent blind mass obedience and communism, the abiding principles of the godless enemy that held its people in slavery.

Nevertheless, exceptional economic growth meant that children born soon after the end of World War II—the first Baby Boomers—would, upon becoming adults, on average have a standard of living almost twice that of their parents. This robust economic growth, combined with labor's relatively high degree of political muscle, gave an extra push to a new development in human history: unlike all previous generations, for the first time in human history, a generation came of age without fear of dire material privation. The parents of Baby Boomers had witnessed the extreme material hardship of the Great Depression. For post–World War II Americans, soon followed by Western Europeans, abundance had been achieved, the most fundamental economic problem overcome.[11] This unparalleled prosperity was striking: car ownership jumped from 13,000 to 44 million between 1900 and 1950—an average of one per household; the share of homes without bathtubs and showers dropped from about 40 percent to about 12 percent between 1940 and 1960; and most striking of all, in the mere half-century from 1900 to 1950, life expectancy rose from 46.3 to 68.1 years.

The combination of robust economic growth, labor empowerment, lessened inequality, and freedom from fear of extreme privation set the conditions for a cultural revolution, most visibly expressed in the so-called countercultural or hippie movement. But this was merely the flashy tip of the

---

[11] Political economist John Kenneth Galbraith's *The Affluent Society* (1957) was the first major widely read work in economics to recognize this extraordinary achievement. It became a bestseller with considerable influence on Baby Boomers.

iceberg catching the sun. Massive cultural and socioeconomic effects were to be found much deeper.

The value shift that occurred as this first generation came of age, freed from fear of material privation, was predicted by economist John Maynard Keynes in his essay, "Economic Possibilities for Our Grandchildren" (1930) and by social psychologist Abraham Maslow in his 1954 book, *Motivation and Personality* (1954). Maslow developed a hierarchy of human needs. In a society where material insecurity prevails, humans are first and foremost guided by materialistic goals. Their concern is with physiological survival itself. All other goals, such as political freedom, a sense of belonging, esteem, or self-actualization are secondary to this material survival goal. Until material security is attained, non-materialist goals appear as expensive luxuries. Only when material security has been attained will people feel comfortable or "liberated" to actively pursue higher, non-materialistic goals. Maslow's hierarchy of goals is presented in the form of a pyramid, with material security at the broad base and self-actualization at the peak. This pyramid and Maslow's analysis give theoretical expression to a happier future, often projected by visionaries, where material needs have been satisfied and humans spend their lives creating a good and just society while becoming the most and best each one can be.[12]

Sociologist Ronald Inglehart applied Maslow's general framework to a study of post–World War II youth. He found that this extraordinary victory over the harshness of scarcity generated a shift from materialist to postmaterialist values, from "an overwhelming emphasis on material well-being and physical security toward greater emphasis on the quality of life." He characterizes postmaterialists as follows: "Postmaterialists . . . are Postmaterialists precisely because they take economic security for granted" (1989, 5, 238). Inglehart bases his thesis of a shift from materialist to postmaterialist values upon two hypotheses:

---

[12] Philosopher Herbert Marcuse, in very different terms, had also recognized and celebrated the overcoming of scarcity in his widely read and highly influential *Eros and Civilization*. Freud had claimed in *Civilization and Its Discontents* (1930) that civilization required a repression from which there can be no escape. Humans had traded freedom for security. Marcuse argued against the contemporary relevance of this position, claiming that the scarcity that led Freud to view the need to curtail the pleasure principle no longer prevailed in the rich countries: "The very progress of civilization under the performance principle has attained a level of productivity at which the social demands upon instinctual energy to be spent in alienated labor could be considerably reduced" (1955, 129). For Freud, civilization required that sexuality, in particular, be repressed. Note that as postmaterialist values arose, so too did popular music—rock and roll—that began removing the polite veil over sexuality in music to more explicitly reference sex and even sex acts.

(1) a scarcity hypothesis that one's priorities reflect one's socioeconomic environment so that one places greatest subjective value on those things that are in relatively short supply; and (2) a socialization hypothesis that, to a large extent, one's basic values reflect the conditions that prevailed during one's preadult years. (1989, 56)[13]

Inglehart defined the materialist values as relating to physiological needs, specifically those having to do with physical and economic security. These values encompass the following categories: stable economy, economic growth, fight rising prices, strong defense forces, fight crime, and maintain order. By contrast, the postmaterialist values relate to social and self-actualization needs and have to do with belonging and esteem, as well as intellectual and aesthetic values. They include the following categories: less impersonal society, more say on job and community, more say in government, free speech, ideas count, and beautiful cities and nature.

From extensive surveys of attitudes, values, and behavior carried out over almost two decades, Inglehart found considerable support for his thesis. Those born after World War II placed less importance upon economic and physical security than older cohorts, while giving greater importance to the environment and such non-material needs as community, belongingness, and self-expression. Other postmaterialist values also appear to be associated with the coming of age of the early Baby Boomers, such as greater equality, racial justice, gender equality, and rejection of war and imperialism.

Inglehart has also found that these postmaterialist values are not merely held in youth, to be abandoned with age. A subsequent study found that in 1988, "virtually all of the cohorts were fully as Postmaterialist as they were in 1970" (1989, 86).

Parents of earlier generations had experienced or viewed extreme material privation and thus felt compelled to raise their children under a strict regime. Failure to do so would not have adequately prepared them for a world of potentially pinching scarcity. These parent-workers have been characterized by their deference to authority, their tolerance for rules and hierarchy, and their conformity (Whyte 1956; Braverman 1998; Lewchuk 1993). But parents of

---

[13] Consequently, "fundamental value change takes place gradually, almost invisibly; in large part, it occurs as a younger generation replaces an older one in the adult population of a society." The socialization hypothesis does not mean that no further value changes occur beyond adolescence. The implication is only that "human development seems to be far more rapid during preadult years than it is afterward, and the great bulk of the evidence points to the conclusion that the statistical likelihood of basic personality change declines sharply after one reaches adulthood" (Inglehart 1989, 69).

post–World War II generations, raising their families in unparalleled affluence in a robust economy, were more willing to indulge their children. They were more willing to raise their children according to the permissive codes of pediatrician Benjamin Spock, whose *Baby and Child Care* (1946) was one of America's bestselling post–World War II books.

It appeared that the highly optimistic vision which in 1930 John Maynard Keynes imagined coming to fruition in a hundred years was arriving well in advance. Keynes wrote:

> . . . the Western World . . . [is] capable of reducing the economic problem, which now absorbs our moral and material energies, to a position of secondary importance. . . . [T]he day is not far off when the Economic Problem will take the back seat where it belongs, and . . . the arena of the heart and head will be occupied, or re-occupied, by our real problems—the problems of life and of human relations, of creation and behaviour and religion. (1930, viii)

Unprecedented affluence put people at ease. Not only could they be less strict with their children, but they could also "lighten up" on themselves. Yet, if Inglehart's research conclusions hold, it is especially with the children—this first generation raised in such affluence—that the greatest impact would occur. Did this unprecedented affluence generate a discipline problem? Was this behind the long-term decline in SAT scores that began in 1965? As will be seen in the next chapter, a discipline problem did appear in some workplaces, a problem that would nourish a political backlash.

As further evidence for his thesis, Inglehart notes studies revealing that the postmaterialists are underachievers economically. As would be expected, they are typically born to richer and better educated parents. But when this advantage was factored out, their incomes wound up substantially below those of Materialists. Although they were more highly educated and held more prestigious jobs, "in the postwar generation, among those whose education continued beyond the age of 18, Postmaterialists earn less than Materialists." They are not as motivated by income, placing greater emphasis upon "interesting, meaningful work and working with congenial people" (Inglehart 1989, 172, 162).

Inglehart interprets these findings as suggesting that the shift from materialist to postmaterialist values entails the loss of an engine for dynamic economic growth. He notes that "nations with relatively high proportions of postmaterialists show significantly lower rates of economic growth than those of nations with high proportions of Materialists" (Inglehart 1989, 175).

Postmaterialist values notably included decreasing conformity. Young people no longer felt such a strong need to adhere strictly to social norms. They dressed more causally, young women went braless, and men grew long hair and beards; they experimented with alternative lifestyles, religions, and mind-altering substances. Sociological and psychological treatises came forth that challenged the conformity of modern life, notably sociologist David Riesman's *The Lonely Crowd* (1950), urbanist William Whyte's *Organization Man* (1956), sociologist Paul Goodman's *Growing Up Absurd* (1960), and psychiatrist R. D. Laing's *The Divided Self* (1965). The wide popularity of novels such as J. D. Salinger's *The Catcher in the Rye* (1951) and Albert Camus's *The Stranger* (1942) captured in fictional form the alienation of the young from straight-laced society and their rebellion against conformity.

In 1965, philosopher Jesse Glenn Gray wrote an essay, "Salvation on the Campus: Why Existentialism Is Capturing the Students," that appeared in *Harper's Magazine*. He noted that students were being drawn to thinkers, especially existentialists, who spoke of the need for authenticity and rejection of unjust social institutions. They were guided toward idealism and sought personal freedom. A few years later, in 1969, historian Theodore Roszak explored this movement in greater depth in his widely read book, *The Making of a Counter Culture: Reflections on the Technocratic Society and Its Youthful Opposition* (1995).

As will be seen in the next chapter, the Cultural Revolution unleashed by abundance and greater equality helped set the stage for a reaction that would stop and reverse the 40-year trend toward greater equality and re-establish greater insecurity. The quasi-utopian future that visionaries had imagined and that seemed to be aborning over the three decades following World War II was smothered in early infancy by a resurgence of laissez-faire ideology and the public policies it legitimated.

11

Simon Kuznets's Happy Prognosis
Crushed in an Ideological Coup

People getting their fundamental interests wrong is what American po-
litical life is all about. This species of derangement is the bedrock of
civic order; it is the foundation on which all else rests.
> —Thomas Frank, *What's the Matter with Kansas?* (2005, 1–2)

As noted in Chapter 1, Simon Kuznets, appealing to empirical evidence, suggested in his 1955 Presidential Address to the American Economic Association that, although inequality increases in the early stages of economic development, beyond some point it can be expected to decrease. His tentative conclusions came near the midpoint of the unprecedented decline in inequality between the 1930s and 1970s. But Kuznets and those who rallied to his optimistic scenario did not fully grasp why inequality exists and why it can be expected to increase as long as economic growth creates more wealth for an elite to appropriate. Their understanding was grounded too narrowly in mainstream economics. They failed to grasp that inequality is political and that ideology has always played a critical role in maintaining or increasing it.

Since the rise of civilization and the state, ideology has legitimated elite control of practically everything, typically including the state. Until recent centuries, a landed aristocracy held this control. But with the rise of capitalism, the aristocracy had to share control with and eventually yield dominant control to a capital-owning bourgeoisie. The socioeconomics that this wealth-generating bourgeoisie set in motion led to industrialization, urbanization, and egalitarian ideals that enabled workers to organize and successfully demand a voice in governance.

The franchise that workers fought for and won began in the nineteenth century, when propertied males gained the right to vote, and since then it has expanded, legally, if not in fact, to the entire adult citizenry. It has enabled enfranchised workers peacefully to use the state to improve their conditions. Given that they are far more numerous than the elite, workers have possessed the electoral muscle at the ballot box to transform social institutions and hold on to an ever-greater share of output. In terms of potential power, their historical relationship to the state has been completely reversed. Historically, the state and elites (backed by the state monopoly over violence) extracted as much surplus as possible from producers. With democratization of the franchise, however, the state became the sole instrument that could limit, or even potentially end, this exploitation. The state had been radically transformed from "the executive committee of the ruling class," as Marx and Engels described it, to a representative government chosen by majoritarian vote. With the franchise, the masses could potentially call on the state to limit, if not eliminate, the elite's ability to capture disproportionately large shares of income, wealth, and privilege.

With democratization of the ballot box and greater constraints on the state's use of violence against workers, the fortunes of elites came to depend more fully upon controlling ideology. And because the masses could now, in principle, dominate the state and rewrite the social script, the elite's ultimate ideological coup would be to convince them that the state is their enemy, that it must, at all costs, be reduced in size and limited in function. This ideological strategy was first used, especially in Anglo-Saxon nations, to restrain the influence of the aristocracy and free the bourgeoisie's activities from government control.[1] Since the democratization of the franchise, generating distrust of the state has been used to discourage workers from using government to their advantage. This argument has been fashioned with ever greater finesse into the basis for an ideological triumph. Over the past 45 years, it has helped reverse the previous 40 years of declining inequality.

This chapter surveys the dramatic ideological reversal since the 1970s that has legitimated altered rules of the game, enabling elites to capture substantially greater shares of wealth, income, and privilege. The elite's use of laissez-faire ideology, combined with its deflecting attention to cultural issues, defines contemporary politics.

---

[1] As will be recalled from Chapter 7, so long as a landed elite controlled the state, its rulers drew their legitimacy from religion above, claiming a divine right or mandate to rule. The bourgeoisie reformulated the state's right to rule as coming from below, from a social contract made by the ruled.

Industrial Dynamism and Relative
Labor Peace

Following World War II, many US industries held substantial monopoly power around the world. Much of the productive capacity of Europe and Japan had been shattered by the war, putting US industries in a privileged position. In the early 1950s, with 6 percent of the world's population, US industry produced 60 percent and exported 29 percent of the total manufactured output of all Western industrialized countries. They produced 93 percent of all automobiles. US firms were at the technological frontier in practically all sectors, and benefited from economies of scale made possible by the huge, wealthy, and well-integrated US economy (Lawrence 1983).

Institutional changes achieved during the 1930s and 1940s enhanced workers' power while maintaining relative peace between employers and employees. The widespread labor strife of the Depression years had led to the creation of a legal framework for collective bargaining. Between the mid-1930s and the late 1940s, legislation at both the federal and state level had established an institutional apparatus to deliver social security, minimum wages, unemployment insurance, and workers' compensation. Because workers fought for better deals on these matters in the political arena as well as at the bargaining table, labor strife within firms was somewhat attenuated.

Nevertheless, in the late 1940s, widespread strike activity and strong inflationary pressures—the latter supposedly due to excessive wage gains— caused public support for unions to decline. Significant setbacks followed. Most notably, the Taft-Hartley Act of 1947 restricted union actions, especially by outlawing sympathy strikes ("secondary boycotting"). It made illegal the massive nationwide strikes that have periodically paralyzed Western European economies and enabled their workers to better maintain their political power. State right-to-work laws in the United States also curbed workers' bargaining power. Still, the workers' political power remained adequate to channel a considerable portion of the fruits of economic dynamism into wages.

Despite this lessening in public support for labor, an implicit post–World War II accord existed between industry and workers. Industry accepted trade unions in the economic and political spheres. Workers, in turn, accepted the basic institutional framework of capitalism, including free trade and international capital mobility. Relative peace between capital and labor, along with the favorable international competitive position of US industry, meant that competitive pressures were mild for much of the US economy.

For a quarter century after World War II, the US economic machine churned out goods and services at an extraordinary rate. Output per worker increased at about 3.3 percent a year in the private sector, and approximately 3 percent overall. As mentioned in Chapter 10, the standard of living doubled in a mere 25 years. Children coming to adulthood during this period would, on average, be twice as well off materially as their parents. Such productivity growth was considerably higher than the approximately 1.8 percent annual rate over the preceding 50 years, a rate at which it took approximately 40 years for living standards to double.

The climate of relative social solidarity that had developed during the 1930s and the war years was visible across the political landscape. Between 1964 and 1979, a large number of national laws were passed that were meant to protect workers and consumers: 62 health and safety laws and 32 laws to protect the environment and regulate energy use (Parenti 1999, 111). Workers covered by corporate pension plans increased from 10 percent in 1950 to over 55 percent by 1979. Substantial gains were also forthcoming in paid vacations, sick leave, and health benefits.

Labor's power and a sense of social solidarity were reflected in President Lyndon Johnson's declaration of War on Poverty in 1964. Supportive policy measures provided the elderly and the poor with healthcare (Medicare and Medicaid), assured nutrition for the poor in the form of food stamps, assisted the poor with public housing and rent subsidies, helped poor children with preschooling (Project Head Start), and extended job training to the poor under the Job Corps. Government was becoming what economic journalist Ezra Klein would later call "an insurance conglomerate protected by a large standing army" (2011).

Even the Republican Party, which traditionally represented the interests of the elite, turned leftward. Indeed, Republican presidents Richard Nixon and Gerald Ford were significantly further left than were later Democratic presidents Bill Clinton and Barack Obama. Nixon, for instance, put through Congress the Occupational Safety and Health Administration, the Consumer Product Safety Commission, the Mine Enforcement and Safety Administration, and the Environmental Protection Agency. He even proposed a negative income tax, which, had it passed Congress, would have guaranteed everyone a basic income. Despite being a Republican president,

Nixon represented a continuation of the egalitarianism that had emerged in the 1930s.

A More Humanized Capitalism

> *The outstanding faults of the economic society in which we live are its failure to provide for full employment and its arbitrary and inequitable distribution of wealth and incomes.*
>
> —John Maynard Keynes, *The General Theory of Employment, Interest, and Money* (1936, 372).

Capitalism has always been plagued by crises during which output plummeted, banks closed, business firms went bankrupt, and workers lost their jobs. Suffering for the least well off has always been severe, sometimes including chronic hunger and even starvation.

During the Great Depression, British economist John Maynard Keynes offered a remedy for these crises. The gist of his argument is that if aggregate demand—the demand for all that is for sale within an economy's markets—is maintained at a level that generates full employment, crises need not occur. Government must serve as guarantor of adequate aggregate demand. It would do so through stimulative fiscal and/or monetary policy if demand should weaken, threatening unemployment. It would undertake contractionary fiscal and/or monetary policy to reduce excess aggregate demand that threatens inflation.

This policy prescription seems simple enough, but the dominance of laissez-faire ideology hindered its implementation, prolonging the Great Depression for 10 years. Then, massive government spending during World War II generated the aggregate demand necessary to lift the economy out of the Depression almost overnight. Unintentionally, it proved Keynes's theory correct.

Keynesian economics came to be widely embraced in the 1960s. President John Kennedy brought Keynesian economists into his administration and convinced Congress to cut taxes in 1963 to stimulate aggregate demand and reduce unemployment. This action also worked as Keynes predicted, helping Keynesian economics gain wider acceptance. Indeed, in 1971, Republican president Richard Nixon declared, "I am now a Keynesian," a political crime for which he was branded a traitor to his party.

The two principal failings of capitalism had long been identified as its boom-bust character and its failure to eliminate poverty even as it created extraordinary wealth. Keynesian aggregate demand management promised to eliminate the problem of crises. As data collection improved, increasingly sophisticated computer models stood to provide government policy makers with better guidance on fine-tuning aggregate demand to maintain full employment and price stability. This would keep the economy on its optimal growth path. Because the economy would no longer suffer crises and the related loss of output, growth would be sustainably robust, producing a "growth dividend" that could finance the elimination of capitalism's second failing—the scourge of poverty.

Keynesian economics and the War on Poverty endeavored to put a human face on capitalism. Government policies were to eliminate the blights of boom and bust, unemployment, and poverty. This humanized capitalism would generate economic dynamism and prosperity for all. It was a unique period of optimism in America as well as in Western Europe.

Abundance, Postmaterialist Values, and Labor Discipline

The optimism was short-lived. As the United States entered the 1970s, it was jolted by several shocks that are discussed in the following. In addition, rising standards of living, along with postmaterialist values, resulted in a labor discipline problem. It was exacerbated by the fact that labor markets had become especially tight after 1965, when President Johnson held out against raising taxes to cool an economy that was overheated by expenditures for the war in Vietnam. Had he increased taxes, parents might have joined their children in protesting the war. With the economy in overdrive, getting a job was relatively easy, and wages were rising.

Raised in unprecedented affluence, the first postwar generation entered the job market in the mid-1960s. But a significant proportion of them proved reluctant to work hard in uninteresting jobs merely for the money to buy more consumer goods. As noted in the previous chapter, many young people looked upon traditional material values with disdain. In their place they celebrated self-expression, richer interpersonal relations, and meaningfulness in work as in other domains of life. This "countercultural" movement drew strength from antiwar activism, as well as influential books such as philosopher Herbert Marcuse's *One Dimensional Man* (1964) and sociologist Philip Slater's *The Pursuit of Loneliness* (1970). These were the Baby Boomers whom French filmmaker Jean-Luc Godard referred to as "the children of Marx and Coca-Cola" (Priestland 2012, 179).

Many young adults, then, were unwilling to accept monotonous, dangerous, or otherwise degrading work. Their recalcitrance was aggravated by the fact that, by the 1960s, the labor movement had become sufficiently powerful politically to force the creation of far more generous welfare systems in all developed countries. Not only did the level of affluence dampen the age-old fear of starvation, but government stood by to safeguard all citizens from such a fate. Government became the people's guarantor of economic security. Over the course of the twentieth century, the costs of social welfare measures in wealthy countries increased taxes from about 10 percent of national income to between a third and a half.

Emboldened by a sense of security, labor became aggressively militant in demanding higher wages, shorter work weeks, safer workplaces, greater voice in decision-making, and better health and vacation benefits. Labor's combativeness was such that by 1969 the number of strikes in the United States was at its highest level since World War II. By 1970 the number of days of labor time lost due to militancy was the highest since 1946. And their militancy paid off. Employers generally ceded to their demands. This militancy spread even to public-sector workers in the late 1960s, who began to strike in violation of legal constraints against doing so. Striking public school teachers, postal workers, garbage collectors, and city office workers generally met with success.

Labor's privileged position was novel in the history of humanity. Fear of unemployment and privation had always compelled producers to perform unsafe and unpleasant work. But, if that fear were to dissipate, how could workers be motivated to work assiduously, especially in boring and unfulfilling jobs under the control of managers who bossed them about? A positive incentive, an attractive carrot, might help, but the character of work had not substantially changed. Workers were free politically and, now, free from the threat of destitution, but they were not free in the workplace. They continued to be ruled over by bosses, with no say over choosing their managers and little say over the work process.[2]

---

[2] This period witnessed a surge of interest in workplace democracy, whereby workers democratically elect a firm's management and the firm's assets would be worker-owned or held in trust (Azzellini 2015; Wisman 1991).

The consequent labor-discipline problem was encapsulated in what became known as the "Lordstown syndrome." The mostly young workers who staffed a General Motors plant in Lordstown, Ohio, chafed at the mindlessness of the work and believed their participation in decision-making could improve both operational effectiveness and product quality. Their disgruntlement led to poor worker discipline, high absenteeism, and high turnover. Lordstown was unique only in that it represented an extreme instance of an increasingly pervasive problem. A strike at Lordstown in 1972 became a national news story. It exposed the dissatisfaction of a new generation of workers with the monotonous drudgery of the assembly line, even at high wages (Loomis 2018). This severe labor-discipline problem has been identified as a cause of the productivity slowdown that appeared after 1966 (Bowles, Gordon, and Weisskopf 1991).

In 1971, the devaluation of the dollar and the revocation of its convertibility into gold put upward pressure on prices as the costs of imports rose and US firms faced less intense foreign competition. Nonetheless, despite postmaterialist behavior and rising inflationary forces, the economy was booming in 1973, even as poor harvests worldwide led to grain shortages and increases in the price of food. The Organization of Petroleum Exporting Countries (OPEC) began cutting output in 1974, pushing up prices for all products whose production depended upon oil. Shortages and higher prices emerged for other raw materials. A wage-price spiral (where workers demand higher wages in expectation of higher prices while businesses raise prices in anticipation of higher wages) was set in motion, and the inflation rate reached 12.3 percent by late 1974.

The economy crashed in late 1973, and the ensuring severe recession lasted until the spring of 1975. It was the worst downturn since the Great Depression, pushing unemployment to 9 percent and rekindling worker insecurity. Six years later, the recession from mid-summer 1981 to late fall 1982 drove unemployment to 10.8 percent, and the redisciplining of labor shifted into high gear.[3] President Ronald Reagan made the tough-on-labor message clear in 1981 when he fired illegally striking members of the Professional Air Traffic Controllers Organization.

---

[3] Between 1979 and 1982, weekly take-home pay fell by more than 8 percent, and by 1982, 44 percent of new contracts required workers to accept wage freezes or cuts (Parenti 1999, 120).

Labor's comfortable sense of financial security was crushed. Students became more focused on preparing for high-paying jobs. During the 1960s and early 1970s, when unemployment was low and wages were rising, college students could major in practically any subject and expect to land a high-paying job. By the mid-1970s, their easygoing confidence in an effortlessly prosperous future disappeared. Between 1968 and 1996, the percent of American college freshmen who viewed the "development of a philosophy of life" as important fell from 82 to 42 percent, while the percent seeking to "be well off financially" rose from 40 to 74 percent. Young people became jaded concerning the potential for making the world more humane, and the proportion believing that "keeping up with political affairs" was important fell from 52 percent to 30 percent (Macionis 1999).

The crushing of the optimism that emerged in the 30 years following World War II is one of the great tragedies of modern US economic and social history. Ironically, although material living standards as measured by real per capita income almost tripled from $10,850 in 1960 to more than $31,000 by 2015 (Hungerford 2016, 10), a widely shared sense of material insecurity developed after the mid-1970s. Rich nations had overcome the problem of scarcity that had always plagued humanity, but the promise of human liberation was for the most part thwarted. Damage has been done not only to the prospect of happiness, but also to the potential for avoiding ecological devastation, a topic that will be explored in the next chapter.

Stagflation and the Delegitimation of Keynesian Economics

Politics, n. A strife of interests masquerading as a contest of principles. The conduct of public affairs for private advantage.
— Ambrose Bierce, *The Unabridged Devil's Dictionary* (2009, 271)

Failure to raise taxes to cool an overheated economy during the Vietnam War pushed the inflation rate to over 6 percent by 1971, matched by an unemployment rate also at 6 percent. This mix came to be called "stagflation," a neologism to describe low growth with high unemployment and high inflation.

Keynesian aggregate-demand management appeared impotent to handle this mix. If government decreased aggregate demand to reduce inflation, it would slow the economy and raise unemployment yet higher. If it were to increase aggregate demand to stimulate the economy and decrease unemployment, it would generate yet more inflation. The Keynesian approach offered no good solution to the crisis—the economy seemed trapped between the devil and the deep blue sea.

Republican President Nixon faced the early stage of stagflation in 1971 as he was beginning to prepare for his 1972 re-election campaign. Rather than risk the political costs of reducing inflationary pressures by cooling the economy (reducing aggregate demand) and thereby raising unemployment, Nixon instituted wage and price controls—a policy that traditional conservatives abhorred because it challenges the legitimacy of the free-market system. If government needs to intervene to control wages and prices, then clearly the free-market system does not operate as its ideology claims. Workers were also opposed to wage and price controls, finding the policy unfair because, if profits were not also regulated, productivity gains would flow into the pockets of wealthy shareholders.

Nixon's wage and price controls were soon abandoned. Although the severe recession of 1973–1975 sent unemployment soaring, it failed to brake inflation significantly. Productivity growth remained weak. By 1979, inflation hit 13.3 percent with unemployment at 5.8 percent.

Stagflation created an opening for the resurgence of the ideology of laissez-faire that the Great Depression had substantially delegitimated. It came forth under the banner of "supply-side economics." Supply-side economics argued that the problem is to be found, not on the demand side as Keynesian economics contended, but instead with the forces that influence supply. It claimed that an overbearing government was choking the economy with high taxes on the rich that discouraged hard work, saving, and investment, while welfare sapped the incentives of the unemployed actively to seek employment, and regulations stifled initiative, innovation, and efficiency. Ronald Reagan ran for the Republican nomination for president in 1980 under the banner of supply-side economics, which his campaign rival, George H. Bush, labeled a "riverboat gamble" and "voodoo economics." Later, as president, Bush would also succumb to the ideological appeal of this magical thinking.

Laissez-Faire Ideology and Resurging
Inequality

*Politics is the process by which a society chooses the rules that will
govern it . . . who wins depends on the distribution of political power
in society.*

     —Daron Acemoglu and James Robinson, *Why Nations Fail*

               (2012, 79)

With Keynesian economics delegitimated,[4] by the mid-1970s, a revival of
laissez-faire ideology focused on delegitimizing government intervention
that had reduced inequality and benefited the non-elite for four decades. This
ideological revival was destined to happen eventually, given that the elites'
wealth and superior education provided them with disproportionate influence over the media and the political sphere. The specific trends and events
that facilitated this reversal are addressed in the following.

 The political climate of the 1960s and, subsequently, the interventionist
Republican Nixon administration frightened conservatives. They feared
that leftist egalitarian politics would spell the end of capitalism. Corporate
America's profits trended downward between 1960 and 1980 (Taylor 2011,
58), and were especially squeezed between 1966 and 1973, when real profits
declined an average of 3.1 percent annually, while average real worker compensation increased 4.4 percent (Bowles, Gordon, and Weisskopf 1991).

 The alleged threats to capitalism, combined with signs of national decline,
prompted pundits to proclaim the end of the American century. The loss of
Vietnam, the United States' first lost war, challenged military supremacy. The
dollar was devalued in 1971 and lost its gold backing, signaling the decline of
what, since World War II, had been the world's key currency—one as good
as gold. OPEC organized to cut the supply of oil, dramatically increasing its
price. Iran took American hostages in 1979, and the United States was hum-
bled by its impotence to free them. The United States and its people no longer
seemed to be masters of the universe. Fueling this decline, conservatives
argued, were the disincentives to work and the labor-discipline problems
brought about by welfare, union power, and labor legislation. Prime evidence

---

[4] As Chicago School economist John Cochrane has put it, "When inflation came in the nineteen-
seventies, that was a major failure of Keynesian economics" (quoted in Cassidy 2010, 31). As early as
1980, economist Robert Lucas wrote, "At research seminars, people don't take Keynesian theorizing
seriously anymore; the audience starts to whisper and giggle to one another" (1980, 19).

was that in 1970 the United States lost more working days per person to strikes than any other developed country (Priestland 2012, 185).

Intractable labor problems were not the only impediment to economic dynamism. High taxes, especially on the rich, allegedly reduced entrepreneurial energies and the motivation to save and invest, resulting in stagnation and anemic tax revenues. The infamous "Laffer Curve," advocated in 1974 by supply-side economist Arthur Laffer, purported to show that higher tax rates lower government revenues because higher tax rates stifle work and investment incentives, thereby decreasing economic growth and the tax base.

Other broad social trends were also viewed as contributing to the nation's decline. The use of recreational drugs became more widespread, as did relatively lenient attitudes toward sexual promiscuity. Both were presented as evidence of moral degeneracy, and pundits recalled the claim that decadence had brought down Rome. Conservatives courted industrial workers who repudiated postmaterialist values. They were depicted as constituting part of "the silent majority" (an expression first used by Nixon in 1969) whose country was being taken over by idle dope-smoking hippies, braless women, militant blacks, and leftists.

The 1960s and early 1970s were a period of pervasive protest by the young. They demonstrated against the Vietnam War, imperialism, racism, poverty, sexism, and even capitalism. They also demanded that their universities address these issues in the curriculum. Domestic terrorism also characterized this period. In 1972, there were 1,900 domestic bombings. Terrorist groups included the Weathermen, the Black Liberation Army, and the Symbionese Liberation Army (Burrough 2015). Many believed that, without a reorientation of policy, far more violent chaos lay ahead.

The swing toward the right was abrupt, offering support for political economist Albert Hirschman's claims that politics tends to be cyclical and that reversals are extreme (2002). This was made evident in the previous chapter. In the presidential election of 1912, 75 percent of the vote went to candidates who called themselves "progressive" or "socialists." Hundreds of socialists were elected between 1880 and 1920. Following World War I, politics turned drastically to the right and then again radically to the left during the Great Depression. The most recent extreme swing was to the right and began in the mid-1970s, bringing an explosion in inequality that continues as this is being written. This latest shift of income, wealth, and privilege toward the rich set in motion a self-reinforcing process since it meant that the rich commanded ever more resources with which to influence public opinion and policy. And research reveals that expenditures on creating and disseminating ideology yield high returns (Glaeser and Saks 2006).

The following subsections address the ways in which, over the past 45 years, the wealthy have gained greater control over think tanks, educational institutions, media, politicians, and the courts. These initiatives improved the likelihood that their self-serving ideology would be well crafted and broadly circulated. The aim of the elite has been to make their belief system more persuasive to a majority of the electorate, empowering politicians who would change the rules of the game in their favor. The coup de grâce would be convincingly to portray the state as the enemy. Mainstream economists' turn away from Keynesianism toward laissez-faire doctrines provided this ideology with scientific legitimacy.

Explosion of Corporate Lobbyists

In 1971, only 175 US corporations had registered lobbyists in Washington; today there are nearly 12,000. Political action committees increased from 89 in the 1970s to almost 1,600 by 2014. These increases come from groups representing corporate and financial interests, not labor or environmental concerns (Federal Election Commission 2009). Corporations spend $34 on lobbying for every dollar spent by labor unions and public-interest groups combined. Large corporations keep as many as 100 lobbyists on retainer. Of the organizations engaged in lobbying, 95 of the top 100 represent corporate interests (Drutman 2015). Money spent on lobbying yields high returns. Political economists Brian Kelleher Richter, Krislert Samphantharak, and Jeffrey F. Timmons find that, for every dollar spent on lobbying, tax benefits equal between 6 and 20 dollars (2009). The political consequence, former vice president Al Gore claims, is that "the United State Congress, the avatar of the democratically elected national legislatures in the modern world, is now incapable of passing laws without permission from the corporate lobbies and other special interests that control their campaign finances" (quoted in Freeland 2013, B1).

Politicians must seek financial campaign assistance from the super-rich and the corporations they predominantly own. Whereas the richest 0.01 percent of the population provided between 10 and 15 percent of total contributions in the 1980s, this amount rose to 40 percent in 2012 (Scheidel 2017, 417). Increasingly, politicians can count themselves among the rich.

In 2013, the median net wealth of members of Congress was over one million dollars, compared to the median net worth of an American household of
$56,335 (Sitaraman 2017, 254).[5]

Explosion of Conservative Think Tanks

Political scientists Jacob Hacker and Paul Pierson (2010, 357) claim that in
the 1970s, corporate leaders unleashed "a domestic version of Shock and
Awe" to take back power from a progressive left that had been improving
wages and working conditions since the 1930s.

The proliferation of conservative think tanks helped in this power
takeback by disseminating conservative, free-market ideology and helping
guide it into public policy. Between 1970 and 2000, they increased in number
from 70 to more than 300. Whereas most earlier think tanks sought to produce intellectually objective research, over two-thirds of the new ones defend
specific conservative positions (Sitaraman 2017, 252).

Corporate leaders created new national organizations such as the Business
Roundtable in 1972 to fund militant free-market think tanks and action
groups. The Heritage Foundation was founded in 1973 as the first think
tank with political advocacy as its explicit goal (Troy 2012, A13). Later that
same year, the American Legislative Exchange Council was founded, to be
followed by the Cato Institute in 1977 and the Manhattan Institute in 1978.[6]

Over the past four decades, conservative think tanks have come overwhelmingly to outnumber and overpower their liberal counterparts. By the
mid-1990s, there were two conservative think tanks for every liberal one
(Rich 2005, 206). While the five largest conservative think tanks each had
total expenses greater than $10 million, only the largest liberal think tank, the
Center on Budget and Policy Priorities, can claim this distinction. In fact, by

---

[5] A 2014 study of members of Congress found that, regardless of their personal wealth, Republican
lawmakers favored the same economic policies. The voting of Democratic legislators, by contrast,
correlated with their wealth such that richer Democrats more often supported lower taxes on the
wealthy and decreased business regulation (Kraus and Callaghan 2014). Only about 2 percent of
members of Congress and only about 3 percent of state-level legislators arose from the working class
(Drutman 2014).

[6] Think tanks advocating a laissez-faire stance were not new. The oldest, the Hoover Foundation,
was founded in 1919 and the American Enterprise Institute in 1943. The highly secretive free-market
Mont Pelerin Society had its first American meeting in 1958. In his 1980 presidential campaign, 22 of
Reagan's 76 economic advisors were members (Muller 2003, 382).

2006 the arch-conservative Heritage Foundation alone had larger expenses than the four largest liberal think tanks combined.

Some of the most intellectually venerable thinks tanks that had generally aligned with a Keynesian perspective, such as the Brookings Institution, replaced senior management with more conservative leaders. It had been the tradition at Brookings to be funded by no-strings-attached grants from foundations and wealthy benefactors. Over recent decades, however, Brookings has sought funding from outside interests, including corporations that designate the specific projects they wish to subsidize. This policy change enabled the organization's revenues to soar from $32 million in 2003 to $100 million in 2013. Lobbyists are increasingly encouraging their clients to donate to Brookings so that their issues are more likely to get research attention. Many academics now challenge the independence or non-partiality of Brookings's research (Hamburger and Becker 2014).

Expansion of Laissez-Faire Influence on Education

From the 1830s to the 1970s, the United States possessed the world's best public education system. But since the late 1970s, as more of the increasingly wealthy elite have sent their children to private schools, public-sector support for education has weakened. This is most striking at the level of higher education. Beginning in the 1980s and accelerating after 2000, under the influence of laissez-faire ideology, state and federal officials began demanding tangible measures of higher education outcomes, arguing that taxpayers should be getting their money's worth (Geiger 2019, 339). Education was represented as a private rather than a public good whose costs should be paid for by its direct beneficiaries, the students themselves. Guided by this ideology, between 1990 and 2010, state support declined from 26 to 7 percent of the University of Virginia's operating budget; at the University of Michigan, from 48 to 17 percent; at Berkeley, from 47 to 11 percent (De Vise 2011, A1). In 1975, the federal government spent 1 percent of GDP for education and training, but by 2015 this allocation had fallen to 0.7 percent (Hungerford 20016, 8). This parallels a falling of the United States behind other countries where higher education is almost wholly publicly financed. Although the United States had long boasted the highest percentage of 25- to 34-year-olds holding college degrees, by 2010 it had fallen to twelfth place among 36 wealthy nations (Lewin 2010, A11). The World Economic Forum ranked the United States fifty-second among 139 nations in the quality of its university math and science instruction in 2010 (Williams 2011).

Due to declining state support, the average cost to students (in constant 1982–1984 dollars) of attending a public college or university more than doubled between 1982 and 2009, from $6,440 to $12,861 per year (OECD 2011).[7] This increase has disproportionately harmed working-class students (Goldrick-Rab 2017). A result has been yet greater inequality, which in turn further reduces state support—a vicious circle. While wealthy parents can compensate for their childrens' short time horizons by paying for their college tuition, poorer children have no compensating mechanism except state-funded or private student loans that may burden them for decades after they graduate.

Historically, higher education has been offered by nonprofit institutions. However, for-profit higher-education institutions have dramatically expanded over the past 40 years.[8] Whereas only 1 percent of American students were enrolled at a for-profit college in 1980, this statistic jumped to 13 percent by 2017 (Doran 2017). The rapid expansion in for-profit education is easy to understand: it is exceedingly profitable. Profits recently represented 19.4 percent of their income (Geiger 2019, 321).

As government funding for higher education has decreased, and the wealthy have concurrently become ever wealthier, privately supported foundations have increasingly funded higher education. Often political strings are attached. Perhaps the most egregious instance is that of the former BB&T Charitable Foundation (merged with Sun Trust in 2019 to form Truist), which offered grants of up to $2 million to a school on the condition that it establish a course on capitalism in which Ayn Rand's extreme right-wing classic novel, *Atlas Shrugged*, is required reading. About 60 schools, including several campuses of the University of North Carolina, signed on (Lubove and Staley 2011, G3). Other foundations that have played an important role in funding research and education, such as the Ford Foundation, have also shifted to the right (Perelman 2007, 63).

---

[7] Incidentally, over this same period, states spent six times more on prisons than on higher education (Gopnik 2012, 73).

[8] Professor of education Roger Geiger notes that in 2002, under the George W. Bush administration, guided by laissez-faire ideology, "A for-profit-sector lobbyist was placed in charge of the higher education division of the Department of Education, and she gutted the restrictions on recruiters" (2019, 321).

Free expression is also under assault in American higher education. There has been a dramatic rise in the percent of professors who are hired, most frequently on one-year contracts, as adjuncts and term faculty not eligible for tenured status. In 1969, about 78 percent of faculty were tenured or on the tenure track, but only 27 percent held this status in 2018 (Flaherty 2018). Non-tenured faculty must take care not to express views that displease administrators and threaten the renewal of their contracts.

Historically, academia has been the most intellectually independent component of the knowledge industry, if not of society generally. Its institution of tenure protected that independence in two important ways. First, in principle, tenured professors cannot be fired for researching and expressing ideas that others find offensive or dangerous. Because they have guaranteed jobs for life, they can write and teach practically what they wish. They can expose students to ideas that may be highly idiosyncratic and unorthodox, thereby opening minds to novelty and creative thinking.

Second, tenure guarantees professors the privilege of dedicating their professional lives to pursuing whatever intellectually excites them without time limits. It has been an institutionalized procedure whereby societies set some promising minds loose to see if something important might come forth. History suggests that societies that take this gamble get back very good returns. The dramatic decline in faculty tenure is compromising academic independence and threatening intellectual freedom. To the extent it does so, political freedom and long-term economic dynamism are jeopardized (Wisman and Duroy, 2020).

Ironically, as Americans have continued to grow collectively wealthier, exploding inequality and job insecurity have left students more stressed and more focused on "careerist" education that presumably offers a smoother path to desirable jobs.[9] And this support for a careerist reorientation of higher education comes from surprising quarters, indicating how free-market ideology has infiltrated practically all of society. Political scientist David Kirp, a member of the Barack Obama Presidential Transition Team, reported that

the Obama administration [hoped] to advance the goal of equal opportunity in higher education by adopting a market-driven rating system designed to

[9] The explosion in tuition has heightened the belief in the need for a careerist education among students and parents alike to get their money's worth. Unbeknown perhaps to both parents and students, studies reveal that liberal arts graduates have a higher probability of rising into senior management positions in US corporations (Ginsberg 2013, 176).

give students a clearer picture of colleges' costs and outcomes. . . . The message is plain—the dollar-and-cents return on investment is what counts. . . . Market values trump everything, including learning how to think . . . [further] . . . to Washington policymakers, a university is little more than a vocational training ground. (2015, 120)

This careerist attitude toward education is further evidence that postmaterialist values are in their death throes. Economist Claude Hillinger observes that "largely unnoticed, the elites have done away with the idea of a liberal education that would empower the population by giving them an understanding of social and political realities. Instead, we have what is essentially vocational training" (2014, 137).

The Media Moves to the Right

Freedom of the press, including all information media, is critical to social and political freedom. For this reason, the Federal Communications Commission (FCC) was established in 1934 to ensure the fairness of radio broadcasts as they expanded and gained widespread influence. It obliged broadcasters to provide balanced information on news, election coverage, and political advertising. However, in 1976, the Supreme Court ruled in *Buckley v. Valeo* that money spent on advertising in political campaigns is constitutionally protected under the free speech clause and that no legal obligation requires the presentation of opposing views.

Further, over the past 45 years, due substantially to deregulation, the traditional media—newsprint, television, and radio—have become concentrated in the hands of a few large corporations. By the beginning of the 2000s, the majority of US media had become controlled by just five companies. About one-third of Americans now listen to radio stations owned by a single company. Deregulation of radio in 1996 practically ended local ownership (Blethen 2004, B7). A result of this increased media concentration is that favorable depictions of government programs or criticisms of laissez-faire ideology and the corporate power structure have become increasingly marginalized.[10] Reporters Without Borders, a news media advocacy

---

[10] Some of the most notable media have shifted to the right over the past 45 years. Major newspapers such as the *New York Times* and *Washington Post*, that had generally represented a centrist Democratic perspective, have put more conservative managers in charge (Perelman 2007, 63).

organization that annually constructs a Worldwide Press Freedom Index, reports the United States at forty-eighth among all countries (Reporters Without Borders 2019).

Courts Politically Empower Corporations

Since the 1970s, US Supreme Court decisions have revealed a pronounced pro-corporate bias. Whereas business won 28 percent of its cases in the court headed by Chief Justice Earl Warren between 1953 and 1969, its success has risen to 64 percent under the court led by Chief Justice John G. Roberts Jr. (Cohen 2020b, B2).[11]

In 1942, the Supreme Court ruled that "commercial" speech was not protected by the First Amendment. Corporations were not to be considered as "persons." However, a number of subsequent rulings, most notably *Rubin v. Coors Brewing* in 1995, invalidated most commercial speech restrictions (Bhaghwat 2010). The ideological coup de grâce occurred on January 21, 2010, in *Citizens United v. Federal Election Commission*. The Supreme Court overturned two precedent decisions and concluded that corporations have the same First Amendment rights to free speech as individuals. Accordingly, they can spend as much money as they wish to support or oppose political candidates.

In this climate, federal agencies also acted in favor of business. In 1949, the Federal Communications Commission (FCC) issued a "fairness doctrine" requiring that holders of broadcast licenses present contrasting views on controversial issues of public importance in a manner that the FCC judged to be equitable and balanced. Reagan's FCC eliminated this doctrine in 1987, and in August 2011, the language that implemented the doctrine was eliminated.

Granting corporations free speech under the First Amendment means augmenting the political voice and influence of the rich. Corporations are overwhelmingly owned by the very rich. In 2020, according to Federal Reserve data, the wealthiest 1 percent of Americans owned 51.8 percent of stocks and mutual funds, and the richest 10 percent of the population owned 87.2 percent, leaving the bottom 90 percent in possession of only 12.8 percent

[11] Journalist Adam Cohen provides elaborate details of the Court's turn to the right in his recently published *Supreme Inequality: The Supreme Court's Fifty-Year Battle for a More Unjust America* (2020a).

(Pisani 2020). Of financial bonds, 60.6 percent are owned by the richest 1 percent, and 98.5 percent by the top 10 percent, leaving only 1.5 percent for the bottom 90 percent (Koechlin 2013).

Most corporate chief executive officers (CEOs) can count themselves among the very wealthy and have become far more so over the past several decades. In 1980, CEOs heading corporations in the Standard and Poor 500 earned 42 times as much as the average worker. By 2013 the ratio had risen to 331 times more (Dill 2014). Whereas CEO compensation has risen by 940 percent since 1978, worker compensation has increased by only 12 percent (Meyerson 2019, 4).

The argument that such incomes are necessary as incentives is unconvincing. Between 1948 and 1975, the economy boomed, even as marginal income tax rates remained above 70 percent, suggesting that CEOs of that period were nonetheless highly motivated. Productivity growth between 1950 and 1970 was twice as high as it was between 1990 and 2010, when marginal income tax rates were less than 40 percent (Piketty 2014, 511). This should not be surprising. Humans are motivated to be recognized as the very best, meaning that what counts is the relative rather than absolute level of pay. As seen in Chapter 2, in terms of the dynamics of sexual selection that underlie all competition, it is sufficient to be the best or among the best to be highly attractive to mates and thereby hold the greatest potential that their genes will be carried into the future.

Part of the reason that corporations are willing to pay such astronomical salaries is traceable to the fact that, since 1980, the highest marginal income tax rate has been all but halved from 70 to 37 percent, meaning corporations are no longer obliged to hand over most of exorbitant CEO salaries to government.

Contributions by corporations and a wealthier elite have made political campaigns far more expensive. In constant dollars, the total amount spent in presidential elections increased from $225 million in 1980 to $6.4 billion in 2016 (Sultan 2017). The average inflation-adjusted cost of winning a House seat increased fourfold, from $360,000 in 1986 to $1.6 million in 2012 (Steinhauser and Yoon 2013). The high cost of political office, along with the decline of unions, has forced politicians of both parties to seek corporate financial support, making them highly sensitive to business interests. This pro-business bias is then expressed in the nomination and approval of conservative high court justices.

The Ultimate Ideological Coup: The State
as Enemy

Since the rise of civilization, the state was the problem for workers, extracting their surplus and protecting elites' ability to do the same. By the end of the nineteenth century, in advanced industrial nations, democratization of the franchise created the possibility that workers might be freed of this exploitation. Democratically and peacefully, the majority could use government to redistribute wealth, income, and privilege. In earlier history, the state protected the elites' property and ability to appropriate workers' surplus; now it could be democratically compelled to ensure that workers share in their surplus. With democracy, the state had thus become the elites' potential enemy.

The egalitarian policies enacted between the 1930s and 1970s made this opposition plain. Progressive government policies gnawed away at upper-class wealth, income, and privilege. Advanced capitalist countries were becoming more equal. To reverse this trend toward greater equality, a promising ideological strategy for elites would be to convince everyone else that government was also their enemy, and thus that its reach and powers should be restricted.

In the United States, this strategy has met with exceptional success. It gained momentum with the rise of supply-side economics in the 1970s and reached takeoff velocity with the election of Ronald Reagan. In his first inaugural presidential address in 1981, Reagan declared that "government is not the solution to our problem; government is the problem." Grover Norquist, a leading Reagan supporter and head of Americans for Tax Reform, declared the goal to be "to cut government in half in twenty-five years, to get it down to the size where we can drown it in the bathtub" (Dreyfuss 2001). The new rallying cry was "starve the beast"—with the intention to reduce the tax revenues that fund progressive policies.

This was little more than ideology, as academic and politician George Cabot Lodge explains: "In spite of their rhetoric, the Republican presidents of the last thirty years have regularly every year increased the power, reach, and cost of government" (2010, 86). However, they have done so in ways that have stealthily shifted more of society's resources to the wealthy. If the political party of the elite did not actually reduce the size of government, it deployed its superior control over ideology to give the impression that it had. Elites pressured political leaders to dismantle programs that were not to their benefit and augment those that were. The wealthy found an effective cheerleader in the *Wall Street Journal*, which tirelessly campaigned to turn Americans against government. In an infamous editorial, it went so far as to advocate raising taxes on the working class so as to get their "blood boiling with tax rage" (Krugman 2003, 4).

Reagan's head of the Office of Management and Budget, David Stockman, publicly divulged the ideological strategy to camouflage tax cuts that redistribute income to the elite. In an unguarded moment, he characterized the supply-side theory behind the tax cuts of 1981 as a "Trojan horse" to re-craft fiscal policymaking to benefit the wealthy: "It's kind of hard to sell 'trickle down,' so the supply-side formula was the only way to get a tax policy that was really 'trickle down.' Supply-side is 'trickle-down' theory" (quoted in Greider 1981, 46).[12]

Nevertheless, despite Stockman's revelation, the strategy of convincing a large part of the population that government is the problem worked. It worked so well that some members of the Tea Party absurdly cried later, "Keep government out of my Medicare!" A poll found that, when asked to identify the cause of their high personal indebtedness, 23 percent blamed government (cited in Rose 2010, 211). In the mid-1950s, three-quarters of Americans agreed with the statement, "You can trust the government to do the right thing most of the time." Only 10 percent did so in 2012 (Wade 2012, 33).

The right had long decried the incompetence of government. In 1962, for instance, Chicago economist Milton Friedman blamed the federal government for having created the Great Depression: "The fact is that the Great Depression, like most other periods of severe unemployment, was produced by government mismanagement rather than by any inherent instability of the private economy" (1962, 38). But it is only after the 1970s that the charge of government ineptitude gained traction within the greater population.

It should be noted that government is not identified as the problem when it comes to national defense, from which the wealthy reap huge profits, while the costs in lost lives, mutilated bodies, and troubled minds are overwhelmingly borne by the far less affluent young. Political scientist Sheldon Wolin

---

[12] Tax cuts favoring the rich have occurred in most rich countries since the 1980s. Economist Thomas Piketty writes that "in many cases, tax cuts for the rich were financed by the privatization of public assets, which in the end amounted to a free transfer of ownership: the wealthy paid $10 billion less in taxes and then used the $10 billion to buy government bonds. The United States and Europe have continued to pursue this same strategy to this day, increasing inequality and encouraging concentration of private wealth" (2020, 616).

writes, "That the patriotic citizen unswervingly supports the military and its huge budgets means that conservatives have succeeded in persuading the public that the military is distinct from government. Thus the most substantial element of state power is removed from public debate" (2010, 199).[13]

An early victory in the anti-government tactic was California's Proposition 13, a property-tax amendment to the state constitution. Although consistently presented as being in the interest of "ordinary families," it launched a tax-cutting campaign in 1979 that essentially benefited the well-to-do. Proposition 13 was the harbinger of a sharp change in attitudes toward taxation, not only in the United State, but in Europe as well. The progressivity of income taxes began to decline practically everywhere, even in relatively egalitarian Sweden. At the same time, the familiar idea that the unemployed and poor were to blame for their condition began to regain currency in Europe. However, disillusionment with government as the source of society's ills runs deepest in the United States (Pharr and Putnam 2000, 8).[14]

Another dynamic reinforces the anti-government animus of the wealthy. Public-sector workers tend to hold more egalitarian views than their counterparts in the private sector (Priestland 2012, 4). When politicians reduced the budgets of public-sector agencies, the quality of their services declined, sometimes quickly and sharply. This outcome provided further evidence of the inefficiency of government, leading to calls for steeper cuts or the privatization of public services. This ideology of "government as the problem" has so thoroughly permeated US political culture that many Americans do not even recognize the very substantial government-sponsored benefits they get. For instance, 44 percent of those who receive Social Security, unemployment benefits, and Medicare claim that they "have never used a government program" (Krugman 2013, 9).

The response of the federal government in bailing out Wall Street in 2008 enraged many Americans, once again creating mistrust of government. The Tea Party movement accused government of causing the Great Recession by forcing banks to issue mortgage loans to those who would not otherwise qualify, especially minorities. In the fall of 2011, Speaker of the House John Boehner proclaimed that "job creators in America, basically, are on strike"

---

[13] As discussed in Chapter 3, in-group favoritism, out-group animosity appears to be genetically "hard-wired" into the human species.

[14] Political economist John Roemer accuses some economists of complicity in generating anti-government ideology: "Incredible as it might seem, it is now becoming increasingly popular in certain circles of economists in the United States to say that the productivity of government investment is zero" (2011, 77).

because they have been "slammed by uncertainty from the constant threat of new taxes, out of control spending, and unnecessary regulation from a government that's always micromanaging, meddling, and manipulating" (quoted in Frank 2011, 8).

Although most Americans believe greater equality would be to their benefit, they do not believe government capable of achieving it. As Roemer wrote, the argument "for inequality, which is currently most prevalent in the United States, is one of futility: Even if the degree of inequality that comes with laissez-faire is not socially necessary in the sense that the incentive argument claims, attempts by the state to reduce it will come to naught because the government is grossly incompetent, inefficient, or corrupt" (2011, 77).

Mainstream Economics Turns Rightward

Wittingly or not, mainstream economists helped fuel the resurgence of laissez-faire ideology. It was ominous that in 1975, economist Arthur Okun published a treatise entitled *Equality vs. Efficiency: The Great Tradeoff*. The title said it all, and the book drew a great deal of attention just as political discourse was turning rightward. Its take-away message was that greater economic equality means less economic dynamism. Although this was not Okun's intention—he actually supported Keynesian measures—his book was ideally suited to legitimate rising inequality, especially given the low productivity growth of the 1970s. Okun's work was symptomatic of the shift in the economics profession away from Keynesianism toward a free-market approach. This movement has been so substantial and ideology-laden that Nobel laureate Joseph Stiglitz claimed that mainstream economics, widely known as neoclassical economics, had abandoned any semblance of scientific inquiry to become "capitalism's biggest cheerleader" (2010, 238). For economist Paul Krugman, "What the top 1 percent wants becomes what economic science says we must do" (2013, 27–28). Political economist Luiz Carlos Bresser-Pereira agrees, asserting:

> Neoclassical economics played the role of meta-ideology as it legitimatized, mathematically and "scientifically," neoliberal ideology and deregulation. . . . Neoliberalism . . . should not be understood merely as radical economic liberalism but also as an ideology that is hostile to the poor, to workers and to the welfare state. [Further], neoclassical macroeconomists

and neoclassical financial economists built models that have no correspondence to reality, but are useful to justify neoliberalism "scientifically." (2010, 2, 3)

Predictably, this "science-based" disdain for the least privileged and the welfare state mirrors its political expression. For instance, US senator Jim DeMint declared that "there are two Americas . . . [but] [i]t's not so much the haves and the have-nots. It's those who are paying for government and those who are getting government" (quoted in Chait 2009, 46). In an infamous 2012 presidential campaign speech, Republican Mitt Romney made the same claim, declaring that 47 percent of the country constitutes a "taker class," paying little or nothing in taxes themselves while expecting the productive classes to subsidize free healthcare, food, and housing.

Economists advanced arguments in favor of privatizing prisons, social security, and government services generally. The pre-1980s concern with poverty and inequality all but disappeared. The 1995 recipient of the Nobel Prize in Economics, Robert Lucas, declared, "Of the tendencies that are harmful to sound economics, the most seductive, and in my opinion the most poisonous, is to focus on questions of distribution" (2004), thereby arguing for exempting inequality from serious scientific investigation by the economics profession. Reinforcing the ideology that individuals alone are responsible for their fates, and that, with hard work, anyone can make it to the top, mainstream economics turned more forcefully toward methodological individualism by putting rational choice theory at the foundation of their science. People make free choices and get their just deserts.

The Nobel Memorial Prize in Economic Sciences is the highest honor that can be bestowed upon an economist. It is noteworthy that it was created in 1968 by Sweden's central bank, which was recommending that the country turn away from its social-democratic orientation and pursue more market-friendly policies. In this light, it is not surprising that the prize has been given predominantly to those who study rational self-interested interactions in free markets, as opposed to those who study the economics of social democracy (Offer and Söderberg 2016).

Although it is true that neoclassical economics legitimates inequality, it is not true that all, or even most, neoclassical economists favor rising or substantial inequality. Much of the difference between what the science does and what its practitioners value is traceable to their methodological stance—their approach to "economic science."

Some believe that the issues surrounding inequality fall outside the domain of economic science. They shy away from the topic on grounds that it involves value judgments which are presumed to be beyond the realm of positive or scientific economics. Values, as Milton Friedman so famously put it, involve "differences about which men ultimately only fight" (1966, 5). Many textbooks in economics insist on a distinction between positive and normative economics, viewing the former as science and the latter as the domain of ethics.

The fact that mainstream economists nurture an image of their science as value-free makes it vulnerable to the charge of serving as ideology. The general inability to appreciate the extent to which economics is value-laden follows from the behavioral assumptions made, the narrow focus of most research, and the relative lack of concern with history in general and the history of the discipline in particular.

A cornerstone of mainstream economics is the criterion of Pareto efficiency: the ideal or optimal allocation of resources occurs where nobody can be made better off without making someone else worse off. This statement, taken alone, can be considered value-free, but it is not generally expressed outside a context in which ownership of the means of production is taken as given. Within this context, an allocation of resources can be ideal only insofar as the given distribution of ownership of the means of production is also ideal. Further, because the mainstream's focus is typically upon markets, Pareto efficiency ignores externalities, those benefits or costs that are not captured in market-generated prices.

Many economists, perhaps a majority, would wish for greater equality. However, their embrace of mainstream doctrine frequently leads them to oppose specific measures that promise to lessen inequality. A good example is the minimum wage. There is a high degree of consensus among mainstream economists that minimum wage legislation will result in reduced demand for low-cost labor, and, thereby, harm those it is intended to help. From the narrow focus of the functioning of markets, the logic is impeccable, but this narrow focus is precisely the shortcoming of their analysis. Seen in a broad perspective, higher minimum wages are widely credited with lessening inequality. Adam Smith was right in holding that, over the long haul, higher wages bring forth greater productivity. Low wages, especially when they keep full-time workers beneath the poverty line, result in socially perverse forms of behavior and outcomes. Low wages induce relative poverty that diminishes work effort, lessens family cohesion, weakens communities, and handicaps children, who are less likely to develop adequate human capital. Such externalities make the statistical study of the full socioeconomic consequences of minimum wages seemingly intractable, and so empirical research rarely takes into account their long-term societal impact. The upshot is that the narrow focus of economic orthodoxy on markets alone provides policymakers with a powerful justification to vote against increases in minimum wages.

Free trade is another example. Mainstream economists find the logic of trade theory incontrovertible. And, with qualifications, it can rightly be argued that free trade typically benefits both the exporting and the importing country, as it enables each to exploit its comparative advantages. However, it is also true that lowering trade barriers often brings about higher domestic inequality. Facing this outcome, neoclassical economists typically respond that public policies can be used to neutralize adverse within-country effects, so that there are some winners and no losers. But seldom is there adequate political support for such counterbalancing policies. Because the reparative or mitigating strategies they recommend are often politically impractical, and because they cannot conveniently abandon, or even slacken, their commitment to free trade, mainstream economists wind up legitimating policies that result in greater inequality. Their values are foiled by what they embrace as their science.

Although striving to be free of ideology, neoclassical economics has proven to be every bit as ideological as the earlier classical school of political economy. For instance, it legitimates inequality with equal if not greater adroitness, thanks to its presumed heightened status as "science," and its far more formalistic mode of expression makes much of its doctrine opaque to non-economists. Moreover, as political scientist Robert Wade puts it, "economists, who constitute the most influential profession in shaping norms of public policy, are trained to presume that inequality is an *inevitable* outcome of the market as a coordinating mechanism, and a *necessary* outcome for the market to function as an incentive mechanism" (2014, 118).[15] The result, in Stiglitz's terms, is that economics as taught "in America's graduate schools . . . bears testimony to a triumph of ideology over science" (2002).

---

[15] Further, Wade observes that "mainstream politicians and mainstream economists in Anglophone countries have been very relaxed about people becoming 'filthy rich,' as though a structure of income distribution with high concentration at the top has no society-wide costs" (2013, 5).

As this book attempts to show, a broad view of human history reveals the centrality of power and politics in all matters economic. Few universities include the study of this history in the required curriculum for obtaining a doctorate in economics. Yet, a look at the discipline's own history discloses that, in any age, the conventional school of economics tends to support the power and privilege structure of the political world in which it flourishes. In state socialist nations, the mainstream economics was Marxist-Leninist. Scholastic economics served the social structure of late medieval Europe. Mercantilist economics espoused the rising power of the bourgeoisie and the nation-state. And since the beginning of modern economics with Adam Smith, mainstream economics has supported the institutions and power structure of capitalism.

During the 40-year period between the 1930s and 1970s in the United States, when progressive politics prevailed, mainstream economics was more accommodating to government intervention into the workings of the economy. Afterward, when politics turned to the right, so too did economics, and it became less receptive to intervention. Economic science, at least in its mainstream expression, appears to be led by politics as opposed to leading society forward by offering policymakers sound, scientifically grounded advice.

Re-Empowered Laissez-Faire's Consequences

> *There are two things that are important in politics. The first is money, and I can't remember what the second is.*
>
> —Senator Mark Hanna, 1895, quoted in
> Ganesh Sitaraman, *The Crisis of the*
> *Middle-Class Constitution: Why Income*
> *Inequality Threatens Our Republic* (2017, 170)

Because of the elite's durable command over society's dominant ideology, the losers—the overwhelming majority of the electorate—have not used the political process to stop the extraordinary reallocation of income, wealth, and privilege toward the rich over the past 45 years. Through the democratic process, they could have forced the development and enactment of compensatory measures to relieve workers harmed by globalization and technological change. They could have modified the legal framework in which these dynamic processes take place (e.g., trade agreements, patent law, and antitrust laws). They could have restructured taxes in favor of ordinary people, and vastly expanded and improved public services that benefit them, such as vocational retraining, healthcare, education, day care, transportation, and recreational facilities. Instead, a majority of voting citizens have bought into the rich's ideology that such measures are not affordable, cannot be competently provided by government, and would not work either to their own benefit or that of the country.

The consequence, Robert Reich, Secretary of Labor during the Clinton administration, reports, is this: "As inequality has widened, the means America once used to temper it—progressive income taxes, good public schools, trade unions that bargain for higher wages—have eroded" (2008, 4). Additionally, "as money has risen to the top, so has political power. Politicians are more dependent than ever on big money for their campaigns" (2010, n.p.). On average, the richest 1 percent received 25 times the income of the bottom 50 percent in 1980 (in approximate figures, $400,000 vs. $15,000 a year). They received 80 times as much in 2015 (about $1.3 million vs. $15,000 a year) (Piketty 2020, 525).

And to please these rich political donors, political leaders permitted labor protections to erode both in the legal code and in the courts, where they appointed and approved judges more attuned to business than labor. Organized labor has declined from 34.7 percent of the workforce in 1954 to 10.3 percent today (6.2 percent in the private sector). Although the cause of the decline of unions in the United States is often attributed to the decline of the manufacturing sector, it should be noted that in Canada, where manufacturing has equally weakened, unions remain strong.

Two widespread misconceptions make it easier to convince a majority of the voting public that their best interest is represented by the ideology and policies advocated by elites: Americans underestimate the degree of inequality, and they mistakenly take it for granted that everyone has unparalleled opportunities to get ahead. People on average estimate that the richest 20 percent own almost 60 percent of all wealth, while in fact they own about 85 percent. More striking, they believe that the bottom 40 percent own 8 to 10 percent of wealth, while in fact they hold only 0.3 percent (Norton and Ariely 2011).

Although the United States was long that country in which vertical mobility was most feasible, this is no longer true. Nevertheless, the conservative mantra is that the United States is the land of equal opportunity. Perfect equality of opportunity would mean that the earnings of children would be unrelated to the earnings of their parents; in other words, the correlation would be zero. For comparison, in a perfectly rigid caste system, the correlation would be one—children would have exactly the same status ranking as their parents. The correlation in the United States is about 0.5, the highest among the Organisation for Economic Co-operation and Development (OECD) countries, surpassed only by China and some Latin American countries (Deaton 2013, 207).[16]

One of the most striking examples of the elite's command over ideology is the drastic reduction of the inheritance or estate taxes, sometimes informally called "death taxes." Counter to the ideological claim, estate taxes do not principally hurt small businesses and farmers. In fact, according to the Joint Committee on Taxation, 99.8 percent of estates pay no estate tax at all. The exempted amount increased from $650,000 per person in 2001 to $5.49 million per person in 2017 (Huang and Cho 2009).

As the wealthy have gained ever-greater shares of income, wealth, and privilege, they have pushed government to create more rent-seeking possibilities (opportunities to gain income by manipulating the political setting, rather than by creating new productive wealth). One consequence is that the financial sector has dramatically grown since the 1970s, increasing its political influence. As Simon Johnson, former chief economist at the International Monetary Fund, put it,

> . . . the American financial industry gained political power by amassing a kind of cultural capital—a belief system . . . [such that] the attitude took hold that what was good for Wall Street was good for the country . . . [and] crucial to America's position in the world. . . . Faith in free financial markets grew into conventional wisdom—trumpeted on the editorial pages of *The Wall Street Journal* and on the floor of Congress. (2009)

Politicians went to work changing the rules of the game, especially through deregulation, to the benefit of the financial sector. Their actions set the stage for a massive financial meltdown that would unleash the worst economic downturn since the Great Depression (Wisman 2013b).

---

[16] With his "Great Gatsby Curve," economist Alan Krueger reveals that as inequality rises, vertical mobility declines (2012).

Further, tax cuts favoring the rich have been accompanied by rising public indebtedness. As a result, net public property (property owned by the American people minus public debt) has declined from about 15 percent of total property to about minus 5 percent. This means less capital available to spend on public goods such as education, medical care, and infrastructure. Negative public wealth also means, Piketty observes, that ". . . private individuals own, through their financial assets, not only all public assets and buildings, on which they collect interest, but also a right to draw on future tax receipts." Thus, they "own not only tangible assets but also taxpayers" (2020, 609, 613).

Why No Post–Great Recession New Deal?

Equality had become a synonym for mediocrity, failed government programs, and coddled incompetence. Equality came to be seen as the enemy of economic competitiveness, and the survival of American affluence came to depend on getting rid of it.

—Christopher Newfield, *Unmaking the Public University* (2011, 67)

The Great Recession triggered by the financial crisis of 2008 was the greatest economic catastrophe since the Great Depression. Why did it not follow the Great Depression script of egalitarian social reform? The Great Depression gave rise to a strong and long-lasting egalitarian political reaction to the laissez-faire ideology that had justified the inequality-generating institutional changes of the 1920s. The hardship of the Great Recession, by contrast, left this ideology practically unscathed. Instead, malaise was largely channeled into a form of populism that enabled the rules of the game to continue to be reformulated to direct yet more income, wealth, and privilege to an elite. Since the beginning of the crisis of 2008, inequality has continued to surge.

Why such radically divergent reactions to systemic dysfunction and severe hardship? Three reasons stand out. First, the crisis beginning in 2008 proved to be less grave, due in part to wiser public policy responses. Second, although the welfare net that developed in the wake of the earlier crisis has become less protective, it remained substantial enough to attenuate the hardship accompanying the Great Recession. And, third, the elite's command over ideology had become more entrenched and sophisticated and therefore better able to survive the later crisis practically intact.

Two calamitous public-policy mistakes followed the stock market crash of 1929. The Federal Reserve System permitted the money supply to contract, creating a liquidity crisis that led to bank failures, deflation, and massive bankruptcies. In addition, Congress blamed unfair foreign competition for the crisis and passed the Smoot-Hawley Tariff Act of 1930, the most protectionist legislation in US history. Both of these reactions helped transform a financial crisis into a full-blown global depression. In terms of financial stability, the immediate response to the severe crisis that began in 2008 was much more astute. The Federal Reserve massively injected liquidity into the banking system and bailed out banks, precluding a collapse of the financial system as well as the deflation and devastating bankruptcies that had characterized the early 1930s. World leaders also forestalled a rush to protectionism. At the G20 meeting in London in 2009, they committed to avoid the mistakes of the Great Depression era by coordinating fiscal and monetary expansion and eschewing trade barriers. Only when the threat of deep depression seemed averted did voices increasingly call for fiscal austerity.

The Great Depression was far harsher for the general population than would prove to be the case during the Great Recession. Whereas unemployment reached 25 percent in the former, and perhaps even 50 percent (Gans 2014, 56), it rose only to 10 percent in the latter. Moreover, no public safety net existed until a weak and fragmentary one emerged late in the Great Depression. By contrast, a considerable public support system was in place to limit suffering during the Great Recession.

Laissez-faire ideology legitimated public policies that enabled upsurges in inequality prior to both crises. The ideology held sway only for a decade prior to 1929, however, while it predominated for three decades prior to 2008. Thus, in the later period, it had time to become far more deeply entrenched in politics and social attitudes, supported by social institutions such as education, media, think tanks, and popular entertainment.[17] Moreover, while socialism was seen by many as a more just alternative to capitalism in the

---

[17] Psychologists John Blanchar and Scott Eidelman cite empirical research revealing that the longer a doctrine exists, the more firmly it is embraced (2013, 238). And laissez-faire has long had powerful media support. For instance, since 1843, *The Economist*, an international weekly magazine-format newspaper, has been the most virulent proponent of laissez-faire. Currently, almost one million Americans subscribe, and according to its own statistics, they are the richest of all periodical readers (Mishra 2019, 77).

1930s, the collapse of the Soviet Union in 1991 all but eliminated it from political discourse.

Both Political Parties in Thrall to Wall Street

Barack Obama's campaign promises led supporters to expect substantial policy measures to reverse inequality, and he was elected president on a wave of progressive optimism. But his initial steps upon entering the White House betrayed these expectations. He hired the same Wall Street professionals and proponents, such as former central banker Timothy Geithner and economist Lawrence Summers, who had participated in setting the underlying conditions for the crisis, to formulate how to deal with it. Rather than nationalizing failing financial services organizations, they rescued them, sparing their wealthy owners from massive losses while letting homeowners go bankrupt on loans they had been fraudulently sold. No mortgage executives were held accountable, and mortgage companies were permitted to foreclose on residential properties instead of being compelled to modify or refinance even the loans that were originated dishonestly. About 9 million households lost their homes. At the end of Obama's presidency, 63.7 percent of households owned their own homes, the lowest level since 1965 (the peak was 69.2 in 2004) (Jackson 2017). Black households were especially pummeled. By 2014, almost half of their wealth had vanished (Heideman 2017), a crushing blow given that net median white household wealth is 13 times greater than that of black households (*The Economist* 2016).

The failing auto industry and its owners were bailed out at a final taxpayer loss of $10 billion due to the lack of provisions requiring repayment. Indeed, the wealthy were generally spared the pain of the crisis. By the end of Obama's second year, the S&P 500 stock index had risen almost 60 percent, recovering most of its losses after its 2007 peak. By the end of his second term, it was 166 percent higher than the 2007 level.

The median jobless rate during the Obama years was 7.7 percent, higher than it had been during any previous postwar administration. In the absence of a commensurate jobs program, unemployed workers were left idle. Many grew discouraged and dropped out of the job market; some never returned. Labor-force participation fell from 65.7 to 62.8 percent (half of the decline due to demographics), the lowest in four decades. (Jackson 2017).

Corporate balance sheets recovered quickly, while small "Main Street" businesses and American households floundered. Although Democrats held majorities in both houses of the US Congress during his first two years (2009–2010), Obama faced the threat of filibusters in the Senate. But rather than attempting to skirt Congress by appealing directly to voters with a strategy like Franklin Delano Roosevelt's fireside chats in the 1930s, he futilely tried to appease Republican opposition. Income inequality, as measured by the Gini coefficient, rose more during the Obama years than during any other administration over the past 40 years (Regalia 2015). Obama failed to push hard for his campaign promise to permit the expiration of George W. Bush's tax breaks for the richest Americans, even though Democratic majorities held both congressional houses. His failure to veto this bill made them permanent.[18] Economist Emmanuel Saez reports that 52 percent of income gains between the financial crisis in 2008 and 2016, Obama's years as president, accrued to the wealthiest 1 percent of households, while the average household's income remained about the same as in 1999 (2016).

The fact that Obama ended up embracing the same politics that had generated inequality over the preceding 35 years was the proverbial straw that broke the camel's back. Many sof his former supporters wound up supporting Trump in the presidential election of 2016.[19]

The Democrats' disappointing response to their unique opportunity to put American society back on a progressive track is symptomatic of the extent to which a wealthy elite's money and ideology have enabled them to capture government. Whether Democrats or Republicans have controlled the White House or Congress has made relatively little difference to who is winning in America. Since Jimmy Carter took office in 1977, income, wealth, and privilege have shifted toward an elite, no matter which party has been in power.[20]

[18] Most of the highly regressive 2001 Bush tax cuts were made permanent in January 2013 with strong bipartisan support in both houses of Congress and signed into law by Obama. The repeal of the estate tax in 2001 was also passed with strong bipartisan support.

[19] The Public Religion Research Institute conducted a poll in June 2016 that found 49 percent of voters in agreement with the statement, "Because things have gotten so far off track in this country, we need a leader who is willing to break some rules if that's what it takes to set things right" (Galston 2018, 74). During the 2016 election campaign, Donald Trump received the greatest support in those counties with the highest levels of economic distress, as well as those where the mortality rates were highest from alcohol, drug abuse, and suicide (Burns 2018).

[20] The election of Jimmy Carter began the shift of the Democratic Party rightward. It was especially President Bill Clinton (1993–2001) who pushed the party toward the right in his campaign pledge to end welfare "as we know it." He also advocated, and in 1997 signed into law, tax credits for higher education which benefited the well-off. Obama further expanded these in 2009. Reagan's 1986 overhaul of the tax system raised the capital gains rate from 20 to 28 percent. Early in his second term, Clinton cut the rate to 15 percent.

The only difference is that Republican policies have been more overtly crafted to benefit the elite. Government under both parties has let down a majority of Americans, and many were ready for anything but more of the same. Although the Republican Party is seen as the party of the well-off, due to its support of cultural stances that are anathema to the Democratic Party, it was stronger at the end of the Obama administration than at any time since 1928 (Time Staff 2017). Donald Trump's appeal was that he seemed and professed not to belong to the establishment, including the Republican Party on whose ticket he ran, that had betrayed ordinary Americans.[21]

The fact that both parties are beholden and in service to monied interests is a direct outcome of the surging inequality which has provided elites with ever greater resources for crafting and disseminating ideology, supporting candidates, and influencing government policies. Since election campaigns are funded by private money, and organized labor has largely been sidelined, candidates in need of massive amounts of money to run for office are trapped. They must appeal to wealthy interests to get and stay elected.[22] There have been counterexamples, such as Senator Bernie Sanders and some other candidates for the presidential election of 2020, but they are the exceptions that prove the rule.

Just as the Republican Party has embraced cultural issues to gain political support, so too has the Democratic Party, as it has become more beholden to corporate and wealthy individuals for campaign contributions. It has generally embraced free-market capitalism and shifted away from social welfare to policies related to identities of gender, race, ethnicity, and sexual orientation.

[21] According to a *Washington Post* analysis of those participating in the attack on the US Capitol on January 6, 2021, in an attempt to overturn Trump's election loss, "Nearly 60 percent [of the 125 defendants] facing charges . . . showed signs of prior money troubles, including bankruptcies, notices of eviction or foreclosure, bad debts, or unpaid taxes over the past two decades. . . . The group's bankruptcy rate—18 percent—was nearly twice as high as that of the American public. . . . A quarter of them had been sued for money owed to a creditor. And 1 in 5 of them faced losing their home at one point. . . . Financial problems were also apparent among people federal authorities said were connected to far-right nationalist groups, such as the Proud Boys" (Frankel 2021).

[22] Democrats as well as Republicans are dependent on the rich and the corporations they own. In the 2014 elections, for example, about 32,000 individuals—0.01 percent of the population—accounted for 30 percent of all political contributions (Olsen-Phillips et al. 2015). Business firms often hedge their bets, investing in politicians of both parties to ensure that, no matter who is elected, they will have access. Research reveals that politicians almost always respond to the will of their contributors, not constituents (Bonica et al. 2013).

How Do the Elite, with So Few Electoral Votes, Win Elections?

Although both parties have been substantially captured by monied interests, the Republican Party is generally the party to which the elite gravitate. But how could they rally sufficient support to get their candidates elected, given that they not only constitute a very small fraction of the voting public, but also officially embrace political programs that are blatantly beneficial to themselves and disadvantageous to the majority? For instance, the Republican Party has long advocated slashing programs that aid lower-income households, such as food stamps, unemployment benefits, funding for public education, public transportation, and publicly provided healthcare. And, proving their allegiance to the rich elite, Republicans have ever advocated cutting taxes for the wealthy. So how do they get their candidates elected?

It should be noted that the right has a long history of demonizing the least privileged as lazy and morally handicapped by dependency on welfare. As a Tea Party bumper sticker puts it, "Keep Working. Millions on Welfare Are Counting on You." American society is presented as providing exceptional opportunities for vertical mobility to those who are willing to work. The least fortunate are told to buck up and fend for themselves as industrious Americans have always done.

This idea of fluid vertical mobility has deep roots in US culture. For much of its history, thanks to the abundance of cheap land available to workers and migrants fleeing Europe's rigid class structure, there was greater social mobility in America than anywhere else. This made Americans more prone to accept personal responsibility for their successes or failures. The rich have earned their high status, and the poor are answerable for their poverty. This ideology also found early support in mainstream religion. The United States has been a predominantly Protestant country, and, as discussed in Chapter 7, for much of its history, Protestantism found the poor to blame for their fate. In addition, neoclassical economics' claim that economic actors get their just deserts reinforces the view that, with effort, anyone can make it in America.

The right also exploits the fact that for many voters, cultural issues trump economic ones. This comes about, in part, because economic issues are complex and hotly contested. Some professional economists endorse the "trickle-down" theory that tax cuts for the rich and corporations, cuts in welfare, and deregulation will generate economic dynamism, increase employment, and raise wages. So, even when other economists contest these supposed results, voters find reason to support a political party that also happens to endorse, or seemingly support, their stances on hot cultural issues such as abortion, gay rights, race, immigration, gun control, and creationism—issues freighted with an emotional energy that economic matters lack.[23] And some issues, such as racism and immigration, are both cultural and economic.

Many Americans, and especially the least privileged, have been depoliticized and fail to vote. They are preoccupied by the difficulties of getting by from week to week, coping with long workdays, job insecurity, soaring health costs, and poor education for their children. A Federal Reserve survey reveals that about 40 percent of Americans would face difficulty paying for an unexpected emergency expense of $400 (Nova 2019). Voting is held on Tuesdays, a workday, unlike Sundays in most countries. And why vote if it seems to make little difference who wins? In the election of 2008, for instance, fewer than half of eligible voters with incomes less than $15,000 voted, whereas more than four-fifths of those with incomes over $150,000 did so (Bonica et al. 2013, 111).

---

[23] Behavioral economists find that people systematically make decisions that run counter to their own interests, driven more by emotions than economic reason. In *What's the Matter with Kansas?* (2005), Thomas Frank provides wide-ranging evidence for this view.

12

Inequality, Conspicuous Consumption, and the Growth Trap

In the long run men inevitably become the victims of their wealth. They adapt their lives and habits to their money, not their money to their lives. It preoccupies their thoughts, creates artificial needs, and draws a curtain between them and the world.

—Herbert Croly, *The Promise of American Life* (quoted in Nguyen 2015)

Few people would assert that a man with fifty thousand a year is likely to have a very much happier life than if he had only a thousand; but to climb from the place in society which belongs to £1,000 a year to that which belongs to fifty thousand is a source of almost ceaseless delight to nearly every pattern of man, and to his wife. This satisfaction is, however, not net social gain: for something must be deducted for the chagrin of some of the many men and their wives who will be passed on the way.

—Alfred Marshall, "The Social Possibility of Economic Chivalry" (1907, 8).

Humans, like all sexually reproducing animals, have always competed for mating success. Excluding coercion, they have had to possess physical traits and exhibit behavior that make them sexually attractive. Through the dynamics of Darwinian sexual selection and gene-culture co-evolution, the genes of those who succeed in attracting mates have gone into the future gene pool, ensuring that these physical and behavioral characteristics endure.

But what is sexually attractive? Inherited physical characteristics have always been significant, but, among humans, culturally determined attributes have generally been more important. What is attractive is what is valued by society and therefore provides high status. As was seen in Chapter 3, for 95 percent of the human story, individuals won prestige by being, for example, aggressive warriors, efficient hunters or gatherers, skillful toolmakers, captivating storytellers, or mellifluous singers—in short, by contributing to the well-being of the group or community. Due to a strong innate sense of fairness, where projectiles were handy and the weak could form coalitions against the strong, individuals had to channel their competitiveness into behavior that was socially approved because it was communally beneficial. Bullying, bragging, and attempting to appropriate disproportionate political power or wealth were strongly discouraged, or even chastised, and as a result such behavior was unappealing to potential mates.

As was seen in Chapter 5, what became most sexually attractive radically changed 5,500 years ago with the rise of states and civilization. With superior military organization and technology, physical force and ideology enabled some to subjugate others and seize their surplus. The highest status was accorded to those possessing wealth and political power. They would be attractive to mates because their material possessions and social privileges could better ensure that their children would survive. Conspicuous consumption of luxury goods and services among elites competing for the pinnacle of status conveyed degrees of wealth. The subjugated and exploited workers typically retained little or no surplus with which to participate in spending for show.

This began to change in the latter part of the nineteenth century when workers in advanced capitalist societies organized to threaten the elites' states with violence and gained the power to retain a portion of their surplus. In social contexts where wealthier elites stepped up their conspicuous consumption, as they did during America's Gilded Age, those below began to emulate them. This was penetratingly analyzed by political economist Thorstein Veblen in *The Theory of the Leisure Class* (1899).

Prior to industrialization, workers' principal source of social status among themselves was their work. Diligence, skill, and productivity were attractive to potential mates because they signaled the worker's ability to provide for the well-being of children. However, industrialization hid work inside factories, narrowed the range of tasks, and reduced others' ability to observe workers' effort, resourcefulness, and efficiency. How much one could consume became a proxy for income, which presumably was a measure of how hard and well one worked. In the search for social status, workers were left with few options beyond their ability to consume goods and services. And the greater the degree of inequality, the greater the pressure to consume more in order to maintain relative status. Heightening this pressure, the urbanization that went along with industrialization reduced the potential to maintain one's reputation and status through participation in the life of a community (Wisman and Davis 2013).

This chapter explores how the devaluation of work and community, combined with high levels of inequality, intensify the struggle for status through conspicuous consumption. This has nourished a vision of material progress which identifies rising levels of output as the key to human happiness. Society has become caught in a growth trap that limits human potential and lays waste the natural environment.

The Urgency of the Ecological Challenge

But now human use, population, and technology have reached that certain stage where Mother Earth no longer accepts our presence with silence.

—Dalai Lama XIV, "Universal Responsibility
and the Environment"

Until recent centuries, because population was sparse and technology rudimentary, human activity did not upset global environmental equilibria. This does not mean that earlier societies did not produce ecological devastation, such as hunting species into extinction, deforestation, severe soil erosion, and polluted waterways.[1] Some even did so to the point of causing their civilizations to collapse (Diamond 2005). But their ecologically harmful actions were local and never attained a globally catastrophic scale.

Now, however, earth has entered a new geological era, the Anthropocene, whose name reflects the pervasive human impact on the whole earth, from the floor of the ocean to the edge of space. Humans have altered 75 percent of the land environment and well over half the marine environment (Fears 2019). Since 1970, there has been a 68 percent drop in the average

---

[1] Long before the rise of civilization, humans allegedly hunted to extinction about half of all huge animals. Humans arrived in Australia about 40,000–45,000 years ago, and the subsequent disappearance of its megafauna may have been the first extermination. Similar human-driven extinctions of megafauna have been claimed for practically every part of the world into which humans migrated (Martin and Greene 2007).

populations of almost 4,400 mammals, amphibians, birds, fish, and reptiles (Brulliard 2020). The destruction threatens to end the planet's ability to support human life. Extreme ecological devastation thus joins nuclear weapons as monstrosities of humanity's own making that menace the human species.

Ironically, this peril results from extraordinary economic success. Extreme global poverty has fallen by 50 percent since 2000. *Homo sapiens* has finally arrived at a point where it is possible to envision victory over the problem of material scarcity, or at least over the problem of dire material privation, in the very near future. Humanity appears to be nearing a state of the world predicted by economist John Maynard Keynes: "For the first time since his creation man will be faced with his real, his permanent problem—how to use his freedom from pressing economic cares, how to occupy the leisure . . . to live wisely and agreeably and well" (1930, 367). However, Keynes's sanguine forecast ignored the human struggle for social status through competitive conspicuous consumption.

Although per capita GDP has increased sixfold since Keynes expressed his optimism, people, even those who live in wealthy countries struggle for ever more material goods, still working long hours, which, including time preparing for and getting to and from work, eats up most of their days. Keynes failed to anticipate this eventuality because he did not see that the pursuit of status makes a struggle over inequality the driving force of human history. Moreover, he did not grasp the intensity of the quest for status because he was unaware that it is biologically driven by sexual competition. Given humanity's age-old evolutionary heritage, the institutions of modern capitalist societies have unleashed a consumption arms race that locks the human species in a growth trap with devastating environmental consequences.

The ecological challenge is a world challenge. An adequate response requires international cooperation, and that, in turn, requires that the nations of the world successfully address a free-rider problem. Reducing emissions of CO_2 and other pollutants is a global public good. The benefit to any country of curbing its emissions is only a fraction of the costs it would bear in doing so, and thus its self-interest militates against undertaking such reductions unless all others do so as well.

The free-rider problem is widely recognized, and strategies for dealing with it are not lacking. For instance, an especially promising one is offered by economist William Nordhaus, who proposes a climate club, the members of which would agree to cut their emissions by the required amount.

Non-members and cheating members would suffer punitive tariffs on their exports to member countries. Setting these penalties at the right level would encourage world-wide compliance by making it in each nation's self-interest to do so (2015).

But why, when nations meet on the climate issue, do they not adopt Nordhaus's proposal or some equally promising strategy? The reason is a second stumbling block—high levels of inequality. Inequality impedes necessary responses to degradation of the environment through two dynamics. First, as noted earlier, higher inequality leads to greater environmental degradation by raising consumption, as lower-income households seek to imitate the consumption spending of those above them. Inequality encourages households to pursue social certification and status through consumption, because high levels of consumption serve as a proxy for how rich they are and how hard they work. Rising inequality strengthens this dynamic, as does the degree to which people introject the ideological view that their status is solely dependent upon their own efforts. The attitudes, institutions, and behavior generated by this focus on consumption reduce the potential for people to achieve status or validation through environmentally friendlier domains such as work and community.

Second, inequality impedes responses aimed at reducing environmental damage by augmenting the political power of those whose interests would be harmed by mitigating or remedial measures—principally the wealthy. They benefit more from pollution (taken in the broadest sense of environmental damage) because, if the cost of pollution is not included in the price of their much greater consumption, that consumption is less expensive. It has been estimated that consumption by the richest 7 percent of the world's population produces 50 percent of the world's greenhouse gas emissions (Sayer 2015, 323). According to Global Footprint Network, "if everyone in the world consumed at the level of US citizens, it would require five earths to support them sustainably, or three earths at European levels of consumption" (cited in Sayer 2015, 315). Further, the elite overwhelmingly own the means of production, and the lack of pollution controls entails that their assets yield higher profits. The elite are also better able to live in places and manners that shield them from pollution's most harmful consequences.

Although these two dynamics affect all modern societies, this chapter will focus predominantly on the United States, the wealthiest large economy and the world's greatest polluter in per capita terms.

Inequality, Social Respectability, Conspicuous Consumption, and the Environment

In modern civilized communities the lines of demarcation between so-cial classes have grown vague and transient, and wherever this hap-pens the norm of reputability imposed by the upper class extends its coercive influence with but slight hindrance down through the social structure to the lowest strata. The result is that the members of each stratum accept as their ideal of decency the scheme of life in vogue in the next higher stratum, and bend their energies to live up to that ideal.
—Thorstein Veblen, *The Theory of the Leisure Class* (1899, 84, 85)

Might environmental pessimism be overblown? Might the normal course of advanced socioeconomic development set in motion forces that restrain or even reverse environmental damage? Three such forces appear to be at work. First, as people become wealthier and other needs are better satisfied, a cleaner environment comes to be more greatly valued. Second, new technol-ogies continually evolve that are less resource-intensive and less polluting. Some, in fact, can scrub away environmental damage. Third, the more in-tensely polluting sectors, such as manufacturing, decline in relation to the aggregate economy as a less polluting service sector expands. Admittedly, globalization compromises this third effect by exporting manufacturing to countries where labor costs are lower and environmental standards less stringent. But these countries might also become wealthy enough for all three reasons to come into play there as well.

Unfortunately, however, inequality sets in motion dynamics that challenge these optimistic expectations. Social institutions in modern societies have evolved to channel the pursuit of status into high consumption. This compet-itive consumption is stronger the more unequal the society and the greater its presumed potential for vertical social mobility, especially where inequality is increasing.

Because this consumption arms race typically uses more resources, it results in more ecological spoliation. There are exceptions. Status might be acquired by "going green." This is especially true in certain visible con-sumption domains such as electric or hybrid automobiles and solar panels on homes. Energy economists Marcello Graziano and Kenneth Gullingham have found that the most important determinant of a homeowner's decision whether to install photovoltaic solar panels is whether other houses in the neighborhood have done so (2014). It is thus both good business and good ecology for the installing firm to put a sign on the front lawn stating, "This house has gone solar." Competitive ecological behavior is to be encouraged.

However, far more status competition occurs in highly polluting luxury goods and services such as huge homes, expensive automobiles, and travel. A striking example is private jets that emit six times more carbon per passenger than normal commercial jets. The number of private jets increased tenfold between 1970 and 2006 as the elite took larger shares of income (Anderson et al. 2008). Conspicuous consumption, as will be recalled from Chapter 2, is a signal that one is rich enough to squander money and therefore rich enough to make a promising mate. As philosopher of art Denis Dutton expresses it, "The best way for an individual to demonstrate the possession of an adaptive quality—money, health, imagination, strength, vigor—is to be seen wasting these very resources" (2010, 156). Thus, the general thrust of status competition biases consumption toward those goods and services that are strikingly expensive. These goods also tend to be highly polluting in their production and maintenance, which may also provide the lavish private spender a sort of devil-may-care panache. The "flash" potential of private goods and services—their power to display the owner's wealth and insouciance—erodes support for public substitutes that are less taxing of the environment.

People are generally unaware that the dynamic of sexual selection is the ultimate driver of their struggle for high social status. Nevertheless, they typically recognize that status strongly motivates their behavior. Some minimal level of social status is a prerequisite for respectability in the eyes of others. And the approval of others is, in turn, necessary for self-esteem or self-respect, the sense of one's own worth that philosopher John Rawls identified as "perhaps the most important primary good," such that without it nothing else has much value (1999, 440). It is exceedingly difficult to maintain self-respect and pursue one's endeavors without social confirmation that one is of value. Or, as Veblen put it, "Only individuals with an aberrant temperament can in the long run retain their self-esteem in the face of the disesteem of their fellows" (1899, 39).[2]

---

[2] Although Veblen believed that social sciences needed to be reformulated in terms of Darwinian principles, he fully missed Darwin's dynamic of sexual selection, suggesting that he may not have read, or read carefully, the works of one of his greatest intellectual heroes. For a discussion, see Wisman 2019.

A widely held belief that, through hard work, vertical social mobility is possible increases pressure to show status through consumption. In precapitalist hierarchical societies, status was ascriptive, ascribed by birth, by the status of one's parents. This was the individual's identity, and little, if any, vertical mobility was feasible. Not only were there practically no avenues for raising one's status, but attempts to do so were discouraged, if not punished. High-status individuals were believed to be naturally superior humans, as those of lower status were believed to be inferior, or not even fully human. In an important sense, everyone's status was as it should be. An extreme instance, as noted in Chapter 4, was Hinduism's caste system. *Dalits,* or "Untouchables," until recently in their history, generally shared their society's belief that their grim existence at the bottom of the social structure was due to poor karma. Because karma is the sum result of behavior in previous incarnations, their current status is justly deserved.

Capitalism has progressively broken down rigid class stratification and created greater potential for vertical social mobility. As explored in Chapter 6, this transformation began in the early stages of capitalism as a rising commercial class—a bourgeoisie—began to accumulate wealth and to demand social recognition commensurate with its new command over society's resources. This bourgeoisie petitioned for equal status with the aristocracy. Its success in doing so entailed that the ground for status shifted from one's birth to one's achievement. Ascriptive status began to yield to performative or achievement-based status. Through diligent hard work and cleverness, one might rise in social standing. As will be recalled from Chapter 7, hard work was a central virtue in Protestantism, the new variant of Christianity that legitimated capitalist values, institutions, and the behavior of the bourgeoisie. Practicing the virtue of hard work brought vertical mobility more nearly within reach.

Vertical mobility developed most fully in those capitalist countries that were essentially composed of immigrants who had left behind worlds with more rigid status barriers. Thus, not surprisingly, considerable vertical mobility was found in countries populated by immigrants such as the United States, Canada, Australia, New Zealand, and Israel. Nevertheless, the potential for vertical mobility, and belief in its possibility, expanded in practically all nations.

It should be noted, however, that in terms of people's behavior, more important than the actual degree of vertical mobility is what is believed to be the case. That is, people's behavior can be expected to correlate more with their belief about the extent of vertical mobility that can be achieved than it would correlate with the extent that exists in reality. As noted in Chapter 11, although the United States used to be the society in which vertical mobility was greatest, this is no longer true. Yet the outdated belief is kept robustly alive for obvious ideological ends. Because Americans generally have more faith in the potential for vertical mobility than do people in other wealthy societies, polls show that they are less concerned with the gap between the rich and the poor (Glendon and Benson 2016, 4; Wisman 2009).

In societies in which the potential for vertical mobility is believed to be substantial, class distinctions become blurred. Although individuals may have a general sense of where they fall in terms of their society's distribution of income or wealth, they have little sense of belonging to a class. Indeed, the extent to which this is true in the United States is suggested by the fact that most Americans describe themselves as middle-class participants in a fluid society.

A belief in equal opportunity for upward mobility inculcates a sense that everyone is responsible for his or her social status. If one works diligently, one can move up.[3] Therefore, individuals are more prone to internalize responsibility for their successes or failures. This places considerable pressure on people to demonstrate high status. To the extent they succeed in doing so, they appear to possess the virtue of hard work.

However, as noted earlier, with industrialization and urbanization, workers were pushed and pulled from agriculture and petty businesses into factories, and from small communities into urban slums, with the consequence that how hard they worked was no longer as directly observable by those outside the workplace. What more easily caught attention was how much they consumed, which came to stand as a proxy for the income that presumably resulted from the quantity and quality of their labor. As Veblen wrote, "To sustain one's dignity—and to sustain one's self-respect—under the eyes of people who are not socially one's immediate neighbors, it is necessary to display the token of economic worth, which practically coincides pretty closely with economic success" (1919, 393). He clarified, "The only practicable means of impressing one's pecuniary ability on these unsympathetic observers of one's everyday life is an unremitting demonstration of ability to

---

[3] As noted in Chapter 4, in the most class-rigid of societies, Hindus also believed that they could move up in status, but not in this lifetime. Only by behavior proper to one's caste in this lifetime might higher status—a higher caste—be attainable in a future incarnation. It is an ingenious legitimation of the status quo.

pay"(1899, 86–87).[4] If a household consumes at the level of those with higher status, then it might acquire that status and the good reputation that accompanies it.

It should be noted that social status today results far more from hard work than was the case at the time Veblen was writing. At the end of the nineteenth century, Veblen viewed people as struggling to exhibit leisure status, that is, to be above work. He noted, for instance, that

> wealth acquired passively by transmission from ancestors or other antecedents presently becomes even more honorific than wealth acquired by the possessor's own effort. . . . The leisure class stands at the head of the social structure in point of reputability; and its manner of life and its standards of worth therefore afford the norm of reputability for the community. (1899, 29, 84)

The reason is that labor had come "to be associated in men's habits of thought with weakness and subjection to a master. It is therefore a mark of inferiority" (1899, 36).

However, in wealthy societies today, and even to some degree in less wealthy ones, these attitudes toward work and leisure are no longer prevalent. As economist Thomas Piketty points out, in the wake of workers gaining the franchise, elites increasingly appealed to merit to justify inequality (2020, 709ff). Consequently, everyone feels compelled to work. Even the very rich work. Some of this change has taken place over the past 50 years. In the 1960s, people admired the idle lives of the so-called jet-setters. Today, they would be more readily looked upon as having flawed characters, or even as debauched.

There are, of course, other, more aesthetically sophisticated means by which those successful in earning a good deal of money can demonstrate their virtue and status. But, as Veblen noted, the "cultivation of the aesthetic faculty requires time and application, and the demands made upon the gentleman in this direction therefore tend to change his life of leisure into a more or less arduous application to the business of learning how to live a life of

---

[4] With an acuity that also marks the much later work of Veblen, Adam Smith understood that the rich are always competing among themselves for the very pinnacle of status by flashing their wealth: "With the greater part of rich people, the chief enjoyment of riches consists in the parade of riches, which in their eye is never so complete as when they appear to possess those decisive marks of opulence which nobody can possess but themselves" (1776, 172).

ostensible leisure in a becoming way" (1899, 75–76). They typically take, therefore, the easier route of conspicuous consumption.

The greater the inequality in income and wealth, the greater the amount that must be consumed by everyone below the very wealthiest to maintain or improve their relative status. This effect will be more powerful where class distinctions are blurred and where a belief in the potential for vertical mobility is strong. In those societies where relatively little potential for vertical mobility is believed to exist, individuals understand their class status as more fixed and known. They possess the status of their parents, which was that of their grandparents, and so on. Should their status be low, it is not the result of a personal failing. It is their "born-to" identity. Moreover, if an individual were to attempt to signal greater status through consumption, it would more readily be viewed as negative, as "showing off." Rather than signaling virtue, it would signal a character flaw. Note again, for instance, the negative judgment frequently made of the consumption practices of the self-made wealthy, the so-called *nouveaux riches* or *parvenus* who have not had occasion to learn what constitutes "good taste."

This tendency to imitate the behavior of the elites is supported by game theory. A winning strategy is to replicate the behavior of high-status winners even if the copied behavior is not clearly the source of the winner's success (Low 2001, 154). Imitating successful people is rational insofar as it saves on learning costs. Natural selection would favor those learners who have been successful in evaluating effective behavior and then imitating it. Conspicuous consumption, therefore, is irrational for society, but it is not irrational for the individual—Adam Smith's invisible hand fails!

Participation in conspicuous consumption, Veblen argued, is socially compelled "through popular insistence on conformity to the accepted scale of expenditure as a matter of propriety, under pain of disesteem and ostracism" (1899, 111). So powerful is this compulsion that "no class of society, not even the most abjectly poor, foregoes all customary conspicuous consumption. . . . Very much of squalor and discomfort will be endured before the last trinket or the last pretense of pecuniary decency is put away" (1899, 85).[5]

---

[5] When the Federal Reserve Bank of Philadelphia examined the relationship between lottery winners and bankruptcies in a Canadian province, they found that neighbors of lottery winners are disproportionately likely to go bankrupt, and these bankruptcies are more likely the larger the lottery prize. Moreover, the larger the lottery win, the more money bankrupt neighbors spent on big-ticket luxury purchases (Lee 2017).

More fluid modern social life has also eroded the power of traditional or inherited sources of identity beyond class membership, such as community, ethnicity, religion, and even gender. Although the residual force of traditional sources of identity is weakest in the immigrant countries such as the United States, this force is rapidly weakening around the globe. The consequence is that individuals feel ever more responsible for not only their status, but also their very self-identity. People experience a greater sense of individuality, so much so that determining and demonstrating one's self-identity becomes a project. Consumption acts as a signaling device for identity, a means to define oneself and to project this definition to others. Maintaining if not improving this identity becomes a never-ending project.

Although inequality is great within countries, it is far greater internationally. The world's wealthiest one percent owns 40 percent of the world's net worth, whereas the bottom 50 percent own but 1.1 percent (Davies et al. 2008). This inequality is increasing. International inequality fuels an international "demonstration effect," whereby the elites in relatively poor countries emulate the consumption standards of their counterparts in the rich countries, stimulating imitative consumption within the poor countries. Thus, when the world's most elite raise their consumption standards, it puts pressure on the world to follow suit, with obvious negative environmental consequences.

An Intensified Struggle for Status Stability with Rising Inequality

From whence . . . that emulation which runs through all the different ranks of men, and what are the advantages which we propose by that great purpose of human life which we call bettering our condition? To be observed, to be attended to, to be taken notice of with sympathy, complacency, and approbation, are all the advantages which we can propose to derive from it.
    —Adam Smith, *The Theory of Moral Sentiments* (1899, 84, 85)

Over the past 45 years, inequality has exploded in the United States and Great Britain, as well as increasing significantly in continental Europe. Rising inequality fosters higher levels of status anxiety, which people have attempted to assuage through more consumption (Wilkinson and Pickett 2019, 202,

236). Surveys confirm that, with rising inequality, Americans have become more aware of their relative positions and have come to see higher levels of consumption as necessary to live a good life (Dwyer 2009, 289). Evidence indicates that, in order to increase consumption, US households have saved less, have become more indebted, and have increased work hours.

It is instructive to track the response to rapidly expanding inequality up to the onset of the Great Recession that began in 2008, because the crisis shocked many families into monitoring their spending more carefully. Over the prior three decades, the personal saving rate fell from 11.4 percent in 1980, to 8.8 percent in 1990, to 4.2 percent in 2000, to 3.7 percent in 2005 (Bureau of Economic Analysis 2020).

As inequality increased, households took on more debt. Average consumer debt in 2003 dollars for Americans over 15 years of age increased from $712 in 1980 to $3,261 in 2003 (Adkisson and McFerrin 2005, 447). Supporting a link between inequality and indebtedness, economist Robert Frank (2007) reports that in those parts of the United States where inequality rose most sharply over a 10-year period, personal bankruptcy rates also rose the most. More striking, in the late 1990s, when inequality was soaring, the economy booming, and unemployment low, personal bankruptcy was four times greater than it was in the 1970s, before the explosion in inequality.

This increased indebtedness held for the rich as well as the poor. However, as expected from a Veblenian perspective, the indebtedness of lower- and middle-income households grew significantly more, relative to income, than did that of wealthier households. New credit instruments, such as home equity loans and mass-marketed credit cards, greatly facilitated this emulative consumption. Nonetheless, as inequality increased, those in the highest income decile became about 50 percent more indebted. This appears to have been driven by the dramatically larger share of income accruing to the ultra-wealthy, the top one-hundredth of one percent. Their income shares soared from about 0.9 in the mid-1970s to 6 percent in 2005, surpassing the previous peak attained in 1929 (Piketty and Saez 2006). Equally astonishing, the economic expansion of the Clinton years provided the top one percent with 45 percent of total growth in pre-tax income, the Bush expansion with about 75 percent, and the first term of Obama (2009–2013) with 95 percent (Wade 2013, 18).

These super-rich households are ever in competition for the very acme of status, dramatically increasing the consumption of extremely expensive and flashy goods and services (private jets, mansions, thoroughbred horse farms, yachts, and positional goods such as waterfront property and elite school educations for their children).[6] A February 2008 Pew survey suggests that this intensified inequality-driven status competition among the wealthy caused anxiety. It found that "the proportion of wealthy Americans who say they are very satisfied with their housing and cars, in particular, has declined considerably since 2001" (Pew Research Center 2008).

The explosion in consumption by these super rich put pressure on those below by making them less satisfied with their belongings and lifestyles. This pressure, which contributed to a profusion of "McMansions" across the United States,[7] is reinforced by media advertising and programming that continually keep the consumption standards of the rich and famous on public display (Schor 1999; Frank 2001). Americans are more targeted by advertising than peoples of other cultures, and this bombardment has become ever more intense. It has been found that advertising as a percent of GDP significantly increases as inequality increases (Wilkinson and Pickett 2019, 112), presumably because it pays greater returns.

In addition to saving less and taking on more debt to preserve their relative status, households increased their work hours. As inequality rose dramatically between 1970 and 2002, work hours per capita in the United States rose about 20 percent, due to increased individual hours worked and the rise of dual-earner households. By contrast, in the European Union where (with the exception of Great Britain) income inequality rose significantly less, work hours fell 12 percent (OECD 2004).[8] Inequality also appears to influence whether women married to working men take jobs. Economist Yongjin Park

---

[6] This may help explain the explosion in tuition at elite private colleges and universities. Public colleges have had to raise tuition as public funding has shrunk. But rising inequality has made ever-wealthier parents less sensitive to college costs. As the elite schools have competed for the most talented professors and administrators, all schools below have had to also raise salaries or risk losing their relative standing, thereby being forced to raise tuitions. So intense is the status competition for entry into elite schools that over the past few years extremely wealthy families have been charged with bribery and fraud to gain entrance for their children (Medina, Benner, and Taylor 2019).

[7] In the decade preceding the financial crisis of 2008, an elite enriched by exploding inequality placed massive investment funds in real estate, not only generating a bubble in real estate prices, but also dramatically stimulating the construction of ever-larger dwellings, so-called McMansions. In their struggle to maintain their relative status, those in lower income brackets also sought larger dwellings. Between 1973 and 2019, even as household size shrank, the median size of new houses increased from 1,525 square feet to 2,322 (US Census Bureau 2019). The negative environmental consequences of heating and cooling these outsize homes will endure for years.

[8] This relationship is supported by another transnational study that found "increased inequality induces people to work longer hours [and] . . . the underlying cause is the Veblen effect of the consumption of the rich on the behaviour of those less well off" (Bowles and Park 2005, F410). The average hours worked annually per capita in the United States in 2015 were 1,877, but only 1,535 in France, with less inequality and a GDP that is 67 percent of the American GDP (Ingraham 2016, G3).

finds that women are more likely to work outside the home where there is greater inequality in men's incomes (2010).

The United States is the only wealthy country that does not legally require employers to provide paid leave. Even when US workers held far more political power than they do today, they did not strongly pressure government to make leave mandatory. The relatively high conspicuous consumption pressures in the United States may help explain why. Veblen contended with his customary insight that increased productivity would lead to greater conspicuous consumption among Americans, rather than fewer work hours (1899, 111).[9]

A "free-to-choose" interpretation does not adequately capture the dynamics of the intensified struggle to maintain status or social respectability as inequality increases. In his last major work, *The Revolt of the Elites* (1996), historian Christopher Lasch noted that, as economic elites take an ever-greater share of income and wealth, they tend to isolate themselves in social enclaves such as gated communities, exclusive clubs, and private schools. They tend to work in jobs, live in neighborhoods, and move in circles where they literally do not encounter those who are struggling to stay on their feet. Because of elites' disproportionate political power, this withdrawal from the wider society and from direct contact with the concerns of other citizens erodes support for public services on which the majority depend—services such as public schools, parks, transportation, public safety, and a clean environment. As former Secretary of Labor Robert B. Reich has put it, "members see no reason why they should pay to support families outside the gates when members are getting everything they need inside . . ." (2001, 199). Communities have increasingly become commodities, "marketed, evaluated, and purchased like any other" (2001, 198), thereby intensifying the segregation of the population according to income and privilege. Between 1990 and 2010, neighborhood segregation by income among families with children rose by about 20 percent (Badger 2016). Whereas in 1970, 64.7 percent of households lived in middle-income neighborhoods, this had fallen to 40.5 percent by 2012 (Reardon and Bischoff 2016).

No longer sharing lives together, the social skills and other cultural advantages of children from wealthy households are no longer as readily

---

[9] Almost three decades ago, economist Juliet Schor noted that "since 1948 . . . the level of productivity of the U.S. worker has more than doubled. In other words, we could now produce our 1948 standard of living . . . in less than half the time. . . . In 1990 the average American owns and consumes more than twice as much as he or she did in 1948, but also has less free time" (1993, 2).

appropriated by their less privileged peers. In the 1950s, sociologist Robert Putnam writes, "affluent kids and poor kids lived near one another, went to school together, played and prayed together, and even dated one another. . . . Nowadays, by contrast, fewer and fewer of us . . . are exposed in our daily lives to people outside our own socioeconomic niche" (2016, 37).

With less political support, public services decay, encouraging those beneath the elites, especially those with children, to do what is necessary—save less, borrow more, and work more hours—to enable them to live in neighborhoods with better public schools and safe recreation centers. As those who can afford private alternatives opt out of consuming public services, however, political support for the latter further deteriorates, as does quality. A vicious cycle is set in motion: increasingly inferior public services motivate well-to-do households to switch to private ones, causing a further decline in the support for and quality of public services. This dynamic lends support to the argument that government is inefficient and that such services should accordingly be privatized. The end result is higher economic, political, and racial inequality. And households respond by ramping up consumption to maintain their relative social status, further despoiling the environment.

At some point, increased inequality, and especially an increasingly sequestered elite, may prevent society from addressing and solving collective problems, such as inadequate infrastructure or ecological degradation. This appears to be the case with the United States today. In his study of societies that collapsed due to environmental destruction, anthropologist Jared Diamond found that "failures to solve perceived problems because of conflicts of interest between the elite and the masses are much less likely in societies where the elite cannot insulate themselves from the consequences of their actions" (2006, 431). Where they were isolated, elites continued to do well, even as environmental desecration generated wars and plunged the masses into starvation. For instance, the ancient Mayan kings in the Yucatan peninsula saw their forests disappearing, soil eroding, and productivity declining, but their own immediate self-interest in competing for the highest status precluded their undertaking measures that might have saved their civilizations and themselves. A more striking example, noted in Chapter 3, is Easter Island's 397 colossal legless human male statues that were constructed as a devasted ecology doomed the civilization to collapse (2006, 79–135). The statues on Easter Island are a monument to extreme inequality and ruinous competition among the elite for status.

Debased Alternatives to Consumption

I confess I am not charmed with the ideal of life held out by those who think that the normal state of human beings is that of struggling to get on; that the trampling, crushing, elbowing, and treading on each other's heels, which form the existing type of social life, are the most desirable lot of humankind, or anything but the disagreeable symptoms of one of the phases of industrial progress.
　　　—John Stuart Mill, *Principles of Political Economy* (1909, 748)

A tendency for humans to accumulate material wealth is often presumed to be universal, a direct result of human nature itself. However, as was seen in Chapter 3, a glance at human evolution reveals this to be false. Prior to the adoption of agriculture 10,000 years ago, almost all humans were nomadic, precluding any significant accumulation of material wealth beyond a few primitive weapons, tools, clothing, and jewelry. Further, attempts to accumulate wealth or political power were socially repressed and even punished. Competition for status and mates had to be expressed through other forms of behavior more beneficial to the community. It is only in the last 3 percent of the human story, since the rise of states and civilization about 5,500 years ago, that substantial accumulated material wealth even became possible. The rise of the state created institutions that directed the pursuit of status in such a way that what was beneficial to a select few was no longer necessarily beneficial for society.

Population generally kept pace with increases in output, leaving standards of living stagnant, albeit highly unequal. Only in the last few centuries has it been recognized that sustainable economic growth is possible: that someone's increase in wealth did not have to mean someone else's decrease, and that, with appropriate institutions, greater productivity could make everyone wealthier. The project of deliberately and fundamentally altering societies' institutions to promote economic dynamism increasingly became a political focus. This was the intent of Adam Smith's advocacy of laissez-faire economics. Yet the idea that economic development was possible spread slowly. When Smith was envisioning rising living standards, historian Edward Gibbon, famous for his treatise on the fall of the Roman Empire, claimed that there was an upper limit to the economic output that could be attained during times of peace and favorable climate, such that only a small surplus would be available to a few (2010). Even political economists from

Adam Smith to John Stuart Mill viewed the potential for economic progress as limited and destined to end in a stationary state. Moreover, as historian Richard Tawney noted, "The idea of economic progress as an end to be consciously sought . . . had been unfamiliar to most earlier generations of Englishmen, in which the theme of moralists had been the danger of unbridled cupidity, and the main aim of public policy had been the stability of traditional relationships" (1926, 206–7).

Nevertheless, the view that greater wealth was possible did spread, and, as it did, it generated a "material progress vision," according to which it is economic growth that will make the good and just society possible (Wisman 2003). Therefore, society should consider economic growth as its highest priority. This has promoted a preoccupation with material progress as the key to improved human welfare. Largely neglected were such essential components of human well-being as more creative and fulfilling work; greater equality in the distribution of opportunity, education, income, and wealth; stronger and more supportive communities; more time for family, friends, and reflection; and a sustainable environment. All of these essentials could be treated as subsidiary issues because maximum material progress was held to be the key to a better future. For the sake of society's maximum economic growth and everyone's greatest possible consumption, the creative destruction of capitalism must be fully unleashed—even if it results in ever more intense competition, insecurity, stress, and environmental destruction.

However, a substantial body of interdisciplinary work in what has come to be called "happiness research" finds that, above a fairly low threshold, the feeling of contentment does not grow stronger in step with higher incomes and higher levels of consumption. Although average degrees of satisfaction are considerably lower in very poor countries than in rich ones, after a certain income level has been attained, further increases do not raise subjective well-being (E. Diener, Diener, and Diener 1995; Veenhoven 1993; Easterlin 2001, 2002). In terms of income and consumption, what appears to be important is one's relative as opposed to absolute position. A notable study by economists Sara Solnick and David Hemenway (1998) finds that, when asked whether they would prefer to live less-well-off in a rich society or near the top in a poorer society, 50 percent claimed they would give up half their real income to live in a society where they were better off than most others. In terms of evolutionary biology, this makes sense. As was seen in Chapter 2, it is relative status that determines the probability of attracting sexual partners and thus sending one's unique set of genes into future generations.

This preoccupation with material accumulation directs people's attention away from the interrelated domains of work and community in which fulfillment and self-esteem are more richly nourished. Nevertheless, at some level these domains continue to be recognized as important. In extensive interviews, sociologist Robert Bellah and colleagues found Americans in agreement that

> ... two of the most basic components of a good life are success in one's work and the joy that comes from serving one's community. And they would also tend to agree that the two are so closely intertwined that a person cannot usually have the one without having the other. (2007, 196)

Work

Happiness research finds that, above a certain material threshold, it is in the realm of work that well-being is most readily achieved. Gunnar Myrdal, 1974 Nobel laureate in economics, wrote that "most people who are reasonably well off derive more satisfaction in their capacity as producers than as consumers. Indeed, many would define the social ideal as a state in which as many people as possible can live in this way" (1968, 136). More recently, political scientist Robert E. Lane reported, "It is in work, not in consumption and, as research reports show, not even in leisure, where most people engage in the activities that they find most satisfying, where they learn to cope with their human and natural environments, and where they learn about themselves" (1991, 235).

Substantial evidence reveals that humans experience a strong sense of well-being when they are involved in working on a project, whether alone or with others, that they find interesting and worthwhile. Indeed, they often become totally immersed in the activity, not unlike athletes do in sports. When in this state they are highly energized, they feel in control, there is a loss of censorious self-consciousness, intrusive negative or pessimistic thoughts fall away, time flies, the activity seems worth doing for its own sake, and they report being happy or being "in their element," at one with their work. Psychologist Mihaly Csikszentmihalyi has chosen the term *flow* for this experience (1993). He likens flow to Abraham Maslow's "peak experiences" (1954) and the outward-looking state that philosopher Bertrand Russell described in *The Conquest of Happiness* (1930, 229).

Having a job—working—is very important for social respect and self-identity. A World Values Survey found that "only 22 percent of respondents agreed that a job is just a way of earning money, and 63 percent said that they would enjoy having a paying job even if they did not need the money" (Alesina, Glaeser, and Sacerdote 2001, 239). In reviewing the literature on the economic psychology of well-being, psychologists Edward Diener and Martin Seligman find two of the six major underlying factors to be: living in a democratic and stable society that provides material well-being, and having rewarding and engaging work and an adequate income (2004, 25).[10]

In good workplaces, work provides a medium in which self-esteem can especially flourish. In work we contribute to society's wealth, as opposed to drawing upon it via consumption, and thus we have grounds for a sense that we are participating in achieving society's well-being. Possessing a degree of control over the work process provides a sense of accomplishment and pride when tasks are completed. Lane points to "evidence that exercise of discretion on the job, which is not so much a right as a requirement of complex tasks, has more substantial effect on self-esteem than any exercise of familiar political rights has ever had" (1991, 198). A national survey taken in 2012 revealed that British workers were significantly happier if they had "more responsibility and control over their work . . . [and that] employees with little control in the workplace have a 23 percent higher risk of heart attacks" (Priestland 2012, 271). Moreover, in work we can aid our fellow workers and bask in their appreciation of our assistance and our skills. It is also noteworthy that workers whose jobs permit them a significant degree of autonomy tend to be culturally liberal, whereas those whose jobs are micromanaged tend to be more authoritarian (Kitschelt 1994, 12–18).

Inequality, however, reduces the potential for work to serve as a means for achieving fulfillment. Because inequality propels households toward consumption to maintain their social standing, where there is a trade-off between work quality and income, inequality encourages workers to choose the latter. The labor market reinforces this tendency.[11] As Lane points out, "In

---

[10] The other four are: to have supportive friends and family, to be reasonably healthy and have treatment available in case of health problems, to have important goals related to one's values, and to have a philosophy or religion that provides guidance, purpose, and meaning to one's life (2004, 25).

[11] So too does mainstream economics. Economist Tibor Scitovsky notes that the ". . . effects of work are completely missing from the economist's numerical index of economic welfare . . . work which produces market goods may be an economic activity, but the satisfaction the worker himself gets out of his work is not an economic good because it does not go through the market and its value is not measurable" (1976, 17).

the labor market where workers are free to choose, there is poor information on quality of work life, the default values of money are strong, family benefits flow from money but not from intrinsic [work] satisfaction" (1991, 406). Consequently, work becomes a means to higher consumption, as opposed to an outlet for creativity and self-expression. Two centuries ago, well before the disastrous environmental consequences of runaway consumption came to light, philosopher Friedrich Hegel pointed to the central importance of rewarding work for a full life, contending that "recognition from his professional peers . . . would save the individual from the temptation to seek recognition through the display of wealth, and from the 'bad infinity' of unlimited wants" (1958, para 250–55).

Community

Inequality reduces *social capital*, a term used to describe the quality of relationships among people who belong to communities inside and outside their places of work. A high level of social capital enriches the experience of belonging while enabling the community to function more effectively. This accords with the evolutionary dynamic of group selection that was addressed in Chapters 2 and 3.

One of the reasons why inequality reduces social capital, economist George Irvin reports, is because "poorer people are more likely to feel out of place participating in community groups, more likely to feel ill at ease and to think that they will make fools of themselves and be looked down upon" (2007, 15). This retreat from social participation not only reduces the well-being of the community but also inflicts pain on those who feel excluded. "Brain scans reveal that the pain of feeling excluded by others stimulates the same areas of the brain as does physical pain" (Wilkinson and Pickett 2019, 57).

An important component of social capital is trust. The European and World Values Survey has found that trust is higher in countries with less inequality. The General Social Survey conducted by the US government has also found that trust is higher in states with less inequality (Wilkinson and Pickett 2011, 53–54). Sociologists Richard Wilkinson and Kate Pickett report that, on a scale of 1–100, as inequality increased, trust in other people and social institutions in the United States fell from 60 percent in 1960 to less than 40 percent in 2004 (2011, 54). In a more recent June 2014 Gallup Poll of trust among Americans, only 30 percent expressed confidence in the Supreme

Court and 7 percent in Congress, while 73 percent claim that corruption is rampant in government (Gylfason 2015, 332). As trust has fallen, more gated communities have sprung up, sales of home security systems have soared, and sport-utility vehicles (SUVs)—tank-like vehicles for the jungle of rage-filled highways—have soared. Among the young, even the adventurous practice of hitchhiking has disappeared.

As interaction declines between people of different classes, they grow farther apart and see one another as less trustworthy. Even members of the same class are circumspect with regard to one another. In their survey of studies on trust, Wilkinson and Pickett find that "with greater inequality, people are less caring of one another, there is less mutuality in relationships, people have to fend for themselves and get what they can—so, inevitably, there is less trust. . . . High levels of trust mean that people feel secure, they have less to worry about, they see others as co-operative rather than competitive" (2011, 56, 57). Planet Ark Environmental Foundation has found that more equal societies tend to have greater social cohesiveness and public spiritedness, resulting in greater recycling of waste materials (2004).

Also working against the sense of community is the fact that greater inequality generates more criminal activity. Research by economist Morgan Kelly finds that inequality has "a strong and robust impact on violent crime" (2000, 530). This research is supported by that of economists Pablo Fajnzylber, Daniel Lederman, and Norman V. Loayza, who find in a study of 39 countries between 1965 and 1995 that violent crime rates and inequality were positively correlated "within countries and, particularly, between countries, and this correlation reflects causation from inequality to crime rates, even after controlling for other crime determinants" (2002, 1).

The belief in the potential for vertical mobility that came with the breaking of inherited status promised more equality of opportunity. However, where inequality is great, an extreme adherence to this belief can work against community spirit. This appears to be the case in the United States, where individuals promptly take credit for their economic successes and do not hesitate to describe the less fortunate as responsible for their economic failures. The World Values Survey has found that 71 percent of Americans versus 40 percent of Europeans believe that the poor could work their way out of poverty; "54 percent of Europeans believe that the poor are unlucky, whereas only 30 percent of Americans share that belief"; and "sixty percent of American respondents, but only 26 percent of Europeans, say that the poor are lazy" (Alesina, Glaeser, and Sacerdote 2001, 237, 242, 243). These differences may also help explain Americans' stronger embrace of laissez-faire political ideology (Lipset 1997). It has been found that in the United States, those individuals who anticipate future growth in their own income are more prone to oppose measures that would redistribute income in favor of the less well-off (Alesina and La Farrara 2001). Other evidence also suggests the greater extent to which Americans hold individuals responsible for their own fates. For instance, economists Alberto Alesina, Edward Glaeser, and Bruce Sacerdote "find an extremely strong relationship in the United States between supporting capital punishment and opposing welfare" (2001, 242). Not surprisingly, in the United States, according to Pew Research Surveys, 71 percent of Republicans, who strongly embrace laissez-faire ideology, support the death penalty versus 34 percent of Democrats (Berman 2016, A3).

In undervaluing the potential for work and community to provide social validation and personal fulfillment, inequality feeds the material progress vision, the view that ever greater material abundance is the key to happiness. Because a high level of consumption confers high status, people leave their communities and sacrifice job satisfaction for higher pay. Not only does the pursuit of status through consumption impair the potential for happiness, it reduces community well-being. It also condemns the environment to spoliation.

Inequality and Political Opposition to Ecological Safeguards

The flaw in the pluralist heaven is that the heavenly chorus sings with a strong upper-class accent.
—Elmer E. Schattschneider, *The Semisovereign People*
(1975, 35)

The accelerating degradation of the global environment clearly demonstrates that measures to slow it have been inadequate. This is substantially because the wealthy, who possess disproportionate political power, have self-interested reasons to minimize, if not deny, the threat and thereby preclude effective intervention. As noted earlier, there are two reasons for their opposition to curbing pollution. First, much pollution results from negative externalities, such that some costs of production are not included in the market price of output. This means that the social costs of production exceed market prices. Because the rich consume more per capita than do the less well off, they proportionately benefit more from prices that do not include the cost of pollution to all humanity. The British Oxfam reports "the richest 10 percent of people produce half of the planet's individual-consumption-based fossil fuel emissions, while the poorest 50 percent—about 3.5 billion people—contribute only 10 percent" (Colarossi 2015). In the United States, 38.5 percent of total consumer spending is done by the wealthiest 20 percent of the population ("Consumer Expenditure Survey" 2008). In 2007, the wealthiest 10 percent held 45.9 percent of total home equity and 25.5 percent of the value of vehicles (Gilbert 2011, 91). The carbon emissions due to the consumption of a rich person are 10 times those of a poor person (Wilkinson and Pickett 2011, 218). Viewed internationally, the United States produces 24.0 tons of carbon per person annually, whereas India produces 1.6 tons (Wilkinson and Pickett 2011, 220). A striking measure of the differences in purchasing power is that in 2017, the world's richest eight individuals owned as much wealth as the world's poorest half, or 3.6 billion people.

The second reason the wealthy gain more from pollution is because they hold practically all ownership claims to industries, many of which have higher profits because, as explained earlier, they can largely foist the environmental costs of production onto society. Due to this concentrated ownership, the interests of the very wealthy and corporate America are typically the same, such that the unparalleled expansion of corporate lobbyists in Washington and corporate campaign contributions are merely extensions of the rich's political power. This fusion of the elite and corporate power serves to block legislation that would curb environmentally destructive activities.

In addition to benefiting from pollution, elites can better shield themselves from its harmful consequences. The least privileged suffer the most. Numerous studies have found that the poorer a neighborhood, the greater the likelihood that its air is polluted. In the United States, African American populations are disproportionately found near waste sites (Szasz and Meuser 1997, 101, 109).[12] And, because the rich are less afflicted by environmental devastation in their everyday lives, they are less likely to consider it a matter of personal importance. Given their disproportionate political power, the

[12] According to the World Health Organization (WHO), air pollution in urban areas for most of humanity is getting worse, with poor urban dwellers suffering most. In low- or middle-income countries, 98 percent of urban areas with more than 100,000 residents breathe air that falls short of the WHO's air-quality standards. For instance, whereas WHO's health ceiling for particulate matter (PM2.5) is 10, New Delhi, the world's most polluted mega-city, clocks in at 122. Air pollution causes life-shortening health problems such as heart disease, cancer, and severe asthma (Mooney and Brady 2016).

relative indifference of the wealthy means weaker public measures to protect the environment.

The rich cannot, of course, shield themselves from the negative consequences of environmental devastation that affects the entire planet, such as global warming or destruction of the ozone layer. But, as Diamond reminds us, elites in past civilizations persisted in competing for status through conspicuous consumption even when they had before their eyes the plain evidence of severe environmental decline that portended the collapse of their societies. Thus, they undermined the foundations upon which their own livelihoods and privileges depended (2006). And today, the trial facing *Homo sapiens* is far more daunting than the ones that confronted the individual civilizations studied by Diamond. Their collapses due to environmental destruction were local, and the earth could recover from such wounds. But now it is the entire earth that is under siege, with the additional challenges of toxic chemicals and global warming.

Several decades ago, when greater environmental optimism still held sway, research suggested that there appears to be an *environmental Kuznets curve* for a number of pollution variables: an inverted U-shaped curve seemed to capture the relationship between rising per capita income and environmental degradation (Grossman and Krueger 1995, 1996). According to this theory, in the early stages of economic development, mounting per capita income worsens pollution, but, at a more advanced stage, rising per capita income correlates with falling pollution. But given the conspicuous-consumption arms race driven by inequality, and accelerated by rising inequality, there is no automatic dynamic that would bring this about. It could occur only if inequality were lowered, empowering those who are more directly affected by pollution to compel political leaders to enact adequate environmental laws.

Those who would win from measures to protect the environment are many, each gaining a little from such actions, while those who would lose are fewer in number but have considerable stakes in the outcome. As economist Mansur Olson (1971) noted, it is far easier to organize a smaller group with a common interest in rent-seeking (gaining income by manipulating the political setting, rather than by creating new productive wealth), and even more so when they have the resources to make political campaign contributions and engage in relentless lobbying. The American Political Science Association notes that "citizens with lower or moderate incomes speak with a whisper that is lost on the ears of inattentive governmental officials, while the advantaged roar with a clarity and consistency that policy-makers readily hear and routinely follow" (2004, 651).

Adding to their political advantages, the elite benefit from the fact that their behavior and views are emulated. In Veblen's words:

> The fact that the usages, actions, and views of the well-to-do leisure class acquire the character of a prescriptive canon of conduct for the rest of society gives added weight and reach to the conservative influence of that class. It makes it incumbent upon all reputable people to follow their lead. (1899, 200)

Other observers agree. Resource ecologist Bobbi Low writes, "We . . . are likely to adopt wrong (sometimes blatantly wrong and illogical) explanations if they are proposed by someone 'of status'" (2001, 178). Evolutionary biologists David Sloan Wilson and John Gowdy point out that ". . . few people are aware that they copy the speech patterns and mannerisms of high-status individuals" (2015, 44). Further, as psychologists Jim Sidanius and Shana Levin note, the

> behavioral asymmetry thesis [of social dominance theory] suggests that dominants will behave in a more group-interested fashion than subordinates due to the consensual endorsement of hierarchy-enhancing legitimizing ideologies. Moreover, under certain circumstances, not only will subordinates not behave in as group-interested a fashion as dominants, but they will actually work against their own group's interests. (2001, 318)

An international study has found that, controlling for per capita income, a more equal distribution of political power, as gauged by degree of political democracy, civil rights, and literacy, correlates with stronger environmental quality (Boyce 2007). This is supported by a study of the 50 American states that reveals a correlation between more equal distribution of political power and stronger environmental policies (Boyce et al. 1999). According to a recent survey by the Pew Research Center, 88 percent of Democrats view climate change as a very serious threat, but only 31 percent of Republicans agree (Dennis 2020). Not surprisingly, the administration of Republican president Donald J. Trump vigorously rolled back the environmental measures put in place by his predecessors. At this writing, the administration of his successor,

Democratic president Joe Biden, is attempting to reinstate regulations intended to safeguard the environment.

Imprisoned by Inequality in the Growth Trap

> *It is scarcely necessary to remark that a stationary condition of capital and population implies no stationary state of human improvement. There would be as much scope as ever for all kinds of mental culture, of moral and social progress; as much room for improving the Art of Living, and much more likelihood of its being improved, when minds ceased to be engrossed by the art of getting on.*
> —John Stuart Mill, *Principles of Political Economy* (1909, 751)

As noted at the beginning of this chapter, the threat of ecological catastrophe results, ironically, from our species' extraordinary success in the primordial struggle with nature to overcome dire material privation. There are many ways to gauge *Homo sapiens*'s achievement. Population, the foremost metric in biology for the success of a species, exploded from 2.4 million humans when agriculture was being adopted, about 10,000 BC, to 300 million in AD 1, to 1.6 billion in 1900, to 7.7 billion today. Looking ahead, population is projected to reach 9.8 billion by 2050 and 11.2 billion by 2100. Between 1900 and 2018, world average life span increased from 31 to 72.3 years. But increasing population and rising affluence are placing unsustainable burdens on our environment. Moreover, inequality-driven conspicuous consumption, which Veblen correctly viewed as "indefinitely expansible" (1899, 111), hastens humanity toward catastrophe.

The world's poor urgently need the fruits of material progress. However, the material progress vision, and the social institutions and attitudes related to it, have locked the materially privileged into a never-ending pursuit of ever greater material possessions. In wealthy countries, greater consumption appears to yield no further increase in happiness. Worldwide, it threatens humanity's very future.

This material progress vision that views unlimited economic growth as the road to human progress has fostered a view that inequality is unimportant. For instance, economist Martin Feldstein states: "I want to stress that there is nothing wrong with an increase in well-being of the wealthy or with an increase in inequality that results from a rise in high incomes" (1999, 35–36).

Citizens may be unconcerned about inequality if their incomes are rising. As economist Henry Wallich comments, "Growth is a substitute for equality of income. So long as there is growth there is hope, and that makes large income differentials tolerable" (1972, 62). Some see inequality as a positive characteristic in the mistaken belief that it augments the potential for growth. Many mainstream economists have embraced such views and, accordingly, pay little attention to inequality.

As this chapter has demonstrated, however, inequality greatly impairs society's ability to avoid ecological disaster in two principal ways: it propels a consumption arms race, and it puts disproportionate political power in the hands of those who benefit most and suffer least from pollution. With lessened inequality, social institutions could more readily be redesigned to privilege, not consumption, but rather the workplace and the community, where—according to happiness research—people find greatest fulfillment. Both working and taking part in the life of the community can provide status and, thus, potential success in attracting mates. And economic growth need not end. So long as it is environmentally benign, or better, reduces the malign effects of current or past harm, growth can continue indefinitely.

Should workers ultimately succeed in freeing themselves from the elite's laissez-faire ideology, what public policies might they require their elected servants to implement? Although a detailed exploration is beyond the scope of this book, a few measures might be mentioned to provide a sense of the possibilities. Excise taxes on luxury goods and services could be formulated to discourage conspicuous consumption. The resulting higher prices would dissuade many consumers. Others, more strongly influenced by the enhanced display value that higher prices confer on luxury items, would channel more revenue into state coffers, making additional funds available to address environmental damage. Because consumption can serve as a proxy for how hard one works and how much one contributes to society, making all salaries public would eliminate the need to signal income through consumption (Carens 1981). Returning to the progressive tax rates prevailing prior to 1981 would more equally distribute the ability to consume, reducing large gaps that induce households to consume more to maintain their relative social standing.

Government could become the employer of last resort, guaranteeing jobs at living wages for everyone willing and able to work. Unemployment and poverty would be vastly reduced, and welfare would be needed only for those who are unable to work. To compete with government guaranteed work, employers would have to offer more interesting work as well as salaries at least equal to the living wage. Moreover, guaranteeing employment would dramatically reduce insecurity. As discussed in Chapter 10, a strong sense of material security among the first generation to come of age following World War II led them to become what Ronald Inglehart called postmaterialists, caring less about earning income with which to buy consumer goods and more about doing "interesting, meaningful work and working with congenial people" (1989, 162). Indeed, with equal educations, on average postmaterialists earned less than materialists.

Workplace democracy, where workers elect their managers, would humanize workplaces and enable workers to structure their jobs to be more rewarding. Their formation could be encouraged by government-backed financing. Progressive corporate income taxes could reduce firm size to enable greater worker participation in decision-making. Worker-controlled firms would have little incentive to relocate, leaving communities in ruin.

All of these briefly mentioned measures would privilege work and community as sites where social validation could be earned and self-respect nurtured. Participation in work and communities could thus provide status, reducing the dependence upon consumption. All of these measures would leave in place capitalism's two principal institutions of private property and markets. The reasons for doing so are addressed in the next chapter.

13

The Problem Is Inequality, Not Private Property and Markets

A State divided into a small number of rich and a large number of poor will always develop a government manipulated by the rich to protect the amenities represented by their property.
—Harold Laski, *A Grammar of Politics* (215, 134)

Money becomes evil not when it is used to buy goods but when it is used to buy power . . . economic inequalities become evil when they are translated into political inequalities.
—Samuel P. Huntington, *American Politics: The Promise of Disharmony* (1983, 38)

Inequality exists because individuals are biologically compelled to seek competitive advantage. The successful gain status and, therefore, a greater likelihood of sending their unique genes into future generations. However, to prevail in this reproductive contest, the competitive advantage over others need not be large. It need only signal the best options to those choosing mates. Of course, not everyone will end up with the individuals who have the very highest status. Instead, they will mate with the best ones available to them, given their own competitive ranking within their gender.

A strong sense of fairness also evolved among humans to restrain competitive behavior. Its success in doing so meant that, for the 97 percent of history when humans lived as nomadic hunter-gatherers, they enjoyed a high degree of economic and political equality. For instance, this sense of fairness compelled gifted and successful hunters to be exceedingly modest and generous. They were expected to refrain from excessive boasting, and they could not distribute their kill for personal advantage because group welfare depended upon it being shared out equally. These hunter-gatherers' precarious material conditions and egalitarian social practices precluded the stronger from developing ideologies to legitimate exploitation of the weaker.

The superior force of the stronger did not create inequality until the rise of the state 5,500 years ago. For inequality to be sustainable, the weaker must be led to believe that it is in their interest, and thus fair. Manipulating the sense of fairness to benefit the stronger is the essence of ideology. Ideology deceives the losers into believing that conditions contrary to their best interests are fair.

In contemporary society, part of what impairs losers' ability to free themselves from the elite's ideology is the lack of a clear conception of viable alternatives to the status quo. With the overwhelming majority of votes, workers possess the political power democratically to shape society to meet their needs. But what order could they create that would improve their lives while preserving, if not enhancing, the economic dynamism and general political freedom made possible by highly unequal capitalism? According to the elite's ideology, there is no superior alternative. Contemporary capitalism is the best for everyone. Most progressives appear more or less to accept this conclusion. Accordingly, they direct their attention to offering marginal alterations that would soften capitalism's hard edges.

The message that there are no attractive alternatives was driven home by the collapse of state socialism in Eastern Europe three decades ago. This lack of alternatives was the core argument set forth in political scientist Francis Fukuyama's highly influential book, *The End of History and the Last Man* (1989). In terms of social systems, he claimed, humanity had reached the "end of history." Contemporary capitalism is the ultimate and best form of human social organization.[1] Central to this widely embraced claim has been the view that any alternative would more greatly empower the state in resource allocation, or, at the extreme, replace private property and markets with state ownership and central planning. But, as the twentieth-century experiences in Eastern Europe revealed, that outcome ultimately resulted in inadequate economic dynamism and a chilling lack of basic freedoms. The result is that Fukuyama's popular view has helped legitimate the expansion of capitalism into practically every corner of the planet, frequently in its crudest laissez-faire expression.

---

[1] Yet, although many still find capitalism unfair and even cruel, as economist Thomas Piketty puts it, "the fall of communism led to a certain disillusionment concerning the very possibility of a just society . . . it extinguished all hope of truly fundamental socio-economic change" (2020, 648, 831).

Critics of this historical interpretation point out that Eastern European socialism, as well as that of China, emerged in societies that had never known democracy. State socialism was imposed upon them by totalitarian political regimes. Democratic socialism, by contrast, freely chosen through the democratic process of open discourse and majoritarian decision-making, would avoid the despotism of past state socialism. However, many advocates of democratic socialism mistakenly reject capitalism's core institutions of markets and private property.[2] Disallowing these institutions inadvertently reinforces the power of the elite's ideology by deflecting attention from the root problem of inequality in ownership and control of the means of production. It also fails to recognize the importance of private property and markets for economic dynamism and freedom.

This chapter examines in detail why the refusal of private property and markets is misguided. More specifically, it reveals how this rejection impedes the development of an attractive and viable alternative model to laissez-faire capitalism that exploits the considerable advantages these institutions offer. It then provides a sketch of an alternative that continues to draw upon the merits of private property and markets while greatly empowering labor and promoting greater freedom.

Capitalism's Unique Dynamic Character

The bourgeoisie, during its rule of scarce one hundred years, has created more massive and more colossal productive forces than have all the preceding generations together.

> —Karl Marx and Friedrich Engels, "Manifesto of the Communist Party" (1848, 477)

Ever since capitalism came to be recognized as a new economic system, it has had vociferous critics. None of them was more insightful and wide-ranging than Karl Marx, arguably "the most influential philosopher of the last two centuries" (Cockshott and Cottrell 1997, 330). Marx's criticism of capitalism included judging private property and markets as dehumanizing social

---

[2] For instance, until recently, both the French Socialist and British Labor Parties held that only by nationalization and state ownership of productive property could societies advance beyond the injustices and malfunctioning of capitalism.

institutions that should be jettisoned. Many critics of capitalism agree. This chapter reveals why they are mistaken.

Marx was correct in locating the central problem of capitalism in the fact that a small class holds a virtual monopoly of ownership and control of the means of production. However, his insistence that private property and markets are pernicious has deflected attention from the central problem of inequality in the ownership and control of productive wealth. This misdirection has obstructed the conception of a viable and attractive alternative.

Marx called the early evolution of capitalism "primitive accumulation." At that stage, two new classes arose. One comprised the people, relatively few in number, who own and control productive wealth in the form of resources and capital (understood as stored-up labor); the other was composed of the masses of workers who, although legally free, had been dispossessed of all economic assets except their ability to labor. In order to survive, workers had to find owners of productive wealth willing to employ them—to allow them to use tools and resources. Marx wrote that, with the dissolution of feudalism, workers "became sellers of themselves only after they had been robbed of all their own means of production, and of all the guarantees of existence afforded by the old feudal arrangements." Consequently, workers "can work only with [the capitalists'] permission, hence live only with their permission" (1867, 1:786; 1875a, 526). This separation of workers who are juridically free—neither slaves nor serfs—from control and ownership of the means of production is the *differentia specifica* of capitalism, the core characteristic that defines it. It is from this extreme inequality in ownership and control of the means of production that the negative consequences of capitalism flow.

Marx believed that the separation of workers from control and ownership of the means of production would characterize capitalism until its end. Because of the rigidity of these class relations, they could be broken only by revolution. Workers would be immiserated until they took command through revolution.[3]

Although varying in its forms, the inequality in ownership and control of productive wealth that characterizes capitalism has been common to all post-primitive social formations since the birth of civilization about 5,500 years

---

[3] This position surprisingly survived despite his awareness and rich description of the manner in which workers struggled successfully for reforms within capitalism during his lifetime, such as limits to child labor and a shortened workday. Although Marx did in a short speech avow that in America, England, and perhaps Holland, workers might "attain their goal by peaceful means" (1875b, 523), this view never got further expression in his theoretical or polemical work.

ago. In every case, because small elites held ownership and control over productive wealth, they disproportionately controlled political power and used it to capture the greatest possible surplus from producers (what remains after the workers' most basic material needs are met). Even the twentieth century's experiments in state-sponsored socialism involved an elite's control over the means of production, enabling them to take a disproportionate share of income and privilege for themselves, albeit to a far lesser degree than found under slave, feudal, and capitalist regimes.[4]

But Marx recognized more amply than any other social thinker that capitalism evolved as a social exploitation machine with distinctive characteristics: its unparalleled capacity for sustainably producing wealth, and the extraordinary dynamism by which it not only destroys what is inherited from the past, but continually transforms itself. Indeed, its dynamic capacity for change is so prodigious that Marx believed it would ultimately self-destruct to the advantage of the formerly exploited workers. Of all the social systems in which the producers have been exploited, only capitalism creates the conditions in which workers can potentially stop the elite's extraction of their surplus.

Contrary to the expectations of Marx and many of his followers, workers gained this potential without revolution. This came about, as was seen in Chapter 9, in the nineteenth century when workers' threats of violence and revolution forced elites to grant them the franchise. With the franchise, they could in principle dispossess the elite and reconfigure society to their interests.

Yet, Marx often identified capitalism's principal institutions of markets and private property as dehumanizing, even as they helped set the stage for full human liberation in the self-destruction of capitalism that he predicted. This stance encouraged many of his followers to insist that building a more humane future would require replacing private property and markets with social ownership and central planning. Although attempts to do just this took place in Eastern Europe, China, and Cuba, it is widely accepted today that the long-term performance of these experiments was poor.

Nevertheless, the conviction that capitalism's principal institutions of markets and private property must be wholly or at least substantially abandoned remains strong among many critics. This repudiation of private

---

[4] State socialist rulers' control over the state and productive wealth led some to label these societies "state capitalists" (e.g., Howard and King 2001; R. D. Wolff 2015).

property and markets prevents them from satisfactorily addressing the core problem of inequality in ownership and control of productive wealth.

But the major faults of capitalism are not due to its principal institutions of markets and private property. They are due instead to the specific form of inequality in productive wealth that evolved concomitantly with them. It is inequality in the ownership and control of the means of production that enables the elite to use these institutions to exploit workers and destroy the environment. Because many critics confuse the instruments of exploitation with the cause, they fail to appreciate the progressive roles these institutions can play in a dynamic, free, and humane economy.

From the Origins of Inequality to Capitalism

Hitherto, every form of society has been based ... on the antagonism of oppressing and oppressed classes.
—Karl Marx, "Economic and Philosophic
Manuscripts of 1844" (1844, 483)

As social beings, humans labor together to transform elements of the natural world. For the far greatest part of the human experience, nomadic hunter-gatherers carried out production cooperatively and without private ownership of resources. Because stone weapons were available to all and the weak could form coalitions against bullies, material and political inequality could not develop. The development of agriculture about 10,000 years ago laid the foundations for the eventual rise of the state and civilization. As productivity in agriculture improved, cultivators could produce more than was necessary for their own subsistence. Advances in metallurgy in Eurasia about 5,500 years ago enabled a small group to command costly and superior military technology not available to cultivators. These superior weapons, combined with superior military organization and ideology, enabled a warrior elite to subjugate producers and expropriate their surplus. Thereby the state was born. Grounded in religious beliefs, ideologies evolved to legitimate rulers' privileges.

The state, with its comparative advantage in violence, enabled elites and the state itself to maximize their capture of producers' surplus. Differing subsequent historical conditions supported varying systems of exploitation such as slavery, debt bondage, feudalism, and over recent centuries, capitalism. Although all of these exploitative (Marx), or extractive (Acemoglu and Robinson 2012), societies might experience periods of growth and dynamism, as was explored in Chapter 6, only capitalism had an incentive structure and a set of socially transformative dynamics that, in the historical context of competition among European nation-states, could permit sustainable economic growth. However, Marx believed that capitalism's self-transforming properties fated it to give way to a non-exploitative future, a society without elites capable of raking off the surplus.

As was seen in Chapter 9, the material and social conditions that would permit workers to gain political power came forth with industrialization and urbanization during the nineteenth century, much as Marx anticipated. Most notably, workers gained the franchise and thus the political power to alter the social structure in ways that would dramatically improve their lives. The democratization of the franchise defanged radical workers' movements, foiling the expectations of Marxists that the proletariat, the working class, would overthrow capitalism and institute socialism. With the vote, grievances would be settled by more peaceful means. The state was transformed from the ruling class's executive committee into a social agency that could limit, or in the extreme eliminate, the elites' capturing of disproportionate shares of income, wealth, and privilege. The fact that workers have done so only to a very limited extent attests to the persuasive power of the elite's ideology.

The Mistaken Indictment of Markets and Private Property

Wherever there is great property, there is great inequality. For one very rich man there must be at least five hundred poor, and the affluence of the few supposes the indigence of the many.
—Adam Smith, *The Wealth of Nations* (1776, 670)

Criticisms of capitalism fall into two broad, albeit overlapping, categories: those that center on the consequences of inequality in ownership and control of the means of production, and those that converge on the alleged repercussions of the most fundamental capitalistic institutions, markets and private property. This second category of criticism often shares a perspective associated with the romantic opposition to modernity.[5]

The principal failings of capitalism that derive from inequality in ownership and control of the means of production include poverty, debased and alienated work, and macroeconomic instability. Those supposedly resulting from markets and private property include inequality, masked social relationships, self-interest, greed, the destruction of community, alienation, individualism, the rise of instrumental rationality, and ecological devastation. These two groups of adverse effects will be addressed in turn.

Capitalism's Extreme Inequality in Productive Wealth Ownership and Control

For Marx, the fundamental character of capitalism is its specific form of inequality, where an elite owns and controls capital (stored-up labor) and natural resources, forcing legally free workers to contract with them in labor markets if they are to work and survive. The result is that ". . . the worker sinks to the level of a commodity and becomes indeed the most wretched of commodities" (Marx 1844, 70). For the right to work, workers must pay their employers the high price of their surplus labor (that portion of their labor which produces output in excess of the workers' subsistence needs). Many of the faults found with capitalism are the direct result of this special form of inequality. They include poverty, debased and alienated work, and macroeconomic instability.

Poverty
Because of the elite's monopoly ownership of productive wealth, workers retain only their labor power. During early capitalism, the elite-controlled

---

[5] Economist Albert Hirschman writes:

> For as soon as capitalism was triumphant and 'passion' seemed indeed to be restrained and perhaps even extinguished in the comparatively peaceful, tranquil and business-minded Europe of the period after the Congress of Vienna, the world suddenly appeared empty, petty, and boring and the stage was set for the Romantic critique of the bourgeois order as incredibly impoverished in relation to earlier ages—the new world seemed to lack nobility, grandeur, mystery, and above all, passion. Considerable traces of this nostalgic critique can be found in subsequent social thought from Fourier's advocacy of passionate attraction to Marx's theory of alienation, and from Freud's thesis of libidinal repression as the price of progress to Weber's concept of *Entzauberung* (progressive disintegration of the magical vision of the world). (1997, 132–33)

state capped wages at bare subsistence, ensuring that the least well-off would live in poverty. As was seen in Chapter 6, this kind of law was proclaimed in the mid-fourteenth century, in the wake of the demographic collapse due to the Black Death that created a labor shortage and put upward pressure on wages. As seen in Chapter 7, ideology, fueled by Protestantism from the sixteenth century on, insisted that poverty both goads workers to use their time productively and saves them from debauchery—the "utility of poverty" argument. Chapter 8 addressed how mercantilist thought and, later, classical political economy gave "scientific" status to this ideological doctrine.

As capitalist technology advanced, by the early nineteenth century it became increasingly labor-displacing, with new machinery replacing workers, thereby continually generating unemployment and putting downward pressure on wages (provoking the Luddite revolts that smashed machinery in English textile mills). Those losing their jobs fell into extreme poverty; those still employed earned lower wages and became more impoverished or, in Marx's term, "immiserated."

Defenders of capitalism, if not of its inequality, correctly claim that over the long term the material living standards of everyone, including the poorest workers and those who are out of work, have dramatically improved. However, capitalism continues to generate unemployment, job insecurity, and, for the least fortunate, poverty. Indeed, the state's commitment to fighting price instability commits it to tolerating a non-inflationary level of unemployment (more technically called the *non-accelerating inflation rate of unemployment*, or NAIRU). This level is also called by its more nakedly ideological name of *the natural rate of unemployment*, as if it were set by nature rather than politics. The preservation of unemployment benefits elite owners of productive wealth by holding down wages and limiting worker demands for better work conditions.

Today, rapid globalization has joined technological change in continually displacing workers and putting downward pressure on wages. A current fear is that robotization will dramatically accelerate the pace of labor-saving technological change.

Alienation and Debased Work
Because workers are alienated from ownership, control, or ready access to productive wealth, they are forced to accept the work conditions that its owners offer. The latter are interested only in profit maximization (competition gives them no choice), and thus better work conditions would exist

only if the improvements enhanced profits. Adam Smith was among the first to recognize the resulting debasement of labor. He noted that, because of the division of labor in factories, workers are rendered "as stupid and ignorant as it is possible for a human creature to become" (1776, 734). With this remark, Smith launched the discourse on worker alienation.

Marx deepened this discourse by arguing that, because workers lack control over the work process, they are hindered from expressing their creativity and sociality in work. Consequently, work is "not the satisfaction of a need; it is merely a means to satisfy needs external to it" (Marx 1844, 74). Workers become alienated from the products of their labor, in particular the stored-up labor in capital that is used to exploit them:

> The *alienation* of the worker in his product means not only that his labour becomes an object, an *external* existence, but that it exist *outside him*, independently, as something alien to him, and that it becomes a power of its own confronting him; it means that the life which he has conferred on the object confronts him as something hostile and alien. (Marx 1844, 72)

With the advance of "machinofacture," the worker is reduced to a mere "appendage of the machine" (Marx and Engels 1848, 479). Because the labor process is debased, the worker has little incentive to work hard. Consequently, as economic historian Douglass North puts it, "the 'discipline' of the factory system is nothing more than a response to the control problem of shirking in team production" (1982, 178).

Macroeconomic Instability

Due to capitalism's inequality in productive wealth, the elite has usually been successful in taking all the increased output resulting from economic growth for itself. But as it succeeds in doing so, workers who spend most if not all of their income receive relatively less, creating a weakness in demand for the economy's output, and thus a dearth of investment potential in the real economy. Seeking an adequate return on their capital, the elite turn ever more to speculative activity in financial and real estate markets, creating bubbles that, when they burst, crash the economy into recession, or worse, depression. These dynamics were in full evidence in the financial crises of both 1929 and 2008 (Wisman 2013b, 2014b).

Many critics of capitalism fail to recognize that what is required for eliminating capitalism's poverty, debased and alienated work, and macroeconomic instability is eliminating its cause in the extreme inequality in ownership and control of productive wealth. Even when some do, they are prone to extend their criticism beyond this inequality in productive wealth to the fundamental institutions of markets and private property.

Charges against Markets and Private Property

In precapitalist societies, markets were usually strictly constrained by laws and customs. Land was the most important form of productive property, and it was generally not readily alienable (available to be bought or sold). Most labor was tied to the land, ruling out labor markets. Moreover, as was seen in Chapters 6 and 7, markets were viewed negatively. The rise of capitalism entailed the slow dissolution of traditional constraints. Freer markets and alienable private property abetted the rise of the new capitalist class to dominance over the traditional landlord class as its members progressively gained monopoly ownership and control of the means of production, and, consequently, the power to extract surplus output from workers. For a variety of reasons addressed in the following, Marx and many critics of capitalism have frequently viewed these institutions of markets and private property, not only as social institutions used by elites to exploit workers, but as intrinsically undesirable.

Markets Lead to Inequality: Economist Joseph Stiglitz has written that "markets, by themselves . . . often lead to high levels of inequality" (2012, xiii). But markets are never to any substantial extent "by themselves." To exist more than marginally, they require legally binding property rights, which in turn cannot exist without government to define and enforce them. Note, for example, that during the so-called Dark Ages in Europe, when substantial state power disappeared, so too did significant market activity.

Where the state is controlled by an elite, property rights and markets come to be defined, regulated, and enforced in ways that enable an elite to use them to capture society's surplus. Thus, the problem is not with private property or markets per se, but with the manner in which they are legally defined and enforced to steer resources disproportionately to elites. Because critics of capitalism have so frequently viewed markets as a source of exploitation and inequality, as opposed to an institution captured by elites to extract surplus, they have been blinded to their extraordinary power for social coordination.

Marxist theorist Leon Trotsky understood this power: "economic accounting is unthinkable without market relations" (quoted in Eagleton 2012, 24).

Markets Mask Social Relationships: Marx claimed that markets create an illusion that he termed "commodity fetishism." Through the division of labor and the social institution of the market, individuals produce for the needs and desires of others. But the mediation of markets between individuals leads them to view themselves as related to the commodities they buy and sell rather than to each other through their labor. In this manner, markets have an effect on social consciousness such that "the relation of the producers [workers] . . . is presented to them as a social relation, existing not between themselves, but between the products of their labour . . . [and thus] a definite social relation between men themselves . . . assumes . . . the fantastic form of a relation between things" (Marx 1867, 1:83). Thus, an elemental social relationship, whereby individuals work for each other, is mystified by this "commodity fetishism."

This charge seems true. But would this not be true of any mechanism that coordinates humans working for each other in a highly complex economy where there is extensive division of labor and workers do not exchange their products face to face?[6] Further, to date, nothing has been identified that could execute the task of orchestrating fabrication, transportation, and trade with the efficiency of markets. But suppose government administration of production and distribution without markets were equally efficient, would it not also, in a highly complex economy, perpetuate the illusion of commodity fetishism? If workers were paid in labor tokens or certificates, as some socialists suggest (e.g., McNally 1993; Cockshott and Cottrell 1997), and used them to purchase consumer goods, would it not still be the case that "the social relations between individuals in the performance of their labor do not appear as their own mutual personal relations but are separated and disguised from

---

[6] Marx anticipated an ultimate end to the division of labor, and implied that work would be a means of achieving creative fulfillment and maintaining direct ties with others. Precisely how such an economy might work in the complex modern world of abundance is never made clear. Indeed, his characterization of the freedom of a post-division of labor world sounds fully premodern, while, ironically, at the same time modernly individualistic. Marx wrote that conditions will prevail such that it is "possible for me to do one thing today and another tomorrow, to hunt in the morning, fish in the afternoon, rear cattle in the evening, criticize after dinner, just as I have a mind, without ever becoming hunter, fisherman, shepherd or critic" (1845, 160). The premodern romantic ring of these activities is striking, while the emphasis on individual autonomy (individualism) is strikingly modern. Its ring of freedom reminds us that "one of the most fundamental traits of modernization is a vast movement from fate to choice in human affairs" (Berger 1986, 86). It is noteworthy that opponents of markets appear to view individualism negatively only when it is interpreted as excessive egoism, especially in pursuit of money. Where it means individual autonomy, it is generally viewed positively.

them under the shape of the social relations between the products of labor"? (Marx 1867, 1:84).

Individualism, Self-Interest, Greed, and Destruction of Community: In the first half of the eighteenth century, Montesquieu expressed concern that commerce would monetize all human relations, resulting in a decline in hospitality and other "moral virtues" (Hirschman 1997, 80). Nineteenth-century social critic Thomas Carlyle lamented that the expansion of markets was reducing interpersonal relationships to a "cash nexus" (Thompson 2015, 227). In a similar vein, Marx and Engels famously declared that under capitalism, "all that is solid melts into air" (1848, 476), and the destruction of traditional social relationships "left remaining no other nexus between man and man than naked self-interest, than callous 'cash payment' . . . [and] drowned [all earlier values] in the icy water of egotistical calculation" (1848, 475). Later, Engels claimed that the capitalist market system leaves humans all alone in a vicious world, as it "isolates everyone in his own crude solitariness . . . [it unleashes] a horde of ravenous beasts who devour one another" (1975, 423). Many subsequent critics of capitalism have embraced the views of Montesquieu, Carlyle, Marx, and Engels: market society makes humans more individualistic and self-interested, if not greedy, and thereby inimical to the bonds of community.

Many of these critics yearned for a society of cooperative social relationships, and markets are by their very nature arenas of competition. However, markets are hardly the sole locus of competition in social life. Ultimately, as was explored in Chapter 2, human behavior is driven by a self-interested, competitive quest for advantage in sexual reproduction. In pursuit of this advantage, humans seek certification of their value in the approbation of others. Accordingly, they compete for recognition, for honors, for jobs, and much else. It needs to be highlighted that this self-interested competition can be expressed in seemingly altruistic ways, such as in generosity, community spiritedness, or just niceness. Any behavior that is socially valued and a source of status has the potential of making its actors sexually attractive and more successful in competing to send their unique genes into future generations. And, for biological beings, that is what ultimately counts.

Arguably, no one competes more arduously than Olympic athletes. The fact that they do not do so primarily for material rewards does not make their pursuit less self-interested. Indeed, their motivation appears far more akin to that of Schumpeter's entrepreneur, who possesses an "impulse to fight, to prove oneself superior to others, to succeed for the sake, not of the fruits of success, but of success itself" (1934, 93). These forms of competition are generally looked upon favorably by critics of markets. But they are no less driven by individual self-interest than the pursuit of profits or high incomes, even if they are dressed up—as they often are in the case of the Olympic games—as undertaken for the supposedly more praiseworthy values of perseverance, excellence, and national glory.

Markets and the Illusion of Free Workers: The evolution of capitalism enlarged the realm of freedom, and its markets were important social instruments for this expansion. This was recognized by eighteenth-century Enlightenment thinkers who held freedom, starting with the liberty to think for oneself, to be among society's highest goals. Classical economists, in particular, came to see markets as a powerful social institution for furthering human freedom. Freedom is evident in every market transaction, since no trade takes place without the willing agreement of buyer and seller alike. Therefore, some argued, to foster individual self-determination, markets should be introduced into practically all domains of social interaction.

Marx challenged this presumed freedom as an illusion for wage workers. Due to the poverty or near-poverty imposed by subsistence wages, they had no free choice in consumption since they could only afford the least expensive commodities that enabled them to survive. And due to elite ownership of productive wealth, workers were not meaningfully free in labor markets. The availability of a "reserve army of the unemployed," in Marx's phrase, prevented wages from rising above the subsistence level. Moreover, capitalist competition reduced wages—as well as working conditions—to the same low subsistence level everywhere. With wages and working conditions the same far and wide, the workers' only choice was to work for the capitalist class or starve.

Extreme inequality in the ownership and control of productive wealth had always enabled elites to extract surplus from workers, whether as slaves, serfs, or wage workers. What is unique to worker exploitation under capitalism is that the coercion is invisible, hidden by the fiction of freedom in labor markets. But this compulsion is not due to markets. It results from the social relations of capitalist production, that is, social relations in the system where workers lack ownership, control, or easy access to productive wealth.

Labor markets mask the fact that workers must pay the high price of surrendering their surplus output to the owners of productive wealth for the privilege of a job. The ideology of labor markets presents instead the contrary: it describes workers receiving wages from the owners, who receive returns in the form of profits, interest, and rents that, within the system, appear to be entirely just. Under the regimes of feudalism or sharecropping, it is clear what the producer must render in surplus value. But under capitalism, "The wage-form . . . extinguishes every trace of the division of the working day into necessary labour and surplus labour, into paid labour and unpaid labour" (Marx 1867, 1:591). As was seen in Chapter 8, neoclassical economics' marginal productivity theory of the distribution of income makes all of this look scientifically proper. All market actors receive compensation equal to the value they contribute to society's output, and, because everyone freely accepts the contract, the outcome appears just. This illustrates how mainstream economics, wearing the mantle of science, serves an ideological purpose, first by hiding the social relations underlying exploitation, and then by justifying the consequent allocation of income.

Money and Alienation: Where markets exist to any substantial extent, money, the universal equivalent, will also exist. However, throughout history, money has been viewed with suspicion, if not outright condemned. Biblically, "the love of money is a root of all kinds of evil" (Timothy 6:10). Marx went beyond attacking the love of money to attacking money itself:

> Money degrades all the gods of man—and turns them into commodities. Money is the universal self-established *value* of all things. It has, therefore, robbed the whole world—both the world of men and nature—of its specific value. Money is the estranged essence of man's work and man's existence, and this alien essence dominates him, and he worships it. (1844, 50)

However, as noted earlier, it is not readily conceivable how a complex society could function without money, or without a sophisticated accounting system in which fungible units (e.g., labor tokens) would serve as money in all but name.

Further, there is a social consequence of money that is seldom recognized. As social historian Yuval Harari states it, "Money is the only trust system created by humans that can bridge almost any cultural gap, and that does not discriminate on the basis of religion, gender, race, age or sexual orientation. Thanks to money, even people who don't know each other and don't trust each other can nevertheless cooperate effectively" (2015, 186). Money and markets link disparate peoples together. They serve, as Voltaire recognized, as instruments for overcoming particularism (Muller 2003, 186).

Private Property and Alienation: Legions of capitalism's critics have found fault with the institution of private property. Philosopher Pierre-Joseph Proudhon famously asserted that "property is theft" (1840).[7] Because Marx and Engels claimed that private property alienates humans from themselves, it would cease to exist in his ideal future: ". . . the theory of the Communists may be summed up in the single sentence: Abolition of private property" (1848, 484). Marx had earlier written that "private property has made us so stupid" and that "communism is the positive transcendence of private property, or human self-estrangement, and thus the real appropriation of human essence by and for man . . . and is therefore the complete *emancipation* of all human senses and attributes" (1844, 84, 87).

Because the evolution of capitalist private property separated workers from their traditional ties to the means of production, they were proletarianized, becoming commodities themselves, undifferentiated stocks of labor power. But the proletarianization of labor is not attributable to private property as such; it is due to an elite's near-monopoly ownership of productive wealth. Buildings, machines, raw materials, and other productive assets that were owned by the workers, whether individually or collectively within the firm, would still constitute private property. And workers could equally experience alienation with state ownership, even if the state held productive wealth "in the name of the people," as the twentieth-century state socialist societies indisputably demonstrated.

Like markets, private property cannot exist to any substantial extent without the state. Like markets, how it functions depends upon how it is defined, regulated, and enforced by the state. In this sense, private property is social, and rejecting it merely divulges a failure adequately to grasp its social embeddedness in politics.

Instrumental Rationality: Marx and Engels claimed that markets nourished not just "naked self-interest" but also "egotistical calculation." Constantly contriving, in the marketplace, to achieve one's selfish aims at the best price or with the least effort fostered an increasing dominance of instrumental reason applied to all things. There appears to be evidence for this view. It is plausible that markets do not actually make people more self-interested.

---

[7] In fact, Proudhon was not against private property per se. What he opposed was capitalist property that removed the worker from ownership and control of productive wealth. He advocated for their reunion. His support for private property stemmed from his fear of the state's tremendous power: "he conceived of the idea of opposing to this power a similar 'absolutist' power'—that of private property" (Hirschman 1997, 128).

Instead, markets make them more conscious of their self-interest and more aware of the need to be rational and calculating about satisfying their desires. It seems credible that in a world in which markets mediate a considerable amount of human interaction and encourage people continually to assess the best "deal," their consciousness and behavior would appear—both to themselves and to others—more transparently self-interested and, at the same time, more astute in achieving their ends.

Adam Smith noted, evidently without disapproval, that in commercial society, "every man . . . lives by exchanging, or becomes in some measure a merchant, and the society itself grows to be what is properly a commercial society" (1776, 22). Many others have taken note of the expansion of means-ends rationality that accompanies the expansion of markets, some with unease (e.g., sociologists Alfred Tönnies, 1887, and Max Weber's "iron cage," 1905), and some positively (e.g., economist Joseph Schumpeter, 1962, philosopher Alfred Sohn-Rethel, 1978).

Tönnies saw humans in their modern market-based setting as having moved from community (*Gemeinschaft*), where relationships are based upon shared values and ends, to a craftily self-interested existence in an impersonal society (*Gesellschaft*), where relationships are contractual and transitory. His assessment of the change was to a considerable extent unfavorable.

Although Schumpeter celebrated the rise of the pragmatic style of reasoning that emanated from markets, he also seemed to lament the ways of thinking that were supplanted:

> Capitalism develops rationality and adds a new edge to it. . . . [I]t exalts the monetary unit—not itself a creation of capitalism—into a unit of account. That is to say, capitalistic practice turns the unit of money into a tool of rational cost-profit calculations. . . . And thus defined . . . this type of logic or attitude or method then starts upon its conqueror's career subjugating—rationalising—man's tools and philosophies, his medical practice . . . his outlook on life, everything in fact including his concepts of beauty and justice and his spiritual ambitions. (2006, 123–24)[8]

---

[8] Schumpeter's concern has often been expressed. As historian Jerry Muller notes, ". . . from [Justus] Möser and [Edmund] Burke down to Jürgen Habermas in our own day, intellectuals have repeatedly expressed concern that the modes of thought and action characteristic of the market would permeate all human relations" (2003, 397).

Strongly influenced by Marx and Weber, Sohn-Rethel argued that, because there is a "real abstraction" (exchange of equivalent values) within markets, their expansion is responsible for the mental practices that give birth and dynamism to philosophy and science. He draws on the expansion of markets in Classical Greece and the Renaissance as prime examples.

However, as Weber made clear, although it was the expansion of markets that nurtured instrumental rationality and the centrality of efficiency, modern complex society requires it, with or without markets. Thus, if bureaucratic planning rather than markets were to serve the coordinating function for a highly complex society, the result would be the same dominance of means-end rationality. Incidentally, Weber characterized this bureaucratization of society as "the polar night of icy darkness" (1921b, xvi).

Market Externalities and Ecological Devastation: Markets are far from perfect mechanisms for resource allocation. They almost always engender third-party effects, or externalities, meaning that not all costs and/or benefits are captured by market prices. When externalities are positive, they have a free-lunch sort of quality that benefits society. But often they are negative, and some cause long-term damage to the natural environment. Public policy could, in principle, reallocate the cost of such negative externalities, for instance, by taxing carbon emissions. As was explored in Chapter 12, the extent to which public policy does not currently address negative externalities results in good part from extreme inequality. This inequality gives elites disproportionate political influence, and, just as they use that influence to capture rents, so do they manipulate the political setting to thwart policy proposals under which they would bear the cost of negative externalities that are not reflected in market prices. Markets per se are not to blame. Negative externalities are an economic effect that could be corrected by public policy—were it not for inequality.

* * * * *

It is indisputable that the evolution of private property and markets has dramatically transformed society and human consciousness. This observation is fully in keeping with Marx's powerful claim that humans create themselves: "[by] acting on the external world and changing it, he at the same time changes his own nature" (1859, 177). Consequently, "since for the socialist man *the entire so-called history of the world* is nothing but the begetting of man through human labour, nothing but the coming-to-be of nature for man, he has the visible, irrefutable proof of his *birth* through himself, of his process of *coming-to-be*" (1844, 92).[9] Marx may have overstated the extent to which human behavior is culturally determined. However, it is beyond serious doubt that innate human proclivities are steered and channeled by human-created social institutions. Further, as discussed in Chapters 2 and 3, gene-culture coevolution reveals that cultural creations lead to biological changes in the human species, making Marx's contention yet more profoundly true.

It is hard to make a credible claim that the consequences of the humanly created institutions of private property and markets have been more negative than positive for their creators.[10] Their positive consequences merit serious attention. Although elites have used them to expropriate workers' surplus, they have been able to do so only because of their near-monopoly ownership and control of productive wealth, which has given them inordinate influence over the state's definition and enforcement of property rights and markets. Nonetheless, these institutions have served as powerful instruments for the production of unprecedented wealth and freedom. In terms of freedom, they serve to decentralize and disperse decision-making and power. And, with the franchise, workers could in principle redefine property rights in their favor.

---

[9] However, Marx also famously wrote: "Men make their own history, but not of their own free will; not under circumstances they themselves have chosen but under the given and inherited circumstances with which they are directly confronted. The tradition of the dead generations weighs like a nightmare on the minds of the living" (1852, 174). Marx's project was to clarify how humans could take control and escape this nightmare.

[10] It is important to point out that Marx and Engels also suggested positive consequences of markets. For instance, they noted how markets decreased parochial prejudices and spread intellectual achievements around the world: "The intellectual creations of individual nations become common property. National one-sidedness and narrow-mindedness become more and more impossible, and from the numerous national and local literatures, there arises a world literature" (1848, 477). Separately, Marx observed: "What is wealth other than the universality of individual needs, capacities, pleasures, productive forces, etc., created through universal exchange?" (1857, 488). This raises the question, as political scientist David Miller notes, of "how developed individuality is to be preserved in the absence of the market mechanism that first brought it into existence. . . . [Marx] praises capitalism for creating the developed individual but . . . fails to show that communism contains mechanisms that will preserve this achievement. . . . [Moreover], the developed individual he admires is precisely the alienated individual he elsewhere pillories. . . . In this view, Marx's whole notion of alienation is part of a romantic anticapitalist outlook that should be jettisoned forthwith" (1987, 193, 198).

Further Distracting from the Need to Focus on Productive Wealth Ownership

Marx's penetrating study of capitalism reveals its dynamics more fully than did the analysis offered by any other observer. His core insight was that the dispossession of workers from any ownership, control, or unhindered access to productive wealth forced them, for their very survival, to seek owners willing to employ them. Yet, as noted earlier, Marx, his followers, and many other critics have extended their attacks to capitalism's two principal institutions of private property and markets. In doing so, they divert attention from the central issue of extreme inequality in the ownership and control of productive wealth. This diversion impedes the generation of an attractive alternative to capitalism that preserves the positive economic and social benefits of these social institutions. Regrettably, other elements within Marx's analysis, even some that represent conceptual breakthroughs, also had this consequence.

For example, at times Marx anthropomorphized capital, seemingly giving it autonomous power, as if it acted on its own behalf. To cite one of many such statements: "Capital is dead labour, that vampire-like, only lives by sucking living labour, and lives the more, the more labour it sucks" (Marx 1867, 1:257). Many other critics of capitalism refer to capital in a similar manner, albeit rarely so colorfully. But this is a distraction. It takes the spotlight away from the critical point that capital is almost exclusively owned and controlled by an elite class.

This tendency has a parallel among both Marxist and non-Marxist critics of capitalism who identify corporate power as the problem. The drawback is, again, that this way of thinking deflects attention from the fact that power ultimately lies with those who own corporations.[11] Although CEOs generally run publicly traded firms with considerable independence from their owners, the latter have a decisive power: in Hirschman's terms (1970), they can exit (sell their ownership shares) or use their voices (organize to vote out the CEOs at annual shareholder meetings). Yet the concentration and exercise of corporate power is continually flashed before the public, while its ownership remains more hidden in the shadows. Although most people are

---

[11] This ownership has always been extremely concentrated. In the United States, for instance, in 2020, according to Federal Reserve data, the wealthiest one percent of Americans owned 51.8 percent of stocks and mutual funds, and the richest 10 percent of the population owned 87.2 percent, leaving the bottom 90 percent in possession of only 12.8 percent (Pisani 2020).

aware of the concentration of corporate power, they greatly underestimate its concentrated ownership (Politizane 2012; Norton and Ariely 2011).

This digression from the root problem is also evident in the especially virulent attacks on the financial sector of the economy. Marx wrote: "The credit system ... constitutes enormous centralisation, and gives to this class of parasites the fabulous power, not only to periodically despoil industrial capitalists, but also to interfere in actual production in a most dangerous manner—and this gang knows nothing about production and has nothing to do with it" (1894, 3:544–45). In another passage, Marx took note of "a new aristocracy of finance, a new sort of parasites in the shape of promoters, speculators and merely nominal directors; a whole system of swindling and cheating by means of corporation juggling, stock jobbing, and stock speculation" (1894, 3:438). But companies operating in the financial sector are owned by the same elite that own productive corporations. Their growth and behavior are a consequence of the politically determined rules of the game— that is, the laws and regulations written at the direction of the elite—and not an inherent characteristic of the financial sector in itself. The passages quoted here make it appear that the managers of financial services companies are ultimately responsible for social and economic dislocations, when in fact they are merely agents in the service of the wealth-owning elite.[12]

The financial sector operates according to rules set by the state, predominantly in service to the elite. It may be, as Marx suggests, that the wealthy have created a Frankensteinian monster that works against their collective interest, as happens in financial crises that destroy a portion of their wealth. Nothing ensures that members of the elite always conduct their affairs in their own best interest.[13] But, under capitalism, they have protected their income, wealth, and privileges well enough to maintain near-monopoly ownership of the means of production.

The functions performed by the financial sector are vitally important in any complex economy. How it is owned, organized, and controlled (by an

---

[12] Notwithstanding the fact that these agents themselves often become part of the elite, thanks to the property rights the elite has pushed through government.

[13] As noted in Chapter 12, anthropologist Jared Diamond (2011) reveals how elites in civilizations that collapsed enabled environmental devastation to advance to the point that they took themselves as well as their societies to total ruin. Economic and social historian Bos Van Bavel reveals instances where a bourgeoisie, after having broken aristocratic power and created robust economic growth, ended up using its wealth to acquire political power to alter institutions enabling rent-seeking that sent their economies and their own well-being into decay.

elite class, its workers, or the state) depends upon who controls political power and thus sets the rules of the game.

Markets and Private Property without Exploitation

> *The form of association . . . which, if mankind continues to improve, must be expected in the end to predominate, is not that which can exist between a capitalist as a chief, and work people without a voice in the management, but the association of the laborers themselves in terms of equality, collectively owning the capital by which they carry on their operations, and working under managers elected and removable by themselves.*
>
> —John Stuart Mill, *Principles of Political Economy*
> (1909, 772–73)

Marx defined the separation of legally free workers from control, ownership, or unhindered access to the means of production as the *differentia specifica* of capitalism, its defining characteristic. An elite, backed by a state it disproportionately controls, uses its command of productive wealth to extract as much surplus as possible from the workers. This extraction takes place through the social institutions of private property and markets, but these institutions are not in and of themselves coercive. Private property becomes a tool of coercion when its unequal ownership forces those who are not owners to become subservient and exploitable.

Because Marx and other critics of capitalism have extended their attacks to private property, markets, and institutions such as corporations and the financial sector, attention has been sidetracked from the core problem of unequal ownership of, control over, and access to productive wealth. This detour impairs the development of an attractive alternative vision that would directly address the issue of inequality.

Such a vision could entail two principal components. First, suppose that workers, exercising their franchise, demand that Congress enact a law under which government must guarantee everyone a job, at a living wage, with benefits such as healthcare, retirement, paid vacation time, and parental leave. Imagine that the law also provides for the training necessary to enter the regular job market. This would eliminate poverty and welfare for those able to work while appealing to the value that everyone who can work should do so.[14]

Second, suppose that taxes, financing, regulations, and property rights are modified in favor of democratic worker-managed firms (Wisman 1991). Within these firms, the private property of productive units could be held in trusteeship, much as is the case with private colleges and universities in the United States. Workers could elect their managers with renewable term limits[15] (as is not the case in colleges and universities beyond many departments). Democratically controlled workplaces would enhance community both at work and in localities that would be more stable, especially since they would be less threatened by profit-driven firm relocations. Productive units in each industry could stand in market competition with each other, as is the case with American higher education.

Progressive income taxes,[16] wealth taxes, and inheritance taxes, as well as public spending, could be structured to limit inequality. Progressive taxes on firm revenues could be designed to encourage the breakup of huge firms into more readily worker-managed sizes. In societies in which the material problem of pinching scarcity has been overcome, any loss of efficiency would be bearable. Moreover, there is good reason to believe that worker-managed firms would be more efficient, partially offsetting forgone economies of scale.

Together, these reforms would eliminate the core source of exploitation that Marx identified within capitalism—the separation of workers from ownership, control, and ready access to the means of production. Guaranteed employment would eliminate job insecurity and poverty. Paired with retraining as appropriate, it would enable everyone to remain productive members of society with the social standing and self-respect this provides. Workplace democracy, where a firm's assets are held in trust (as in higher education), would empower workers with control over the tools and resources with which they work. In such a world, private property and markets would continue to exist, but no longer as instruments of exploitation. Workplace democracy would, John Stuart Mill wrote, relieve workers "from the necessity of paying, out of

[14] This is not a novel idea. As noted in Chapter 10, in the United States from Roosevelt in the 1930s until 1978, proposals were advanced in the political sphere to guarantee jobs for all those willing and able to work.

[15] For a discussion of how such firms might be structured, see Ellerman (1991).

[16] Economist Thomas Piketty writes that "According to our estimates, the optimal top tax rate in the developed countries is probably above 80 percent. . . . The evidence suggests that a rate on the order of 80 percent on incomes over $500,000 or $1 million a year . . . would not reduce the growth of the US economy" (2014, 512, 513).

the produce of their industry, a heavy tribute for the use of capital" (1909, 773–74). Further, if job tenure were instituted, the commodification of labor power would generally be of short duration, much as the pre-tenure probation period for many professors in academia.

Colleges and universities in the United States produce a world-class product, making for a highly successful export industry that is the envy of the world. US higher education thus provides an impressive example of a highly dynamic industry that is intensely competitive, thrives without being profit-driven, and is significantly worker-controlled. Moreover, there is no reason to believe that an economy modeled in this way would be any less dynamic and self-transforming than current capitalism.[17] Indeed, it may lead to greater dynamism. Guaranteed employment, appropriate retraining, and greater equality may be expected to further the democratization of education and raise achievement levels (Coady and Dizioli 2017), outcomes that promise to advance the rate of growth in productivity. Note, also, that guaranteeing jobs would eliminate the depreciation of human capital that accompanies unemployment as well as associated crime, decayed neighborhoods, and broken or dysfunctional families.[18]

Today's advanced capitalist societies depict themselves as grounded in human freedom. Yet they do not include workplaces as sites in which freedom should prevail, even though workers spend almost one-half of their waking time at work and preparing for and getting to work. Nor do they include freedom from the scourge of unemployment. The dominance of the elite's self-serving ideology of laissez-faire economics has succeeded in keeping these freedoms out of public discourse to such an extent that they are rarely even mentioned, much less debated. No contemporary political party—and, remarkably, no present-day labor movement—expresses substantial support for either guaranteed employment or workplace democracy.

The United States' original conception of freedom—the one that prevailed between the Declaration of Independence and the Civil War—viewed it as depending upon participation in the public sphere by citizens who governed themselves individually and collectively in work as well as in politics. The

---

[17] Opponents to worker control of firms will argue that workers are not competent to make the complex decisions that firms must make. But it will be recalled that the supposed incompetence of citizens was the principal argument offered by elites against political democracy. In both instances, the challenge is to elect competent managers rather than directly involving all workers in all decision-making. The relative economic and social success of political democracies proves it possible and desirable.

[18] For further discussion, see Wisman and Pacitti (2018).

economic independence of small farmers and artisans cultivated a sense of civic virtue. The freedom they celebrated depended upon "free labor," not in the capitalist sense of being free to sell one's labor power to the employer of choice, but, instead, being free from economic dependency, free from being bossed about, free to exercise control over the tools and resources with which they worked. In the prevailing American ideal, the objective of wage labor was temporary, a means to amass savings with which to purchase tools and resources and become independent and become one's own boss. The end of the frontier and cheap land, combined with industrialization and soaring inequality in productive wealth, began to massively proletarianize American workers, obscuring the authentic ideal and eroding the practice of economic freedom.

Contemporary economic and social dysfunction reveals an urgent need for a modern social vision that encompasses job security and freedom in the workplace. If widely embraced, credibly explained, and ardently advocated by progressives, a political platform based on workplace democracy and guaranteed employment at living wages, with reskilling where necessary, holds promise of being highly attractive to electorates. Democracy and freedom would be extended from the political domain to work life because no one would receive directives from anyone whom they have not democratically participated in selecting. The curse of unemployment and the misfortune of inadequate professional education would be eliminated. Moreover, such an arrangement would not appear all that different from classical capitalism, retaining its dynamic potential as well as its two principal institutions of private property and markets, without concentrating power in the state. It would constitute the next major step in the historical unfolding of freedom.

Whether an economy with guaranteed employment and workplace democracy as described here would still qualify as capitalism is a fair question. However, there is no canonical definition of capitalism that all accept. It is true that Marx understood capitalism to be a system in which an elite class owns the means of production and workers are compelled to bribe them for jobs by giving up their surplus labor. Accordingly, for Marx and many Marxists, a society in which work was guaranteed, workers controlled the means of production, and the two institutions that most characterize capitalism—free markets and private property—still prevailed, would no longer be capitalism. Such a system would have a resemblance to the institutional structure of capitalism, but without its exploitation because workers would be reunited with the tools and resources that make their work possible. It should be noted, however, that capitalism as a social system does not necessarily define the size of the productive wealth-owning class—it could be a few people or everyone.

In contrast to observers on the left, it is common for proponents of contemporary capitalism to define the system by its two principal institutions. Many of them would likely accept historian Jerry Muller's suggestion: "A working definition of capitalism is 'a system in which the production and distribution of goods is entrusted primarily to the market mechanism, based on private ownership of property, and on exchange between legally free individuals'" (2003, xvii). Libertarian economist Ludwig von Mises claimed that "the market is . . . the focal point of the capitalist order of society; it is the essence of capitalism" (quoted in Berger 1986, 188). Thus, according to the understanding of these non-Marxists, an economy with guaranteed employment and workplace democracy would still be capitalism, although clearly not capitalism in its classic form. In any case, it would not be the opposite of capitalism. Sociologist and theologian Peter Berger argued with good reason that "a society dominated by market mechanisms would not usefully be called socialist" (1986, 174).

Decentralized Power

> In each city, isn't the ruling group master? . . . And each ruling group sets down laws for its own advantage. . . . And they declare that what they have set down—their own advantage—is just for the ruled, and the man who departs from it they punish as a breaker of the law and a doer of unjust deeds.
> —Plato, Thrasymachus's Speech in *The Republic* (1968, 338d–9a)

For Marx, the state served as the executive committee of the ruling class. This was usually true, because the state needed the support of those who were rich and powerful enough potentially to usurp the rulers' power. Consequently, elites had to be appeased. However, if the state could muster adequate power—if it could gain "totalitarian" power, in the informal sense of exercising complete control and tolerating no opposition—it could further its own interests even at the expense of the wealthiest class.[19] It could

---

[19] The extent to which the state might become highly autonomous has been addressed by Marxist philosopher Antonio Gramsci, political philosopher Nicos Poulantzas, and sociologist Ralph

expropriate their property, tax their wealth and income, or take a greater portion of society's surplus, leaving less for elites to extract from producers. Left unchecked, the state gravitates toward absolute power.[20] What Marx describes as the Asiatic mode of production was just this, a state relatively, albeit never entirely, free of the constraints of the wealthy. The pharaohs' power seems to have been near absolute. So too, the Soviet state held almost total power, constrained only by the Communist Party, whose elite members enjoyed considerable privileges and from whose membership the rulers of the state were drawn.[21]

Part of the broad appeal of capitalism is that its states' power has generally been more limited than those under alternative economic systems. In early capitalism, the state was constrained by both the traditional aristocracy and the rising bourgeoisie, and in mature capitalism by capitalists and workers. Thus, in the capitalist system, the constraints imposed by the state's disparate counterparties have generally left room for greater freedoms.

Nothing legitimates and empowers the state to amass more power than war or the threat of war. Because leaders receive greater loyalty and respect from followers when external aggression threatens, they face an all but irresistible temptation: they can benefit if they can convincingly keep alive a perception of external aggression (Wisman 2014a). They can even be expected to craft measures against other powers that will provoke a limited amount of real threat.[22]

Milliband. Mussolini coined the word "totalitarian" to capture his ideal of "nothing against the state, nothing without the state, nothing outside the state" (quoted in Berger 1986, 236).

[20] Marx and Engels could envision that the state would eventually "wither away" under communism because they failed to understand that humans are innately competitive. They are so, as Darwin later made clear, due to the dynamics of sexual selection. For the same reason, they were unable to appreciate that the institutions of private property and markets could serve to both channel and limit the negative consequences of competitiveness.

[21] Revolutionary anarchist Mikhail Bakunin, a participant in the First International, in 1873 prophetically claimed of Marx's vision: "The actual 'proletarian government' will . . . be in the hands of a 'privileged minority.' . . . That minority, the Marxists say, will consist of workers. Yes, perhaps of former workers. And these, as soon as they become rulers or representatives of the people, will cease to be workers and will begin to look upon the entire world of manual workers from the heights of the State. They will no longer represent the people, but themselves and their own pretensions to rule the people. . . . But these selected men will be ardently convinced, and at the same time, learned socialists. The term 'scientific socialism' . . . proves that the alleged People's State will be nothing else but the quite despotic rule over the popular masses by a new and not very numerous aristocracy of real and spurious savants" (quoted in Nomad 1939, 199).

[22] Two twentieth-century examples especially stand out. The hostility of the West, and especially the United States, toward the Soviet Union after 1917 and Cuba after 1961 made the threat of foreign aggression convincing to the peoples of these societies, thereby legitimating their suspensions of freedoms as necessary.

The experiences of concentrated state power in the past, such as the twentieth-century examples of state socialism in Eastern Europe and fascism in Germany and Italy, or contemporary ones as in Egypt, Saudi Arabia, and Iran, testify to the social costs of a too-powerful state. Their rulers' relatively unchallengeable power has resulted in severe abuses of human rights and limits on the freedom and flexibility necessary for sustainable economic dynamism that does not deplete natural resources. China, with its highly totalitarian rule and expanding capitalist institutions, may be an anomaly, but its recent economic success makes it harder to assume that capitalism is a bulwark against authoritarian government.

Historical and actual experience suggest, then, that societies must take care not to grant too much power to the state. The state is a terrifying social institution, albeit a necessary one. It is terrifying because it has a massive comparative advantage in violence, and thus in coercion. However, the state has almost always had to appease elites. Accordingly, its powers have most consistently been used against workers. In societies where workers have substantially shared political power, states have been far more benign for all their citizens. But worker political power is currently in retreat. As a consequence of exploding inequality over the past 45 years, elites have gained increasing control over the state. This trend has resulted in public policies that tend to reduce freedom as well as workers' welfare.[23]

Further Reflections

Democracy is first and foremost about equality: equality of power and equality of sharing in the benefits and values made possible by social cooperation.
    —Sheldon Wolin, *Democracy Incorporated* (2010, 61)

Within states where workers have the franchise, the elite's ideology has dominated in varying degrees. When the elite's command of ideology weakened, political parties representing the interests of workers managed to change the rules of the game sufficiently to result in general improvements for workers' welfare. But only once in the history of modern capitalism has the elite's

---

[23] The United States, where inequality recently has most increased, now ranks poorly on many freedom indexes. On freedom of the press in 2020, for instance, it ranks 45th (Reporters without Borders 2020).

ideological power been weakened to the point that workers could use the state not just to improve their conditions, but to reduce inequality in income, wealth, and privilege. This occurred between the 1930s and 1970s, in the wake of the Great Depression's substantial delegitimation of the elite's laissez-faire ideology. The high level of inequality came to be viewed as unfair. However, given the elite's dominion over essentially everything, it was only a question of time before they reasserted their control over ideology. As detailed in Chapter 11, inequality has persistently—and dramatically—increased since the 1970s. Major political parties in today's rich capitalist countries have all bought into (or been purchased by) the interests and ideology of the elite. The parties differ only in the degree to which they have done so.

This chapter has argued that a paramount impediment to gaining freedom from the elite's self-serving ideology is the lack of an attractive alternative. The failure to envision a more egalitarian social order has significantly been due to the tendency among critics of capitalism to find fault with its core institutions of markets and private property. But these institutions per se are not the issue. It is, instead, that the rules of the game governing markets and private property are biased toward the elite, to whom they shepherd income, wealth, and privilege. The root problem is extreme inequality in the ownership of productive wealth, combined with an ideology that has come to seem self-evident. These advantages provide elites with disproportionate control over government, enabling them to write the rules of the game in their favor.

The attacks on markets and private property spread blame over the entire capitalist system. It is the corporations and their CEOs, or the banks and their leaders, or international trade. Inequality appears only as one among multiple problems. In fact, however, inequality is the source of all these other problems. With blame splayed all about, it is little wonder that many people believe nothing can be done.

Especially harmful to recognition of the root problem of inequality is the tendency to locate blame in the moral failings of key actors. Economist Jeffrey Sachs writes:

> At the root of America's economic crisis lies a moral crisis: the decline of civic virtue among America's political and economic elite. A society of markets, laws, and elections is not enough if the rich and powerful fail to behave with respect, honesty, and compassion toward the rest of society and toward the world. America has developed the world's most competitive market society but squandered its civic virtue along the way. Without

restoring an ethos of social responsibility, there can be no meaningful and
sustained economic recovery. (2011, 3)

As noted earlier, blaming actors for social problems is understandable from
an evolutionary viewpoint. For the first 95 percent of human history, identifi-
able social institutions did not exist. When something went wrong, it was due
to the immoral actions of individuals. This generated a bias to look for fault
in individuals, as opposed to the social institutions that channel their behavior into socially harmful expressions.

In contemporary rich capitalist societies, no major political parties that
can win elections represent worker interests in a significant way. And the
voices that attempt to represent workers fail to gain acceptance because, on
the one hand, their proposals are too diverse and unfocused, and, on the
other, the positions they espouse appear too extreme or frightening. Those
expressing such positions frequently attack capitalism lock, stock, and barrel,
including private property and markets. Such voices are too easily slammed
by the elite's ideological trump card—the claim that they lead to socialism
and totalitarianism. Moreover, many workers have net wealth in property,
mostly in their homes, pension funds, automobiles, and household items,
all of which give them a stake in the status quo. Restructuring capitalism
to guarantee employment and favor workplace democracy would preserve
private property and markets while redirecting, as opposed to augmenting,
state power.

14

What Future for Inequality?

It is our responsibility to design social institutions that reap maximum benefits from individual instincts for sexual competitiveness. In the terminology of game theory, we may not be able to keep individuals from playing as selfish competitors in the mating game, but we can choose, to some extent, which mating game our society plays. . . . Discovering better ways of managing human sexual competitiveness should be the explicit core of social policy.
—Geoffrey Miller, *The Mating Mind* (2001, 430)

The system isn't broken; it was built this way!
—Occupy Wall Street slogan

This book argues that the struggle over inequality is the underlying force driving human history. Other forces identified by historians and social scientists as the principal engines of history, such as religion, war, demographics, class conflict, technological advances, and great men, have themselves been propelled by the struggle over inequality. This argument has been constructed upon three principal supporting claims. First, the essential driving force for inequality is the biological imperative to send one's unique set of genes into future generations. The genes that exist at any moment are those whose carriers competed successfully for mates. Because high social status results in greater success in mating, humans have evolved to seek status for competitive sexual advantage. The qualities that provide status are predominantly determined by a society's culture and institutions.

Second, inequality underlies all politics—the various ways in which people organize relationships within and between groups. Humans biologically evolved as social beings, and, in addition to their propensity to compete, they evolved with a strong sense of fairness. Politics is the social process that strives to resolve the tension between competition and fairness. Politics influences behavior by shaping the social institutions or setting the rules of the game that define how competition can be conducted.

Third, although physical violence and intimidation (the threat of violence) remain the trump cards in creating, maintaining, or increasing inequality, ideology is the political weapon that is continually in service. Manipulating humans' innate sense of fairness is the essence of ideology.[1] Ideology hoodwinks the losers into seeing conditions that are contrary to their best interests as fair and just.

For most of history since the rise of the state and civilization, the elite's ownership and control of productive wealth has been the proximate cause of inequality. The privileges of early elites were preserved by an ideology that convincingly presented their sovereignty as the will of the gods and the natural order of the world. Therefore, the elites' monopoly ownership and control of productive wealth was as it should be. Since the rise of capitalist societies, inequality in productive wealth has been portrayed as creating a dynamic economy whose benefits trickle down to everyone. Those who accumulate wealth earned it (or their forebears earned it), and it is fair because anyone could do the same and everyone benefits. This ideology gains strength because the less well-off naturally tend to imitate the behavior and beliefs of elites, the successful people. It also helps to preserve inequality that ordinary people greatly underestimate the extent to which productive wealth is owned by the elite. What draws their attention is the tip of the iceberg—the elite's conspicuous wealth in mansions, yachts, private planes, clothing, and jewelry. Attention is also deflected from the concentrated ownership of productive wealth by progressives' focusing more often on inequality in income, to the relative neglect of inequality in wealth. In fact, the latter is immensely greater, and more important for political influence, than the former.

The struggle over inequality is the defining issue of history to date, and, so long as humans remain a sexually reproductive species, it will also be the defining issue of humanity's future[2] (Chapter 12 explored the relationship between inequality and the existential threat of environmental devastation,

---

[1] Suggesting the extremes to which some attempt to push ideology, historian David Hackett Fischer writes that many American conservatives argue that fairness is "hostile to capitalism, destructive of national security, and dangerous to liberty," and that unfairness is virtuous and inseparable from freedom (quoted in Woodard 2012). They also frequently claim that life is unfair—some are born healthy, attractive, and strong and others not—as if to minimize the importance of socially generated unfairness.

[2] This might no longer be true in a futuristic scenario wherein humans, to gain immortality and/ or survive ecological destruction, have transformed themselves into non-biological or non-carbon-based forms that would reproduce asexually.

and Chapter 13 mapped a path toward a more egalitarian society.) But what will be the future trajectory of inequality, and thus of *Homo sapiens*? The key question is whether the ideology that justifies inordinate shares of income, wealth, and privilege for the elite can be delegitimated in the eyes of the majority. If most voters see it as unfair, then they can democratically elect representatives who will enact egalitarian public policies.

Might this delegitimation occur? No one, of course, knows. Social causation is of such complexity, that the future is unpredictable. Accordingly, this concluding chapter will refrain from speculating about the society to come, and simply offer some grounds for both pessimism and optimism.

Grounds for Pessimism

The violence and injustice of the rulers of mankind is an ancient evil, for which, I am afraid, the nature of human affairs can scarce admit of a remedy.

—Adam Smith, *The Wealth of Nations* (1776, 460)

Although humanity existed for 97 to 98 percent of its history, first as nomadic foragers and then as early agriculturalists, without significant economic or political inequality, there can be no return to that era, nor, of course, would such a return be desirable. And since the rise of the state and civilization 5,500 years ago, inequality has almost always been as extreme as possible. Elites have continually claimed for themselves practically all surplus output, leaving producers with barely enough to survive. Given this history, can there be any realistic hope for a future of greater equality?

With the maturation of capitalism, Marx saw that industrialization and urbanization brought workers together in factories and slums where they could organize to fight collectively for a better deal. They struggled for and progressively won the right to vote and, with it, the potential to wrest political power from the elite. Due to their overwhelming numbers, the enfranchised workers could conceivably rewrite the social script—the rules of the game—to their best advantage. The legacy of civilization's extreme inequality could, in principle, be brought to an end, and humanity could return to the equality and freedom of its beginnings, this time with material abundance. But workers did not substantially rewrite the script because the elite's ideology convinced enough of them that flattening inequality would not be to their benefit. Producers' working conditions and lives improved, but only to the extent necessary to quell their rebelliousness.

Despite workers' gains, greater economic equality in Western Europe and the United States had to wait until the mid-twentieth century. The Great Depression sufficiently delegitimated the elite's laissez-faire ideology, such that between the 1930s and 1970s, inequality decreased as never before. It was roughly midway through this exceptional period, in 1955, that Simon Kuznets provided the support of economic science for the view that increasing equality would characterize humanity's future. He hypothesized that inequality increases in the earlier phase of economic development, but at some point it starts to decrease. His well-deserved stature in the economics profession inspired great optimism among the proponents of greater equality.

But two decades later, Kuznets's sanguine prognosis was contradicted by the facts. Laissez-faire ideology returned in full force during the 1970s to justify public policies that enabled inequality to explode. What optimists such as Kuznets failed to appreciate is the principal historical role of the elite's ideology in influencing politics to maintain regimes of usually extreme inequality.

In premodern times, because producers usually lived at bare subsistence, any change in the allocation of economic output that left them less would, obviously, be life-threatening. It would result in desperation and potentially provoke rebellion. In the far richer and more complex political systems of developed countries, few live at bare subsistence, and, usually, the consequences of rule changes are neither so painful nor so immediately obvious. Moreover, the changes are packaged and sold as in everyone's best interest. Elites win with a tax cut favoring them here, a financial or environmental deregulation there, altered property rights (such as those enabling great private ownership of knowledge), all purported to stimulate investment, boost economic dynamism, and create more jobs and higher wages. Cuts in government spending on social programs are justified as necessary to balance governmental budgets and nudge the unemployed to seek jobs more energetically. As these changes in public policy accumulate over the course of decades, the redistributional consequences become significant. Because this rewriting of the rules of the game occurs piecemeal, it sneaks up on the less fortunate, who may only take heed and react when a severe crisis pushes them into dire straits.

It is plausible that the prevailing ideology can only be effectively challenged during and after an especially grave crisis—one that harshly reduces living standards and financial security—an event as extreme as the Great Depression of the 1930s. Prior to the latest surge in inequality, economist Jeffrey Williamson pointed out that the greatest increases in inequality in the United States culminated in 1860, 1914, and 1929, and that "each of these pinnacles was followed by a major upheaval—civil war and slave emancipation, world war, or unparalleled depression . . ." (1980, 51). However, it should be noted that politics in the wake of severe crises can shift to the right as well as to the left, as European fascism of the 1920s and 1930s and the post-2008 Great Recession's turn to right-wing populism in the United States confirm.[3] Studying legislative elections in 20 advanced democracies between 1970 and 2014, political economists Manuel Funke, Moritz Schularick, and Christoph Trebesch determined that extreme right-wing parties find rising support in the wake of financial crises (2015).

As noted earlier, only once—during the Great Depression of the 1930s—was the ideology of the elite adequately delegitimated, such that there was a politically driven decrease in inequality for a substantial period. But suppose political skills for dealing with crises improve, and the elite's ideology adjusts to the lessons of the Great Depression and other social catastrophes that invalidate established principles. A deeper understanding of crises can generate responses that effectively limit their destructiveness. As discussed in Chapter 11, this was the case with the global crisis that began in 2008. Governments massively stimulated economies, and world leaders committed to avoid the mistakes of the early 1930s by abjuring protectionism and coordinating fiscal and monetary expansion. Only when the threat of depression seemed averted and the established ideology came through relatively unscathed did politicians serving the interests of the elite proceed to implement fiscal austerity measures that permitted inequality to continue its upward trajectory. In this light, the delegitimation of the elite's ideology in

---

[3] Political parties representing the interests of elites often support positions that deflect attention from the core issue of inequality. This is, of course, necessary to garner enough electoral support to win, given that elites constitute a very small part of the electorate. Historian Robert Paxton has characterized fascism as "a form of political behavior marked by obsessive preoccupation with community decline, humiliation, or victimhood and the compensatory cults of unity, energy, and purity" (2004, 218). The rhetoric of authoritarian politicians such as former president Donald Trump, France's Marine Le Pen, and Viktor Mihály Orbán, prime minister of Hungary, has insistently expressed these themes.

the 1930s and the consequent sustained 40-year decline in inequality appears to be a historical singularity.

As to the future, under an ideological canopy, more and more measures could be launched that further enhance the elite's ability to capture ever more income, wealth, and privilege. For instance, for the sake of deficit reduction, selective cutting of government spending could continue the decline in quantity and quality of public services that began over 40 years ago. The vicious cycle of worsening public goods and improving private goods could continue, turning those who are not rich against government, the only social agency that can come to their aid. Elite-driven policies could ensure that real wages continue to stagnate, or decline in purchasing power as they fail to keep pace with inflation, or decline relative to owners' returns as they fail to keep pace with productivity gains. Pensions could continue to erode as consumer debt rises and savings contract. Social Security benefits could be cut, or the system privatized. Developments like these would tend to lengthen the economic distance between a small wealthy elite and the rest of the population. Could inequality continue to rise until the masses live near the subsistence level, as they did prior to the second half of the nineteenth century?

Impoverishment on such a large scale would spell the end of democracy. Fearing that democracy could result in redistribution, elites would prefer authoritarian regimes that would exclude most of the population from any actual political participation.[4] Moves in this direction are currently under way in the United States. Behind the ideological ruse of fighting voter fraud, conservative state policymakers have been curbing electoral accommodations and setting up substantial impediments to voting for many of society's less privileged. These obstacles specifically target low-income, minority, and young voters—precisely the groups most likely to vote for liberal and progressive candidates. Voter identification laws have been the most prevalent tool used to limit the franchise.[5]

In light of this dynamic, it is not surprising that the rise of inequality over the past several decades in most countries of the world has led to what sociologist Larry Diamond claims is a "democratic recession," where the worldwide number of democratic states has decreased and the quality of democratic

---

[4] Recall from Chapter 9 that, less than four decades after the French Revolution established universal male suffrage, fewer than 1 percent of males were eligible to vote.

[5] These measures are being taken in tacit agreement with former Republican president Donald Trump's public avowal that with higher "levels of voting . . . you'd never have a Republican elected in this country again" (Milbank 2020).

governance has declined (Frum 2017). Freedom House reports that 2019 was the fourteenth consecutive year of decline in global freedom (2020).

But might elites come to realize that great inequality is not in fact in their enlightened long-run interest? Recent research has found the age-old claim that greater inequality fosters economic dynamism to be mistaken. Instead, greater inequality causes economies to grow more slowly (Alesina and Rodrik 1994; Berg and Ostry 2013; Bernstein 2013; Dabla-Norris et al. 2015; Easterly 2002; Persson and Tabellini 1994).[6] Drawing on extensive research, Wilkinson and Pickett (2009, 2019) report that more unequal societies score lower on practically every measure of quality of life. Even within the United States, states with higher levels of inequality typically have more severe social problems.

Although elites, living in gated communities, sending their children to private schools, and playing in country clubs, can shield themselves from many social problems afflicting the greater society, slower economic growth will constrain their ability to extract more surplus. And at some point, they will no longer be protected from ecological devastation. As Rousseau recognized long ago, elites can become victims of their own ideology (2013, 257).

Anthropologist Jared Diamond has found ample evidence for Rousseau's claim. As noted earlier, he reminds us that elites have pursued their immediate self-interest even when they had before them evidence of severe environmental devastation, the decline of their civilization, and the long-run ruin of the foundations upon which their own privileges and livelihoods depended (2005). Diamond's investigations suggest that elites tend not to recognize and act upon their enlightened long-term self-interest because they are forever caught up in the present moment of an unremitting contest among themselves for the pinnacle of status. As will be recalled from Chapter 6, this was the dynamic that economic and social historian Bas van Bavel found in three early market societies where rent-seeking elites, competing for status through conspicuous consumption, eventually brought their economies to ruin.[7] This outcome is supported by modeling conducted

---

[6] Andrew G. Berg of the Institute for Capacity Development and Jonathan D. Ostry of the International Monetary Fund find that the principal reason why lessened inequality is favorable to economic growth is the increasing role played by human capital. Access to the education necessary for its formation is more readily found in more equal societies. In a recent and highly influential book, economist Robert J. Gordon has argued that inequality is one of the principal "headwinds" braking growth and condemning the US economy to relative stagnation in the years to come (2016).

[7] Van Bavel reports that, about three to four centuries after the rise of market societies, where markets evolved for the factors of production (land, labor, and capital) as well as for output, increasing inequality permitted elites to gain increasing political power, which they used to change the rules of the game to enable their rent-seeking. The result was that the Gini coefficient for wealth inequality

by systems scientists Safa Motesharrei, Jorge Rivas, and Eugenia Kalnay, whose results predict that societies collapse when elites consume increasing portions of aggregate incomes (2014).

Authors of other noteworthy research papers reach similarly disheartening conclusions. In his magisterial study of inequality leveling, political scientist Walter Scheidel finds "little solid evidence for leveling by peaceful means" (2017, 377). Alberto Alesina and Roberto Perotti find strong empirical support for a positive association of inequality, political instability and civil unrest (1996). As a result of expanding inequality, could the United States become a failed state? Might other rich states do so as well? Political economists Daron Acemoglu and James Robinson remind us that "countries become failed states . . . because of the legacy of extractive institutions, which concentrate power and wealth in the hands of those controlling the state, opening the way for unrest, strife, and civil war" (2012, 376). Economist Thomas Piketty's research leads him to conclude that "there is no natural, spontaneous process to prevent destabilizing, inegalitarian forces from prevailing permanently" (2014, 21).

Grounds for Optimism

. . . an ideal picture of a society which may not be wholly achievable, or a guiding conception of the overall order to be aimed, is . . . not only the indispensable precondition of any rational policy, but also the chief contribution that science can make to the solution of the problems of practical policy.
    —Friedrich von Hayek, *Law, Legislation and Liberty* (1982, 1:65)

Despite the reasons for pessimism outlined in the preceding section, there is a case to be made for optimism about a more egalitarian future. The fatalism that currently characterizes much writing on prospective social, political, and economic conditions in developed countries may stem from a myopic view. A deeper historical perspective may be more instructive.

---

reached as high as 0.85 for Florence by 1427 and Amsterdam by 1630, or even higher for Iraq in the early tenth century. At these levels, their economies began declining (2019, 72–73, 128, 194–95). Similar levels of wealth inequality are now found in today's rich market economies. The distribution of private wealth in the United States, as well as in Germany, the Netherlands, and Sweden, is in the range of 0.8 to 0.9 (Saez and Zucman 2016).

Awareness that extreme inequality might be eliminated only arose during the past 250 years, a period that represents less than 5 percent of civilized history. The ideal of equality only began receiving significant attention in the second half of the eighteenth century, the era of the French and Scottish Enlightenments, Adam Smith, Thomas Jefferson, and the American and French revolutions. It arose alongside the recognition that sustainable social and material progress is possible. From a historical perspective, socioeconomic equality and progress are recent concepts.

A sophisticated, fully developed concept of ideology—based on the insight that certain doctrines serve to legitimate inequality—is even younger, dating to Marx in the mid-nineteenth century, although its embryonic expression existed during the Enlightenment period. Indeed, the intellectual foundations for contesting ideology were laid in the seventeenth century, notably with philosopher René Descartes's contention that supposed statements of fact must withstand critical examination. Reason, rather than faith, must guide humans. This was revolutionary. Only reason can lead to truth, and, as Goethe would later proclaim, *die Wahrheit wird euch frei machen*—the truth will set you free.[8]

As will be recalled from Chapter 8, early defenders of capitalist inequality recognized the danger of educating workers. They feared that, if workers were given educations, they would grow discontent with their demanding menial labor, low wages, and rude living conditions. Among those who preferred that the poor be kept ignorant were otherwise progressive thinkers such as political economist and philosopher Bernard de Mandeville and the notable French Enlightenment luminaries Denis Diderot and Louis-René Caradeuc de La Chalotais. Nonetheless, since the nineteenth century, the rising political power of the working class has increasingly democratized education. In principle, as even its opponents recognized, schooling gives people cognitive and rhetorical skills they can use in analyzing and exposing how ideological doctrines legitimate exploitation.

This is not to suggest that it is easy to question well-established patterns of thought that are embedded in the culture. Further, the laissez-faire ideology that legitimates inequality in developed countries has become ever more sophisticated, and the scientific-sounding arguments supporting it

---

[8] Although developed independently, many of these views and the optimism they advance parallel those that are extensively addressed by cognitive scientist Steven Pinker in his recent bestselling book, *Enlightenment Now* (2018).

seem authoritative. As discussed in Chapter 8, neoclassical economics' use of technical terminology and quantitative methods makes it opaque to ordinary people. Just as earlier inequality was accepted as the will of the gods whose reasons are beyond human comprehension, today it is accepted by many because economic science declares it necessary through reasoning that seems beyond lay comprehension.

Still, the continuing expansion of formal education, and the spread of knowledge acquired through online and personal contact with other people and other ways of thinking, holds the potential for nourishing more critical reflection and articulating more compelling arguments. As the world becomes more cosmopolitan, superstition, institutional religion, and unthinking assent to dogmatic statements progressively decline.[9] Over time, this trend may liberate people from ideology that represents as fair social institutions that work against their interests.

What propelled the democratization of education was the successful struggle of workers for a better deal and, especially, the right to vote in democratic elections. The franchise still provides the greatest hope for a future of lessened inequality. Where elections have been relatively fair, worker welfare has substantially improved, even if the persuasiveness of the elite's ideology has impeded the implementation of durably egalitarian policies. Those 40 years of declining inequality between the 1930s and 1970s stand as a reminder that the prevailing ideology can be delegitimated and that the elite's wealth, income, and privilege can be reduced, peacefully, through the democratic process. The improvement in general welfare during this period is striking, as was seen in Chapter 10. With the further spread and deepening of education, more workers may learn of this success, and the knowledge may embolden them to recreate it.[10] They already have the electoral power. Only ideology blocks them.

[9] Since the Enlightenment, in rich countries there has been a progressive decline in religion's importance in people's lives. Indicators of religiosity have been found to decline as per capita GDP increases, although the United States is an outlier (McCleary and Barro 2006). And even in the United States, rapid changes are reported to be occurring. In a new book, sociologist Ronald Inglehart reports a rapid decline in the expressed importance of God in American lives, falling, on a scale of 1 to 10, from 8.2 to 4.6 in a little over the decade preceding 2017 (2021). In October 2019, the Pew Research Center published results of a poll showing the share of Americans claiming "none" as their religious affiliation increasing from 16 percent to 26 during the preceding 12 years (Pew Research Center 2019b).

[10] Voters might come to realize that wealthy economies grew far more robustly between the end of World War II and the mid-1970s, while inequality was decreasing, than it has over the past 45 years as inequality has exploded.

The question of the future of inequality should be assessed within an understanding of its origins and the dynamics underlying its expression over the full trajectory of the human story. The human species has existed for 200,000 years, and, for the first 97 percent of that period, humans lived essentially free from exploitation in egalitarian social groups. Only the past 5,500 years, since the rise of civilization and the state, have witnessed the exploitation of producers and the burgeoning of extreme inequality. Thus, the preponderance of the human story reveals that, unlike sexual competition, there is nothing *naturally necessary* at the origin of political and economic inequality. They are cultural creations.

Although extreme exploitation and inequality have characterized human history since the rise of the state and civilization, so too has extraordinary progress. In developed countries, this progress has advanced geometrically, continually accelerating and, in contemporary times, providing extraordinary improvements in the lives of practically everyone.[11] Advancements in technology are stunning and gaining speed. But stunning, too, is the social progress achieved over the past few centuries. Slavery, the most abject condition for workers, everywhere in existence since the rise of the state and civilization, has become everywhere illegal and, apart from the atrocity of sex trafficking, has largely disappeared from the face of the earth. Since World War II, the colonialism that demeaned and exploited conquered peoples has also been eradicated. People are progressively becoming conscious of implicit and institutional racism. Polygamy and harems have practically died out as monogamy has become almost everywhere the norm. There is increasing recognition that gender equality is a crucial issue of justice and fairness that can no longer be deferred. Violence of humans against humans has declined over the full course of history (Pinker 2011). The pace of advances has been especially impressive over recent decades. Democratic societies where all adults were legally enfranchised only came about in the twentieth century. Extreme global poverty has fallen by 50 percent since 2000, less than a generation. *Homo sapiens* has finally arrived at the point where it is possible to envision victory over the problem of scarcity—at least in the sense of ending dire material privation—in the near future. Between 1990 and 2017, a mere 27 years, the world's infant mortality rate was more than halved, decreasing from 65 to 29 deaths per 1,000 live births. Over the past 60 years, global life

---

[11] Economist Bradford De Long estimates that world per capita income doubled every 6,000 years prior to 1750, after which it has doubled every 50 years (De Long 1998).

expectancy increased by 40 percent, from 52 to 73 years, and global literacy doubled from 42 to 86 percent.

Such spectacular improvement in human flourishing does not, of course, mean that conditions will continue to get better for everyone in the future. In particular, it does not necessarily mean that lower-status people will reject the elite's self-serving ideology, free themselves from exploitation, and overcome immoderate inequality in wealth, income, and privilege. Nevertheless, recent social, political, and economic progress, especially the democratization of knowledge, provides grounds for optimism.

There is strong contemporary evidence that, with the help of world leaders, activists, academics, pollsters, and journalists, awareness of inequality is growing in developed countries. In 2013, as noted in Chapter 1, President Barack Obama called increasing inequality the "defining challenge of our time." Pope Francis identified economic inequality as "the root of social evil" (O'Leary 2014). Occupy Wall Street drew a great deal of attention to the fact that the top 1 percent had made off with virtually all economic gains over the past several decades. Abroad, beginning at the end of 2018, a massive and sustained popular revolt against rising inequality was led in France by the *gilets jaunes* (named for the yellow road-safety vests many of them wore).

Information about the socially harmful consequences of extreme inequality is increasingly appearing in the academic and popular press. Note the extraordinary and surprising success of economist Thomas Piketty's dense and lengthy treatise on inequality, *Capital in the Twentieth-First Century* (2014). A world-wide polling in 2014 by the Pew Research Center found Americans and Europeans ranked inequality as the "greatest danger in the world," above nuclear holocaust or environmental degradation (2014). In the United States, Bernie Sanders, a democratic socialist who advocates substantial redistribution, came close to capturing the Democratic Party's 2016 and 2020 nominations for president. The Pew Research Center has found that as collective memory of Eastern European state socialism fades, the percent of American adults 30 and younger who have a favorable view of socialism has risen to 50 percent (Pew Research Center 2019b). A 2019 YouGov poll revealed that 70 percent of millennials claim they would vote for a socialist (Kight 2020).

Greater economic equality cannot, of course, end competition, nor would that be desirable. Competition is not only mandated by our biology, it fuels progress. But to do so, it must be properly channeled by social institutions. Competition can be redirected by remodeling social institutions, for example, shifting incentives away from excessive individual wealth accumulation and consumption toward less materialist expressions such as creativity, workmanship, contributions to community, or generosity. Such a reorientation of competition is urgently needed to counter the threat of ecological devastation.

The ultimate block to a more egalitarian future is the elite's ideology that inequality is good for everyone and thus fair. The ultimate question, therefore, is whether that ideology will be delegitimated. There is unprecedented urgency that this occur. Humanity has reached a unique juncture where its extraordinary successes have given birth to two, and possibly three, Frankensteinian monsters that each alone threatens to end the human story. The first is the result of nation-state competition that has created, and continues to create, weapons of such massive destructiveness that much life, including human, would perish if they were unleashed. The second is the result of organizational and technological prowess that has enabled both population and per capita consumption to explode, putting devastating pressures on the natural environment necessary for the survival of our own and every other species. The third potential monster is yet in the making. It is the creation of robots with such powers that they could sometime in the future decide to enslave, or seemingly more likely, eliminate their no-longer-useful creators.[12]

Taming these human-created monsters will require increasing social coordination—just what is threatened by high or, worse, increasing inequality.

As this book goes to press, the coronavirus pandemic continues to depress economic growth and exacerbate inequality. While elites are doing well with, to date, bullish capital markets, many of the less fortunate, including minorities and service-industry workers, are experiencing high unemployment and reduced standards of living. In addition, inequities in the distribution of vaccines may widen the gap between rich and poor countries. Whether this crisis will generate widespread solidarity among non-elites, and lead them to contest the laissez-faire ideology that has legitimated their loser status over the past 45 years, remains an open question.

---

[12] But does not the threat posed by robotization indicate that it is technological change rather than inequality that is the defining issue of history? No. How technology unfolds has always depended upon politics that define and enforce its ownership and control. For instance, technology can create massive unemployment or give everyone less work and greater abundance. It always depends upon the rules of the game—social institutions—set by politics.

References

Abrams, Paula. 2009. *Cross Purposes: Pierce v. Society of Sisters and the Struggle over Compulsory Public Education*. University of Michigan Press.

Acemoglu, Daron, and James A. Robinson. 2000. "Why Did the West Extend the Franchise? Democracy, Inequality, and Growth in Historical Perspective." *The Quarterly Journal of Economics* 115(4): 1167–99.

Acemoglu, Daron, and James A. Robinson. 2006. *Economic Origins of Dictatorship and Democracy*. Cambridge; New York: Cambridge University Press.

Acemoglu, Daron, and James A. Robinson. 2012. *Why Nations Fail: The Origins of Power, Prosperity and Poverty*. 1st ed. New York: Crown Publishers.

Acocella, Joan. 2017. "The Hammer: How Martin Luther Changed the World." *The New Yorker*, October, 67–73.

Addio, Anna Cristina d'. 2007. "International Transmission of Disadvantage: Mobility or Immobility across Generations? A Review of the Evidence for OECD Countries." Working Paper 52. OECD Social, Employment and Migration Working Papers. Paris: OECD. http://www.oecd.org/els/38335410.pdf.

Alcock, John. 1978. "Evolution and Human Violence." In *War: A Historical, Political and Social Study*, edited by L. L. Farrar Jr., 23–40. Santa Barbara, CA: ABC Clio Press.

Alesina, Alberto, and Dani Rodrik. 1994. "Distributive Politics and Economic Growth." *The Quarterly Journal of Economics* 109(2): 465–90.

Alesina, Alberto, and Edward L. Glaeser. 2006. *Fighting Poverty in the US and Europe*. New York: Oxford University Press.

Alesina, Alberto, Edward Glaeser, and Bruce Sacerdote. 2001. "Why Doesn't the United States Have a European-Style Welfare State?" *Brookings Papers on Economic Activity* 32(2): 187–278.

Alesina, Alberto, and Eliana La Farrara. 2001. "Preferences for Redistribution in the Land of Opportunities, Working Paper 8267." *National Bureau of Economic Research*.

Alesina, Alberto, and Roberto Perotti. 1996. "Income Distribution, Political Instability, and Investment." *European Economic Review* 40(6): 1203–28.

Alford, John R., and John R. Hibbing. 2004. "The Origin of Politics: An Evolutionary Theory of Political Behavior." *Perspectives on Politics* 2(4): 707–23.

Allison, Graham. 2016. "How Trump and China's Xi Could Stumble into War." *Washington Post*, April 2, 2016, sec. B.

American Political Science Association. 2004. "American Democracy in the Age of Rising Inequality." Task Force on Inequality and American Democracy. http://www.apsanet.org/content_2471.cfm.

Anderson, Benedict. 2006. *Imagined Communities: Reflections on the Origin and Spread of Nationalism*. Rev. ed. London; New York: Verso.

Anderson, Nick, and Susan Svrluga. 2016. "Georgetown Plans to Apologize for Its Role in Slavery." *Washington Post*, September 2, 2016. https://www.washingtonpost.com/

news/grade-point/wp/2016/09/01/georgetown-panel-urges-university-to-apologize-for-its-role-in-slavery/.

Anderson, Perry. 2013. *Passages from Antiquity to Feudalism*. 1st ed. New York: Verso.

Anderson, Sarah, Sam Bollier, John Cavanagh, Chuck Collinns, and Robert Weissman. 2008. "High Flyers: How Private Jet Travel Is Straining the System, Warming the Planet, and Costing You Money." *Institute for Policy Studies*, June 24, 2008. https://ips-dc.org/high_flyers/.

André, Jean-Baptiste, and Nicolas Baumard. 2011. "The Evolution of Fairness in a Biological Market." *Evolution* 65(5): 1447–56.

Andrews, Evan. 2014. "10 Things You May Not Know about Genghis Khan: History Lists." *History.Com*, April 29, 2014. http://www.history.com/news/history-lists/10-things-you-may-not-know-about-genghis-khan.

Andrews, Helena, and Emily Heil. 2015. "The Ashley Madison Lead Isn't Rocking D.C.—Yet." *Washington Post*, August 20, 2015, sec. C.

Appleby, Joyce. 2011. *The Relentless Revolution: A History of Capitalism*. Reprint ed. New York: W. W. Norton.

Aristotle. 1962. *The Politics of Aristotle*. Edited and translated by Ernest Barker. New York: Oxford University Press.

Aronson, Elliot. 1989. "The Rationalizing Animal." In *Readings in Managerial Psychology*, edited by Louis R. Pondy, David M. Boje, and Harold J. Leavitt, 4th ed., 134–44. Chicago: Chicago University Press.

Atack, Jeremy. 2014. "Capitalism's Promised Land." In *The Cambridge History of Capitalism: The Rise of Capitalism: From Ancient Origins to 1848*, edited by Larry Neal and Jeffrey G. Williamson. Vol. 1, 533–73. Cambridge: Cambridge University Press.

Azzellini, Dario, ed. 2015. *An Alternative Labour History: Worker Control and Workplace Democracy*. Reprint ed. London: Zed Books.

Bacevich, A. J. 2013. "How Manning and Snowden Made Secrecy Impossible." *Washington Post*, August 18, 2013, sec. B.

Bacon, Francis. 1620. *The Philosophical Works of Francis Bacon*. Edited by Robert Leslie Ellis. London: Longman, 1861.

Badger, Emily. 2016. "Study: Upscale Neighborhood Best Gift Parents Can Buy Kids. *Washington Post*, May. https://www.highbeam.com/doc/1P2-39623314.html.

Bailyn, Bernard. 2013. *The Barbarous Years: The Peopling of British North America—The Conflict of Civilizations, 1600–1675*. New York: Vintage.

Balkin, J. M. 2003. *Cultural Software: A Theory of Ideology*. New Haven, CT: Yale University Press.

Barber, Nigel. 1991. "Women's Dress Fashions as a Function of Reproductive Strategy: Sex Roles." *Sex Roles* 40(5–6): 459–71.

Bastiat, Frédéric. 1850. "The Law," June 1850. http://bastiat.org/en/the_law.html.

Baumeister, Roy F., and Kathleen D. Vohs. 2004. "Sexual Economics: Sex as Female Resource for Social Exchange in Heterosexual Interactions." *Personality and Social Psychology Review* 8(4): 339–63. https://doi.org/10.1207/s15327957pspr0804_2.

Becker, Sascha O., Steven Pfaff, and Jared Rubin. 2016. *Causes and Consequences of the Protestant Reformation*. Orange, CA: Chapman University, Economic Science Institute. http://www.chapman.edu/research-and-institutions/economic-science-institute/_files/WorkingPapers/becker-pfaff-rubin-reformation-survey.pdf.

Bell, Daniel. 1988. "The End of Ideology Revisited—Part II" *Government and Opposition* 23(3): 321–31.

Bellah, Robert N., Richard Madsen, William M. Sullivan, Ann Swidler, and Steven M. Tipton. 2007. *Habits of the Heart: Individualism and Commitment in American Life*. 1st ed., with a new preface. Berkeley: University of California Press.

Bellamy, Edward. 1888. *Looking Backward*. New ed. New York: Dover Publications.

Belonsky, Andrew. 2018. "Video: Helen Keller Tells It." *In Case You're Interested* (blog). June 27, 2018. https://incaseyoureinterested.com/2018/06/27/video-helen-keller-tells-it/.

Berg, A., and J. Ostry. 2013. "Inequality and Unsustainable Growth: Two Sides of the Same Coin?" *International Organizations Research Journal* 27(2): 792–815.

Berger, Peter L. 1967. *The Sacred Canopy: Elements of a Sociological Theory of Religion*. New York: Anchor.

Berger, Peter L. 1986. *The Capitalist Revolution: Fifty Propositions about Prosperity, Equality, and Liberty*. New York: Basic Books.

Berger, Peter L., and Thomas Luckmann. 1967. *The Social Construction of Reality: A Treatise in the Sociology of Knowledge*. New York: Anchor.

Berghahn, Volker R. 1993. *Germany and the Approach of War in 1914*. 2nd ed. New York: Bedford/St. Martins.

Berman, Mark. 2016. "Death Penalty." *Washington Post*, September 30. https://www.washingtonpost.com/news/post-nation/wp/2016/09/30/states-arent-using-the-death-penalty-as-much-now-americans-are-abandoning-it-too/

Bernstein, Irving. 1966. *The Lean Years: A History of the American Worker, 1920–33*. Boston: Penguin Books.

Bernstein, Jared. 2013. "The Impact of Inequality on Growth." *(blog)*. http://www.americanprogress.org/issues/economy/report/2013/12/04/72062/the-impact-of-inequality-on-growth/.

Berry, John Widdup. 1976. *Human Ecology and Cognitive Style: Comparative Studies in Cultural and Psychological Adaptation*. Beverly Hills, CA; New York: John Wiley & Sons.

Berwick, Robert C., and Noam Chomsky. 2017. *Why Only Us: Language and Evolution*. Reprint ed. Cambridge, MA: MIT Press.

Betzig, Laura L. 1986. *Despotism and Differential Reproduction*. New York: Aldine.

Betzig, Laura L. 1993. "Sex, Succession, and Stratification in the First Six Civilizations: How Powerful Men Reproduced, Passed Power on to Their Sons, and Used Power to Defend Their Wealth, Women, and Children." In *Social Stratification and Socioeconomic Inequality*, edited by Lee Ellis, 1:37–74. Westport, CT: Praeger.

Bhaghwat, Ashutosh. 2010. "A Brief History of the Commercial Speech Doctrine (With Some Implications for Tobacco Regulation)." *Hastings Science and Technology Law Journal* 2: 103–16.

Bierce, Ambrose. 2009. *The Devil's Dictionary: Easyread Super Large 18pt Edition*. ReadHowYouWant.com.

Black, Sandra E., and Kenneth L. Sokoloff. 2006. "Long-Term Trends in Schooling: The Rise and Decline (?) Of Public Education in the United States." In *Handbook of the Economics of Education*, edited by E. Hanushek and F. Welch, 1:69–105. Elsevier. https://doi.org/10.1016/S1574-0692(06)01002-6.

Blakey, Roy G. 1917. "The War Revenue Act of 1917." *The American Economic Review* 7(4): 791–815.

Blanchar, John C., and Scott Eidelman. 2013. "Perceived System Longevity Increases System Justification and the Legitimacy of Inequality." *European Journal of Social Psychology* 43: 238–45.

Blanning, Tim. 2008. *The Triumph of Music*. Cambridge, MA: Harvard University Press.

Blethen, Frank A. 2004. "Stop the Media Mergers." *Washington Post*, September 19, 2004, B7.

Bloch, Marc. 1970. *French Rural History: An Essay on Its Basic Characteristics*. Translated by Janet Sondheimer. Berkeley: University of California Press.

Blount, Sally. 1995. "When Social Outcomes Aren't Fair: The Effect of Causal Attributions on Preferences." *Organizational Behavior & Human Decision Processes* 63(2): 133–44.

Boehm, Christopher. 1997. "Impact of the Human Egalitarian Syndrome on Darwinian Selection Mechanics." *The American Naturalist* 150(S1): S100–21.

Bogaard, Amy, Mattia Fochesato, and Samuel Bowles. 2019. "The Farming-Inequality Nexus: New Insights from Ancient Western Eurasia." *Antiquity* 93(371): 1129–43.

Bogart, Dan, and Gary Richardson. 2011. "Property Rights and Parliament in Industrializing Britain." *The Journal of Law & Economics* 54(2): 241–74.

Boix, Carles. 2006. "The Roots of Democracy." *Policy Review* 135: 3–21.

Boix, Carles. 2015. *Political Order and Inequality: Their Foundations and Their Consequences for Human Welfare*. New York: Cambridge University Press.

Bonica, Adam, Nolan McCarty, Keith T. Poole, and Howard Rosenthal. 2013. "Why Hasn't Democracy Slowed Rising Inequality?" *Journal of Economic Perspectives* 27(3): 103–24.

Borton, Hugh. 1968. *Peasant Uprisings in Japan of the Tokugawa Period*. 2nd ed. New York: Paragon Book Reprint.

Boserup, Ester. 1965. *The Conditions of Agricultural Growth*. London: Routledge.

Bourdieu, Pierre. 1984. *Distinction: A Social Critique of the Judgement of Taste*. Translated by Richard Nice. Cambridge, MA: Harvard University Press.

Bowles, Samuel, and Herbert Gintis. 2002. "The Inheritance of Inequality." *Journal of Economic Perspectives* 16(3): 3–30.

Bowles, Samuel, and Herbert Gintis. 2007. "Power." Working Paper 2007-3, University of Massachusetts. http://scholarworks.umass.edu/econ_workingpaper/37/.

Bowles, Samuel, and Herbert Gintis. 2013. *A Cooperative Species: Human Reciprocity and Its Evolution*. Reprint ed. Princeton, NJ; Oxford: Princeton University Press.

Bowles, Samuel, David Gordon, and Thomas E. Weisskopf. 1991. *After the Waste Land: A Democratic Economics for the Year 2000*. 1st ed., 2nd printing. Armonk, NY: M. E. Sharpe.

Bowles, Samuel, and Yongjin Park. 2005. "Emulation, Inequality, and Work Hours: Was Thorsten Veblen Right?" *Economic Journal* 115(507): F397–412.

Boyce, James K. 2007. "Inequality and Environmental Protection." In *Inequality, Collective Action, and Environmental Sustainability*, edited by Jean-Marie Baland, Pranab Bardhan, and Samuel Bowles, 314–48. Princeton, NJ: Princeton University Press.

Boyce, James K., Andrew R. Klemer, Paul H. Templet, and Cleve E. Willis. 1999. "Power Distribution, the Environment, and Public Health: A State-Level Analysis." *Ecological Economics* 29(1): 127–40.

Boyd, Robert, and Peter J. Richerson. 2009. "Culture and the Evolution of Human Cooperation." *Philosophical Transactions of the Royal Society B: Biological Sciences* 364(1533): 3281–88.

Braudel, Fernand. 1982. *The Structures of Everyday Life: Civilization and Capitalism, 15th–18th Century*, Vol. 1. 1st US ed. 2 vols. New York: Harper & Row.

Braverman, Harry. 1998. *Labor and Monopoly Capital: The Degradation of Work in the Twentieth Century*. Anv. ed. New York: Monthly Review Press.

Bresser-Pereira, Luiz Carlos. 2010. "The Global Financial Crisis and a New Capitalism?" *Journal of Post Keynesian Economics* 32(4): 499–534.

Brody, David. 1993. *Workers in Industrial America: Essays on the Twentieth Century Struggle*. New York: Oxford University Press.

Brookman, Fiona. 2003. "Confrontational and Revenge Homicides among Men in England and Wales." *Australian & New Zealand Journal of Criminology* 36(1): 34–59.

Brosman, Sarah, and de Waal, Frans B. M. 2002. "A Proximate Perspective on Reciprocal Altruism." *Human Nature* (Hawthorne, NY) 13(1): 129–52.

Brulliard, Karin. 2020. "Humans Are Decimating Wildlife, and the Pandemic Is a Sign, Report Says." *Washington Post*, September 11. https://www.washingtonpost.com/science/2020/09/10/wildlife-population-plunge/.

Bureau of Economic Analysis. 2020. "Bureau of Economic Analysis (BEA NIPA), U.S. Department of Commerce, NIPA Tables. 2010." https://apps.bea.gov/iTable/index_nipa.cfm.

Burns, Harry. 2018. "How Well GDP Measures the Well-Being of Society." *Khan Academy*, March 21, 2018. https://www.khanacademy.org/economics-finance-domain/macroeconomics/macro-economic-indicators-and-the-business-cycle/macro-limitations-of-gdp/a/how-well-gdp-measures-the-well-being-of-society-cnx.

Burrough, Bryan. 2015. *Days of Rage: America's Radical Underground, the FBI, and the Forgotten Age of Revolutionary Violence*. New York: Penguin Press.

Buss, David M. 1989. "Sex Differences in Human Mate Preferences: Evolutionary Hypotheses Tested in 37 Cultures." *Behavioral and Brain Sciences* 12: 1–49.

Buss, David M. 1994. *The Evolution of Desire: Strategies of Human Mating*. 1st ed. New York: Basic Books.

Buss, David M. 2011. *Evolutionary Psychology: The New Science of the Mind*. 4th ed. Boston: Pearson.

Butler, Joseph. 1736. *Bishop Butler's Analogy of Religion, Natural and Revealed, to the Constitution and Course of Nature*. Edited by George R. Crooks. New York: Harper & Bros.

Byrne, Edmund. 2010. *Work, Inc.: A Philosophical Inquiry*. Philadelphia: Temple University Press.

Camus, Albert. 1942. *The Stranger*. Translated by Matthew Ward. New York: Vintage.

Cantillon, Richard. 1755. *Essai sur la nature du commerce en general*. Edited by Henry Higgs. New York: A. M. Kelley.

Cantoni, Davide, Jeremiah Dittmar, and Noam Yuchtman. 2017. "Religious Competition and Reallocation: The Political Economy of Secularization in the Protestant Reformation." Working Paper 23934. National Bureau of Economic Research. https://doi.org/10.3386/w23934.

Carens, Joseph H. 1981. *Equality, Moral Incentives, and the Market: An Essay in Utopian Politico-Economic Theory*. Chicago: University of Chicago Press.

Carey, Alex. 1996. *Taking the Risk Out of Democracy: Corporate Propaganda versus Freedom and Liberty*. 1st ed. Urbana: University of Illinois Press.

Cassidy, John. 2010. "After the Blowup." *The New Yorker*, January 11, 2010. http://www.newyorker.com/reporting/2010/01/11/100111fa_fact_cassidy.

Chace, James. 2005. *1912: Wilson, Roosevelt, Taft and Debs—The Election That Changed the Country*. Reprint ed. New York: Simon & Schuster.

Chait, Johathan. 2009. "Wealthcare." *The New Republic*, September 23. https://newrepublic.com/article/69547/the-gop-overreaching-health-care

Childe, V. Gordon. 1936. *Man Makes Himself*. Nottingham: Coronet Books.

Cicero, Marcus Tullius. 1913. *De Officiis (On Duties)*. Translated by W. Miller. Cambridge, MA: Harvard University Press.

Clark, Gregory. 2009. *A Farewell to Alms: A Brief Economic History of the World*. Princeton, NJ: Princeton University Press.

Clark, John Bates. 1908. *The Distribution of Wealth*. New York: Augustus M. Kelley.

Clausewitz, Carl von. 1989. *On War*. Translated by Michael Eliot Howard and Peter Paret. Reprint ed. Princeton, NJ: Princeton University Press.

Coady, David, and Allan Dizioli. 2017. "Income Inequality and Education Revisited: Persistence, Endogeneity, and Heterogeneity Working Paper WP/17/126." International Monetary Fund. https://www.imf.org/~/media/Files/Publications/WP/2017/wp17126.ashx.

Coase, Ronald. 1960. "The Problem of Social Costs." *The Journal of Law and Economics* 3(1): 1–44.

Cochran, Thomas C., and William Miller. 1961. *The Age of Enterprise: A Social History of Industrial America*. 1st ed. Harper & Row.

Cockshott, W. Paul, and Allin F. Cottrell. 1997. "Value, Markets and Socialism." *Science & Society* 61(3): 330–57.

Codrescu, Andrei. 2019. "The Posthuman Dada Guide." 2019. https://www.goodreads.com/work/quotes/6381689-the-posthuman-dada-guide-tzara-and-lenin-play-chess.

Cohen, Adam. 2020a. *Supreme Inequality: The Supreme Court's Fifty-Year Battle for a More Unjust America*. 1st ed. New York: Penguin Press.

Cohen, Adam. 2020b. "Perspective | The High Court Has Been Siding with the Rich against the Poor since Nixon." Washington Post. April 8, 2020. https://www.washingtonpost.com/outlook/2020/04/08/high-court-has-been-siding-with-rich-against-poor-since-nixon/.

Consumer Expenditure Survey. 2008. Washington, DC: Bureau of Labor Statistics. https://www.bls.gov/cex/csxann08.pdf

Conwell, Russell H. 2004. *Acres of Diamonds*. Edited by John Wanamaker. New York: Executive Books.

Coogan, Gertrude Margaret. 2018. *Money Creators: Who Creates Money, Who Should Create It*. New York: Pickle Partners.

Cooper, Anthony Ashley, Third Earl of Shaftesbury. 1714. *Shaftesbury: Characteristics of Men, Manners, Opinions, Times*. Edited by Lawrence E. Klein. Cambridge: Cambridge University Press. http://public.eblib.com/choice/publicfullrecord.aspx?p=144633.

Courtwright, David T. 2019. *The Age of Addiction: How Bad Habits Became Big Business*. Cambridge, MA: Belknap Press.

Creel, H. G. 1951. *Confucius: The Man and the Myth*. London: Rutledge and Kegan Paul.

Crippen, Timothy, and Richard Machalek. 1989. "The Evolutionary Foundations of the Religious Life." *International Review of Sociology Series 1* 3(3): 61–84.

Csikszentmihalyi, Mihaly. 1993. *The Evolving Self*. New York: Harper Collins.

Cummins, Denise. 2005. "Dominance, Status, and Social Hierarchies." In *The Handbook of Evolutionary Psychology*, edited by David M. Buss, 676–97. New York: John Wiley & Sons Inc.

Curle, Adam. 1949. "Incentives to Work: An Anthropological Perspective." Human Relations 2(1): 41–47.

Dabla-Norris, Era, Kalpana Kochhar, Nujiin Suphaphiphat, Frantisek Rika, and Evidiki Tsounta. 2015. "Causes and Consequences of Income Inequality: A Global Perspective Era Dabla-Norris; Kalpana Kochhar; Nujin Suphaphiphat; Frantisek Ricka; Evridiki Tsounta." IMF Staff Discussion Note No. 15/13, June.

Darwin, Charles. 1859. *On the Origin of Species*. Cabin John, MD: Wildside Press.

Darwin, Charles. 1871. *The Descent of Man and Selection in Relation to Sex*. London: John Murray.

Darwin, Charles. 1887. *The Life and Letters of Charles Darwin*. London: John Murray.

Davies, James B., Susanna Sandstrom, Anthony Shorrocks, and Edward N. Wolff. 2008. "The World Distribution of Household Wealth." Working Paper Series DP2008/03. World Institute for Development Economic Research (UNU-WIDER). http://ideas.repec.org/p/unu/wpaper/dp2008-03.html.

Davis, David Brion. 1999. *The Problem of Slavery in the Age of Revolution, 1770–1823*. New York: Oxford University Press.

Dawkins, Richard. 1976. *The Selfish Gene*. New York: Oxford University Press.

De Long, J. Bradford. 1998. "Estimates of World GDP, One Million B.C. –Present." Working Paper. https://delong.typepad.com/print/20061012_LRWGDP.pdf.

De Vise, Daniel. 2011. "Investment in Public's Ivory Towers Is Eroding." *Washington Post*, December 27, 2011: A1.

de Waal, Frans B. M. 2009a. *Peacemaking among Primates*. Cambridge, MA: Harvard University Press.

de Waal, Frans. 2009b. "The Origins of Fairness." New Scientist 204(2734): 34–35. https://doi.org/10.1016/S0262-4079(09)63003-7.

Deane, Phyllis. 1965. *The First Industrial Revolution*. Cambridge: Cambridge University Press.

Deaton, Angus. 2013. *The Great Escape: Health, Wealth, and the Origins of Inequality*. Princeton, NJ: Princeton University Press.

DeGrazia, Sebastian. 1962. *Of Time Work and Leisure*. New York: Twentieth Century Fund.

Dennett, Daniel C. 1995. *Darwin's Dangerous Idea: Evolution and the Meanings of Life*. New York: Simon & Schuster.

Dennett, Daniel C. 2006. *Breaking the Spell: Religion as a Natural Phenomenon*. New York: Penguin Books.

Dennis, Brady. 2020. "Most Americans Believe the Government Should Do More to Combat Climate Change, Poll Finds." *Washington Post*, June 23. https://www.washingtonpost.com/climate-environment/2020/06/23/climate-change-poll-pew/.

Desai, Raj, and Harry Eckstein. 1990. "Insurgency: The Transformation of Peasant Rebellion." *World Politics* 42(4): 441–65.

Dewey, Caitlin. 2015. "Ashley Madison Faked Female Profiles to Lure Men in, Hacked Data Suggest." *Washington Post*, August 30, 2015, sec. E.

Diamond, Jared. 1987. "The Worst Mistake in the History of the Human Race." *Discover Magazine*, May, 64–66.

Diamond, Jared. 1998. *Why Is Sex Fun? The Evolution of Human Sexuality*. New York: Basic Books.

Diamond, Jared. 1999. *Guns, Germs, and Steel: The Fates of Human Societies*. New York: W. W. Norton.

Diamond, Jared M. 2005. *Collapse: How Societies Choose to Fail or Succeed*. New York: Viking.

Diamond, Jared. 2012. *The World until Yesterday: What Can We Learn from Traditional Societies?* New York: Viking Adult.

Dickmann, Mildred. 1981. "Paternal Confidence and Dowry Competition: A Bioculture Analysis of Purdah." In *Natural Selection and Social Behavior*, edited by Richard D. Alexander and Donald W. Tinkle, 417–38. New York: Chiron Press.

Diener, E., M. Diener, and C. Diener. 1995. "Factors Predicting the Subjective Well-Being of Nations." *Journal of Personality and Social Psychology* 69(5): 851–64.

Diener, Ed, and Martin Seligman. 2004. "Beyond Money: Toward an Economy of Well-Being." *Psychological Science in the Public Interest* 5(1): 1–31.

Dill, Kathryn. 2014. "Report: CEOs Earn 331 Times as Much as Average Workers, 774 Times as Much as Minimum Wage Earners." *Forbes*, April 15. https://www.forbes.com/sites/kathryndill/2014/04/15/report-ceos-earn-331-times-as-much-as-average-workers-774-times-as-much-as-minimum-wage-earners/.

Dimont, Max I. 2004. "Jews, God, and History." Google Books, Chapter 6. https://www.google.com/books/edition/Jews_God_and_History/Lm5U0YSPmBUC?hl=en&gbpv=1&dq=Though+Protestantism+ had+begun+as+a+strictly+religious+reform+movement,+ the+people+behind+the+new+economic+forces+seized+the+Reformation+and+bent+it+to+their+own+economic+needs.&pg=PT201&printsec=frontcover.

Dittmar, Jeremiah E., and Ralf R. Meisenzahl. 2016. "State Capacity and Public Goods: Institutional Change, Human Capital, and Growth in Early Modern Germany." Working Paper. https://www.federalreserve.gov/econres/feds/state-capacity-and-public-goods-institutional-change-human-capital-and-growth-in-early-modern-germany.htm

Dobb, Maurice. 1947. *Studies in the Development of Capitalism*. New York: International Publishers.

Dobb, Maurice. 1967. "Marx's Capital and Its Place in Economic Thought." *Science and Society* 31(4): 527–40.

Doran, Leo. 2017. "Who Goes to For-Profit College?" *InsideSources*, March 7. https://www.insidesources.com/goes-for-profit-college/.

Douglas, Paul Howard. 1996. *Real Wages in the United States, 1890–1920*. New York: Houghton-Mifflin.

Dower, John W. 2010. *Cultures of War*. New York: W. W. Norton.

Dreyfuss, Bob. 2001. "Grover Norquist: 'Field Marshal' of the Bush Plan." *The Nation*, April 26. https://www.thenation.com/article/grover-norquist-field-marshal-bush-plan/.

Drutman, Lee. 2014. "Congress Has Very Few Working Class Members. Here's Why That Matters : Sunlight Foundation." June 3. https://sunlightfoundation.com/2014/06/03/white-collar-government/.

Drutman, Lee. 2015. "How Corporate Lobbyists Conquered American Democracy." *The Atlantic*, April 20. http://www.theatlantic.com/business/archive/2015/04/how-corporate-lobbyists-conquered-american-democracy/390822/.

Dubey, Oeindrila, and S. P. Harishz. 2015. "Queens." Working Paper, New York University. https://www.nber.org/system/files/working_papers/w23337/w23337.pdf

Dubofsky, Melvyn. 1986. "Not So 'Turbulent Years': A New Look at the 1930s." In *Life and Labor: Dimensions of American Working-Class History*, edited by Charles Stephenson and Robert Asher, 205–23. Albany: State University of New York Press.

Dubofsky, Melvyn. 1996. *Industrialism and the American Worker, 1865–1920*. Wheeling, IL: Harlan Davidson.

Duby, George. 1974. *The Early Growth of the European Economy*. Ithaca, NY: Cornell University Press.

Dumazedier, Joffre. 1968. "Leisure." In *International Encyclopedia of the Social Sciences*, 9:248–49. New York: Macmillan.

DuPlessis, R. S. 1997. *Transitions to Capitalism in Early Modern Europe*. Cambridge: Cambridge University Press.

Dutton, Denis. 2010. *The Art Instinct: Beauty, Pleasure, and Human Evolution*. 1st ed. New York: Bloomsbury Press.

Dwyer, Rachel E. 2009. "The McMansionization of America? Income Stratification and the Standard of Living in Housing, 1960–2000." *Research in Social Stratification and Mobility* 27(4): 285–300. https://doi.org/10.1016/j.rssm.2009.09.003.

Eagleton, Terry. 2012. *Why Marx Was Right*. Reprint ed. New Haven, CT: Yale University Press.

Easterlin, Richard A. 2001. "Income and Happiness: Toward a Unified Theory." *Economic Journal* 111(473): 465–84.

Easterlin, Richard A. 2002. *Happiness in Economics*. Cheltenham, UK: Edward Elgar.

Easterly, William R. 2002. *The Elusive Quest for Growth: Economists' Adventures and Misadventures in the Tropics*. Reprint ed. Cambridge, MA: MIT Press.

Edsforth, Ronald. 1998. "Made in the U.S.A.: Mass Culture and the Americanization of Working-Class Ethnics in the Coolidge Era." In *Calvin Coolidge and the Coolidge Era*, edited by John Earl Haynes, 244–72. Washington, DC: Library of Congress.

Ehrlich, Paul R. 1968. *The Population Bomb*. Reprint ed. Cutchogue, NY: Buccaneer Books.

Elias, Norbert. 1939. *The Civilizing Process: Sociogenetic and Psychogenetic Investigations*. Rev. ed. Oxford; Malden, MA: Blackwell.

Ellerman, David. 1991. "The Democratic Firm: A Cooperative-ESOP Model." In *Worker Empowerment: The Struggle for Workplace Democracy*, edited by Jon D. Wisman, 83–100. New York: Bootstrap Press.

Emler, Nicholas. 1994. "Gossip, Reputation, and Social Adaptation." In *Good Gossip*, edited by R. F. Goodman and A. Ben-Ze'ev, 117–38. Lawrence: University Press of Kansas.

Engels, Donald W. 1980. *Alexander the Great and the Logistics of the Macedonian Army*. New ed. Berkeley: University of California Press.

Engels, Friedrich. 1975. "Outlines of a Critique of Political Economy." In *Karl Marx–Friedrich Engels Collected Works*, 3:418–43. Moscow: International.

Engerman, Stanley L., and Kenneth L. Sokoloff. 2005. "Colonialism, Inequality, and Long-Run Paths of Development." Working Paper 11057. National Bureau of Economic Research. http://www.nber.org/papers/w11057.

Enrigue, Álvaro. 2018. "The Curse of Cortés." *The New York Review of Books*, 65(9): May 24. https://www.nybooks.com/articles/2018/05/24/mexico-curse-of-cortes/.

Evergreen Garden Care. 2020. "Gardening Popularity—Is It Growing or Declining?" *lovethegarden*. https://www.lovethegarden.com/uk-en/article/gardening-popularity-it-growing-or-declining.

Fajnzylber, Pablo, Daniel Lederman, and Norman V. Loayza. 2002. "Inequality and Violent Crime." *Journal of Law and Economics* 45(1): 1–40.

Fanon, Franz. 1967. *Black Skin, White Masks*. Translated by Lam Markmann. New York: Grove Press.

Farndon, John. 2010. *The World's Greatest Idea*. London: Icon Books.

Fawcett, Henry. 1863. Manual of Political Economy. London: Macmillan.

Fears, Darryl. 2019. "One Million Species Face Extinction, U.N. Report Says. And Humans Will Suffer as a Result." *Washington Post*, May 7. https://www.washingtonpost.com/climate-environment/2019/05/06/one-million-species-face-extinction-un-panel-says-humans-will-suffer-result/.

Federal Election Commission. 2009. "Number of Federal PACs Increases." http://www.fec.gov/press/press2009/20090309PACcount.shtml.

Fehr, Ernst, Helen Bernhard, and Bettina Rockenbach. 2008. "Egalitarianism in Young Children." *Nature* 454(August): 1079–83.

Feldstein, Martin. 1999. "Reducing Poverty Not Inequality." *Public Interest,* (137 Fall): 33–41.

Feltman, Rachel. 2014. "Switch to Farming Weakened Skeletons: Human Bones Became Less Dense as Ancestors Settled, Studies Show." *Washington Post*, December 24, sec. A.

Ferguson, Niall. 2012. *Civilization: The West and the Rest*. Illustrated edition. New York, N.Y.: Penguin Books.

Fieder, Martin, and Susanne Huber. 2012. "An Evolutionary Account of Status, Power, and Career in Modern Societies." *Human Nature* 23: 191–207.

Finley, Moses I. 1980. *Ancient Slavery and Modern Ideology*. Edited by Brent D. Shaw. Rev. ed. Princeton, NJ: Markus Weiner.

Fisher, Helen. 1994. *Anatomy of Love: A Natural History of Mating, Marriage, and Why We Stray*. New York: Ballantine Books.

Flaherty, Colleen. 2018. "About Three-Quarters of All Faculty Positions Are off the Tenure Track, According to a New AAUP Analysis," *Reports and Publications*, October 12. https://www.insidehighered.com/news/2018/10/12/about-three-quarters-all-faculty-positions-are-tenure-track-according-new-aaup.

Flannery, Kent, and Joyce Marcus. 2012. *The Creation of Inequality: How Our Prehistoric Ancestors Set the Stage for Monarchy, Slavery, and Empire*. Cambridge, MA: Harvard University Press.

Flannery, Tim. 2020. "The First Mean Streets." *The New York Review of Books*, March 12. https://www.nybooks.com/articles/2020/03/12/early-cities-first-mean-streets/

Fogel, Robert W. 1994. "Economic Growth, Population Theory, and Physiology: The Bearing of Long-Term Processes on the Making of Economic Policy." Working Paper 4638. National Bureau of Economic Research. http://www.nber.org/papers/w4638.

Fogel, Robert William, and Stanley L. Engerman. 1995. *Time on the Cross: The Economics of American Negro Slavery*. W. W. Norton.

Foner, Eric. 1995. *Free Soil, Free Labor, Free Men: The Ideology of the Republican Party before the Civil War*. Oxford: Oxford University Press.

Forster, Nathaniel. 1767. *An Enquiry into the Causes of the Present High Price of Provisions. In Two Parts: I. Of the General Causes of This Evil. II. Of the Causes of It in Some Particular Instances*. Independence, KY: Gale ECCO, Print Editions.

Fox, Robin, and Lionel Tiger. 1997. *The Imperial Animal*. New Brunswick, NJ: Transaction.

Frank, Robert H. 2001. *Luxury Fever: Why Money Fails to Satisfy in an Era of Excess*. New York: Free Press.

Frank, Robert H. 2005. "Positional Externalities Cause Large and Preventable Welfare Losses." *American Economic Review* 95(2): 137–41.

Frank, Robert H. 2007. *Falling Behind: How Rising Inequality Harms the Middle Class*. Berkeley: University of California Press.

Frank, Robert H. 2011. *The Darwin Economy: Liberty, Competition, and the Common Good*. 1st ed. Princeton, NJ: Princeton University Press.

Frank, Thomas. 2005. *What's the Matter with Kansas? How Conservatives Won the Heart of America*. Reprint ed. New York: Holt Paperbacks.

Frank, Thomas. 2011. "Easy Chair: More Government, Please." *Harper's Magazine*, December, 8–12.

Frank, Thomas. 2012. *Pity the Billionaire: The Hard-Times Swindle and the Unlikely Comeback of the Right*. Rev. ed. New York: Picador.

Frankel, Todd C. 2021. "A Majority of the People Arrested for Capitol Riot Had a History of Financial Trouble." *Washington Post*, February 11. https://www.washingtonpost.com/business/2021/02/10/capitol-insurrectionists-jenna-ryan-financial-problems/.

Frankfort, Henri, H. A. Frankfort, John A. Wilson, Thorkild Jacobsen, and William A. Irwin. 1977. *The Intellectual Adventure of Ancient Man: An Essay on Speculative Thought in the Ancient Near East*. 1st ed. Chicago: University of Chicago Press.

Frankfurter, Felix. 1916. "The Constitutional Opinions of Justice Holmes." *Harvard Law Review 29*(6): 683–702.

Franklin, Benjamin. 2017. *The Complete Works of Benjamin Franklin: Letters and Papers on Electricity, Philosophical Subjects, General Politics, Moral Subjects & the Economy, American Subjects before & during the Revolution*. Oxford: Madison & Adams Press.

Fraser, Steve. 2015. *The Age of Acquiescence: The Life and Death of American Resistance to Organized Wealth and Power*. New York: Little, Brown.

Freedom House. 2020. "Freedom in the World 2020." https://freedomhouse.org/sites/default/files/2020-02/FIW_2020_REPORT_BOOKLET_Final.pdf.

Freeland, Chrystia. 2013. "Book Review: 'The Future: Six Drivers of Global Change' by Al Gore." *Washington Post*, February 22. http://www.washingtonpost.com/opinions/book-review-the-future-six-drivers-of-global-change-by-al-gore/2013/02/22/3c9f5f50-76bf-11e2-95e4-6148e45d7adb_story.html.

Freuchen, Peter. 1961. *Book of the Eskimos*. 1st ed. Cleveland, OH: World.

Freud, Sigmund. 1930. *Civilization and Its Discontents*. New York: Dover Publications.

Fried, Morton H. 1967. *The Evolution of Political Society: An Essay in Political Anthropology*. New York: McGraw-Hill Humanities/Social Sciences/Langua.

Friedman, Gerald. 1988. "Strike Success and Union Ideology: The United States and France, 1880–1914." *The Journal of Economic History* 48(1): 1–25.

Friedman, Milton. 1962. *Capitalism and Freedom*. Chicago: Chicago of University Press.

Friedman, Milton. 1966. *Essays in Positive Economics*. Chicago: University of Chicago Press.

Friedman, Milton, and Rose Friedman. 1980. *Free to Choose*. New York: Harcourt.

Friedman, Milton, and Rose D. Friedman. 1988. "The Tide in the Affairs of Men." In *Thinking about America: The United States in the 1990s*, edited by Annelise Anderson and Dennis L. Bark. Stanford, CA: Hoover Institution Press.

Frum, David. 2017. "How to Build an Autocracy." *The Atlantic*, March. https://www.theatlantic.com/magazine/archive/2017/03/how-to-build-an-autocracy/513872/.

Fukuyama, Francis. 1989. "The End of History?" *The National Interest* 16: 3–18.

Funke, Manuel, Moritz Schularick, and Christoph Trebesch. 2015. "Going to Extremes: Politics after Financial Crises, 1970–2014." SSRN Scholarly Paper ID 2676590. Rochester, NY: Social Science Research Network. http://papers.ssrn.com/abstract=2676590.

Furness, E. S. 1920. *The Position of the Laborer in a System of Nationalism*. Boston: Houghton-Mifflin.

Galbraith, James K. 2019. "Inaugural Godley-Tobin Memorial Lecture, Eastern Economic Association." *Review of Keynesian Economics* 7(1): 1–5.

Galbraith, John Kenneth. 1957. *The Affluent Society*. New York: Mentor Books.

Galbraith, John Kenneth. 1982. "Recession Economics." *The New York Review of Books*, 29(1): February 4. https://www.nybooks.com/articles/1982/02/04/recession-economics/

Galenson, David W. 1984. "The Rise and Fall of Indentured Servitude in the Americas: An Economic Analysis." *The Journal of Economic History* 44(1): 1–26.

Galston, William A. 2018. *Anti-Pluralism: The Populist Threat to Liberal Democracy*. New Haven, CT: Yale University Press.

Gans, Herbert J. 2014. "Seeking a Political Solution to the Economy's Problems." *Challenge* 57(5): 53–64.

Garfield, Zachary H., Christopher von Rueden, and Edward H. Hagen. 2019. "The Evolutionary Anthropology of Political Leadership." *The Leadership Quarterly* 30(1): 59–80.

Garfinkel, Yosef. 2003. *Dancing at the Dawn of Agriculture*. 1st ed. Austin: University of Texas Press.

Garraty, John A. 1978. *Unemployment in History*. 1st ed. New York: Harper & Row.

Geary, David C., Jacob Vigil, and Jennifer Byrd-Craven. 2004. "Evolution of Human Mate Choice." *Journal of Sex Research* 41(1): 27–42.

Geiger, Roger L. 2019. *American Higher Education since World War II: A History*. Princeton, NJ: Princeton University Press.

Geoghagen, Arthur T. 1945. *The Attitude towards Labor in Early Christianity and Ancient Culture*. Washington, DC: Catholic University of America.

George, Henry, and Bob Drake. 1879. *Progress and Poverty*. 1st ed. New York: Robert Schalkenbach Foundation.

Gernet, Jacques. 1979. "Imperial Justice." In *China, Yesterday and Today*, edited by Molly Joel Coye and Jon Livingston, 2nd ed., 60–62. New York: Bantam.

Gibbon, Edward. 2010. *The Decline and Fall of the Roman Empire*, Vol. 1–6. New York: Everyman's Library.

Gilbert, Dennis. 2011. *The American Class Structure in an Age of Growing Inequality*. 8th ed. Los Angeles: Sage.

Ginsberg, Benjamin. 2013. *The Fall of the Faculty*. Reprint ed. Oxford: Oxford University Press.

Gintis, Herbert, Samuel Bowles, Robert Boyd, and Ernst Fehr. 2005. "Moral Sentiments and Material Interests: Origins, Evidence, and Consequences," 1–39. In *Moral Sentiments and Material Interests: The Foundations of Cooperation in Economic Life*. Cambridge, MA: MIT Press.

Glaeser, Edward L., and Raven E. Saks. 2006. "Corruption in America." *Journal of Public Economics* 90(6–7): 1053–72.

Glendon, Robert J., and John M. Benson. 2016. "Income Inequality: The Public and the Partisan Divide." *Challenge* 59(1): 4–11.

Godwin, William. 1793. *Enquiry Concerning Political Justice, and Its Influence on Morals and Happiness*. Los Angeles: HardPress.

Goff, Jacques Le. 1997. *La civilisation de l'Occident médiéval*. Paris: Flammarion.

Goldin, Claudia, and Robert A. Margo. 1992. "The Great Compression: The Wage Structure in the United States at Mid-Century." *The Quarterly Journal of Economics* 107(1): 1–34.

Goldmann, Lucien. 1973. *The Philosophy of the Enlightenment*. Cambridge, MA: MIT Press.

Goldrick-Rab, Sara. 2017. *Paying the Price: College Costs, Financial Aid, and the Betrayal of the American Dream*. Reprint ed. Chicago: University of Chicago Press.

Goodman, Paul. 1960. *Growing Up Absurd: Problems of Youth in the Organized Society*. New York: NYRB Classics.

Goody, Jack. 1998. *Food and Love: A Cultural History of East and West*. London: Verso.

Gopnik, Adam. 2012. "The Caging of America." *The New Yorker*, January 30. Gopnik, Adam. 2012. https://www.google.com/search?client=firefox-b-1-d&q=Gopnik%2C+Adam.+2012.+%E2%80%9CThe+Caging+of+America.%E2%80%9D+

Gordon-Childe, V. 1947. *History*. London: Cobbett Press.

Gordon, Linda. 2017. *The Second Coming of the KKK: The Ku Klux Klan and the 1920s and the American Political Tradition*. New York: Liveright.

Gordon, Robert J. 2016. *The Rise and Fall of American Growth: The U.S. Standard of Living since the Civil War*. Princeton, NJ: Princeton University Press.

Gottschall, Jonathan. 2008. *The Rape of Troy: Evolution, Violence, and the World of Homer*. Cambridge; New York: Cambridge University Press.

Gould, Lewis L. 1996. *Reform and Regulation: American Politics from Roosevelt to Wilson*. Heights, IL: Waverland.

Gowen, Annie. 2018. "'We Don't Have Any Fear': India's Angry Young Men and Its Lynch Mob Crisis." *Washington Post*, August 28. https://www.washingtonpost.com/world/asia_pacific/we-dont-have-any-fear-indias-angry-young-men-and-its-lynch-mob-crisis/2018/08/26/9a0a247a-a0aa-11e8-a3dd-2a1991f075d5_story.html?utm_term=.348c94271fea.

Graeber, David. 2012. *Debt: The First 5,000 Years*. Reprint ed. Brooklyn, NY: Melville House.

Gray, Jesse Glenn. 1965. "May 1965 Issue Salvation on the Campus Why Existentialism Is Capturing the Students By J. Glenn (Jesse Glenn) Gray." *Harper's Magazine*, May: 53–59. https://harpers.org/archive/1965/05/salvation-on-the-campus/

Graziano, Marcello, and Kenneth Gullingham. 2014. "Spatial Patterns of Solar Photovoltaic System Adoption: The Influence of Neighbors and the Built Environment." *Journal of Economic Geography* 15(4), October: 815–39.

Green, Anna. 2008. *Cultural History*. London: Palgrave Macmillan.

Greenberg, Robert. 2006. *How to Listen to and Understand Great Music*, 3rd ed. Chantilly, VA: Teaching.

Greider, William. 1981. "The Education of David Stockman." *The Atlantic Monthly* 248(5): 27–54.

Grossman, Gene M., and Alan B. Krueger. 1995. "Economic Growth and the Environment." *The Quarterly Journal of Economics* 110(2): 353–77.

Grossman, Gene M., and Alan B. Krueger. 1996. "The Inverted-U: What Does It Mean?" *Environment and Development Economics* 1(1): 119–22.

Gylfason, Thorvaldur. 2015. "Social Capital, Inequality, and Economic Crisis." *Challenge* 58(4): 326–42.

Habeeb, Mark. 2018. "The Middle East Leads the World in Income Inequality." *AW*. January 14, 2018. https://thearabweekly.com/middle-east-leads-world-income-inequality.

Hacker, Jacob, and Paul Pierson. 2010. Winner Take All Politics: How Washington Made the Rich Richer—and Turned Its Back on the Middle Class. New York: Simon & Schuster.

Haines, Elizabeth L., and John T. Jost. 2000. "Placating the Powerless: Effects of Legitimate and Illegitimate Explanation on Affect, Memory, and Stereotyping." *Social Justice Research* 13(3): 219–36.

Hamburger, Tom, and Alexander Becker. 2014. "Brookings's New Reality." *Washington Post*, October 31, 2014, sec. A.

Hamlin, Kimberly A. 2014. "Sexual Selection and the Economics of Marriage: 'Female Choice' in the Writings of Edward Bellamy and Charlotte Perkins Gilman." In *America's Darwin: Darwinian Theory and U.S. Literary Culture*, edited by Tina Gianquitto and Lydia Fisher, 151–80. Atlanta: University of Georgia Press.

Harari, Yuval Noah. 2015. *Sapiens: A Brief History of Humankind*. 1st ed. New York: Harper.

Harford, Tim. 2016. "A Beautiful Theory." *Forbes*. December 14. 2006/12/10/business-game-theory-tech-cx_th_games06_1212harford.

Harms, Robert. 1999. *Games against Nature: An Eco-Cultural History of the Nunu of Equatorial Africa*. 2nd ed. Cambridge: Cambridge University Press.

Harris, Marvin. 1989. *Our Kind*. New York: Harper & Row.

Harris, Marvin. 1991. *Cannibals and Kings: Origins of Cultures*. Reissue ed. New York: Vintage.

Harvey, David. 2003. *The New Imperialism*. Oxford: Blackwell Publishers.

Haskins, Ron. 2012. "Decisions That Doom the Future." *Washington Post*, March 30, https://www.washingtonpost.com/opinions/the-myth-of-the-disappearing-middle-class/2012/03/29/gIQAsXlsjS_story.html?tid=a_inl_manual

Hauser, Marc D., M. Keith Chen, Frances Chen, and Emmeline Chuang. 2003. "Give unto Others: Genetically Unrelated Cotton-Top Tamarin Monkeys Preferentially Give Food to Those Who Altruistically Give Food Back." *Proceedings: Biological Sciences* 270(1531): 2363–70.

Hayek, Friedrich A. 1982. *Law, Legislation and Liberty*. Vol. 1. 3 vols. London: Routledge and Kegan Paul.

Hayek, Friedrich A. 1991. *The Fatal Conceit: The Errors of Socialism*. Chicago: University of Chicago Press.

Heckscher, Eli. 1934. *Mercantilism*. 2 vols. London: George Allen and Unwin.

Heckscher, Eli. 2007. *International Trade, and Economic History*. Edited by Håkan Lingren, Mats Lundahl, and Ronald Findlay. Cambridge, MA: MIT Press.

Hegel, Georg Wilhelm Friedrich, and T. M. Knox. 1821. *Hegel's Philosophy of Right*. London: Oxford at the Clarendon Press, 1958.

Heideman, Paul. 2017. "Assessing Obama," *Jacobin,* January 20. http://jacobinmag.com/2017/01/barack-obama-presidency-trump-inauguration.

Henrich, Joseph, Robert Boyd, and Peter J. Richerson. 2012. "The Puzzle of Monogamous Marriage." *Philosophical Transactions of the Royal Society of London B: Biological Sciences* 367(1589): 657–69.

Hertz, Tom. 2007. "Trends in the Intergenerational Elasticity of Family Income in the United States." *Industrial Relations* 46(1): 22–50.

Herztberg, Frederick. 1966. *Work and The Nature of Man*. New York: Mentor Books.

Hicks, John Donald. 1960. *Republican Ascendancy, 1921–1933*. New York: Harper.

Hicks, John R. 1973. *A Theory of Economic History*. Oxford: Oxford University Press.

Hill, Sarah E., Christopher D. Rodeheffer, Vladas Griskevicius, Kristina Durante, and Andrew Edward White. 2012. "Boosting Beauty in an Economic Decline: Mating, Spending, and the Lipstick Effect." *Journal of Personality and Social Psychology* 103(2): 275–91.

Hillinger, Claude. 2014. "Is Capital in the Twenty-First Century, Das Kapital for the Twenty-First Century?" *Real-World Economics Review*, no. 69: 131–37.

Hirschman, Albert O. 1997. *The Passions and the Interests*. Twentieth anniversary ed. Princeton, NJ: Princeton University Press.

Hirschman, Albert O. 2002. *Shifting Involvements: Private Interest and Public Action*. Twentieth anniversary ed. Princeton, NJ: Princeton University Press.

Hobart, Michael E. 2018. *The Great Rift: Literacy, Numeracy, and the Religion-Science Divide*. Cambridge, MA: Harvard University Press.

Hobbes, Thomas. 1651. *Leviathan*. London: Oxford University Press.

Hobsbawm, E. J. 1968. *Industry and Empire: An Economic History of Britain since 1750*. 1st American ed. London: Weidenfeld & Nicolson.

Hodgskin, Thomas. 1832. *The Natural and Artificial Rights of Property Contrasted*. London: B.S. Fabernoster Row.

Hofstadter, Richard. 1989. *The American Political Tradition: And the Men Who Made It*. Reissue ed. New York: Vintage.

Hofstadter, Richard. 1992. *Social Darwinism in American Thought*. Reprint ed. Boston: Beacon Press.

Holden, C., and M. Mace. 2009. "Phylogenetic Analysis of the Evolution of Lactose Digestion in Adults." *Human Biology* 81: 597–619.

Holt, Charles F. 1977. "Who Benefited from the Prosperity of the Twenties?" *Explorations in Economic History* 14(3): 277–89.

Homer. 1847. *The Iliad of Homer*. Princeton: George Thompson.

Homer. 1944. *The Odyssey*. New York: Walter J. Black.

Houle, Christian. 2009. "Inequality and Democracy: Why Inequality Harms Consolidation but Does Not Affect Democratization." *World Politics* 61(4): 589–622.

Houlgate, Stephen. 2005. *An Introduction to Hegel: Freedom, Truth and History*. 2nd ed. Malden, MA: Wiley-Blackwell.

Howard, M. C., and J. E. King. 2001. "'State Capitalism' in the Soviet Union." *History of Economics Review* 34(1): 110–26.

Huang, Chye-Ching, and Chloe Cho. 2009. "Ten Facts You Should Know about the Federal Estate Tax." *Center on Budget and Policy Priorities*. February 23, 2009. https://www.cbpp.org/research/federal-tax/ten-facts-you-should-know-about-the-federal-estate-tax.

Huber, Evelyne, Dietrich Rueschemeyer, and John D. Stephens. 1993. "The Impact of Economic Development on Democracy." *Journal of Economic Perspectives* 7(3): 71–85.

Hume, David. 1742. "Of the Middle Station of Life." In *Selected Essays*, edited by Stephen Copley and Andrew Edgar. Oxford: Oxford University Press.

Hume, David. 1748. *An Enquiry Concerning Human Understanding*. Cambridge, MA: The Harvard Classics, 1909. http://www.bartleby.com/37/3/11.html.

Hume, David. 1955. "Of Refinement in the Arts." In *David Hume: Writings on Economics*, edited by Eugene Rotwine and Margaret Schabas, 32–40. New Brunswick, NJ: Transaction.

Hungerford, Thomas. 2016. "We're Not Broke: America's Real Spending Problem and How to Fix It." *Challenge*, 1–19.

Hunt, Alan. 1996. *Governance of the Consuming Passions*. New York: St. Martin's Press.

Huntington, Samual P. 1983. *American Politics: The Promise of Disharmony*. Cambridge, Massachusetts: Harvard University Press.

Hutton, Timothy J., and Jeffrey G. Williamson. 1995. "The Impact of Immigration on American Labor Markets Prior to the Quotas." Working Paper 5185. National Bureau of Economic Research. http://www.nber.org/papers/w5185.

Images and History. 2018. "Otto von Bismarck: Great Social Reformer?" *Images and History* (blog). January 21, 2018. https://imagesandhistory.wordpress.com/2018/01/21/otto-von-bismarck-great-social-reformer/

Inglehart, Ronald. 1989. *Culture Shift in Advanced Industrial Society.* Princeton, NJ: Princeton University Press.

Inglehart, Ronald F. 2021. *Religion's Sudden Decline: What's Causing It, and What Comes Next?* 1st ed. New York: Oxford University Press.

Ingraham, Christopher. 2016. "Wealth and Leisure Go Hand in Hand, except in the U.S." *Washington Post*, February 28, sec. G.

Interrante, Joseph. 1979. "You Can't Go to Town in a Bathtub: Automobile Movement and the Reorganization of Rural American Space, 1900–1930." *Radical History Review* 1979(21): 151–68. https://doi.org/10.1215/01636545-1979-21-151.

Irvin, George. 2007. "Growing Inequality in the Neo-Liberal Heartland." *Post-Autistic Economics Review*, (43): 1–23.

Jackson, Brooks. 2017. "Obama's Final Numbers." *FactCheck.Org.* September 29. https://www.factcheck.org/2017/09/obamas-final-numbers/.

Jäntti, Markus, Bernt Bratsberg, Knut Røed, Oddbjørn Raaum, Robin Naylor, Eva Österbacka, Anders Björklund, and Tor Eriksson. 2006. "American Exceptionalism in a New Light: A Comparison of Intergenerational Earnings Mobility in the Nordic Countries, the United Kingdom and the United States." Working Paper 1938. IZA Discussion Paper. Bonn, Germany: Institute for the Study of Labor (IZA). http://ideas.repec.org/p/iza/izadps/dp1938.html.

Jencks, Christopher. 2015. "The War on Poverty: Was It Lost?" *The New York Review*, April, 82–85.

Jenkins, J. Craig. 1982. "Why Do Peasants Rebel? Structural and Historical Theories of Modern Peasant Rebellions." *American Journal of Sociology* 88(1): 487–514.

Johnson, E. A. J. 1932. "Unemployment and Consumption: The Mercantilist View." *Quarterly Journal of Economics* 46(4): 698–719.

Johnson, Simon. 2009. "The Quiet Coup." *The Atlantic*, May. http://www.theatlantic.com/magazine/archive/2009/05/the-quiet-coup/307364/.

Jones, Adam G., and Nicholas L. Ratterman. 2009. "Mate Choice and Sexual Selection: What Have We Learned since Darwin?" *Proceedings of the National Academy of Sciences of the United States of America* 106 (Supplement 1), June: 10001–8.

Jones, Eric Lionel. 1987. *The European Miracle: Environments, Economies, and Geopolitics in the History of Europe and Asia.* 2nd ed. Cambridge; New York: Cambridge University Press.

Jones, Eric Lionel. 2000. *Growth Recurring: Economic Change in World History.* 2nd ed. Ann Arbor: University of Michigan Press.

Jost, John T., and Brenda Major. 2001. *The Psychology of Legitimacy: Emerging Perspectives on Ideology, Justice, and Intergroup Relations.* Cambridge: Cambridge University Press.

Jost, John T., Brett W. Pelham, Oliver Sheldon, and Bilian Ni Sullivan. 2003. "Social Inequality and the Reduction of Ideological Dissonance on Behalf of the System: Evidence of Enhanced System Justification among the Disadvantaged." *European Journal of Social Psychology* 33(1): 13–36.

Junger, Sebastian. 2016. *Tribe: On Homecoming and Belonging.* New York: HarperCollins.

Kanazawa, Satoshi. 2009. "Evolutionary Psychological Foundations of Civil Wars." *The Journal of Politics* 71(1): 25–34.

Kanazawa, Satoshi, and Mary C. Still. 1999. "Why Monogamy?" *Social Forces* 78(1): 25–50.

Kane, John, and Haig Patapan. 2012. *The Democratic Leader: How Democracy Defines, Empowers and Limits Its Leaders*. Oxford: Oxford University Press.

Keegan, John. 2004. *A History of Warfare*. London: Vintage.

Keeley, Lawrence H. 1997. *War before Civilization: The Myth of the Peaceful Savage*. Reprint ed. New York: Oxford University Press.

Kennedy, David M. 2001. *Freedom from Fear: The American People in Depression and War, 1929–1945*. Reprint ed. New York: Oxford University Press.

Keynes, John Maynard. 1930. "Economic Possibilities for Our Grandchildren." In Keynes, *Essays in Persuasion*, 358–73. New York: W. W. Norton.

Keynes, John Maynard. 1936. *The General Theory of Employment, Interest, and Money*. New York: Harcourt, Brace & World, 1965.

Kight, Stef W. 2020. "70% of Millennials Say They'd Vote for a Socialist." *Axios*. October 28. https://www.axios.com/millennials-vote-socialism-capitalism-decline-60c8a6aa-5353-45c4-9191-2de1808dc661.html.

Kirp, David L. 2015. "It's All about the Money: How America Became Preoccupied with Higher Education's Bottom Line." *The American Prospect*, Spring: 119–21.

Kitschelt, Herbert. 1994. *The Transformation of European Social Democracy*. Cambridge: Cambridge University Press.

Klein, Ezra. 2011. "The U.S. Government: An Insurance Conglomerate Protected by a Large, Standing Army." February 14. http://voices.washingtonpost.com/ezra-klein/2011/02/the_us_government_an_insurance.html.

Klein, Richard G. 2009. *The Human Career: Human Biological and Cultural Origins*. 3rd ed. Chicago: University of Chicago Press.

Koechlin, Tim. 2013. "The Rich Get Richer: Neoliberalism and Soaring Inequality in the United State." *Challenge* 56(2): 5–30.

Komlos, John. 2007. "On English Pygmies and Giants: The Physical Stature of English Youth in the Late 18th and Early 19th Centuries." In *Research in Economic History*, edited by Alexander J. Field, Gregory Clark, and William A. Sundstrom, 25:149–68. London: Emerald Group.

Kraus, Michael W., and Bennett Callaghan. 2014. "Noblesse Oblige? Social Status and Economic Inequality Maintenance among Politicians." PLOS ONE 9(1): e85293. https://doi.org/10.1371/journal.pone.0085293.

Krueger, Alan B. 2012. "The Rise and Consequences of Inequality in the United States." Presented at the Center for American Progress (CAP), Washington, DC, January 12. https://pages.wustl.edu/files/pages/imce/fazz/ad_10_1_krueger.pdf.

Krugman, Paul. 2003. "The Tax-Cut Con." *New York Times*, December 22. www.rci.rutgers.edu/~jdowd/krugman-taxcuts.pdf.

Krugman, Paul. 2013. "The 1 Percent's Solution." *New York Times*, April 25, sec. Opinion. http://www.nytimes.com/2013/04/26/opinion/krugman-the-one-percents-solution.html.

Kuhn, Thomas S. 1970. *The Structure of Scientific Revolutions*. 2nd ed. Chicago: University of Chicago Press.

Kuijper, Bram, Ido Pen, and Franz J. Weissing. 2012. "A Guide to Sexual Selection Theory." *Annual Review of Ecology, Evolution, and Systematics* 43(1): 287–311. https://doi.org/10.1146/annurev-ecolsys-110411-160245.

Kuran, Timur. 2004. "Why the Middle East Is Economically Underdeveloped: Historical Mechanisms of Institutional Stagnation." *The Journal of Economic Perspectives* 18(3): 71–90.

Kuznets, Simon. 1955. "Economic Growth and Income Inequality." *American Economic Review* 45(1): 1–28.

Lachmann, Richard. 1987. *From Manor to Market: Structural Change in England, 1536–1640*. Madison: University of Wisconsin Press.

Laing, R. D. 1965. *The Divided Self: An Existential Study in Sanity and Madness*. Reprint ed. New York: Penguin Books.

Lal, Deepak. 2001. *Unintended Consequences: The Impact of Factor Endowments, Culture, and Politics on Long-Run Economic Performance*. Cambridge, MA: MIT Press.

Landes, David S. 1969. *The Unbound Prometheus*. Cambridge: Cambridge University Press.

Landes, David. 1998. *The Wealth and Poverty of Nations*. New York: W. W. Norton.

Lane, Robert E. 1991. *The Market Experience*. Cambridge; New York: Cambridge University Press.

Lane, Robert E. 2001. *The Loss of Happiness in Market Democracies*. New ed. New Haven, CT: Yale University Press.

Lantican, Clarita P., Christina H. Gladwin, and James L. Seale. 1996. "Income and Gender Inequalities in Asia: Testing Alternative Theories of Development." *Economic Development and Cultural Change* 44(2): 235–63.

Lasch, Christopher. 1996. *The Revolt of the Elites and the Betrayal of Democracy*. New ed. New York: W. W. Norton.

Laski, Harold J. 2015. *A Grammar of Politics*. New York: Routledge.

Lawrence, R. Z. 1983. "Is Trade Deindustrializing America? A Medium-Term Perspective." *Brookings Papers on Economic Activity* 1: 129–70.

Lawton, Graham. 2020. "Human Evolution: The Astounding New Story of the Origin of Our Species." *New Scientist*, April. https://www.newscientist.com/article/mg24532760-800-human-evolution-the-astounding-new-story-of-the-origin-of-our-species/.

Leakey, Richard, and Roger Levin. 1978. *People of the Lake: Mankind and Its Beginnings*. New York: Avon Books.

Lebergott, Stanley. 1964. *Manpower in Economic Growth: The American Record since 1800*. New York: McGraw Hill.

LeBlanc, Steven A., and Katherine E. Register. 2004. *Constant Battles: Why We Fight*. New York: Macmillan.

Lee, Frederic. 2009. *A History of Heterodox Economics: Challenging the Mainstream in the Twentieth Century*. 1st ed. London; New York: Routledge.

Lee, Richard Borshay. 1979. *The !Kung San: Men, Women and Work in a Foraging Society*. 1st ed. Cambridge; New York: Cambridge University Press.

Lee, Timothy B. 2017. "Study: Lottery Winners' Neighbors Tend to Spend Themselves into Bankruptcy." *Vox*, February 23. https://www.vox.com/2016/2/23/11095102/inequality-lottery-bankruptcy-study.

Lepenies, Philipp H. 2013. "Of Goats and Dogs: Joseph Townsend and the Idealisation of Markets—a Decisive Episode in the History of Economics." *Cambridge Journal of Economics*, 38(2): March: 447–57.

Lewchuk, W. 1993. "Men and Monotony: Fraternalism as a Managerial Strategy at the Ford Motor Company." *Journal of Economic History* 53(4): 824–56.

Lewin, Tamar. 2010. "Once a Leader, U.S. Lags in College Degrees." *New York Times*, July 23, 2010, sec. Education.

Lindert, Peter H., and Jeffrey G. Williamson. 2016. *Unequal Gains: American Growth and Inequality since 1700*. Princeton, NJ: Princeton University Press.

Lipset, Seymour Martin. 1997. *American Exceptionalism: A Double-Edged Sword.* New York: W. W. Norton.

Livingston, James. 2009. "Their Great Depression and Ours." *Challenge* 52(3): 34–51.

Locke, John. 1689. *The Second Treatise of Government*. London: Dent & Sons, 1975.

Lodge, George. 2010. "The Need for Ideological Consciousness." Challenge 53(2): 76–89.

Long, A. A. 1974. *Hellenistic Philosophers: Stoics, Epicureans, Skeptics*. London: Duckworth.

Loomis, Erik. 2018. *A History of America in Ten Strikes*. New York: The New Press.

Lopreato, Joseph. 1984. *Human Nature and Biocultural Evolution*. Boston: Allen & Unwin.

Losurdo, Domenico. 2014. *Liberalism: A Counter-History*. Translated by Gregory Elliott. London; New York: Verso.

Low, Bobbi S. 2001. *Why Sex Matters: A Darwinian Look at Human Behavior*. Princeton, NJ: Princeton University Press.

Lubove, Seth, and Oliver Staley. 2011. "Gifts to Colleges Now Coming with Strings Attached." *Washington Post*, May 15, sec. G.

Lucas, Robert E. 1980. "The Death of Keynesian Economics." *Issues and Ideas*, 18–19.

Lucas, Robert, Jr. 2004. "The Industrial Revolution: Past and Future." *Annual Report*, Federal Reserve Bank of Minneapolis, vol. 18 (May): 5–20.

Lumsden, Charles, and Edward O. Wilson. 1983. *Promethean Fire: Reflections on the Origin of Mind*. Cambridge, MA: Harvard University Press.

MacEachern, Scott. 2010. *The Origin of Civilization*. Chantilly, VA: The Great Courses.

Machiavelli, Niccolo. 1513. *The Prince*. New York: The Modern Library.

Macionis, John J. 1999. *Sociology*. 7th ed. Upper Saddle River, NJ: Prentice Hall.

Malinowski, Bronislaw. 1922. *Argonauts of the Western Pacific*. New York: Dutton.

Malinowski, Bronislaw. 1992. *Magic, Science and Religion and Other Essays*. Prospect Heights, IL: Waveland Press.

Malthus, Thomas Robert. 1798. *On Population*. Edited by Gertrude Himmelfarb. 1st ed. New York: Modern Library, 1960.

Malthus, Thomas Robert. 1803. *An Essay on the Principle of Population*. 2nd ed. London: J. Johnson.

Malthus, Thomas Robert. 1820. *Principles of Political Economy: Considered with a View to Their Practical Application*. London: William Pickering.

Mandeville, Bernard. 1714. *The Fable of the Bees*. Edited by P. Harth. Harmondsworth, Middlesex, England; New York, NY: Penguin, 1970.

Mann, Michael. 1993. *The Sources of Social Power: The Rise of Classes and Nation-States,* Vol. 2, *1760–1914*. Cambridge: Cambridge University Press.

Mann, Michael. 2012. *The Sources of Social Power: A History of Power from the Beginning to AD 1760*. 2nd ed. Vol. 1. Cambridge: Cambridge University Press.

Marcuse, Herbert. 1955. *Eros and Civilization*. Boston: Beacon Press.

Marcuse, Herbert. 1964. *One-Dimensional Man: Studies in the Ideology of Advanced Industrial Society*. 1st ed. London: Routledge.

Marmor, Theodore R. 2014. "How Social Insurance Protects Americans from Growing Economic Risks." Scholars Strategy Network. February 28, 2014. https://scholars.org/contribution/how-social-insurance-protects-americans-growing-economic-risks.

Marshall, Alfred. 1890. "Some Aspects of Competition." *Journal of the Royal Statistical Society* 98: 612–43.

Marshall, Alfred. 1907. "The Social Possibility of Economic Chivalry." *Economic Journal* 13(49): 58–68.

Martin, Paul S., and Harry W. Greene. 2007. *Twilight of the Mammoths: Ice Age Extinctions and the Rewilding of America.* 1st ed. Berkeley; London: University of California Press.

, Karl. 1843. *Critique of Hegel's Philosophy of Right.* Translated by Joseph O'Malley. Cambridge: Cambridge University Press, 1977.

Marx, Karl. 1844. "Economic and Philosophic Manuscripts of 1844." In *The Marx-Engels Reader,* edited by Robert C. Tucker, 2nd ed., 66–125. New York: W. W. Norton, 1978.

Marx, Karl. 1845. "The German Ideology." In *The Marx-Engels Reader,* edited by Robert C. Tucker, 2nd ed., 146–202. New York: W. W. Norton, 1978.

Marx, Karl. 1847. "The Poverty of Philosophy." http://www.marxists.org/archive/marx/works/subject/hist-mat/pov-phil/ch02.htm.

Marx, Karl. 1852. "Chapter 7, The Eighteenth Brumaire of Louis Bonaparte." In *The Eighteenth Brumaire of Louis Bonaparte. Karl Marx 1852.* http://www.marxists.org/archive/marx/works/1852/18th-brumaire/ch07.htm.

Marx, Karl. 1857. *Grundrisse.* London: Penguin, 1993.

Marx, Karl. 1859. *A Contribution to the Critique of Political Economy.* Moscow: Progress, 1970.

Marx, Karl. 1867a. *Capital: A Critique of Political Economy.* Vol. 1. 3 vols. New York: International, 1967.

Marx, Karl. 1867b. *Capital: A Critique of Political Economy.* Translated by Samuel Moore and Edward Aveling. Vol. 1. New York: The Modern Library, 1906.

Marx, Karl. 1875a. "Critique of the Gotha Program." In *The Marx-Engels Reader,* edited by Robert C. Tucker, 2nd ed., 525–41. New York: W. W. Norton, 1978.

Marx, Karl. 1875b. "The Possibility of Non-Violent Revolution." In *The Marx-Engels Reader,* edited by Robert C. Tucker, 2nd ed., 522–24. New York: W. W. Norton, 1978.

Marx, Karl. 1894. *Capital: A Critique of Political Economy.* Vol. 3. 3 vols. New York: International Publishers Company, Incorporated.

Marx, Karl, and Friedrich Engels. 1848. "Manifesto of the Communist Party." In *The Marx-Engels Reader,* edited by Robert C. Tucker, 2nd ed., 469–500. New York: W. W. Norton, 1978.

Marx, Leo. 2000. *The Machine in the Garden: Technology and the Pastoral Ideal in America.* 35th anniversary ed. New York: Oxford University Press.

Maryanski, Alexandra. 1994. "The Pursuit of Human Nature in Sociobiology and Evolutionary Sociology." *Sociological Perspectives* 37(3): 375–89.

Maslow, Abraham H. 1954. *Motivation and Personality.* Edited by Robert Frager, James Fadiman, Cynthia McReynolds, and Ruth Cox. 3rd ed. New York: Longman.

Mazumder, Bhashkar. 2005. "Fortunate Sons: New Estimates of Intergenerational Mobility in the United States Using Social Security Earnings Data." *Review of Economics and Statistics* 87(2): 235–55.

McCleary, Rachel M., and Robert J. Barro. 2006. "Religion and Economy." *Journal of Economic Perspectives* 20(2): 49–72.

McCloskey, Deirdre N. 2007. *The Bourgeois Virtues: Ethics for an Age of Commerce.* Chicago: University of Chicago Press.

McElvaine, Robert S. 1993. *The Great Depression: America 1929–1941.* Reprint ed. New York: Times Books.

McNally, David. 1993. *Against the Market: Political Economy, Market Socialism and the Marxist Critique.* London: Verso.

McPherron, Shannon P., Zeresenay Alemseged, Curtis W. Marean, Jonathan G. Wynn, Denné Reed, Denis Geraads, René Bobe, and Hamdallah A. Béarat. 2010. "Evidence for Stone-Tool-Assisted Consumption of Animal Tissues before 3.39 Million Years Ago at Dikika, Ethiopia." *Nature* 466(7308): 857–60.

Meadows, Donella H. 1972. *The Limits to Growth: A Report for the Club of Rome's Project on the Predicament of Mankind*. 2nd ed. New York: Universe Books.

Medina, Jennifer, Katie Benner, and Kate Taylor. 2019. "Actresses, Business Leaders and Other Wealthy Parents Charged in U.S. College Entry Fraud." *New York Times*, March 12, sec. U.S. https://www.nytimes.com/2019/03/12/us/college-admissions-cheating-scandal.html.

Menand, Louis. 2016. "He's Back: Karl Marx, Yesterday and Today." *The New Yorker*, October, 90–97.

Mercier, Hugo, and Dan Sperber. 2011. "Why Do Humans Reason? Arguments for an Argumentative Theory." *The Behavioral and Brain Sciences* 34(2): 57–74; discussion 74-111.

Merton, Robert K. 1936. "The Unanticipated Consequences of Purposive Social Action." *American Sociological Review* 1(6): 894–904.

Meyerson, Harold. 2019. "How to Really End Shareholder Capitalism." *The American Prospect*. September 18. https://prospect.org/api/content/eaeb93ac-da4b-11e9-9b46-12f1225286c6/.

Milanovic, Branko. 2016. *Global Inequality a New Approach for the Age of Globalization*. Cambridge, MA: Belknap Press of Harvard University Press.

Milbank, Dana. 2020. "Stop Fretting about Trump and Do Something about It. Right Now." *Washington Post*, July 26. https://www.washingtonpost.com/opinions/2020/07/24/stop-fretting-about-trump-do-something-about-it-right-now/.

Mill, John Stuart. 1869. "Thornton on Labour and Its Claims." *Fortnightly Review*, May: 505–18.

Mill, John Stuart. 1909. *Principles of Political Economy*. 7th ed. Clifton, NJ: Augustus M. Kelley.

Miller, David. 1987. "Marx, Communism, and Markets." *Political Theory* 15(2): 182–204.

Miller, Geoffrey. 2001. *The Mating Mind: How Sexual Choice Shaped the Evolution of Human Nature*. Reprint ed. New York: Anchor.

Miller, John P. 2018. "Ancient Symbols in Rock Art." *Bradshaw Foundation*. http://www.bradshawfoundation.com/ancient_symbols_in_rock_art/.

Mishel, Lawrence, Jared Bernstein, and Sylvia Allegretto. 2007. *The State of Working America*. Ithaca, NY: Cornell University Press.

Mithen, Steven. 1999. *The Prehistory of the Mind: The Cognitive Origins of Art, Religion and Science*. 1st ed. London: Thames & Hudson.

Mokyr, Joel. 1990. *The Lever of Riches: Technological Creativity and Economic Progress*. New York: Oxford University Press.

Mokyr, Joel. 2004. *The Gifts of Athena: Historical Origins of the Knowledge Economy*. Princeton, NJ: Princeton University Press.

Montgomery, David. 1987. *Workers' Control in America*. Cambridge: Cambridge University Press.

Mooney, Chris, and Dennis Brady. 2016. "Air Pollution Getting Worse in World's Cities, WHO Reports." *BostonGlobe.com*, May 13, 2016. https://www.bostonglobe.com/news/nation/2016/05/12/air-pollution-getting-worse-world-cities-who-reports/rZEaeKUWHgAbjLgiZ66DBL/story.html.

Moore, Barrington. 1966. *The Social Origins of Dictatorship and Democracy: Lord and Peasant in the Making of the Modern World*. Boston: Beacon Press.

Moran, Timothy Patrick. 2005. "Kuznets's Inverted U-Curve Hypothesis: The Rise, Demise, and Continued Relevance of a Socioeconomic Law." *Sociological Forum* 20(2): 209–44.

Morgan, Kelly. 2000. "Inequality and Crime." *Economics and Statistics* 84(2): 530–39.

Montesquieu, Charles de Secondat baron de. 1748. *The Spirit of Laws*. New York: Colonial Press, 1899.

Motesharrei, Safa, Jorge Rivas, and Eugenia Kalnay. 2014. "Human and Nature Dynamics (HANDY): Modeling Inequality and Use of Resources in the Collapse or Sustainability of Societies." *Ecological Economics* 101(May): 90–102.

Moyer, Justin Wm. 2015. "Motorhead Frontman's Life Rocked, like Music." *Washington Post*, December 30, 2015, sec. C.

Muller, Edward N., and Mitchell A. Seligman. 1987. "Inequality and Insurgency." *The American Political Science Review* 81(2): 425–52.

Muller, Jerry Z. 2003. *The Mind and the Market: Capitalism in Western Thought*. Reprint ed. New York: Anchor.

Muller, Jerry Z. 2013. "Capitalism and Inequality." *Foreign Affairs*, 9(2), April: 30–51.

Mumford, Lewis. 1961. *The City in History*. New York: Harcourt, Brace, Jovanovich.

Myrdal, Gunnar. 1968. *The Political Element in the Development of Economic Theory*. New York: Simon & Schuster.

Neal, Larry, and Rondo Cameron. 2016. *A Concise Economic History of the World*. 5th ed. Oxford: Oxford University Press.

Neel, James V. 1980. "On Being Headman." *Perspectives in Biology and Medicine* 23(2): 277–94.

Newfield, Christopher. 2011. *Unmaking the Public University: The Forty-Year Assault on the Middle Class*. Cambridge, MA: Harvard University Press.

Nguyen, Trung. 2015. *Naturalopy Precept 19: Liberty*. EnCognitive.com.

Nietzsche, Friedrich. 1878. *Human, All-Too-Human: Parts One and Two*. North Chelmsford, Massachusetts: Courier Corporation, 2012.

Nietzsche, Friedrich. 1887. *On the Genealogy of Morals*. New York: Vintage Books, 1969.

Nisbet, Robert A. 1973. *The Social Philosophers*. New York: Thomas Y. Crowell Company.

Noell, E. 2006. "Smith and a Living Wage: Competition, Economic Compulsion, and the Scholastic Legacy." *History of Political Economy* 38(1): 151–74.

Nomad, Max. 1939. *Apostles of Revolution*. Boston, MA: Little Brown.

Nordhaus, William. 2015. "Climate Clubs: Overcoming Free-Riding in International Climate Policy, Presidential Address to the American Economic Association." *American Economic Review* 105(4): 1339–70.

North, Douglass C. 1982. *Structure and Change in Economic History*. New York: W. W. Norton.

North, Douglass C. 2010. *Understanding the Process of Economic Change*. Princeton, NJ: Princeton University Press.

North, Douglass C., and Robert Paul Thomas. 1971. "The Rise and Fall of the Manorial System: A Theoretical Model." *The Journal of Economic History* 31(04): 777–803.

Norton, Michael I., and Dan Ariely. 2011. "Building a Better America—One Wealth Quintile at a Time." *Perspectives on Psychological Science* 6(1): 9–12.

Nova, Annie. 2019. "Many Americans Who Can't Afford a $400 Emergency Blame Debt." *CNBC*, July 20, 2019. https://www.cnbc.com/2019/07/20/heres-why-so-many-americans-cant-handle-a-400-unexpected-expense.html.

O'Leary, Naomi. 2014. "Pope Francis' Stunning Critique of Capitalism." *HuffPost*, January 23, 2014. https://www.huffpost.com/entry/pope-francis-evangelii-gaudium_n_4342964.

Obama, Barack. 2013. "Remarks by the President on Economic Mobility." *Whitehouse. gov*. December 4, 2013. https://obamawhitehouse.archives.gov/the-press-office/2013/12/04/remarks-president-economic-mobility.

OECD. 2004. *OECD Employment Outlook 2004*. Paris: Organization for Economic Cooperation and Development.

OECD. 2011. *Education at a Glance 2011*. Paris: OECD Publishing. http://www.oecd-ilibrary.org/education/education-at-a-glance-2011_eag-2011-en.

Offer, Avner, and Gabriel Söderberg. 2016. *The Nobel Factor: The Prize in Economics, Social Democracy, and the Market Turn*. Princeton, NJ: Princeton University Press.

Okun, Arthur. 1975. *Equality and Efficiency: The Big Tradeoff*. Washington, DC: Brookings Institution Press.

Olenda, Ken. 2015. "The Civil Rights Struggle in Selma." *Socialist Worker (Britain)*. 2015. http://socialistworker.co.uk/art/39888/The+civil+rights+struggle+in+Selma.

Olsen-Phillips, Peter, Russ Choma, Sarah Bryner, and Doug Weber. 2015. "The Political One Percent of the One Percent in 2014: Mega Donors Fuel Rising Cost of Elections." *OpenSecrets Blog*. April 30. https://www.opensecrets.org/news/2015/04/the-political-one-percent-of-the-one-percent-in-2014-mega-donors-fuel-rising-cost-of-elections/.

Olson, Mancur. 1971. *The Logic of Collective Action: Public Goods and the Theory of Groups, Second Printing with New Preface and Appendix*. Rev. ed. Cambridge, MA: Harvard University Press.

O'Mara, Margaret. 2017. *Pivotal Tuesdays: Four Elections That Shaped the Twentieth Century*. Reprint edition. University of Pennsylvania Press.

Oriana. 2016. "Dante Mad in Inferno; Milking the Apocalypse; Give Us This Day Our Daily Crap; Secret Life Ff Pronouns; Saliva Protects against Cavities." Oriana-Poetry *(blog)*. November 6, 2016. http://oriana-poetry.blogspot.com/2016/11/dante-mad-in-inferno-milking-apocalypse.html.

Otterbein, Keith F. 1994. *Feuding and Warfare: Selected Works of Keith F. Otterbein*. Langhorne, PA: Gordon and Breach.

Padden, R. C. 1970. *The Hummingbird and the Hawk: Conquest and Sovereignty in the Valley of Mexico 1503–1541*. New York: Harpercollins College Division.

Panksepp, Jaak. 2004. *Affective Neuroscience: The Foundations of Human and Animal Emotions*. Oxford University Press.

Parenti, Christian. 1999. "Atlas Finally Shrugged." *The Baffler* 13: 108–20.

Park, Yongjin. 2010. "The Second Paycheck to Keep Up with the Joneses: Relative Income Concerns and Labor Market Decisions of Married Women." *Eastern Economic Journal* 36: 255–76.

Paxton, Robert O. 2004. *The Anatomy of Fascism*. New York: Knopf.

Perelman, Michael. 2007. *The Confiscation of American Prosperity: From Right-Wing Extremism and Economic Ideology to the Next Great Depression*. New York: Palgrave Macmillan.

Perelman, Michael. 2012. "The Power of Economics Versus the Economics of Power." *Challenge* 55(6): 53–66.

Persson, Torsten, and Guido Tabellini. 1994. "Is Inequality Harmful for Growth? Theory and Evidence." *American Economic Review* 84: 600–21.

Pérusse, Daniel. 1994. "Mate Choice in Modern Societies: Testing Evolutionary Hypotheses with Behavioral Data." *Human Nature* 5(3): 255–78.

Peters, Mike. 2018. "The Most Potent Weapon in the Hands of the Oppressor Is the Mind of the Oppressed." *The Most Potent Weapon in the Hands of the Oppressor Is the Mind of the Oppressed* (blog). October 18. https://www.redpepper.org.uk/the-most-potent-weapon-in-the-hands-of-the-oppressor-is-the-mind-of-the-oppressed/.

Petsoulas, Christian. 2001. *Hayek's Liberalism and Its Origins: His Idea of Spontaneous Order and the Scottish Enlightenment.* London: Routledge.

Pettegree, Andrew. 2015. *Brand Luther: How an Unheralded Monk Turned His Small Town into a Center of Publishing, Made Himself the Most Famous Man in Europe—and Started the Protestant Reformation.* 1st ed. New York: Penguin Press.

Pew Research Center. 2008. "Economic Discontent Deepens as Inflation Concerns Rise." Pew Research Center for the People and the Press *(blog).* February 14. http://www.people-press.org/2008/02/14/economic-discontent-deepens-as-inflation-concerns-rise/.

Pew Research Center. 2014. "Greatest Dangers in the World." Pew Research Center's Global Attitudes Project *(blog).* October 16. https://www.pewresearch.org/global/2014/10/16/greatest-dangers-in-the-world/.

Pew Research Center. 2019a. "Stark Partisan Divisions in Americans' Views of 'Socialism,' 'Capitalism.'" Pew Research Center *(blog).* June 25. https://www.pewresearch.org/fact-tank/2019/06/25/stark-partisan-divisions-in-americans-views-of-socialism-capitalism/.

Pew Research Center. 2019b. "In U.S., Decline of Christianity Continues at Rapid Pace." Pew Research Center's Religion & Public Life Project *(blog).* October 17. https://www.pewforum.org/2019/10/17/in-u-s-decline-of-christianity-continues-at-rapid-pace/.

Pharr, Susan J., and Robert D. Putnam. 2000. *Disaffected Democracies: What's Troubling the Trilateral Countries?* Princeton, NJ: Princeton University Press.

Phillips, Kevin. 2008. "Too Much Wealth, Too Little Democracy." *Challenge,* 45(5), September–October: 6–20.

Pieper, Josef, and James V. Schall. 1963. *Leisure: The Basis of Culture.* 1st ed. San Francisco: Ignatius Press.

Piketty, Thomas. 2014. *Capital in the Twenty-First Century.* Cambridge, MA: Harvard University Press.

Piketty, Thomas. 2020. *Capital and Ideology.* Translated by Arthur Goldhammer. Cambridge, MA; London: Harvard University Press.

Piketty, Thomas, and Emmanuel Saez. 2006. "The Evolution of Top Incomes: A Historical and International Perspective." Working Paper 11955. National Bureau of Economic Research. http://www.nber.org/papers/w11955.

Pinkard, Terry. 1996. *Hegel's Phenomenology: The Sociality of Reason.* Cambridge: Cambridge University Press.

Pinker, S. 2003. "Language as an Adaptation to the Cognitive Niche." In *Language Evolution: States of the Art,* edited by S. Kirby and M. Christiansen, 16–37. New York: Oxford University Press.

Pinker, Steven. 2002. *The Blank State: The Modern Denial of Human Nature.* New York: Penguin Press.

Pinker, Steven. 2011. *The Better Angels of Our Nature: Why Violence Has Declined.* New York: Viking.

Pinker, Steven. 2018. *Enlightenment Now: The Case for Reason, Science, Humanism, and Progress.* 1st ed. New York: Viking.

Pisani, Bob. 2020. "Wealth Gap Grows as Rising Corporate Profits Boost Stock Holdings Controlled by Richest Households." *CNBC.* August 27. https://www.cnbc.com/2020/08/27/wealth-gap-grows-as-rising-corporate-profits-boost-stock-holdings-controlled-by-richest-households.html.

Planet Ark. 2004. *The Recycling Olympic Report.* Sydney: Planet Ark Environmental Foundation.

Plato. 1968. *The Republic of Plato.* Edited by Alan Bloom. 2nd ed. New York: Basic Books.

Polanyi, Karl. 1944. *The Great Transformation: The Political and Economic Origins of Our Time.* Boston, MA: Beacon Press.

Politizane. 2012. *Wealth Inequality in America.* Youtube. http://www.youtube.com/watch?v=QPKKQnijnsM&feature=player_embedded#t=15.

Pollan, Michael. 2002. *The Botany of Desire: A Plant's-Eye View of the World.* New York: Random House Trade Paperbacks.

Pope, James G. 2016. "Why Is There No Socialism in the United States? Law and the Racial Divide in the American Working Class, 1676–1964." *Texas Law Review* 94(7): 1555–90.

Popper, Karl. 1966. *The Open Society and Its Enemies.* Vol. 2. 2 vols. London: Routledge.

Pounds, Norman John Greville. 1974. *An Economic History of Medieval Europe.* New York: Longmans.

Powell, Adam, Stephen Shennan, and Mark G. Thomas. 2009. "Late Pleistocene Demography and the Appearance of Modern Human Behavior." *Science* 324(5932): 1298–1301.

Priestland, David. 2012. *Merchant, Soldier, Sage.* London: Allen Lane.

Proudhon, Pierre-Joseph Laura. 1840. *What Is Property? An Inquiry into the Principle of Right and of Government.* Charleston, SC: Forgotten Books.

Prum, Richard O. 2017. *The Evolution of Beauty: How Darwin's Forgotten Theory of Mate Choice Shapes the Natural World—and Us.* New York: Doubleday.

Pryor, John B. 1987. "Sexual Harassment Proclivities in Men." *Sex Roles* 17(5): 269–90.

Purzycki, Benjamin Grant, Coren Apicella, Quentin D. Atkinson, Emma Cohen, Rita Anne McNamara, Aiyana K. Willard, Dimitris Xygalatas, Ara Norenzayan, and Joseph Henrich. 2016. "Moralistic Gods, Supernatural Punishment and the Expansion of Human Sociality." *Nature* 530(7590): 327–30.

Putnam, Robert D. 2016. *Our Kids: The American Dream in Crisis.* Reprint ed. New York: Simon & Schuster.

Quinn, Annalisa. 2017. "An Incredible Meet Cute, Told a Little Too Incredibly." *Washington Post*, October 1, sec. B.

Rae, J. 1895. *The Life of Adam Smith.* London: Macmillan.

Rawls, John. 1999. *A Theory of Justice.* Rev. ed. Cambridge, MA: Belknap Press.

Reardon, Sean F., and Kendra Bischoff. 2016. "The Continuing Increase in Income Segregation, 2007–2012." *Stanford Center for Education Policy Analysis.* http://inequality.stanford.edu/sites/default/files/increase-income-segregation.pdf.

Rees, Albert, and Donald P. Jacobs. 1961. *Real Wages in Manufacturing, 1890–1914.* Princeton University Press. https://www.jstor.org/stable/j.ctt183pp5r.

Regalia, Martin. 2015. "Obama's Economic Legacy: 'Just the Facts.'" *U.S. Chamber of Commerce*. September 11, 2015. https://www.uschamber.com/above-the-fold/obama-s-economic-legacy-just-the-facts.

Reich, Robert B. 2001. *The Future of Success*. New York: Knopf.

Reich, Robert B. 2008. *Supercapitalism: The Transformation of Business, Democracy, and Everyday Life*. Reprint ed. New York: Vintage.

Reich, Robert B. 2010. "The Root of Economic Fragility and Political Anger." OpEdNews. July 13, 2010. https://www.opednews.com/articles/The-Root-of-Economic-Fragi-by-Robert-Reich-100713-774.html.

Reinhart, Carmen M., and Belen Sbrancia. 2011. "The Liquidation of Government Debt." NBER Working Paper No. 16893. http://www.nber.org/papers/w16893.

Remoff, Heather. 2016. "Malthus, Darwin, and the Descent of Economics." *American Journal of Economics and Sociology* 75(4): 862–903.

Reporters without Borders. 2019. "2019 World Press Freedom Index." https://rsf.org/en/ranking.

Reporters without Borders. 2020. "2020 World Press Freedom Index." https://rsf.org/en/ranking_table.

Rich, Andrew. 2005. *Think Tanks, Public Policy, and the Politics of Expertise*. Cambridge; New York: Cambridge University Press.

Richardson, Lewis Fry. 1960. *Statistics of Deadly Quarrels*. Pacific Grove, CA: Boxwood Press.

Richter, Brian Kelleher, Krislert Samphantharak, and Jeffrey F. Timmons. 2009. "Lobbying and Taxes." *American Journal of Political Science* 53(4): 893–909.

Riesman, David. 1950. *The Lonely Crowd: A Study of the Changing American Character*. New Haven, CT: Yale University Press.

Roach, John. 2004. "Brain Study Shows Why Revenge Is Sweet." *National Geographic News*. August 27, 2004. http://news.nationalgeographic.com/news/2004/08/0827_040827_punishment.html.

Robertson, David Brian. 2000. *Capital, Labor, and State*. Lanham, MD: Rowan and Littlefield.

Robinson, Joan. 1962. *Economic Philosophy*. New York: Doubleday.

Roemer, John. 2011. "Ideological and Political Roots of American Inequality." *Challenge* 54(5): 76–98.

Roll, Eric. 1974. *A History of Economic Thought*. 4th ed. Homewood, IL: Richard D. Irwin.

Rosanvallon, Pierre. 2013. *The Society of Equals*. Cambridge, MA: Harvard University Press.

Rose, Nancy E. 2013. "Bring Back the WPA: Lessons from the Job Creation Programs of the 1930s." In *Employment Guarantee Schemes: Job Creatin and Policy in Developing Countries and Emerging Markets*, edited by Mathew Forstater and Michael J. Murray. 155–179. New York: Palgrave Macmillan.

Rose, Stephen. 2010. *Rebound: Why America Will Emerge Stronger from the Financial Crisis*. New York: St. Martin's Press.

Rosenberg, Nathan, and L. E. Birdsell, Jr. 1987. *How the West Grew Rich: The Economic Transformation of the Industrial World*. New York: Basic Books.

Roszak, Theodore. 1995. *The Making of a Counter Culture: Reflections on the Technocratic Society and Its Youthful Opposition*. Berkeley: University of California Press.

Rousseau, Jean Jacques. 1755. *Discourse upon the Origin and Foundation of Inequality among Mankind*. New York: Oxford University Press, 1994.

Routh, Guy. 1975. *The Origin of Economic Ideas*. White Plains, New York: International Arts and Sciences Press.

Rubin, Jared. 2014. "Printing and Protestants: An Empirical Test of the Role of Printing in the Reformation." *Review of Economics and Statistics* 96(2): 270–86.

Russell, Bertrand. 1930. *The Conquest of Happiness*. Edited by Daniel C. Dennett. 1st ed. New York: Liveright.

Sachs, Jeffrey. 2011. *The Price of Civilization: Economics and Ethics after the Fall*. London: The Bodley Head.

Saez, Emmanuel, and Gabriel Zucman. 2016. "Wealth Inequality in the United States since 1913: Evidence from Capitalized Income Tax Data." *The Quarterly Journal of Economics* 131(2): 519–78.

Saez, Emmanuel. 2016. "U.S. Top One Percent of Income Earners Hit New High in 2015 amid Strong Economic Growth." Equitable Growth *(blog)*. July. http://www.equitablegrowth.org/u-s-top-one-percent-of-income-earners-hit-new-high-in-2015-amid-strong-economic-growth/.

Sahlins, Marshall. 1974. *Stone Age Economics*. New Brunswick, NJ: Aldine Transaction.

Salinger, J. D. 1951. *The Catcher in the Rye*. New York: Little, Brown and Company, 1991.

Sayer, Andrew. 2015. *Why We Can't Afford the Rich*. Bristol: Policy Press.

Schattschneider, Elmer E. 1975. *The Semisovereign People: A Realist's View of Democracy in America*. Revised edition. Hinsdale, Ill: Wadsworth Publishing.

Scheidel, Walter. 2017. *The Great Leveler: Violence and the History of Inequality from the Stone Age to the Twenty-First Century*. Princeton, NJ: Princeton University Press.

Schiffman, Richard. 2017. "Professor Caveman." *The Atlantic*, April. https://www.theatlantic.com/magazine/archive/2017/04/professor-caveman/517815/.

Schivelbusch, Wolfgang. 1993. *Tastes of Paradise: A Social History of Spices, Stimulants, and Intoxicants*. Translated by David Jacobson. New York: Vintage Books.

Schmitt, David P. 2005. "Fundamentals of Human Mating Strategies." In *The Handbook of Evolutionary Psychology*, edited by David M. Buss, 258–91. New York: John Wiley & Sons.

Schor, Juliet. 1993. *The Overworked American: The Unexpected Decline of Leisure*. Reprint ed. New York: Basic Books.

Schor, Juliet B. 1999. *The Overspent American: Why We Want What We Don't Need*. 1st ed. New York: Harper Perennial.

Schumpeter, Joseph A. 1934. *The Theory of Economic Development*. Translated by R. Opie. Cambridge, MA: Harvard University Press.

Schumpeter, Joseph A. 1954. *History of Economic Analysis*. New York: Oxford University Press.

Schumpeter, Joseph A. 1962. *Capitalism, Socialism, and Democracy*. 3rd ed. New York: Harper Torchbooks.

Schumpeter, Joseph. 2006. *Capitalism, Socialism and Democracy*. New ed. London; New York: Routledge.

Schuster, Jack H., and Martin J. Finkelstein. 2008. *The American Faculty: The Restructuring of Academic Work and Careers*. Johns Hopkins University Press. Johns Hopkins University Press.

Scitovsky, Tibor. 1976. *The Joyless Economy: The Psychology of Human Satisfaction*. Oxford: Oxford University Press.

Scott, James C. 1987. *Weapons of the Weak: Everyday Forms of Peasant Resistance*. New Haven, CT: Yale University Press.

Scott, James C. 2013. "Crops, Towns, Government." *London Review of Books*, 35(22): 13–15, November 21, 2013.

Scott, James C. 2017. *Against the Grain: A Deep History of the Earliest States*. 1st ed. New Haven, CT: Yale University Press.

Sejnowski, Terrence J. 2018. *The Deep Learning Revolution*. Cambridge, MA: MIT Press.

Shapin, Steven. 2014. "Libel on the Human Race." *London Review of Books*, 36(11): 26–29, June 5, 2014.

Sheets-Johnstone, Maxine. 1990. "Hominid Bipedality and Sexual Selection." *Evolutionary Theory* 9(1): 57–70.

Sidanius, Jim, and Shana Levin. 2001. "Legitimizing Ideologies: The Social Dominance Approach." In *The Psychology of Legitimacy: Emerging Perspectives on Ideology, Justice, and Intergroup Relations*, edited by John T. Jost and Brenda Major, 307–31. Cambridge: Cambridge University Press.

Simons, Walter. 2003. *Cities of Ladies: Beguine Communities in the Medieval Low Countries, 1200–1565*. Philadelphia: University of Pennsylvania Press.

Sinclair, Upton. 1906. *The Jungle*. Unabridged ed. Mineola, NY: Dover Publications.

Sitaraman, Ganesh. 2017. *The Crisis of the Middle-Class Constitution: Why Income Inequality Threatens Our Republic*. New York: Alfred A. Knopf.

Slater, Joanna. 2019. "Indian Father 'Hires Assassins to Kill Daughter's Husband Because He Was from Lower Caste.'" *The Independent*, August 26. https://www.independent.co.uk/news/world/asia/indian-couple-father-assassins-caste-wedding-amrutha-varshini-pranay-perumalla-a9071206.html.

Slater, Philip. 1970. *The Pursuit of Loneliness: America's Discontent and the Search for a New Democratic Ideal*. 3rd ed. Boston: Beacon Press.

Smiley, Gene. 1998. "New Estimates of Income Shares during the 1920s." In *Calvin Coolidge and the Coolidge Era*, edited by John Earl Haynes, 215–32. Washington, DC: Library of Congress.

Smith, Adam. 1759. *The Theory of Moral Sentiments*. Indianapolis: Liberty Classics, 1976.

Smith, Adam. 1763. *Lectures on Jurisprudence*. Edited by Ronald Lindley Meek, D. D. Raphael, and P. G. Stein. Glasgow Edition of the Works and Correspondence of Adam Smith 5. Oxford: Clarendon Press, 1976.

Smith, Adam. 1776. *An Enquiry into the Nature and Causes of the Wealth of Nations*. New York: The Modern Library, 1937.

Sohn-Rethel, Alfred. 1978. *Intellectual and Manual Labour: Critique of Epistemology*. London: Macmillan.

Solnick, Sara, and David Hemenway. 1998. "Is More Always Better? A Survey on Positional Concerns." *Journal of Economic Behavior & Organization* 37(3): 373–83.

Solon, Gary. 1992. "Intergenerational Income Mobility in the United States." *American Economic Review* 82(3): 393–408.

Sombart, Werner. 1976. *Why Is There No Socialism in the United States?* Translated by P. M. Hocking and C. T. Husbands. 1st ed. New York: Palgrave Macmillan.

Spencer, Herbert. 2008. *A System of Synthetic Philosophy: First Principles*. Vol. I. New York: Obscure Press.

Spock, Benjamin, M. D., and Robert Needlman, M. D. 1946. *Dr. Spock's Baby and Child Care*. 9th ed. New York: Pocket Books, 2011.

Spruyt, Hendrik. 1994. *The Sovereign State and Its Competitors*. Princeton, NJ: Princeton University Press.

Srinivasan, T. N. 1977. "Development, Poverty, and Basic Human Needs: Some Issues." *Food Research Institute Studies*, no. 02. http://ideas.repec.org/a/ags/frisst/135545.html.

Stanford, Craig B. 2001. *The Hunting Apes: Meat Eating and the Origins of Human Behavior*. Princeton, NJ: Princeton University Press.

Steckel, Richard H., and John Wallis. 2007. *Stones, Bones, and States: A New Approach to the Neolithic Revolution*. National Bureau of Economic Research. https://www.google.com/search?q=stones%2C+bones%2C+and+states&ie=utf-8&oe=utf-8.

Steinhauser, Paul, and Robert Yoon. 2013. "Cost to Win Congressional Election Skyrockets." *CNNPolitics.com*. July 11. http://www.cnn.com/2013/07/11/politics/congress-election-costs/.

Stigler, George J. 1941. *Production and Distribution Theories*. New York: Macmillan.

Stigler, George J. 1982. *The Economist as Preacher and Other Essays*. Chicago: University of Chicago Press.

Stiglitz, Joseph. 2002. "Joseph Stiglitz: There Is No Invisible Hand." *The Guardian*. December 20. http://www.theguardian.com/education/2002/dec/20/highereducation.uk1.

Stiglitz, Joseph E. 2010. *Freefall: America, Free Markets, and the Sinking of the World Economy*. Reprint ed. New York: W. W. Norton.

Stiglitz, Joseph E. 2012. *The Price of Inequality: How Today's Divided Society Endangers Our Future*. 1st ed. New York: W. W. Norton.

Stoelhorst, J. W., and Peter J. Richerson. 2013. "A Naturalistic Theory of Economic Organization." *Journal of Economic Behavior & Organization, Evolution as a General Theoretical Framework for Economics and Public Policy* 90(June): S45–56.

Stone, Lawrence. 1969. "Literacy and Education in England 1640–1900." *Past & Present*, no. 42: 69–139.

Sultan, Niv M. 2017. "Election 2016: Trump's Free Media Helped Keep Cost Down." *OpenSecrets News*. April 13. https://www.opensecrets.org/news/2017/04/election-2016-trump-fewer-donors-provided-more-of-the-cash/.

Suttle, B. 1987. "The Passion of Self-Interest: The Development of the Idea and Its Changing Status." *American Journal of Economics and Sociology* 46(4): 459–72.

Suzman, James. 2017. *Affluence Without Abundance: The Disappearing World of the Bushmen*. New York: Bloomsbury USA.

Suzman, James. 2021. *Work: A Deep History, from the Stone Age to the Age of Robots*. New York: Penguin Press.

Swarens, Tim. 2018. "How Many People Are Victims of Sex Trafficking?" *Indianapolis Star*. January 11. https://www.indystar.com/story/opinion/2018/01/11/human-trafficking-statistics-how-many-people-victims/1013877001/.

Sweezy, Paul M. 2001. "Marxism and the Social Sciences." Monthly Review 53(4). http://monthlyreview.org/archives/2001/volume-53-issue-04-september-2001/.

Szasz, Andrew, and Michael Meuser. 1997. "Environmental Inequalities: Literature Review and Proposals for New Directions in Research and Theory." *Current Sociology* 45(3): 99–120.

Tawney, R. H. 1926. *Religion and the Rise of Capitalism*. New York: Harcourt, Brace & World.

Taylor, Lance. 2011. *Maynard's Revenge: The Collapse of Free Market Macroeconomics*. Cambridge, MA: Harvard University Press.

Taylor, Rebe. 2008. "The Polemics of Making Fire in Tasmania: The Historical Evidence Revisited." *Aboriginal History* 32: 1–26.

The Economist. 2016. "A Reflection on Barack Obama's Presidency," December 24. https://www.economist.com/news/christmas-specials/21712062-barack-obamas-presidency-lurched-between-idealism-and-acrimony-some-his.

Thomas, Keith. 1964. "Work and Leisure in Pre-Industrial Society." *Past and Present* 29: 50–66.

Thompson, E. P. 1963. *The Making of the English Working Class*. New York: Vintage.

Thompson, William. 1850. *An Inquiry into the Principles of the Distribution of Wealth Most Conducive to Human Happiness*. London: William S. Orr.

Thompson, Willie. 2015. *Work, Sex, and Power*. London: Pluto Press.

Thornton, William Thomas. 1869. On Labour: Its Wrongful Claims and Rightful Dues. Its Actual Present and Possible Future. Reprint edition. Macmillan and CO.

Thurnwald, Richard. 1932. *Economics in Primitive Communities*. London: Oxford University Press.

Tierney, Brian. 1959. *Medieval Poor Law: A Sketch of Canonical Theory and Its Application in England*. Berkeley: University of California Press.

Tilly, Louise A., and Joan W. Scott. 1988. *Women, Work and Family*. 1st ed. New York: Routledge.

Time Staff. 2017. "10 Historians on What Will Be Said about President Obama's Legacy." *Time*. January 20. http://time.com/4632190/historians-obamas-legacy/.

Tocqueville, Alexis de. 1835. *Democracy in America*. Edited by Henry Reeve. Vol. 1. 2 vols. New York: Vintage.

Tocqueville, Alexis de. 1840. Democracy in America. Translated by Henry Reeve. Vol. 2. 2 vols. New York: Vintage.

Tokumitsu, Miya. 2017. "The United States of Work." *New Republic*. April 18, 2017. https://newrepublic.com/article/141663/united-states-work.

Tolstoy, Leo. 1961. *Anna Karenina*. New York: Signet Classics, New American Library.

Tönnies, Ferdinand. 1887. *Community and Society: Gemeinschaft und Gesellschaft*. New York: Harper & Row.

Tooby, John, and Leda Cosmides. 2005. "Conceptual Foundations of Evolutionary Psychology." In *The Handbook of Evolutionary Psychology*, edited by David M. Buss, 5–67. New York: John Wiley & Sons.

Trefil, James. 2014. "Struggling to Understand the Unknowable." *Washington Post*, December 7, sec. B.

Trembley, Rodrigue. 2010. "A Long Economic Winter Ahead | Dissident Voice." July 7, 2010. http://dissidentvoice.org/2010/07/a-long-economic-winter-ahead/.

Trivers, Robert. 1985. *Social Evolution*. Menlo Park, CA: Benjamin Cummings.

Troy, Tevi. 2012. "Less Politics More Thought in Think Tanks." *Washington Post*, March 16, A13.

Tuchman, Barbara W. 1978. *A Distant Mirror: The Calamitous 14th Century*. New York: Alfred A. Knopf.

Tuchman, Barbara W. 1987. *A Distant Mirror: The Calamitous 14th Century*. Reissue ed. New York: Random House Trade Paperbacks.

Tucker, Josiah. 1966. "A Brief Essay on Trade." In *A Select Collection of Scarce and Valuable Tracts on Commerce*, edited by R. J. McCulloch, 31–48. New York: A. M. Kelley.

Turgot, Anne-Robert-Jacques. 2010. *Turgot on Progress, Sociology and Economics*. Edited by Ronald L. Meek. Cambridge: Cambridge University Press.

Turner, Frederick Jackson. 1921. *The Frontier in American History*. New York: Holt.

Tylecote, Andrew. 2016. "Institutions Matter: But Which Institutions? And How and Why Do They Change?" *Journal of Institutional Economics* 12(3): 721–42.

US Census Bureau, M. C. D. 2019. "Characteristics of New Housing." https://www.census.gov/construction/chars/highlights.html.

USDA. n.d. "Lincoln's Milwaukee Speech | National Agricultural Library." Accessed November 24, 2017. https://www.nal.usda.gov/lincolns-milwaukee-speech.

van Bavel, Bas. 2015. "History as a Laboratory to Better Understand the Formation of Institutions." *Journal of Institutional Economics* 11(1): 69–91.

van Bavel, Bas. 2016. *The Invisible Hand? How Market Economies Have Emerged and Declined since AD 500.* Oxford: Oxford University Press.

van Bavel, Bas. 2019. "Open Societies before Market Economies: Historical Analysis," *Socio-Economic Review* 18(3): 1–21.

van Zanden, Jan Luiten. 1995. "Tracing the Beginning of the Kuznets Curve: Western Europe during the Early Modern Period." *Economic History Review* 48(4): 643–64.

Vanek, Joann. 1980. "Work, and Family Work, Leisure, and Family Roles: Farm Households in the United States, 1920–1955." *Journal of Family History* 5(4): 422–31.

Vatter, Harold G. 1985. *The U.S. Economy in World War II.* New York: Columbia University Press.

Veblen, Thorstein. 1899. *The Theory of the Leisure Class: An Economic Study of Institutions.* New York: The Modern Library, 1934.

Veblen, Thorstein. 1919. "Some Neglected Points in the Theory of Socialism." In Veblen, *The Place of Science in Modern Civilization*, 387–408. New York: B. W. Huebsch.

Veblen, Thorstein. 1919. "The Socialist Economics of Karl Marx II." In Veblen, *The Place of Science in Modern Civilization*, 431–56. New York: Russell & Russell.

Veblen, Thorstein. 1920. "Review of The Economic Consequences of the Peace by John Maynard Keynes." *Political Science Quarterly* 35(3): 467–72.

Veenhoven, R. 1993. *Happiness in Nations: Subjective Appreciation of Life in 56 Nations, 1946–1992.* Erasmus University of Rotterdam, Department of Social Sciences, RISBO, Center for Socio-Cultural Transformation.

Verba, Sidney, and Gary R. Orren. 1985. *Equality in America: The View Form the Top.* Cambridge: Harvard University Press.

Bierce, Ambrose. 2000. *The Unabridged Devil's Dictionary.* Atlanta: University of Georgia Press. https://www.jstor.org/stable/j.ctt17573xj.

Verbruggen, Jan F. 1997. *The Art of Warfare in Western Europe during the Middle Ages from the Eighth Century.* 2nd ed. Rochester, NY: Boydell Press.

von Mises, Ludwig. 1988. *Socialism: An Economic and Sociological Analysis.* Translated by J. Kahane. 6th edition. Indianapolis: Liberty Classics.

von Mises, Ludwig. 1990. *Economic Freedom and Interventionism.* Edited by Bettina Bien Greaves. New York: Foundation for Economic Education. http:// www.mises.org/ efandi/ ch9.asp.

von Rueden, Christopher, Michael Gurven, Hillard Kaplan, and Johathan Stieglitz. 2014. "Leadership in an Egalitarian Society." *Human Nature* 25(4): 558–66.

de Waal, Frans B. M. 2009a. *Peacemaking among Primates.* Cambridge, MA: Harvard University Press.

de Waal, Frans. 2009b. "The Origins of Fairness." *New Scientist* 204(2734): 34–35. https:// doi.org/ 10.1016/ S0262- 4079(09)63003-7.

Wade, Nicholas. 2009. *The Faith Instinct: How Religion Evolved and Why It Endures.* New York: Penguin Press.

Wade, Robert. 2012. "Why Has Income Inequality Remained on the Sidelines of Public Policy for So Long?" Challenge 53(3): 21–50.

Wade, Robert. 2013. "How High Inequality Plus Neoliberal Governance Weakens Democracy." Challenge 56(6): 5–37. https://doi.org/10.2753/0577-5132560601.

Wade, Robert Hunter. 2014. "The Strange Neglect of Income Inequality in Economics and Public Policy." In Toward Human Development: New Approaches to Macroeconomics and Inequality, edited by Edward Giovanni, Andrea Cornia, and Francis Steward, 99–121. Oxford: Oxford University Press.

Wallich, Henry C. 1972. "Zero Growth." Newsweek, January 24, 1972: 61–62.

Waltzer, Michael. 1974. The Revolution of the Saints: A Study in the Origins of Radical Politics. New York: Atheneum.

Waterman, A. M. C. 2008. "The Changing Theological Context of Economic Analysis since the Eighteenth Century." History of Political Economy 40(5): 121–42.

Wax, Amy L. 2004. "Evolution and the Bounds of Human." Law and Philosophy 23(6): 527–91.Weber, Max. 1905. The Protestant Ethic and the "Spirit" of Capitalism. New York: Penguin Classics.

Weber, Max. 1921a. Economy and Society: An Outline of Interpretive Sociology. Edited by Guenther Roth and Claus Wittich. New ed. Berkeley: University of California Press.

Weber, Max. 1921b. Political Writings. Edited by Peter Lassman. Translated by Ronald Speirs. Cambridge: Cambridge University Press.

Weber, Max. 2003. General Economic History. Mineola, NY: Dover Publications.

White, Lynn. 1966. Medieval Technology and Social Change. London; New York: Oxford University Press.

White, Lynn. 1969. The Dynamo and Virgin Reconsidered: Machina Ex Deo. Cambridge, MA: MIT Press.

Whyte, William H. 1956. The Organization Man. Rev. ed. Philadelphia: University of Pennsylvania Press.

Wiessner, Polly. 1982. "Risk, Reciprocity and Social Influences on !Kung San Economics." In Politics and History in Band Societies, edited by E. Leacock and R. B. Lee, 61–84. Cambridge: Cambridge University Press.

Wilkinson, Richard, and Kate Pickett. 2009. The Spirit Level: Why Greater Equality Makes Societies Stronger. Reprint edition. New York: Bloomsbury Press.

Wilkinson, Richard, and Kate Pickett. 2019. The Inner Level. London: Penguin Press.

Willensky, Harold. 1961. "The Uneven Distribution of Leisure: The Impact of Economic Growth on 'Free Time.'" Social Problems 9: 32–56.

Williams, George C. 1996. Adaptation and Natural Selection. Reprint ed. Princeton, NJ: Princeton University Press.

Williams, Ray. 2011. "Why America Is in Decline." Psychology Today. March 11. http://www.psychologytoday.com/blog/wired-success/201103/why-america-is-in-decline.

Williamson, Jeffrey G. 1980. American Inequality: A Macroeconomic History. New York: Academic Press.

Williamson, Jeffrey G. 1991. Inequality, Poverty, and History: The Kuznets Memorial Lectures. Cambridge, MA: Blackwell.

Wilson, David Sloan. 2003. Darwin's Cathedral: Evolution, Religion, and the Nature of Society. 1st ed. Chicago: University of Chicago Press.

Wilson, David Sloan. 2007. Evolution for Everyone. New York: Delacorte.

Wilson, David Sloan. 2015. Does Altruism Exist? Culture, Genes, and the Welfare of Others. New Haven, CT: Yale University Press.

Wilson, David Sloan, and John M. Gowdy. 2013. "Evolution as a General Theoretical Framework for Economics and Public Policy." *Journal of Economic Behavior and Organization*. 90 (June): S3–10. https://doi.org/10.1016/j.jebo.2012.12.008.

Wilson, David Sloan, and John M. Gowdy. 2015. "Human Ultrasociality and the Invisible Hand: Foundational Developments in Evolutionary Science Alter a Foundational Concept in Economics." *Journal of Bioeconomics* 17(1): 37–52.

Wilson, Edward O. 1978. *On Human Nature*. Cambridge, MA: Harvard University Press.

Wilson, Edward O. 1989. "The Biological Basis of Culture." *International Review of Sociology Series 1* 3(3): 33–60.

Wilson, Edward O. 2014. "On Free Will." *Harper's Magazine*, September 2014. https://harpers.org/archive/2014/09/on-free-will/

Wilson, Margo, and Martin Daly. 1988. *Homicide*. New York: Aldine Transaction.

Wilson, Margo, Martin Daly, Stephen Gordon, and Adelle Pratt. 1996. "Sex Differences in Valuations of the Environment?" *Population and Environment* 18(2): 143–59.

Wisman, Jon D. 1989. "Straightening Out the Backward-Bending Supply Curve of Labor: From Overt to Covert Compulsion and Beyond." *Review of Political Economy* 1(1): 94–112.

Wisman, Jon D. 1991. *Worker Empowerment: The Struggle for Workplace Democracy*. New York: Bootstrap Pr.

Wisman, Jon D. 1998. "Christianity, John Paul II, and the Future of Work." *International Journal of Social Economics* 25(11–12): 1658–71.

Wisman, Jon D. 2001. "Rethinking the Social Character of Social Science." In *Crossing the Mainstream*, edited by Amitava Krishna Dutt and Kenneth P. Jameson, 277–96. Notre Dame, IN: University of Notre Dame Press.

Wisman, Jon D. 2003. "The Scope and Promising Future of Social Economics." *Review of Social Economy* 61(4): 1–21.

Wisman, Jon D. 2009. "Household Saving, Class Identity, and Conspicuous Consumption." *Journal of Economic Issues* 43(1): 89–114.

Wisman, Jon D. 2013a. "Government Is Whose Problem?" *Journal of Economic Issues* 47(4): 911–38. https://doi.org/10.2753/JEI0021-3624470406.

Wisman, Jon D. 2013b. "Wage Stagnation, Rising Inequality and the Financial Crisis of 2008." *Cambridge Journal of Economics* 37(4): 921–45.

Wisman, Jon D. 2013c . "Why Marx Still Matters." *International Journal of Pluralism and Economics Education* 4(3): 229–42.

Wisman, Jon D. 2014a. "9/11, Foreign Threats, Political Legitimacy, and Democratic Institutions." *Humanomics: The International Journal of Systems and Ethics* 30(1): 22–40.

Wisman, Jon D. 2014b. "The Financial Crisis of 1929 Reexamined: The Role of Soaring Inequality." *Review of Political Economy* 26(3): 372–91.

Wisman, Jon D. 2017. "Exploding Inequality Is Killing Democracy." *E-International Relations*, January. http://www.e-ir.info/2017/01/04/exploding-inequality-is-killing-democracy/.

Wisman, Jon D. 2019. "The Darwinian Dynamic of Sexual Selection That Thorstein Veblen Missed and Its Relevance to Institutional Economics." *Journal of Institutional Economics* 15(1): 49–72.

Wisman, Jon D. 2020. "A Brief Sketch of the Economic Causes of War and Peace." Working Papers. American University, Department of Economics. https://ideas.repec.org/p/amu/wpaper/2020-01.html.

Wisman, Jon D., and Mike Cauvel. 2021. "Why Has Labor Not Demanded Guaranteed Employment?" *Journal of Economic Issues*, 55(3): 677–97.

Wisman, Jon D., and Matthew Davis. 2013. "Degraded Work, Declining Community, Rising Inequality, and the Transformation of the Protestant Ethic in America: 1870–1930." *American Journal of Economics and Sociology* 72(5): 1075–104.

Wisman, Jon D., and Aaron Pacitti. 2018. "Guaranteed Employment and Universal Child Care for a New Social Contract." *Theory and Action* 11(2): 1–41.

Wittfogel, Karl. 1957. *Oriental Despotism: A Comparative Study of Total Power*. 1st ed. New York: Vintage.

Wolff, Edward N. 2010. *Recent Trends in Household Wealth in the United States: Rising Debt and the Middle-Class Squeeze—An Update to 2007*. SSRN Scholarly Paper ID 1585409. Rochester, NY: Social Science Research Network. http://papers.ssrn.com/abstract=1585409.

Wolff, Richard D. 2015. "Socialism Means Abolishing the Distinction between Bosses and Employees." *Truthout*. June 22. http://www.truth-out.org/news/item/31567-socialism-means-abolishing-the-distinction-between-bosses-and-employees.

Wolin, Sheldon S. 2010. *Democracy Incorporated: Managed Democracy and the Specter of Inverted Totalitarianism*. Princeton, NJ: Princeton University Press.

Woodburn, J. 1980. "Hunters and Gatherers Today and Reconstruction of the Past." In *Soviet and Western Anthropology*, edited by Ernest Gellner, 95–117. London: Duckworth.

Woodard, Colin. 2012. "To Understand America, Look at New Zealand." *Washington Post*, February 19, 2012. https://www.washingtonpost.com/entertainment/books/fairness-and-freedom-a-history-of-two-open-societies-new-zealand-and-the-united-states-by-david-hackett-fischer/2012/01/24/gIQAsRcYKR_story.html

Wrangham, Richard. 2019. *The Goodness Paradox: The Strange Relationship Between Virtue and Violence in Human Evolution*. New York: Pantheon.

Wright, Quincy. 1942. *A Study of War*. Chicago: Chicago University Press.

Wynn, Neil A. 1986. *From Progressivism to Prosperity: World War I and American Society*. New York: Holmes &Meier.

Zahavi, Amotz. 1975. "Mate Selection—a Selection for a Handicap." *Journal of Theoretical Biology* 53: 205–14.

Zahavi, Amotz, and Avishag Zahavi. 1999. *The Handicap Principle: A Missing Piece of Darwin's Puzzle*. Oxford; New York: Oxford University Press.

Zelditch, Morris, Jr. 2001. "Theories of Legitimacy." In *The Psychology of Legitimacy: Emerging Perspectives on Ideology, Justice, and Intergroup Relations*, edited by John T. Jost and Brenda Major, 33–53. Cambridge: Cambridge University Press.

Zieger, Robert H. 1995. *The CIO: 1935–1955*. Chapel Hill: University of North Carolina Press.

Index

For the benefit of digital users, indexed terms that span two pages (e.g., 52–53) may, on occasion, appear on only one of those pages.